Charity and the Great Hunger in Ireland

Charity and the Great Hunger in Ireland

The Kindness of Strangers

Christine Kinealy

BLOOMSBURY

LONDON • NEW DELHI • NEW YORK • SYDNEY

Bloomsbury Academic

An imprint of Bloomsbury Publishing Plc

50 Bedford Square
London
WC1B 3DP
UK

1385 Broadway
New York
NY 10018
USA

www.bloomsbury.com

Bloomsbury is a registered trade mark of Bloomsbury Publishing Plc

First published 2013
Reprinted 2013, 2014 (twice)

British Library Cataloguing-in-Publication Data
A catalogue record for this book is available from the British Library.

ISBN: HB: 978-1-4411-7660-8
PB: 978-1-4411-4648-9
ePDF: 978-1-4411-1758-8
ePUB: 978-1-4411-3308-3

Library of Congress Cataloging-in-Publication Data
A catalogue record for this book is available from the Library of Congress.

Typeset by Deanta Global Publishing Services, Chennai, India

Do Barry Quest, 1945–2012

A chuisle mo chroí

CONTENTS

ACKNOWLEDGEMENTS

In researching and writing this book over the period of many years, I have incurred a number of debts. I apologize in advance if there are any omissions or if my words do not do full justice to the amount of support that I have received.

Inevitably, in a book of this size and scope, I have many people to thank for their professional assistance. Various librarians and archivists have given their time generously. This includes Dr Beth Pattterson, Bruce Lancaster and Kathleen Juliano, all of Drew University Library. Chris Anderson of the Methodist Archive at Drew University steered me towards many interesting religious sources. I benefitted greatly from the generosity and passion of people associated with the Great Hunger Collection at Quinnipiac University, namely, Grace Brady, Charles Getchell, Turlough McConnell, Claire Tynan, Dr David Valone and Robert Young. I am especially grateful to President John Lahey for his vision and hospitality.

I should like to thank Dr Maureen Watry, head of Special Collections and Archives at Liverpool University, Justin Cavernelis-Frost, archivist at the Rothschild Archive in London and the staff of the Baring Archive also in London, for their guidance when using their records. The staff in the National Library of Ireland gave me much assistance, and Honora Faul pointed me to a number of lesser-known sources. I am also grateful to Victoria O'Flaherty, director of the National Archives, St Kitts, for searching the relevant records on my behalf. Karla Ingemann, Records Officer of the Bermuda Archives, assisted me in researching the relevant records. Special thanks go to Alan Delozier, archivist at Seton Hall University, New Jersey, for his invaluable help.

A number of people have read and commented on drafts of chapters, for which I am much indebted. Francine Sagar, as usual, has proved to be an insightful and perspicacious commentator. Other readers include Dr Elias Ortega-Aponte, Dan Moran, Gregory Fox, Niamh Hamill, Eibhlín Walsh, Kevin Hall and Siobhán Kinealy. Their comments and diverse insights have been extremely valuable. Cassie Brand assisted in a number of ways, not least of which was in helping me put together the Bibliography. Many other friends and colleagues have provided support and encouragement, including Bernadette Barrington, Angela Farrell, David Sexton, Nick Carter, Timothy Collins, Linda Swerdlow, Stanley Goldstein, Susan Bailey, Don Mullan, Kristin Leary, Honora Ormesher, Margaret (Peggy) Terry, Dr Anne Rodda,

Dr Lauretta Farrell, Mandi Huizenga and Dr Stephen Butler. Thanks are due also to Michael Greenwood and Rhodri Mogford of Bloomsbury Publishing, for their patience and belief in this project.

My wonderful children, Siobhán, Ciarán – and now Sarah – have kept me grounded, while my Irish collie, with his regular demands to be fed, walked and petted, has provided a much-needed distraction from the intense process of writing. My thanks and love to the late Barry Quest, who accompanied me to many of the relevant archives and libraries. His energy and brilliance are sorely missed.

Finally, my gratitude goes to people whom I have not met; the thousands of individuals who gave their money and their time to assist the Irish poor during the dark years of famine. They are the heroes of this story.

Cover Image Note

An illustration from a later famine in Ireland. From 'Harper's Weekly', 28 February 1880.

Introduction

The Irish Famine of 1845–52 was the first national disaster to attract international sympathy and sustained large-scale financial donations.[1] The earliest place where money was raised on behalf of the Irish poor was Calcutta in India at the end of 1845. This action was started by British residents. Following the second and more devastating appearance of potato blight in 1846, fund-raising for the Irish poor took place throughout the world. Donations were raised in every continent, cutting across national boundaries and economic, political and gender divisions. Those who contributed included Christians, Jews, Muslims and Hindus. The response was unprecedented in terms of its diversity, magnitude and geographic extent. Financial contributions were made by the rich and influential, including Queen Victoria, the Sultan of Turkey, the president of the United States and Pope Pius IX. However, subscriptions also came from the poorest and most marginalized groups in society, such as ex-slaves in the Caribbean, the Choctaw Nation in Oklahoma, as well as convicts and 'fallen women' in London. In regard to the latter group, their individual names were not recorded, but their sacrifice was immense.

When the potato blight first appeared in 1845, Ireland was covered by a network of relief provision. A state system of poor relief, the Irish Poor Law, had been introduced in 1838. By 1845, 118 of the country's 130 workhouses were providing relief. At the same time, 800 medical charities were in operation throughout the country. While the workhouses were new and untested, medical charities were well established.[2] The catastrophe of the Famine, however, exposed the limitations of both organizations as their institutions proved inadequate to deal with the multiple demands being placed on them.

In the early decades of the nineteenth century, political economists, politicians and others debated the role of the government in assisting the poor. A general consensus was that poverty was the fault of the individual and caused by moral failure; external assistance would only serve to increase the demands made by the poor and perpetuate a culture of dependency. Therefore, in the terminology of the time, many poor were deemed 'undeserving' of assistance. Both the English Poor Law, which had been amended in 1834 to make it more frugal, and the even more stringent Irish Poor Law of 1838, were under-pinned by these approaches. Nonetheless, concurrent with attempts to reduce welfare provision, philanthropy – defined by Brian Harrison as 'any organization devoting money, time, thought, or energy to relieving the miseries of the poor, the neglected, or the oppressed' – was expanding rapidly.[3] By 1869, there were so many private charities (an estimated 700 in London alone) that the Charity Organization Society was established in order to coordinate their activities.[4] At the same time, similar debates to those that informed Poor Law legislation had been taking place in the United Kingdom about the role of philanthropy. The general consensus was that charity should only be given to those who were morally 'deserving' and capable of self-improvement. Indiscriminate charity, it was agreed, did more harm than good.[5]

Within Ireland, philanthropy reflected religious tensions in society. While women played a key role, charitable organizations were mostly controlled by a small elite group of middle class Protestant men.[6] Moreover, as the historian Margaret Preston has suggested, Irish philanthropy, as in Britain, was permeated by notions of race, class and religion, which deemed the Irish poor to be inferior and different.[7] The draconian terms of the 1838 legislation had made it clear that the Irish poor were regarded as even less deserving than the poor in Britain.[8]

Many Victorians regarded charity as important for bringing about social amelioration.[9] Charity, however, clearly reflected existing 'hegemonic social relationships' while helping to maintain social divisions.[10] The historian Howard Wach has even suggested that charity, on both sides of the Atlantic, consolidated middle-class hegemony.[11] Ultimately, philanthropy represented another form of political brokering among the elites, while reflecting their own socio-economic needs, not those of the poor.[12] Even the admirable Society of Friends, when organizing clothing collections in 1847, drew clear distinctions between what was or was not suitable for the Irish poor to wear, one request asking for donations of clothes and bedding that were 'old', 'coarse', 'unserviceable' or condemned'. Some items of clothing were rejected as being inappropriate for poor people.[13] Starving or otherwise, social distinctions were to be maintained.

Initially, the governments of both Sir Robert Peel and Lord John Russell had responded to the widespread distress caused by the potato failures with a number of special relief measures. Tragically, they proved to be both inadequate and inappropriate. Moreover, the regulations governing official relief were strict and inflexible. In the case of food distribution and sale, the Commissariat was only allowed to deal with local Relief Committees, regardless of how inefficient or insolvent they were. The committees had been instructed not to sell food below the local market price, which placed it beyond the reach of even those employed on the public works, where wages were kept deliberately low. In a major change in direction, after August 1847, all relief was made the responsibility of an extended Poor Law.

The consequences of transitioning to different relief measures had not always been thought out in advance by the government or the Treasury. In early 1847, the public works were arbitrarily closed, even though soup kitchens had not yet been opened. It was left to private charities to provide relief in the interim. No thought had been given to the vessels in which the soup would be cooked: the Society of Friends and the Irish Relief Association intervened to provide cauldrons. The amended Poor Law of 1847 provided for the dismissal of Boards of Guardians who were judged not to be doing their duty. However, their removal added to the problems of the unions so affected, which tended to be the most impoverished ones, and the Poor Law Commissioners asked the British Relief Association if they would provide grants to assist with the change-over from elected to paid Guardians.[14] Again and again, private charity, either by its own volition or at the request of the British government, intervened to provide a vital life-line to the poor. Regardless of limitations, private charity, especially during the Famine years, proved effective in saving lives. Fewer bureaucratic checks meant that financial overheads could be kept low, while providing relief more directly and efficiently than official channels could do.

A number of relief committees were especially convened to raise funds for Ireland. The two main organizations were the Central Relief Committee and the British Association for the Relief of Distress in Ireland and the Highlands of Scotland. The Central Relief Committee was formed in Dublin by the Society of Friends in November 1846. Shortly afterwards, sister committees were formed in London and New York. The British Relief Association was formally constituted on 1 January 1847 in London, by bankers and businessmen, many of whom had no direct relationship with Ireland. In total, the Central Relief Committee raised over £200,000 worth of relief, and the British Relief Association, over £400,000. Most of their charity was distributed by volunteers.

The name of Count Strzelecki is known to scholars of the Famine. Paul de Strzelecki, a Polish explorer and Agent for the British Relief Association, worked tirelessly in Ireland for three years on behalf of the sick and starving poor, a task for which he refused to accept any payment. He was assisted by numerous English and Irish men and women who are less well known, but who contributed their time and also risked their lives. At the beginning of 1847, for example, two young noblemen, Lord Robert Clinton and Lord James Butler, offered their services free of charge to the Association. They each were put in charge of large areas in the west of Ireland where they laboured to bring food to the poor. English and Irish Quakers traversed the country to help provide relief and set up soup kitchens. All of the relief workers were assisted by members of the Royal Navy and the Coast Guard who gave their services for no payment.

The story of private charity was also a tale of heroism as these people not only worked without recompense to help the poor of Ireland, they faced considerable dangers by being in the front-line of providing relief to debilitated and diseased people. The additional tragedy of relief officials themselves being ill was lamented by Strzelecki in February 1847, he explaining 'the working out of the new relief is impeded by the number of efficient persons who are on the sick list, and on whom the duty of carrying it out devolved; so, critical as the situation of the country is at the present juncture, it may still become more critical, as the epidemic continues'.[15] In April 1847, Count Strzelecki himself fell sick. He attributed his recovery to having experienced epidemics in other countries. Others were not so fortunate; an estimated 13 members of the Society of Friends died while providing relief, while the same number of Catholic priests died in Liverpool while tending to sick famine immigrants.[16]

The agents of the various relief agencies who travelled throughout Ireland provided powerful eye-witness accounts of the chaos, the devastation, and the need of the Irish poor for external support. Their first-hand accounts provided an important counter-point to the negative commentary appearing in papers such as the *Times* and *Punch*.[17] Furthermore, their testimonies were a reminder that those who suffered were not simply statistics, but were individuals, deserving of sympathy and support. The Agent in Belmullet sent the following to the British Relief Association in London, 'to give you an idea of the progress of the Famine':

The first day I landed here I noticed a chimney sweep in the crowd, a sturdy little fellow who did not beg, but was going about with his brush in his hand seeking work. I fancy he was a stranger in the place. I often met him; he never asked me for anything. This morning I was out about half-past six, and passing down the street I saw a poor creature on the pavement, nearly naked, and moaning sadly. I stirred him up with my stick, but he could not rise, nor did I recognize him, till someone reminded me it was the poor sweep, but so altered I had not known him. Six days had done this. A little food and clothing have brought him round, and he will live if he gets food for the future; but had I not come across him, I believe he would have soon expired. There are hundreds of similar cases.[18]

More importantly, the interventions of charities did save lives, as the Poor Law Commissioners acknowledged in July 1848. The Commissioners informed the committee of the British Relief Association that without their 'munificent assistance, the new Irish Poor Law would in some Unions of Ireland have been practically a dead letter, *and thousands might have died of starvation*'.[19] In addition to his duties for the Association, Count Strzelecki introduced a scheme whereby children would be provided with clothing and food. It proved to be spectacularly successful and, unusually, popular both with the poor and with relief officials. A government official in the Tralee Union in County Kerry reported:

. . . it was a great comfort to me, after seeing the terrible destitution of the country, to witness so many little children happy and healthy amidst the dreadful desolation which surrounded them, and I sincerely wished in my heart that the subscribers to the Association Fund could witness the real good, almost unmixed with evil, it has caused . . . in those schools where I found the children at study, I found them comparatively clean, which is a great improvement in the habits of a population, and almost an education of itself – their hair was combed, and, though in rags, there was an appearance of tidiness upon them which I was surprised at.[20]

This sentiment was echoed by a Catholic priest in Skibbereen, a town which in 1847 had become synonymous with poverty and suffering, who claimed 'Since the children are fed, matters are now becoming quite cheering'.[21] Feeding the schoolchildren was widely regarded as having a beneficial influence on both the children and their families. The impact was acknowledged by the British Relief Association who reported:

It cannot but be a subject of congratulation, that, at a period when apathy and hopeless resignation to their fate seemed to be much prevailing amongst the Irish peasantry, charitable relief, which too frequently tends to foster such evils was, under this system of administration, the means of infusing a better spirit into the character of the labourer.[22]

There was considerable collaboration between charities, both in terms of sharing personnel and giving financial assistance to smaller organizations. At the beginning of 1847, for example, the Irish Relief Association, the Society of Friends and St Jude's Relief Committee in Liverpool shared a 'relief ship' that took 300 tons of corn, meal and ingredients for soup from Liverpool to the west coast of Ireland.[23] When the vessel encountered problems off the coast of Killybegs in Donegal, the British Association undertook to distribute the cargo to the ports for which it was destined.[24] This cooperation was not unusual and ensured that as little of the money raised as possible was spent on administrative or transport costs.

The British Relief Association Agent who was based in Wexford praised the work of the local Society of Friends: they, he believed, 'have the best appointed and regulated soup kitchens I have seen, issuing 600 quarts and half a pound of bread, gratis, to individuals chosen under the immediate superintendence of members of their own body'. The Friends had supplied food to the poorest regions, including the mining districts of Ballimaheen, near Kilmacthomas, 'places that, but for active and immediate help, would have equalled Skibbereen'.[25]

The various charities realized that it was not just food that the poor needed. As the Famine progressed, people required medicines, clothes, fuel and coffins – items not provided by the various relief schemes introduced by the government. Again, private charity helped. The need for clothes was particularly acute in the harsh winter of 1846 to 1847, when the primary form of relief required working out of doors, six days a week, twelve hours a day. The bad weather also hampered relief officials. Strzelecki's movements were hindered by the snow falls and frosts in February 1847, forcing him at times to complete his journey on foot. His concern, however, was for the poor, as he informed his superiors in London:

> This state of the weather is rendering the aspect of the misery of the people still more aggravating, as amongst thousands which I meet, I have not seen one who had a clothing corresponding to the bitter cold which is experienced; on the contrary, what is beheld is the emaciated, pale, shivering, and worn-out farm people wrapt in most wretched rags, standing or crawling in snow, bare-footed.[26]

The main charities were successful in attracting donations of clothing. Occasionally, the garments were not appropriate. One agent for the British Relief Association commented wryly that, 'the parcels sent by charitable persons contain the most absurd articles, ladies' old ankle boots, with fringe at the tops, old liveries, pinafores, garters, etc etc'.[27] Nonetheless, the British Relief Association's Agent in County Donegal reported that the people of Arranmore Island were 'the best clothed people I have ever met'. He attributed this to a 'liberal contribution' from the Society of Friends and the Ladies' Society of Belfast. Although clothed, the local people had no food. The island was surrounded by plentiful fish – cod, ling and turbot – but the poor had no fishing tackle, it having been pawned. The Agent provided ten shillings for the purchase of fishing tackle, which was then to be re-sold to the local people at a reduced rate.[28] His actions demonstrated how the various charities were able to intervene in practical ways.

The majority of charitable donations was raised and distributed in 1847. In that year, the overwhelming need was for immediate assistance. The two main charities also desired to provide more practical, long-term aid to the Irish poor. At the end of 1847, the Quakers used their remaining resources to provide seeds and equipment such as spades and fishing tackle to the poor. In February 1848, Strzelecki sent four bakers from Dublin to the distressed regions to teach local contractors how to bake bread. Upon doing so, he remarked, 'It is a melancholy reflection, when one reviews the obstacles which are to be met with introducing here an art which is familiar to the whole world'.[29]

The role of Charles Trevelyan, Permanent Secretary at the Treasury, remains contested and controversial.[30] That he played a pivotal role in managing the day-to-day provision of government relief is indisputable. As a civil servant, Trevelyan was able to serve under the administrations of both Peel and Russell. In August 1847, at the commencement of a third year of shortages, he decided to take a holiday, which he felt was justified, 'after two years of such continuous hard work as I have never had in my life'.[31] Trevelyan's strong work ethic was matched by his dogmatism and evangelical religious beliefs. His position at the Treasury also meant that government relief became as much an exercise in accounting as in saving lives. However, it was not just in the area of official relief that Trevelyan held sway. Despite being the public face of government relief, Trevelyan supported the intervention of private charity. When, at the end of 1846, the government was debating its role in relation to that of private charitable endeavours, Trevelyan agreed to support the latter on two conditions: first, that wealthy Irish people would lead by example, and secondly, that the Treasury should have substantial control over any monies so raised.[32] His demands were acceded to; consequently, Trevelyan's vision permeated the distribution of private as well as public relief. However, his involvement was not without criticism. Trevelyan favoured the publication both Queen's Letters in 1847, appealing for church collections on behalf of Ireland and the Highlands of Scotland. In advance of the second Letter, Trevelyan wrote to the London *Times* asking for generosity for 'the unhappy people in western districts of Ireland, who will again perish by thousands this year if they are not relieved'.[33] He also endorsed the charitable works undertaken by the Society of Friends and the London-based organization that became known as the British Relief Association.[34] Trevelyan's public interventions on behalf of the various charities drew some criticism in Britain. The *Standard* suggested that the government should shoulder full responsibility for alleviating the distress, rather than throwing it, as Trevelyan was attempting to do, on the few who were 'pious and humane . . . in order to spare the hard hearted and niggardly'.[35] The *Spectator,* in turn, accused the Treasury Secretary of being 'too close to the misery of the wretched people'.[36] Whatever Trevelyan's motivations or intentions, his actions suggest that even those closest to official relief measures understood the need for them to be augmented by private charity.

Occasionally, the giving of emergency relief through charity was disliked for having a demoralizing impact on the recipients. The *Times* was generally hostile to interventions in Ireland, whether from the government or from charities. On 12 October 1847, while applauding British people for their generosity, the paper pointed out that, 'public opinion is decidedly averse to this repeated "begging" for Ireland'. While not doubting that the distress in Ireland was genuine, it suggested that giving charity would only serve to keep Ireland in 'permanent national degradation'.[37] From the perspective of the government, there was always a concern that private charity given during the Famine would be provided too liberally and without necessary checks and balances, or that it would demoralize local relief efforts. In a few instances, these fears appeared justified. At the beginning of May 1847, Captain Loney RN, British Relief Association agent for Sligo, Leitrim and Boyle, found there was widespread reluctance to introduce a new poor rate to enable the Temporary Relief Act to become operative. In his estimation:

Two things have conspired to foster this inactivity – the continuance of the public works, and the very great facility of obtaining donations from charitable associations, on the product of which they have been subsisting

for some time past. For the Committee must know that the supplies from
the Sligo depot have been entirely gratuitous for some weeks, and are
so large as seriously to affect the merchants of this place, whose stores
are now, and have been, well stocked since the closing of the depot to
sales. I am of opinion that a less liberal system would have stimulated
the Committee to exertion, and hastened the operation of the new relief
measures, while not a single life would be sacrificed.[38]

The idea of combining charity with moral improvement was most evident
in the work of various evangelical groups, who were active in Ireland after
1845. Adopting a providentialist interpretation of the Famine, the suffering
of Irish Catholics became an opportunity to save their souls. In September
1847, one evangelical newspaper affirmed, 'it may be hoped too, that the
late, terrible calamity may awaken the Irish people to a sense of moral
degradation of the labouring poor, and greater efforts may be made to
educate and Christianize the poor, deluded Papists'.[39] A few weeks later, they
commented, 'The great evil of Ireland is Romanism – an hierarchy holding
an allegiance to a foreign prince and having no identity of interest in any
social reform or amendment in Ireland, but who are deeply interested in
perpetuating the ignorance of the Romish population everywhere'.[40]

Several of the groups associated with church missions had large funds
available and worked in some of the poorest districts in Ireland, where
they undoubtedly saved lives. Nevertheless, the taint of 'souperism', that
is providing food in exchange for conversion to Protestantism, cast a long
and dark shadow on the giving of relief by non-Catholic organizations.
Writing at the commencement of the sesquicentenary commemorations
in 1995, Dr Robert McCarthy, Rector of Galway Parish and Proctor of
Tuam, suggested, 'This is perhaps the moment to face squarely the charge of
"souperism" which is still levied against the Church of Ireland in relation to
its actions during the famine period'.[41] The work of the proselytizers divided
communities at the time of the Famine, and left a rancorous legacy that
lasted long after good harvests had returned to Ireland.

Regardless of the proselytizing activities of a number of evangelicals,
within Ireland the work of the various charities was widely praised.[42] The
work of Quakers was especially singled out. In August 1848, the *Dublin
University Magazine* applauded the Friends in general, and Jonathan Pim
in particular, for 'that high energy, those great sacrifices, and that Christian
zeal which, undaunted by the over-whelming extent of a visitation such as
the world has never seen the like of before, devoted, time, wealth, strength,
talent, everything to the preservation of our fellow beings and God's
creatures.[43] The Quakers, despite their individual exertions, believed their
involvement had only been possible due to the generosity of unknown
donors. This point was made by the Dublin committee when thanking
people in New York for their fund-raising efforts, 'Whilst we sensibly feel
the large responsibility which devolves upon us, in endeavouring, as we are

bound to do, to carry out faithfully and with due promptitude the designs of those who are thus pleased to make us the almoners of their bounty, we can gratefully appreciate the confidence of a community to whom we are comparatively unknown'.[44]

Most of the financial donations to Ireland were concentrated in the early months of 1847 in response to the second, disastrous failure of the potato crop. The contributions from the United States were particularly magnanimous and, as the Famine intensified, they became even more important. As early as 3 June 1847, the Society of Friends were admitting that donations from Ireland and Britain, while previously generous, were drying up, forcing them to rely on their American donors for support.[45] However, even as donations were flooding in from the US, the Treasurer of the Relief Committee in New York warned that the large-scale immigration of destitute poor from Ireland would reduce the amount of funds collected:

> Considering the vast amount of taxes which this City is obliged to pay for the support of foreign poor, our citizens are displaying a noble generosity on this occasion — but when it shall appear, as soon it must, that their taxes will be greatly increased this year by the increasing influx of destitute emigrants, we cannot expect that the stream of their bounty will continue to flow in this channel, great and direful as is the calamity which has called it forth.[46]

By the end of 1847, most donations to Ireland had dried up, while the various relief committees were winding up their activities. The Central Relief Committee and the British Relief Association remained active, but in a much-reduced way. It is impossible to know how much was raised. The American traveller and philanthropist, Asenath Nicholson, who distributed relief alongside other organizations at the height of the Famine, stated in her account, published in 1851, that the Quakers had received and distributed £200,000 (over half of which had been raised in the US), the British Relief Association had dispensed about £400,000, and other relief organizations, £200,000. She estimated that the amount raised by local relief committees in Ireland exceeded £300,000. In total, she believed private relief exceeded one and a half million sterling, while government relief was ten million sterling.[47] Fifty years later in 1896, William Patrick O'Brien, published his account of the Famine. He calculated that by September 1847, when the Temporary Relief Act was replaced by the Poor Law, the British government had expended £7,330,491 while private subscriptions were just below £1,500,000. The latter was an under-estimate because it did not take into account non-monetary donations, and the many contributions had not been recorded. In addition to these, donations from the United States had been estimated to be £1,107,266, of which £200,000 had come from Irish immigrants.[48] O'Brien provided an early example of giving prominence and praise to the work of the Quakers.

Regardless of the crucial role played by various charities, relatively little has been written about their involvement, with the exception of the Quakers. Yet many of the main charitable organizations left comprehensive accounts of their work and some included detailed lists of their donors.[49] These accounts provide an impressive record of world-wide generosity. They are also a testament to the professionalism and probity of the main relief organizations, and a lasting tribute to the kindness of those who gave.

The precise amount of money raised from charitable benevolence is difficult to estimate accurately, but it probably was in the region of two million pounds, constituting international philanthropy on a scale previously unknown.[50] More importantly, the money raised proved to be vital to the survival of the Irish poor, at a time when government relief was inadequate, provided with parsimony and reluctance, and constrained by views of the Irish poor as undeserving of assistance. Although it is impossible to quantify, private charity saved thousands of lives. The importance of these interventions was recognized at the time. In August 1848, the *Dublin University Magazine* averred, 'Never before had any civilized people experienced such suffering – never had there existed a feeling of universal sympathy, accompanied by exertions for their relief, on so gigantic a scale'.[51]

Even as people were still crowding into Irish workhouses, a narrative was being shaped concerning the generosity or otherwise of those who gave to Ireland. Thomas D'Arcy McGee, a member of Young Ireland who had fled to the United States in 1848 due to his political activities, wrote of the Famine in his book *A History of the Irish Settlers in North America,* published in 1852.[52] He claimed:

> The Czar, the Sultan, and the Pope, sent their roubles and their Pauls. The Pasha of Egypt, the Shah of Persia, the Emperor of China, the Rajahs of India, conspired to do for Ireland, what her so-styled rulers refused to do – to keep her young and old people living in the land.[53]

McGee's particular praise was reserved for his new home, 'America did more in this work of mercy than all the rest of the world'.[54]

McGee's claims were repeated verbatim in a book published in the United States in 1878, written by the Rev James J. Brennan entitled, *A Catechism of the History of Ireland,* in answer to the question, 'Who did send assistance to Ireland?' Brennan's Catechism provided the answer:

Recent events:
    Q: Was anything done to relief the distressed?
    A. Yes, but not by the English, 'whose ships, laden to the gun whales, sailed out of Irish ports, while the charity of the world was coming in'. In 1846 food to the value of fifteen million pounds was shipped to England, and in 1847, the 'famine year', the produce of the country

amounted to forty-four million nine hundred and fifty-eight thousand one hundred and twenty pounds, an amount sufficient to feed twice the population of Ireland.[55]

Myth has played a part in shaping how private charity has been remembered. In popular memory, the British Queen is remembered for her parsimony, and the Turkish Sultan for his thwarted generosity. A widely-held belief is that Queen Victoria only gave £5 (the so-called 'fabled fiver') for famine relief, while making a much larger donation to an animal home in England. In reality, the Queen was the largest single donor to famine relief.[56] Apart from the actual monetary amount, her contribution was important in encouraging others to give.

The origin of these myths and controversies are unclear, although they both seem to be politically motivated. In 1880, as another famine raged in Ireland, Charles Stewart Parnell, leader of the Home Rule Party, toured America. On the day of his arrival, he stated, 'In 1845, the Queen of England was the only sovereign who gave nothing out of her private purse to the starving Irish. The Czar of Russia gave, as did the Sultan of Turkey, but Queen Victoria sent nothing.'[57] Parnell's comments drew anger from across the Atlantic, notably from his political protagonist and defender of Unionism, Lord Randolph Churchill. Churchill cabled his disagreement with Parnell. The disagreement dragged on, with Parnell telling a public meeting that Churchill was wrong.[58] In 1995, when the sesquicentenary of the appearance of blight was being commemorated, these arguments about Victoria's contribution were repeated, causing heated debates in the press.[59]

The Sultan of Turkey, Abdul Medjid Khan, proved to be a generous benefactor to Ireland, giving £1,000 for famine relief. His initial offer of £10,000 had been reduced so as not to offend British royal protocol. Contemporary documents record the Sultan's donation and the response of people in Ireland. However, there is a popular myth that the Sultan, dismayed at not being able to give the higher amount of money, offered to supplement his contribution with supplies of food, an offer that the British government rejected. This decision is supposed to have forced the food-laden ships from Turkey to dock surreptitiously in Drogheda. However, the claims of a blockade in Dublin forcing ships to sail to Drogheda have not been substantiated. Nor does it accord with the fact that the British government, keen to encourage charity, had agreed to pay the freight on relief ships coming to Ireland.

The story about the Sultan being prevented from sending food-laden ships to Ireland again seems to originate with Parnell. During his American tour in 1880, when accusing Queen Victoria of doing nothing during the Famine, he referred to the British government not allowing the Sultan's ships to dock. This accusation was also immediately refuted by cable by Lord Churchill.[60] The debate about the Sultan has intruded into Irish politics in the twenty-first century.[61] When visiting Turkey in 2010, the then president of Ireland, Mary McAleese, caused controversy by claiming:

> The Sultan of the Ottoman Empire sent three ships, full of foodstuffs, to Irish ports in Drogheda. Irish people never forgot this unique generosity initiative. The symbols in the Turkish flag, the crescent and the star, have become the symbols of the region. Moreover, we see the Turkish symbols on the uniforms of the soccer team.[62]

The persistence of the myth has even inspired one Turkish film-maker to produce a fictionalized account.[63] Significantly, while early accounts of the young Sultan speak about his generosity to Ireland, there is no reference to the elusive relief ships.[64]

The myths that surround some of the charitable donations to Ireland should not be allowed to overshadow the truly magnificent contributions of people throughout the world. As the *Dublin Magazine* pointed out in 1848, it was not just the 'civilized' world that had given to Ireland:

> The Sultan of Turkey ... the people of India ... enfranchised negroes ... red men ... and even enslaved negroes ... contributed from their poverty, for the relief of those whose condition was, in this respect, one of greater distress that their own.[65]

The value of this generosity was noted by the General Relief Committee of New York City, who raised thousands of pounds in 1847, which they forwarded to the Quakers in Dublin. In their published proceedings in 1848, they seemed to be appealing to future generations so that such kindness should be remembered:

> Whether we look at the kindly instinct and Christian principle which gave it birth, or at the thousands who it saved from starvation – or the new bond of cordial friendship with which it connects us beyond the sea ... in all of these aspects, it is right that the act should be fairly represented and not lightly forgotten.[66]

The following chapters seek to provide a fair representation of the challenges facing those who came to the assistance of Ireland during the Famine. Furthermore, the generosity of these donations has to be set against a backdrop of what, in Europe, was described as the 'hungry forties' – a decade defined by unemployment, underemployment, credit crises, food shortages and revolution. Chapter 1 examines the debates that took place in the early nineteenth century regarding poverty and the responsibility for alleviating it. It also looks at the coming of the Famine and the various relief measures introduced. Chapter 2 looks at some of the earliest charitable interventions to assist the Irish poor, which took place following the first appearance of blight, in places thousands of miles from Ireland. It also explores a sometimes forgotten aspect of this benevolence, that is, how Irish people came to the assistance of their fellow country men and women.

The Society of Friends played a leading role in providing aid throughout the Famine. Their interventions were welcomed at the time and have subsequently been much praised. Their work, at the centre of an international fund-raising network, is examined in Chapter 3. Chapter 4 looks in detail at the work of their sister organization in the United States, the General Relief Committee of New York, which supplied the Dublin committee with large amounts of food and monetary assistance in 1847. It examines several of the donors and their donations in depth.

News of the suffering resulted in a number of prominent individuals making donations to Ireland, although each for different reasons. This elite group included Queen Victoria, the Sultan of Turkey and the President of the United States. Just as important as their individual donations was the encouragement their involvement gave to others. Chapter 5 examines the contribution and impact of the donations of influential members of international society and the debates and controversies that resulted from their involvement.

Chapter 6 looks at the diverse and important roles played by the Catholic Church throughout the Famine. The early intervention of Pope Pius IX and his appeal to the international Catholic community on behalf of Ireland was unusual, and it resulted in large amounts of money being collected for Ireland. The Catholic clergy played a vital, if sometimes overlooked, role in distributing this relief.

Charitable benevolence was regarded as being particularly suited to women, allowing them to be 'agents of social improvement'.[67] The multiple tasks undertaken by women are the focus of Chapter 7. Despite having no specialized training, individually and collectively, women demonstrated their abilities as fund-raisers, administrators and care-givers. Moreover, the women who actually worked with the poor not only witnessed unimaginable horrors, but they were also daily exposed to the very real dangers of disease and death. The work of women during the Famine – in Ireland, Britain, American and elsewhere – moved them from being simply agents of change to savers of lives.

Chapter 8 looks at the vital part played by the British Relief Association for the Relief of Distress in Ireland and the Highlands of Scotland in providing assistance. The Association was the largest organization involved in Famine relief, recording over 15,000 individual donations. Chapter 9 explores in greater depth the contribution to the Association made by people, many of whom had no connection with Ireland.

The United States was a major source of fund-raising. Even before the Famine, there were a number of established Irish communities throughout the country, but the donors were drawn from all sections of society. Chapter 10 explores some of the ways in which donations were raised and distributed.

It also shows how, occasionally, relief efforts became tied in with the politics of the day, in particular, the transatlantic anti-slavery campaign, the Irish Repeal movement and American electoral ambitions and disagreements.

In Victorian society, religious conversion and philanthropy were closely linked, reflecting a widely-held belief that poverty resulted from moral failure.[68] Chapter 11 deals with one of the most controversial aspects of charitable interventions: that of proselytizers who sought to convert the Irish poor. As this chapter demonstrates, the reality was far more complex than simple conversion. Proselytism was pervasive during the Famine, especially in some western districts but, for the most part, souperism was imported into these areas and not practiced by Anglican ministers who lived among the people. Moreover, the evangelical impulse to win converts was not just confined to the Church of Ireland, but evident among other, smaller Protestant denominations.

This work tells many incredible stories, but predominantly two separate, yet intertwined ones, prevail: one is concerned with suffering and one with generosity. The generosity of strangers to Ireland at the time of the Famine remains a largely untold story. With the passage of time, many who gave so much to the Irish poor have been forgotten. So, if, at times, it seems that too much detail in terms of names and places has been provided in the account that follows, this has been done in order to give a small measure of recognition to the thousands of people who contributed, some famous at the time, most of whom are forgotten today. The pages that follow only skim the surface of this remarkable story. Their involvement saved lives and deserves to be remembered. It is the story of those remarkable interventions with which this book is concerned. The chapters that follow are a testimony to those people who demonstrated the true value of the kindness of strangers.

A Note on Money, Currency Values and the Rate of Exchange:

Before 1971, British money was measured in pounds (£ or *l*), shillings (s.) and pennies (d.). The pound was divided into twenty shillings **or** 240 pennies.

'£1 in 1846 = £100 in today's terms'[69]

The rate of exchange between sterling and US dollars in 1847 (based on bills sold in February of that year) was that £100 was approximately equivalent to $469.[70]

1

'Apparitions of death and disease'.[1] Official responses to the Famine

Regardless of widespread poverty, Ireland in 1845 did not appear to be a country about to undergo a sustained and deadly subsistence crisis. While dependence on a single crop, the potato, was high, consumption of this vegetable had a number of advantages. It was prolific and extremely nutritious (especially when consumed with buttermilk), and it enabled the concurrent cultivation of grain, much of the latter being grown for export. Since 1801, Ireland had been part of the United Kingdom, with the parliament in Westminster governing the largest empire in the world at the time. The creation of the United Kingdom had signalled the end of Irish self government. At the same time, it had provided the Westminster Parliament with an opportunity to legislate on behalf of the Irish and to demonstrate the benefits of a unitary British state. In the succeeding decades, however, legislation that treated Ireland as a colony rather than as an equal partner within the Union had been passed.[2] Moreover, Catholics, the majority population in Ireland, had remained excluded from full political participation in the Westminster Parliament until the granting of Catholic Emancipation in 1829. The condition of Ireland, its people and its land, was well known to the government and administrators in London as a result of a number of detailed enquiries undertaken in the 1830s and 1840s. One investigation into Irish poverty had taken three years to complete and had led, eventually, to the establishment of a Poor Law in 1838. By 1845, therefore, the country contained a network of relief institutions and administrators. In many ways, the Irish poor were better understood and better served than the poor in many other European countries.

1741 – The Year of Slaughter

Debates on the roles of private charity and assistance to the poor had been taking place since the late eighteenth century, coinciding with rapid population growth in both Britain and Ireland. The Irish population had been growing rapidly since the mid-eighteenth century; it had more than trebled in the period between 1745 and 1845, reaching over eight million by the time of the 1841 census.[3] Ironically, both dates were framed by a famine. In 1740–41, the famine (known in Irish as *Bliain an Áir*, or the Year of Slaughter) had been caused by bad weather, a severe frost followed by drought, which had destroyed the oat and potato crops. The shortages had an immediate impact on a society that was overwhelmingly agrarian, as well as politically and socially fractured. Exact mortality levels are not known, with some estimates as high as 38 per cent.[4] Clearly, the impact of the mid-eighteenth century famine had been devastating.

Private charity was a traditional response to natural disasters. During the famine of 1740–41, the Catholic Church, which represented approximately 80 per cent of the population, was under the restrictions of the repressive Penal Laws. Instead, power lay in the hands of a small Anglican elite known as the Protestant Ascendancy. Despite being the church of a minority, the Anglican or Established Church was affluent. It made a series of interventions to help the poor, providing relief in the form of free food and fuel. Relief was particularly important in Dublin, which contained a large population of 100,000 people, many of whom were corn eaters. Hugh Boulter, Archbishop of Armagh and Primate of the Church of Ireland, fed the poor of the city at his own expense.[5] By April 1741, he was providing food for 4,400 people each day. His generosity was not unexpected as, since his appointment to this position in 1725, Boulter had intervened on a number of occasions to make cheap food available to the poor.[6] Outside the church, other individuals provided relief, one of the most elaborate schemes taking place in Celbridge, County Kildare, where the ornate Conolly Folly was built in 1740 to give employment. The structure, which was 140 feet high, had been commissioned by Katherine, the widow of William Conolly. It cost £400 to build and the workers were paid a half-penny a day.[7] The motivations for providing private charity were mixed – fear of riots, philanthropic patronage, Christian charity and the workings of a moral economy that imposed a social responsibly on the 'haves' to assist the 'have-nots' in times of distress.

Just as remarkable as the private charitable interventions was the response of Dublin Castle, the centre of British administration in Ireland. In January 1740, the Duke of Devonshire, in his capacity as Lord Lieutenant of Ireland, prohibited grain exports from Ireland to anywhere except Britain. The closing of the ports had widespread support even from merchants, who feared the alternative was rioting.[8] This type of intervention would prove to be illuminating in the light of debates concerning food imports and exports during the Great Famine, 100 years later. Even more imaginatively, the Charitable Musical Society planned to raise funds by holding a concert. Devonshire, who was in London at the time, personally sought out George Frideric Handel and invited him to Dublin to perform in the charity concert. Handel agreed, using the occasion as an opportunity to unveil his new piece, the *Messiah*.[9] Despite these impressive actions, private charity and government intervention in the 1740s' subsistence crisis remained piecemeal and uncoordinated. Moreover, despite individual measures to alleviate the suffering, the death toll proved to be high, between 300,000 and 480,000 people dying in a country with a population of approximately 2,400,000.[10]

Other food shortages followed in the late eighteenth century. There were partial crop failures in 1745, 1753, 1756, 1766, 1769, 1772, 1782 and 1795. In general, the impact of these failures was localized, with little excess mortality. An exception was 1782–83, when extremely wet weather ruined much of the grain crop. Again, private charity helped to alleviate the condition of those affected; public subscriptions were opened and the Catholic Church made a door-to-door collection.[11] The scale of the shortages, however, made government intervention necessary.[12] Regardless of protests by merchants and some politicians, in 1783, the Lord Lieutenant placed an embargo on the export of corn, potatoes, flour and associated products, from Ireland. The Corn Laws (restrictive legislation that kept the price of grain stuffs artificially high) were temporarily suspended and £100,000 was made available as a bounty to merchants who imported oats and wheat. The impact of these interventionist measures was to stabilize food prices and reduce the risk of famine. Continued bad weather in 1783 prolonged the subsistence crisis into the following year. Again, the response was prompt and, measured against relief measures in the 1840s, generous and effective. The Dublin House of Industry, which had been established by the government in 1703 to remove beggars and vagabonds from the streets, was full.[13] In 1783, it was allowed to give outdoor relief for the first time in its history, while government money was made available to feed a further 9,000 people daily. It took ten days to establish this scheme, which provided an unfavourable comparison with the lethal delays that accompanied the opening of public works in 1846 and soup kitchens in 1847. Moreover, each person was given one pound of bread, one herring and a pint of beer daily, again, the amount and quality being superior to the diet provided to the poor in the late 1840s.[14] Despite some excess mortality, overall the response of the authorities, both the Irish Parliament and Dublin Castle, to the 1782–84 food shortages proved effective and a sustained subsistence crisis did not transform into a famine.[15] Crop failures continued following the passage of the Act of Union, the most serious shortages occurring in 1817, 1822 and 1831.

Poor relief

At the time of the union, a major difference between Ireland and the rest of the United Kingdom was the lack of a national, state system of poor relief. In England, state intervention to the poor dated back to the sixteenth century.

By the early nineteenth century, two distinct Poor Laws existed in Britain, one for England and Wales and one for Scotland, both of which recognized the principle that the poor had a right to relief. In Ireland, however, no system of relief was in place, despite the repeated associations of Ireland with poverty and intermittent subsistence crises. In the early decades of the nineteenth century, a major concern of successive British governments, political economists and social commentators had been poverty and population growth. These two issues had become indelibly linked largely due to the writings of a prominent political economist, Rev Thomas Malthus (1766–1834). His *Essay on the Principle of Population* (1798) had warned of the danger of rapid population growth, especially among the poorer classes.[16] Although not initially concerned with Ireland, to many, his proposition that population increase would outstrip food production appeared a perfect fit. Malthus's credibility grew with the commencement of census-taking throughout the newly created United Kingdom – in England, Wales and Scotland in 1801, and in Ireland in 1821.

After 1800, but more especially following the final ending of the Napoleonic Wars in 1815, a key question for the enlarged Westminster Parliament became, whether a system of Poor Laws should be extended to Ireland. An imperative was provided by the fact that in the early decades of the nineteenth century, Irish population grew from approximately five-and-a-half million in 1800, to seven million in 1821 (the first decennial census) to over eight million in 1841. For those who wanted to apply a Malthusian analysis, this demographic increase was alarming. Malthus himself had warned a parliamentary committee in 1826 of the danger of Irish population increase for Britain:

> It is vain to hope for any permanent and extensive advantage from any system of emigration which does not primarily apply to Ireland, whose population, unless some other outlet is opened to them, must fill up every vacuum created in England and Scotland, and to reduce the labouring classes to a uniform state of degradation.[17]

Malthus appeared to be suggesting that the Union between Britain and Ireland had not only not raised the standard of living of the Irish, but that it was having a negative impact on living standards in Britain.

An early intervention in the debate was made in 1828, in the form of a direct appeal to the then Prime Minister, Irish-born Arthur Wellesley, better known as the Duke of Wellington, and (in British eyes) the hero of the Battle of Waterloo.[18] The appeal, signed from 'A member of a Parochial Poor Relief Committee', marshalled Malthus's arguments to show that if a scheme was not devised to assist the Irish 'helpless poor', Ireland would become even more impoverished and indigence would spread throughout the British Empire as a result of emigration.[19] Although the author believed that some government intervention was necessary, he did not accept that the British Poor Laws (Scotland was distinct from England and Wales) should be extended to Ireland. Moreover, using an argument that would be invoked 20 years later, he was critical of absentee landlords for ignoring their charitable duties while being a drain on Irish resources.[20]

The late 1820s and 1830s coincided with the debates on a Catholic Emancipation Act followed by ones on the 1832 Representation of the People Act. The passage of both pieces of legislation changed the political face of the United Kingdom, the former giving Catholics the right to sit in the Westminster Parliament, and the latter leading to a more general reform of the parliament and an extension of the franchise. One of the first significant acts passed by the reformed Westminster Parliament was the Poor Law Amendment Act of 1834, which made the existing English and Welsh Poor Laws more stringent.[21] The Act represented a major change in the provision of a welfare system that had been in place and evolving since the sixteenth century. Overall, it signalled a more authoritarian and less sympathetic approach to the giving of poor relief, while encouraging a move, as far as practicable, away from outdoor relief (generally in the recipient's home) to indoor relief in specially designated institutions.[22]

At the same time that changes were taking place in the English and Welsh systems of relief, attention was being given to the relief of poverty in Ireland. In 1833, the government appointed a Royal Commission to investigate this issue. It was chaired by the Anglican Archbishop of Dublin, Richard Whately, who was also an eminent political economist. The Commission sat for three years during which time it carried out an exhaustive and detailed enquiry. Its conclusions were that, for part of each year, two-and-a-half million Irish people lived in poverty. It suggested that a Poor Law, based on the recently amended English model, was not suited to Ireland, but that Irish poverty needed to be tackled at its roots, with an innovative programme based on public works and assisted emigration.[23] The suggestion that there should be extensive and costly government intervention in the affairs of Ireland was out of line with the prevailing attitudes regarding the relief of the poor. The response of the Whig government was to ignore the report and its findings and to send instead an English Poor Law Commissioner, George Nicholls, to Ireland. His remit was to investigate the extent of destitution (as opposed to poverty) in Ireland and to report on the suitability of extending the English Poor Law to the country. Following his short, six-week tour, Nicholls reported that 100,000 Irish people fell into the category of destitution and therefore required some form of assistance. Furthermore, and not surprisingly, Nicholls, a champion of the amended system of English poor relief, suggested that it should be extended to Ireland.[24]

The 1838 Poor Law

Nicholls's recommendations regarding the suitability of a Poor Law for Ireland were welcomed by the Whig government as they allowed it to bypass Whately's report. Consequently, on 31 July 1838, 'An Act for the more Effectual Relief of the Destitute Poor in Ireland' became law.[25] Though closely modelled on the amended English Poor Law of 1834, the Irish Poor Law contained three substantive differences. In the latter, all relief had to be provided within a workhouse, no allowance being made for outdoor assistance; there was no legal right to relief for the Irish poor; there was to be no Irish Law of Settlement (which meant that paupers in England and Wales could only obtain assistance if they had established a 'residency' in the locality). These three aspects of the Poor Law each proved problematical during the time of the Famine. There was a further subtle, but no less significant, difference in terms of language. While the 1834 English Poor Law amended laws 'relating to the poor', the Irish legislation was solely concerned with 'the destitute poor'.[26]

The Irish Poor Law was placed under the jurisdiction of the English Poor Law Commission in London, with George Nicholls being given special responsibility for it. The legislation was implemented speedily. The country was divided into 130 new administrative districts, known as Poor Law Unions, which were subdivided into electoral divisions. Each Union had its own workhouse and, architecturally, they were to be forbidding buildings. All relief was to be provided within these institutions and they acted as a physical embodiment of the intended harshness of the system. Once inside, families were separated, there being five distinct categories, each living in separate areas, men, women, boys, girls and children aged under 2 years. The daily life of the inmates, who were referred to as 'paupers', was strictly regulated and intended to be part of the deterrent system. The diet was to be monotonous and, if possible, inferior to that of the nearest prison. An extensive system of punishments existed for those who transgressed the many rules of workhouse life.[27]

While the discussions on the Poor Law had focused on the people at the bottom of the social scale, poverty in Ireland was not simply confined to the group that had been the subject of so much public discussion and debate. On the eve of the Famine, a significant number of landowners were experiencing financial difficulties and 'one owner in every twelve was insolvent'.[28] This indebtedness, together with increased fiscal burdens after 1845, hampered the ability of a number of landowners to provide relief to their tenants. Additionally, the Poor Law had introduced a new form of taxation, known as the poor rates. Poor rates were paid by both occupiers and landowners. In 1843, the rate was amended to make landowners responsible for paying the rates on small plots of land valued at less than £4.[29] This change was to have a significant impact following the introduction of the 1847 Poor Law Extension Act when responsibility for paying for all relief passed to ratepayers, this legislation proved to be an incentive to evict.

The remit of the 1838 legislation extended beyond simply providing poor relief. Significantly, each workhouse was to contain an infirmary, although it was only to be for the use of sick inmates. Prior to the Poor Law, medical charity had been voluntary. Most of the medical institutions in the country had their roots in the eighteenth century. At that stage, charitable interventions mirrored wider divisions within society. According to historian Laurence Geary, medical charities 'were imbued with a strong Anglican ethos and bias'.[30] Moreover:

> Medical charity in the eighteenth and nineteenth century were rarely, if ever, the disinterested offspring of charity or philanthropy. It would be unduly cynical to deny genuinely charitable, humanitarian, idealistic or religious motives to those who established, funded and administered medical institutions for the relief of the sick poor in Ireland and elsewhere, but it would be equally disingenuous, and evasive, to ignore the worldly considerations of self and family, commerce and society that compelled individuals to contribute their time and money to those institutions. Medical charity was both social lubricant and social obligation.[31]

Some of the attitudes that had been evident during the debates on the Poor Law underpinned a new approach to the giving of charity. Outside periods of extraordinary distress, charity to people deemed to be able bodied was frowned upon and regarded as demoralizing, while charity to the sick was regarded as more acceptable. The Act of Union had contributed to the departure of a number of nobility and gentry from Dublin, which had a significant impact on local charities. The government initially agreed to meet this deficit for a period of 20 years; a commitment which actually extended to 40 years.[32] The introduction of the Irish Poor Law contributed to a significant decline in charitable interventions as the funding of workhouse relief (and each workhouse contained an infirmary) became the responsibility of local taxpayers.

In the years following the passage of the Poor Law legislation, Ireland experienced two periods of extended food shortages, in 1839 and 1842. On both occasions, the government decided that it was beyond the capability of the workhouse system to deal with periods of extraordinary distress. Instead, extraordinary relief measures were put in place. Significantly, Nicholls had warned that a self-financing Poor Law would not be suitable to deal with a period of famine on the grounds that, 'Where the land has ceased to be reproductive, the necessary means of relief can no longer be obtained from it, and a Poor Law will no longer be operative'.[33] His advice was ignored after 1845.

By 1845, 118 of the planned 130 workhouses were providing relief. The deterrent aspect appeared to be working as they contained few inmates.[34] Overall, the Irish Poor Law and the debates that preceded it demonstrated the unsympathetic and inflexible attitude of the British government to Irish poverty.[35] Furthermore, by making the Irish legislation far more stringent than the English and Scottish Poor Laws, a point was made that Ireland may have been part of the United Kingdom, but she was not regarded as an equal partner within the Union.

The blight

Potato blight was first detected in Ireland in late August 1845. It arrived relatively late in the harvest period and its appearance was irregular, so less than 50 per cent of the crop was destroyed. The British government, under the leadership of Sir Robert Peel, responded promptly to the news and put in place a number of traditional relief measures that were to prove effective. As in 1839 and 1842, these arrangements were intended to exist side by side with the Poor Law, a distinction being drawn between ordinary and extraordinary destitution.[36] The impact of the food shortages was not expected to be felt until spring 1846, which gave Peel's government time to prepare. The relief measures were varied. A Scientific Commission was sent to Ireland to investigate the cause and remedies for the mysterious disease. Their reports demonstrated how little people, even leading scientists, understood about the nature of the blight. Some attributed its spread to atmospheric factors, while remedies for preserving the seed potatoes ranged from soaking in a saline solution to sprinkling with either sulphuric or hydrochloric acid. Nothing, however, proved efficacious.[37]

The government encouraged the formation of local relief committees to oversee the sale of food, and employment on specially constituted public works. These schemes were to be paid for by money raised through local subscriptions, the government providing a 100 per cent matching grant for all money thus raised.[38] More controversially, the government intervened in the market place and imported food from the United States to Ireland. Recognizing that such a measure would not be popular, especially with merchants, they decided to keep it a secret for as long as possible. The government enlisted the London-based company of Barings Brothers to purchase corn on their behalf. They, in turn, employed the merchant N. J. Cummins to act in Ireland. Charles Trevelyan, Permanent Secretary of the Treasury, was put in charge of overseeing the whole operation. Throughout the process, the need for secrecy was emphasized.[39]

Towards the end of 1845, reports appearing in the Irish press were copied by newspapers elsewhere, suggesting that the severity of the food shortages had been exaggerated. The *Irish Railway Gazette* of 29 November proclaimed, 'the extent of the potato failure in Ireland has been greatly exaggerated. All authentic accounts report the crop fully one-third above an average'. The paper estimated that even if one-third had been lost to blight, the amount remaining was still above average.[40] Privately, Cummins, the merchant hired to import corn to Ireland, admitted that 'Reports on the state of crop are conflicting'.[41] Nevertheless, the government used the uncertainty as an opportunity to reduce their purchase of food. Initially, they had ordered £100,000 worth of corn and grain but, in February 1846, they halved this quantity.[42] Also, it had been agreed to make these purchases overseas, but in April, the governments decided that the corn should be purchased within the United Kingdom's markets. They were advised against this action by the Barings' representative, on the grounds that prices had climbed so high and their budget was limited.[43]

A consequence of the food shortages in Ireland was that it precipitated the repeal of the Corn Laws in June 1846, which allowed a gradual reduction in the high duties on imported corn. In the short term, repeal did not ease the situation in Ireland and, in the longer term, it meant that Ireland lost her protected position within the British markets.[44] However, if the repeal of the Corn Laws brought no immediate benefit to Ireland, news of it caused excitement in America, with one paper declaring, 'if such should be its effect, the Americans will be able to contribute of their abundance to the distress of their Irish brethren without being taxed by Great Britain for the privilege'.[45] Repeal had a further consequence. This action did not have the support of many within the Tory Party and it resulted in Peel being ousted as Premier. Peel was replaced by Lord John Russell, leader of the Whig Party. Traditionally, the Whigs were viewed as being more sympathetic than the Tory Party to Irish interests. Increasingly also, while the Tory Party was regarded as the party of the landed interest, the Whigs were allying themselves with the professional and merchant middle classes. When Russell became Premier, he did so as the leader of a minority party within parliament. The majority Tory Party, however, had split into two warring factions, the Peelites and the Protectionists. Similar divisions were taking place in Irish politics. In summer 1846, the Young Ireland group formally left the Repeal Association, creating two rival nationalist groups. Moreover, the 70-year-old Daniel O'Connell was physically and mentally declining. He died in May 1847 in Genoa, far away from his beloved country. Sadly, when Ireland needed strong representation, her leaders were fighting.[46] At the same time that blight was making its second appearance in Ireland, British and Irish politics were weak and fractured.

1846

Few, if anybody, died of starvation during the first year of food shortages in Ireland. The reappearance of potato blight in the summer of 1846, earlier and in a more virulent form than in the previous year, transformed the temporary food shortages into a major subsistence crisis. The second potato blight resulted in over 90 per cent of the crop being destroyed. Apart from the magnitude of the loss, the cumulative effect of two years of shortages left the poor with few resources, either physical or material. Faced with this gloomy situation, the widespread expectation was that the new Whig government would intervene to compensate for the shortages. This hope seemed to be realized when Lord John Russell informed the House of Commons in August 1846 that he would employ the 'whole credit of the Treasury . . . to avert Famine and maintain the people of Ireland'.[47] In retrospect, it appeared a hollow promise.

Several members of the new Whig Government regarded the relief measures of the previous year as having been too generous and suggested that Irish reports of suffering had been embellished.[48] Continuity was provided in that the Treasury was to oversee the new relief measures. In effect, this meant that Charles Trevelyan, since 1840 the leading civil servant at the Treasury, was given a primary role in administering assistance to Ireland. Trevelyan allied himself with a 'moralist' circle in British politics who viewed the food shortages in providentialist terms.[49] His brusque manner, dogmatic approach and tendency to micro-manage were disliked by others involved in the relief operations, who privately coined the word 'Trevelyanisms'.[50] Nonetheless, Trevelyan had a number of powerful allies. The new Whig Chancellor of the Exchequer, Sir Charles Wood, shared Trevelyan's providentialist view of the Famine and, together, they were able to ensure a stringent and minimalist approach to the giving of relief. This parsimony worried other relief officials. At the beginning of 1847, Henry Labouchere, Chief Secretary in Dublin Castle, appealed directly to the Prime Minister, requesting him to ask Trevelyan to release more funds for Irish relief purposes.[51] Quite literally, the lives of many Irish poor had become dependent on one civil servant and the machinations of a weak government in London.

Although a number of Peel's policies were reintroduced in autumn 1846, the priorities of the new government were different. Despite the large shortfall in food production, the Whigs decided not to intervene in the market place, but to leave food supply to market forces. Even Peel's limited interventions in the previous year had angered merchants and proponents of free trade. Nonetheless, as the Irish political economist, Isaac Butt, pointed out, there were many restrictions of the importation of foodstuffs, including the remaining Corn Laws and the Navigation Acts. A sharp increase in freight charges had also added greatly to the cost of bringing food into Ireland.[52] The food depots established in the previous year were to remain open but, with few exceptions, they were to be stocked from private enterprise or charitable donations.[53] Food was to be sold via the local relief committees but, regardless of the sharp increase in prices, it was not to be sold below the local market price. Sir Randolph Routh remained in charge of the Commissariat Department, which looked after the distribution of food in these depots. Routh was Scottish, a fact disliked by some in Ireland. An editorial in the *Tuam Herald* warned, 'We don't know who this worthy knight is but it is quite clear he knows nothing about either the wants or the wishes of the Irish people'.[54]

Ireland was not the only country experiencing food shortages in the late 1840s. The potato disease had appeared in many parts of Europe, including the Highlands of Scotland, although generally in a less virulent form than in Ireland. Additionally, corn harvests were poor in 1846 and 1847, which proved to be particularly serious in countries in which bread was the staple diet of the poor. Moreover, a credit squeeze and an industrial downturn meant that the urban poor were suffering too. Many governments responded to the impending crises by intervening in the marketplace and openly purchasing food for their poor.[55] Multiple calls were made on American generosity from parts of Europe that were suffering from a combination of harvest failure and an industrial downturn. A letter from Basle in Switzerland, dated 13 April 1847, which was published in a number of American newspapers, explained that there was no grain or potatoes in the cantons. They asked that, 'the Americans who have hastened so zealously to the help of the Irish, might now think of the poor sister republic, oppressed in every possible way and send it something of their superfluity'.[56]

Public works

The Whig government decided that public works, based on hard physical labour, were to be the main means of providing relief in the second year of food shortages. There were some changes from the way in which they had operated in the previous year. Under Peel, public works had been financed from the Grand Jury 'cess' (a tax payable by occupiers); after August 1846, they became a charge on Poor Law taxation. As far as possible also, a daily rate of pay was to be replaced by piece work, that is, payment based on output. Furthermore, the authority to make decisions in regard to the workforce was removed from the local committees and given to the Treasury, in effect, to Trevelyan.[57] By October, many of the public works – the government's prime agency for providing relief – were still in the process of being established and remained untested as a form of relief. The workhouses were also starting to fill up: as early as November, for example, the Sligo Union stopped making further admissions.[58] As reports of suffering and mortality reached the Irish and British press, the reality of this ineffectiveness became more fully appreciated. These narratives of disease, dislocation and death were picked up by the international press, and they prompted a call for charitable interventions.

Although originally the public works had been intended for men, by the end of the year women were seeking employment on them. Visiting Quaker, William Bennett, observed:

> It was melancholy and degrading in the extreme to see the women and girls withdrawn from all that was decent and proper and labouring in mixed gangs on the public roads. Not only in digging with the spade, and with the pick, but in carrying loads of earth on their backs, and wheeling barrows like men, and breaking stones, are they employed. My heart often sank within me . . .[59]

Even those who gained employment found that this was not an end to their problems. In Bruff in County Limerick, following a desperate request by the local relief Committee, employment was provided for 60 women on the works. When they were paid and found that their wages did not exceed one-and-a-half pence a day, they did not return.[60] The hard physical demands made upon hungry bodies, combined with low wages and inadequate clothing, had disastrous results. Dysentery (also known as the flux or the bloody flux), resulting in severe diarrhoea, was one outcome.[61] The low wages, at a time of rising food prices, also undermined the effectiveness of public works. The Irish Relief Association reported that, 'in many instances, the supply of provisions is either wholly inadequate to the demand, or they are sold at such a price as to place it beyond the power of the people'. Additionally, 'many thousands' were too infirm to seek employment. In these cases, the Irish Relief Association stepped in to either sell food at a reduced rate or give it gratuitously.[62] Charity was propping up the official relief measures, but even this combination was not enough to save lives.

The suffering of the people in two small towns in west Cork, Skibbereen and Schull, embodied the failure of government relief. By November 1846, deaths in Schull were averaging 25 a day: by early February 1847, this had risen to 35 a day.[63] Mortality in the area was so extensive that the local Coroner was too busy to attend the inquests on death of three men from starvation. It was found that 'On the examination of the bodies, after being exhumed, there was found no trace of food in the stomach or intestines'.[64] Following a visit to Skibbereen in December 1846, a local magistrate, Nicholas Cummins of Ann Mount, Cork, felt compelled to write to the Duke of Wellington describing the condition of the people. He had been expecting to encounter 'frightful hunger', but nothing had prepared him for what he witnessed. A copy of Cummins's letter was sent to the London *Times,* which was published in the paper on Christmas Eve.[65] As a consequence of this and other appeals, the small town of Skibbereen achieved a grim notoriety for the suffering of its people. One outcome was that donations for the local poor were raised from within Ireland and further afield.

An unforeseen problem, which added to the difficulties both of the poor and the relief providers, was the weather. At the end of 1846, the winter snow hampered the movement of both government and private relief officials, while impeding the progress of those employed in the public works, many of whom were inadequately clothed. The coming of warm weather proved to be problematic also. On 25 March 1847, Strzelecki reported from Westport that:

The sudden warmth of the weather and the rays of a bright sun, accelerate prodigiously the forthcoming end of those whose constitutions are undermined by famine or sickness. Yesterday, a countrywoman, between this and the harbour (one mile distance), walking with four children, squatted against a wall on which the heat and light reflected powerfully;

some hours after, two of her children were corpses, and she and the two remaining ones taken lifeless to the barracks. Today, in Westport, similar melancholy occurrences took place.[66]

Weather continued to hinder the availability of food supply even following the harvest. A shortage of water in September 1847 meant that the mills could not work to full capacity, thus increasing the price of flour.[67]

By the end of 1846, most of the 130 workhouses were full. The 1838 legislation had deemed that when they reached their capacity, the Boards of Guardians were not permitted to give additional relief. The large number of workhouse inmates put pressure on local ratepayers, especially in areas where they were being called on to finance other forms of relief. It was not only workhouses that were unable to cope with the pressures resulting from the second failure of the potato crop. Medical institutions were finding it impossible to meet the demands placed on them as multiple diseases increased; moreover, 'The philanthropic response of most communities simply collapsed under the onslaught of sickness and disease that befell them from the winter of 1846 onwards'.[68] The impact was devastating as fever hospitals throughout the country were so deeply in debt that they were threatened with closure. And so, in desperation, they appealed to the government. The government, however, refused all applications on the grounds that they had not allocated any funding to assist hospitals or dispensaries.[69] It was a short-sighted response with lethal consequences. The spread of fever resulted in the Temporary Fever Act being amended in April 1847, taking responsibility for emergency fever hospitals from the Poor Law Guardians and giving it to relief committees that had been established by the Relief Commission. Hospitals were then able to obtain funding from a combination of voluntary subscriptions and government grants.[70]

By the end of 1846, it was clear that the public works had failed. Administrative difficulties, the high cost and the consequent neglect of the land resulted in a decision to bring the works to an end. Overall, they had proved more expensive than had been anticipated and more difficult to administer than expected. Yet, despite low pay and back-breaking labour, the provision of works had never kept up with the demand for employment. Tragically, despite the existence of public works, people were dying – in their thousands.

The inadequacy and inappropriateness of the relief measures caused dismay among some of the Irish elites. On 14 January 1847, a meeting of 'peers, members of Parliament and landed proprietors' was convened in the Rotunda Rooms in Dublin. The meeting was well attended, and included 26 Irish Members of Parliament, they representing the main political parties. Regardless of political differences, a number of resolutions were agreed. The representatives were deeply critical of the policies of the British government, including the fact that massive amounts of food were being exported from the country.[71] In the preceding months, the corporations of Dublin, Belfast,

Cork and Derry, among others, had been requesting that the ports be closed, and thus available food be kept in the country. This demand had been ignored. Instead, vast amounts of foodstuffs had continued to leave Ireland, while the cost of food imported had been kept artificially high.[72] The committee's resolutions, which were embodied in a Memorial to the government, included:

> 5. That we recommend that Relief Committees should be allowed to sell food under first cost to the destitute, in their respective neighbourhoods, and that their doing so should not disentitle them to Government contributions in aid of their funds.
> 6. That while we affirm, that it is the clear and paramount duty of the State to take care that provision be made for the destitute, we regret that the means hitherto adopted for that purpose have, on the one hand, proved incommensurate with the evil, and on the other hand, have induced the expenditure of vast sums of money upon useless or pernicious works.

The meeting concluded by agreeing that the Famine was an Imperial disaster and therefore should be met from the resources of the Empire.[73]

As official relief floundered, it was increasingly obvious that private charity was providing a safety net when government relief failed. On 17 January 1847, the resources of the Rev Crosthwaite from Durrus Glebe in Bantry were stretched even more than usual as 400 men in the parish who were employed on the public works had not been paid for four weeks, due to an administrative oversight by one of the officers of the Board of Works.[74] The local workhouse was full and taking no more admissions. Crosthwaite had fed as many of them as he could and believed his interventions, only possible due to money sent from England, had saved them from death.[75] This was not the only inefficiency associated with the local public works. In his capacity as chairperson of the Relief Committee, Crosthwaite had provided the Engineer with a list of 700 men to be employed on two roads. When the Engineer eventually processed the list, Crosthwaite realized that the Engineer had engaged all on the same road, which was ten miles from where many of the poor lived. The appeal of the Relief Committee to change this was ignored and so, in the words of the minister, 'The poor creatures have still the alternative of walking ten Irish miles every morning, or else lie down and die'.[76] Crosthwaite predicted that the public works would soon close.[77] He was correct.

At the beginning of 1847, the British government announced that the public works were to be brought to an end. Instead, a series of relief measures were to be introduced that would lead to the Poor Law becoming responsible for both permanent and temporary relief. In the interim period, government soup kitchens would be opened. At the same time, other measures were to be implemented, that would facilitate cheap food becoming available: there was to be a complete remission of corn duty; the Navigation Laws would be suspended; and sugar duties would be reduced. The government continued to refuse to import foodstuffs itself, however, which was in marked contrast to the action of other governments in Europe, who were facing shortages due to a poor grain harvest. The French government, for example, reduced duties on grain and flour, and imported 100,000 barrels of flour, in order to stabilize food prices.[78]

The closure of public works was announced in January 1847. They were to be replaced, in the short term, by soup kitchens. In the longer term, the Poor Law was to be amended and made responsible for all relief. Yet, even after the decision was made, the numbers continued to increase, from approximately 570,000 when the announcement was made, to 734,000 by March. Taking into account families who relied on having a member employed on the works, this figure meant that in the region of 3,000,000 people depended on them. The public works, inadequate though they were, together with private charity, had provided a tenuous lifeline to millions of people during the winter of 1846–47. The Treasury, anxious to bring this expensive and cumbersome relief project to an end, announced on the 10 March that, on 20 March, there was to be a minimum 20 per cent reduction in people employed, to be swiftly followed by further reductions. This direct intervention by the Treasury, in which they effectively bypassed the Board of Works, was prompted by their belief that: 'All effectual control in the increase in the number of persons employed, and over the manner in which the work is executed in them, has, for the present, been lost'.[79]

Moreover, further justifications were that the relief works were keeping people away from their normal agricultural pursuits and encouraging them to be 'idle', by allowing them to earn an income in return for very little labour.[80] This abstract rationale for closing the public works paid no account of the dozens of letters received by the Board of Public Works in the early months of 1847, and forwarded to the Treasury, outlining the starving condition of the people, even of those employed on the works. Instead, policy was based on a perception of Ireland and the Irish poor that prevailed in the corridors of Whitehall and Westminster, and in the columns of the *Times*, but bore no relation to the eyewitness testimony of officials working in Ireland.

The closure of the public works at a time when many soup kitchens remained inoperative meant that there was a hiatus in the provision of government relief. The Grand Jury in County Kerry described the Treasury's decision as equivalent to signing a 'death warrant' on the poor of Ireland.[81] This sentiment was echoed by the *Nation* newspaper, which condemned the arbitrary lay-offs, predicting the outcome would be even more 'death from starvation', while condemning the British government's 'utter apathy to the tremendous responsibility with which they are trifling'.[82] In the absence of government relief, it was left to private resources to fill the starvation gap. For Count Strzelecki of the British Relief Association, the impact of the closure was to increase demands made on charitable resources. Throughout April, he doubled the grants that he was making available to local Poor Law officials.[83] In the absence of government relief, private charity was the only buffer between life and death.

The government directed that, on 20 March 1847, 20 per cent of the people employed on the works were to be struck off, and that further reductions should be made as the soup kitchens opened. Again, private charity acted as a safety net. The committee of the British Association asked their agents to pay special attention to areas where the relief works had started to close and to extend their activities and provide additional relief if necessary.[84] In these and other ways, even where government relief was being provided, it often was being propped up by the intervention of private charity. Despite various official relief measures and thousands of pounds of private charity, the suffering and starvation of the poor continued in the summer of 1847. An American philanthropist and abolitionist who was travelling through Connaught was disturbed by what she witnessed, writing, 'I could scarcely believe that these creatures were my fellow-beings. Never had I seen slaves so degraded'.[85]

The Temporary Relief Act, popularly referred to as the Soup Kitchen Act, provided for the establishment of soup kitchens and the distribution of food to the poor. Only cooked food could be provided, and each person requiring it had to attend the place of distribution in person. For logistical and financial reasons, the food was often soup. The British government employed the services of a French chef, Alexis de Soyer, to visit Dublin and create a soup recipe and soup kitchens, to help feed the poor. On 5 April 1847, Soyer's 'model' soup kitchen was opened in Dublin, amidst great fanfare. The Lord Lieutenant, the Lord Mayor of Dublin and hundreds of other dignitaries attended, as did members of the British and Irish press. They were all invited to sample the soup. Not surprisingly perhaps, they pronounced it to be 'delicious'.[86]

Soyer had devised a number of different recipes – copies of which appeared in several Irish newspapers. They included a number of meatless recipes. Soyer believed that the farinose content would be good for people who had not eaten for a while, and that a fish-based recipe was appropriate for people who lived on the coast.[87] Sadly, he appeared unaware that many fishermen had pawned their equipment in the first year of shortages and little fish was available to the poor during the years of shortages. The Temporary Relief Act faced other problems. The British Relief agent in the south-east warned at the beginning of May that the poor in Arklow, 'do not look so well as they did when I was here last; many of the old people as well as the young are dropping off; they have generally a paler and more sunken appearance, and more cases of swollen ankles'.[88] The Nation denounced the recipes as 'soup-quackery', which had been 'taken by the rich as a salve for their consciences'. Perhaps more damningly, Soyer's recipes were criticized in the medical journal, The Lancet. The Lancet estimated that the amount of soup being provided by Soyer's recommendations was less than one-quarter of the required daily amount.[89] In the House of Commons also, Lord George Bentinck queried the sufficiency of food being provided in the government's soup kitchens. He was answered:

> A ration was to consist either of 1½ lb. of bread (the newspapers stated it at ½ lb. so that there was a material difference), or 1 lb. of biscuit, or 1 lb. of meal or flour, or any other grain, or one quart of soup thickened with a portion of meal, according to any known receipts, and one-quarter ration of bread, or biscuit, or meal, in addition. He hoped the noble Lord would agree with him in thinking that this allowance of food was sufficient.[90]

Like other relief measures, the Temporary Relief Act was highly bureaucratic, which was justified on the grounds of reducing opportunities for fraud. It utilized the administrative structure of the Poor Law, with each electoral division appointing a Relief Committee, which was charged with drawing up lists of people requiring relief. The lists were then scrutinized by Inspecting Officers appointed by the Relief Commissioners. A Finance Committee oversaw the expenditure within the Union. In early May 1847, as the relief was changing from the public works to the government soup kitchens, the Dublin Quakers pessimistically predicted:

> From the present aspect of things around us, we cannot venture to antici- pate an early termination or even diminution of our labours, but must rather contemplate increasing claims for help for several months to come, in consequence of the continued impoverishment of those classes border- ing on the wholly destitute, whose means of support are abridged by the failure of employment, arising from the non-consumption to so large an extent of the ordinary products of their industry.[91]

By July, the Temporary Relief Act was operational in 1,800 electoral divi- sions and over 3,000,000 people were receiving free daily rations of food. As the soup kitchens spread, the British Relief Association reduced its involvement, on the grounds that no further private assistance was neces- sary.[92] Regardless of initial problems with the transition to government soup kitchens, by early July, three million people, who represented approx- imately 40 per cent of the Irish population, were dependent on this relief. Yet charity was still providing some support, Joseph Bewley and Jonathan Pim, the secretaries of the Friends' Relief Committee in Dublin, explaining to one of their American benefactors:

> Not-withstanding the enormous supply of gratuitous food, we are still daily receiving from various parts of the country appeals for help, no less touching and ardent, and but a little less urgent than at any period during the last six months.[93]

The Friends pointed out it was not simply from the poorest members of society who were requesting aid, but:

> The solicitations for help are chiefly on behalf of those who in ordinary times have been far removed from want; small farmers, decent tradesmen and others, who are not quite arrived at the point of complete destitution entitling them to be placed on the public relief lists, or who would shrink from the exposure of their necessities, inseparable from a system of legislative relief.
>
> The case of the small farmers commends itself especially to our care; hard-working, industrious men, with families, possessing perhaps four or five acres of ground, which they have with great difficulty managed to sow with grain or green crops, and in so doing exhausted all their little resources. They are generally refused public assistance, as not completely destitute; but the alternative of selling their farms at a ruinous price is such as not to be resorted to but in the very last extremity, and hence they are willing rather to struggle with starvation for the few months which may elapse ere they can reap the fruit of their labours.[94]

The observations of Bewley and Pim provide an insight into a group that was often beyond the reach of official relief measures, that is, small farmers whose livelihood had also been taken from them. Not entitled to government relief, they turned to private charity in order to survive. Tellingly, the two Quakers explained they considered it a 'privilege' to be able to help such people.[95]

As food prices rose, supplies became increasingly out of the reach of the poor. In some cases, the hunger of the people made them desperate and willing to steal. The British Relief Association agent in Belmullet, County Mayo, reported in April 1847 about meal being shipped there, 'Not a bag can come ashore unattended by an armed guard; and, at one time, the people had nearly overpowered the soldiers, who were unwilling to be harsh with such diseased and famished assailants'.[96] It was not only food prices that increased. Freight charges on food imported into the country had more than tripled throughout 1846. In March 1847, the boat-owners on the Royal Canal between Dublin and Longford raised their freights from 11s.8d, to 17s. a ton, a circumstance that inflated the cost of foodstuffs being brought into the country.[97]

A further problem with the way in which relief was provided was that the various types of relief required the expenditure of a large number of calories. The poor had to walk great distances in order to avail themselves of the relief – to the public works, to the soup kitchens, to the workhouses and to emigration depots. Writing some years later, Octave Thanet observed:[98]

> In all the letters and reports of the time distances are mentioned. Always the people are walking from remote homes to the works or the village

or the soup kitchen. Miles on miles, thousands of miles, must have been traversed in torment that winter. To me, there is nothing ghastlier in all the famine than this vision of incessant motion; of a squalid procession whose life is dribbling away with every step . . . The skeletons crawled along the street and sometimes dropped dead on their way to the soup kitchen.[99]

Throughout the winter of 1846–47, newspapers in America were carrying weekly reports of the suffering in Ireland, many of which made gruelling reading. One from County Mayo stated:

Men are not infrequently, it is stated, found dead in the ditches by the wayside. Some are so changed by want as not to be recognizable by their friends – their looks wolfish and glaring as madmen; without clothes or food of any kind, they roam around in search of food until death seals their misery.[100]

In March 1847, reports of suffering in Ireland in American papers appeared next to an account of the annual revenues of Great Britain which was 'in the highest degree satisfactory', with income exceeding expenditure by almost three million pounds.[101] To counter accusations of exaggeration that appeared in sections of the British press, eyewitness testimonies proved invaluable. Elihu Burritt, an American philanthropist, pacifist and abolitionist, who was travelling by foot in the south-west of Ireland, sent reports to the American press of what he described as 'apparitions of death and disease'. He concluded, 'Were it were not for giving them pain, I should have been glad if the well-dressed children of America could have entered these hovels with us, and looked upon the young children wasting away unmurmuringly, by slow, consuming destitution'.[102] In 1847, Burritt published his experiences in *A journal of a visit of three days to Skibbereen, and its neighbourhood*, with the view of bringing the awfulness of the suffering to a wider audience.[103]

For some individuals, however, as food became scarcer and more expensive, opportunities for making profit became apparent. The American Consul in Belfast, Thomas Gilpin, believed that the Famine, together with the repeal of restrictive import legislation, provided opportunities for American shippers. At the beginning of 1847 he observed that while no American ships had visited Belfast between May 1843 and June 1846, by the beginning of 1847, 14 had landed with full cargoes.[104] One American individual who sought to benefit personally was Robert Loughead, the Consul in Derry. This Consulate had opened in 1830 and Loughead's appointment lasted from October 1845 to April 1854, after which he was moved to Dublin where he remained until his death in 1855.[105] Because remuneration for holding this position was low, the person appointed required private income.[106] Following the second failure of the potato crop, while reporting about the mortality around him, Loughead was simultaneously urging his son, a merchant seaman, Capt. James A. Loughead, to send supplies of foodstuffs to him from the US, pointing out:

> [T]here is a chance now of Making Money. [P]urchase immediately on receipt of this **Letter** . . . for there is nothing here but starvation. Dozens dying a day with hunger; let it be sent by Glasgow, Sligo, Belfast, Liverpool, but to Londonderry if possible.

In a postscript, Loughead demanded that the letter be kept a secret, except to those immediately involved. Only a few months later, as food prices dropped, Loughead wrote to his son lamenting that they opportunity for profit had passed.[107] The American Consul played a dual role. While privately urging his son to send supplies to be sold for personal profit, Loughead was acting publicly as a conduit for distributing charity to the local poor, sent from America.[108]

Despite the palpable evidence of widespread deaths by the beginning of 1847, no attempt was made to keep official records of mortality. This omission was challenged by a number of diverse people. In parliament, George Bentinck and Benjamin Disraeli, leaders of the 'Protectionist Party', who had split from Peel over the repeal of the Corn Laws, repeatedly requested that records be produced. Russell's explanation for refusing was that, 'In Dublin, especially, there had never been known a pressure of business so severe as that which now unhappily prevailed in the offices connected with the Government'. To this, Bentinck's ally, Benjamin Disraeli, responded:

> The remark made by the noble Lord on the state of the public service might be very just; but he could not help saying, that if returns were moved for the quantities of pigs and poultry consumed within a given time, there would not be the least objection raised to any such return. Now there was, however, a remarkable and unprecedented mortality afflicting the sister kingdom, and the difficulties placed in the way of obtaining an exact statement of the deaths appeared to be insuperable.[109]

Less publicly, but just as powerfully, the writer, Maria Edgeworth, who was actively involved in providing relief in her locality, was concerned that Irish MPs were not providing leadership on this matter:

> Mr. Tuite, who was here yesterday, told us that in the House of Commons the contradictory statements of the Irish members astonished and grieved him, as he knew the bad effect it would have in diminishing their credit with the English. Two hundred and fifty thousand is the report of the Police up to April.[110]

Throughout the summer of 1847, there were reports that abundant crop yields were expected in Ireland, especially of potatoes and corn.[111] In July

1847, some newspapers were including positive reports concerning the approaching harvest. Although only one-sixth of the usual area was under potato cultivation, the remainder was planted under green crops, while the corn crops were more abundant than ever before. This gave hope that following harvest, there would be enough food to feed all those who survived until that time.[112]

A General Election was held in the United Kingdom in August 1847. It was called a year before the official dissolution of parliament. The Conservative Party, still split between Protectionists and Peelites, won a majority of seats, although it was 42 fewer seats than in the previous election. The Whigs increased their support, but they were still almost 30 seats behind the Conservative Party.[113] The Repeal Party gained 16 seats, giving it a total of 36. The increase largely reflected a tribute to the recently dead Daniel O'Connell. Young Ireland had also campaigned in the election, they being more overtly critical of the Whig government's relief policies than their former repeal colleagues.[114] Overall, the outcome meant that the Whigs remained in power, Russell again leading a minority government that depended on support from Peel and his followers. At a time when strong government was needed, British politics were still suffering the fallout of having a deeply divided Conservative Party, while in Ireland, the death of O'Connell had consolidated the discord between Young Ireland and Old Ireland.

The Poor Law Extension Act, 1847

In August 1847, the British government announced that the Irish Famine was over and declared that if any more relief was required it had to come from Irish, not British – or even Imperial – taxation. This changeover was facilitated by the introduction of the Poor Law Extension Acts, under which both permanent and extraordinary relief were to be consolidated. The Acts provided for outdoor relief to be provided to reflect this extended role.[115] Manifestly, the Famine was not over: in 1848, over one million people were still dependent on a minimal form of poor relief for survival. This announcement by the government, however, effectively marked the end of most of the fund-raising activities that had taken place throughout the world in the previous 12 months.

The change to the Poor Law meant that the responsibility for financing relief was to be borne by local ratepayers. In some of the poorest unions, this placed a heavy burden on people whose resources were much diminished. In recognition of this difficulty, the 22 poorest unions were officially designated 'distressed' and were to be offered minimal support. One of the most controversial aspects of the new legislation was the 'Quarter-Acre Clause', which deemed that anybody who occupied more than this quantity of land was not eligible to receive relief.[116] Smallholders who had held on to their land during the previous two years of shortages, were now forced to give it up if they wanted Poor Law relief – the only form of assistance which was now available from the government. Lord Palmerston, an Irish landowner and a member of the government, explained the motivation for such harsh requirements:

> It is useless to describe the truth that any great improvement in the social system in Ireland must be founded on an extensive change in the present state of agrarian occupation, and that this change implies a long, continued and systematic ejectment of small holders and squatting cottiers.[117]

The fact that the new relief measures had a secondary purpose of bringing about social change was recognized at the time:

> In addition to this temporary relief there enters into the government scheme a plan for permanently changing the social condition of Ireland. It is proposed to create a class of small landed proprietors constituting a middle class in society, heretofore unknown in that country; and which, if it can be affected, will do much toward both a moral improvement and an amelioration of the physical condition of the people.[118]

The new system was responsible not only for the poor, but for the sick poor. From 1 October 1847, emergency fever hospitals and dispensaries, which had been established under the Central Board of Health and financed by the Relief Commission, were now to be funded from the poor rates. Thus, despite the pressures caused by the Famine, the Poor Law was made fully responsible not only for the poor but also for the sick poor, and for both permanent and temporary relief to both categories of persons. Again, it seemed that the Union between Britain and Ireland was one in name only as the government abnegated responsibility of the most vulnerable in society. The Poor Commissioners apprehensively appealed to the Irish guardians to ensure that sick fever patients, who numbered about 13,000 at the time of the change, should be adequately cared for.[119] Unfortunately, 'The directives and ordinances of the Central Board of Health were probably breached more often than observed'.[120] Again, an inappropriate policy meant that those who were already suffering suffered even further.

At the end of 1847, although provisions were more plentiful than they had been in the preceding year, the people were without the means to purchase them. Perhaps, even more worryingly, the change to Poor Law relief had also left the poor vulnerable, the Quakers noting, 'in many districts the provisions of the poor law, under which all destitute persons are entitled to maintenance, are very imperfectly carried out'.[121] One visitor to Ireland observed the changes in Irish workhouses:

> Before the Famine they were many of them quite interesting objects for a stranger to visit, generally kept clean, not crowded and the food

sufficient. But when the famine advanced, when funds decreased, when the doors were besieged by imploring applicants, who wanted a place to die so that they might be buried in a coffin, they were little else than charnel houses, while the living, shivering skeletons that squatted upon the floors, or stood with arms folded against the wall, half-clad, with hair uncombed, hands and face unwashed, added a horror if not a terror to the sight.[122]

The Quakers were aware that the transition to a different form of relief had caused many difficulties and that there were various groups, including small farmers, who fell outside the remit of the new system. They warned:

It is obvious, therefore, that there is a wide field before us for the exercise of benevolence, and that a long time must elapse, before the traces of famine can be expected to disappear. A brief outline of our accounts furnished to thy respected predecessor, about a month since, would inform you of the probable balance that is at our disposal.[123]

James Hack Tuke, a Quaker from Yorkshire who had first travelled to Erris in County Mayo at the end of 1846, returned in the autumn of 1847. His detailed account of what he witnessed was harrowing. He observed:

Ten thousand people within forty-eight hours journey of the metropolis of the world, living, or rather starving, upon turnip-tops, sand-eels, and sea-weed; a diet which no one in England would consider fit for the meanest animal he keeps.[124]

The introduction of the amended Poor Law in 1847 forced various charities to review their position, although for the most part, their money had already been spent.

The changeover to Poor Law relief in the autumn of 1847 meant that the services of the British Relief Association were again called on, on the grounds that, 'the transition from the one system to the other, it was obvious, would be attended with considerable difficulty, out of which much additional pressure of a temporary character might probably arise'.[125] Again, private charity was called on to provide essential relief when the government was failing to do so.

The beginning of 1848 brought no relief from suffering, with a higher number of applications for Poor Law relief occurring in February than in January. The geographical impact of the distress was changing, with it becoming mostly confined to the unions of Kilrush, Ennistymon, Ballina, Belmullet, Castlebar, Ballinrobe, Westport and Clifden. The distress was exacerbated by the spread of typhus fever and by the inclement weather. In 1848, Strzelecki reported that the condition of the poor in parts of Connaught and Munster was worse than in the previous two years.[126] Strzelecki estimated that, by this stage, 99,000 holders of land had been evicted and were homeless. Many did not want to take shelter in the workhouse due to 'domestic separation', that is the separation of families; therefore, they took outdoor relief, even though they had no home. He was aware of the suffering that had accompanied the evictions, but hoped that the consolidation of property would ultimately benefit Ireland.[127] Yet his despair was palpable. In March 1848, the usually moderate Strzelecki reported that, 'The Inspectors of Ballina and Belmullet write to me that, notwithstanding all their efforts, this district is a disgrace to any civilized country'.[128]

Most of the burden for financing both the Temporary Relief Act and the amended Poor Law fell on owners of land, especially those estates contained many small occupiers. For some officials in London, Irish landowners were just as much a barrier to economic progress as potato growers at the other end of the social scale and similarly undeserving of sympathy.[129] The Quakers believed that the large number of absentee landlords in many of the poorest districts contributed to the difficulties of providing both government and private relief. In contrast, several agents of the British Relief Association complained that the people who were resident and sat on the Relief Committees were inefficient and often hampered the distribution of relief. Matthew Higgins, the agent in Belmullet, reported, 'the men we have to work the committee there are so ignorant, so dishonest, and so quarrelsome'.[130] Apart from demands on their time, from 1845 heavy financial burdens were being placed on Irish landowners, whatever their income level. In 1848 and 1849, the Encumbered Estates Acts were passed, which forced landowners who were in debt and unable to meet their financial obligations to sell their properties.[131]

Blight reappeared on the potato crop of 1848, although other foodstuffs were healthy. A fourth year of shortages, combined with widespread disease and extensive homelessness, kept pressure on the strained resources of the Poor Law. Unlike two years earlier, however, there was little charitable money to prop up the government's relief measures. On 1 September 1848, Lord John Russell and his family visited Dublin. To readers of the *Nation*, he was the English Prime Minister who had introduced four coercion bills to Ireland in a period of nine months.[132] He was also the Prime Minister who was presiding over the most devastating famine in the modern era. According to the historian Donal Kerr, the nine months that followed the Whigs' coming to power in June 1846 witnessed the highest level of excess mortality ever known within Ireland.[133]

In 1849, the distress in some of the unions in Connaught and Munster was even more severe than in 1847. The suffering was exacerbated by homelessness. Even readers of the hard-hearted *Times* were kept informed of the continuing misery:

> While hundreds of thousands were deprived of food and health by the failure of the potato crop, about 90,000 holders of land had lost their hearths by evictions and voluntary surrender and become houseless, some

taking refuge in the workhouses others took outdoor relief – in a state of emancipation, sickness and nudity hardly credible.[134]

Newspapers in America were also reporting the dismal scenes in Ireland:

Horrors accumulate in the West. Famine and disease are sweeping away the people in myriads. The Protestant clergy, joined by the Roman Catholic, implore aid for their miserable flocks; the gentry and middle classes are fast sinking to the lowest level; some affluent people hear the appeals on behalf of the utterly destitute, but their donations are instantly swallowed up, while the cries continue for 'more', 'more', and death seems the only certain means of relief.[135]

In February 1849, the government made a small grant of £50,000 to assist the poorest unions in Ireland. They simultaneously made it clear that no more public money would be forthcoming. Ireland's responsibility for financing the relief was consolidated shortly afterwards with the introduction of the Rate in Aid tax, which levied an additional rate on all Poor Law unions, for redistribution to the poorest ones. It was unpopular both with those having to pay the new tax and with distributors of relief. For Edward Twistleton, the Poor Law Commissioner for Ireland, it was a final straw, leading to his resignation, he explaining he could not implement the legislation, 'with honour'.[136] In June 1849, as distress showed no signs of abating, members of Parliament and the Queen raised a private subscription, which was entrusted to Count Strzelecki. In that month, there were 200,000 inmates in the workhouses, 770,000 people were receiving outdoor relief and 25,000 were in hospital. Strzelecki, who revisited the western districts, reported that those on outdoor relief were, 'in a state of emaciation, sickness and nudity hardly credible, crowding together and crouching under heaps of rotten straw of their unroofed cabins, under bridges, burrowing on the roadside, or in the ditches of the cold and wet bogs'.[137] In 1849, the prisons were overcrowded, leading to legislation allowing the prison dietary to be reduced. The rationale was that prisons had superior diets to local workhouses leading people to commit crimes in order to avail themselves of the superior quantities of food.[138]

Although the main charitable bodies had ceased their involvement in late 1847 or in 1848, instances of private charity were still taking place in some areas. In October 1848, the non-commissioned officers and privates of the 6th Royals, stationed in Nenagh, were distributing 'in charity a large quantity of soup and bread daily to about forty poor creatures'.[139] These individual acts of generosity provided a small glimmer of hope in a dark cavern of misery and hopelessness.

It was not until 1852 that the blight fully disappeared from Ireland. By this time, the population had fallen by over 25 per cent. The impact of seven years of food shortages continued to resonate for far longer, however.

Even after good harvests had returned to the country, the Irish population continued to fall. In 1841, the population of Ireland had been in excess of eight million people; by 1901 it had fallen to just over four million. What made the tragedy more extraordinary was the fact that, since 1800, Ireland had been part of the United Kingdom, which was at the centre of the vast, powerful and resource-rich British Empire. Unfortunately, the resources of that Empire had not been deployed to mitigate the sufferings of the poor in Ireland. Thankfully though, as the following chapters demonstrate, thousands of people, many of whom had no direct connection with Ireland, had come to the rescue of the starving poor. The story of charitable interventions during the Famine is remarkable not only in terms of its generosity, but also in terms of its impact. Without this intervention, the death toll in Ireland would have been far higher during those tragic years.

2

'Some great and terrible calamity'.[1] Relief efforts from near and afar

The news that a potato blight had appeared in Ireland in 1845 prompted the formation of fund-raising committees in two distant and distinct locations: Calcutta in India and Boston in the US. Reports that blight had attacked the Irish potato crop reached India in November 1845, although details about the extent of the loss were vague.[2] Follow-up accounts in the local newspapers suggested (incorrectly) that over two-thirds of the crop had been destroyed. These accounts prompted English-born residents to organize a fund-raising committee.[3] In Boston, relief efforts became tied up with demands for political independence, a committee being formed at the initiative of the local Repeal Association. The Boston Repealers were led by American-born John W. James.[4] The food shortages in Ireland were cited as the most recent example of British misrule. At a meeting in early December, at which $750 was collected, one speaker claimed that due to 'the fatal connection of Ireland with England, the rich grain harvests of the former country are carried off to pay an absentee government and an absentee propriety'.[5] The fund-raising efforts were short lived, however, drying up at the beginning of 1846 when it was suspected that reports of the distress had been exaggerated.[6]

India

In December 1845, newspapers in Calcutta recorded that 'some gentlemen at the head of the community have formed a provisional committee for the relief of the distressed Irish to act until a public meeting could be called'.[7] In Calcutta, the founders of the relief committee were motivated by reasons that were very different from those in Boston, the predominant one being the desire to assist their fellow subjects 'at home'. Thus, Irish unity with Britain and the wider Empire, rather than separation from it, was the main impetus behind these fund-raising efforts. The organization of the Indian relief effort was modelled on a similar action that had taken place there in 1822, when Ireland had been experiencing severe food shortages. At that time, 'a very large sum was realized by public subscriptions'.[8] An estimated £37,000 had been sent to the western counties of Ireland from Calcutta, Bombay and Madras.[9] In 1845, the expectation was that, as had been the case in 1822, the impact of the crop failure would not last for more than one season.

On 29 December 1845, a public meeting was held in the Town Hall in Calcutta and a Provisional Committee was appointed. An appeal was made to 'British Residents and other inhabitants of this country to . . . follow a noble example, afforded here on a former and like melancholy occasion, in 1822, by subscribing liberally to supply the wants of our Irish fellow subjects'.[10] The newspaper, the *Bengal Hurkaru,* which in the previous few years had reported extensively on the activities of both Daniel O'Connell and the Orange Order, saw some good in the potato failure, suggesting that it had taken 'some great and terrible calamity' to bring Irish people together. A further outcome, they believed, would be to bring Ireland more closely into the Imperial family.[11]

Within days of being established, the Committee published the 'Provisional Resolutions by the Committee':

1 That subscriptions be solicited generally from all classes of society throughout the Presidency of Bengal.

2 That the proceedings be communicated by the committee to all the civil and military stations, and that the smallest donations be gratefully received.

3 That several houses of Agency and the Union Bank be requested to receive the contributions.

4 That the proceedings in general be inserted in all the Calcutta papers and that lists of contributions be also published from time to time.

5 That a meeting of the inhabitants of Calcutta at the Town Hall be called at the earliest possible day for which due notice can be given for the purposes of giving fuller efficiency to the wishes of the subscribers here and arranging for the careful administration of the funds at home.

The Calcutta Committee, which was headed by Sir Lawrence Peel, an English judge, and Sir James Grant, an English Civil Servant, demonstrated that the fund-raising activities were not confined to people of Irish extraction. Peel, a former British MP and relative of the British Prime Minister Sir Robert Peel, had been in India since 1840. During his 15-year stay, he would donate all of his official income of £8,000 a year to public charities.[12] An Irish member of the committee was William O'Shaughnessy, Esq., a medical doctor with the

East India Company who had been born in Limerick.[13] Although a number of Indians gave their support to the Calcutta Committee, membership was limited to British and Irish settlers.[14]

From the outset, the Committee made it clear that even the smallest donations would be welcome. They appealed to other Europeans and to the 'native community' to become involved in their philanthropic activities.[15] A direct request was made to Sir Hugh Gough, a high-ranking, Irish-born officer in the British Army, to support to the Committee. At this stage, approximately 40 per cent of the British army serving in India was Irish-born and they were regarded as a valuable source of potential funds. Irish soldiers were also at the forefront of some of the fiercest battles taking place in India. The onset of famine in Ireland coincided with the Anglo-Sikh War. Irish losses were particularly severe at the Battle of Sutledge at the beginning of 1846. This conflict had been under the command of Generals Gough and Henry Hardinge, the latter being an English military Commander and Governor General of India. In a number of Catholic churches in Calcutta, prayers were said for the slain Irish soldiers. The congregations were reminded of the generosity of Irish soldiers to their families at home and that, without this resource, 'hundreds of poor families must be deprived by the late battles, in which so many Irish soldiers perished. This misfortune cannot but greatly aggravate the distress they must endure from the failure of the potato crop'.[16] Irish soldiers who survived the Battle of Sutledge raised £840 for the relief of their countrymen. They entrusted this money to Lord Gough for transmission home.[17]

In January 1846, the Calcutta Committee formally constituted itself as the Irish Relief Fund. It was also referred to as the Calcutta Relief Fund or the Indian Relief Fund. The central committee was based in Calcutta, but a network of support organizations were established throughout India. The Committee met regularly in the early months of 1846, with details of its meetings and the subscriptions raised being reported in the local press. To expedite the distribution of their funds in Ireland, they appointed a Board of Trustees in Dublin to oversee its allocation. At the behest of the committee in India, the Irish board involved Catholics and Protestants, including, Daniel Murray, the Catholic Archbishop of Dublin and Richard Whately, the Anglican Archbishop. The other Trustees were the Duke of Leinster, Lord Cloncurry, the Rev Dr Blake, Archdeacon Torrens, Rev Dr Whelan, Dr Kane, Father Mathew and Dr Robert Graves of the Meath Hospital in Dublin. A Catholic businessman, Thomas L. Synnott, was appointed Secretary of the Fund.[18] Synnott was also working with the Mansion House Committee.[19] The money, raised almost 7,000 miles away, was to be distributed in Ireland as these men saw fit. At the end of April, a meeting of the Trustees was held at the Dublin home of the Duke of Leinster, to consider the best way of dispensing the money. It was agreed that, as far as possible, aid should be given to those groups beyond the reach of government relief.[20]

By 10 January 1846, 29,633 rupees had been donated to the Irish Relief Fund in India.[21] A month later, the amount raised in Bengal alone had risen to 60,000 rupees.[22] The contributors were diverse, with women among the first donors.[23] Large amounts were given by Irish soldiers in the British army and by British residents in the country. A number of donations from Catholic soldiers were made through Bishop Carew or other local priests. One gift of 29 rupees, made through Rev J. McCabe, came from 'Catholic Irish Soldiers and Sepoys at Barrackpore'.[24] Additional donations were made by native Indians, including those who were themselves poor, and by other European residents in the country. At the beginning of 1846, for example, donations were received from a number of Freemason Lodges, the Bishop of Madras, German and Russian merchants in Calcutta and from the French Consulate. Numerous small contributions were received from low-skilled and low-paid native workers, often made in the small currency of annas [there were 16 annas to one rupee]. The donors included 'Sirkars [book-keepers], Podars [book-keepers], Daitories, Peons Piyadus, [messenger or office boys or a native policeman], Burkhudasas, Coolies [unskilled labourers], Bheeties [water carriers] and Furrashes [carpet sweepers]. The donations from these poor Indians amounted to over 99 rupees.[25] The Military Board in Bombay reported that its office workers had 'subscribed the sum of 218-8-0 rupees for the relief of the destitute Irish. A good part of this has, much to their credit, been spontaneously given by the native clerks who have nobly imitated the example of their European brethren of that department'.[26]

The work of the Calcutta Committee continued throughout 1846. In March, a further remittance of £2,000 was sent to Ireland.[27] It came from the region known as the Bengal Presidency, which included West Bengal, Assam, Bihar, Meghalaya, Orissa, Tripura, Penang and Singapore. The generosity of people in India was debated in Irish newspapers; a number of the more conservative ones having denied that external aid was necessary. In contrast, the *Dublin Evening Post* responded to donations from the Calcutta committee by asserting, 'in India, as in Ireland, the lies of the *Evening Mail* have been estimated at their proper value'.[28] Donations from India continued. In April, it was estimated that the subscription for the distressed Irish amounted to 74,422 rupees; by July it had risen to 77,287 rupees.[29] Reports in Ireland suggested that, at this stage, donations totalled over £6,000.[30] Throughout 1846, the Indian Fund distributed money in counties Galway, Limerick, Clare, Tipperary, King's, Cork, Meath, Waterford, Mayo, Waterford, Kilkenny, Longford and Armagh.[31] Most of the funding was issued directly to local parish priests, many of whom recorded their gratitude in the columns of the Irish newspapers.[32] However, at the same time that the Calcutta Committee was being thanked publically, it was also being criticized by the influential *Freeman's Journal* for not allowing correspondence to the Trustees to be made public. Although praising the work of the Calcutta Fund, the newspaper believed that these letters contained 'statistical information of the utmost importance to be made known' yet, rather than being shared, it was being 'thrown into the drawers or the waste paper receptacles of the trustees'.[33] These comments are a reminder of the challenges faced by charities when trying to balance public and private interests, while focusing on their primary objective of saving lives. The importance that fund-raising in India had been to the government's policies in Ireland following the first potato failure was evident when, in August 1846, the Relief Commission issued a circular to local committees comprised of 17 questions, one of which concerned the amount of donations that they had received from government and other sources, the Calcutta Relief Fund being regarded as the most important source of private charity.[34]

In the summer of 1846, news from Britain was dominated by the fall of Sir Robert Peel's Tory government and its replacement by a Whig administration led by Lord John Russell. The new government was barely in place when the potato blight returned to Ireland, destroying over 90 per cent of the potato crop. The grain harvest was also poor, making a second year of shortages inevitable. This gloomy prognosis, which was quickly transmitted around the world, prompted international fund-raising activities that again extended to India. Official approval of the work of the Calcutta Fund was reinforced by a donation of £200 from the Prime Minister in November 1846.[35]

The relief offered by the Whig government following the second appearance of blight, which was more frugal than that of the previous year, had a disastrous impact. Increasingly, private charity provided a crucial lifeline for the poor. As early as October 1846, Synnott was receiving multiples requests for assistance from the Indian Fund, the appeals pointing to the fact that the public works – the fulcrum of the Whigs' relief measures – were still not operative.[36] The opening of the works did not alleviate the situation. Requests made to the Relief Commission in Dublin Castle by the local parish priest in Moycullen in County Galway for assistance for 500 of his parishioners, who were too weak to seek employment on the public works and who were 'almost dead for want of food', had been consistently ignored. In desperation, he appealed to the Calcutta Relief Fund. A subvention received in December 1846 allowed him to give assistance to the local poor.[37]

By the end of 1846, the funds of the Indian Relief Fund were exhausted.[38] During its twelve months' existence, it had raised approximately £14,000. The calls made on its limited resources had been plentiful, with the Committee in Dublin receiving over 2,000 grant applications. In January 1847, the Duke of Leinster informed Archbishop Murray that the small amount of remaining funds should be transferred to the General Central Relief Committee for all Ireland.[39]

At the beginning of 1847, large-scale mortality was being reported from Ireland. The Calcutta Relief Fund had intended to disband but, again, people in India responded to the tragic news with more fund-raising. In July 1847, the Calcutta committee sent £2,500 to Ireland, but asked that it be entrusted to the General Central Relief Committee for them to distribute as they saw fit.[40] In Bombay, a new committee was formed in response to the news, raising over £3,000 in just one week.[41] Assistance to Ireland came from diverse and unexpected sources. The Freemasons of India, who had donated intermittently since 1845, promised to raise a further £5,000 for famine relief, while 'the wealthy Hindoos [sic] of High Castes who have latterly been admitted to the Order by the authority of the Grand Lodge of England' promised that they would raise a separate subscription for the Irish poor.[42] Despite unrest in the country, military and civil stations in the districts of Mofussill and Dwarkanath were contributing. In May, the Bombay Relief Committee reported that:

> The Sepoys of some of the native regiments have subscribed as largely as the same grade, rank and file, in European regiments; the native employees in all the Company's [East India Company] departments of service, jagheradars [sic, more usually, *jagheerdar* – a noble] and native princes, have all, where it has been known to them, come forward most liberally, often most so where the means have been the shortest.[43]

Again, assistance was explained in terms of the unity of the British Empire, the donations being described as, 'evidence of the vital unity of feeling which binds together the members of England's mighty empire'. The writer went on to say:

> These mutual acts of kindness and fellow feeling tend to strengthen the attachment both of the mother country and her dependencies, and are amongst the best pledges of its perseverance.[44]

The report concluded by pointing out that large amounts of grain were available in India at low cost if the Irish Famine was to continue.[45] The Bombay Committee was offered the purchase of 40,000 tons of grain by the Collector at Rumachee in the Scinde for use of the 'famishing Irish', but they did not possess sufficient means to purchase it.[46] The Famine did continue, but these food resources remained untouched, the imperial government choosing not to avail itself of them. The harvest of 1847 marked an end to a series of extraordinary relief measures introduced by the British Government in the previous two years. Instead, the Irish Poor Law, paid for by local taxation, was made responsible for both ordinary and extraordinary relief. The harvest also signalled the closing of many fund-raising activities, including in India. The early charitable interventions from Calcutta and elsewhere were not forgotten by Irish people. In 1877, when there was famine in large parts of India, an 'Indian Relief Fund' was formed in Ireland, which sent money to the poor of India, just as India had sent money to the starving of Ireland 30 years earlier.[47]

Australasia

Support for the Irish poor came from other far-flung parts of the British Empire. The use of parts of Australia as a penal colony for convicts from Britain and Ireland had commenced in 1788. A disproportionately high number of Irish men and women had been transported there. By the 1830s, the Australian colonies were pulling away from their convict roots and the majority of settlers were voluntary immigrants. New South Wales became the first state to abolish the transportation system in 1840.[48] Reports of the potato failure in Ireland had been appearing in Australian papers throughout 1846 but, because of the great distances involved, it could take up to five months for information to be received in the Australian colonies.

In the wake of the second failure, one of the earliest overseas meetings took place in Melbourne in New South Wales in November 1846, on behalf of the 'distressed Irish'. Melbourne had only been established as a colonial settlement in 1835. The meeting had been convened by the local Mayor, but he was prevented by illness from attending. Although attendance was described as 'limited', £11.17s.9d. had been collected.[49] Sydney, the first settlement in Australia, had become the colony's first city in 1842. The population responded to the news from Ireland by establishing a Relief Fund on behalf of the starving Irish and Scotch in August 1846. Smaller settlements in the region undertook to open their own subscriptions lists on behalf of the Sydney collection, generally collected under the umbrella of the New South Wales' Irish Relief Fund.[50] At its first meeting, the Sydney Committee called on other districts to convene their own public meetings. Meetings followed in North Brisbane and Cambooya.

Large sums of money were raised in Australia. Two subscriptions totalling over £1,362 were made in Melbourne in August and October 1846.[51] At the beginning of September, £720 was remitted by the Sydney Committee, followed by £1,140 in mid-October and £1,500 in January 1847. Adopting a similar approach to that of the Calcutta Fund, the money was entrusted to the two Archbishops of Dublin, the Rev Drs Murray and Whately, to be distributed 'without distinction of creed or county'.[52] As had been the case in India, sympathy was often expressed in terms of a shared imperial responsibility, while the proceeds of collections were described as being 'sent home'.[53] The Treasurers of the Melbourne Committee, John Geoghan and John Shannessy, also made clear their pride in being able to make these donations, regarding it as:

> . . . advantageous to the cause of emigration into this district to urge the munificence of this contribution as an indication of the encouraging prosperity which has attended the colonists who have selected it as their adopted country.[54]

As the distress continued, the emphasis shifted to using the money raised to finance emigration to Australia.[55] The Sydney committee explained, 'Whatever sum may be raised, it ought to be distinctly understood it is contributed on the condition that we shall be entitled to the services of the emigrants'. They expected to raise a large sum for this purpose.[56] By the end of 1847, £2,000 had been collected by the Sydney Committee, which they sent to the British Relief Association headquarters in London. At the same time, they stipulated that their funds should be used only to fund emigration to New South Wales. The Association felt unable to comply with this request on the grounds that they had been founded to provide, 'immediate relief to the starving population of Ireland and Scotland'.[57] Disheartened, the Sydney Committee considered keeping their remaining surplus of £300 to distribute among local charities rather than sending it to Ireland.[58] Nonetheless, a second donation of £126.4s.5d. and a third of £268.12s.2d. were sent to the London Committee from Sydney; out of the latter, they requested that £39 should be reserved for Scottish relief.[59] The British Relief Association transferred the initial donation of £2,000 to the MP, Francis Scott, who undertook to use it to assist emigration to Australia.[60] In September 1848, Australian colonists responded positively to news that the Government had initiated a scheme to send Irish orphans aged 14 to 18 to the colony.[61]

Fund-raising in Australia was not confined to the largest towns, as the responses in Berrima, Bathurst and Goulburn demonstrated. In Berrima, a town lying on the road between Sydney and Goulburn, a public meeting had been convened as early as 28 September 1846 to discuss the situation in Ireland. Even before this formal gathering, the police chief had received donations of £14.8s.6d., which he had forwarded to the Sydney committee.[62] Many of the speakers at the Berrima meeting were Irish, including the Catholic priest, the Rev John Grant, who said it was 'the duty of all British subjects to contribute as far as their circumstances will allow'. He also noted that people of all denominations had supported the meeting. A collection of £50 was raised.[63] A further meeting was held in the Court House, chaired by the local Police Magistrate in late July 1847. A resolution was passed that, 'this meeting deeply sympathizes with the sufferings of our fellow-subjects in Ireland and Scotland'. It was agreed to open subscription lists, 'to enable parties subscribing to send their donations either for emigration, or to be sent home for the express purpose of assisting in relieving the immediate wants of the people'. A sum of £10.4s. was raised.[64] All of the donations from Berrima were forwarded to the Sydney Committee.

Bathurst in New South Wales, which had been established by British settlers in 1815, was one of the oldest inland towns in Australia. A meeting took place in Poplar's Hotel on 11 August 1847 to discuss ways in which they could assist the Sydney Relief Fund. One speaker pointed out that the involvement of the district in the project had been delayed; nevertheless, he believed that their endeavours would be 'very efficient, as the harrowing details of distress which they had heard from time to time would stimulate them to liberality'. In common with the approach of the Sydney committee, another speaker suggested that emigration was the best way of 'affording tangible and permanent relief' to the Scottish and Irish poor.[65] Disagreement ensued though, when it was suggested that the money raised could be most effective if used to assist emigration to North America rather than to Australia, the latter being far more expensive. The proposer pointed out:

> The expense of forwarding one immigrant to Australia would be greater than that of sending four or five to British America, or the United States; and as the meeting had been called for the purpose of considering how to rescue the poor of these countries from the very jaws of death, this charitable purpose should not be thwarted by any selfish views of personal advantage.[66]

Following a heated discussion, it was decided that they should allow the Sydney committee to use the money raised as it saw fit. The meeting closed with a collection of £58. This included £3 from the local Catholic priest, Fr Viventius Bourgeois, who had previously donated £34.[67]

On 21 July 1847, an English-born Anglican minister, William Sowerby, dedicated his sermon in Goulburn, New South Wales, to the poor in Ireland and Scotland.[68] Goulburn, one of Australia's earliest inland cities, was a small community, first settled in 1825, which by the 1840s had a population of approximately 1,200. According to Sowerby, the rationale behind the sermon was that, 'so much ignorance, as to the real state of these people, prevails among our population; and also, that considerable misapprehension exists, as to the motives of those who are exerting themselves on behalf of their fellow creatures'.[69] He felt compelled to talk about this topic because 'many of us are connected by the nearest and dearest ties' in what he referred to as 'our common Fatherland'.[70]

The fund-raising efforts of the inhabitants of Goulburn had commenced in the previous year. The local population had first heard of the shortages twelve months earlier but, like many others, believed that it would be a temporary problem. Nonetheless, 'a very large sum' had been raised by a small group of locals, with 'each establishment entering into a generous rivalry to out-vie its neighbour in this charitable and humane undertaking'.[71] Initially, they had been afraid that their exertions would arrive too late to help the suffering people, but 'arrival after arrival [of newspapers] from Great Britain brought out to us accounts of disease and starvation, to which history scarcely affords a parallel'.[72] Additionally, the local population had received reports of the suffering in private letters. In his sermon, Sowerby read from a letter from Beerhaven [sic] in County Cork, dated 27 February 1847, which outlined the misery of the people, despite the exertions of private individuals and the state.[73] In response to the distressing news, meetings had been held throughout New South Wales, including one in Goulburn on 17 July 1847.[74] The people of Goulburn appointed a committee to receive contributions, either in cash or in produce. In regard to the latter, they recommended that people consult one of the printed circulars issued by the Sydney Committee, which had been widely distributed, and in which they listed articles suitable for donation. The Treasurer of the Committee, a 'Mr Sullivan', could offer further advice if needed.[75]

Goulburn's sermon and the response to it provide an insight into the changing relationship between the colonies and the metropole, revealing a shifting balance of power between the former and the latter. Colonial assistance to the Scottish and Irish poor in the United Kingdom suggested that the Imperial core was not invincible. Sowerby warned:

> If the inhabitants of Ireland and the North of Scotland become one vast mass of paupers, England must eventually be involved in the same calamity, and all the three kingdoms must fall, either carrying with them in their overthrow this, and every other dependence of the British Crown, or at any rate, seriously damaging their prosperity.[76]

Unlike respondents from other parts of the world, the colonists in New South Wales wanted to do more than simply send donations. According to Sowerby:

> It has occurred to a great number of influential and good men in this Colony, that the most permanent mode of relief we can hold out, is to offer a shelter, a refuge, and a home upon our shores, to as many of these unfortunate beings as our means, when devoted to that purpose, will permit. And surely no country can be in a condition to offer to such greater advantage than this . . . In the amazing superabundance with which we are blessed, let us impart some share to their famishing bodies.[77]

Clearly, not only did the Australian colonies have an abundance of food, there was also a great demand for labour, and their available territory was vast. Charity to Ireland provided a showcase to display the advantages of emigrating to Australia.

During previous periods of shortages, fast days had been held in the colonies, similar to the one that had taken place in the United Kingdom on 24 March 1847. Sowerby felt aggrieved that, although it had been done before, in this instance, 'It has not been deemed expedient by those who rule in the Church in this Colony, that a day of fasting and humiliation should be set apart for the purpose of deprecating the wrath of Almighty God'.[78] Sowerby suggested that individual prayer and humiliation was still possible.[79] However, he decided not to hold a special collection in his church, but to refer people to the work of the Committee and urged that people should not be governed by any prejudice but should give according to their means.[80]

Not all Australians were pleased with the efforts being made on behalf of Ireland. A number of colonists in the State of South Australia were dissatisfied with the response from their local government. South Australia was unusual because it had not been founded as a penal colony, but as a free settlement in 1836. When hearing of a contribution by the Assembly in Barbados, a local newspaper complained, 'we know that although the colonists here contribute nobly, individually and collectively, the plethoric treasury of South Australia has given nothing; and that, apparently for the supercilious reason that her rulers have been "otherwise engaged"'.[81]

Like Australia, Van Diemen's Land (later Tasmania) had been used as a penal colony for British and Irish convicts. At the beginning of 1847, the island's press, noting that subscriptions in Sydney, Port Philip and Adelaide amounted to over £5,000, called on local people to form their own committees. They suggested that the Governor, Sir Thomas Denison, could take a lead in this matter.[82] The response of the colonists was enthusiastic. The island's capital, Hobart, was at the forefront of fund-raising. By May, the town's Irish and Scotch Relief Committee had raised three separate donations amounting to £1,260 in total, which were sent the British Home Secretary on behalf of 'starving Irish and Scotch peasantry'.[83] Cornelius O'Driscoll, who was the Treasurer of the Committee, had founded the Colonial Bank in Hobart in 1840, and donations were channelled through it.[84] Not all colonists were in favour of this type of intervention. One local newspaper, the *Courier*, suggested that by the time the money arrived, the crisis would probably be over. Furthermore, referring to articles in the London *Times*, the paper reminded its readers that the amount of money in Irish saving banks was increasing.[85] In 1849, Van Diemen's Land would become directly enmeshed in the political affairs of Ireland, when it was decided that the leaders of the Young Ireland rebellion were to be sent there.[86] In addition to fund-raising, therefore, the Australian colonies, through the orphan emigration scheme, political transportation and more general emigration, played a significant part in the affairs of Ireland, despite being thousands of miles away.

The Irish helping the Irish

The assistance of the Irish to each other during the Famine has often been overlooked. When the young Quaker William E. Forster visited Ireland at the end of 1846, he mused, 'I have no doubt whatever, in any other country, the mortality would have been far greater; that many lives have been prolonged, perhaps saved, by the long apprenticeship to want in which the Irish peasant has been trained and by that loving touching charity which prompts him to share his scanty meal with his starving neighbour'. He acknowledged this could not persist as 'One class after another is falling into the same abyss of ruin'.[87]

Many narratives of the Famine, however, have criticized landlords, especially absentee ones who, not experiencing the distress first-hand, appeared indifferent to the suffering of their tenants. Radical MP William

Smith O'Brien, himself a landowner, introduced a bill in the House of Commons on 18 March 1847, proposing a tax on absentee landlords. It was defeated by 70 to 19 votes.[88] Members of the Society of Friends were particularly critical of the apathy of some landowners.[89] Even the gentle Count Strzelecki, writing from Clifden, aired his frustrations:

> The disorder and moral disorganization amongst the gentry and land-owners, to whom the Government and the charitable institutions mainly look for support and cordial, honest, and straightforward co-operation in carrying out the relief for the poor, increases tenfold the actual calamity of Ireland in general, and of this part in particular; for none of them, at least as far as this barony is concerned, has or possesses an actual stake or interest in that co-operation; every one of them – from Mr ***, who is in possession of 500,000 acres, to the lowest – is involved, lives on an allowance, and has his estate managed by the agency for his creditor; so that the poor are placed between a landlord who is unable to give them assistance, and the agent who has no interest in giving them any, and looks to the Government to do it, which again is wholly unqualified in dealing with the details of relief or distribution.[90]

However, the response of landlords to the deteriorating situation in Ireland varied greatly, and not all landowners were indifferent to their tenants' suffering. An overlooked aspect of famine relief is how Irish people, both in Ireland and elsewhere, sought to alleviate the distress. Landowners who were resident were frequently members of the Boards of Guardians that looked after the local workhouses, and they were expected to be involved in the specially formed relief committees that looked after the extraordinary relief measures introduced between 1845 and 1847. Apart from administrative responsibilities, the financial burden on resident landowners and clergy increased substantially after 1845.

In addition to poor rates, relief committees relied on locally raised subscriptions in order to be eligible for government funding. A substantial part of their work, therefore, especially after 1846, was to garner contributions from both resident and absentee landlords.[91] As early as October 1846, the Bruff Relief Committee in Limerick made a desperate plea to local landowners, 'to solicit your aid in the present unprecedented calamity'. Within only two months, the price of Indian corn meal had quadrupled, while wages on the public works remained so low that people were pawning or selling their possessions. The Bruff Committee explained, 'it is heart-rending to witness the appalling sufferings of multitudes around us – sufferings only equalled by their patience'. The committee appealed to landowners to:

> subscribe munificently to this 'Relief Fund' upon which your own poor people must mainly depend on in this eventful crisis. The amount you give will not only determine the government grant, but will influence

contributions of other landed proprietors ... [while] enlarged benevolence and active sympathy in this present siltation, will, we trust, serve to knit the hearts of the tenantry and labourers to their legitimate patrons, and forever obliterate the prejudices entertained in England against the Irish landlords.[92]

As the Quakers observed, absentee landlords who behaved badly placed further responsibilities on those who were resident. This point was made by Richard Davis Webb during a visit to Belmullet in County Mayo in May 1847. He praised George Vaughan Jackson, a small landowner, who was travelling 100 miles each week to assist three different relief committees.[93] Moreover, not all absentees were neglectful. At the end of 1846, the local Anglican minister in Bantry pointed out that even though the Earl of Bandon no longer owned land in the parish, he had sent £10 to the Relief Committee and £20 for the local public works, in addition to his usual Christmas gifts to the tenantry. Furthermore, Bandon was providing funds to the Schull Relief Committee.[94] At the other end of the country, landowners William Sharman Crawford MP in County Down and Lord George Hill in County Donegal were praised for their work on behalf of their tenants, which included reducing rents and selling grain below market price – something that Relief Committees were forbidden from doing.[95] Similarly, in County Leitrim, John Robert Godley, the High Sherriff of the County, donated £20 to his local relief committee in Killegar and reduced rents by 15 per cent.[96] These actions were being repeated throughout Ireland, but were overshadowed by narratives of death or Irish apathy. Additionally, the transfer to Poor Law relief following the harvest of 1847 signalled that Irish taxpayers, not British or imperial ones, were solely responsible for financing relief. The young Marquis of Sligo was widely regarded as a compassionate landlord. Although he had not received any rent since the first appearance of blight, he had not evicted any tenants. In 1848 though, he was forced to borrow £1,500 to pay his poor rates, and evicted some tenants, explaining that the additional fiscal burden meant that he was now 'under the necessity of ejecting or being ejected'.[97]

While the multiple contributions of landowners were crucial in allowing the relief committees to perform their duties, it is clear that more could have been done by some in Ireland. Lord Londonderry and his wife made contributions of £20 and £10 to their local relief committees at the beginning of 1847. The following year, the Londonderrys expended £15,000 renovating their home in Mount Stewart. When attacked in the local press for his parsimony, Londonderry responded that 'My conscience acquits me of ever having acted wrongly as a proprietor, a landlord or a Christian'.[98] The editor of the *Londonderry Standard* responded that 'His Lordship is then in a most enviable state of inward blessedness for we imagine that some of the Apostles themselves could scarcely have made such a declaration'.[99]

In addition to supporting the government's relief measures, a number of Irish people played an active role in the various charitable endeavours taking place within Ireland and among Irish communities elsewhere. Several of these committees were modelled on bodies that had been formed to deal with the shortages in 1821 and 1822, most notably the Mansion House Committee in Dublin and the Tavern Committee in London. The Irish Relief Association had been involved during the shortages of 1831 and was reconstituted following the second harvest failure in 1846.

By responding to the first appearance of potato blight, the Mansion House Committee became the first private organization to become involved in Famine relief in Ireland. It had been reconvened in October 1845 by the Lord Mayor of Dublin, John Arabin, whose official home was the Mansion House in Dawson Street. Its members included the Duke of Leinster, Daniel O'Connell MP and Henry Grattan MP. Daniel Murray, the Catholic Archbishop of Dublin, was a member, although Archbishop Whately was not.[100] The Chairman was Lord Cloncurry who, sometime later, was made a Trustee of the Calcutta Relief Fund. The secretary was Thomas Synnott, who also worked on behalf of the Calcutta Committee. Many members of the Committee were Catholic and known to be sympathetic to Repeal, leading the conservative Dublin *Packet* to accuse them of being 'factional' and exaggerating the distress in Ireland.[101]

One of the first actions of the Mansion House Committee was to organize a deputation to the Lord Lieutenant, Lord Heytesbury, requesting the government to respond to the shortages with measures appropriate to Ireland. They pre-empted this by warning of, 'the awful state of the kingdom was likely to become reduced to, if the Government did not at once step into prevent, as far as possible, by all human means, the dreadful scourge of anticipated famine and pestilence'.[102] Their recommendations included public works that were of 'national utility', 'closing the ports' to stop the exportation of food, a tax on absentee landlords, establishing public granaries, and banning the use of grain in distillation.[103] Many of these measures had been utilized, with success, during earlier periods of food shortages.[104]

The delegation was met 'very coldly' by the Lord Lieutenant. The blunt opinion of the *Freeman's Journal* was that his response could be summed up by the phrase, 'They may starve'.[105] Heytesbury's official reply was regarded as so unsatisfactory by the Committee that they decided to meet regularly and to each contribute £5 towards expenses. They developed a practical strategy to the shortages, based on ascertaining the extent of loss, searching for an antidote to the disease, and suggesting ways to provide the people with food and employment. On 8 November, the Committee sent out over 3,500 questionnaires to assess the situation in the country. This was to enable them to write directly to the British Prime Minister, Sir Robert Peel, 'pointing out to him the exact state of this country, and the pressing and imminent danger of famine, and to take immediate and efficacious precautions to avert the otherwise certain and impending calamity'. They also suggested that the ports should be 'opened' to allow food to freely enter the country.[106] The letter warned Peel that, 'Whilst you hesitate, if hesitate you shall, the people of Ireland are about to die in countless numbers'.[107] Peel's response was to appoint a Scientific Commission, based in Dublin Castle, which would carry out its own research. At the beginning of December, on behalf of the Committee, Synnott had attended on the Scientific Commissioners with the results of their early enquiries. He had been met with the 'utmost courtesy and kindness' but it had been made clear that no cooperation was possible.[108] Nonetheless, to further support the work of the Scientific Commission, the Mansion House decided to send out a second questionnaire on 10 December 1845 and to make available a synopsis of their findings.[109] When the 'men of science' left Ireland, they had spent less than three weeks in the country and had come up with no practical solutions of how to mitigate the impact of the potato disease.[110] No account appears to have been taken of the Mansion House Committee's detailed research by the government officials.[111] Nonetheless, the members of the committee believed that their persistence in providing full details of the extent of the potato failure had resulted in early and successful intervention by Peel's government.[112] In September 1846, at a meeting chaired by Daniel O'Connell, it was agreed that there was no need for the Mansion House Committee to resume its fact-finding activities, he trusting in the new Whig government to provide relief.[113]

Faith in the relief policies of the Whig administration was short lived as the public works and other measures quickly proved inadequate and inappropriate to deal with such a large-scale famine. On 23 December, a meeting was convened in the Music Hall in Dublin at which Daniel O'Connell and other local dignitaries were present, including Archbishop Murray and the Provost of Trinity College. Their concern was with the 'unparalleled distress' of poor in the city. To help alleviate the suffering, it was agreed to form the Metropolitan Relief Committee. One speaker, Rev Creighton, a Presbyterian minister, was vocal in his criticism of 'the conduct of the government, who allowed the poor to perish sooner than interfere with the interests of the general trader', but he was admonished for 'travelling into political economy'.[114] At a meeting held only a week later, and chaired by Daniel O'Connell, an overtly political resolution was passed calling attention to the insufficiency of food in the country and warning:

if immediate, active and persevering attention be not paid to the awful symptoms by which we are surrounded, those who are guilty of any neglect in these particulars will be responsible before man, and we venture to add before an all-just Providence, for the destruction by famine and disease of millions of lives in Ireland.[115]

The discussions highlighted the increasingly uneasy relationship between political responses and charitable ones.

The Mansion House provided the headquarters for the Metropolitan Relief Committee. As was common practice, every few days lists of subscribers were published in the newspapers. The membership of the committee was diverse and both clerical and lay. Trustees including the Very Rev Dr O'Connell, the Mayor, John O'Connell MP, Isaac Butt, QC and the abolitionist, James Haughton.[116] The Metropolitan Committee appealed to the wealthier parishes of Dublin to donate to the poorer ones. They also asked for people outside of Dublin to contribute, which resulted in subscriptions from Britain and France.[117] Again, people with few resources donated to the Committee: the clerks and bookkeepers of Messrs Classon and Duggan gave one day's pay, which amounted to £1.16s.6d.; Dr Phelan, the Governor of the House of Industry, contributed £1; and the Governor and Officers of Richmond Bridewell donated a day's pay of £4.15s.[118] In January 1847, the committee had sufficient resources to finance the opening of private soup kitchens in the city. The impact of these grants was considerable; they enabled St Luke's Parish, for example, to provide 1,400 rations of soup, three times a week, between January and April.[119] Other, more established charities were appealing to the Metropolitan Committee for assistance; they awarding the Sick and Indigent Room Keepers Society a grant of £100.[120] The Trustees hoped that by taking care of the capital's poor, the resources of the newly formed General Central Relief Committee could be applied in total to the more remote districts in Ireland.[121]

Within only weeks of being established, the Metropolitan Committee was experiencing financial problems. At the end of February, they announced, 'with deep regret', that due to lack of funds they were unable to respond to the 'increasing and alarming destitution' in the city. The Trustees made an urgent appeal for more subscriptions.[122] By March, the Committee was finding it impossible to meet the demands placed on them. They passed a unanimous decision asking the government to immediately put the Temporary Relief Act, which provided for the opening of soup kitchens, into effect in the city.[123]

The General Central Relief Committee for All Ireland was formed in Dublin in late 1846 and worked out of an office in College Green. The Chairman was the Marquis of Kildare, and the large committee comprised of 31 influential men, including the, now, 71-year-old Daniel O'Connell, his son John and William Smith O'Brien. These three men were leaders of the two rival nationalist groups in Ireland, Young Ireland and Old Ireland.[124] O'Connell's health, however, was failing, and his involvement in this and other charitable endeavours was brief, he spending the final months before his death in May 1847, travelling to Rome in order to meet with the Pope.[125] The General Relief Committee encouraged people from everywhere in the British Empire to contribute. In this they were successful, receiving donations from all over the world, including £3,472 from Toronto, £441 from Buenos Ayres, £470 from Grahamstown in the Cape (South Africa) and £296 from Delhi in India. Money was also raised within Ireland, including

£42 sent by Lord George Paget on behalf of the officers and privates stationed at Portobello barracks in Dublin.[126] The brewer, Arthur Guinness, also contributed to the Committee.[127] By February 1847, they had raised almost £2,000.[128] The names of their subscribers were updated weekly in the columns of the *Freeman's Journal*.[129] Lists of the donations made were printed in the same paper.[130] At the beginning of 1847, in recognition of the still deteriorating condition of the poor, the committee decided to meet on a daily basis.[131] In April, the funds of the Committee were augmented by the British Relief Association, who gave them £10,000, part of the proceeds from the first Queen's Letter.[132] Like other relief bodies, the General Central Relief Committee started to wind down its activities with the approach of the 1847 harvest. In its July report, it reported optimistically that the potato crop was 'unusually luxuriant'.[133] In its twelve months of existence, the Committee had dispersed 1,871 individual grants. Of this money, the largest amount, £20,835, had been distributed in Connaught. In Ulster, £11,300 had been granted, primarily in counties Cavan and Donegal.[134] Despite the relative smallness of the grants, they had made a difference to the lives of the poor. Writing from Kilmeena in Westport, the local Rector, Thomas Hardiman, thanked the Committee for two grants totalling £70. He went on to say:

> There never was, in Ireland, or any other country, a body that has done so much good in so short a space of time, and with such inadequate resources, as has been confessedly accomplished by the 'Central Committee' since its establishment – what a pity that those noble-hearted individuals, who have thus given the strongest proof of their ability and disinterested zeal for the cause of the poor, should not be sustained by all classes of the community.[135]

In May 1849, as the impact of the Famine showed no signs of abating in many parts of Ireland, the General Relief Committee briefly re-formed. They explained that they did so because 'the year 1849 is likely to be the most memorable epoch in the annals of British misery'.[136] Realizing that private charity alone could not save the poor, they decided to appoint a delegation to travel to London, 'to lay the condition of the people and the country before the Minister, and if needs be, before the Throne'.[137] Shortly afterwards, a small subscription was raised by individual members of the British government on behalf of Ireland. It was a small token gesture; the greater message was that the Irish poor were to rely on their own resources.

A number of relief organizations were founded in Belfast, a predominantly Presbyterian town, which lay at the centre of the thriving linen trade. The Belfast General Relief Fund was established to raise subscriptions in the town of Belfast to help the poor in all parts of Ireland. Its secretaries included Rev Dr Drew, an Anglican minister, while Sir Arthur Chichester was Chairman, and the Mayor of Belfast, W. Johnson, was

President.[138] At its first meeting on 2 January, it drew up a number of guidelines, including:

> first, that the relief be afforded to alleviate the present distress in Ireland without restrictions to any locality—secondly, that the sum raised be entrusted to a committee, to be elected from the subscribers—and thirdly, that this sum be expended solely in supplying food.[139]

By the end of January, the committee had raised over £4,000, and money was still flowing in. An unusual contribution had been given by the young Earl of Belfast, whose donation of £80 had resulted from the sale of his own musical compositions.[140] Unexpectedly, shortly after being founded, the committee began receiving requests to give relief locally. The potato failure and a downswing in industrial production had greatly increased destitution within the town, which had been exacerbated by an influx of poor people. A consequence of the deteriorating situation in Belfast was that, throughout 1847, thousands of people were being kept alive by a privately operated soup kitchen. Nonetheless, the town's graveyards were overflowing.[141] The demands made on the Relief Fund became so great that the committee was having to work seven hours a day, yet still could not keep up with requests for assistance.[142] In total, the Belfast Relief Fund raised £7,073.1s.9d. They gave Belfast and the adjoining Ballymacarrett, a grant of £1,600.13s.11d.[143] They also made two grants, each of £1,000, to enable the local soup kitchen to remain open. The Belfast Committee did not only provide relief in the form of food. In 1846 and early 1847, over 11,000 poor people were deported from Scotland and England to Belfast as a consequence of British Laws of Settlement, which meant that these new immigrants had no right to relief. The Belfast committee provided £900 to enable these people to return to their homes in other parts of Ireland. On 12 May, the committee announced that it was disbanding. During its brief existence, it had received 176 applications for assistance from Ulster and made 90 grants; from Leinster, it had received 39 applications and made 14 grants; from Munster, it had received 133 applications and made 65 grants; and from Connaught, 90 applications had been received and 41 grants issued.[144]

The money that was being raised so generously in Ireland and throughout the world in 1846 and 1847 would not have found its way to the poor without the dedication of Irish officials and volunteers who distributed the charity. One group that was directly involved in overseeing relief operations in the poorest districts, and were doing so without compensation, were the officers of the Coast Guard, the Navy and the Commissariat. They were singled out for praise by the Quakers for their efforts on behalf of the starving.[145] Matthew Higgins of the British Relief Association commended the officers and men assisting him in Belmullet, who often worked till dark and on Sundays to get food to the people.[146] Without their involvement, the distribution of relief, both government and private, and the operation of soup kitchens, would not have been possible. Moreover, this was done at considerable personal risk to their health. Diseases, including fever, dysentery and cholera, each had a lethal impact on people who were mal-nourished, and for those who were involved in the distribution of relief, there was a real risk of contagion. Sadly, as the Famine progressed, some of those who had been providing relief themselves came to require assistance.

Irish people overseas proved assiduous in their benevolence, both as members of fund-raising committees and as donors. Irish-born Jacob Harvey, who was secretary of the General Relief Committee in New York, estimated that the amount of money remitted by 'the laboring Irish, male and female' in 1846 had reached a million dollars, 'part of the earning of poor Irish emigrants, sent in one year to help their poorer friends at home, and all done quietly, regularly and systematically, without any parade of public meetings or committees'.[147] In Liverpool, a local newspaper reported that 'the Post Office was besieged by Irish labourers, sending small sums of money home to their afflicted kinsfolk'.[148] When visiting the Aran Islands in Galway Bay in March 1847, Lord James Butler, Agent for the British Relief Association in Galway, was surprised to find that, 'a considerable sum of money has been sent to the island by people who have emigrated; more than 140*l* within the last few days; and a great desire for emigration exists'.[149] A number of individuals and groups in Ireland joined the fund-raising efforts. William John Campbell Allen, a successful Belfast merchant, arranged for the shipment of corn to Ireland for free distribution.[150] His wife was involved with the Belfast Ladies' Relief Committee, which was providing relief to all parts of Ireland. The Royal Irish Art Union organized an exhibition of Old Masters on behalf of the poor. Officers at one of Dublin's army garrisons put on an amateur dramatic performance, which raised £15.[151]

Involvement in Famine relief came about in unexpected ways. Two students at Oxford, one of whom was Irish, responded to the ubiquitous reports of the Famine by undertaking their own research. Frederick Hamilton-Temple-Blackwood, 1st Marquis of Dufferin and Ava, was part of the Anglo-Irish Ascendancy. He and George Boyle, the Earl of Glasgow, had become close friends at the University of Oxford. In January 1847, Dufferin expressed an interest in visiting a famine district in Ireland and, towards the end of February, he and Boyle travelled to Dublin. Dufferin was aged only 20 and Boyle, 21. In Ireland, they were recommended to go to Skibbereen, which they did.[152] Skibbereen had come to the attention of the British public at the end of 1846 due to a series of letters that had appeared in the press describing the desperate condition of the poor. Within weeks, the name of Skibbereen had become a shorthand for the suffering in Ireland. Nonetheless, when Dufferin and Boyle arrived there, they were not prepared for the scenes they witnessed. The young men stayed in the district for 24 hours. Dufferin recorded his painful impressions in a letter, which was published in 1847 as a short pamphlet. He admitted:

> We have found everything but too true; the accounts are not exaggerated – they cannot be exaggerated – nothing more frightful can be conceived. The scenes we have witnessed during our short stay at Skibbereen, equal anything that has been recorded in history, or could be conceived by the imagination.[153]

The proceeds of this pamphlet were donated to the poor of Skibbereen. Back at Oxford University, Dufferin threw himself into raising subscriptions for Ireland, but when he attempted to convene a public meeting, he was discouraged from doing so by the Anglican Bishop of Oxford.[154] Nonetheless, he informed his mother that:

> The news we have brought back [from Ireland] has made a great impression upon the men here. They are squeezing out money from every possible sponge, principally innocent old fathers and warm-hearted mothers; they are selling their pictures, their pianos, and have passed some very statesmen-like decisions with regard to their kitchen arrangements . . . I hope that before we have done that £1,000 will be poured into Ireland.[155]

To this sum, Dufferin added his own, at the time, anonymous contribution of £1,000.[156] In addition, the young student's personal account of his experiences provided a powerful testimony to the awfulness of the suffering in Skibbereen.

Sir Robert Peel, Prime Minister during the first year of shortages, had predicted that:

> There will be no hope of contributions from England for the mitigation of this calamity. Monster meetings, the ungrateful return for past kindness, the subscriptions in Ireland to repeal rent and the O'Connell tribute, will have disinclined the charitable here to make any great exertions for Irish relief.[157]

Peel's analysis proved to be incorrect as multiple collections were made and committees established in Britain, much of the money being channelled through the two main relief organizations or through the churches. One of the smallest, but most poignant, donations for Ireland came from convicts on board the *Warrior* hulk – a prison ship – at Woolwich. The prisoners had observed boxes in the dockyard for the relief of the distressed inhabitants of Ireland and Scotland, and asked if they could make their own contribution. Permission was granted, on the understanding that the donation must be voluntary on the part of every convict. The sum collected, in small donations of pennies and halfpennies, amounted to 17 shillings.[158]

The donation by the Woolwich prisoners was especially extraordinary in the light of the conditions that they were enduring. In January 1847, the radical MP for Finsbury in London, Thomas Slingsby Duncombe, had requested that a select committee be held looking into the condition of the Woolwich prisoners, which he had found to be, 'both distressing and disgusting'.[159] Duncombe, described by one newspaper as a 'dandy demagogue', was known for being outspoken in defence of those groups he regarded as oppressed.[160] In 1844, he had opposed the imprisonment of the aged Daniel O'Connell.[161] In a debate in the House of Commons on the condition of the prisoners on the Woolwich hulk, Duncombe had pointed out that, even when dying, these men were viscously, and sometimes fatally, flogged. He added, 'the medical treatment was so brutal, both as regarded the treatment of the prisoners while living and after death, as to be a disgrace to any country calling itself a civilized and Christian country'.[162] It was these ill-treated English prisoners who sent their precious small coins to assist the poor of Ireland. The situation in Woolwich and in Ireland begged the question, how could such brutality and suffering exist in a country that regarded itself as 'civilized'? However, the actions of the English convicts revealed that humanity could exist in the depths of brutality.

From the first donations that had been made in Calcutta at the end of 1845 to the contribution of convicts in Woolwich, it had been apparent that concern for the starving people of Ireland was transcending political, religious and national boundaries. Moreover, poverty itself was proving no barrier to giving aid to the Irish poor. The early charitable responses to the potato failures not only crossed traditional divides, but challenged assumptions about the poor being undeserving of assistance. Furthermore, rather than being indifferent to the suffering of their own people, it showed that many among the Irish elites were working tirelessly to save lives. Worryingly, however, the multiple demands that were being placed on these and other charities had also exposed the limitations of official relief.

3

'A labour of love'.[1]
Quaker Charity

The reappearance of potato blight in 1846 transformed what had been a year of shortages into a far more serious subsistence crisis. Government intervention, in the form of public works, was slow to be established and proved inadequate to cope with the emerging crisis. The vacuum in relief provision was partly filled by private charity. Fund-raising on behalf of Ireland had commenced as early as October 1845, however, following the second crop failure, a number of organizations were formed with the intention of not simply raising money, but becoming directly involved in the distribution of relief. As a consequence, government and private relief were operating side by side. Despite the dedication and professionalism of the men and women who worked on behalf of the Irish poor, by the end of 1846, thousands were already dead or beyond salvation. Within this landscape of disease, death, desolation and despair, a small number of charities worked to save lives.

The Dublin Committee

One of the first groups to respond to the unfolding tragedy was the Society of Friends, also referred to as Quakers or Friends. Despite the relative smallness of their communities in Britain and Ireland, Quakers, together with Unitarians, were disproportionately prominent in the charitable world within the United Kingdom.[2] The Friends also had a reputation for being in the forefront of campaigns for social justice, including the abolition movement, to end slavery. When dealing with victims of the Famine, they brought a degree of compassion and openness that was absent at many levels of government relief. Not only did they add dignity to the giving of charity, importantly, they did not combine relief with trying to win religious converts. Their approach won them praise and gratitude both at the time and in subsequent decades.

A number of Quaker communities in Ireland had started to provide food rations in the autumn of 1846. In Cork City, a delegation of Friends had met with local commissioners on 11 November requesting the use of a space in the market to open a soup kitchen. They intended to erect a boiler capable of making 100 gallons of soup daily for a period of four months. The soup was to be made from, 'the best description of beef, and good split peas'. Money had already been donated for this purpose and some Cork Friends had agreed to provide monthly subscriptions.[3] At this stage, they viewed their intervention as being short term only. As the condition of the country deteriorated, several Dublin Quakers suggested that the situation demanded a more coordinated response. Although, at the time of the Famine, Quaker numbers in Ireland were small – totalling only about 3,000 – Quakers were part of a worldwide network of fellow religionists. Many were successful bankers or merchants, which provided them with valuable international contacts. In mid-November 1846, Joseph Bewley convened a meeting in Dublin. Subsequently, a Central Relief Committee of 21 members was established in Dublin. Auxiliary committees were formed in Cork, Clonmel, Waterford and Limerick.[4] The Secretaries of the Dublin Committee, Joseph Bewley and Jonathan Pim, attended their offices daily in an effort to keep up with the demands being placed on them and to coordinate the activities of committees both in Ireland and elsewhere. A visitor from England who called into the Dublin offices in March 1847 observed that some members were working 'day and night'.[5]

The Quakers recognized that people needed immediate access to food – food that was either free or cheap – a very different approach from the philosophy underpinning the relief measures of the Whig government. Although the Quakers quickly established a network for providing relief, their resources were limited in terms of finance and manpower. To maximize their effectiveness, the Quakers worked with local relief committees and other volunteers to establish soup kitchens. They agreed to supply all soup boilers free of charge.[6] Finding suitable premises was a further challenge and, again, the Quakers took a lead role. In Limerick, they got permission for the unused *Monte de Piété* (which had been built to house a charitable pawn service for the poor) to be converted to a soup depot.[7] The Friends also offered to act as a conduit for the distribution of clothing and of fabric from which clothes could be made. This latter provision was particularly important in the freezing winter of 1846–47. In each of these endeavours, they aimed to encourage local efforts and, as far as possible, avoid providing gratuitous relief.[8]

The lack of clothing of the Irish poor was an area in which the intervention of charities proved crucial. In the first year of shortages, many poor had pawned what few possessions they had, including items of clothing.[9] In December 1846, Quakers travelling throughout Ireland reported that the nakedness of many people meant they were unable to work, while they were more vulnerable to illness in what was proving to be an especially cold winter.[10] In February, as the freezing conditions continued, the Dublin Clothing Committee appealed to the 'Brethren and Sisters of England', informing them, 'Starvation has produced raggedness in those who *had* clothing, and nakedness in those who previously had nothing better than rags to cover them, by day or by night'. The appeal went on to say that it did not matter if the materials were coarse, as long as they were 'warm and strong'. It also reassured potential benefactors that precautions had been taken against donated items being pawned.[11]

From the outset, the Friends wanted to promote Irish involvement in relief provision, especially in poorer areas. A report from Clonmel provides an insight into their important role in initiating local participation:

> A very important meeting took place here to-day. It originated with the Society of Friends (male and female), whose character for humanity and benevolence is so well known and appreciated. On this painfully-interesting occasion, the great principle of charity was well sustained, all sects and classes having cheerfully promised to co-operate with the good men who set on foot a subscription for the purpose of establishing in Clonmel a *soup depot,* where a substantial nutritious article might be obtained by all in need of it at a merely nominal price.[12]

In Waterford, the Rev John Sheehan, described as 'an influential Roman Catholic priest', publicly praised the work of the local Society of Friends. By December, over 400 of the most destitute people were being fed a daily ration of one pound of bread and a quart of soup – described as 'excellent soup'. The number being about to be increased to 600 on four days of the week, a scheme that was to remain in place for six months, until the harvest period. Sheehan's praise was fulsome:

> God bless the Friends; for what they have done may God reward them ... nothing but the purest and most benevolent feelings have activated them in giving this charity – and I have never found the slightest attempt at interference with the religious principles of the recipients of their charity.[13]

Similar praise was heaped on the Friends for their work during this 'distressing emergency' at a conference for clergymen of all denominations held in Exeter Hall in London in mid-January 1847.[14]

It was not just rural districts that were making claims on the Quakers. Within Dublin itself, there was also widespread poverty; the food shortages had put pressure on the towns and cities in Ireland, as people swarmed in looking for relief or employment. The main Dublin Quaker soup kitchen was in the centre of the city, at Charles Street, Upper Ormond Quay. Within days of opening, it was serving 1,000 quarts of soup a day. In March 1847, cooked rice was included some days of the week due to the prevalence of disease; rice was believed to have beneficial medical effects.[15] Following the opening of the government's soup kitchens under the Temporary Relief Act, the demand reduced drastically. However, as proved to be the case elsewhere, there was a delay in official relief becoming available; consequently, the Quakers did not fully close their soup depots until July 1847. By this stage, the Friends had sold 54,880 quarts of soup, while 48,357 quarts had been provided for gratuitous distribution.[16] At this time also, the Society of Friends and other charitable bodies were optimistic that the approaching harvest would be healthy and mark an end to famine.[17]

Women Friends were involved in providing aid in a variety of ways, as the following report from Dublin shows:

> Clothing was distributed by Susanna Pim, while Isabelle Pim was involved with the Kingstown Industrial Society which supplied new nets to fishermen. Food was also distributed by Mary Greenwood Pim and by Ruth Pim of the Liberty Infant School. In the rural areas the Moss family was distributing aid in Kilteman and the Barringtons near Bray.[18]

On 25 November, shortly after the creation of the Dublin Committee, a sister group was formed in London. It viewed its role as primarily a fund-raising one and, from the outset, it worked closely with the Dublin Friends. One of the secretaries of the London Committee was Charles Tylor, who was editor of the Quaker magazine, *The Friend,* which had been founded in 1843. The other secretary was Rickman Godlee, a barrister at Middle Temple.[19] A Ladies' Committee was also formed in London, its main purpose being to gather clothes for the poor in Ireland. Additionally, they raised money which they used to promote industries, such as sewing and weaving, among women.[20] The London Committee commenced its work by issuing two appeals. The first, on 2 December, was directed at Friends in England, the second, on 2 January, was made to Friends in North America.[21] The American Appeal stated:

> That brotherly love and sympathy which have so long prevailed between us and our friends in America, induce us to communicate with you on a subject which is a present exciting a very deep and lively interest in the minds of the Friends of this country.
>
> You are, doubtless, already aware of the existence of the awful calamity which has overspread a large part of Ireland . . . notwithstanding the large and comprehensive measures for providing employment for able-bodied labourers, and the partial efforts made in some quarters to raise collections for the distressed, it was felt there was a part which Friends had to perform, and to which they were called to apply themselves with earnestness and zeal.[22]

The London Committee employed two vessels, the *Albert* and the *Scourge,* to take food to the west of Ireland. Freight was paid by the Treasury and the

Admiralty allowed free use of the vessels, on the condition that they were accompanied by representatives from the Friends.[23] By the end of 1847, the London Committee had raised a total of £45,051.13s.8d., of which £42,726.2s.0d. had come from subscriptions, and £300 from bank interest, while the British Treasury paid freight charges on items sent to Ireland, which amounted to £2,025.11s.8d. This money represented donations from approximately 3,600 individuals and groups.[24] Inevitably, a high portion of the donors were Quakers, but the two committees were impressed by how many donors were non-members.[25] The funds of the London Committee were distributed thus[26]:

	£ s. d. (pounds, shillings and pence)
To the Dublin Committee	17,888...9...4
Sundry small grants	65...0...3
Claddagh Fisherman	100...0...0
Purchase of Provisions	17,488...3...8
Clothing for Ladies Committee	1,020...0...0
Sundry Expenses	236...17...8
Cargoes from America	2,025...11...8
Balance	6,226...11...4
Total	45,051...13...8

In March 1847, deputations of Friends from all over Ireland and representatives from the London Committee travelled to Dublin to meet with the Central Relief Committee. The London Committee reported that the visit 'had the effect of most fully confirming the conviction we had previously entertained, of the very judicious, effective, and energetic character of the measures of our friends in Dublin'.[27]

American generosity

The Friends were not only successful in garnering support in Britain, but also they proved to be effective in fund-raising in North America, with donations coming from all sections of society. An appeal by the Central Relief Committee had first appeared in the American press at the end of 1846. By 1847, eyewitness accounts from Friends travelling in the western districts provided powerful testimony to the extent of suffering in Ireland.[28] Quakers in the United States proved to be some of the earliest and most generous individual donors. By February 1847, the Dublin Committee had received £2,250 from Friends in America.[29] This sum included $83,000 from Friends in Philadelphia,[30] while Friends in Hopkinton, Rhode Island, had sent $350.[31] However, it was a man, who had no direct connection with either Ireland or the Society of Friends, who played a pivotal role in coordinating relief efforts in the US. In February 1847, the General Relief Committee was formed in New York, led by Myndert Van Schaick, a successful businessman of Dutch origin. Its members were drawn from various religious and ethnic backgrounds. A prominent role was played by an Irish-born Quaker, Jacob Harvey, who offered his services as secretary to the committee. Although the work of the committee was originally intended to be limited to the city, they received contributions from twenty-four states in total and thus became a major conduit for sending relief to Ireland. The New York Committee decided that, unless a donation had been specified by the donor, they would entrust all of their charity to the Friends in Dublin.[32]

On 1 May 1847, Friends from all over Ireland gathered in Dublin. When listing the donations they had received, special tribute was paid to the generosity of America: the sum of £13,083.9s.1d. had been provided in cash, and over 20 vessels, many carrying whole cargoes of provisions, had either arrived or were on the way to Ireland, with more to follow. They passed a resolution that:

> In recording this extraordinary, if not unparalleled, manifestation of sympathy and liberality, we are bound to offer our grateful and cordial acknowledgments on behalf of the suffering poor of this afflicted country, for whose help these munificent supplies have, from the concurrence of several causes at the present time, proved peculiarly seasonable. We have also to record the grateful sense we entertain of the confidence thus placed in our fidelity and discretion, and to express how deeply we feel the responsibility which devolves upon this Committee to carry out, in the most prompt and efficient manner, such measures of relief as may best comport with the designs of the generous donors.[33]

Shortly after, Jacob Harvey felt compelled to correct a report that had appeared in the London *Times*. The paper had suggested that the American donations had come from Irish people in that country. Harvey pointed out that:

> This remark does great injustice to Americans . . . The Irish, as a body, have done their duty nobly towards their suffering friends at home, and this fact has been made known to the world; they do not wish, therefore, to receive the praise which properly belongs to American philanthropists, and I wish it to be known in England that the great public movement in favour of Ireland throughout the Union is most essentially American.[34]

On 18 May 1847, the Dublin Quakers reported that while the supplies from the United States were having an impact, they saw no prospect of a reduction in demand for aid:

> It would be impossible for us to say at present, what portion of these large supplies have been actually distributed; and some of our correspondents do not hesitate to assure us that the large distribution thus made, has been instrumental, under Providence, in saving thousands of lives. The demands for assistance continue to be as heavy as at any former period, and we fear are likely to be so, for some considerable time to come.[36]

The donations from the New York committee had an immediate and beneficial impact, the Dublin Committee writing on 19 May explaining:

> . . . in the course of the few days which have elapsed since the first arrival, many thousand barrels of your excellent meal have been allotted in free grants in some of our most remote and distressed districts of the country; and some of the correspondents do not hesitate to assure us *that the large distribution thus made, has been instrumental under Providence in saving thousands of lives.*[35]

A month later, there had been no easing up of the demand for relief. At that stage, the Dublin Committee had provided assistance to every county in Ireland, the highest amounts going to the remotest districts in Connaught, Munster and Ulster. The relief so given totalled £60,000. Of that amount, about £50,000 had come from donations raised in Britain and Ireland. Increasingly though, the Friends were relying on donations being received from the US.[37] They described the work being done by the Committee in New York, through which so much relief was channelled as 'a labour of love'.[38]

Dependence on donations from the United States became even more important as local sources of funding dried up. On 3 June 1847, the Dublin Committee estimated that contributions from Britain and Ireland had reached £50,000, but that 'latterly, we are chiefly, indeed almost wholly, working with the supplies so bountifully entrusted to us from your favoured land'.[39] Support from the New York Relief Committee raised the morale of the Friends in Ireland, they admitting that it had served:

> . . . not only to strengthen our hands by your munificent and most seasonable supplies, but to animate us to pursue our engagements, in which, from the commencement of our labours to the present time, we have been surrounded with difficulties and discouragements, of which we are compelled to say we can as yet see no prospect of an early termination.[40]

In addition to the large contributions provided by the committee in New York, overseas donations came from Boston, Philadelphia and Nantucket in the US, and from Madrid in Spain.[41] People in Canada also proved generous supporters of the Friends. As had been the case in India, some residents there viewed raising money for Ireland and Scotland as being part of their Imperial duty to come to the assistance of their suffering 'fellow countrymen'.[42] An Irish Relief Fund based in Toronto acted as a conduit for a network of relief committee established throughout Upper Canada, the proceeds to be forwarded to the Central Committee of the Quakers in Dublin. In addition to raising money, they urged people to donate foodstuffs, ready for transport as soon as navigation was possible. By April 1847, the Toronto committee had raised over £2,000. They engaged two men to travel to Buffalo and, when there, to purchase foodstuffs to be sent to Ireland immediately through either Boston or New York, deciding that as food was urgently needed in Ireland, they should not wait until their frozen ports were navigable. They urged other relief committees to do the same.[43] The people in Canada realized that the distress in Ireland and Scotland would result in a large increase in immigration. The Toronto committee predicted that Irish landlords, in order to avoid high taxes, would 'use every means to induce the indigent to emigrate'.[44] To help these emigrants find work in Canada, rather than become a burden on local charity, the committee formed an Emigrant Settlement Society. They also considered whether part of the money being raised should be used to assist poor immigrants.[45] A newspaper in Canada West, reporting on the creation of this Society, called for similar action in their territory.[46] Regardless of these justifiable concerns, money and food continued to be sent to Ireland from all parts of Canada. At the beginning of September, the *Georgian* arrived in Ireland carrying a cargo of flour from the committees in Toronto, London and Montreal, with a promise of more to follow.[47] The foodstuffs were entrusted to the Society of Friends.[48] The practical interventions regarding emigration, however, were an acknowledgement that charitable assistance to the Irish poor was not simply confined to the island of Ireland.

Friends themselves were liberal contributors: members of the Society of Friends in Ireland gave £4,826.16s.6d., while members of the London Committee donated £37,398.5s.11d. Individual donors in Ireland included Arthur Guinness and Son, who made two donations of £100 each.[49] The London Committee received donations from a number of MPs included Viscount Morpeth (£100) and George Moffatt (£50). Multiple donations came from Yorkshire, included £5 collected in a Presbyterian meeting house in Bradford. Again, people with little to give gave. Operatives at the Kate's Grove Iron Works in Reading contributed £28.3s.3d.[50] Friends in the United States were especially responsive, Philadelphia alone raising over $3,000. This was in addition to large amounts of money raised by the Irish Relief Committee in the city. Abolitionists in Boston made a number of donations, which totalled over $200. Others who gave chose to remain anonymous.[51]

The desire to help Ireland appeared to remove boundaries and distinctions, while distance did not deter this spirit of ecumenicalism and unparalleled generosity.

To facilitate the giving of private charity, the government had promised to pay the cost of freight on ships bringing relief to Ireland from America and Britain. In total, the government paid over £33,000 in freight charges on behalf of the Quakers.[52] However, in return for the government paying freight, the foodstuffs coming in to the Quakers had to be channelled through the Commissariat depots. This arrangement gave the Treasury a measure of control over the storage and pricing of the foodstuffs so received. The Treasury had a similar agreement with the British Relief Association.[53] The government also interfered in less visible ways. Most of the Indian corn sent to Ireland was shipped in barrels, which kept it dry during the journey. However, upon arrival in Ireland, the government insisted that it be transferred into sacks, the sacks being sold for half a crown (2s/6d.) each. Asenath Nicholson was perplexed by this arrangement. She was receiving aid from America for personal distribution, it being transmitted to her through the Quakers. She found that she was forced to recover the cost of the sacks through the sale of the meal, thus throwing a further burden on the purchaser. She pointed out:

> The meal sent from New York was of the best kind, the hull being taken off and the meal kiln-dried, which had it been left in barrels would have remained for a year or more in good order. This, the government being unacquainted with the nature of the article, probably did not understand. If the inquiry be made – why did the government interfere with donations sent to the 'Dublin Central Committee', as donations – the answer can only be that they must have acted on one of two principles: that as they paid the freight of American grants, they had a right to use a little diction in the arrangement, in order to secure a partial remuneration, or they must have acted upon the principle, that their interference would forward the exertions making on behalf of their subjects.[54]

For Nicholson, the unbearable part of this arrangement was that the cost of purchasing the sacks had to be passed on to the poor and so food was 'taken from their hungry mouths to pay for sacks'. And for her, this one example of unnecessary interference helped to explain why 'the poor were so little benefitted by the bounties sent them from abroad'.[55]

Eyewitness testimony

An early concern of the Dublin Committee had been in regard to obtaining accurate information concerning the levels of distress, especially in the remote regions. They also wanted to find suitable channels through which they could distribute their relief. These issues were resolved when a number of English Friends offered to travel to the west of Ireland to assess the situation. Their eyewitness accounts were published in many newspapers and starkly confirmed the reality of the suffering. In addition, their journeys stimulated local involvement, especially among the upper classes.[56] The Quaker's involvement and first-hand testimony proved invaluable in saving lives in the winter of 1846–47 and beyond.

The first person to offer his services was William Forster of Norwich. Forster had decided on this course of action even before he knew that the Friends had established committees in Dublin or London. His son, William Edward Forster, on vacation in Galway, had sent home reports of what he was witnessing, which had made his father determined to travel there himself.[57] Forster arrived in Dublin on 28 November accompanied by Joseph Crosfield. The members of the Central Relief Committee were glad to find that 'his views were found to harmonize fully with those of the Dublin Committee, and he was warmly encouraged to pursue the course he proposed'.[58] Forster's plan was to visit the most impoverished areas in Ireland and to obtain information about the extent and nature of the destitution. He commenced his journey on 28 November and completed it on 14 April 1847.[59] During Forster's early weeks in Ireland, a number of Irish Quakers acted as his guides, including Dr Bewley of Moate and Marcus Goodbody of Clara.[60] However, hard snow falls hindered the early part of their travels. Forster had been provided with money to distribute as he saw fit which, in most cases, entailed opening a soup kitchen without delay.[61] Despite having experience of working with the English poor, he was shocked by conditions in Ireland. He informed his wife:

> I have not the nerve – there is no need to tell my weakness – to look upon the suffering of the afflicted; it takes too much possession of me, and almost disqualifies me for exertion . . . It was enough to have broken the stoutest heart to have seen the poor little children in the union workhouse yesterday- their flesh hanging so loose from their little bones, that the physician took it in his hands and wrapped it around their legs.[62]

For part of his visit, Forster had been accompanied by his 27-year-old son, William Edward Forster. William Edward had visited Ireland following the second crop failure in 1846 when he had stayed at the home of Daniel O'Connell in Derrynane. He returned to the country in January 1847 with his father.[63] His visits made a deep impression. Everywhere he and his father were greeted with cries of 'the hunger is upon us'. He wrote, 'no colouring can deepen the blackness of the truth'. Despite the suffering, William Edward had been impressed by the charity of the Irish poor towards each other, but he realized this charity would disappear, simply because, 'One class after another is falling into the same abyss of ruin'.[64]

Forster was also accompanied by a number of Friends during parts of the journey, many of whom were much younger than him. His first companion, 26-year-old Joseph Crosfield, a native of Liverpool, published a brief account of travelling with Forster, which was published under the title 'Distress in Ireland'.[65] Others included 22-year-old William Dillwyn Sims, whose mother Lydia had been a well-known abolitionist.[66] Sims published an account of the two weeks he had spent with Forster.[67] Another young Friend who accompanied Forster for part of his journey was James Hack Tuke, a 27-year-old Quaker from York. Tuke, who was interested in the care of the mentally ill, had accompanied Forster and Crosfield to the United States in 1845, visiting asylums while there.[68] The crisis in Ireland brought these three men together again. Tuke praised Forster's endurance and perseverance, writing:

> To the younger men who, from time to time, went out for a few weeks to assist in the work, it was no light task; but for a man of William Forster's temperament, advanced in years and whose intense sympathy caused him to realize sympathy with an acuteness into which few could enter, the daily strain of living and working in the midst of scenes of death and starvation was at times almost overwhelming.[69]

Tuke's graphic and compassionate accounts of what he witnessed provided powerful testimony regarding the desperate condition of the people. From Donegal, he reported that some of the local population was surviving on cabbage or seaweed.[70] When visiting Connemara in 1847, Asenath Nicholson spent some time with Tuke, travelling with him from Rossport to Ballina. She observed 'many a poor suffering one received not only a kind word but a shilling or half-crown as we passed along'.[71] In the autumn of 1847, Tuke returned to Ireland. He again visited some of the remotest western districts of County Mayo including Belmullet. Regardless of his earlier experiences in Ireland, his reports reveal his horror at the scenes he was witnessing. He wrote, 'Human wretchedness seems concentrated in Erris; the culminating point of man's physical degradation seems to have been reached in the Mullet'.[72] Even people who were still alive, he described as 'living skeletons'.[73] Tuke published his experiences as a *Visit to Connaught in 1847*, which he had first sent as a letter to the Central Relief Committee. In it, he gave an account of a number of heartless evictions by a local landowner, John Walshe. Walshe retaliated by criticizing Tuke's narrative, which resulted in his visiting the area again in 1848, to prove the veracity of his statement.[74] Tuke caught what was referred to as 'Irish famine fever' in 1848. Ironically, he had contracted the fever not in Ireland, but in England, while assisting Irish immigrants to Yorkshire.[75]

A number of English Quakers assisted in bringing food to Ireland. Edmund Richards of Gloucester and George Hancock of Liverpool travelled to the west of Ireland in February 1847 to oversee the distribution of the cargos of the *Scourge* and the *Albert* in some of the remotest coastal districts.[76] They undertook this journey in response to a stipulation by the Admiralty that a member of the Society of Friends had to be on board the relief ships from England.[77] George, a young man at the time, was the son of Dr Hancock, an abolitionist and friend of Garrison.[78] Despite the numerous reports that had been published in the British press describing conditions in the west of Ireland, he was appalled by the scenes he beheld.[79] Richards wrote from Belmullet that, 'the fearful state of starvation and destitution of the barony of Erris is such as no language can pourtray [sic]'. He estimated that out of the population of 30,000 people, 18,000 were without subsistence.[80]

Another English Quaker, William Bennett, travelled to Ireland in March 1847. His purpose was to give out seeds for crops, primarily turnips, swedes and 'mangels' (also known as mangle-wurzels),[81] they having been paid for from his own resources and by some private donations from Friends. Bennett wanted to encourage diversity from dependence on the potato. He was accompanied by his eldest son. Initially, the Quakers in Dublin had been concerned that his intervention might act as a disincentive to local exertions, but they were reassured by his cautious approach.[82] Only a few months later, the British government decided to distribute green-crop seeds, in an effort to revive Irish agriculture. William Todhunter, a Friend, was asked to manage some of the distribution process on behalf of the Commissariat. His ingenious idea was to use the postal system as a quick and efficient means of delivering the seeds.[83]

The Ladies' Clothing Society in London (of which Bennett's sister was a member) had provided Bennett with £50, three large bales of clothing and a box of arrowroot and ginger.[84] Although he journeyed to Ireland in March, during his first few days he experienced a heavy snow storm.[85] Early in his travels, he observed a corpse on the road side, which he regarded as evidence of 'the extreme distress'.[86] In Ballina, he was reunited with a number of English Friends including William Forster. Bennett praised the older man for his dedication to his mission.[87]

From Erris, a remote district in County Mayo, Bennett wrote,

language utterly fails me in attempting to depict the state of the wretched inmates . . . My hand trembles while I write. The scenes of misery and degradation we witnessed still haunt my imagination . . . the lines of this day can never be effaced from my memory. These were our fellow creatures. . . .[88]

Bennett published his experiences in *Narrative of a Recent Journey of Six Weeks in Ireland*, which was based on letters he had written to his sister.[89] The proceeds of his book were donated to Irish relief.[90]

A number of Irish Quakers, including James Perry, Jonathan Pim and Richard Davis Webb, toured the west of Ireland on behalf of the Dublin Committee in the spring of 1847.[91] Perry and Pim, who travelled together

to Galway, found that most of the relief in the city was being provided
through private means and distributed by local Protestant clergymen as well
as in a number of Catholic convents. Their visit coincided with the Treasury
directive that employment on the Public Works had to be cut by at least 20
per cent. As a consequence, the two Friends estimated that during their two-
week visit, they would need to distribute £10,000.[92] Webb, a printer, was also
an ardent abolitionist. He had, together with James Haughton and Richard
Allen, founded the Hibernian Anti-Slavery Society in 1837. In 1847, Webb
had been asked by the Central Relief Committee to investigate allegations
of misappropriations of their funds.[93] Such occurrences were rare. At the
beginning of 1848, Webb undertook a second visit to the impoverished west.[94]
From Erris he reported that, 'Death has fearfully thinned many families since
my last visit'.[95] The various Quaker narratives from the west had confirmed
that fishermen were particularly badly affected and so they were targeted for
support, especially those in Claddagh in Galway and parts of Mayo, Dublin,
Cork and Arklow. Some of the money was provided in order to promote new
fisheries. However, the destruction of shell fish beds by scavenging, hungry
people, the distance from markets and poor management meant that few
had survived.[96] In 1849, Webb again acted as a troubles shooter on behalf of
the Dublin Committee, travelling to Belmullet to investigate whether their
money was being wasted in support of a local fishery. He concluded that no
further funds should be given to support this endeavour.[97]

The various English and Irish Quakers who traversed Ireland following
the second potato failure not only provided vital emergency relief, but also
created a body of invaluable eyewitness testimony. William Forster, and
the various Friends who joined him on his mission, kept detailed records
of their experiences, which were reported not only in the Quaker press, but
also in secular newspapers in Ireland, Britain and America.[98] Forster's early
reports of conditions in the west won praise in the Irish newspapers for
verifying that descriptions of famine had not been exaggerated.[99] Moreover,
the accounts of these men not only brought the attention of the public to
the suffering of the Irish poor, but also left members of the government in
no doubt as to the severity of the crisis and the limitations of official relief
measures. By visiting the cabins of the poor, and providing accounts of the
distress of individuals and their families, the Friends afforded substance
and authenticity to the unfolding tragedy in Ireland. Their appeals for
further intervention, however, while answered by donors on both sides
of the Atlantic, were largely unheeded by those groups with whom most
responsibility lay – absentee landowners and politicians in London.

Longer-term improvement

When the Society of Friends had first become involved in providing
emergency relief, they had anticipated their involvement would last a few

months only. This had been extended to the harvest of 1847. While a number of charitable organizations did wind up their activities at this period, the Friends remained involved with famine relief, although the nature of their involvement changed. A constant debate within the Quaker committees had been over how to balance the immediate needs of the poor with a desire to bring about longer-term improvements in their situation. In early meetings, therefore, there had been 'considerable discussion' as to whether part of the funds should be used to promote industry and thus 'the permanent improvement of the condition of the Irish poor', but this had been decided against. The reason given was:

> The immediate pressure of actual want in many parts of Ireland was then so severe, and all the existing means for its relief so entirely inadequate, that it was concluded that we could not at that time with propriety extend the application of our funds to any objects beyond the supply of food and clothing to the hungry and destitute.[100]

In the spring of 1847, as government soup kitchens began to be opened, the Central Relief Committee had started to close their own soup establishments, believing there was little point in the duplication. The Friends decided to end their involvement totally when the amended Poor Law of August 1847 was implemented and outdoor relief became available. They resolved to use any leftover money for industrial purposes or for assisting those who were not eligible for Poor Law relief. At this stage, they had provided over 9,000 individual grants.[101]

The two main charities, the British Relief Association and the Society of Friends, were aware of the other's activities and expressed great respect for each other. In general, the Friends were more liberal in their provision of relief, whereas the British Relief Association observed government guidelines more closely. In districts where the Friends were active, Strzelecki recommended that the Association should be cautious about intervening and preserve their resources. This was evident in the summer of 1847 when he cautioned against 'the present glut of relief'.[102] Within a few weeks, as the work of various charities came to an end and the extended Poor Law came into operation, the 'glut' was replaced by a dearth in many districts.

Commenting on the careful balance of relief provided by government, landowners and private charity, the Quakers explained:

> We shall enlarge our scale of assistance if circumstances appear to demand it, and the means at our disposal admit: but in the present state of the country, we find constant need of careful discrimination, to preserve the funds entrusted to us from going into the pockets of the land-holders, who are by recent legislative measures charged to a certain extent with the maintenance of the destitute in their respective districts. This law is as

yet imperfectly carried out, and pending the perfecting of its machinery in the several localities, very large assistance is required in societies like ours to preserve the people from starvation, but great care is required that we do not needlessly assume burdens which properly belong to the owners of property, and may be levied by a rate. On the other hand, even when these measures are in full operation and faithfully administered, there is often a great mass of distress which cannot be reached by any public system of relief, and which it is our office to search out and administer to, if possible, through the hands of trustworthy and intelligent agents.[103]

At the beginning of 1848, despite the appalling conditions over winter, the Central Relief Committee still had 'a large reserve in money and food'. Problems with the Poor Law, however, meant that many people were not eligible for any assistance, the Friends resolved to use this money to:

... carry out some objects of great importance in promoting productive employment, yielding an immediate maintenance to the hands engaged and those depending upon them, and having a tendency, as we hope, permanently to improve their condition. Amongst these the most prominent objects are the encouragement of fisheries on our western and southern coasts, and the introduction of a better system of agriculture in some of the most neglected districts of the West.

We are also issuing considerable supplies of clothing, which, to an almost naked population, is essential to the preservation of health; and whilst we endeavor as little as possible to issue food gratuitously to the destitute for whom a resource is provided under the Poor Law, we contribute under careful restrictions, to the nourishment of those recovering from sickness, and some other classes of suffering persons whose condition cannot be reached by any system of legislative relief.[104]

Following this decision, the Dublin Committee immediately put in place plans to support 'the cultivation of land, the improvement of fisheries, and the encouragement of manufactures'.[105] The London Committee also agreed to use part of their funds to help promote industrial pursuits in Ireland. In particular, they were keen to help the fishermen in Claddagh, Galway and, to this end, had engaged a fishing captain from Falmouth to travel there and assist them.[106]

On 5 May 1848, the London Committee published their Third Report which they addressed to the Subscribers of the London Relief Fund. It commenced by explaining that:

Although a considerable balance of the funds entrusted to our care still remains unapplied, we are unwilling longer to delay the fulfillment of the intention expressed to us in a former circular.[107]

For over 18 months, the Dublin and London Committees had worked unstintingly to offer relief directly to the Irish poor and to provide a safety net when other forms of relief failed. They were now going to use the diminished resources at their disposal to make available loans and grants with which they hoped to help bring about permanent improvement in the lives of the poor.

Abolition and controversy

The involvement of the Quakers was not without a degree of controversy. The Society of Friends was well known for its early championing of the cause of abolition. As fund-raising efforts spread, a pressing question arose as to whether they would accept money from slave-holding states in the US. The final report of the Central Relief Committee recorded a number of donations received from Charleston. By the 1840s, Charleston in South Carolina was a centre of cotton production that depended on slave labour. The city had a small, but well-established Irish community which responded swiftly to the news from Ireland. On 19 February, $1,000 was sent to the Dublin Committee with the request that it be distributed 'in such a way as in your judgement is the best calculated to do the most good'.[108] Rather than hold a public meeting, the collection had been organized by the local Hibernian Society. Four days later, they sent an extra $300.[109] A number of smaller donations were sent subsequently.[110] In November 1847, the Hibernian Society passed a resolution thanking the Central Relief Committee 'for the very judicious and efficient manner in which you have appropriated the funds sent you'.[111] The final report of the Society of Friends, however, did not record that the donations from Charleston, and other slave-owning areas, had caused a rift within their committee, several members strongly opposing the accepting of such donations.[112] Following a number of intense discussions, the majority of the Dublin Committee voted on behalf of accepting this donation.[113]

The decision to accept donations from districts which condoned slavery offended a number of Irish abolitionists. Dublin-born Richard Allen, who was a founding member of the Central Relief Committee, was also prominent in the anti-slavery movement and a personal friend of the outspoken American abolitionist, William Lloyd Garrison. Allen played a leading role in the debate about whether the Friends should accept money from slave-holding states. At a meeting in March 1847, Allen had tried to impress on the committee how awful slavery was, but felt that he had failed in this mission.[114] He followed this up with a long letter to the Central Committee outlining his concerns. For him, the question was 'fraught with future consequences of good or evil'. Allen acknowledged the sympathy of leading slave-holders including Henry Clay, John Calhoun and others towards the Irish poor. He proposed that their donations should not be accepted, even though it would have provided thousands of pounds worth of relief, but acknowledged:

> The reaction which our refusal to receive those contributions will probably excite – that the swell of sympathy will fearfully recoil at such a cutting rebuke; that the slave states will be thoroughly convulsed; that rage will take the place of apparent gentleness, cursing of blessing; that we may have to bear a great amount of obloquy both at home and abroad; that our motives will be impugned; that we shall be called hypocrites, and accused of aggravating the dreadful state of misery in this country.[115]

In regard to the slave-holders, he asked:

> Shall we, by accepting his blood-stained contributions to the sacred cause of suffering humanity, stamp him with the seal of Christian fellowship; or by firmly yet kindly rejecting the money, as that to which he has no claim, and which belongs to his down-trodden brother, shall we teach him his true position?[116]

Allen pointed out that they had recently declined £70 sent to them by Lord John Russell on behalf of the Queen's Theatre, leading him to ask 'Is the money obtained from the theatre more tainted in our view than the proceeds of slavery?'[117]

The debate was taken up on the other side of the Atlantic. American abolitionist, Henry C. Wright and Irish abolitionist, Richard Davis Webb, jointly wrote an appeal that was published in the Boston *Liberator* on 30 April 1847 in regard to the Friends accepting the money from slaveholders, for the starving Irish. Wright was travelling in Europe between 1842 and 1847. The letter proposed:

> Ireland is in a most deplorable state. It is awful to contemplate, that, while I am writing these few lines, many are actually famishing for want of a little of the bread that perisheth. I trust the American people will go on nobly as they have begun, and by such practical operation, draw the bonds of human brotherhood closer, and spread that sentiment, 'We are all brethren, though seas roll between'. But, as to the slaveholding portion of your people, even to save life, we cannot touch that money stained with the slaves' blood. It is every moment crying to God for Vengeance. I fear we must say to the Friends' Relief Committee, as it was said to the Free Church, 'SEND BACK THAT MONEY!'[118]

The controversy was picked up by one of the leading Irish American newspapers, the Boston *Pilot* which claimed to be anti-slavery, but opposed to the abolitionists. The paper described the correspondence in the *Liberator* concerning donations to Ireland as 'absurd, ungenerous, base and unmanly'.[119] It reaffirmed the claim that American slaves were better looked after than Irish peasants, adding:

> Slavery, in the abstract, is a moral evil, it is true; we wish it were abolished, but in the right and legitimate way . . . Many of the Southern planters themselves, are not in favor of slavery; they acknowledge it to be in a certain point of view a moral evil. But they inherited their property, and are they to become beggars merely to gratify a mass of bigots? . . . They treat their slaves with the utmost kindness, allow them every reasonable privilege, and would to God that the slaves, the myriads of *white slaves* of England were as comfortable, as happy, and as well provided for. The Southerner heard of the distress of Ireland; his heart bled at the recital of her woes; he instantly opened his purse as a Christian and a man. But because he is the owner of slaves, his money should be rejected, and the poor Irish must die with hunger. The Southern slaves are infinitely better off in their present condition than millions of the British subjects . . .
>
> What say ye to this, philanthropists of the Dublin Central Relief Committee? What a comment for you! Who is the greater slave, the well fed and well clothed blacks of this country, or the white subjects of England, whom political and social oppression is constantly starving to death, not only in Ireland but on your own soil, under your own eyes?[120]

Caroline Wells (Healey) Dall, an American feminist, social reformer and abolitionist, entered the debate, criticizing the writings of Wright, Webb and Haughton directly. In a long letter to the *Liberator,* she explained her dismay:

> In the copy of the *Liberator* just received, I have been pained by an expression of opinion on the part of Henry C. Wright, and Jas. Haughton, with reference to the contributions taken up for destitute Ireland, at the South. As I am well known to be a faithful enemy to the institution of slavery, as I have done what few anti-slavery persons can pretend to—namely—lived two years in a slave State—in open opposition to the institution, and acting constantly in frank violation of the law,— instructing a class of 13 adult blacks in the alphabet of our language and religion, I feel that I have a right to speak out on this subject, which cannot be gainsaid . . .
>
> Slaveholders are a class of men; they vary like any other class. Some of them are weak, wicked, cruel . . . but more, far more, are ignorant and well meaning. They never think of slavery as a sin, they hardly know that any one so regards it, and the majority of those, who pass wicked laws, do it under the influence of others, persuaded that it is necessary to civil peace, and the protection of property. Many of these men are kind-hearted and affectionate, and would feel the distress of Ireland as much as you and I, and when they put their hands into their pockets, had no

more idea of buying 'golden opinions' for themselves than I have, though I say it, that should not say it. Shame on James Haughton for accusing them of it. Little enough do they care what Ireland thinks of them . . .

   That class of men, who thought of the sufferings of the Irish, and sent something to their relief, are the most hopeful class at the South. The very benevolence which prompted this act, if not despised, may yet work out their salvation . . . The slaveholders of the South, are they not as much as the slave its victims? and must we not love them into better things?[121]

Tellingly, the final report of the Society of Friends did not refer to these acrimonious debates. The debate on abolition, however, revealed how difficult it was to keep charity and politics separate, even when the ultimate purpose was to save lives.

The cost of giving

The withdrawal of the Quakers and other charitable groups from providing relief inevitably placed more responsibility for saving the lives of the poor on official measures, which after 1847 meant the Poor Law. Unfortunately, financial difficulties, combined with a dogmatic approach to giving relief, meant that levels of evictions, emigration, disease and death – all indicators of extreme suffering – changed little. The government's relief measures were not succeeding, yet, publicly, they adhered to the conviction that Ireland's salvation depended on forcing her to rely on her own resources. Privately, the government and its agents at the Treasury appeared less certain. In June 1849, Charles Trevelyan (now Sir) wrote to the Dublin Committee asking them what their plans were to help to alleviate the 'great distress which still prevailed'. To entice the Quakers to become involved again, they were offered the derisory sum of £100 from Treasury funds. The response of the Friends was telling in terms of how they viewed responsibility for saving lives:

> . . . after full deliberation we were of opinion that, in the event of undertaking the distribution of relief as heretofore, the sum which we could hope to collect would be utterly inadequate for such an object; that even if sufficient funds were placed at our disposal, we could no longer calculate on the assistance of many of our most efficient agents and correspondents, and that the relief of destitution, on an extended scale, should in future be entrusted to the arrangements which parliament had provided for that purpose.[122]

In 1852, the Dublin Quakers published a final report of their proceedings, entitled, *Transactions of the Central Relief Committee of the Society of Friends during the Famine in Ireland in 1846 and 1847*. It was over

500 pages long and provided an early account of the workings of private charity. The committee apologized for a delay in its appearance, explaining it had arisen partly as a result of the death of Joseph Bewley in the previous year. The final report provided a remarkable record of an incredible period in Quaker history. Much of the information it contained was heart-wrenching. It listed the many donors to Quaker relief. In total, the Dublin Committee had received contributions in excess of £200,000. Nonetheless, the Friends believed that their interventions had not been a success.[123] Such an admission was a melancholic reflection on the fact that, despite the tireless efforts of the Friends, and the generosity of those who supported them, over a million people had died.

The personal cost of Quaker involvement was high. The reports of the Friends who undertook journeys to the west of Ireland in 1847 reveal the pain and trauma of witnessing such suffering first-hand. In addition to the mental toll, there was a real physical and financial price to working so hard, in what often appeared to be a hopeless cause. Writing in March 1847, Jonathan Pim confessed, 'I cannot go on no longer on the present plan. My business is totally neglected. My health, neither of body or mind, would bear it'. Poignantly, Pim did collapse from exhaustion shortly afterwards.[124]

A number of Friends made the ultimate sacrifice, by paying with their lives. Abraham Beale who worked on behalf of the Cork Committee in both the city and surrounding rural areas died of typhus fever in August 1847, which he caught while working with the poor.[125] A contributing factor, however, was that, 'the painful effect on his mind of tales of sorrow beyond his power to relieve, was too much for him, and worn down in mind and body he was unable to withstand the attacks of disease'.[126] For Asenath Nicholson, Beale's name, 'left a sweet and lasting remembrance'.[127] Henry Perry of Blackrock, Treasurer of the clothing committee and a manager of a soup kitchen in Dublin, died in 1848.[128] In the US, Jacob Harvey, Secretary of the New York Relief Committee, died, it was suspected, from exhaustion, as did William Todhunter in Ireland.[129] Todhunter had accompanied Forster for part of his visit to the west in 1847.[130]

Overall, the contribution of the Society of Friends was remarkable for its selflessness, compassion and effectiveness. Their role was recognized at the time, the *Dublin Freeman's Journal* commenting:

> Their exertions have been taxed to the uttermost, involving a duty and responsibility such as never had been imposed on similarly constructed bodies in the history of the world. . . Testimonies of their promptitude and liberality have been afforded by all the representatives of local wretchedness; and it must be a consolation and a keen satisfaction to the minds of those gentlemen who have made such sacrifices of time and thought in the cause of charity, that their labours should be rewarded by the universal gratitude of their country'.[131]

The Quakers won the praise of all who worked with them. Even the independently minded Asenath Nicholson, who had occasionally criticized their dogmatism, admired their approach to giving relief:

> These men, moved by high and lofty feelings, spent no time in idle commenting on the Protestant or the papist faith – the Radical, Whig or Tory politics, but looked at things as they were, and faithfully recorded what they saw. Not only did they record, but they relieved.[132]

After 1846, the Society of Friends gave 5,375 individual grants, provided 157 boilers, distributed 7,848 tons of food and donated £20,700.15s.6d. in monetary grants.[133] Importantly, the Friends had not only saved many lives, but also had brought compassion and dignity to the giving of charity at a time of desperation and devastation.

4

'An ocean of benevolence'.[1] The General Relief Committee of New York

Throughout the final months of 1846, newspapers in the United States were carrying reports from Ireland that chronicled the deteriorating state of the people. In the wake of the first appearance of blight, there had been a number of sporadic suggestions that America should send aid to Ireland, but the second failure of the potato crop provoked a widespread response. For some Irish Americans, however, the reaction was not quick enough: in November, the Boston *Pilot* admonished its readers, asserting, 'We confess we have been astonished at the apathy and indifference with which the people of this country have regarded the horrible conditions of their fellow beings in Ireland'.[2] The formation of the Central Committee of the Society of Friends in Dublin in November, and their circular to Friends throughout the world, confirmed the gravity of the situation and resulted in a number of donations being made from all parts of the United States. In New York, the Quakers' circular prompted a number of 'benevolent gentlemen' to ascertain 'the exact losses with a view to institute measures of providing relief'.[3] The outcome of this investigation was the founding of a committee that put New York at the forefront of international fund-raising efforts for Ireland. Interestingly, the man responsible for this initiative had no direct connection to Ireland.

The General Relief Committee

Myndert Van Schaick, a member of one of New York's oldest Dutch families, was a successful businessman associated with bringing drinking water to New York. Reports of the worsening conditions in Ireland prompted him to take a more professional approach to providing aid. He commenced by opening a subscription list on 7 February.[4] He invited fellow members of the New York elite to assist. His request was followed by a meeting on 12 February in Prime's Building in Wall Street, which was provided free of charge. This in turn led to the formation of a 'special committee' consisting of Jacob Harvey, George Griffin, Theodore Sedgwick and John Jay, all of whom were successful businessmen. Van Schaick acted as both Chairman and, briefly, as Treasurer of the Standing Committee (see Appendix for membership). On 12 February, the *ad hoc* committee issued an appeal on behalf of the Irish poor, which they entitled, an 'Address to the Public'. It pointed out that four million people were on 'the verge of starvation', and that 'Neither the energy of the father, nor the tenderness of the mother, avail anything – young and old, the strong and the feeble, are involved in this common ruin'.[5] The justification of American involvement was explained thus:

> It is to God alone that we can ascribe the fertile soil, the boundless prairies, the infinite mineral wealth, which makes our country the garden of the world . . . Our fellow citizens, generally of the agricultural and commercial classes, are making large gains by the advance in foreign prices. What is death to Ireland is but augmented fortune to America; and we are actually fattening on the starvation of another people.[6]

The appeal concluded by stating, 'every dollar that you give, may save a human being from starvation!'[7]

The committee, together with John A. King, a former Assemblyman, convened a public meeting at the Tabernacle (the United Church of Christ) on Broadway on 15 February.[8] The Tabernacle had been founded in 1832 by Lewis Tappan, a leading abolitionist.[9] The meeting was attended by the cream of New York society and cut across divides of religion and nationality. It was chaired by Robert Minturn, a wealthy merchant. According to one newspaper, 'he expressed in a beautiful manner the duty the people here owe in connection with the great claim Ireland presents to us'.[10] Among religious leaders who addressed the gathering was Rev (later Bishop) Jonathan Wainwright of St John's Episcopal Chapel.[11] The following day, local newspapers reported that 'the standing committee for the relief of sufferers in Ireland, have permission to occupy an office on the second floor of Prime's Buildings, no. 54 Wall Street, opposite the Merchant's Exchange, where attendance will be given from 10.00 am to 2.00 pm each day, to receive contributions for that object'.[12] A further large meeting was held in the Tabernacle on 23 February. Van Schaick was confirmed as President, together with a committee of 22 vice-presidents and five secretaries.[13] The committee included local politicians and businessmen including John Jay, James King and Stewart Brown. The new organization was to be known as the General Relief Committee of New York. Van Schaick called on the public, without reference to 'customs or creed', to support their work and thus help the starving in Ireland.[14] He pointed out, 'The Irish cabin of 1847 – without food for the living, or coffins for the dead – exhibits a picture more heart-touching than perhaps misery ever before presented to the eye of philanthropy'.[15] During his speech, Van Schaick, alluding to the political situation in Ireland, criticized absentee landowners:

On the liberal aid of the Irish absentees, who have habitually deserted their home to spend abroad that overflowing wealth which should have enriched, or at least saved from want, their native land – who have broken asunder those ties of patronage and reciprocated affection that should consecrate the relation of landlord and tenant – we have no reason to suppose that the Irish peasantry can confidently rely in this extremity of their need. England has nobly headed the list of charity for the relief of her suffering sister, thus redeeming in part the debt, ancient and vast, which she owes to Ireland.[16]

Questioning how a famine on such a scale could exist in the centre of civilization, he alluded to the condition of Southern slaves, a motif that was present in much of the American fund-raising:

How would the world exclaim, with England at its head, should our Southern negro slaves be fed solely on the potato, and be left, upon a failure of that crop, to starve and die in masses by the road side, or in crowded and nauseous hovels, without even a poor candle for the last rites of their religion, and there to be gnawed by rats or buried with no covering save their rags![17]

According to Van Schaick, in the preceding year Irish house servants and labourers in the United States had contributed over one million dollars, which he attributed to a 'deep-seated love of country'.[18]

However, he also made the oft-repeated point that Americans were benefitting financially from the food shortages in Europe:

That Ireland, the hospitality of whose people has been long proverbial, now stricken by the hand of Providence, and filled with the starving, the dying, and the dead, has a peculiar right to sympathy and aid; and that to this Republic, whose wealth is increased by their want, it especially belongs to contribute of the abundance where with God has blessed us, to the necessities of the Irish people.[19]

From the outset, it was apparent that American relief efforts would cut across economic and political boundaries and would involve people who had no direct connection with Ireland. The ecumenical nature of the New York committee was enshrined in the resolution that 'customs' or 'creed' does not 'absolve us from the duties of common brotherhood'.[20] Religious diversity was also manifest in the committee's composition. Van Schaick, the President of the General Relief Committee, was a former Democratic Assemblyman and Senator. He was a member of one of the city's oldest and wealthiest Dutch families and belonged to the Dutch Reformed Church.[21] He was also a noted philanthropist who had no direct association with Ireland. Responding to a donation from Pensacola in Florida, Van Schaick outlined some of the reasons for his involvement:

> We hope that our operations will save some lives, will heal some broken hearts, and in the performance of a Christian duty will exhibit the character of American freemen in no disadvantageous light abroad.[22]

When he resigned his position, he offered further insights into his personal motivations for working on behalf of the Irish poor:

> Supposing that I might be able to accomplish some good to a greatly abused and suffering people, my employment has been to me a source of unmixed gratification and happiness, and now that I am about to resign my trust into the hands of another, I cannot leave my post without conveying to the true and disinterested friends of Ireland my ardent hope that the education of the people with Bible in hand, and irrespective of religious dogmas and sectarian interests, may be made to constitute one of the measures, as it is an indispensable preparation by which the population are to be enabled to provide for their own subsistence, without depending too much on human aid, advice or direction, which is quite as likely to be selfish, as disinterested.[23]

One of the secretaries of the General Relief Committee was an Irish-born merchant, Jacob Harvey, whose family were members of the Society of Friends in Limerick.[24] He worked in this capacity until his premature death in 1848, which was mourned by people on both sides of the Atlantic.[25] Another founding member of the committee was August Belmont. He had been born in Europe but, following emigration, had changed his surname from Schoenberg to avoid anti-Jewish prejudice. In the US, he acted as agent for the Rothschild Banking House. In addition to offering administrative support, Belmont made a personal donation of $500.[26] Some years later, he became embroiled in controversy with the Irish American community as a result of looking after the 'Fenian Fund'.[27]

The committee moved quickly, sending letters to the clergy of all denominations in the city, asking them to make collections in their respective churches.[28] As donations started to pour in from the rest of the country George Barclay, James Reyburn and Robert Minturn took responsibility getting the relief to Ireland.[29] Minturn, of the shipping agents 'Grinell, Minturn and Co.', took charge of commissioning the ships to carry the foodstuffs to Ireland. The fact that the cargoes arrived intact was later attributed to his careful choice of sailing vessels.[30]

It was decided that all food and money raised would be sent to the Central Relief Committee of the Society of Friends in Dublin. On 24 February, Van Schaick wrote to Jonathan Pim and Joseph Bewley, Secretaries of the Dublin Committee, addressing them as 'Christian Friends'; they responded by addressing him as 'Respected Friend'. Van Schaick's letter included an initial donation of £3,000 ($14,066.67), he explaining 'our fellow-citizens of every name and creed, deeply sympathizing with the distresses of the Irish people, have with the greatest alacrity come forward to contribute their mite towards the alleviation of a misery, which we fear, no human aid can reach in all its depths and recesses'.[31] Although the New York Committee preferred to provide aid in food, they felt that sending cash would provide more immediate relief and help remote districts. The majority of the food aid was to be given to families who were totally destitute, but the Committee had agreed that a smaller portion would be sold to 'poor families who are still able to buy at such reasonably reduced rates as may be consistent with the humane intention of the contributors'.[32]

The initial response to the appeal was so great that the committee was forced to meet daily. By the end of February, they had raised over $45,000.[33] By March, that amount had more than doubled, rising to over $105,000.[34] At the end of the month, Van Schaick informed the Dublin Committee that:

The cry of Ireland for assistance will be answered with great liberality from every quarter of this country – even I hope from the defaulting States, who in their infancy are unable to pay the debts which they were induced to contract by their evil counselors.[35]

By mid-April though, donations were beginning to slow down, which Van Schaick attributed to two reasons, 'because all tides ebb and flow' and 'the unusually great numbers of poor people that have been landed on our shores from British traders since 1 April'.[36] On 11 May, Van Schaick confirmed that the charitable impulse in New York was slowing down and informed the committee in Dublin, 'This City is filling fast with foreign poor, and I am sitting frequently the whole morning in this room, without receiving any money excepting occasionally a remittance coming in from the country or from a distant state'.[37]

Regardless of the reduction in donations, by 18 May the total had reached $144,450.30.[38] By 25 June, the committee had raised $156,581.65 in cash on behalf of 'the famishing poor of Ireland without distinction of sect, creed or opinion'.[39] At this point, James Reyburn took over as Treasurer, although Van Schaick remained as Chairman. On 2 February 1848, Reyburn reported that $19,037.37 had been received.[40] In total, $171,374.24 in cash had been collected; $156,581.65 had been received by Van Schaick in the early months up to 25 June 1847, and $14,792.59 added in the following twelve months, when Reyburn was Treasurer. During this period, donations in the form of provisions amounted to $242,042.79 in value.[41] However, the freezing weather in the west of the country meant that the canals and rivers were not navigable and so much of the foodstuffs could not be transported until spring.[42]

The New York committee worked closely with the Quakers in Dublin. As Van Schaick explained to one of the American donors, 'In the impartiality, judgment and discretion of the Central Committee of the Society of Friends, all our committee have unlimited confidence'.[43] Bewley and Pim, in turn, responded:

> . . . we sensibly feel the large responsibility which devolves upon us, in endeavoring, as we are bound to do, to carry out faithfully and with due promptitude the designs of those who are thus pleased to make us the almoners of their bounty. We can gratefully appreciate the confidence of a community to whom we are comparatively unknown.[44]

The impact of the American donations in Ireland was considerable, as Jonathan Pim, writing from County Mayo at the end of March, explained:

> Your assistance comes at a most opportune time, as I quite think that the coming month will be really the period of trial; and I trust that your contributions, stimulating our Committee and the other bodies to whom they may be sent, to increased exertions to meet the crisis, will be the means of greatly lessening the suffering, and of saving many lives.
>
> I enclose a copy of a circular which we have sent out a few days since, and wilt give thee some idea of our course of action. I also send a copy of the Government instructions under the new act, which will enable thee to form some opinion of its object and probable effects. If we can get on tolerably well over the coming month, I shall have great hopes that our difficulties will be greatly lessened by the general working of the new act.
>
> Your contributions are truly noble, and are felt and acknowledged by all here to be such. They put many of our rich people here to shame – or at least they ought to do so. The warm and generous sympathy which extends throughout the Union, springing from those brotherly feelings which a common language, a common origin, and kindred institutions naturally inspire, will, I trust, have effects long outlasting the misfortunes which have drawn it forth and may hereafter tend to neutralize the jealousies, which conflicting interests must occasionally produce.[45]

Similar sentiments were expressed by the Quakers in Dublin, who acknowledged:

> We can truly say that the munificence of your City and its vicinity, and of the citizens at large in many other parts of the United States as exhibited by the immense supplies of food they are sending for our starving people, surpass all the expectations that we had ventured to form on the subject.[46]

The General Relief Committee decided to publish their proceedings in a pamphlet.[47] One purpose was to show the donors that their contributions had been received and to let them know how these contributions were being utilized in Ireland. A further reason for making the information available was to disabuse some people in Britain of the idea that there had been a selfish motive behind the donations.[48] The report also explained that initially the committee had intended to act only on behalf of New York City, but:

from being the representatives of a single City, they became the almoners as will appear from the contributions they now acknowledge, of large numbers of their fellow- countrymen in the states of Connecticut, Massachusetts, Vermont, New Hampshire, New York, New Jersey, Pennsylvania, Maryland, Virginia, North Carolina, South Carolina, Georgia, Florida, Alabama, Mississippi, Kentucky, Tennessee, Arkansas, Indiana, Illinois, Wisconsin, Iowa, Michigan and Ohio, as well as residents of Canada and the District of Columbia – and of officers and sailors attached to our navy on foreign stations – and of the Choctaw tribe of Indians in the far West.[49]

Occasionally, special requests had been made on behalf of particular districts in Ireland. In early March, the Irish Relief Committee of Salina and Syracuse donated $1,200. In the accompanying letter, James Lynch, on behalf of the Committee, stated:

The committee have the utmost confidence in the prudence and humane feeling of that society, and feel assured that they will make a fair and impartial distribution of everything sent them; but some of the members of our committee are particularly acquainted with the province of Munster, and believe that the greatest destitution and distress prevails in the counties of Cork, Kerry and Tipperary, and would (if not inconsistent with the action of the Committee of Friends in Dublin) wish one-half of our contributions sent to the starving poor of Cork, Kerry and Tipperary.[50]

A donation of $210 from the inhabitants of Morganton, North Carolina, requested that one-half be sent to the parish of Inniscoffey, County Westmeath and the other half to the parish of Milltown, in same county. Van Schaick apologized to the Dublin Committee for special requests, but explained, 'It is difficult for us to avoid giving you some trouble in this way. But we make no promises, and keep these local feelings as much as possible at a distance from our system of operations'.[51] Nonetheless, on 29 April, Van Schaick wrote to the Dublin Friends:

I have promised two old Irish gentlemen who came to this room abounding in sympathy and thankfulness, that I would say to you that a letter had been received from Thos. Swanton of Cranlieth, county Cork, representing the extreme destitution and misery of the large parish of Skufl [sic], East Skull [sic], a half parish, containing 8000 inhabitants, is particularly recommended to your attention, Though I clearly see the danger and the impropriety of interfering with your system by giving special instructions, yet less than this I could not do at the request of 'two gray haired old men'.[52]

The suffering and mortality in Schull and Skibbereen, the two small towns which achieved international notoriety in early 1847, had become a powerful clarion call for external charity to be given to Ireland.[53] The Dublin Committee acknowledged that this was one of the poorest districts in Ireland and responded by sending members of their Cork Society to the areas to distribute relief as requested.[54]

As was frequently noted in 1846 and 1847, a number of Americans were becoming wealthy because the food shortages in Ireland and other parts of Europe had doubled the value of food exports from the US. Philip Hone, a former Mayor of New York and noted diarist, confessed to feeling guilty for eating sumptuous dinners while the Irish were starving. He attributed the recent increase in American's prosperity to a sharp increase in food and freight prices.[55] Hone was one of the founding members of the General Relief Committee of New York.[56] In February, he made a personal donation of $25 to the Committee.[57] Hone was given a chance to something practical to help Ireland when he was asked, in spring 1847, by the Lisburn-born merchant prince, Alexander Turney Stewart, to preside over a raffle for a rosewood piano. It was to be held in Stewart's show-case store, the Marble Palace in New York City.[58] Like Hone, Stewart was involved in fund-raising for Ireland, being a member of the General Standing Committee of the New York Relief Committee.[59] The piano had been donated by Horatio Worcester, a piano forte maker also based in Broadway.[60] The raffle raised $1,275.[61] Stewart personally contributed 'generously' to the day's proceedings.[62] The raffle was not the end of Stewart's involvement in famine relief. An early biography stated that in 1847 he chartered a ship which he filled with provisions and sent as a gift to Ireland. Nor was this the last time that Stewart demonstrated that he had not forgotten his roots.[63] During the industrial downswing in Ireland in 1863, he arranged for a ship loaded with foodstuffs to be sent to unemployed mill workers and weavers in the Lisburn and the Maze districts. In addition, he offered a free passage to New York to those who wanted to emigrate.[64]

As news reached the United States of the cost of foodstuffs in Ireland, appeals were made that assistance should be given as far as possible in provisions rather than money, so that food prices in Ireland did not rise further. In Ireland, Indian corn was selling at 74 shillings a bushel, double the price of that in the States.[65] Money donations in New York were collected at 54 Wall Street, while provisions or clothing to be sent to Ireland were to be left at the store of Joseph Naylor at 18 Broadway, and marked 'relief for Ireland'.[66] Inspired by the activities in New York City, Brooklynite R. J. Todd offered to receive or collect provisions in that town until a vessel could be obtained to carry them to Ireland.[67] The donations received by the New York Committee up to 27 May 1847 were primarily used to fund the sailing of 14 ships, either fully or partly loaded with provisions. The cargoes consisted largely of Indian corn, flour, cornmeal, barley and beans, with smaller quantities of cheese, pork and beef. Cartons of clothes were also included. The New York committee left it to the Committee in Dublin to 'determine the best course to pursue in applying our consignments so as to save life, and shed some small rays of comfort into the abodes of your desolate people'.[68] Once the foodstuffs arrived in Ireland, they were transported to the interior by inland navigation.[69] The Irish committee had asked if the first cargoes could go to Dublin, which had good links via inland navigation to some of the remotest parts of Ireland.[70] Subsequent ships were sent to Liverpool in England, the port being the centre of the transatlantic trade and enjoying close trading links with Dublin.[71] The initial cargoes arrived in April.[72] Part of the money raised was used to offset freight charges, but this became unnecessary when the government announced that, on production of a consular certificate, they would pay freight charges on aid sent to Ireland and Scotland.[73] The request for the government to pay these charges had been made by the London Committee of the Society of Friends.[74] As soon as a cargo arrived, it was:

> Taken charge of by the agents of Government, at their respective ports of destination, so as to relieve us from all expenses attending the landing, storage, costs of agency and transporting it to the distressed districts, an arrangement which will contribute essentially to facilitate the proper distribution whilst it will divest these operations of almost all cost.[75]

Importantly, the agreement of the Treasury meant that the cargoes from America could be distributed without 'delay, risk or expense'. Moreover:

> The food put on board at New York, may be considered as laid down at most at the doors of the sufferers for whom it is intended, without any material diminution from the expenses, attending its transport across the Atlantic, or the cost and delay inseparable from its conveyance into the remote and mountainous districts of this country, where the distress is of the most severe character, and the channels of internal communication very imperfect.[76]

The Quakers were permitted to make use of the many Commissariat Depots used during the previous year's shortages, for the holding and distributing of food. The British Treasury, however, refused to pay any insurance charges.[77] The Quakers were appreciative of these arrangements, praising, 'the liberal spirit on the part of our Government, to which we are indebted for such important facilities, and as the fact of so many of the vessels delivering their cargoes to the agents of Government, would, in itself, if unexplained, furnish occasion of uneasiness'.[78]

By the beginning of 1848, the freight charges paid by the British government for goods coming from North America totalled £42,673.17s.6d.[79] This amount represented 119 ships, which had sailed from a variety of ports, including 36 from New York, 27 from New Orleans, 18 from Philadelphia, six from Charlestown, five from Baltimore, Savannah and Mobile, four from Boston, four from Wilmington, three from Toronto, two from Montreal and Alexandria (Virginia), and one each from Newark and Richmond. An overwhelming number of these cargoes – 63 in total – were consigned to the Society of Friends in Ireland, while smaller amounts were sent to the Mayor of Cork (four shiploads), the Mayor of Belfast (two shiploads), the General Central Relief Committee in Dublin (four), the Irish Relief Association (four) and the Dublin Parochial Association (two). Single cargoes were also sent to the Archbishop of Tuam and the Archbishops of Armagh and Dublin. The Rev P. Murphy in Wexford received two consignments.[80] Four shiploads destined for Belfast were delivered to the care of 'Mr Allen', while two shiploads sent to Cork had been consigned to local individuals – to a 'Mr Barry' and 'Misses Cox', respectively. The Cox sisters of Dunmanway in West Cork had achieved some notoriety in the United States when their appeal for aid had been read out at a public meeting by the American Vice-President and widely reported.[81] Four shiploads were designated for Scotland, with three being sent to the Highland Destitution Committee and one to the Glasgow Relief Committee.[82]

Donors and donations

Donations to the New York Committee were not only made in money or provisions. More unusual contributions included the proceeds of a concert by the Musical Society, a gift of a piano, expensive jewellery, a barge (which proved to be useful for conveyed foodstuffs), an offer by the French Consulate to convene a meeting of French citizens, and the assistance of the Mercantile Library Association.[83] As was generally the case, aid to the committee cut across social and political groups. The 'Descendants of the Pilgrims' donated $10 and 'officers, cadets and labourers at West Point' contributed $312.43.[84] A 'Relief Ball' held in Castle Garden, the Emigrant Receiving Station in New York City, raised $1,420.25. The Jury and Clerk in the case of 'Griffin versus Mutual Life Insurance' gave $2. The Temperance inhabitants of Norfolk, Litchfield County in Connecticut, contributed $475 on the 26 February 1847. They requested that breadstuffs to that value should be given to the Rev Theobald Mathew, the Irish Temperance leader, to be used by him in such manner as he deemed fit.[85] A number of journals and papers including the *Journal of Commerce* and the *Tribune* organized collections, while staff in the office of the *New York Observer* gave $17.[86]

Women were significant contributors to the committee, although many gave anonymously. One of the largest individual donations came from a 'Lady' who gave $1,000. Other donations from women included $133 received from 'the Ladies of Burlington, Vermont'.[87] 'The ladies of Monticello, Sullivan County' held a donations party which raised $5.[88] Teachers and Scholars of Madame Chegary's French School, a seminary for young women, raised $47.25.[89] Mrs Van Cortlandt, a resident of Sing Sing, New York, organized a collection amounting to $45.50.[90] Children and young people also joined in the fund-raising. This included 'two little self-denying girls', of Rhinebeck, Duchess County in New York, who gave $10.[91] The boys of Ward School No. 3 in the 10th Ward raised $1.54 in one-cent coins.[92] Amenia Seminary, a private Methodist co-educational secondary school and college, located in Duchess County, raised $20.[93] The principal of the school was Erastus Otis Haven, who had an illustrious career as an educationalist.[94] Pupils of a George P. Quackenbos donated $7. Two of the smallest donations came from 'a little boy' and 'a little Irish emigrant, both of whom contributed 50 cents.[95] Pupils of St Matthew's Lutheran Academy in Walker Street, NYC, raised $14.[96] A school for young ladies, run by Charlotte M. Havens and located at 263 Ninth Street, New York City, held a fair that raised $287. The donors stipulated that $50 of this was for 'the Scotch'.[97] Charlotte's younger sister, Catherine, later noted in her diary:

> . . . four years ago there was a dreadful famine in Ireland, and we gave up our parlor and library and dining room for two evenings for a fair for them, and all my schoolmates and our friends made things, and we sent the poor Irish people over three hundred dollars. My brothers made pictures in pen and ink, and called them charades, and they sold for fifty cents apiece; like this: a pen, and a man, and a ship, and called it, "a desirable art" – Penmanship. The brother, who used to be so mischievous, is studying hard now to be an engineer and build rail-roads. He draws beautiful bridges and aqueducts.[98]

Donations came from rich and influential citizens. Van Schaick contributed $500, as did a number of other businessmen.[99] The large sum of $2,000 came from the Board of the New York Stock and Exchange Board.[100] Theodore Frelinghuysen, then Chancellor of the University of the City of New York and a successful politician known for his evangelical views, donated $5.[101] Horace Greeley, founder of the *New York Tribune*, gave $6.50.[102] Greeley, known for his radical politics, was an avid champion of the Young Ireland group and their demands for an independent Ireland.[103]

In June, the Washington City company of Corcoran and Riggs donated $5,000.[104] William Wilson Corcoran, one of the owners, had been born in Georgetown, Washington in 1798.[105] His father, Thomas, had emigrated from Limerick to Baltimore in 1783.[106] William Wilson Corcoran was a renowned philanthropist and art collector. Although not a Catholic, in 1851 he gave $500 to Father Mathew's temperance movement.[107] This marked the beginning of a friendship between the men, leading to a meeting in Ireland in 1853, when Father Mathew cautioned, 'I now hope that you will not visit Ireland until next July, at which season the beloved country of your ancestors will appear in all its beauty'.[108]

Many well-known people gave their support to the fund-raising. Irish-born Richard Pakenham, who had been appointed Envoy Extraordinary and Minister Plenipotentiary to the United States of America in December 1843, gave £100, which was the equivalent of $469.[109] William Colville Emmet, son of the Irish-born veteran of the 1798 rebellion, Thomas Addis Emmet, contributed $400, which was followed a few weeks later by an additional $25.[110] A number of musical concerts were held in New York and the surrounding areas. A performance of the oratorio of Handel's *Messiah* was given at the New York Tabernacle on 27 February 1847, and 'In a rare show of unanimity, both the Sacred Music Society and the American Musical Institute generally volunteered to pool their resources, as did the conductors'.[111] Dr Edward Hodges, a noted organist, was one of the organizers. Unfortunately, terrible weather kept potential audience members at home and the hall was virtually empty.[112] The concert raised a disappointing $24.[113] Kip & Brown, Proprietors of the Greenwich & Broadway Stages, donated the proceeds of one day's performance, which amounted to $295.46.[114]

The poor of the City also contributed, as did various groups of workers, with donations for the 'hands of Philip Hone' ($360), 'clerks, Maiden Street' ($6), 'hands in Bowne and Co.'s bindery' ($30), 'Workmen and hands of Mrs G. B. Miller and Co.'s Manufactory' ($27.50), 'the workmen in the employ of Peckham and Runville'($76.26), 'workmen in the employ of Moses G. Baldwin, manufacturers and jewellers, 145 Reade Street' ($32), 'the hands of Pearse and Brooks, paper mills' ($57), 'the hands of the manufactory of H. P. Leake, 164 Broadway' ($100), 'the men employed in Allaire Iron Works, New York' ($157), 'lithographers of New York' ($5), 'the employees of the Eerie railroad at Pierpoint' ($100) and 'workmen in the employ on NY dyeing and printing establishment on Staten Island', ($106.50).[115] Donations were made also by police of the First Ward ($71), the officers and crew of the US steamer Michigan gave $10, 'workers in the employ of the New York Screw Company' ($60), 'the agents and drivers of the Harlem Railroad Company' ($76).[116] French residents and workmen gave $637.55. The money was donated on their behalf by Victor De Launay who, with his brother, owned a company in New York and Le Havre. B. P. Haatmgs & Co., of Detroit, sent a donation made by 'A Committee of Miners on south side of Lake Superior', who raised funds to pay expenses on 60 bbls (barrels) of flour to be transported to Ireland.[117] The officers and workmen of the Dry Dock Navy Yard in Brooklyn gave $530.61, which was used to purchase 120 barrels of corn meal to be transported on the *Victor*. On its arrival in Dublin, the Society of Friends wrote to the workers in the Navy Yard thank them for their generosity.[118] A donation of $57.42 was raised from Moira in Franklin in New York, the covering note explaining that it was 'mainly contributed by those who depend upon their daily labor for their daily bread'. Van Schaick responded, 'May their bread never fail and their cup be always full'.[119]

Inevitably, Irish groups and societies were prominent in the relief efforts. The Irish Relief Committee of Galena in Illinois sent $1,000.[120] A ball organized by the Independent Sons of Erin raised $420.[121] The Hibernian Providence Society in New Haven, which had been founded in 1842, donated $200.[122] An interesting donation of $385 was made by the Benevolent Order of Bereans.[123] This newly formed Protestant secret society was similar in outlook to the Orange Order and was known for its anti-Catholic views.[124] They had links with the larger American Protestant Association.[125]

Public figures were important in assisting in promoting the work of the New York Committee. Local mayors, in particular, acted as a conduit for many donations.[126] Andrew Hutchins Mickle, a tobacco merchant and former Mayor of New York from 1846 to 1847, gave $40 on behalf of 'Tammany Hall'.[127] While later remembered as an example of institutionalized corruption, Tammany Hall (also known as the Society of St Tammany), was renowned at the time for helping immigrants, especially Irish immigrants. It had close links with the Democratic Party and both were a known for holding pro-slavery views.[128] In addition, the Society donated the proceeds of a ball held on St Patrick's Day, which raised $200.[129] In contrast, the Friendly Sons of St Patrick in New York forsook their annual ball in 1847 and instead donated the $215 worth of food 'to their suffering brethren in Ireland'.[130] The money was channelled through James Reyburn, who had been President of the Friendly Sons since 1843 and was Treasurer of the Irish Emigrant Society.[131] It was Reyburn who replaced Van Schaick as Treasurer of the General Relief Committee.

Church involvement

Public lectures proved to be a popular way of raising money for Ireland. At the end of March, Rev Henry Giles, a Unitarian minister who had been born in County Wexford, lectured before the Society of the Young Friends of Ireland in the Broadway Tabernacle. It brought in $ 378.50.[132] Giles, a noted orator, had earlier raised money for the Philadelphia Relief Fund by giving a public lecture.[133] However, Giles was not the only Irish-born man of the cloth to lecture. John Hughes, the flamboyant Irish-born Bishop of New York, lectured at the Tabernacle on 20 March.[134] Hughes's father had emigrated to the United States in 1816 and John had joined him a year later. Hughes entered the priesthood in 1820 and he had been ordained a bishop in 1838.

In the intervening period, he had gained a reputation as an outspoken and effective defender of the Catholic Church, his robust approach earning him the nickname 'Dagger John'.[135] When anti-Catholic rioting had erupted in Philadelphia in 1844, Hughes had taken an uncompromising stand, warning the perpetrators that if the violence spread to New York, the city would become 'a second Moscow'.[136] Hughes's topic was 'On the antecedent causes of the Irish Famine in 1847'. He commenced by saying, 'The year 1847 will be rendered memorable in the future annals of civilization by two events; the one immediately preceding and giving occasion to the other; namely, Irish famine and American sympathy and succor'.[137]

Despite his deeply held religious views, Hughes did not take a providentialist view of the food shortages, instead warning:

> Let us be careful, then, not to blaspheme Providence by calling this God's famine. Society, the great civil corporation which we call the State, is bound, so long as it has the power to do so, to guard the lives of its members against being sacrificed by famine from within, as much as their being slaughtered by the enemy from without.[138]

Although he defended the rights of property, he qualified this, saying:

> still the rights of life are dearer and higher than those of property; and in a general famine like the present, there is no law of Heaven, nor of nature, that forbids a starving man to seize on bread wherever he can find it, even though it should be the loaves of proposition on the altar of God's temple.[139]

Hughes's strong defence of his countrymen and their human rights was a powerful call to the people of New York to act.[140] The lecture raised $529.11, of which $4.50 was deducted for advertising.[141] The lecture was noticed outside the New York area. One Washington newspaper observed:

> The tickets were a dollar each, and the proceeds, quite handsome, were appropriated to the great object. The bishop is a very agreeable speaker; his voice is clear and musical. He is about fifty years of age, of dark complexion, Milesian features, stoops slightly, and has very much of that air which somehow always characterizes the Romish ecclesiastic.[142]

Inevitably, Catholic congregations, some of which were newly formed, contributed. One of the largest individual donations came from St Patrick's Cathedral in New York City who gave $1,350.87 in March 1847, followed by an additional $20.[143] On St Patrick's Day 1847, a collection was made in St James's Catholic Church in New York which raised $100. On the same day, the Temperance Society attached to the church collected $94.[144] The pastor of the Church was Rev John Smith, who, like Hughes, had been born in County Tyrone.[145] Many other Catholic congregations, predictably perhaps, raised money for Ireland. St Joseph's Catholic Church on Sixth Avenue ($800), St Mary's Catholic Church, Grand Street ($2,250.72), St Peter's Catholic Church ($1,083), the Nativity Catholic Church, a Jesuit church on Second Avenue ($2,060.62), Wallabout's Catholic Church, Brooklyn ($125.60), St Nicholas (German) Catholic Church on Second Street ($42.23), and St Peter's Catholic Church, Staten Island ($143) all contributed to the General Relief Committee. The recently opened St Francis of Assisi Church, in Midtown Manhattan, raised $22. This church had been established in 1844 by Father Zachary Kunz, a Hungarian Franciscan priest. The majority of the congregation was poor German immigrants.[146] These fund-raising efforts benefited from the fact that in the preceding decade a number of new Catholic churches had been built in the US, reflecting the large-scale Catholic immigration to the country even before the Famine and European revolutions of 1848.

The ecumenical nature of the response was evident in the donations received from diverse religious congregations, including Baptists, Episcopalians, Dutch Reformed, Presbyterians, Methodists, Congregational Christians and Unitarians.[147] A number of local synagogues also contributed.[148] Rev William Stevens Balch of the Universalist Church in Bleeker sent $38.55 to the Relief Committee.[149] Balch, who had been at Bleeker Street since 1841, was a renowned journalist, politician, teacher, historian and educationalist, who helped to found St Lawrence University. Even before the influx of immigrants caused by the Famine, he worried about the undemocratic influence that Catholic immigrants were having on American politics, leading him to write in 1842, *Native American Citizens: Read and Take Warning!*[150] Nonetheless, he felt moved to donate to Irish suffering. A number of churches made more than one donation. St Paul's Episcopal Church in Ossining, New York, built with local marble quarried by inmates of nearby Sing Sing Prison, donated one week's Offering of $59.[151] They made a subsequent donation from their Sunday collection of $5.[152]

An unusual donation came from the *John Wesley,* a Bethel Ship moored in New York. Bethels were discarded ships that were reused as floating chapels for resident and visiting seafarers. The *John Wesley* had been made into a floating Methodist Chapel in 1845, especially for the use of sailors.[153] The ship was moored at the foot of Carlisle Street, on the North River.[154] The *John Wesley* was the first Bethel Ship to be fitted out and dedicated for this purpose. It flew American, Norwegian, Danish and Swedish flags.[155] The pastor was the Swedish-born O. G. Hedstrom, and his congregation was described as being comprised of 'wayward sailors'. On 7 March, they donated $11.25 to the General Relief Committee.[156] The following day, the sailors made an additional donation of $6.[157] Further donations were made, bringing the seamen's contribution to over $22. The congregation

on the *John Wesley* had been informed of the suffering in Ireland and
Scotland during a sermon by Rev George Lane, a Methodist minister
on 7 March.[158] Hedstrom wrote on their behalf to a local evangelical
newspaper, pointing out:

> Let our neighbours and brethren know on the other side of the Atlantic
> that the poorest of us think of them and pray for them; trusting that the
> merciful father of us all will, for the sake of our Lord Jesus Christ, cause
> his face to shine upon them, and give them fruitful seasons again, that
> their hearts may rejoice in him.[159]

It was not only Christian communities who contributed. A number of
synagogues made collections. At this time, there were less than 50,000 Jews
throughout the US, with approximately 13,000 of them residing in New
York City.[160] Members of the Franklin Street Synagogue collected $80.[161]
The Crosby Street Synagogue, which was the third to have been built in the
City, donated $175.[162] The donation was the outcome of a specially convened
meeting, for the purpose of 'taking measures for the relief of the famishing
thousands of their fellow mortals in that unfortunate and destitute country,
Ireland'.[163] The prayer and address were delivered by Jacques Judah Lyons,
the *hazan*, or prayer leader. Lyons, who had been born in Surinam in Dutch
Guiana, had joined the Congregation Shearith Israel of New York City
in 1839. In his address, he made an impassioned plea for the Irish poor:

> A nation is in distress, a nation is starving. Numbers of our fellow-
> creatures have perished, *dreadfully, miserably* perished from hunger and
> starvation. Millions are threatened with the same horrid fate, the same
> dire calamity. The aged and the young, the strong and the feeble alike are
> prostrated. The heart of civilization is touched by the distress and woe
> of the sufferers. Relief, and if not relief at least alleviation, is the first
> sentiment to which utterance is given, and in obedience to that sentiment
> are we, my brethren, assembled this evening . . .[164]

Lyons was followed by Jonas B. Phillips, the Assistant District Attorney, who
delivered a speech of 'great beauty and eloquence'.[165]

Other contributions

Many small towns assembled their own committees to raise money on behalf
of the General Relief Committee. This included the New Haven Irish Relief
Committee, which gave several donations, committees based in Morristown,
New Jersey ($114.75), Waterbury, Connecticut ($460), Morgantown,
Virginia ($220), Toledo, Ohio ($331–71) and Plattsburg in New York ($50).

Further donations came from the Ninth Ward of New York City ($397.70), the Haverstraw Irish Relief Society ($220), committees formed in Honesdale, Pennsylvania ($1,000), in Onondaga, New York ($1,200), the Citizens of Chicago ($1,687.44), South Bend, Indiana ($111.75), Montgomery, Alabama ($575.62) Jonesboro, Alabama ($350), Wooster, Ohio ($117.84), Danville, Kentucky ($363–30), Louisburgh, North Carolina ($36.25), Tallahassee, Florida ($800), Petersburgh, Virginia ($722.88) and Mackinac Island, Michigan ($200).[166] The Mayor of Cleveland, Ohio sent $121.16.[167] On 4 May, the large sum of $1,302.64 was received from Vicksburgh in Mississippi.[168] The citizens of Quincy, Florida raised $125.81, the proceeds of one meeting.[169] It had been chaired by Charles H. Dupont, a local lawyer, businessman and Democratic politician. Dupont was also a plantation owner who kept 108 slaves.[170]

The population of Richmond, Virginia provided relief in the form of foodstuffs, giving 2,600 barrels and 150 bags of kiln dried corn meal, in addition to 324 barrels of Indian corn, two barrels of peas, two hogsheads and one box of bacon, 40 barrels of flour as well as 16 boxes of clothing.[171] George Barclay, a member of the New York Committee who was in charge of provisions, responded:

The people of this country deserve great credit for the prompt and liberal contributions made by them for the relief of our suffering fellow beings in good old Ireland, a country to which I am warmly attached, having spent many happy days there between the years 1815 and 1810, and received very kind attentions.[172]

Similarly, a committee in Milwaukee, Wisconsin, donated flour, to be distributed thus: 50 bbls to Dublin, 50 bbls to Belfast, 50 to Cork, 75 to Waterford, 100 to Galway, 60 to Valencia in Kerry and 50 bbls to Westport, County Mayo. The Milwaukee Committee requested 'these donations to be given in their names to the Roman Catholic and Protestant ministers of the above-named places, or to some other prominent gentlemen'.[173]

One of the largest single contributions was made by the City of Albany, the state capital of New York. On 19 April, their donation of $16,000 was recorded by the General Relief Committee.[174] This was followed by $4,000 on 14 May, $2,000 on 2 July and $400 on 13 September. Their final donation of $282.78 was received on 2 February 1848.[175] The Albany Committee for the Relief of Ireland had been founded in February 1847 in response to the appeal from New York. The chairman of the Albany Committee was Robert M. Jenkins, a successful local lawyer. Other members of the executive committee included Edward Delavan, a wine merchant and temperance advocate, bank presidents Thomas Olcott and John Norton, and James Dexter an attorney. John Ford, also an attorney, served as the committee's Secretary and Theodore Olcott, Director of the Canal Bank, served as Treasurer. The Committee appointed an official collector to each ward within the city, and a circular was issued asking for donations, which could be in cash, food, clothing or provisions (usually grain or flour). The names of individuals who donated over $5 were listed in the local newspapers. Thomas James, a prosperous flour merchant, was a member of a subcommittee that oversaw the collection and transfer of goods from Albany. As was the case elsewhere, fund-raising efforts included special concerts, lectures and church sermons. More unusually, the three Roman Catholic Churches in Albany took part in a 'benevolent race' to raise funds. Together, they donated $5,329 to the Committee.[176]

Due to the size of the first donation from Albany, a complete vessel was able to be filled with provisions and sent to Ireland, it being known as the 'Albany ship'. The Albany ship, which was in fact the British Brig *Minerva*, sailed to Cork and, as requested by the Albany committee, its cargo of 2,000 barrels of meal was distributed among the poor in Dublin, Cork, Tuam and Cashel.[177] The British government paid the freight charges.[178] A second Albany ship, the *Malabar*, sailed at the end of May.[179] It was carrying provisions to Dublin, valued at $24,013.08.[180] The final Albany ship, the *Ashburton*, left for Ireland in the latter part of December 1847. It was carrying 715 barrels of corn meal and $212.78 in cash. Following this shipment, the Albany Committee dissolved itself.[181] In total, the City had raised approximately $25,000 on behalf of the Irish poor. Van Schaick, who was a native of Albany, commented 'I feel proud of the good conduct of the ancient Dutch city'.[182] Undoubtedly, the generosity of the people of Albany helped to save many lives throughout Ireland.

On 10 May, $103.30 was received from Richard H. Coolidge, the Assistant Surgeon of Fort Gibson in the Cherokee Nation.[183] The fort, situated at what was referred to as the 'Indian Frontier', was coping with trouble from the local Cherokee Nation while many of their men had been deployed to fight in the Mexican War.[184] Coolidge, who had been born in New York City in 1816, had been appointed assistant surgeon in the United States Army in 1841. He was highly regarded and, later, promoted for his bravery during the Civil War, but died prematurely in 1866.[185] Captain Silas Casey of the 2nd infantry sent $112, on behalf of the officers, soldiers and Sunday school scholars at Fort Mackinac, Michigan, which had been made on 10 May.[186] A committee for Ireland had also been founded in the frontier town of Fort Wayne in Indiana. The town had grown as a result of the Eerie Canal which had brought German and Irish immigrants to the area. The committee consisted of Allan Hamilton, Hugh McCullough and Henry Colmick, who raised $150.[187]

A donation of $653 was made by members of the US Naval forces serving on the west coast of Africa on board USS *United States*, sent there to suppress the illegal slave trade. Three-quarters of the money raised was for Ireland and one-quarter was for Scotland.[188] The captain, Joseph Smoot, was a hero of the War of 1812.[189] The author, Herman Melville, had enlisted as a seaman on this frigate in 1843.[190] The Commanding Officer of the *USS United States* explained their motivation:

> The distressing accounts brought from the United States, of the sufferings of the poor in Ireland and Scotland, have caused a deep feeling of concern for their unfortunate condition, which has been manifested in a substantial manner by the officers and crew of this ship.
>
> Without having been prompted, they came forward and offered to raise a contribution in money. The amount collected might have been larger, but for the necessity of limiting and regulating subscriptions made by seamen, in consequence of the unequal donations which they would other-wise make. It was therefore found proper to fix the amount which each should give.
>
> A bill drawn upon the Hon Secretary for the sum of $653 is herewith enclosed. We are aware that it is but the 'widow's mite' when compared with the amount subscribed by our kind hearted people at home; yet, we trust that it will effect some good, and that it may reach its destination in time to relieve the sufferings of many individuals.[191]

The Ireland Relief Committee of Nashville, Tennessee proved to be both active and generous, raising a number of large contributions for the Irish poor. On 15 April, the New York committee noted the receipt of $1,200, forwarded by a subcommittee comprised of William Gowdy, Benjamin Litton and William Eakin.[192] This was not their first donation for Ireland. On 27 March, they had sent $2,500 to the Central Relief Committee of the Society of Friends 'to be distributed among the suffering Irish in such a way as in your opinion may be productive of the greatest relief'.[193] The accompanying letter explained, 'The donors sympathize most heartily with the sufferings of the people of Ireland; and hope that they, in connection with their fellow countrymen of other states, may be able to alleviate them in some considerable degree, until more permanent means of relief may be found'.[194] An Irish relief committee had been founded in Memphis which, throughout April, sent several separate donations. By 21 April, the Memphis committee had donated $1,376 which, by the middle of May, had reached $2,374.61.[195] The Memphis committee suggested that because so much aid was going to the south of Ireland, a portion of their funds should go to 'Belfast and to Londonderry'.[196] Van Schaick reassured them that:

> Concerning the mode, time, amount and plan of distribution to each locality, the best judges in Ireland are that Committee of Quakers. As they are entirely disinterested and conscientious in their proceedings, they will do perfect human justice to all parts of the Island. I shall take care to give them extracts from your letter concerning your views, which they will treat with candor and respect, and will conform to, if it be possible and consistent with duty.[197]

He added:

> I glory in your liberality to the abused and suffering people of Ireland, and in the consideration that it is an offering of that divine sensibility of soul which is not confined to country, but would extend its beneficence to every oppressed and famishing people, and not merely to a sect or a party.[198]

An example of disproportionate generosity by people who had few resources themselves was provided by the Navy Yard in New York where the officers and workmen raised $530.61. They had already given $604. The accompanying letter explained:

> Upon any occasion, to be the medium of presenting a donation for the relief of the distressed and the unfortunate, would afford me pleasure; but in the performance of the duty now devolving upon me I experience the more satisfaction in saying that I believe none have contributed more willingly, or in a spirit of truer philanthropy than those at this Yard; for it is not of their abundance, but of their penury, that many have responded to the appeal which has been made in behalf of the famishing people whom your Committee seek to relieve.[199]

Van Schaick thanked them, saying, 'Your noble contribution from your generous and valiant associates and men will largely aid in the blessed work of our meek and humble friends in Dublin'.[200]

Impressively, it was groups who were themselves poor that proved to be most generous in relative terms. One of the most remarkable donations to Ireland was made by people who were themselves disenfranchised, impoverished and marginalized. Captain William Armstrong, the Indian agent near Fort Smith in Arkansas, sent $10, 'a large portion of which was contributed by our red brethren of the Choctaw nation'.[201] This donation was reported in sections of the American press.[202] Van Schaick, when writing to the committee in Dublin at the end of May, referred to the donation from 'the children of the forest, our red brethren of the Choctaw nation'.[203] On 21 May, the New York committee recorded receipt of $170 from Captain Armstrong, noting again, 'A large portion of this sum was contributed by our red brethren of the Choctaw nation'.[204] Their generosity was reported in the Irish newspapers in June.[205]

The Choctaws were not alone in their generosity. The Cherokee Nation held a meeting in Tahlequah on 5 May to raise money for the hungry in Scotland, explaining, 'the very considerable number of the descendants of Scotsmen among the Cherokee is calculated particularly to awaken our sympathy towards that people'.[206] The Chief was himself named John Ross (his Cherokee name being *Coowescoowe*). English-educated Ross had led the Cherokee Trail of Tears from their ancestral homes in 1838, a move that he had strongly resisted. During the journey, thousands died, including Ross's wife.[207] The money raised by the Cherokees was forwarded to the Scottish Relief Committee in Philadelphia.[208] When urging people to contribute, reference was made to the Choctaw's support for Ireland, and an appeal was made to other parts of the Nation to become involved.[209] Within a month, the Cherokees had raised $245.25.[210]

The generosity of the Choctaws and Cherokees was described in the press in terms of their civilizing encounters with the white man. The US *Gazette* acknowledged their intervention, averring:

> Among the noble deeds of disinterested benevolence which the present famine has called forth, none can be more gratifying to enlightened men than the liberality of our red brethren in the Far West . . . The unexpected contribution is the more acceptable that it comes from those upon whom the white man has but little claim . . . Christianity has taught them that 'God hath made of one blood all nations of men to dwell upon the face of the earth'.[211]

N. Chapman, of the Philadelphia committee, was less equivocal, informing Chief Ross:

> How sensibly they are affected by this act of truly Christian benevolence on the part of the Cherokee nation. Especially are we gratified by the evidence it affords of your people having already attained to higher and purer species of civilization derived only from the influence of our holy religion, by which we are taught to view the sufferings of our fellow beings wherever they exist as our own.[212]

The work of the General Relief Committee was not without controversy. In March 1847, Congress agreed to the *Jamestown* and the *Macedonian* being used to take supplies to Ireland, although they declined to pay any charges associated with the voyages. In May, articles appeared in various New York newspapers written by Commodore DeKay, criticizing the New York committee for refusing to use his services on the *Macedonian*. The committee refuted his version of events.[213] They claimed they had rejected his offer on the grounds that it would be quicker to employ a number of smaller vessels. Furthermore, if the *Macedonian* was used by the committee, it would be impossible for the British Treasury to pay the freight charges.[214] DeKay remained unsatisfied, publishing more critical articles and blaming the New York committee for the delay in the *Macedonian* sailing to Ireland. The committee again repudiated DeKay's accusations, but now in more detail, explaining that DeKay had expected the committee to pay salaries to him and his officers, which they considered an inappropriate use of the monies that had been raised.[215] In retrospect, the committee believed that their judgement had been correct and that they had sent relief:

> in the most rapid, direct and economical manner, and with as little ostentation as possible, than to devote any portion of a fund so sacred, under circumstances so imperative to the transmission of any part of these

provisions in a costly manner, for the gratification of personal, municipal or national feeling.[216]

Nonetheless, DeKay's complaints added a bitter note to what had been a glorious and charitable venture on behalf of the starving poor in Ireland.

The approach of the 1847 harvest was watched with trepidation, not only in Ireland, but also by those who were involved in fund-raising elsewhere. News from Ireland throughout summer appeared to be positive, with a large, healthy harvest expected.[217] In August, Reyburn informed the Dublin committee 'we are all alive to the prospect of your harvest – the result of which will make it necessary to continue or wind up our committee, most of whom are now absent from the city, in order to escape our very hot season'.[218] The hope that the 1847 harvest would mark an end to famine proved to be illusory. The smallness of the potato crop, coinciding with a more general economic downturn, meant that Ireland was facing a third consecutive year of famine. Moreover, the extended Poor Law legislation placed the financial burden for relief onto Irish taxpayers, many of whom had few resources. The transfer to Poor Law relief again put pressure on private charities, although, as was evident from the experience of New York committee, the charitable impulse was slowing down. By the end of 1847, international fund-raising drive had mostly dried up.

The final donation to the General Relief Committee in New York was received on 2 February 1848. It was for $282.78 and came from the Chairman of the Albany Committee.[219] As was the case with other fund-raising organizations, the bulk of the Committee's work had been carried out in the early months of 1847; while $156,581 was raised up to the end of June 1847, the total raised after this date was $19,037.[220] In its relatively brief existence, the General Relief Committee had provided an efficient and effective conduit for getting much-needed food to Ireland. The thousands of people in the United States who came together on behalf of the starving Irish resumed their lives. In the longer term, the contributions of many of them were forgotten. When Van Schaick, the inspiration behind the New York Committee, died in 1865, his long obituary made no reference to his work on behalf of Ireland in 1847.[221] However, he, together with thousands of other Americans, many of whom had no connection with Ireland, and others, whose names have not been recorded or have been forgotten, helped to save the lives of the suffering Irish. Charity, it appears, was more important to them than publicity. Impressively also, differences of religion, class and ethnicity were cast aside in favour of helping a starving people 3,000 miles across the ocean. As the Committee declared in its report, 'Let Ireland's extremity be America's opportunity to teach the nations a magnificent lesson in human brotherhood by her mighty deeds of brotherly love'.[222]

5

'Arise ye dead of Skibbereen'.[1]
Leading by example

By the middle of the nineteenth century, philanthropy had moved away from the traditional role of the wealthiest groups giving to the poorest ones. Also, while religion still played a major role, there had been a growth in more secular charitable organizations, who adopted increasingly systematic approaches to collecting and distributing relief. Many of these bodies were managed by middle-class philanthropists, but their funding came from all classes of society.[2] The involvement of political and religious leaders in the giving of private charity remained important, however, not simply for the amount of money they donated, but for the encouragement their donations provided to others. For these elites, the patronage of charitable endeavours provided another way of maintaining and asserting their political power.[3]

The British monarch

When the potato blight first appeared in 1845, Queen Victoria was aged 26 and had been on the throne for seven years. She had never visited Ireland. Victoria became directly and publicly involved in assisting Ireland at the beginning of 1847. Her participation was diverse and involved more than simply making a donation to the starving Irish. In her capacity as head of state, she was required to issue a Queen's Speech to mark the annual opening of the Westminster Parliament. On 19 January 1847, Victoria delivered her speech in person, from the Throne. It was predominantly concerned with the 'dearth of provisions' in Ireland and in parts of Scotland; however, her opening statement immediately linked Irish suffering with Irish violence:

> In Ireland especially the Loss of the usual Food of the People has been the Cause of severe Sufferings, of Disease, and of greatly increased Mortality

among the poorer Classes. Outrages have become more frequent, chiefly directed against Property; and the Transit of Provisions has been rendered unsafe in some Parts of the Country.[4]

This unfortunate coupling reinforced negative stereotypes of Ireland at a time when the country was in desperate need of external assistance and sympathy.

As head of both church and state, Victoria played an important role in supporting and promoting various charities. Her intention to play a public role in fund-raising for Ireland had become evident early in January 1847. At the beginning of that month, a committee had been formed in London at the initiative of a number of bankers and other prominent people. The British Relief Association for the Relief of Extreme Distress in Ireland and Scotland, as its name suggested, was not confined to assisting in Ireland. Extensive fund-raising activities had already commenced on behalf of both countries and so a key aim of the British Relief Association was to provide 'a competent machinery for administering the public munificence'.[5] Because distress was less extensive in Scotland than in Ireland and, in the former, landlords had responded with 'prompt and systematic exertions', it was decided that one-sixth of all funds raised should go there.[6]

The official report of the British Relief Association recorded that Queen Victoria had requested that her name be placed at the head of the list of donors with a contribution of £2,000.[7] Initially she was to have given £1,000 and the official reason given for doubling it was that Scotland, where the potato crop had also failed, was to be included.[8] Unofficially, one of the Irish members of the Association's committee had suggested that the sum was paltry and should be increased.[9] Following Victoria's contribution, other members of the Royal family, including the King of Hanover, made a donation. Shortly afterwards also, the British Relief Association received a gift from another head of state, the Sultan of Turkey, who gave £1,000.[10]

The Queen's involvement, in fact, pre-dated her much-publicized donation. In October 1846, the monarch ordered three consecutive Sundays of prayers for 'relief from dearth and scarcity now existing in parts of the United Kingdom owing to the failure of some of the crops of the present year'.[11] In consultation with the Archbishop of Canterbury, Anglican priests in England and Ireland were asked to read, for three consecutive Sundays in October, prayers on behalf of the starving poor in Ireland.[12] In Ireland, the days of prayer were to continue until 23 November.[13] In reality, the moving force behind this appeal was not the Queen, but her Prime Minister, Lord John Russell. A call for state religious observances could only be made by the monarch (and, in Ireland, generally through her representative, the Lord Lieutenant), but in reality they were political decisions that involved the Prime Minister.[14] Additionally, Russell, working with the Rev Marcus Gervais Beresford, the Church of Ireland Archbishop of Armagh, had agreed that Friday, 20 November 1846 should be designated as a day of humiliation in the Established Churches in Ireland. The ordering of national days of worship by the state was not unusual and, in theory, was meant to extend to all denominations. This particular response to the food shortages in Ireland, however, reflected the British state's Protestant values.[15] Furthermore, the public religious observances also suggested that the Irish poor were being punished by a force greater than indifferent landlords or an unfeeling and distant British government; God was showing his displeasure.

Queen Victoria's involvement intensified in 1847. Within two weeks of her donation to the British Relief Association, a Queen's Letter was issued. It was read from pulpits in Anglican Churches throughout Britain on 13 January 1847. The Queen's Letter had, in fact, been approved by Russell's Cabinet in December 1846. Again, Beresford, the Bishop of Armagh, seemed to have been a moving force behind the decision.[16] Collections made following the reading of the Letter had reached £50,000 by mid-March, all of which was given to the British Relief Association.[17] The Letter also called for a day of 'fast and humiliation'. The day chosen was 24 March, and its official designation was, 'Fast Day: a public fast and humiliation to obtain pardon of our sins and to send up prayers and supplications to the Divine Majesty for the removal of a grievous scarcity and dearth of divers articles of sustenance and necessaries of life'. Queen Victoria's Letter explained why such a day was necessary:

> He will, if we turn unto Him in due contrition and penitence of heart, withdraw His afflicting hand, have therefore resolved, and do, by and with the advice of our Privy Council, hereby command, That a Public Fast and Humiliation be observed throughout those parts of our United Kingdom called England and Ireland, on Wednesday the Twenty-fourth day of March, One thousand eight hundred and forty-seven, that so both we and our people may humble ourselves before Almighty God, in order to obtain pardon of our sins.[18]

Calling for such days was not without precedents, having been done in both the United States and the United Kingdom on previous occasions of national crisis or national rejoicing.[19] Regardless of the overt religious aspect of such a day, in Britain, it could only be called by a monarch in their capacity as head of the state church. The timing of this one was significant. By the end of 1846, it was evident that the public works were in turmoil; they were unable to keep up with demand for employment and they were failing to save lives. Their closing had been officially announced in January 1847. However, many of the government soup kitchens that were replacing them would not be available until early summer and then, only for a short period until permanent relief became available in the form of an extended Poor Law. In the interim, an even higher number of people were likely to die. Inevitably, private charity was looked on to fill this official void. Significantly, the Queen's Letter called for a day of fasting and concurrent fund-raising had the approval of the Treasury, the evangelical Wood and Trevelyan both wanting to exercise some control over how private relief was distributed.[20] Holding such a day reinforced a providentialist interpretation of the food shortages. Moreover, it provided a powerful (and politically convenient) explanation to the public for the appearance of the blight.

Rev Edward Bickersteth, an English minister who was supporting various proselytizing missions in Ireland, had no doubt why fast and humiliation were necessary:

> In the visitation itself, occasioning this appointment, seldom has there been a judgment more evidently from the hand of God . . . England has sorely neglected Ireland; and, as a neglected child brings disgrace and suffering both on its parents and on itself, so Ireland has proved a cause of shame and trouble to England, while it is full of wretchedness and suffering in itself.[21]

Bickersteth was a veteran of such days and had, during the national fast in 1832, written a guide to how it should be observed, which he reprinted in 1847. On each occasion, over 100,000 copies were distributed.[22]

Calling a day of public fast and humiliation entailed more than saying prayers or attending church. It was usually held on a Wednesday, a work day, and during the course of the day, in addition to prayers being said in public places, sermons and fasts, businesses, public houses and public offices, including banks, were shut. On 24 March, even the London Stock Exchange closed. However, for the poorer, labouring classes who participated, it represented a real financial sacrifice, as they were not compensated for the loss of a day's earnings. An important dimension of the day was that money was raised. By doing so, it provided concrete evidence of sympathy and support by the British Protestant establishment for the Irish (largely Catholic) poor. On the morning of 24 March, the Queen and Prince Albert, the Duchess of Kent, the ladies and gentlemen of the Court, and the domestic household, attended Divine Service at the private chapel in Buckingham Palace. The sermon was preached by the Bishop of Oxford. The Queen Dowager and the Duke of Cambridge attended St James's Chapel Royal, where the Bishop of London preached. The congregation was described as being 'somewhat thin'. It was also noted that although there was a full congregation at St Paul's Cathedral, 'the stalls were empty, the choristers' seats were vacant, and the organ was dumb'.[23]

Traditionally, if parliament was in session, the national fast was observed by the two Houses of Parliament, but separately.[24] On 23 March, Russell announced 'that it was the intention of the Speaker to be in the House at a quarter before eleven o'clock to-morrow to meet such Members as wished to accompany him to attend divine worship'.[25] The following day, the Commons met at half-past ten, and the chaplain read prayers. The House then adjourned to St Margaret's Church, where Dr Buckland and

Archdeacon Dealtry preached. Forty members, including Lord John Russell and Sir Robert Peel, attended. In the House of Lords, at half-past ten the Lords passed in procession to Westminster Abbey, where Dr Wordsworth read the service and the Bishop of St Asaph preached. Those present included four bishops and 14 peers, including the Duke of Wellington and the Lord Chancellor.[26]

The holding of a day of prayer and a public fast was not universally welcomed. Privately, the Queen herself disliked the idea of fast days, regarding them as superstitious. She believed that the 1847 day would be 'disapproved by all enlightened people as a very absurd thing of bygone days'. Even more forcefully, she regarded attributing the Famine to what was in her view, a loving God, was 'almost blasphemous'.[27] A number of Anglicans in Ireland, including Archbishop Whately of Dublin, also disliked the linking of famine with fast.[28] Nor was the day without its critics in Britain. Mark Philips, MP for Manchester, asked if the labourers employed on the public works in Ireland, 'at the rate of 1s. per day, the money so received by them, raised by the taxation of the people of England' would observe the Fast Day and so be paid for not working?[29] He was assured by Henry Labouchere, the Chief Secretary for Ireland, that Irish workers would continue to work on the Fast Day. Philips also asked if English labourers would be punished if they did not observe the day; a question that received no answer from his parliamentary colleagues.[30]

A more forthright criticism of the fast came from the Nonconformist, radical MP John Bright, who pointed out that the fast excluded those who were not members of the Established Church, which was generally the case in both Scotland and Ireland. He suggested:

The Government might, had they not regarded old precedents, have drawn up the proclamation more wisely. Instead of doing honour to the Deity, the document was an insult to religion, and calculated to engender, on the one hand, gross superstition, and gross infidelity on the other. He [Bright] had, since that proclamation appeared, spoken on the subject to persons of almost all religious persuasions, and did not see anything like a feeling that the affirmations in the proclamation were proved, or that there was any reasonable ground, from Scriptural authority, for believing that any advantage could come to this country from a fast ordered by the civil power. He regarded the fast as a useless ceremony which reminded him of days gone by, but which was not in accordance with the enlightened opinions of the present day.[31]

As Bright had suggested, the Fast Day was not observed by all religious denominations. Synagogues remained open throughout the United Kingdom. The Society of Friends chose not to observe the Fast. In England, the Friends produced handbills explaining their reasons for not doing so. Workers employed by the Friends resolved that 'instead of spending the day in idleness, they would occupy themselves with their usual employment, and devote the proceeds of their day's labour to relieve the distress of the starving Irish'.[32]

Several sermons made throughout the day echoed the themes of sin and punishment. Several were published. In the prestigious St James's Church in Westminster in London, the sermon by the Rev Charles Hicks Gaye referred to repeated 'suffering' in 'a particular province of this kingdom'. Directly referring to Ireland, it added, 'It may be that the people have been less thrifty, less steady, less active and industrious than others; and yet, though it were so, this were not a time for remembering it'.[33] Nonetheless, the retributive sermon pointed out that the continual subdivision of land had been unwise, as had dependence on one root crop. It also criticized proprietors who were absentee, and the Irish people for not being law abiding, both faults having been compounded by 'oversights by the rulers'. At this point, Rev Gaye reminded his congregation that these were all secondary causes for the suffering: 'the primary cause is *God*'. Gaye was publicly critical of the scheduling of the day, saying that many were surprised that the Queen's Letter had not been read on an earlier day, and he questioned why there was such a long gap between publishing the Letter and reading it in churches.[34] He concluded by returning to the famines in Scotland and Ireland, warning that conditions were already very bad; he feared one quarter of Irish population could be lost.[35] In Cambridge, the town was described as being 'quiet', with many shops closed for the day, but with services being held, and collections made, by all of the denominations. William Carus, the Dean of Trinity Church, who was known for his anti-Catholic views, used the opportunity to give a sermon suggesting that the Famine was God's retribution for the recent grant to Maynooth Seminary in Ireland.[36]

Regardless of criticisms, many people throughout Britain and Ireland participated in the Fast Day. Generally, Catholic churches did not observe these state-inspired interferences in religious matters, but in the case of the 1847 fast, they urged their congregations to say special prayers.[37] On the other side of the world, a number of colonists in South Australia expressed their disappointment that they had not been invited to join in the Day of Fast, 'in some way that would not only have been pleasing to the royal mind, but, above all, acceptable to the King of kings'.[38] Financially, the Queen's Letter and Fast Day were successful and, in total, over £172,000 was raised. A small number of people suggested that the latter should be repeated; in July, parliament received six petitions containing 387 signatures asking for another day of humiliation to be called.[39]

For a number of MPs, a key question had been who would be put in charge of distributing the money raised. George Alexander Hamilton, who had been born in County Down and was MP for Dublin University, wanted to know if 'either the heads of the Church, or the clergy of the Established Church in Ireland, with whom their brethren in this country deeply sympathized, were to be in any way connected?' At this stage, it had been decided that the

'London Committee' (the British Relief Association) 'which comprised some gentlemen of the highest character in the country, and many of the dignitaries of the Church', would be put in charge. Hamilton was further reassured that, 'the fund would be distributed through the local relief committees in Ireland, comprising, as was well known, the clergymen of the Established Church in each parish within the district'.[40] Sir Robert Harry Inglis MP, who was known for his outspoken defence of the Anglican Church and his opposition to both Catholic and Jewish Emancipation, asked a similar question only a few weeks later.[41] He was reassured by the Home Secretary, George Grey, that the British Relief Association would be the channel for distributing these funds:

> That committee possesses a high character and standing in the country, and they have published the details of the plans upon which they proceed in their distributions. A very large sum has already been disposed of by them, and they are acting in connexion [sic] with the Government. I think that the mode they adopt is most effectual in rendering the money available to the utmost extent.[42]

A second Queen's Letter was issued in October 1847, reflecting the fact that the Famine was far from over in Ireland. Ironically, it coincided with a Thanksgiving Day in Britain, 'for the late abundant harvest', that was held on 17 October. Yet, three days before the public rejoicing, the Prime Minister wrote a confidential letter to the Queen entitled 'Collapse in the City', which warned of an imminent financial collapse of many businesses in England.[43] Nevertheless, on the day of Thanksgiving, a collection for Ireland was made.[44] To encourage donations, a letter from Charles Trevelyan was published in the main newspapers, reassuring people 'that no assistance whatsoever will be given from national funds to those unions which, whether they have the will or not, undoubtedly have the power of maintaining their own poor'.[45]

The second Queen's Letter only raised £30,000. Again, the money collected was entrusted to the British Relief Association.[46] A campaign, led by the London *Times*, had argued that the Irish poor were undeserving of any more charity.[47] Some of the fiercest criticisms of giving charity to Ireland were made in the *Economist*. In a lengthy article, it warned it readers:

> IRELAND is again demanding- and receiving much public attention. Her Majesty's Government, in appointing a day of thanks giving for the abundant harvest have also required the clergy of the Church of England on that day to urge their congregations to subscribe for the relief of the Irish. Never within our recollection has such a demand met with so cold, so repulsive a response. Ever since the order in council was published, the daily journals have teamed with letters from rectors, incumbents, and curates, declaring that they cannot conscientiously comply with her Majesty's recommendation; that their own poor are suffering and

starving; that the Irish do not deserve further relief, and that though they will read the order as desired, they will not press their congregations further to contribute for the relief of the Irish.[48]

It was not just the English press that was critical. In France, the influential *Journal des Débats* reported that 'England is becoming incensed and indignant at this eternal mendicity'. It added 'Ireland has received money from all parts of the globe – she has held out her hand to the entire world – to France, to America, to the Pope, to the Sultan! She has humiliated and dishonoured us by knocking at every door and collecting money in foreign countries and she wants more, in addition. The English operative – the laborious artisan of Sheffield and Manchester, is called to cast the fruit of his labours into that bottomless pit!'[49]

Regardless of such public reproaches, the Queen's involvement did not end in 1847. In 1848, a petition was sent to her directly requesting that she intervene in Ireland, the belief being that both the British press and parliament had turned against further support for the Irish poor.[50] In June 1849, in an attempt to encourage charitable donations, government ministers made a private donation to famine relief. To this, Queen Victoria added £500. The money was entrusted to Count Strzelecki of the British Relief Association to distribute.[51] Two months later, in August 1849, Queen Victoria and her family visited Ireland for the first time. They were warmly welcomed in Cork, Dublin and Belfast. Due to the ongoing distress, it was not to be an official state visit, and most of her time was spent at sea, as she travelled by yacht.[52] A nervous Lord Lieutenant was able to report that 'the people are not only enchanted with the Queen and the gracious kindness of her manner and the confidence she has shown in them, but they are pleased with themselves for their own good feelings and behaviour'.[53] However, there were some undercurrents of tension. Catholic Archbishops John MacHale and Michael Slattery declined to participate in the welcome arranged by Archbishop Murray of Dublin. MacHale refused to sign a welcome address on the grounds that 'I find no allusion whatever to the sufferings of the people, or the causes under the control of the legislative enactment by which their sufferings are still aggravated'.[54] Slattery did not attend a levée in the Queen's honour, and he criticized what he characterized as her indifference to the condition of the Irish poor.[55]

Inevitably perhaps, several nationalists held the Queen accountable for the continuing deaths in Ireland. A ditty sung on the streets in 1849 summed up this feeling:

> Arise ye dead of Skibbereen
> And come to Cork to see the Queen.[56]

The early blaming of Queen Victoria for her indifference to the suffering of her Irish subjects was to become a theme that later generations of nationalists frequently recounted. In 1880, for example, Charles Stewart

Parnell claimed that, 'In 1845, the Queen of England was the only sovereign who gave nothing out of her private purse to the starving Irish. The Czar of Russia gave, as did the Sultan of Turkey, but Queen Victoria sent nothing'.[57] Clearly, a myth had taken root that was choosing to ignore Victoria's varied and prolonged involvement in Famine relief.

The Sultan

Abdul Medjid Khan was aged only 16 when he succeeded his father and became Sultan of the Ottoman Empire in 1839. Like Victoria, therefore, he was a teenager when he acceded to the throne. In Western eyes, the Ottoman Empire was generally regarded as a repressive regime, its unpopularity increasing due to the treatment of Greece during their struggle for independence in the 1820s. However, fearing both Egyptian and Russian incursions into the Ottoman Empire, successive sultans had sought to establish good diplomatic relationships with Britain.[58]

Abdul Medjid Khan's desire to be a modernizing ruler was evident early in his reign when he initiated a reorganization of government. Within only a few years, he had reformed the army, education, the tax system and the Criminal and Commercial Codes. The Sultan's liberal reputation was consolidated when, in 1840, he intervened to stop the persecution of Jews in Damascus.[59] Moses Montefiore, who would later be involved with the British Relief Association, had acted for the British government on the Jews' behalf.[60] At the beginning of 1847, it was revealed that the Sultan was going to abolish slave markets in the Empire.[61] A few weeks later, it was announced that he had promised to build a Protestant chapel for the English workmen employed in iron works near Constantinople.[62] The Sultan's multiple reforms earned him praise from Western commentators. One tribute, written by an English Christian missionary, praised Abdul for being 'kind-hearted' and 'enlightened in the European sense'.[63]

Abdul Medjid Khan's involvement in Famine relief took place early in 1847, when he made a donation of £1,000 to the British Relief Association. He had originally offered £10,000 and some ships laden with provisions, but had been advised by British diplomats that British Royal protocol meant that nobody should contribute more than the Queen. It was suggested that he gave half the sum contributed by Victoria.[64] The Sultan complied with this suggestion.[65] The Sultan's donation was entrusted to the Honourable Mr Wellesley, the Ambassador in Constantinople. He, in turn, accompanied by all Embassy staff, visited 'Babi Ali' (the Turkish seat of government), to convey his thanks and gratitude.[66] This gesture was followed by a letter from the Ambassador expressing the thanks of the Queen, as well as those of the British Empire, for the financial aid from the Sultan to the Irish people.[67] As with all donations received by a government department, it was forwarded to the British Relief Association.

The donation by the Sultan was praised widely in both Ireland and Britain.[68] One English religious journal, in an article entitled, 'A Benevolent Sultan', averred:

> The Sultan has sent the sum of one thousand pounds for the relief of Ireland in the grievous famine under which that country is now suffering. This act of regal munificence on the part of his imperial highness is without precedent. For the first time a Muhomedan [sic] sovereign, representing multitudinous Islam populations, manifests spontaneously a warm sympathy with a Christian nation. May such sympathies, in all the genial charities of a common humanity, be cultivated and henceforth ever be maintained between the followers of the crescent and the cross! Christianity and truth alike triumph by charity, which can adopt every creed into its capacious bosom, and transmute them, through love, into the one religion of perfect love, which is Christ's Gospel.[69]

This article, which juxtaposed the Sultan's Muslim faith with his act of Christian generosity, was replicated in other newspapers.[70] The London *Times* was more restrained, but stated that his response to the 'distressed Irish . . . does him great credit'.[71] The Sultan's response to the suffering of the Irish poor was cited as a proof of his character because, 'when he heard of distress existing in that unhappy country, he immediately conveyed to the British Ambassador his desire to aid in its relief and tendered for that purpose a large sum of money'. When it had been pointed out that he could not give more that the Queen 'he at once acquiesced in the propriety of this resolution'.[72]

Within Ireland, a meeting to thank the Sultan was convened at the Royal Irish Agricultural Society in Dublin, presided over by the Earl of Charlemont, a liberal, reforming landlord. At the meeting, an Address was drawn up, which was signed by many of the principal people in the country. Significantly, the Address acknowledged how important external charity had become to the survival of the Irish poor: 'In this emergency the people of Ireland had no alternative but to appeal to the kindness and munificence of other countries less afflicted than themselves, to save them and their families from famine and death'.[73] The British Relief Association included the Address in its account of proceedings 'as a proof of the gratitude of the Irish for the assistance afforded them at a time of great need'. The Address, which was translated into Turkish, read:

> May it Please Your Majesty,
>
> We the undersigned Noblemen, Gentlemen, and Inhabitants Resident in Ireland, beg most respectfully to approach your Majesty in order to testify our deep-felt thanks and gratitude for the munificent act of benevolence and attention lately displayed by your Majesty towards the suffering and

afflicted inhabitants of Ireland, and to than your Majesty on their behalf for the liberal contribution of One THOUSAND Pounds, lately given by your Majesty, to relieve the wants and mitigate the sufferings of the Irish people.

It had pleased Providence in its wisdom to deprive this country suddenly of its staple article of food, and to visit the poor inhabitants with privations such as have seldom fallen to the lot of any civilized nation to endure. In this emergency the people of Ireland had no alternative but to appeal to the kindness and munificence of other countries less afflicted than themselves, to save them and their families from famine and death; and our Majesty has responded nobly to the call, thereby displaying a worthy example to other great nations of Europe to assist their suffering fellow-creatures in affliction.

For this timely and benevolent act, whereby numbers are relieved and saved from perishing, we beg leave again, on their behalf, to testify our grateful acknowledgements to your Majesty, and to express an ardent hope that the vast territories which acknowledge your sway and participate in your bounties, will be saved from those privations and afflictions which it has been our unhappy destiny to endure.[74]

The Sultan's response to the Irish Address gives some insight into his motivations:

It gave me great pain when I heard of the sufferings of the Irish people. I would have done all in my power to relieve their wants . . . I pray that for the future they may be prosperous and happy and independent of the aid of other nations. In contributing to the relief of the Irish people, I only listened to the dictates of my own heart; but it was also my duty to show my sympathy for the sufferings of a portion of the subjects of her Majesty, the Queen of England, for I look upon England as the best and truest friend of Turkey.[75]

The Sultan's actions were noted further afield. They were praised by the American abolitionist paper, the *National Era,* which had been impressed by the announcement that the slave markets in Constantinople were being abolished. The paper averred: 'The name "*Turk*" may yet become an epithet of refinement, as it has been of cruelty'.[76] An Australian newspaper, repeating a report from an Irish newspaper, pointed out that the Sultan's donation represented the first time that:

In the history of Mohometism [sic] the fact is unprecedented in the head of the Moslem world taking, such a generous interest in the sorrow of a Christian people; indeed we believe that even amongst the potentates of Christendom such acts of disinterested benevolence, if not unknown, are of very rare occurrence. One thing at least is certain, that amidst all the foreign sovereigns of the east or of the west, the Sultan of Turkey is the only one who has shown so practical a sympathy for the Irish people.[77]

Despite the Sultan's explicit expression of admiration for England, as with a number of other private donations, his intervention was used as a way to berate the British government. An example of this occurred in 1849, when one American newspaper reported:

'Royal Etiquette and its Consequences'. Not long ago, while Famine was doing its deadly work in Ireland, the Sultan Abdul Medjid Khan, proposed to make a donation of ten thousand pounds, and to send vessels laden with provisions, for the relief of the starving Irish. But, unfortunately, it was suggested by the Sultan's Ministers that it would not be proper for a foreign sovereign to make so large a donation, and that one thousand pounds, which was just half the sum donated by Queen Victoria for the same purpose, would be sufficient. Accordingly, the munificent benefaction originally intended to be sent, which, money and provisions together, could not have been less than forty or fifty thousand pounds, which was remitted through the British Minister at Constantinople.[78]

In the short term, the Sultan's contribution was not forgotten. In 1849, the leader of Hungarian independence, Lajos Kossuth, fled to Turkey seeking asylum. The Sultan was pressured by the Austrian and Russian governments to return Kossuth and other political refugees to the Hapsburg Empire. By refusing to do so, he was risking war with his belligerent neighbours. His refusal to cooperate led to his being commemorated in a poem, which was published in the Dublin Nation on 13 October 1849:

God bless the Turk! God bless the Turk!
God bless the Turk! For this Christian work,
May his noble shadow never be less!
May Mahomed guard him,
And Allah reward him,
And Suleyman bless him,
And the Houris caress him . . .

Some of the later lines in the poem paid tribute to the Sultan's donations to Ireland:

Let Ireland be grateful,
And pay back the alms
That His Highness bestowed.[79]

In 1853, on the eve of the Crimean War, in answer to the question of why the United Kingdom should support the Turk, who was not a Christian, a correspondent of the Irish *Freeman's Journal* reminded its readers, 'I beg to remind some people (without forgetting his independent hospitality, equal to our own) how very like a Christian he behaved when the famine raged in Ireland'.[80] The nationalist paper added its own explanation of what had happened:

> The conduct of Abdul Medjid on the occasion referred to was that of a good, humane and generous man. A believer in Mahomedanism [sic] he acted in the true spirit of a follower of Christ, and set an example which many professing Christians would do well to imitate. But, while giving the high-minded Sultan the credit which he so nobly deserves, we cannot forget that his benevolent intentions towards the suffering poor of Ireland were most cruelly frustrated by the English Ambassador at the Porte. It was stated repeatedly at the time, without the slightest attempt at contradiction – and we fear the demining allegation is but too true – that that person actually induced the Sultan to reduce his intended donation of several thousand pounds to the same amount as the comparatively small sum contributed by Queen Victoria – enforcing his advice by a representation that the accounts of the Irish famine were greatly exaggerated.[81]

Abdul Medjid Khan died in 1861. Despite the multiple reforms carried out by the Sultan, at the time of his death, the Ottoman Empire was both politically and financially weak. His act of generosity to Ireland in 1847, when he was aged only 23, which combined compassion with political expediency, has lived on as a remarkable act of charity and one that challenges the concept of charity as 'Christian duty'.

The American President and Congress

Sporadic fund-raising activities on behalf of Ireland had commenced in the United States at the end of 1845, but they only really gained momentum following the second potato failure. A meeting convened in Washington on 9 February by the American Vice-President, George Dallas, suggested that sympathy for Ireland had reached the highest political levels. In its wake, meetings were held throughout the States to raise money for Ireland. A number of politicians wanted the federal government to make its own donation for the Irish poor. The debates that ensued showed that relief for Ireland had become enmeshed in American politics, with Congress and even the President being dragged into them. Thus, humanitarian concern for Ireland became tied in with issues concerning the limits of congressional involvement in foreign affairs.

President James K. Polk had taken office in March 1845. He was the eleventh President of the United States and, at the age of 49, the youngest to be sworn in up to that time. From the outset, Polk had pledged that he would serve only one term in office.[82] He was a supporter of Jacksonian Democracy, which laid the foundations for the later Democratic Party. During his Presidency (1845–49), Polk brought the nation into the American-Mexican War over the ownership of Texas, while threatening war with Britain over what became known as the 'Oregon Question'. Polk was descended from Ulster-Scots immigrants. He was Presbyterian and a regular church attender.[83] Polk's election victory in 1844, and that of the Democratic Party, was due largely to the support of naturalized Irish immigrants.[84]

While private American citizens were caught up in the wave of wanting to send aid to Ireland, debates on this topic were taking place within the federal government about the limits of their responsibilities to the Irish poor. On 8 February 1847, the day before a large meeting was due to take place in the American capital, Congressman Washington Hunt from New York, introduced a bill suggesting that the US government provide $500,000 for the purchase of foodstuffs for Ireland and to undertake to transport these goods. Despite widespread support, the bill never passed through the Committee stage. Further attempts followed to revive this proposal. On 26 February, Senator John Crittenden, a Whig politician from Kentucky, proposed that the United States provide $500,000 for famine relief for Ireland and Scotland. Crittenden, whose own family background was Welsh and French, had no direct relationship with Ireland, but he had a reputation for charitable work, especially among the poor.[85] In his speech, he admitted that he wished:

> . . . to discharge what I consider a solemn duty . . . The calamity is no ordinary one. It is not the result of idleness or folly on the part of the people . . . it may be asked, is it any duty of ours to be asked to relieve their suffering, to impose our charity? I think it is . . . who are the sufferers at this time? They are our kindred, bound to us not only by a common humanity, but by a more common bond of brotherhood. We are, to a great extent, the descendants of the people of Ireland . . . this famine fills the world with the voice of lamentation. Are we not bound as men and Christians to listen and respond? I think we are.[86]

Crittenden used the American government's giving of money to Caracas in the wake of the devastating earthquake in 1812, to suggest there was precedent for such an action.[87] Furthermore, he claimed, 'the Irish have not only the claims of humanity on our compassion; they also had the claims of brothers'.[88] One of those giving support was General Lewis Cass of Michigan who made reference to the 'Angel of Death' killing people in Ireland. Cass, a Democrat, had spoken at the Washington meeting. During his speech, he opined that the condition of the Irish poor, 'is a case beyond the reach of private charity . . . It is a national calamity and calls for a national contribution'.[89] Opponents of the bill were unmoved by images of Irish suffering or calls to humanity. Senator John Niles of Connecticut insisted that the food shortages in Ireland were the responsibility of the British government, not the American one. He further suggested that such an action would not only be disrespectful to the British authorities, but that this money could be better spent on American people. Finally, he stated that spending money in this way was unconstitutional.[90]

Inevitably, the move to give government aid to Ireland became tied up with American political debates. Crittenden's initiative was primarily supported by the Whig Party. The Whigs were opposed to the war with Mexico and so they were able to make the distinction between using money to save lives as opposed to killing them. One of the supporters of this intervention was the newspaper proprietor Horace Greeley, a prominent supporter of the Whig Party and an advocate of Irish independence.[91] However, a suggestion that such a move by Congress would be unconstitutional was made by several members of the Democratic Party. The opposition of the Democrats was possibly disingenuous and politically motivated given that they were traditional allies of Irish immigrants. There were exceptions. When Crittenden's bill was passed by the Senate, its supporters included the Democrats John C. Calhoun, an outspoken defender of slavery from South Carolina, Senator Edward Hannegan from Indiana, who had Irish background and was known for his dislike of Britain, and General Cass from Michigan.[92] For the most part, voting was carried out on party lines; 80 per cent of Whigs voted for it, and 84 per cent of Democrats voted against.

Despite opposition, Crittenden's bill was passed by the Senate. Lewis Levin of Pennsylvania, who had opposed the bill, suggested it should next be put before the Ways and Means Committee. Levin was one of the leaders of the American Republican Party, a nativist group founded in 1843 with a clear anti-immigrant and anti-Catholic agenda.[93] The bill never emerged from the Ways and Means Committee; the argument being made that even if they had passed it, the President would then have had to veto the bill on the grounds that it was unconstitutional to use public funds for foreign aid. The National Era had predicted that, 'the Senate bill for the relief of Ireland was referred to the Committee of Ways and Means, with the intention, of course, of extinguishing it'.[94]

Outside of Congress, there was criticism of the bill. Some suspected that Whig support had been a cynical ruse to win the Irish vote, or had been a crude means to embarrass the Polk administration which was already in debt, partly as a result of the Mexican War. The anti-slavery National Era was cynical of everybody's motives, pointing out that 'this bill was introduced, sustained, and carried through, chiefly by the cooperation of rival aspirants for the Presidency'. The paper further demanded:

> Where is it written that the Federal Government shall be the almoner of the Republic? That is shall have the power to take the money from my pocket, to buy clothes or breadstuffs for the poor of other lands? . . . if

it may appropriate money to help the poor in Ireland, why may it not appropriate money to relieve the States of this Union of their heavy debts and thus wipe out the foul blot of repudiation? Or, set apart a fund to be used by the States in aid of the relief of our two and a half million slaves?[95]

The paper concluded by calling on Americans to do something for Ireland and to be 'the almoners of their own bounty', admonishing, 'let the Government mind its own business and not undertake to do what the uncompelled charity of the people will do far better'.[96]

The *Brooklyn Eagle,* a supporter of the Democratic Party, accused the Whigs of being complicit with the British government and opposed to Irish independence. The paper alleged that the Whig Party was 'pretending that they care for Irish interests or Irish sufferings, nobody believes for a moment. It is an empty show and clamour *for the votes of the Irish adopted citizens'.*[97] General Cass was criticized in the *New York Tribune* for not having been consistent enough in his defence of the bill, the paper pointing to the fact that previously he had made a 'beautiful and pathetic speech' on behalf of Ireland, but then refused to vote.[98]

By this stage, President Polk had intervened in the dispute and made it clear that he would have to stop the bill if it proceeded out of the committee stage and was passed in the House as he believed it to be unconstitutional. In his diary he wrote that, despite the more pressing business of war, he had taken time to inform the Cabinet that:

> If the Bill which had passed the Senate a day or two ago appropriating half a Million of Dollars to be donated to the Government of Great Britain for the relief of the suffering poor of Ireland and Scotland should pass the Ho. Repts and be presented to me, I could not approve it. I stated my reasons at some length, the chief of which was the want of Constitutional power to appropriate the money of the public to charities either at home or abroad. I did not formally ask the opinion of the Cabinet on the subject, but no dissent was expressed to the opinion which I had given.[99]

He went on to say that he had, 'all the sympathy for the oppressed Irish & Scotch which any citizen can have'. To reinforce this point, he added, 'A few days ago I contributed my mite ($50) for their relief, but my solemn conviction is that Congress possesses no power to use the public money for any such purpose'.[100] Polk, with the help of James Buchanan, outlined reasons for imposing a veto on the bill if it passed the House, but it never made it beyond the Ways and Means Committee.[101] Whatever the individual or collective reasons for supporting or opposing Crittenden's bill, its progress had been effectively halted. Yet, as an alternative, the President encouraged people to make their own contributions to assist Ireland, pointing out that he had personally given to the Irish poor and that others could do the same.[102]

By insisting that the bill had floundered on a constitutional issue and that he was personally sympathetic to Irish relief, Polk was treading a fine line in not alienating the Irish supporters of his party. Polk's donation was not without its critics. The *Pilot*, a Boston paper that was regarded as a mouthpiece for Irish Catholics, was particularly vocal. The paper's proprietor was Patrick Donahoe (sometimes rendered, Donohoe), who had been born in Ireland in 1811. He claimed that the President's $50 contribution had been '*squeezed out* of his private purse'. Moreover, the paper suggested that Polk had only donated when he heard that his Secretary of State, James Buchanan, had given $100.[103] The Pennsylvanian-born Buchanan liked to boast of his Irish heritage, pointing out that his father had been born in Donegal, in the 'kingdom of Ireland'.[104] The American President was not the only target of the *Pilot's* opprobrium. They also criticized the Governor of Maine whom, they claimed, had contributed only $10.[105]

While Crittenden's bill had raised a number of constitutional issues, his was not the only attempt to give American assistance to Ireland at a government level. The young and flamboyant politician, Daniel Edgar Sickles, introduced a bill into the New York State Assembly to use state funds to purchase food for the Irish poor, but it was also thrown out.[106] Sickles, a Democrat, was closely associated with Tammany Hall politics.[107] But, if party politics had failed to deliver aid on behalf of Ireland, it had not deterred the thousands of American people who desired to do something magnanimous on behalf of the starving Irish. In the early months of 1847, charity in the form of money, food, clothes and seeds flowed to Ireland. Regardless of party squabbles, individual American politicians, including the President and Vice-President, proved to be important participants in this transatlantic outpouring of charity. Furthermore, while Congress had been prevented from making a financial subvention to Ireland, it immediately showed its support by voting to allow two American ships of war to take food to the starving Irish.[108] Polk agreed that, as recommended by the Secretary of the Navy, Captain George DeKay and Captain Robert Forbes should be allowed to command these vessels and 'transport provisions donated by Private contribution to the famishing poor of Ireland & Scotland'.[109] (see also Chapter Ten)

Undoubtedly, Queen Victoria, Sultan Abdul Medjid Khan and President James Polk could each have done more to help the poor in Ireland. Nonetheless, their contributions are noteworthy and their personal interventions undoubtedly made a significant contribution to fund-raising activities. Inevitably, they attracted a disproportionate amount of attention and praise. However, at the same time that these heads of states were making their well-publicized donations, the poorer classes were also making great sacrifices on behalf of Ireland. Moreover, as a visitor from the United States in the early months of 1847 noted, it was 'done without any ostentation on their part; their names and their donations were not paraded in the newspapers, but promptly, generously, and quietly, all appeared anxious to hand in their money'.[110] Donations from other heads of state also provided an opportunity for Irish nationalists to juxtapose foreign generosity with the parsimony of the British government; at the end of July 1847, an article in the *Nation* reported, 'to think that we have begged from the four winds, and are fed by the alms of the Sultan, the President and the Pope, while the government that rules over us, when asked for bread, offered the people, like St John, a book to eat'.[111] For the starving poor in Ireland, however, the origins and motives behind the charitable interventions were probably of no concern as they struggled to survive.

6

'This cruel calamity of scarcity'.[1]
The Role of the Catholic Church

The involvement of the main Irish churches in providing famine relief has often been overshadowed by the less palatable part played by some Protestant denominations in winning converts. Both the Anglican and Catholic Churches, however, played a vital role in fund-raising and in providing assistance. The initial response of the hierarchy of the two main churches tended to be spiritual rather than practical, they both issuing calls for prayers. Following the first appearance of blight, the Roman Catholic Archbishop, Dr Daniel Murray, asked that a special collect (prayer) be said in all Catholic Churches, 'in deprecation of the approaching famine'. Similarly, the Established Church requested that a special prayer for time of famine be said.[2] As the food shortages intensified, the churches faced a number of unexpected devotional challenges. In the approach to Lent in 1847, a number of Catholic Bishops announced that during this period of abstinence, the poor could eat meat if it was being served in the soup kitchens, while those employed on the public works did not have to observe the usual Mass attendance requirements.[3]

Clergy from all the main churches were at the forefront of providing relief. In addition to serving on relief committees, many were the recipients of funds raised elsewhere. Visitors to Ireland noted how many Protestant ministers, assisted by their wives and daughters, managed local soup kitchens.[4] The Quaker, William Bennett, when visiting Killala in 1847, felt moved to write of the local clergy:

I believe we have no idea of the daily exertion, self-sacrifice and agony of spirit they have to go through, whose lot is cast, almost single-handed, in the midst of these fearful scenes of want and suffering, without the power to relieve . . . unless such devoted instruments had been here and there raised up, the country must have become depopulated.[5]

The demands made on the Anglican clergy were more formal than that of other ministers as they were expected by the government to serve on the local relief committees, formed in the wake of the first appearance of blight. At Trevelyan's insistence, Catholic curates had been excluded from membership of these committees. This led Lord Monteagle, a leading Whig politician, to protest to the Viceroy that, 'You also exclude all the Roman Catholic curates. Without them, and here they are laboring like tigers for us working day and night, we could not move a stroke'.[6] The involvement of Catholic priests outside the committees was also praised by Asenath Nicholson, an American Bible Protestant. She noted that, 'They had two drawbacks which the Protestants in general had not. First, a great portion of them are quite poor; and second, they, in the first season of the Famine, were not entrusted with grants as the Protestants were'.[7] Nonetheless, the Catholic clergy were frequently criticized in the British press, led by The *Times*, which accused them of being subversives and agitators. This charge was vigorously denied by MacHale in a letter to the Prime Minister at the end of 1848.[8] Regardless of these restrictions and criticisms, the Catholic Church in Ireland played a vital role in providing famine relief, assisted by the international support of its co-religionists.

Vatican involvement

At the time of the first appearance of the potato blight, the Catholic Church in Ireland consisted of 23 Bishops and four Archbishops. The Archbishops were Archbishop John MacHale of Tuam, Dr William Crolly of Armagh, Michael Slattery of Cashel and Daniel Murray of Dublin. Following the granting of Catholic Emancipation in 1829, an ambitious programme of reform and church-building had been put in place, with Murray playing a pivotal role.[9] Unusually, Murray enjoyed good relations with both the British government and the Vatican. He was a noted philanthropist and in addition to church affairs, he dedicated his time to founding 'religious associations for the education and relief of the poor'.[10] Apart from supporting its own churches, colleges, orphanages and penitentiaries, the Catholic Church maintained 'The Society for Propagating Faith', which raised £7,000 annually and 'The Catholic Book Society', which had circulated five million books in the ten years prior to 1845.[11] At the time blight first appeared in the country, the Catholic Church hierarchy was more concerned with the proposed building of three new universities – the Queen's Colleges, but in their view, 'Godless colleges' – than with the impact of the food shortages on the poor.[12] The outspoken MacHale, an ardent supporter of Daniel O'Connell, was vociferously opposed to them.[13] Murray, however, despite the Vatican's condemnation, spoke in favour of the Queen's Colleges, leading to accusations that he was a 'Castle Catholic', that is, a Catholic who was deferential to the British administration in Dublin Castle.[14]

As proved to be the case with many charitable interventions, most fund-raising by Catholic communities followed the second, and more serious, failure of the potato crop. The intervention by Pope Pius IX on behalf of the Irish poor at the beginning of 1847 provided a direct call to Catholics to assist Ireland. Unusually, despite large amounts of money being raised on its behalf, the Catholic Church in Ireland created no formal committees or structures through which donations could be channelled. Consequently, most of the money raised came directly to the archbishops, primarily Archbishop Murray in Dublin. A smaller number of donations were sent to Rev Paul Cullen, Rector of the Irish College in Rome. This system meant that, unlike with other relief organizations, no central system was maintained of recording the sums of money received, despite the fact that several were large. A further feature of relief to the Catholic Church was that it often continued beyond 1847. Unusually, it was overwhelmingly provided in money rather than in foodstuffs.[15]

Pius IX made a number of public interventions on behalf of the starving poor in Ireland. Italian-born Pius (Pio Nono) served as Pope from 1846 to 1878, making him the longest reigning Pontificate ever. Pius IX had been elected to this position in June 1846, following the death of Pope Gregory XVI. The new Pope was regarded as a political moderate and had been the first choice of liberals within the Church.[16] However, the Pope was not only the leader of the international Catholic Church, but also the temporal head of the Papal States in Italy, and both were regarded by Italian nationalists as an impediment to Italian unification.[17]

Like that of Queen Victoria, the Pope's involvement in famine relief was multifaceted, he providing both financial and spiritual succour. Similar to the Queen's response, his had international significance. Furthermore, in a number of ways, the actions of the Italian Catholic Pope mirrored those of the English Protestant Queen and her government. Sympathy for Ireland in the Vatican was helped by widespread admiration for Daniel O'Connell. When the Liberator died in May 1847, he was *en route* to meet the Pope. His death was marked with a three-day funeral service in Rome, which was a significant accolade for a lay person.[18] Close relations between Ireland and the Vatican were also facilitated by the presence in Rome of Paul Cullen, Rector of the Irish College from 1832 to 1850. The Irish College had been founded in 1628 and was both a seminary and a focus of Irish Catholic interests in Rome. During his time there, Cullen established good friendships in the Vatican, notably with both Gregory XVI and his successor, Pius IX.[19] From the beginning of 1846, Cullen had been receiving reports from Ireland of an impending famine. The Catholic hierarchy, however, was absorbed in its own internal squabbles, especially regarding the establishment of three new universities in Ireland, an issue on which the Irish bishops disagreed.[20] At the same time, the Papacy was – controversially – seeking to establish the Catholic hierarchy in England.[21] Initially, Cullen combined his opposition to the

'Infidel Colleges' in Ireland with a more general criticism of the British government.[22]

In Rome, the early response to news of the crisis came from people who had no connections with the Catholic Church. Following the second appearance of blight, British and Irish residents formed a committee on behalf of the Irish poor, which was chaired by John Harford. John Scandrett Harford, a wealthy banker and abolitionist, had been brought up as a member of the Society of Friends but had converted to Anglicanism.[23] While spending the winter of 1846–47 in Rome, he had witnessed the coronation of Pius IX in his capacity as Chairman of the English community. On hearing of the situation in Ireland, he undertook to collect for the relief of the Irish poor.[24] Harford's committee comprised of men from England, Scotland and Ireland and included John F Folliot, MP for Sligo.[25]

Concurrently with Harford's initiative, at the end of 1846, several leading prelates expressed their willingness to intervene privately 'to use every effort to relieve the effect of the Famine on the impoverished Catholics of Ireland'.[26] At the beginning of 1847, the Vatican became more openly involved in Famine relief, possibly prompted by the public participation of Queen Victoria and the linking of assistance for Ireland with the Anglican Church. Papal sympathy for the Irish poor was genuine, with Pius IX admitting privately that he had been following events in Ireland and that the news had made him 'very sad'.[27] The idea for a Papal subscription was believed to have originated with Cardinal Fransoni, Prefect of Propaganda. At the time, the population of Rome was undergoing their own hardships due to the River Tiber overflowing. Despite their poverty, Fransoni believed that the people would give their 'mite', adding 'I am certain the Father of the Faithful will add something, and give the movement his countenance and support'. He promised to lay the matter before both the Pope and Paul Cullen.[28] On 14 January, Cullen wrote to Archbishop Murray informing him:

> Our good and holy Pontiff, Pius IX, filled with compassion for the suffering of the poor in Ireland, has authorized a public subscription to be made in Rome for their relief, and has commenced the good work by giving as his own contribution 1,000 dollars (£250). Millions of the poor will, I trust, raise their voices to the Throne of Mercy to implore the choicest blessings of Heaven on so tender-hearted a father and to pray for the preservation of so great a Pontiff.[29]

The Pope promised to donate a further 1,000 scudi (or dollars) in April, to which would be added 4,000 scudi from 'the ladies of his family'.[30]

Pius IX's donation was given to the 'English' committee in Rome. Harford thanked Cullen for the Pope's 'munificent' contribution and requested an audience with him in order to thank him personally.[31] A delegation from the committee met with the Pope on 8 February. Cullen and Dr Kirby of the Irish College were also present. Although the group was referred to as 'the

English delegation', the men came from all parts of the United Kingdom. Harford praised the Pope for the 'benevolent and significant manner in which you have signified to us, through Dr Cullen, your charitable and generous intention of contributing one thousand scudi'. Harford said that this donation was not only appreciated in Rome, 'but in every portion of the British empire'.[32] Pius responded that, 'were the means at my command more extensive I should not limit myself to the little I have done in a cause in which I feel the warmest sympathy'. He also promised that he would continue to pray for the suffering Irish.[33]

The Pope's involvement prompted donations to the Vatican from Catholic bishops throughout the world.[34] Fransoni's view was that the money donated by the Catholic Church should, in the first instance, be sent to Archbishop Murray, who would 'know how best to divide this among the four Metropolitans, giving most where there is greatest need and seeing that the suffragan bishops in districts badly affected receive a just allocation'.[35] This approach allayed a fear among the Irish Bishops that if the Papal money was channelled through the British government, it would be forwarded to a relief fund that was controlled mostly by Protestants. Archbishops MacHale and Slattery, therefore, intervened to prevent the donations from the Pope and the other churches in Rome from going into a central fund, successfully securing this money for the Irish Bishops and priests.[36]

A number of subscriptions in Rome were channelled directly through Cullen, he then forwarding them to Murray in Dublin.[37] In addition to monetary donations, Cullen received a number of more unusual gifts, including 2000 'cubic palmi'[38] of marble 'for those suffering hunger in Ireland'.[39] He also was given paintings and a diamond ring, valued at £100.[40] More traditional aid included a contribution of 10 scudi, which was made by the Sacred Congregation of the Index, a body that had been founded in the sixteenth century to create a catalogue of prohibited books.[41] By mid-February, Cullen estimated that donations made to the church in Rome were in the region of £14,000 to £15,000. In comparison, he believed that Harford's committee had collected only £1,000.[42] Large amounts of money continued to be sent to Fransoni and Cullen, they receiving an estimated £3,500 between April and July 1847.[43] The *Dublin Evening Post* praising the Pope for his support, added:

> The amount of the collections may be only as a drop in the ocean of Irish misery, still it will show the clergy and the people of suffering Ireland how deeply the Father of the Faithful and the good people of Rome sympathizes in their afflictions.[44]

The Pontiff's interventions were reported and acclaimed as far away as Sydney in Australia.[45]

The Pope's special interest in the Famine was manifested in a number of other ways. In addition to his financial contributions, he proposed a

Triduum (three days of prayer), which was to include sermons in Italian, English and French, respectively. The Triduum commenced on 25 January 1847 in the Church of St Andrea della Valle and was conducted by Father Gioacchino Ventura, a well-respected priest and orator. The English sermon was delivered on the second day by Dr Paul Cullen, followed by the French sermon by Monseigneur Bourget, the Bishop of Montreal.[46] During the ceremonies, people were said to be crying openly. Several donations were made for Ireland, including gifts of jewellery. Over the three days, the collections raised 1,111 scudi.[47] Only a few months later, following his death, Daniel O'Connell would be revered in a similar way, with Fr Ventura conducting three days of prayers in Rome.[48] To raise awareness of the depth and extent of suffering of the Irish poor, the Vatican even prepared a pamphlet *Breve notizia dell' attuale Carestia in Irlanda* (Brief Notice of the Present Famine in Ireland), which contained heart-rending extracts of newspapers reports from Ireland.[49]

The Pope's intervention did not end there. In late February, Cullen confided in Archbishop Murray that, 'The Pope is having an Encyclical prepared appealing for Irish famine sufferers'. Tellingly, Cullen continued, 'His Holiness is not happy about the slowness of [the British] Parliament to cope with the situation'.[50] In March, Pius IX issued an Encyclical asking Catholics throughout the world to pray on behalf of Ireland. It was a rare gesture by the head of the international Catholic Church. The Papal Encyclical, *Praedecessores Nostros*, was delivered by Pius IX at St Mary Major Basilica on 25 March 1847. Significantly, this Catholic intervention took place the day after the Anglican-led day of fast and humiliation had been held in the United Kingdom. The Encyclical was accompanied by a less formal letter from the Pope asking Catholics everywhere to come to the aid of the Irish.[51] His appeal involved a number of spiritual incentives:

We exhort you to ordain, that in the dioceses or countries subjected to your jurisdiction, as has already been done in our city of Rome, there shall, during three days, be recited public prayers in the temples and other consecrated places, in order that, touched by these supplications, the Father of Pity may deliver the Irish nation from this cruel calamity of scarcity, and keep away so frightful a calamity from the other kingdoms and countries of Europe. And in order that this desire may be more fully and usefully accomplished we accord our indulgence of seven years, for every time, to all those who shall be present at such prayers; and to those who during the three days shall have been present at the prayers, and who, during the week of this triduo, having been purified by the sacrament of penitence, shall receive the most holy sacrament of the Eucharist, we give, by our apostolical authority, plenary indulgence. Next, we recommend more strongly to your charity, venerable brethren, that, by your exhortations, you incite the people submitted to your jurisdiction to aid Ireland with liberal alms. We undoubtedly know that we have no need to remind you of the virtue of alms giving, nor of the abundant fruits which it produces in obtaining . . . Therefore, we recommend you, above all, on the occasion of the public prayers to be ordained for Ireland, to engage; the people submitted to your power to supplicate the Lord, at the same time, in favour of all the Church.[52]

The Pope's support continued beyond the Encyclical. Fr Tobias Kirby, who had been born in Ireland but was based in Rome (and in 1849 would succeed Cullen as Rector of the Irish College), was granted an audience with Pius IX in early August 1847. He reported the Pope as having confided, 'I am exceedingly interested in the cause of Poor Ireland'.[53] A number of more unusual interventions by the Pope won the praise of the London *Times*. Pius had been asked by an English Catholic lady if he would provide his autograph to be exhibited at some fund-raising bazaars in England. The Pope not only supplied his autograph, but added it to a letter, *'scritta di sua mano'* (written by his own hand), together with 'a beautiful rosary of agates, and a carnelian medallion, engraved with a head of our saviour pendant from it'. These items were expected to raise large amounts of money from wealthy Catholic families.[54] When the rosary arrived in England, it was exhibited in a bank in Pall Mall, and a subscription list was opened for the Irish poor.[55]

Surprisingly, given the multiple interventions made by the Pope for the Irish poor, it was left to Dr Cullen to suggest to the Irish Archbishops and Bishops that they should thank him formally. They responded immediately.[56] Further appreciation was expressed in, 'The Address of the Catholics of Ireland to His Holiness Pope Pius IX signed on behalf of the Meeting by the Chairman, John O'Connell, MP for the City of Limerick and City of Kilkenny, Dublin, made in July 1847'.[57] The authors of this address took the opportunity to argue the case for the re-establishment of an independent Parliament for Ireland. They suggested that the ongoing Famine demonstrated this need 'because, after forty seven years' experience of the control of our affairs by others, we find our country and our people reduced down to nearly utter destitution and death!'[58]

The response from Europe

The Pope's prayers and the Encyclical galvanized Catholic Bishops and Archbishops throughout the world to act. Archbishop Murray in Dublin was the main recipient of the financial contributions. Many were sent directly to him, although several were forwarded from Rome. The donations came in a variety of currencies, and Murray requested that, as far as possible, they be transmitted through a London bank, generally Coutts and Co., where they could be converted to sterling.[59] A smaller number of donations were sent directly to banks in Dublin. The letters that accompanied the donations were written in several languages, including French, German and Latin. Dealing with this torrent of international correspondence and donations made in multiple currencies was clearly a daunting task. Murray, who was aged almost 80, brought in the younger Thomas Synnott to assist him.[60] Synnott, a Catholic businessman, had previous experience of working with Murray and of distributing relief in his capacity as secretary of the Mansion House Committee and the India Relief Fund.[61] His efficient work on behalf of the poor in Dublin and elsewhere in the country was widely praised.[62]

Catholic communities throughout Europe proved particularly receptive to the Pope's appeals. The backdrop to this generosity was a series of bad harvests and the onset of an industrial downswing. There was also widespread political unrest, which erupted in a series of revolutions in 1848.[63] Belgium, which had won its independence from the Netherlands, and thus from a Dutch Protestant monarch, was at the forefront of charitable activities for Ireland. Regardless of the fact that Belgium had been seriously affected by the potato blight, experiencing a decline in potato yields of 87 per cent in 1845 and 43 per cent in 1846, large amounts of money were raised, especially in 1847.[64] In the Bruges Archdiocese, 5,000 francs was collected and two separate sums of £240 and £150 were sent to Murray.[65] Despite great poverty existing in his own parishes, Louis Joseph Delebecque, Archbishop of Ghent, sent £940 followed by £150, which had been donated by wealthy members of his congregation. In addition, the Archbishop promised to pray on behalf of the Catholics of Ireland.[66] A collection in the diocese of Malines raised 16,000 francs, which was converted to £680 and sent to Murray through a London bank.[67] Donations also came from the archbishops of Antwerp and Namur, which totalled over £1,000.[68]

Several members of the Catholic Church in France were active even before the Pope's public involvement, with donations being sent to Murray at the beginning of 1847. The fund-raising efforts were led by Baron Augustin Louis Cauchy, a brilliant mathematician, who, with other well-known public persons in Paris, wrote to the Pope asking him to make a universal appeal for the victims of the Irish Famine. In addition, Baron Cauchy and others formed the Paris Relief Committee and suggested that Murray should form a similar body in Dublin.[69] Although the French committee worked closely with the Catholic Church, it remained distinct, sending separate donations to Murray.[70] Several of the letters that accompanied the donations provided an insight into the sacrifices and motivations of the donors. The Bishop of Marseilles sent two contributions of £150, 'despite the many calls on the charity of his flock'.[71] In the archdiocese of Blois, there was much distress caused by a flooding of the Loire River. Nonetheless, the local Bishop, Monseigneur Fabré-des-Essarts, made a donation of 3,500 francs, which was converted to £137. The French Bishop informed Murray, 'If the sum sent is small the prayers that go with it are ardent and sincere'.[72] Not all donations were channelled through the church. Responding to the Pope's appeal, 'un pauvre domestique de France' sent 50 francs to Murray.[73]

A poignant contribution was made by J. T. Mooratz of Paris, who explained to Murray that, 'Before his 16-year-old daughter died three days ago, she said she wished to contribute to the relief of the Irish poor'. He sent £50 for Murray to distribute as he saw fit, as a gift for, 'the repose of his daughter's soul'.[74]

Catholic congregations in Austria and the various German states responded to Pius IX's appeal. Contributions came in various different currencies, including florins, francs, dollars and thalers (silver coins used throughout Europe). Again, jewellery was donated. Johann Peter von Richarz, Bishop of Augsburg, informed Murray that the Pope's letter, together with the promise of Indulgences, had raised 13,000 florins, which was converted to £1,080. Smaller donations followed.[75] The experiences of Bishop Richarz demonstrated the complexity of the process of sending money to Ireland. On 25 December 1847, Richarz wrote to Murray (in English) explaining, 'According to Your Lordship's letter of the 11 November, I took great care to find a banker who would undertake to transmit to You by Your appointed way, the money collected in my diocese'.[76] The money had been raised in florins. Richarz gave it to a local banker, Augustus Frommel, who deducted postage and other expenses amounting to £23. Frommel then obtained Bills of Exchange from Messrs Coutts and Company in London and, following the deduction of their expenses, they lodged the money in the Bank of Ireland in Dublin. Richarz anticipated that his donation would be available by the middle of January 1848.[77] The process of getting the proceeds of Richarz's collection to Ireland had taken almost four months, which represented a significant delay given the need for emergency relief.

Throughout 1847, money continued to be raised by Catholic communities. The Archbishop of Aix-la-Chapelle (Aachen) sent 27,272 thalers (£36), while the Archbishop of Trèves (Trier) raised 2,277 dollars.[78] The latter explained that his diocese was very poor, but that his parishioners, 'pray that the famine may soon end'.[79] Donations continued to be sent to Ireland even following the harvest. In December 1847, a number of donations were made by Franz Arnold Melchers, the Vicar Capitular of Munster and Suffragan. He informed Murray that the Pope's Encyclical had aroused much sympathy for Ireland. In June, he had sent £150, followed by £1,050 in July, £10 in August and £500 in December, which were all transmitted directly to the Bank of Ireland, 'for the relief of these afflicted by the Famine'.[80] Collections having been prompted by the Pope's appeal, other donations came from the dioceses in Paderborn and Bonn, the latter sending the proceeds of three collections which amounted to 1,144 dollars or £161.[81]

A smaller number of donations were received by Murray from Spain, which included 50 francs from Cartagena and £43 from the staff of *Revista Catolica* in Tarragona.[82] In the neighbouring island of Gibraltar, which had been a British colony since 1714, a number of collections were made. Dr Henry Hughes, Bishop in Gibraltar, sent £100 to Ireland.[83] Hughes was an Irish Franciscan Friar, who had been born in Wexford in 1788.[84]

At the end of 1845, accompanied by five Sisters from the Loreto Abbey in Rathfarnham, Dublin, Hughes had travelled to Gibraltar in order to establish Catholic schools there. He had appealed to Murray in Dublin for support in this venture.[85] Other money from this small island included £70 from the 66th Regiment, sent via London, and collections made by local Methodist ministers, to be divided between Ireland and Scotland.[86]

Italy, like Germany, was made up of a number of distinct states and kingdoms, many of which were experiencing political unrest in 1847 and 1848. Some fund-raising efforts had taken place even before the Pope's intervention. The St Vincent de Paul Society in Genoa had collected £5,633, and following the Encyclical, local Catholics donated a further £5,000.[87] Elsewhere, the Bishop of Susa (Savona) set 1,200 francs to Murray, 4,000 francs came from the Bishop of Ivrea, £450 and £150 was sent by Mgr Franzoni, Archbishop of Turin. Franzoni's contributions were sent to Ireland via the Sardinian Legation in London.[88] Donations also came from bishops and archbishops in the dioceses of Sarzana and Brugnato, Mondovi Aosta in Piedmont. The Bishop of Acqui collected £2,600 pounds for famine relief following the reading of Pius IX's letter.[89] Savoy in the north of Italy had been part of the Kingdom of Piedmont-Sardinia since 1815. In July 1847, the Bishop of Annecy sent 2,600 francs to Murray.[90] Only a few weeks later, the Italian states became absorbed in a violent struggle for independence and unity, which overshadowed their concerns for Ireland. Moreover, regardless of their own suffering, Catholics in Ireland became concerned for the personal safety of their spiritual leader, Pius IX.[91]

Despite the large amounts of money being collected and sent to Murray, the sums he was forwarding to his fellow archbishops appeared quite small. At the end of February, MacHale thanked Murray for £240 of 'the Roman money' received for distribution among the poor of Connaught.[92] Around the same time, Dr William Crolly, the Archbishop of Armagh, acknowledged the receipt of £190, given for the benefit of the poor in his province.[93] Two weeks later, Crolly thanked Murray for sending an additional £17 from Rome, while MacHale acknowledged the receipt of £26.[94] In April, Murray sent MacHale a further £25.[95] In September, however, MacHale received £500 from Murray, which had come from Rome. When thanking him, MacHale noted, 'The Holy Father's letter was full of blessings for the suffering poor of Ireland'.[96] The money put in the hands of the Irish archbishops was, in turn, distributed to local parish priests in sums mostly ranging between £5 and £100. Not all the money was distributed to the clergy. Murray gave £5 to Robert Fetherston, a JP in Charleville, whose wife had sought assistance for the poor of Bruree.[97] Even for those who were recipients of this bounty, it was necessary to seek charity from other sources. Fr Michael Enright of Castletown Berehaven in west Cork, who received a number of small sums of money from Murray, ranging from £5 to £10, informed the Archbishop that he was considering using funds from the British Association to feed the pupils of National Schools during the winter of 1847.[98] Elizabeth

Fetherston, in addition to support from Murray, had received subscriptions from England and Scotland and from Quakers in Limerick.[99]

The same Fr Enright, who was cooperating with the British Relief Association, found it more difficult to work with the representatives of the local Protestant church. When sending him a donation of £10 Murray had enquired privately if the Anglican minister and Fr Enright could work together in the distribution of future donations. Enright responded that he was:

> . . . sorry to say that the Rector, Mr O'Grady, refused in the presence of the other gentlemen to act with Fr E. in the distribution of such relief. He has avoided all form of collusion with these gentlemen and will continue to do so; he [Fr. E.] has reason to believe that they are receiving grants themselves, one person admitted as much in an unguarded moment.[100]

Rev O'Grady was subsequently to achieve a more public and positive notoriety through the success of his literary son, Standish, who was born in the town in 1846.[101]

The International response

In addition to the large amounts of money sent to Archbishop Murray and his fellow archbishops from Europe, charity from Catholics came from other parts of the world. Donations had been collected by the Catholic Church in India since the beginning of 1846. A number were made directly to the Irish-born Bishop Patrick Joseph of Bengal. Most of this money was channelled through the Indian Relief Fund, the Irish trustees including both Archbishop Murray and Archbishop Whately.[102] On the other side of the world, substantial collections were made in Canada. In Quebec, a Relief Committee chaired by Andrew W. Cochran raised £1,500 to aid victims of the Famine in Ireland and a further £500 for those in Scotland. Within Ireland, the money was entrusted to Archbishops Murray and Whately, 'to be distributed to deserving official Boards of Relief'. In his accompanying letter, Cochran referred to the gratitude of the residents of Quebec for the support they received from Ireland after the fire in their city – a devastating fire having occurred there in 1845.[103] Also in Quebec, the charitable Independent Order of Odd Fellows raised $1,200, but asked that a portion go to Scotland.[104] William Walsh, Bishop of Halifax in Nova Scotia, sent a number of donations which, by March 1847, amounted to over £1,800. In addition, £31.5s was collected by St Mary's Catechistical Society.[105] Walsh had been born in County Waterford and educated at Maynooth Seminary.[106] When forwarding this money to Murray, Walsh informed him that he was considering establishing a permanent subscription for Ireland, adding that, 'Halifax is now at peace'.[107] Patrick Phelan, the Coadjutor Bishop in the

Diocese of Kingston in Ontario, was also Irish born. He had been born in County Kilkenny but studied for the priesthood in Montreal.[108] In April 1847, Phelan sent an undisclosed amount of money to Murray towards famine relief.[109]

Several small communities in Canada participated. A donation of £52.2s.6d. was collected in Baytown near Ottawa River by Rev P. Telman, the local parish priest. It was sent to Cullen in Rome who, in turn, forwarded it to Murray.[110] The town of Chatham near Miramichi in New Brunswick sent £300, which had been collected by Catholic residents. The money was sent to Murray by John Sweeny, a Catholic Missionary, with a request that it be forwarded to the Dublin Relief Committee. Sweeny further requested that the contribution be acknowledged in the *Tablet,* an English Catholic newspaper.[111]

Multiple donations came from Catholic communities in the United States. The first to organize relief in the United States appears to have been Thomas O'Flaherty, parish priest of Salem, Massachusetts who, as early as December 1845, set up an Irish Charitable Relief Fund and collected over $2,000.[112] Following the failed harvest of 1846, large amounts were collected for the Irish poor. William Tyler, the first Bishop of Hartford, had converted to Catholicism as a teenager.[113] He raised $3,600 from parishes in Connecticut and Rhode Island, which he sent to Ireland in the form of a bill of exchange.[114] The money was to be shared among the four Irish archbishops. Tyler explained to Murray that his diocese was a new one and although the congregation were 'few and poor, they promptly and generously responded to his appeal for their starving brethren in Ireland'.[115] The French-born bishop of Mobile in Alabama, Michael Portier, sent £120 care of MacHale. MacHale informed Murray that he was retaining £50 for Tuam, but was dividing the remainder among the other archbishops.[116] One donation to Murray from the United States was given by mistake. Bishop John Hughes of New York had given support to the General Relief Committee of New York in early 1847, giving them the proceeds of a public lecture. Inadvertently, Murray was the recipient of a draft for £170 that Hughes had intended for Archbishop Whately.[117]

One of the largest individual American donations came from Bishop John Fitzpatrick of Boston. By March 1847, he had raised $20,000. Although he entrusted this money to the Irish archbishops, he asked that they utilize it 'without distinction of creed'.[118] A number of donations came from secular sources. The Albany Committee, which was one of the most active in the US, sent a number of relief ships to the Society of Friends in Ireland. In addition, they sent 2,000 barrels of corn meal 'to be jointly administered by the Catholic and Protestant Archbishops of Ireland'.[119] A number of donations were received from South America. This included £441.10s.1d. from Buenos Ayres, 'towards relief of distress in Ireland', which was sent to Murray.[120] Other contributions came from Montevideo in Uruguay and Caracas in Venezuela.[121] In early 1847, Fr Aidan Devereux, a priest in the

Cape of Good Hope, sent £100 to Archbishop Murray.[122] Devereux, who had been born in Ferns in County Wexford in 1801, had been appointed the first bishop of the eastern district of Cape Colony in December 1847.[123] He died in South Africa in 1851.[124]

Nearer to Ireland, Catholic Churches in Britain were involved in fund-raising. Some of this was directed through the medium of the *Tablet*, which had been launched in 1840. Its editor, Frederick Lucas, constantly urged his readers to raise money for the 'starving poor of Ireland'.[125] Large amounts of money were collected. On 18 January 1847, Bishop Thomas Griffiths, Vicar Apostolic of London, sent £2,000 'for the relief of distress among the poor in Ireland' to Archbishop Murray.[126] Cardinal Nicholas Wiseman, whose parents were Irish, was associated with the intellectual revival of the Roman Catholic Church in England in the mid-nineteenth century. In January, he made four separate donations to Murray of £50, £80, £266 and £93, respectively.[127] Father John Kirk, who had a parish in Lichfield in Staffordshire, sent a number of individual donations. Kirk apologized for their smallness, but pointed out that his parish was a poor one. He had, however, been helped by two brothers, who were lawyers and Protestant, and had given him ten guineas for the Irish poor.[128] Many smaller donations came from parishes throughout England. A number of contributors referred to the poverty of their own parishioners, but their desire to help Ireland.

Some of the largest donations from England came from the Catholic community in Liverpool. The first recorded donation was made by people who were themselves poor. Irish navvies, who were employed constructing the railway to Bury, promised to contribute one day's wages for the Irish poor. In this way, they raised £52 which they gave to the priest of St Joseph's parish in Liverpool to send to Ireland on their behalf.[129] Liverpool was the main port of entry for poor immigrants from Ireland. In the final months of 1846, emigration to the port had been increasing; during a period of six days, from 4 to 9 January, the Select Vestry relieved 7,146 Irish families, consisting of 29,417 persons, of whom 18,376 were children.[130] To cope with the pressure, a number of soup kitchens were opened in the city. Religious tensions emerged, however, as some local evangelicals insisted that no food should be provided on Sundays. This action led Lord Brougham to condemn the perpetrators for 'mixing up religious fanaticism with the cause of charity and benevolence'.[131]

Regardless of the burden being placed on the local rates due to the influx of Irish immigrants, by February 1847, Liverpool had raised £3,000 for famine relief.[132] Most of this money had been collected at a meeting convened by Bishop James Sharples at the Concert Hall in Lord Nelson Street. Liverpool-born Sharples had been consecrated a bishop in Rome in 1843 by Cardinal Fransoni. He collected £2,000, which was subscribed by fewer than fifty persons. C. J. Corbally, a prominent local businessman, acted as Treasurer to the relief fund.[133] The day after the meeting, Corbally sent this money to Ireland to be divided in equal shares to the Archbishops of Cashel and

Tuam. Church collections in Liverpool raised a further £1,000.[134] Additional amounts were contributed by Thomas Cullen, a relative of Paul Cullen who resided in the city. In February 1847, he sent £600, with a promise to send a further £400 before the end of the month.[135]

In addition to financial efforts, Catholic clergy in Liverpool contributed to Famine relief in another way. Despite the personal risk of working with the Famine immigrants, many of whom were malnourished, ill or unwitting incubators of disease, priests were often in the frontline of providing relief with the meagre resources available to them. As many as 14 priests died carrying out these duties. The first victim was Fr Peter Nightingale of St Anthony's Church, who died at the beginning of March 1847. Fr Parker of St Patrick's Church succumbed to typhus in April. He was aged 43. Parker had established the parish in 1844, with the support of a small number of nuns, to look after Irish immigrants.[136] In June, Fr Grayston aged 33, and his colleague, Fr Haggar, aged 29, of the same parish contracted a fever which proved fatal.[137] On 26 May, Dr James Appleton, aged 40, a Benedictine who had left the Presidency of Douai College to work in Liverpool, died.[138] He had contracted fever while working with sick famine immigrants in St Peter's Church.[139] Rev Bernard O Reilly who had been born in Westmeath, Fr Gilbert, O. S. B., aged 27, and Fr William Dale, O. S. B., aged 43, all died of fever, as did Fr Richard Gillow, of St Nicholas parish, aged 36, and Fr Whitaker of St Joseph's Church. The rector of Old Swan, Fr Haddocks, contracted fever but recovered. These priests joined the 15,000 deaths from famine and fever that took place in the city in 1847.[140] A small, simple monument to the 'martyr priests' was erected outside St Patrick's Church in 1898.[141] It was not only priests in Liverpool who gave their lives working with the Famine poor. In Canada, an estimated 13 priests and 17 Catholic nuns died while tending to sick Irish immigrants. The mortality among priest in Ireland was even higher, but like many of their parishioners, their deaths were unrecorded and overlooked as the living struggled to survive.[142]

Another recipient of fund-raising efforts was Fr Mathew, widely referred to as 'the apostle of temperance'. Mathew, despite his international reputation, was disliked by some members of the Catholic hierarchy. However, he used his prominence to appeal directly to leading members of the government to plead for more relief. He also used money that he received from Britain and America to open his own soup kitchen in Cork.[143] These donations included a large grant of $2,557 from Patterson in New Jersey.[144] The Liverpool philanthropist, William Rathbone, who played a pivotal role in assisting with the distribution of the cargo from the relief ship, the Jamestown, in April 1847, privately gave Mathew some subventions to continue his work and provide employment as late as 1848. Mathew responded to this generosity by saying, 'on the part of the rising generation of my generation, I thank you for your ardent desire to infuse into them a spirit of self-respect and industry'. He added a hope that 'a young Ireland, prosperous and happy, will delight your eyes on your next visit to Ireland'.[145]

Catholics within Ireland came to the assistance of their suffering co-religionists. In June 1847, the Christian Brothers in Cork received an anonymous donation via the Rev Peter Cooper of Dublin of £20, which was described as 'the offering of a benevolent lady towards the relief of the destitute children of their schools, for which they offer their grateful acknowledgement'.[146] Cooper was based in St Mary's Parish in Marlborough Street in Dublin, which was part of Archbishop Murray's parish. Among other duties, he was Guardian of St Joseph's Asylum for Aged and Virtuous Females.[147] In Galway, the Patrician Brothers, under Paul O'Connor, had set up the Orphans' Breakfast and Clothing Institute which at one stage was giving breakfast to a thousand children as well as feeding 400 to 500 poor in their homes. The order, also known as the Religious Congregation of the Brothers of Saint Patrick, had been founded in 1808. The Annual Report for 1847 stated, 'It is resolved that while a penny or particle of food remains in the Establishment, or can be obtained by the humblest entreaty, not one of the little creatures will be cast overboard!'.[148]

At the beginning of 1848, the Right Rev Dr James Browne, Bishop of Kilmore in County Cavan, donated the proceeds of collections made over five Sundays at the door of his church, for the relief of the destitute of all religious denominations. To this, Browne added his own contribution, making a total of £27. The local newspaper, the *Anglo-Celt*, when reporting on this matter, noted, 'Amongst the contributors were several Protestants'. They continued, 'the poor of this neighbourhood owe a deep debt of gratitude to his Lordship for his unwearied exertions in their behalf. We trust the noble example thus set will be extensively followed by those who are in a position to "do likewise"'. Unusually, this money was used to release clothing from pawnbrokers, which had been pledged prior to Christmas day. In total, 540 tickets had been issued.[149] Even more unusually, Dr Browne worked closely with a local landowner, Lord Farnham, who was renowned for his Protestant evangelical views, to provide relief to the local poor.[150]

Distinct from the Catholic Church, but working with its blessing, was the Society of St Vincent de Paul, an organization founded in France in 1833 and which regarded charity as a Christian virtue. A branch of the society had been established in Cork in March 1846 and from there had spread to other parts of Ireland. Men and women worked in separate branches of their organization in Dublin and its environs to bring relief to the poorest of the poor.[151] Because of the small size of the Irish society, they applied to their headquarters in France for assistance with providing famine relief. By May 1847, the Vincent de Paul Society in France had sent 153,000 francs or £6,000.[152] Cardinal Tommaso Gizzi, the Papal Secretary of State, congratulated the President of the Society in France for his efforts on behalf of the Irish poor.[153] Support had come from members of the Society in a number of other countries: 'Holland was the main contributor, with Italy, Turkey, France and England also giving donations. People in Mexico, although at war, had contributed'.[154] A large portion of donations received in this way was channelled through an Irish solicitor, Redmond Peter O'Carroll. O'Carroll, although a layman, was the first Spiritual Director of the Superior Council of Ireland.[155] He died in 1847, having contracted typhus fever. The involvement of the St Vincent de Paul Society in Ireland was not without controversy, they being forced to counter accusations that their approach to charity was sectarian and only favoured Catholics.[156]

In addition to their practical and spiritual support for the suffering in Ireland, the archbishops and bishops intervened at a political level. On 26 October 1847, a delegation consisting of the four archbishops met with the Lord Lieutenant, the Earl of Clarendon. Clarendon's arrival in Ireland in the summer of 1847 had coincided with the transfer to an amended system of Poor Law relief. His initial analysis of the crisis appeared optimistic, if callous, he opining:

> In the next two years there will be a grand struggle and the government of Ireland will be a painful, thankless task, but I am convinced that the failure of the potatoes and the establishment of the Poor Law will eventually be the salvation of the country – the first will prevent the land being used as it hitherto has been.[157]

At the meeting in Dublin Castle, the archbishops presented the Viceroy with a Memorial explaining:

> Several of Your Excellency's memorialists are come from those remote districts in which the famine is but too visible in the numbers of the most pitiable objects imploring relief, and they can state, from the intimate knowledge of their condition, that in these localities there are not sufficient available resources to avert an extensive destruction of human life . . . Yet laws sanctioning such unnatural injustice, and therefore injurious to society, not only exist but are extensively enforced with reckless and unrelenting vigour, while the sacred and indefeasible rights of life are forgotten amongst the incessant reclamations of the subordinate rights of property.[158]

The intervention and pleas of the Catholic hierarchy did not alter the course being pursued by the British government and its representatives in Ireland. Moreover, a large portion of the charitable impulse, so evident in the preceding months, had largely dried up. Although donations continued to be made to the Catholic Church, they were on a much reduced scale. Their impact, however, remained significant. As late as January 1849, the Christian Brothers in Cork informed the editor of the *Tablet* that, as a consequence of the generosity of people in England, they were feeding 400 children a day.[159]

Throughout 1848, most of Europe, including Italy and Ireland, experienced revolutionary turmoil. In Ireland, this was to culminate in an easily defeated rising in County Tipperary in July led by Young Ireland.[160] In Italy, the crisis was more prolonged. A backdrop to the Pope's contribution and that of other members of the Catholic Church in Rome had been an unfolding political crisis within the various Italian states, which came to a head in 1848, with attempts to bring about Italian unity and independence. The Papal States, which included Rome, were opposed to the demand for Italian unification. The impact of the unrest on the Vatican had been evident in 1847, leading Fr Kirby to suggest that the British government was cynically taking advantage of the instability by offering to support the Pope.[161] Edward Maginn, an outspoken nationalist bishop, wrote to Cullen on 7 October 1847 from Buncrana in County Donegal to thank the Pope and, at the same time, to extend his sympathy. He concluded by promising that there were plenty of men in Ireland, 'six feet high at least, ready to fight for Pope'.[162] Such proclamations seemed meaningless when, in 1848, the Pope was forced to flee from Rome. From that time until 1850, Pius IX lived in exile in Gaëta in central Italy. Understandably, after 1848, the Pope, a refugee with his own future uncertain, had less involvement with events in Ireland. Sympathy for Pius IX was evident from the collections being made throughout the international Catholic world to enable him to return to the Vatican. Donations to the Pope included multiple ones from Ireland.[163] This generosity seemed cruelly ironic given the continued suffering of the Irish poor. Nevertheless, while the Pope's involvement in Irish affairs may have been shortlived, it had been significant. In 1847, his very public concern had prompted Catholics throughout the world to intervene on behalf of the Irish poor and they had responded generously to this appeal, both with money and with prayers.

Despite having neither a national structure nor an agreed strategy for distributing funds, the Catholic Church in Ireland proved to be an important conduit for distributing funds raised throughout the world on its behalf. Notwithstanding the troubles faced by the Papacy after 1848, its valuable work was able to continue after many other donations to Ireland had dried up. At the same time as saving lives, however, the Catholic Church was also engaged in a battle over souls, as the work of several evangelical churches intensified.[164] In subsequent Catholic narratives of these years, the Famine was reduced to a battle of the faiths. Writing in 1881, Rev C. Davis recalled:

It was in this period of writhing national agony that the arch-enemy of our holy religion prompted his agents in Great Britain and Ireland to attempt the spiritual ruin of the faithful Irish people. What in the past could not be effected by the sword, by confiscation, by corruption, was to be effected by money and want.[165]

In popular memory and public discourse, the struggle against religious conversion became a dominant part of the Famine narrative.[166] As a consequence, cooperation between the churches, at both national and local levels, was overlooked or ignored, as was the generosity and heroism of many Catholics and Protestants who worked to save lives, rather than souls. After 1845, the charity and involvement of the Catholic Church, in Ireland and internationally, made an important contribution to relief efforts. Moreover, by working in close physical proximity with the sick and the dying, many Catholic priests and nuns made the ultimate sacrifice of giving their lives on behalf of the Irish poor.

7

'How good people are!'[1]
The involvement of women

Seven hundred pounds at last we've got,
What with it shall we do?
We'll purchase one huge metal pot.
Some curry powder too.
For water at the boiling point with any curry shaken in,
Will do as well as any joint to fill a poor man's skin.
And no-one can question that this food is not substantial fare,
By it are Norfolk's labourers rude. Supplied by Ducal care.
Thus spoke a miss but then arose, a storm of fierce debate,
Some ladies were for buying clothes and all began to prate
Some thought that tracts would do most good. . .[2]

The unpublished poem above, entitled *A Ladies' Committee in Ireland, 1849*, provides some wry insights into the challenges facing women's relief committees throughout the Famine. Yet, regardless of the difficulties and dangers, women played an important role both as fund-raisers and as givers of relief during these years. Their involvement is not surprising. Throughout the nineteenth century, middle-class women, particularly spinsters, were prominent in all aspects of charitable work, they being particularly skilful at appealing for money. Their involvement was facilitated by the fact that they had so much leisure time.[3] Through their philanthropic work, women gained an entrance from the home to society and an influence beyond the domestic sphere. This pattern was repeated within Ireland where middle-class women 'played a major role in providing charity to the poor and outcast'.[4] Much Irish philanthropy, however, was characterized by the same sectarian divides that permeated national and local politics.[5] Interestingly, the involvement of women in Famine relief was unusual not only for its scale and diversity, but also because, for the most part, it cut across traditional religious divisions.[6]

Women were particularly active in the winter of 1846 to 1847, when the public works were proving to be pitifully inadequate for the needs of the poor. During this period, numerous donations from women, many anonymous, were recorded by both the Society of Friends and the British Relief Association. While women were not permitted to be members of the local relief committees, they were often responsible for carrying out the work of these bodies, in particular, distributing clothing and medical relief and managing the voluntary soup kitchens that covered the country.[7] Despite having a lower profile than the men who were members of the government's relief committees, women came together to form associations to help the poor in many of the cities and towns of Ireland. As a consequence, a network of ladies' associations existed throughout the country. Even though their work was often overshadowed by the activities of the larger organizations, it was no less important in saving lives. Collectively and individually, it is clear that women from diverse backgrounds played a significant role throughout the Famine. Despite a lack of training, they proved to be skilful and fearless in coming to the assistance of the poor, sick and dying.[8]

Charles Trevelyan of the Treasury, who interfered in so many aspects of famine relief, also interfered in the giving of private charity. He recognized that much charitable work was being carried out by women and religious ministers, whom, he assumed, were unfamiliar with financial transactions. To facilitate the giving of small donations in England, he asked the London branch of the Irish Provincial Bank to place an advertisement explaining how the transfer of money could be achieved. Trevelyan further recommended that 'as the persons who would avail themselves of this assistance are mostly ladies and clergymen and other persons not conversant with business, the notice should be of the plainest description, and give the direction of the office in London, and a list of the towns in Ireland in which your branch banks are situated'.[9] Clearly, Trevelyan had underestimated the women's abilities. As their activities in Ireland and elsewhere had demonstrated, women were adept at forming committees, raising funds and assisting the poor. A number of Irish and British women had developed these skills as participants in the anti-slavery movement or in various philanthropic societies. Within these organizations, women had been responsible for the emergence of charity bazaars, which became a popular way of raising money in the nineteenth century.[10] The involvement of women in providing famine relief took them even further into the public sphere of activity and, in the case of Irish women, often brought them face to face with the objects of their benevolence.

The various women's associations were clearly aware of other relief initiatives. By the end of December 1846, women, individually and collectively, were applying to the newly reconstituted Irish Relief Association for assistance. While the overwhelming majority of applications to the Association were made by Anglican ministers, in few instances, it was women who took the initiative; these women included Miss Cox from Dunmanway, Miss Townsend from Castle Townsend, both in County Cork, who each received two boilers; Mrs Smith from Castlebellingham in Louth, one boiler; and the Honourable Miss Plunkett, on behalf of the relief committee in Ballyoney in County Mayo, who received £10.[11] A larger number of applications were made on behalf of women's associations. Requests came from all parts of the country. In Six Mile Bridge in County Clare, for example, a number of women had already made their own donations and had distributed 'collecting cards amongst their friends', thus raising £60. This money had been used to open a soup kitchen two days a week, but it had no boiler. The local (male) relief committee applied to the Irish Relief Association on their behalf. In response, the women were sent a boiler and a grant of £15.5s.[12] A similar appeal was made on behalf of a ladies' committee in Arklow, where the local fishermen were particularly distressed. The women had been collecting subscriptions, but also lacked a boiler.[13] In nearby Baltinglass, more unusually a committee had been formed consisting of both men and women; the Chairman was Rev Henry Scott, while the Secretary was a woman, Miss Jane Chandler. The committee had encouraged a number of local people to agree to give weekly subscriptions, but the local landowner, the Earl of Aldborough, was an absentee and had not made any contribution. They appealed to the Irish Relief Association for support.[14] A committee in the Tubrid parish in County Tipperary, which also consisted of men and women, appointed a 'Miss Muir' as Treasurer. In their application to the Irish Relief Association, they explained that, 'the destitute labourers on the public works seem to move with difficulty in their labour, and their pallid looks and worn frames of body loudly testify to their destitution and want of food'. They had opened a soup kitchen but, as their work increased, required a boiler and additional funding in order to provide good-quality food that was affordable.[15]

Irish women showed similar alacrity when applying to philanthropic societies outside Ireland. Within days of the British Relief Association being formed in London on 1 January 1847, it was receiving appeals from women in Ireland requesting financial support. These early requests included one from Mrs Katherine Donovan, the Honorary Secretary of the Ladies' Committee for Relief of the Poor in Tralee, County Kerry. The highly organized committee of the British Relief Association agreed to send them a form on which to submit their request.[16] The following day, the Association received a letter from the ladies relief committee in Dublin, urging support for some of the remote districts in Ireland. The London Committee resolved to give them £100, subject to the approval of Sir Randolph Routh of the Commissariat Department. But they were also asked to complete the necessary paperwork.[17] These requests were indicative of the extent of the involvement of Irish women in providing assistance.

A number of associations were especially created in response to the crisis. Women in Belfast were in the forefront of these activities. The first women's association formed in the town was the Ladies' Relief Association for Connaught. The association had been the idea of Dr John Edgar, Moderator of the Presbyterian Church of Ireland since 1842 and Secretary of the Assembly's Home Mission. When travelling in Connaught in the autumn of 1846, he had been upset by the poverty of the people and decided to act upon it following his return to Belfast. Interestingly, he chose women as his medium, resulting in the formation of the Ladies' Relief Association in October 1846.[18] By the end of 1847, they had raised £4,615.6s.1d.[19] Virtually all of this money had been used to distribute gratuitous relief to the destitute, with no labour or reading of bibles being required in return. At this stage, Edgar decided that the work of the committee would be more useful if they focused on teaching the poor females in Connaught how to earn their own income.[20] Subsequent donations, therefore, were used to establish Industrial Schools in which the children were taught needlework and knitting. While the children worked, they were also taught to read 'and made familiar with the Scriptures'.[21] If they could not attend school, they were encouraged to read the bible at home. Asenath Nicholson, when visiting the Industrial Schools in Connaught, praised their work, believing that, as a consequence 'an industry, founded on righteous principles, was springing up – and industry that not only rewarded but elevated – the convenient term "lazy Irish" was hiding its slanderous head'.[22] This initiative was also admired by the Society of Friends who gave the Ladies' Industrial Association a grant of £500 in May 1848.[23] A condition of this grant was that an equal amount should be raised from other sources.[24] The success of the Association meant that by the beginning of 1851, it was employing 56 female teachers who were working with 2,000 pupils and their families.[25]

The Belfast Ladies' Association for the Relief of Irish Destitution was formed on 1 January 1847. The first meeting was described as, 'a large and influential assemblage of Ladies of all religious denominations'. It took place in the Commercial Buildings, but, subsequently, weekly meetings were held in the Library of the Royal Belfast Academical Institution.[26] The committee was organized on professional lines, with a number of subcommittees being established, which included the Corresponding, Clothing, Industrial, Collecting and Bazaar Committees.[27] To raise funds, the town of Belfast was divided into a number of districts and subscriptions lists were opened in each of them. In spring, a bazaar was planned to augment these funds. Donations were also sought from Scotland and England. The Association's early commitment to 'sink all doctrinal distinctions' and provide assistance without regard to religion was praised by Nicholson, who observed their work first-hand.[28]

The Belfast Ladies' Association consisted of 115 members, with Miss Knowles as President. One of the most well-known members was Mary Ann McCracken, then aged 77, and a noted social reformer and philanthropist.[29] She was sister to Henry Joy McCracken, who had been executed in 1798 for his part in the rebellion. Mary Ann shared many of his egalitarian ideals, including a commitment to the abolition of slavery.[30] Maria Webb, a fellow abolitionist, was also a founding member of the Ladies' Association. Webb had been born in Lisburn to a Quaker family, but she had moved to Belfast in 1828 following her marriage to William Webb. Maria was Secretary of the Belfast Ladies' Anti-Slavery Society.[31] Within the US, she and her family were well known in anti-slavery circles, their friends including Frederick Douglass. In January 1847, Webb wrote a letter to her American colleagues, which was published in a number of newspapers. She expounded:

> I have been, for the last few weeks, overpowered with business arising out of the arrangements on behalf of the famishing, destitute, state of our own peasantry. I do not mean the peasantry in districts surrounding Belfast, but distant agricultural counties, where things are truly in an awful state . . . Can America do anything to save our poor people from utter starvation?[32]

In December 1847, Webb contacted Maria Weston Chapman in Boston on behalf of the Belfast Ladies' Anti-Slavery Committee. For a number of years, Irish women abolitionists had been sending locally made products to be sold at the Boston Anti-Slavery Bazaar. In that year, however, she apologized for the smallness of the offering, explaining that the Belfast women had been preoccupied with looking after the poor within Ireland.[33] Other members of the Ladies' Association included Mary Ireland who, like Webb and McCracken, was a prominent member of the local anti-slavery movement and therefore accustomed to committee work.[34] Isabella Campbell Allen, wife of the wealthy Unitarian merchant, William Campbell Allen, was Treasurer of the Industrial Committee, a subsection of the main committee, which was responsible for financing and selling locally made linen and knitwear.[35]

By early March 1847, the Belfast Ladies' Association had raised over £2,000 in monetary aid.[36] Initially, they used these resources to assist mothers and their families who were in the greatest need.[37] Aid was provided predominantly in the form of food, clothing and fuel – the latter being especially crucial in such a cold winter. Clothing was also essential, especially for those employed on the public works in freezing, snowy conditions. Large supplies of clothing and clothing materials were given to the Belfast Ladies' Association from England, coming from towns and cities far apart as Newcastle-Upon-Tyne and Worcester. The largest individual donation of clothing came from Carlisle, in the far north of England, where a 'Ladies' Association for the Irish Poor' had been formed. They contributed 1,372 articles.[38]

A few weeks after coming into existence, the Belfast Ladies' Association decided to use part of their funds to support 'industrial pursuits', as a way of helping to preserve a spirit of independence among the recipients. They saw this shift of emphasis as the best way of helping to 'preserve the females from the moral evils which have sometimes arisen from their engaging in company with promiscuous assemblages of persons of the other sex, as labourers on the road or other public works'.[39] They hoped that larger charitable organizations would continue to provide food in these districts. Instead, the Belfast Ladies' Association focused on providing grants, often to be used to purchase flax for spinning or yarn for knitting.[40]

The Belfast Ladies' Association provided assistance throughout Ireland, although most of the demands made on their charity came from Ulster (particularly counties Donegal and Antrim) and County Mayo. However, the women were surprised by the rapidly deteriorating condition of the town of Belfast and the increasing demands being made on them from the local poor. While acknowledging the local suffering, the Association continued to provide general relief, but some of their members helped to establish a separate society for the poor of Belfast.[41]

In addition to their own work in providing aid, the Belfast Ladies' Association received many requests from both men and women seeking financial assistance for their work. The Belfast committee had encouraged other women, especially those in the most distressed districts, to form their own societies. Consequently, they received a number of requests from women, both as individuals and on behalf of local associations, for support. The latter included an appeal from the newly formed ladies' associations of Kilalla and Newcastle.[42] Many appeals for aid were made by Catholic priests and Church of Ireland ministers. Wives of Anglican ministers proved particularly active in distributing relief and providing employment on behalf of relief committees.[43] However, other women with no direct relationship to the churches also proved to be energetic in helping the local poor. On 18 February 1847, a Mrs Hewitson from Rossgarrow near Milford in County Donegal, wife of a former military man, informed the Belfast Association that she and her daughters, together with some local women, had formed an Industrial Committee, of which she was both Treasurer and Secretary. For some weeks they had been providing employment and food to local women, helped by small grants from the First and Second Unitarian Congregations of Belfast and from the Society of Friends. That money was now exhausted. The Belfast Ladies' Association had already sent them one consignment of clothing, which had arrived at the same time as 'a bitter snow storm'. Mrs Hewitson asked for another batch to be sent, explaining:

> The children, in particular, are never half covered, and their few things seldom made to fit . . . Some men are now working on the roads in thin linen jackets; and many starving beings, male and female, some of tender age, are now expecting employment on them, and anxiously imploring a covering from the exposure they are subject to, at such work.[44]

When touring the north of Ireland, Asenath Nicholson stayed with the Hewitson family and praised them highly. She noted that Mrs Hewitson rose at 4.00 a.m. every morning to make food for the local poor, who, '. . . through the day made the habitation a nucleus not of the most pleasant kind. The lower window-frame in the kitchen was of board instead of glass, this all having been broken by the pressure of faces continually there'.[45] Her initial impression of the district, however, had been deceptive. Nicholson had first met Mrs Hewitson and her son near Derry, where they 'took tea at a delightful little mansion on the sloping side of one of Ireland's green lawns, looking down upon a beautiful lake. "And is there", I asked, "on this pretty spot, misery to be found?"[46] Her journey to the Hewitson home quickly revealed that there was, leading Nicolson to admit that her 'heart was tortured with unparalleled scenes of suffering'.[47]

An appeal to the Belfast Ladies' Association was made by ministers in the nearby parish of Templecrone in Dungloe, who had visited the island of Arranmore and were shocked by what they saw. Their request ended on a sombre note:

> Since calmly reviewing and reflecting upon the harrowing and revolting incidents that were crowded into our hurried walk, through but a part of the island, and that on a short Winter's day, we feel astonished and dismayed at the accumulating misery that presented itself to us; and we mourn, as we feel persuaded that such afflictions are but the shadows of things to come, and the beginning of unutterable horrors.[48]

The Belfast Committee responded by sending 'a noble donation' of £60 for the islanders and £5 for the parish in general.[49]

Mrs Hume from Glen Lodge in Killybegs desired to establish a knitting group for local women and asked the Belfast Ladies' Association to provide a grant for this purpose.[50] Her correspondence with the Belfast committee demonstrated her frustrations with the limitations of government relief measures:

> The aid, which has been obtained, by Government employing some on the public works, is very inadequate to the extent of want. The limitations of one only being employed out of a very large family, at 9d a day affords to a laboring man, with six or eight children, a scanty pittance for their support. The females are totally unemployed, in a state of wretchedness and want, and would require some active efforts to relieve them by giving work.

A few weeks later, William Hume J. P. of the same address wrote a frustrated letter to the Relief Commission in Dublin, which he ended by saying:

> I must confess, as a Landlord (not receiving any rent) my inability to assist my poor tenants in their need. But the plan of the Commissary General, I suppose, accords with the views of Government, to procrastinate relief, until starvation and death ensues. This is, I assure you, the general impression.[51]

These letters, outlining dissatisfactions with government relief, reinforced the importance of groups such as the Belfast Ladies' Association. Mrs Hume was awarded a grant of £10 by the Belfast committee; she promised to 'expend it judiciously, so as to cultivate a love for feminine habits of industry amongst our females, who have hitherto known and understood only working in the fields'.[52]

In total, the Belfast Ladies' Association raised £2,617.1s.6d. – a small sum of money compared with that raised by the main charitable bodies.[53] However, their hard work and inclusive approach won the praise of Nicholson, who had the opportunity to meet with many ladies' associations as she travelled throughout the country. She was unequivocal in her approval, writing, '"The Belfast Ladies" Association embraces an object which *lives* and *tells*, and will continue to do so, when they who formed it shall be no longer be on earth'.[54]

At the other end of the country, numerous relief associations were being formed by local women. The Cork Ladies' Relief Society for the South of Ireland was founded in December 1846 in response to the second failure of the potato crop. Their list of patronesses was long and impressive, being headed by Countess of Bandon, the Marchioness of Thomond, Dowager Countess Mountcashel and the Countess Listowel, among others.[55] Such a notable group of patrons showed that awareness of the crisis had reached all levels of Irish society. Miss Wheatley (possibly Whately) was one of the Secretaries of the Society, and the Treasurer was Anna Maria Lee, both from Cork City. They made it clear that their main focus was to help women and children, which they did by giving breakfasts to destitute schoolchildren, and relief to widows and children who had lost the men of their families.[56] Lee also called for each local parish to form their own ladies' committee, and for the members to lead by example, by planting parsnips and carrots. More controversially, she suggested that the committees should seek to collect subscriptions from absentee landlords.[57] The professional way with which the Cork Ladies' Society approached their task was evident from their production of circulars appealing for support.[58] Moreover, any group that applied to them for assistance was asked to complete a questionnaire providing a detailed account of the local destitution and information regarding the existence of soup kitchens, voluntary subscriptions and fund-raising efforts by the local women, etc.[59]

Many small towns in west Cork suffered greatly throughout the famine period and were to become indelibly associated with starvation and suffering. These areas had attracted some private benevolence in the wake of the first crop failure. In May 1846, Lady Carbery, wife of the largest landowner in the area, had made a donation of £100 to the Skibbereen Poor Relief Committee.[60] The second appearance of blight had a devastating effect on the poor in the whole district and prompted many charitable interventions, with relief committees established by women in the towns of Ballydehob and Schull. The Ballydehob Ladies' Association was formed at the beginning of January 1847. Within weeks of its formation, food and clothes had been distributed to 130 families, but many others had been denied assistance due to lack of resources. The Secretary, Jane Noble, appealed to Sir Randolph

Routh, Head of the Commissariat: 'The young mothers and their famished infants . . . present scenes of distraction . . . far beyond my powers of description'.[61] Jane Ellesmere Noble was the daughter of John Noble of Lisnaskea, County Fermanagh. The Famine was to change her life in an unexpected way. On the death of the previous Rector, Rev Robert Traill, who had died of famine fever, John Triphook moved to the Rectory in Schull. He and Jane married in 1848.[62] The death of Rev Traill, who had worked so hard to save the lives of the starving Catholics and Protestants in his district, was much lamented locally.[63]

The Schull Ladies' Association won praise from a government official, Assistant Commissary General William Bishop, who visited the district at the end of January. He informed Routh that out of a population of 9,000, 1,000 were employed on the public works, but 7,000 were in 'extreme destitution'. He reported that, in addition to one small voluntary soup kitchen:

There is a ladies' association, doing much good, at a great personal sacrifice and upon a very limited fund. These ladies visit the cabins where the worst cases of fever and sickness prevail, and by a judicious distribution of nourishment and clothing have doubtless, under Providence, been instrumental in saving many lives.

Bishop assured his superior that any 'small assistance' that could be given to them would:

I am satisfied, be carefully and beneficially disposed of and, perhaps, act as an encouragement for the more general formation of such societies, which may, by their example, do much good in the present moment of affliction.[64]

When Captain Harston visited the Schull district on behalf of the British Relief Association, he provided grants of food and clothing to both the Ballydehob and Schull ladies' committees.[65]

In Kinsale, also in west Cork, the local Ladies' Committee worked closely with the government relief committee, the latter having built special premises to oversee the provision of relief. William Harvey and Joseph Harvey, two Quakers who visited in February 1847, were impressed with the orderly way in which assistance was being given, noting:

Under the same roof there is a soup kitchen, where the 'Ladies' Committee' attend, and with their own hands distribute a considerable quantity each day (about 600 quarts, we believe), partly gratuitous, and partly at 1d. per quart.

When the Quakers visited the area, they met with some of the ladies' committee and found them to be 'active and very useful', one woman showing them her visiting book and relief tickets for distribution among the poor.[66] Tellingly, when the Quakers departed, they left the money entrusted to them with the Kinsale Ladies' Committee, believing 'but for the activity and benevolent care of the Ladies' Committee ... it is probably that many might have perished altogether'.[67]

The nearby town of Dunmanway also suffered greatly. A small group of gentry women worked tirelessly to alleviate the condition of the local poor, making appeals to both England and America. The Dunmanway Indian Meal Ladies' Committee comprised of the sisters Martha and Katherine Cox, Harriet Shuldham, Ellen Jagoe and Anna Maria Galbraith.[68] Its patrons were Lady Carbery and Mrs Major General Shuldham.[69] The Anglo-Irish Cox family had owned land in Dunmanway since 1688. Martha and Katherine were known for their benevolence towards their tenants and they had responded to the potato failure swiftly, immediately lowering rents. On 1 January 1847, the committee sent an appeal to English women. The prognosis of Ireland's condition was grim:

> The Christian Ladies of England are earnestly called upon by their Irish sisters to help them in 'saving alive in Famine the perishing people of Ireland.' The Irish are not regardless of their county's misery and have done what they could to relieve it; but so widespread and so total is the destitution, that it is beyond their power to remove it. In former times, the Irish cottier was ready to divide his last meal with the hungry, and the best potato in the bowl was preserved for the widow and the fatherless; but now there is not one to divide – the daily morsel is consumed at once, and he has nothing left to save the perishing neighbour from dying at his door. Fever and other deadly diseases have set in on famine, and unless we can procure foreign aid, Ireland must soon be one wide field of the dying and the dead.
>
> If you, dear lady, into whose hands these papers may be placed, would make a collection of sums, however small, among friends and neighbours, and send it by Post-office Order on the Cork Post-office, to any of the under-signed Committee, who will gratefully acknowledge them, such aid will save many lives. When were the Ladies of England appealed to in vain?[70]

With small grants from the government and the Irish Relief Association, the Dunmanway women had opened a soup kitchen, but they now needed a larger boiler. On 11 January 1847, they made a request to the Irish Relief Association for two boilers to enable large quantities of soup to be made.[71] Unusually, the application was signed by the women – Harriet Elizabeth Shuldham, Martha Cox, Anastasia Galbraith and Ellen Jagoe – and not by men on their behalf. In their covering letter, they provided an insight into the limitations of the public works, stating that the wages earned by a man would barely support him alone and so their wives and children were suffering. The situation was exacerbated by the fact that local merchants were deliberately overcharging for foodstuffs, and so, 'many been saved by the exertions of a few in underselling the extortionate millers and merchants of this place – and the soup shop saves many more'. The request for boilers was granted, but the women were told if they required further grants they should apply to the Ladies' Association in Dublin.[72]

The enterprising ladies of Dunmanway also extended their appeals to the United States. At a meeting for Ireland, held in Washington on 9 February 1847 and convened by Vice-President George Dallas, theirs was one of the letters read out. Again, it was an appeal by women to women, being addressed to 'The Ladies of America':

Oh, that our American sisters could see the labourers on our roads, able-bodied men, scarcely clad, famishing with hunger, with despair in their once cheerful faces, staggering at their work . . . oh, that they could see the dead father, mother or child, lying coffinless, and hear the screams of the survivors around them, caused not by sorrow, but the agony of hunger, they whose hands and hearts are ever open to compassion would unite in one mighty effort to save Ireland from such misery.[73]

In 1848, in recognition of the munificence of the Cox sisters, the local Catholic priest, Fr James Doheny, presented them with a silver tea service.[74] Yet, only ten years later, the Cox family suffered their own financial difficulties. In 1858, the sisters offered almost 7,000 acres of the estate, including The Manor House, and the town of Dunmanway, for sale in the Encumbered Estates Court.[75]

In other parts of the country, women were providing support to the local poor in a variety of ways. Distress in the seaside town of Arklow in County Wicklow had been exacerbated by the added failure of the local herring industry. The local women formed a committee and were collecting in the region of £10 a week, but could not afford to purchase a boiler for soup. In December, they contacted the Irish Relief Association requesting a boiler.[76] By the beginning of 1847, the situation had deteriorated, the poor having to pawn their clothes, furniture, fishing and agricultural equipment. At their own expense, the Arklow Ladies' Committee paid for information to be collated and forwarded to the Society of Friends.[77] In the west of the country, in Tralee in County Kerry, local women established a soup kitchen. Tickets for the 'good quality meat soup' were sold at half of the cost price and then given to the poor. By February 1847, 950 quarts of soup were being distributed daily.[78]

In the north west of the country, a ladies' committee was formed in the City of Derry and throughout 1847 they made numerous small grants to surrounding areas, notably in County Donegal.[79] In some of the more remote districts in Donegal, in which there were no resident gentry, the destitution was particularly severe. The Quakers who visited the county at the end of

1846 made a point of praising the resident landlords for their labours on behalf of the local poor, although they were apprehensive that this could not continue as rents were not being paid. The Quakers also complimented the ladies of Donegal who had, 'come nobly forward in the cause and, at the sacrifice of much comfort, are much engaged in visiting or attending the poor, employing the women in knitting, spinning, etc'.[80] Other parts of the country were in a similar situation. A minister who visited Derrycarne in Mohill in County Leitrim reported that deaths from starvation had been 'numerous', due to lack of the resident proprietors and the remoteness to the Mohill Relief Committee. He suggested that a small loan be made by the government for the establishment of a soup kitchen, which some 'respectable ladies' would be willing to manage, under the eye of the local constabulary.[81] Throughout Ireland, these selfless women were providing a safety net when no other relief was available to the poorest of the poor.

The largest society formed by women was the Ladies' Relief Committee for Ireland, which met in Fitzwilliam Square, Dublin. Its patron was the Duchess of Leinster. Its members were criticized by the forthright Nicholson, she believing that they 'sheltered themselves behind their old societies – most of them excusing themselves from personal labour, feeling that a few visits to the abodes of the poor were too shocking for female delicacy to sustain'.[82] Nonetheless, the Dublin Ladies' Committee proved effective in establishing strong links with women's committees outside Ireland. A ladies' society in Brooklyn sold articles which had been produced by women in the west of Ireland, on behalf of the Ladies' Relief Committee.[83] Women in London, in turn, proved to be efficient fund-raisers. A bazaar held in Regent's Park in July 1847 brought in £3,000, which the Dublin committee used to purchase clothes for the poor.[84] In total, in a period of two years, the Ladies Relief Association raised almost £12,000.[85]

Other groups of women who came to the aid of the poor were those in holy orders and, in the case of the Established Church, wives of Anglican ministers. Despite their relatively small number, even before the Famine, nuns had tended to the sick. This aspect of their work increased after 1845. The Sisters of Mercy in Limerick, for example, visited 4,737 sick people between 1845 and 1850.[86] This type of involvement was replicated elsewhere. In Cork, ten Sisters caught fever from working with the poor, two of them dying.[87] In addition to working with the sick, nuns also tried to promote industrial activities among the poor, especially females.[88] In 1847, the Presentation Nuns in Limerick opened a lace-making business for impoverished girls.[89] Similarly, 'Irish Needlework' was introduced as a relief measure in the Presentation Convent in Youghal, County Cork. It was from these origins that the making of 'Irish Point' spread to many other centres in Ireland, notably Kenmare, Killarney and New Ross.[90] When members of the Society of Friends visited Galway City in March 1847, they praised both the local Protestant clergy and the local convents for providing relief so efficiently. The Sisters of Mercy were feeding between 500 and 600 poor daily, most of the recipients being girls and children. The Presentation Convent was providing a daily breakfast to 500 girls and children, while the Lombard Street nuns had installed a new boiler, with a capacity for up to 80 gallons, and were giving soup or porridge to young boys. The West Convent was providing the Claddagh fishermen with rations of soup.[91]

Several convents received money from Dr Paul Cullen of the Irish College in Rome. There, subscriptions had been initiated by Cardinal Fransoni, the Prefect of the Sacred Congregation for the Propagation of the Faith. In July 1847, Sister M. Paula Cullen (a cousin of Paul Cullen) of the Mercy Convent in Westport, acknowledged the receipt of £50 sent by the Cardinal. As a result, hundreds were getting a daily meal at the convent.[92] In the same month, Mother Teresa Collins, of the Presentation Convent in Dingle, received £50 from Cardinal Fransoni.[93] Further donations to the Dingle and Westport convents were sent in 1848.[94] In June 1847, the Presentation Convent in Tuam was feeding 300 people a day, but in order to continue, they appealed to Cullen for funding.[95] They also successfully appealed to the Society of Friends. In 1848, the six nuns who ran the Presentation Convent were complimented by Nicholson for restoring the 400 children in their school to health and giving then a 'ruddiness of look and buoyancy of manner'. This had been done by providing them with a daily meal of stirabout (a kind of porridge) and treacle. The children had also been taught knotting, a skill that could be used for making both ornamental and practical items. Following her visit, Nicholson concluded that 'looking upon these happy faces one might feel that Ireland is not wholly lost'.[96]

Other convents that provided relief included the Sisters of Mercy in Tuam, in Birr, King's County, and Charleville in County Cork; the Ursuline Sisters in Elphin; the Sacred Heart Sisters in Roscrea; the Sisters of Charity in Oranmore, County Galway; the Poor Clares in Loughrea and Newry; the Carmelites in Loughrea; and the Dominican Sisters in Athenry.[97] Some of the necessary funds had been contributed by fellow Catholics in England where the *Tablet* newspaper was active in promoting aid for Ireland. Some funding was more direct. The Sisters of Mercy in Limerick received 'large' donations from Right Rev Dr Briggs, Catholic Bishop of Beverly in Yorkshire.[98] The Convent of Mercy in Kinsale received 'liberal donations from Father Mathew and from co-religionists in England, America and Rome'. The Quakers also supplied them with large supplies of rice, maize and biscuits. Because of these contributions, 'Twice a day the nuns distributed food to the children, besides helping a large number of adults, and soup was given daily to all who applied at the convent dispensary'.[99] In February 1848, when most private donations had dried up, the Kinsale nuns appealed to Dr Cullen, for financial support.[100] The Sisters were able to help a practical way: in 1848, they were allowed to visit the infirmary in the local workhouse and nurse patients suffering from fever and cholera.[101] The involvement of nuns was not confined to Ireland. In Montreal in Canada, an order of French-Canadian Sisters of Charity, the Grey Nuns, cared for Irish

Famine emigrants, many of whom were orphans. Inevitably, many were sick resulting in the deaths of the Sisters and doctors who tended them.[102] The historian Donal Kerr has estimated that 17 nuns died in Canada alone working with the Famine poor, but as more records become available, the number could be far higher.[103]

Many Anglican ministers were members of the government's Relief Committees. Frequently, the practical side of their duties appears to have been completed only because of the support of women. Writing on 4 January 1847, an appeal by the Rev Hamilton Maddan in Carrick-on-Suir, elucidated the difficulties of providing relief. The population of the town was approximately 13,000, of whom 4,500 were experiencing 'absolute want' yet many of the landlords were absent or showed no interest in alleviating the situation. Both the workhouse and fever hospital were full and refusing further admissions. Food prices were beyond the reach of most people, even those employed on the public works. Consequently, the main relief appeared to be provided by local women, including Maddan's wife:

> We have opened a soup shop, where Mrs Maddan and other ladies attend every day for three hours; it is, I trust, doing much good; the door is surrounded by hundreds of poor, starving creatures, almost crushing each other to death to get a quart of soup.[104]

A number of women acted independently of a committee structure, demonstrating female agency in relief and philanthropic work. One of the most famous women involved in providing relief was Maria Edgeworth. Born in England in 1767, most of her life had been spent in Ireland. Edgeworth was the author of a number of acclaimed novels, her first being 'Castle Rackrent', published in 1800. Although in her 80-th year in 1847, Edgeworth used her fame to make various appeals on behalf of the local poor. She regarded such interventions as 'much against the grain', yet she wrote to the Quaker committee in Dublin, on behalf of the vicar, Mr Powell, asking them for either brogues or leather with which to make shoes. Her reasons were practically stated, 'men and boys who can get employment in draining especially, cannot stand the work in the wet for want of strong shoes'.[105] The Quakers responded by providing her with £30 for food, offering a soup boiler with a capacity of 80 gallons, in case they did not possess one that was large enough, and sending £10 for 'women's work'. Separately, the Clothing Committee sent her leather for the making of shoes and brogues.[106] To preserve their limited resources, Edgeworth and her land agent decided that relief should only be given to those tenants who were up to date with their rent.[107] She also approved of giving relief to the poor in grain rather than as soup, to 'encourage them to cook at home and not be mere craving beggars'.[108]

Edgeworth made her own financial contribution determining that the proceeds of 'Orlandino', a short story which she was writing to be included

in Chambers' *Miscellany of instructive & entertaining tracts,* should be given
to the poor relief fund. *Orlandino* was the tale of a Protestant drunkard
.(and hence beyond the reach of Father Mathew whom Maria greatly
admired) who was saved by the goodness of children. The story accorded
with Maria's own strict views on temperance.[109] She was delighted with the
outcome, informing her friend Mrs S. C. Hall (the pen-name of the novelist,
Anna Maria Hall):

> Chambers, as you always told me, acts very liberally. As this was to earn
> a little money for our parish poor, in the last year's distress, he most
> considerately gave prompt payment. Even before publication, when the
> proof-sheets were under correction, came the ready order in the Bank of
> Ireland. Blessings on him! and I hope he will not be the worse for me.
> I am surely the better for him, and so are numbers now working and
> eating; for Mrs. Edgeworth's [her step-mother] principle and mine is to
> excite the people to work for good wages, and not, by gratis feeding, to
> make beggars of them, and ungrateful beggars, as the case might be.[110]

Edgeworth's fund-raising efforts were not confined to Ireland. The
Birmingham Relief Committee in England sent her £5 for the 'starving Irish',
leading her to exclaim 'How good people are!'[111]

In April 1847, a number of American newspapers carried an appeal from
Edgeworth, one paper describing her as 'one of the brightest gems Erin has
to boast'.[112] It was dated 11 March and came from her family home in
Edgeworthstown. Her entreaty was to all ladies in America, but in particular, to the ladies of New York. She commenced by affirming that accounts
of the suffering had not been exaggerated: 'I assure you that during my
sixty-six years residence in Ireland, I never knew of distress equal to the
present . . . famine, disease, deaths innumerable are in *all* parts of this kingdom – putrification and pestilence in some. . .' Her appeal was not only for
immediate support, but also for seed to prevent the occurrence of even more
suffering in the future, 'Indian corn for food may be had for money – money
will relieve all of our wants *for the present*– but without seed *our future is
hopeless*'.[113] Her request resulted in large quantities of seed corn being sent
to Edgesworthstown. Again, she was overwhelmed by the generosity of not
only those who donated the corn, but those who helped in its transport – the
Irish porters who carried the seed corn sent from Philadelphia to the shore
for embarkation refused to accept payment. When the *Macedonian* arrived
from New York in July, the cargo was given to the care of the Society of
Friends, with the exception of 50 barrels of foodstuffs sent from Boston for
Edgeworth.[114] An example of generosity which particularly delighted her
was a donation made by 'The children of Boston', who knew her books, and
sent her a £150 worth of flour and rice, inscribed 'To Miss Edgeworth, for
her poor'.[115] These and other contributions led her to write to a friend, 'You
will see how good the Irish Americans have been, and are'.[116]

Edgeworth was more critical of Australian interventions, confiding to a friend:

> Having seen in the newspapers that the Australians had sent a consider-able sum for the relief of the distressed Irish, and that they had directed it to the care of 'His Grace the Archbishop of Dublin', meaning Dr. Murray, I wrote to our Archbishop Whately, playing upon this graceless proceed-ing towards him and, to the best of my capacity, without flattery. I did what I could to make my letter honestly pleasing to His Grace, and I received the most prompt, polite, and to the point reply, assuring me that the Australians were not so graceless in their doings as in their words, that they had made a remittance of a considerable sum to him.[117]

Whately informed Maria that he had forwarded his donation to the Quaker's Central Relief Committee and urged her to apply to them for further assistance.[118]

Maria died in May 1849, aged 82. The Famine was still raging in parts of Ireland. Shortly before she died she wrote a poem expressing her love for her adopted country. Her work on behalf of the Irish poor both before and during the meant that these feelings were reciprocated:

> *Ireland, with all thy faults, thy follies too,*
> *I love thee still: still with a candid eye must view*
> *Thy wit, too quick, still blundering into sense*
> *Thy reckless humour: sad improvidence,*
> *And even what sober judges follies call,*
> *I, looking at the Heart, forget them all!*[119]

It was not only Irish-born women who were involved in the distribution of charity. One of the most remarkable women to be involved was the American traveller, philanthropist and religious maverick, Asenath Nicholson. Like Edgeworth, she was a published author. Nicholson had written an account of her travels through Ireland in 1844 and 1845, as *Ireland's Welcome to the Stranger; or, An Excursion through Ireland in 1844 and 1845, for the purpose of investigating the condition of the poor*. One of her motivations for visiting Ireland in 1844 had been to bring bibles to the poor.[120] Because of this, a reprinted version of her book, published in 1926 was re-titled *The Bible in Ireland* by its editor, Alfred Tresidder Sheppard.[121] However, Margaret Howitt, whose parents had been friends of Nicholson's, objected to this title, pointing out 'although she very honourably gave English and Irish copies of the Douai Testament to Catholics, and Protestant ones to Protestants, nevertheless the distribution of Scriptures was only a secondary motive'.[122] Nicholson's earlier visit meant that she had an informed perspective and knowledge of the country, both before and during the tragedy. In addition to providing relief, she recorded her experiences and observations in *Annals of the Famine in Ireland,* first published in 1851. It provided powerful, personal testimony of the awfulness of the destitution and of a world turned upside down – people eating dogs and dogs eating people.[123] Regardless of her own religious beliefs and commitment to Bible Christianity, Nicholson unequivocally rejected a providentialist interpretation of the Famine, stating 'God is slandered when it is called an unavoidable dispensation of His wise providence'.[124] Moreover, she was critical of the churches, particularly the Established Church, which were using the hunger of the Irish people as an opportunity to win converts, and she especially denounced those who preyed on the vulnerability of children. Furthermore, she was cynical about winning converts in such a paltry way and about the long-term impact of such conversions, 'Rice, Indian meal, and black bread would, if they had tongues, tell sad and ludicrous tales. The artless children too, who had not become adept in deceit, would sometimes tell the story in short and pithy style'.[125] Nicholson's contempt was not confined merely to zealous evangelicals. She was disparaging of overly bureaucratic relief officials and spoiled wealthy women who feigned concern, but in reality avoided the poor. She was also critical of the pampered rich and the idle poor but, she believed, 'The rich are idle from a silly pride and long habits of indulgence; and the poor, because no man *hires* them'.[126]

Nicholson's approach befitted her personality. She worked as an independent provider of relief, initially on the streets of Dublin from January to June 1847, before travelling to the north. She provided relief in the form of bread or soup in some of the poorest streets of Dublin, commencing distribution at 8.00 a.m. in the morning until her supplies ran out.[127] In order to prepare for her day's activities, she rose at 4.00 a.m.[128] Although based in Dublin, she travelled to other parts of Ireland, witnessing the suffering at first-hand, or as she described it, 'misery without a mask'.[129] Much of Nicholson's funding came from donations raised in New York, where she had lived prior to coming to Ireland. Initially, the money was transmitted to her via the committee of the Society of Friends.[130] She rejected the idea of keeping any documentation of her donations as a waste of precious time, 'knowing that a faithful unerring record would be kept in the council chamber above, where the rich and the poor would soon meet before the Maker of them all'.[131] As so often proved to be the case, it was the poor who gave to the poor. One of Nicholson's donations came from the children of a pauper school in New York, which she described as 'an offer richer than all'. Appropriately, she chose to give the money to 'a school in the poorest convent in Dublin [that] was in the greatest state of suffering'.[132] Nicholson's work brought her into contact with other relief associations and she was not afraid to express her opinion on them. She was particularly impressed with the two ladies' committees in Belfast, comparing them with the ones in Dublin. While the latter were effective in raising money, they were less diligent in providing relief because, as Nicholson observed, '*giving* and *doing* are antipodes in her who has never been trained to domestic duties'.[133]

Overall, Nicholson's contribution, individual and quirky as it was, proved to be unique and invaluable. She bore witness to the sufferings of the poor, and to their nobility, patience and generosity – perspectives that challenged the glib stereotypes of some sections of the British press. Impressively also, her descriptions came from first-hand experience of the Irish poor. And she, of all the relief officials, probably spent most time working among the dying and diseased.

The potential involvement of one female donor caused controversy. The renowned English actress, Helen Faucet, was appearing in Dublin but had cancelled her performances due to illness. However, when she heard of the distress she offered to give one special show and donate the proceeds to the Central Relief Committee of the Quakers. The Friends disapproved of theatrical performances. The *Nation*, generally admirers of the work of the Quakers, came to the defence of the actress, commenting that she should have been publicly thanked.[134] A less public donation was made by Lady Lucy Foley, a relative of Lord Edward Fitzgerald, who had been killed during the 1798 rebellion. From her home in Marseilles, she sent Archbishop Murray £100, which she wanted to be used for the relief of the poor in Dublin and its neighbourhood. She included with her donation a personal request that Masses be offered for 'the soul of her adopted son, Francis Marie Harris, an eighteen-year-old cadet in the Navy who died when his ship was on the Tagus; he was a Catholic and received the last sacraments from Catholic priests'.[135]

The activities of other individual women were important. A number of ladies' committees had, as their patrons, ladies of the great houses. Several of these women became directly involved in providing relief. Lady Mary de Vere, mother of the poet, Aubrey, and a member of the Spring-Rice family, helped revive the art of making 'Limerick Lace' as a relief measure in 1847.[136] The English-born Frances Anne Vane, third Marchioness of Londonderry, was an heiress in her own right and married to one of the wealthiest men in Ireland. Despite living in England, Vane took a keen interest in the running of her husband's large property in Country Antrim. During a visit in 1846, she helped to establish an Estate Relief Committee that distributed soup and blankets to those most in need, and she provided turnip and parsnip seeds to all of their tenants. Additionally, Indian corn was sold at a reduced rate and some of the tenants were relieved of having to pay their rents. Vane also followed a more traditional path of women by organizing a bazaar, which raised several thousand pounds. Indicative of her high ranking in society, Queen Victoria and the Duchess of Kent were her patrons.[137] Catherine, the Dowager Marchioness of Sligo, was mother to the largest landowner in County Mayo. Her son George, the third Marquis, had inherited the property in 1845, when aged only 25. He helped his tenants by providing them with cheap corn and potatoes, his mother observing, with satisfaction, that he 'has so good a feeling towards the poor on his estate'.[138] Lady Sligo, although not resident in Westport, maintained a keen interest in local affairs.

Through the Agent, she provided relief intermittently in a variety of ways, her preferred one being through the giving of blankets. She explained, 'it appears to me that the best charity that can be given to the *very* poor is blankets'.[139] However, despite her own charity, she disapproved of too much government relief, opining:

> it would certainly be ruin to the people if they were persuaded they were not to work hard and will be supported in idleness . . . it must be admitted that the lower class are always fond of trusting to anything rather than their own exertions.[140]

Her comments reveal that even among the philanthropically inclined, there was an ingrained belief that the poor were the architects of their own destiny. It was not only women of rank or influence who became involved in providing assistance. Elizabeth Fetherston of Bruree House in Charleville, north County Cork, proved to be both energetic and enterprising on behalf of the local poor. In January 1847, she issued a circular appealing for financial assistance, pointing out that the imminent closure of the public works would add to their suffering. By May, Fetherston had received £37 from women in England and Scotland. She had also appealed to Archbishop Murray in Dublin and to the Quakers in Limerick for assistance.[141]

Women in the United States provided assistance to Ireland in various ways. In July 1847, Rev Alexander Rantoul of Ray in County Donegal received 31 barrels of kiln-dried Indian meal from 'Miss Foster, principal of the Female Seminary, Washington, Pennsylvania, and her pupils'.[142] The Washington Female Seminary was a Presbyterian institution that had been founded in 1836 to provide 'a finishing education for young women of good Christian standing'. Sarah Foster, whose family had emigrated from Ireland in 1764, had become principal in 1840.[143] One of the most active relief committees in the United States was the Brooklyn Committee. Unusually, they also had a separate ladies' committee of which Anna Hifferman [Hefferman?] was Secretary.[144] In March 1847, they organized a fund-raising 'ladies festival for Irish relief' in the Brooklyn Institute. The local newspaper urged attendance promising, 'the smiles of the ladies alone are worth double the price of the ticket'.[145] Invaluable support to the women of Ireland was given by one particular member of the Brooklyn Committee. Throughout 1847, advertisements appeared in the *Brooklyn Eagle* on behalf of a local merchant, R. J. Todd, whose business was located at 88 Fulton Street. He was the recipient of many consignments of goods from the Ladies' Irish Relief Committee in Dublin, which consisted of 'Irish manufactured articles . . . comprising rich Knit Shawls, Hose, Gloves, Household Linen, with many unique, rich, costly and fancy articles'. The Dublin Ladies' Relief Committee were acting as a conduit for the Industrial Society for the Improvement of the Peasantry in Ireland, selling their products that consisted most of shawls, hosiery and gloves. Todd invited the ladies of Brooklyn to visit his store to inspect and purchase them 'by which they can procure many rare items, and aid the cause of starving Ireland'.[146] When much of the charitable relief to Ireland had dried up, Todd continued to promote the work of the Irish women.[147] As late as 1849, he was still selling 'useful and fancy' goods on behalf of the Dublin Ladies' Relief Committee.[148] Elsewhere in the US, women were encouraged to participate in fund-raising for Ireland, while a number of American women, such as those in Binghamton, New York, established an Irish relief committee.[149]

Large amounts of money were raised in the US, much of which was channelled through the General Relief Committee in New York. They, in turn, worked closely with the Society of Friends in Dublin. Jacob Harvey, a secretary of the New York committee, received several applications from women in both Ireland and England asking for his financial support. In each case, he referred them back to the Dublin Committee, whom he believed were more familiar with the situation and better able to judge which requests were deserving of support.[150] A number of American newspapers included reports of donations made by Irish females on behalf of their fellow countrymen. A Chicago newspaper was fulsome in its praise of an Irish girl, Rosa White, who gave her last six dollars to the Irish Relief Fund: 'That sweet girl deserves to be embalmed in the memory of the good, and her sweet name to be inscribed on the tablets of all the poor in heart'.[151] Elsewhere, a servant girl, employed by Mr George Rust of Syracuse House, gave $25 to the New York Relief Committee. The girl explained, 'she needed it for her own use, but her necessities were not to be compared with those of her poor mother and friends in Ireland'.[152] Mary M. Graham, described as 'a hired girl', sent $20 back home. The newspaper recounting these stories explained that it did so because, 'Much is said of the idleness and lack of thought of the people of Ireland, but such instances as these show that, when placed in circumstances where their labour is sure of a reward, they can not only make and save, but, where the occasion demands, give with an unsurpassed liberality'.[153]

The lack of clothing of the Irish poor was frequently cited by officials as an obstruction to those in need being able to access relief. The necessity for having warm clothing was especially acute for those employed on public works in the freezing winter of 1846–47. Many poor had pawned their clothing in order to purchase food. Furthermore, the constant wearing of the same clothes, day and night, inevitably contributed to the spread of diseases.[154] The provision of clothing to the poor was a traditional pursuit of women's charities. For Charles Trevelyan, this was a good arrangement. He praised the fact that, 'the women of the upper and middle classes in England are employing themselves to a considerable extent in the charitable work of making clothes for the destitute Irish'. He asked that Inspecting Officers in Ireland recommend Irish women who would be suitable conduits for the distribution of such clothes.[155] Routh suggested that the clothes should first be channelled through the Ladies' Association in Dublin, who were receiving funding from the British Relief Association to assist them in this work.[156]

The Ladies' Clothing Committee of London was one of the largest providers of clothes for Ireland. The extensive range of its labours was recognized by the fact that they were given £5,324 by the British Relief Association and £4,208 from the Society of Friends.[157] Other women's groups were also active. By March 1847, a ladies' association in Exeter had collected 1,000 items of new clothes together with numerous parcels of second-hand clothing.[158] However, donors were warned against sending clothing of too good a quality, for fear that it would be pawned, rather than used. The agent of the British Association in Belmullet also suggested that shoes were not needed as they were 'as useless to these people as gloves would be to English peasants'. Moreover, he was concerned that the clothes he had already received would mean that the poor would be better dressed than the wealthiest farmers in the locality.[159] A further danger of sending high-quality clothing was identified by the forthright Asenath Nicholson:

> I had boxes of clothing, and I am obliged to acknowledge what common report says here, that the people of the higher classes in general showed a meanness bordering on dishonesty. When they saw a goodly garment, they not only appeared to covet, but they actually bartered, as though in a shop of second-hand articles, to get it as cheaply as possible and most, if not all of such, would have taken these articles without any equivalent, though they knew they were the property of the poor . . . The poor were shamefully defrauded, where they had no redress and none to lift the voice in their favour.[160]

The two largest organizations involved in providing charitable relief – the Central Committee of the Society of Friends and the British Relief Association – assisted in the distribution of clothing. By January 1847, the Friends in Dublin had received so many donations of garments from Ladies' Committees in England that they decided to form a subcommittee for this purpose. By July, the contributions had virtually dried up and so the committee was disbanded. During its existence, the committee had made 668 grants of clothing to the most distressed districts.[161] The transfer to Poor Law relief in August 1847 did not ease the demand for clothing, with the Quakers reporting that it was not only the poor, but those who were previously comfortable who were now in need. In November 1847, a new clothing subcommittee was formed. In the first four months of 1848, 612 grants of clothing were made by the Friends. Most of these items were distributed through the Quaker's auxiliary committees in Waterford and Cork, or through the Ladies' Relief Committee in Dublin.[162] In total, the Dublin Committee received £793.14s.11d. worth of clothing from the Friends, of which they repaid £379.12s.8d., received from sales.[163]

A guiding principle of both government relief and, increasingly, private charities was that the Irish people should become self-sufficient so that a disaster of this magnitude would never occur again. Consequently, a number of ladies' associations used their limited resources to provide longer-term benefits in the form of giving women employment skills, especially those of spinning, weaving and knitting. Several industrial schools were established that were generally under the superintendence of women. Again, they were praised by the Quakers for showing 'much energy and perseverance in conducting them'. Yet again, the Quakers provided valuable financial support giving these ladies multiple loans or grants.[164] They, in turn, were recipients of funds contributed by individual women and ladies' committees.[165]

A number of groups, such as medical officers and religious ministers, who were in the frontline of helping the poor and diseased during the Famine, did so at great risk to their own health. Their contribution and sacrifice was immense, but sometimes overlooked. Women, however, were to the fore in offering support to the providers of relief. The London Ladies' Relief Association for Ireland donated £500 to a committee of 'medical men' in Dublin.[166] The Committee used this money to meet 'the present wants of widows and orphans of those medical practitioners who have fallen victims, or who shall hereafter fall victims to the prevailing sickness, or to the pressure of fatigue and anxiety in discharge of their onerous duties'.[167] Only a few months later, the London Ladies' Committee sent a further £300, which was used to assist the widows and 27 children of seven fallen medical officers.[168]

Another overlooked group which suffered financially during the Famine was the clergy, many of whom experienced a decline in income. Again, it was women who sought to remedy this situation. At the beginning of 1849, encouraged by Archbishop Whately of Dublin, the Dublin-based Ladies' Relief Association formed a separate committee with a view to providing relief to impoverished members of the Anglican clergy. Whately, who became a patron, contributed £100 to assist the committee in getting started. In total, he and his wife gave over £470 to this fund. During its three years' existence, the Ladies' Relief Association distributed £4,600 to Anglican clergy and their families.[169]

As was the case with other private relief associations, donations to the various women's associations dried up at the end of 1847. However, some work did continue. At the beginning of 1848, a number of women's charities, including the Ladies' Industrial Society of Connaught, was still helping to provide clothing to children in the western unions. They were helped by a number of local women, including Lady Booth, in their work.[170] It is clear from the reports of many relief workers that numerous ladies' societies had been established throughout Ireland and were doing valuable work. Many references to their activities were oblique, but always favourable. Overall, the work of the women won admiration from all who observed it. Government officers who were touring the country noted the important roles played by women and the ways in which they were supporting the government's relief measures. An official who visited the Schull area in January 1847 praised the ladies' committee for their 'personal sacrifice' because 'these ladies visit the cabins where the worst cases of sickness and fever prevail, and by a judicious distribution of nourishment and clothing, have doubtless, under Providence, been instrumental in saving many lives'.[171] In Carrikbeg in County Waterford, for example, women were taking it in turns to manage the 'Soup Society' and were making daily reports of their activities to local Relief Committee.[172]

The work of the various ladies' associations in some of the most impoverished parts of Ireland was also commended by other charitable bodies. Captain Harston, the British Association agent in west Cork, reported that, 'The Ladies' Association is much to be praised, for by their exertion they reach very many cases that no Relief Committee could, and are personally daily cognizant for some miles round of the actual state of the inhabitants of the cottages scattered far and wide'. At the time of his visit, however, the women had almost run out of funds, leading Harston to give them a grant from the British Relief Association.[173] This case was not isolated. When an Association agent visited Tuam, he noted that the women had already received a private grant of money but, because their involvement was so valuable, he was going to give them an additional one from the British Association.[174] Members of the Society of Friends who visited some of the most distressed parts of Ireland in the winter of 1846 and 1847 were full of praise for the work of the various ladies' committees that they encountered, acknowledging, 'A very large portion of grants was made to ladies, who were found to be our most efficient almoners'.[175] Clearly, without the, often invisible, support of women, government relief would have been even more ineffective.

The efforts of women in Dungarvan in County Waterford drew fulsome praise from a local newspaper, the *Cork Constitution*. Its prosaic prose provides a reminder of the gender stereotypes prevalent at the time, and how women involved in Famine relief overcame them:

Woman, true to the instincts of her own beautiful – almost spiritual nature, saw that there was one great necessity, which male relief committees, or the desultory employment afforded by the public works, could not possibly remedy, and she immediately proceeds to supply it . . . And what can be so delightful as to find these gentle beings leaving their drawing rooms, their perfumed chambers, their refined and elegant amusements, their lulling music etc., to enter the house of poverty and wretchedness and rags and multi-form misery, where every sight is almost loathsome, every scent pestiferous, every sound the moans of the creature stretched in a bedless dormitory, reduced to a skeleton by emaciating poverty and starvation, and bringing with them the nourishment afforded by these depots? . . . These benevolent ladies have thrown aside every distinction, which in ordinary times the conventionalities of society may, perhaps, act out from them. They feel fully the pressure of the times, the necessity for action, and since the formulation of their plan, no exertion has been spared by them in carrying it out.[176]

The experience of Dungarvan – which was replicated elsewhere in Ireland – demonstrated that women, so often confined to the private sphere, had proved, through their deeds and actions, their important place in the frontline of saving lives in Ireland. However, the various ladies' associations and committees, together with the work of women who acted alone, would not have been possible without the grants, in food, money and clothing that they received from people and relief organizations throughout the world, whose generous interventions saved an untold number of lives.

8

'A gloomy picture of human misery'.[1] The Role of the British Relief Association

Following the second potato failure, private charity moved from being sporadic and localized to being more structured and centralized. Also, rather than simply raise funds, a number of organizations that became involved in the day-to-day distribution of relief were formed. The Society of Friends were in the forefront of providing relief directly, but the largest, and financially most successful, charitable group was the British Relief Association, which was established largely at the initiative of bankers in England, who had no connection with Ireland. As a result of their involvement, London, the seat of government, also became the centre of charitable activities for the Irish poor.

The British Relief Association

'The British Relief Association for the Relief of Distress in Ireland and the Highlands of Scotland' was the largest relief organization involved in Famine relief. It announced the commencement of its activities at the end of 1846 by issuing a public address which stated:

Information having been received of the most distressing character, and of undoubted credibility, of the rapid progress of famine and utter destitution in many remote parishes of Ireland and Scotland, in which there are but few families who can be considered as the resident gentry, and who are therefore exposed to urgent and overpowering demands for the smallest supplies of the necessaries of life, by the famishing population, to an extent far exceeding any means within their power – it has been determined, in dependence upon God's blessing, to form a Committee in London for

the purpose of aiding the efforts made to relieve the multitudes who are
suffering under the present awful calamity.[2]

The address was followed by a circular by the Lord Mayor of London,
John Kinnersley Hooper,[3] to the chief magistrates of England and Wales.
Response to these notices was swift, resulting in the convening of public
meetings and the opening of subscription lists.

Even before any public monies had been received, the founders of the
charity made their own donations, with representatives of the chief banking
houses in London each giving £1,000. News of the formation of the
committee prompted Nicholas Cummins, the Cork J. P. who only a few
weeks earlier had contacted the Duke of Wellington on behalf of the poor in
his district, to write to the *Cork Constitution*:

> I have unbounded satisfaction in being able to assure you of the glorious
> fact that nine names alone in London have this day subscribed for the
> truly noble amount of £8,000. Surely her merchants are princes and her
> traders the most honourable on the earth.[4]

The founders of the Association held their first formal meeting on 1 January
1847 at the headquarters of Rothschild's Bank in St Swithin's Lane in
London.[5] At that time, Rothschild's was the largest international banking
company in the world. Those attending included Irish-born Stephen
Edmund Rice, the eldest son of Thomas Spring Rice, 1st Baron Monteagle
of Brandon and Lady Theodosia Pery. A number of leading English bankers
were also present including Henry Kingscote and John Abel Smith, the latter
taking the Chair.[6] The Lord Mayor of London was invited to serve on the
committee.[7]

The British Relief Association brought together many of the leading
merchant bankers of the day. Thomas Baring, Raikes Currie and Lionel de
Rothschild were all associated with their family banks. Baring and Currie
were also Members of Parliament. Barings Bank had, in the wake of the
first failure of the potato crop, been employed by the government to secretly
import corn into Ireland. They refused to accept any commission for this
task.[8] The bank was also involved in obtaining an eight million pound
loan on behalf of the government for relief in Ireland.[9] Like Baring and
Curry, Sir James Weir Hogg, the Association's auditor, was an MP. Hogg, a
Chairman of the East India Company, had been born in County Antrim and
educated in Trinity College, Dublin. Samuel Jones-Loyd, another successful
English banker and noted philanthropist, was appointed Chairman of the
Association.[10]

Interestingly, and incorrectly, Rothschild was listed as an MP in the official
Report of the Association.[11] Although he had successfully contested the
General Election in 1847, because he was a Jew, he had been unable to take
the Oath of Allegiance and therefore could not take his seat in the House of

Commons. Rothschild was not the only Jewish member of the committee of the Association. Alderman David Salomons, another successful banker, had been the first Jewish sheriff of London and the first Jewish Mayor of London; in both cases, the law had to be changed to allow him to take office. Tellingly, during his mayoralty an inscription that had blamed the Great Fire of London of 1666 on Roman Catholics was removed.[12] Like Rothschild, Salomons had stood for election to the House of Commons, but had also been disbarred from taking his seat. Another prominent member of the English Jewish community offered his services to the Association. Sir Moses Montefiore, a successful financier and philanthropist, has been described as, 'the most famous Jew in the world'.[13] Acting on behalf of the British Foreign Office in 1840, he had helped to achieve the release of Jewish prisoners, falsely accused of ritual killing in Damascus. His successful intervention in this and other humanitarian issues consolidated his reputation as an international statesman who transcended national and religious boundaries.[14] Within days of the British Relief Association being formed, Montefiore volunteered, 'to proceed to Ireland at his own charge, examine into the state of the country and people, and report to the committee from time to time with regard to the distress.'[15]

The British Relief Association saw the value of its work lying in providing relief in districts in which there were 'few families who can be considered as the resident gentry'.[16] In keeping with the enormity of the task that confronted them, the committee met daily, usually at the offices of the South Sea Company, the Governors having consented to their building being used for this purpose.[17] Meeting in the famous South Sea House on Threadneedle Street in London linked them with the commercial hub of the British Empire. The dedication shown by these wealthy and powerful won praise from the young Quaker businessman and philanthropist, William E. Forster, who had travelled with his father to Connemara in the winter of 1846–47. He noted, with approval, 'Rothschild, Kinnaird and some dozen other millionaire city princes meeting every day, and working hard. A far greater sacrifice to them than mere gifts of money'.[18]

From the outset, the members of the Association treated their voluntary work as a business, seeking information from and about distressed regions, establishing guidelines governing the distribution of relief and creating multiple forms regarding the provision of a grant.[19] They asked the British Home Secretary, Sir George Grey, to provide material that could be useful to their labours, thus demonstrating an early willingness to work closely with the government.[20] The Association pointed out that, in this role, it was providing 'a channel' through which benevolent persons could give aid to the poor of Ireland and Scotland, which would be 'secured as far as possible from the danger of being abused'.[21] To this end, assistance was to be provided in food, clothing and fuel, but in no case would money be given.[22]

Official approval of the Association was made evident when they recorded, on 4 January, receipt of a letter from the Prime Minister, apprising them that the Queen was 'pleased to order her name to be inserted as a donor of two thousand pounds towards the object of the fund'.[23] The following day, they received £500 from Prince Albert.[24] Other royal donations followed, including £1,000 each from the Queen Dowager and the King of Hanover, £300 from the Duchess of Kent and the Duke of Cambridge, £200 from the Duchess of Gloucester and £100 from the Duchess of Cambridge and Princess Sophia.[25] Encouraged by this recognition, the Association sent a circular to people occupying high offices of state, including Peers and MPs, asking for contributions. An appeal for aid was inserted in the national newspapers and this request was extended to British communities in India, Singapore and China.[26] In addition to financial assistance, the Association asked for cast-off clothing.[27] Not all of the money and articles so-solicited were intended for Ireland. One-sixth of funds raised were to be used to assist the distress in the Highlands of Scotland where the potato had also failed.[28] To look after Scottish needs, the Earl of Dalhousie and Arthur Kinnaird were enlisted as members of the committee. These two men were to work with committees already established in Glasgow and Edinburgh.[29] Donors who had a particular connection with Scotland or a district within it could request that their contribution be sent there.

From the outset, the British Relief Association worked closely with the British government and their established relief networks. This, in effect, meant working with Charles Trevelyan of the Treasury and with Sir Randolph Routh of the Commissariat Department, who had both played pivotal roles in famine relief since the first appearance of the blight. The government welcomed this cooperation. On 8 January 1847, George Grey admitted that 'extreme destitution' existed in a number of areas, which government measures alone would not mitigate. He asked that the British Relief Association deploy some of their resources to supplement official relief. To assist the Association in their work, he offered to provide any information that would be useful.[30]

A more intriguing call on the funds of the Association was made privately by Charles Trevelyan. On 1 February, he wrote to Jones-Loyd, informing him that government officials were daily witnessing scenes that were 'seriously affecting their health and spirits'. He suggested:

> . . . it would be an act of great charity, not only to the people themselves, but to our officers, who often have to witness the dreadful distress of the people without being able to afford them any immediate relief, if you would place at the absolute disposal of such of our Inspecting Officers as you have entire confidence in, moderate sums of money (say 100*l* at a time) to be employed by them entirely at their discretion.[31]

The requests by Trevelyan and Grey suggest that they were willing to use the privately raised funds of the British Relief Association to finance government operations. They additionally implied that government relief was proving woefully inadequate.

Within weeks of being formed, the British Relief Association had received requests for financial support from a number of organizations in Ireland. This included several ladies' associations, as far apart as Dublin and Kerry.[32] A request for funding was also made by the Rev George Hazelwood who attended their meetings on 9 and 18 January; during the second one, he 'made strong representations that some of their funds should be distributed through Lord George Hill's committee'.[33] The committee in question was the Irish Relief Association, which included a number of well-known evangelicals. The British Relief Association declined to comply with Hazelwood's request.[34] On a number of other occasions, the Association demonstrated that they were anxious not to be accused of any religious bias. Rev Stuart Majeudre of Lougdon [sic] asked them to transmit a donation on his behalf to, 'the Protestant clergyman in Achill'.[35] This was probably Edward Nangle, an evangelical missionary on the island. The committee refused to do so, suggesting to Rev Majeudre that he forward the money directly.[36]

By the beginning of 1847, there were over 1,000 local relief committees in Ireland, working under the auspices of the Commissariat. These committees had been authorized to sell food at the local market price or, in cases of extreme destitution, to give it gratuitously. By working through established committees, the Association believed that they could 'afford relief more promptly, widely and safely, than could be effected in any other way'. Applications to the Association were, therefore, directed to the Commissariat Officers for their approval or otherwise.[37] The Association's own guidelines were:

1 That all grants should be in food and not in money.
2 That no grant should be placed at the disposal of an individual for private distribution.
3 That the grants from the funds should be exclusively for gratuitous distribution (see Appendix for full instructions).[38]

However, within days of commencing its operations, the Association found it impossible to adhere to its own rules regarding only giving grants in food, due to its unavailability in some areas. In these cases, it was decided to allow small grants of money to be issued. The Association's agents were in no doubt as to the real problem for the poor: there was no absolute want of money in Ireland due to the efforts of government and private individuals, but, 'what was wanted was *food,* and more especially CHEAP FOOD'.[39] As the season advanced and more food became available, money grants proved to be less necessary.[40]

On 4 January, only days after its first meeting, the Association received a report on conditions in Skibbereen, the town that had come to symbolize suffering in Ireland. The Committee decided to act immediately and obtain a ship to take food to Ireland.[41] They acted swiftly, with the first vessel, H. M. S. *Dragon,* leaving London on 16 January. The provisions on the ship – flour and peas – had been provided by the company of Messrs Erichsen, which had been advising the Committee on practical matters to do with shipping.[42] Eric Erichsen had previously been employed by Charles Trevelyan to import corn to Ireland. Other companies worked with the British Association, many offering their services gratuitously. This included the Peninsula and Oriental (P and O) Steam Company and the Dublin Steam Packet Company, who provided their vessels free of charge, while the railway companies in Britain and Ireland carried the provisions on their trains at no cost. As was the case with the other main charities, the government had undertaken to defray the cost of freight and shipping charges.[43]

The first cargo of Association's provisions was used to supply food depots in the south-west of Ireland, resulting in the creation of 14 small depots between Cork and Kenmare. Prior to their establishment, relief committees had been forced to travel as far as Cork city in order to obtain supplies. The use of a warehouse and of clerks was provided by the Cork merchants, N. and J. Cummins.[44] The same company offered similar assistance two months later to Captain Forbes of the *Jamestown* when it arrived from Boston. The Association appointed a number of agents to carry out their work. Several of them were senior members of the Royal Navy and familiar with the western coastline. They worked closely with Routh in Dublin to determine where their services were most needed. The coastguard had been instructed to help with the distribution of the Association's foodstuffs. The first agent to arrive was Captain Harston R.N. Acting on government advice, he travelled to west Cork. He quickly discovered that Clonakilty, Bantry and Schull were in need of urgent help, the poor surviving on seaweed. The local fishermen had no clothes except their oiled overalls because they were, 'all pawned; the pawn shops, however, are now closed, in consequence of their owners having no further capital'. News of the imminent arrival of food had an immediate beneficial effect, bringing down the price of meal by a penny per stone.[45] Getting the food inland was more problematic, being hampered by bad weather, the distances to be covered and 'a *slight* risk that the food might be plundered'.[46] Although Harston had been instructed only to sell meal to the local relief committees, within days of arriving he informed the London Association that he would not be abiding by this ruling because he had discovered 'many nooks, and fishing cabins, remote from any large village or town, and away from Relief Committees . . . are consequently left in the most extreme destitution and privation'.[47] By acting in this way, the British Relief Association was assisting those who fell through the rigid guidelines governing official relief. Harston was concerned about the lack of boilers in the area – there being only two to cook food for a population of 9,000. This situation was not unusual and it was mostly left to private charity – the Quakers and, to a lesser extent, the Irish Relief Association – to supply the necessary equipment.[48] Interestingly, Harston believed that it was inappropriate to give soup to the hungry on the grounds that 'it may sustain a strong man sometime, but never recover these poor, weakened, and suffering people'.[49] On 18 April, Harston informed the committee in London that due to '*urgent* private circumstances', he had to resign and return to England. He added, 'The feeling that the benefits and great good conferred by your Association, partly through your agents, alone keep me here . . . I shall remain until I have your sanction to return to England, or my successor arrives'.[50] It was not until 5 May that Harston's successor, Captain Thomas Rodney Eden RN, arrived in Skibbereen. On 11 May, Harston left West Cork for England.[51] His duties were not completely over; when he arrived in London, he briefed the British Relief Association about the awful state of the country.[52] Eden's time in Cork was brief also. In mid-June, he was informed that the Association was terminating its activities in that locality, as government soup kitchens had opened.[53] Eden returned to London to give an account of his activities. His departure marked an end to his involvement with the Irish poor. In July 1847, he commissioned the frigate, *Amphitrite* whose main duty was to capture vessels carrying African slaves to the Americas.[54] Eden died, in January 1858, when the ship was moored in Mazatlan Harbour in Mexico. He was aged only 38.[55]

The British Relief Association did not only operate in the west of the country. One of their agents, Captain Whitmore, looked after East Cork, Waterford and Tipperary. Whitmore, like many of his colleagues, had offered his services for free. In his district, he found pockets of distress, which he attributed to the closure of the public works, inactive Relief Committees and uncaring landlords and middlemen. In these circumstances, he believed that the exertion of individuals could literally make the difference between life and death, and that, for the poor who were not being taken care of by other agencies, the intervention of the British Relief Association was crucial.[56] Regardless of widespread hunger and illness (mostly from fever), Whitmore concluded, 'the destitution in the county of Tipperary is not to be compared with parts of Cork and Waterford, and in no place do I consider them worse off . . . Still, there are cases that under the regulations cannot be provided for, and the Committees I have found glad to use the grants made to them for their relief; the sick in particular are most in need of a little extra food'.[57]

Count Strzelecki and other volunteers

The person who was most closely associated with the work of the British Relief Association was Count Pawel (Paul) Strzelecki.[58] He, like many others who worked for the Association, offered his services for free. Strzelecki had first been introduced to Thomas Baring though Samuel Jones-Loyd. Strzelecki, a noted explorer of Australia, had become a naturalized British subject in 1845, one of his sponsors being Jones-Loyd.[59] On 20 January, he was described to the committee of the Association as 'a Polish gentleman of extensive travel who had offered his personal services gratuitously'. The committee deferred the decision to employ him.[60] However, on the following day, the Association appointed Strzelecki as their main agent in Ireland, thanking him for 'his tender of service'. He was asked to attend their next meeting.[61] Twenty-four hours after doing so, Strzelecki was travelling to Dublin where he was directed to make contact with the Irish administration, notably Sir Randolph Routh.[62] From Dublin, Strzelecki journeyed to the west where he had been charged with looking after counties Donegal, Mayo and Sligo. The extreme weather – snow, rain, hail, frost and bitter cold – was not only adding to the misery of the poor, but hampered Strzelecki's movements. His determination to complete his mission was evident. When, as occurred on a number of occasions, his carriage became stranded due to snow storms or snow drifts, he simply proceeded to his destination on foot.[63]

Strzelecki's initial letters revealed his horror at what he encountered. Writing from Westport in early February, he explained:

> No pen can describe the distress by which I am surrounded. It has already reached such a degree of lamentable extremes that it becomes above the power of exaggeration and misrepresentation. You may now believe anything which you hear and read, because what I see surpasses whatever I read of past and present calamities.[64]

The scenes that he witnessed between Westport and Sligo were just as disturbing:

> . . . in the locality of Ballina, Foxford, Swineford [sic], Castlebar, the desolate aspect of the country is more fearful still. The population seems as if paralyzed and helpless, more ragged and squalid; here fearfully dejected, there stoically resigned to death; there, again, as if conscious of some greater forthcoming evil, they are deserting their hearths and families . . . Of the fate, gloomy and awful, which overhangs the whole population, that of the poor children, and the babies at the breasts of their emaciated and enervated mothers, excites the deepest feelings of commiseration.[65]

Strzelecki's graphic reports provided insights into how famine was causing social bonds to break down:

> Equally painful is to observe that the destitution, which was hitherto impairing but the physical frame of the population, should begin now to extend its baneful influence over the moral feelings, and even those sacred ties for which Irish families have been proverbial: for instances of recklessness of mothers to their children, those of adults to their aged parents, are as frequent as the consequences of such recklessness are melancholy.[66]

Strzelecki was particularly upset by the scenes that he witnessed in Belmullet, where 25,000 people were spread over 400 square miles. He judged the local relief committee to be inefficient, while the only available food was from a Commissariat depot in the western extremity, which meant that people who were hungry, including those who were employed on the public works, had to walk up to 30 miles in order to obtain food.[67] Strzelecki immediately appointed a Special Committee consisting of two Protestant clergymen, a Catholic Priest and the Coast Guard, all local residents, to oversee the distribution of a grant from the Association.[68] Despite the bad weather and other difficulties, by 1 March Strzelecki had provided relief in 65 localities: this included 30 bales of clothing, 1,020 bags of rice and 1,905 barrels of Indian meal. To ensure efficient and prompt distribution, he employed two constables as his assistants, defending the expense incurred in this way as 'unavoidable'.[69]

As Strzelecki travelled through the west, he repeatedly encountered problems with local relief committees. Even after they had received external assistance, he found that many had not acted promptly to distribute relief. In Castlerea in County Roscommon, a member of the local committee had received two grants – on 23 February and again on 21 March – to purchase meal. By the end of March, despite the local people being in 'utmost need', none of them had received any food. This 'painful experience' was repeated elsewhere and Strzelecki admitted his 'utter inability to prevent abuses'. Consequently, he decided to work with officers appointed under the Temporary Relief Act, instead of voluntary local committees. Strzelecki informed his employers in London, 'Whether I did this rightly or not you will determine'.[70] They approved of Strzelecki's actions.[71] By doing so, however, they were helping to move their charitable interventions closer to government relief, namely to Poor Law relief. Regardless of various problems, by 1 April, Strzelecki had overseen the distribution of almost £6,000 on behalf of the British Relief Association: namely, in counties Donegal £1,740; Sligo, £1,193; Mayo £2,953; and Galway, £90.[72] Working in these testing circumstances inevitably took its toll on health. In early April, Strzelecki was laid low with an unidentified 'infectious disease'. He recovered, but some of those who had assisted him in Westport, including the Rev Mr Pounder, the rector of Westport, died.[73]

During the transfer from public works to the Temporary Relief Act, Strzelecki realized that some people would remain unprovided for. A Treasury Minute of 10 March imposing a minimum 20 per cent reduction in the number employed on the public works, even though many soup kitchens were not yet open, added to the number of people who had no supplies or income. Inevitably, pressure on the limited resources of the Poor Law continued. In the Castlerea Union, for example, people were clamouring to get in the workhouse, regardless of the high levels of fever and mortality – 800 of the 1,000 inmates were sick.[74] In this period of transition, Strzelecki regarded the work of the Association as more important than ever, and he appealed to the London Committee to 'apprize me of the *maximum amount* to which I may go in the grants issued'.[75] As the demands placed on the resources of the British Relief Association increased throughout April, Strzelecki requested permission to double the grants he was giving to Poor Law officials.[76] Ironically, the grants were not given to electoral divisions that exhibited the greatest need, but those where the local officials had demonstrated the greatest efficiency. As Strzelecki explained:

> The preference given to such electoral divisions over those where the *greatest destitution* prevails was imperative, for experience has demonstrated to me, that whatsoever the misery is in a district, the grant to alleviate its horrors becomes a dead letter without an efficient Committee.[77]

As a consequence of this approach, distress and mortality occurred, not due to lack of available resources, but due to administrative strictures.

Strzelecki's early and distressing reports resulted in the Association sending, in March, Matthew James Higgins to the impoverished, isolated town of Belmullet. Higgins had offered his services free, yet in some ways appeared an odd choice. He was the only son of landed gentry from Benown Castle, County Meath and had also inherited estates in British Guiana.[78] Higgins was a writer and had contributed to many English papers including the *Times* and the *Pall Mall Gazette*. He was known in the London press by his various pen names, the most frequently used one being *Jacob Omnium* (or JO).[79] His writing skills were greatly admired by other authors including William Thackeray and Anthony Trollope.[80] Before travelling to Ireland, Higgins had been sent detailed instructions by the British Relief Association, the contents of which provide an insight into how they viewed the role of their agents:

> While you will be called upon to act, however, in general conformity with the spirit of these instructions the particular circumstances of the District, and the operations which will be carried out there simultaneously may call for departure from them in many instances. The Committee have therefore thought it proper to repose in you a full confidence and discretion in such cases . . .
>
> With this view they have placed at your disposal for gratuitous distribution a supply of clothing which you will be pleased to allocate to the several relief Committees, and others permitted to purchase said, for distribution amongst the Labourers and their families, who by industry and activity have shown themselves worthy of encouragement.
>
> You will be also empowered to draw freely upon the several Government Provision Stores in relief of the existing distress, and of this Commissary General Sir Randolph Routh has been fully advised.
>
> It is conceived that by making your Grants of provisions for gratuitous distribution to the several Relief Committees simultaneous with the issue of Seed Corn, all temptation to make use of the latter as food (an evil unhappily to be anticipated in the present destitute condition of the District) may be averted.

You will therefore be pleased to consider this as a very important branch of your duty, with the assurance that at so important a crisis, it is the earnest desire of the Committee to render this important operation as effective as possible.

The experience of the Count Strzelecki will be most useful to you, and he has therefore been requested to furnish you with all the information in his power, as to the Districts adjacent to Belmullet, and, if possible, to communicate with you personally.[81]

When Higgins arrived in Belmullet, he was shocked by what he found. Again and again, it appeared that no number of eyewitness testimonies could actually convey the horror of what was happening in Ireland. He reported: 'The streets are full of people in a dying state; at every corner one hears horrible accounts of bodies found in ditches and on dung heaps'. He believed that deaths from starvation and disease 'equal the worst details from Skibbereen'.[82] Like Strzelecki, Higgins was particularly touched by the plight of the children:

I cannot express to you how painful it is to witness the wretched children, actually expiring in the streets, and to be debarred from assisting them; but if I were to do so once, I could not walk about the town.[83]

Higgins immediately arranged for food and clothing to be provided gratuitously in the remote coastal districts of Ballyglass, Dulock, Tullaghan and Berwick. By doing so, he was contravening his instructions, but he justified this on the grounds that 'the destitution of the people in these districts is so utter, that I feel I am but acting as you would wish'.[84] He quickly realized that the people required more than just food and clothing. Wherever he went there were dead bodies, becoming putrid because their relatives could not afford to bury them. One of Higgins' first tasks was to arrange for 24 coffins to be made. He also purchased two coffins from his own money, for a woman whose children had died.[85]

As was so frequently the case, Higgins was frustrated by the inefficiencies of both the local relief committees and the Poor Law Guardians. He rationalized, 'they cannot even understand – nay, most of the Poor Law Guardians are unable to read – the instructions sent around by the Government . . . in the meantime, the people are dying'.[86] The fact that the population in Belmullet was so scattered over inaccessible mountainous terrain led Higgins to despair that 'all you and I do will not prevent numbers from rotting unheeded in their cabins'.[87] Getting food to the remote areas was hindered by the need for it to be guarded during the journey – a point Higgins felt it necessary to explain to the Association in London, 'lest you should imagine I have not done enough'. He elucidated that:

I have no means of sending provisions anywhere – for an escort is absolutely necessary, and I have no means of obtaining one. Indeed, both policemen and soldiers are very much harassed here, and can hardly be expected to do more work. The people are not dangerous, but they fall on the meal and the biscuit, cut open the sacks and scramble for the contents; and this is done chiefly by women and sick creatures, who are much more difficult to be repelled than able-bodied men with whom we could deal harshly.[88]

Higgins was based in Letterbrick, a small coastal town. It had no hospital or dispensary and was 31 miles away from the nearest workhouse. Higgins described some of his experiences in an article that appeared in the *Times* of 22 April 1847. His letter was long and his language was frank, leaving readers in no doubt about the desperate state of the poor. He explained that the British Relief Association, responding to reports of distress in Ireland, had sent him to County Mayo because, 'I had been loudest in my condemnation of the conduct of both Irish and English landlords'. Higgins's experiences in Letterbrick did not comfort him. He was critical of the three local Protestant clergymen, claiming, 'one is insane; the other two are not on speaking terms and will not "act" together in any way'. He described the three Catholic clergy as 'good, simple men – poor, ignorant and possessing little influence over their flocks'. Although the local soup kitchen had been given money by the British Relief Association in advance of his arrival, no food was being provided, 'because the vicar and the curate, having £130 entrusted to them by our association, had quarrelled, and preferred seeing the parishioners starve than make soup for them in concert'.[89]

There were only two large resident landlords. Higgins was scathing about one known as, 'The Mulligan', of whom he said:

He is chairman of a Relief Committee which he never attends; he has given no money nor any food, while he extracts everything he can from the soil. He pays no taxes, builds no cottages or farm buildings, supports no schools or hospitals.

Mulligan was the only Resident Magistrate in the area, but he been accused of having seduced the daughter of a coastguard and therefore was not going out in public. Nonetheless, although his starving tenants were not in arrears, he was 'ruthless' in evicting them. In contrast, the other large landlord, Mr Black, had been active in distributing relief. Of the smaller local landlords, Higgins had praise only for one, the remainder, in his opinion, being as avaricious as Mulligan. Landlord apathy or greed meant that the only food available to the local people was that provided by the government or the British Relief Association, and employment on the public works was in the process of being reduced and would end completely in May. Consequently, many of the poor in Belmullet were without food or medicine or clothes and they were dropping dead on the streets. In the two days prior to submitting this report, Higgins had personally paid for the burial of 20 people, fearing that if he did not do so, their corpses would infect the living.

Higgins concluded his report:

> Lest I may be suspected of caricature or exaggeration, I will, in conclusion, set down what my eyes have seen during the last half hour. I have seen in the court-house an inquest held on the body of a boy of thirteen who, being left alone in a cabin, with a little rice and fish in his charge, was murdered by his cousin, a boy of twelve, for the sake of that wretched pittance of food. A verdict of "willful murder" has since been returned. The culprit is the most famished and sickly little creature I ever saw, and his relatives whom I heard examined, were all emaciated and fever-stricken.[90]

Higgins left Belmullet on 4 May 1847. During his brief period there, he had helped to establish soup kitchens throughout the district on behalf of the British Relief Association. Importantly also, by doing so he had helped to facilitate a transfer to the Temporary Relief Act and government soup kitchens.[91] Despite all that he had done to help the local people, his final letters were dejected. In them, he made a special plea for the district he was leaving, asking that Erris should 'be made an exception to the general relief measures'. Higgins had already been in touch with the Treasury regarding this matter, but explained, 'I am unwilling to write too often to Mr Trevelyan, but I will entreat any of the Committee who are in communication with Government, to impress upon them the necessity of sending a special officer here'.[92]

During his two-month stay in Belmullet, Higgins had worked hard to provide the local people with food, clothing and coffins. However, his endeavours could not prevent the mass mortality he witnessed daily and which distressed him so much. Despite all that he had done, Higgins believed that the area was in 'crisis', with people still dying in the streets.[93] Higgins's unapologetic writings on what he witnessed were a powerful and lasting testament to the suffering of the poor and the indifference of many landlords. When Higgins died in 1868, he was mourned as far away as Australia, being remembered for his handsome looks and his forthright writings.[94] However, during the months he spent in the west of Ireland, for which he received neither compensation nor lasting recognition, he not only saved lives, but he gave a voice and some dignity to people who appeared to have been abandoned by their government, their landlords and their priests.

Unlike Higgins, whose area of responsibility had been small, if problematic, Lord Robert Clinton[95] and Lord James Butler,[96] who had also offered their services to the British Relief Association, were jointly put in charge of counties Galway, Clare, Limerick and north Kerry. Clinton, a younger son of the Duke of Newcastle, was aged only 27 at the time of his volunteering. He had no direct connections with Ireland. Butler's family came from Kilkenny.

When Clinton and Butler met in Galway City, they decided that Butler should take charge of counties Clare and Galway, Clinton the remainder. Arriving in his district in March, Clinton reported that the condition of the poor in north Kerry and Limerick was 'most miserable'. He blamed this largely on the high price of food but also the dependence on public works and the low wages. He concluded his report by asking, 'the state of the poor creatures is quite heart-rending; yet what more can we do?'[97] A few weeks later, Clinton established a large food depot in Tralee, with an auxiliary store in Milltown. He was assisted by a local landlord, Sir W. Godfrey, and by the local Catholic priest, leading Clinton to lament, 'I wish I could find more members of Relief Committees imbued with the same liberal feeling towards their neighbours'. However, by doing so he had exceeded his remit and, in his report, he asked 'I should much wish that the Association should confirm or condemn my conduct in respect to these depots by return of post'.[98] Although it brought his involvement with famine relief to an end, the introduction of the soup kitchens pleased Clinton on the grounds that, 'the free access of food and wholesale nourishment at the present time will, I can assure you, restore life to hundreds who are gradually sinking from insufficiency of food, and enable hundreds of others to resist the attacks of fever'.[99] Clinton's involvement with Ireland was short lived. In 1852, he was elected to the British parliament as a Liberal candidate. His parliamentary career was lacklustre and ended in 1865.[100] He died two years later, aged only 47, his role during the Irish Famine having long been forgotten.

Lord James Butler, of the Butler family of Kilkenny Castle, found the distress in Galway City was not as great as what he had witnessed elsewhere. This opinion changed as he travelled to the west of the county. Butler was repeatedly appalled by what he saw, not merely the devastation, but the whole way of life he witnessed which, he believed, had made such a crisis inevitable. He was shocked by the 'immense population' that had survived in such rocky landscape on the potato, which he referred to as the 'fatal root'. Like Clinton, he believed that it was crucial to use the resources of the Association to establish food depots in the most remote districts, leading him to ponder 'why people should have ever settled in such a spot if a mystery'. Unlike his fellow agents, Butler repeatedly demonstrated more concern with preventing abuse than with saving lives. He repeatedly warned against too lavish expenditure by the British Relief Association warning, 'it is necessary to be very careful about granting large sums, even should the funds at their disposal equal those of the Empire'.[101] Butler was critical of the way in which a number of local committees were handling their funds. He was particularly disapproving of the Roundstone Committee, admitting, 'one or two remarks made by them put me on my guard'. Although they had received grants from the Association, he judged their accounts to be 'unsatisfactory and incorrect'. When returning to Galway City, Butler met with representatives from the Society of Friends – James Perry, Jonathan Pim and R. Barclay Fox, who were travelling through the country to see if their aid had been properly distributed. Butler described the grants made by the Quakers as having been 'most liberally made' and wryly predicted that 'little satisfaction awaits them at Roundstone'.[102] The involvement of Butler, like that of Higgins, was brief, he being replaced by a Naval Officer in May.

Royal naval involvement

At the insistence of the Treasury, the closure of the public works had commenced on 20 March, a decision which had placed additional pressure on the British Relief Association and other charitable bodies. In April, however, the funds of the Association received a boost when the entire proceeds of the Queen's Letter, which amounted to almost £172,000, were entrusted to them. This action was a strong indicator that both the Treasury and the Home Office were happy with the way in which they were providing relief. It also reinforced the need of the Association to work in close collaboration with Trevelyan. The increase in income meant that more agents could be sent to Ireland. The timing was judicious as the closure of the public works and the transition to the Temporary Relief Act was placing a strain on the limited resources of many charities. The type of agents chosen indicated a change of direction by the British Relief Association. The early agents had been volunteers, mostly drawn from the leisured classes, who had offered their services for free. Their backgrounds had not prepared them for the work they had undertook to do, yet they conscientiously represented the British Relief Association and their donors. After April, the men sent to Ireland were mostly naval officers, the Association working with the Admiralty on this matter. Thus, in April, County Donegal was placed under Captain Lewis Jones R. N., Counties Roscommon and Longford under Captain Parker R. N., and Dr Loney R. N. was sent to counties Sligo and Leitrim.[103] In recognition of the fact that they would need to act quickly, the British Relief Association issued them with a set of instructions which were to act as guidance principles.

> The Committee are aware that famine has already established itself in many Districts so undeniably, that it would be a vain attempt on the part of their Agent to define with any accuracy the classes of persons to be relieved out of a free Grant. But they wish you to bear in mind for application, whenever practicable, the principle that few Grants ought to be limited to those who are unable to labour.

While urgent cases of necessity were to be responded to, the agents were advised to act with an eye to economy as famine was likely to last for some months. They were to work with local agencies, but were warned to:

> take care to make it fully understood by the Relief Committees and other local bodies with whom you communicate, that you are assisting in the

administration of a voluntary Relief Subscription arising from English Charity necessarily limited in extent, and therefore not only justifying, but requiring economy in its distribution, but yet so large to deserve the warmest thanks of the Irish people to the Contributors.[104]

Captain Jones was one of the new agents appointed to help with the transition from the public works to the government soup kitchens. His movements in Donegal were hampered by the weather – in this case, high winds throughout May. As was the case elsewhere, he encountered instances of both good and bad practices. He found the Glenties Union to be particularly poorly managed. However, Jones felt compelled to report on the actions of a benevolent landlord, John Hamilton of Fintown near Glenties. Hamilton had inherited his lands when only 7-years old. Even before the Famine, he had a reputation as a caring landlord, a reputation that continued throughout his life.[105] In response to the food shortages, he was active in providing employment by obtaining government loans under the Drainage Acts.[106] Jones said of him:

> Mr Hamilton, the proprietor of Fintown, received me with the kindest hospitality, sharing with me his house and larder . . . The population is about 1,000; a good number are on the public works, others have been employed on their own lands, and Mr Hamilton has constantly kept twenty to thirty on his own grounds. He has by his exertions, and the generosity of friends, stored a quantity of meal, some of which have been sold, but none hitherto given gratuitously; amongst other donations, he has to thank your Association for a grant of 20*l.* The provisions are stored in the lower part of his house, so that he is living in one room, and in every way meets the exigencies of the day with cheerfulness and confidence. You will perhaps bear with me and excuse my going somewhat into detail; but if afforded me the most gratifying pleasure to witness the noble and exemplary conduct of this young man, and, at any rate, to come into contact with one so nobly doing his duty, of a class so much abused, whether rightly or not it is not for me to say; but at any rate here is one, the only gentleman in the district, keeping his people together; not one in the poor-house, and only two have been; here he is, by his exertions and cheerfulness, keeping 1000 persons in heart, and checking despondency.[107]

Jones praised other landowners, including Sir James Stewart of Rathmelton. In contrast, his characterization of the local people was harsh:

> The people always have lived in dirty, wretched, miserable pig-holes of places; but, with these places, and plenty of potatoes (14 lbs a day for each member of a family), they were satisfied and content, leading a lazy, indolent life.[108]

When he travelled to the Inishowen peninsula in the north of the county, Jones again encountered resident landlords who were looking after the poor, leading him to conclude that 'the inestimable advantage of the presence of old established resident landlords, and most particularly so in the present crisis, when the representatives of these families are men of such sound principles'.[109] In contrast, he found the inhabitants of Dunglow and Mullaghberg near Ballyshannon to be 'wretched', reporting that, 'They belong to nobody, and nobody seems to take much interest in their welfare; they are, therefore, for the present, in the hands of the British Relief Association to keep them in existence'.[110] Jones's work in Ireland ended in June. He returned to naval duties at the end of 1847 and was honoured for his services in 1861 (K.C.B.) and 1873 (G.C.B.).[111] When he died in 1895 at the age of 98, his obituary made no mention of his brief involvement with the British Relief Association.[112]

William Loney, also of the Royal Navy, was placed in charge of Sligo, Leitrim and Boyle. Loney had been born in Tipperary in 1817 and appointed a surgeon in the Navy in 1839. He had offered his services after reading a letter in the *Times* in February 1847 by Commander Caffin, R. N., Commander of Her Majesty's steam sloop *Scourge,* describing the appalling poverty he had witnessed in Cork. Caffin had suggested that naval surgeons should be employed in Ireland to oversee the distribution of medicine and food. Loney, who was working in the Marylebone Dispensary in London at the time, immediately offered his services to the Director of the Medical Department of the Navy. At the beginning of March, he was told to hold himself in readiness for being sent to Ireland at very short notice.[113] In early April, Loney was invited to meet Stephen Spring Rice, the Honorary Secretary of the Association, at South Sea House. The following day, Loney left to take up duties in Ireland. His instructions, sent to him on 14 April, were:

> You will proceed as soon as practicable & take charge of a sub-district in that under the directions of Count Strzelecki. It is thought expedient to leave to that gentleman, who has already gained great knowledge of the local circumstances, a power of instructing you to make grants in cases which he has investigated; but it is not intended to restrict you from making grants on your own responsibility.[114]

Loney was disappointed on arrival in the north-west of Ireland to find that his main duties consisted of overseeing the distribution of provisions and clothes and not looking after the sick.[115] His reports to the Association indicated his concern with medical matters. Loney reported that the people had such a deep-rooted fear of infection that they abandoned their relatives who were suffering from fever. He believed that the situation could be eased through the establishment of district hospitals at relatively little expense.[116] On 12 June, Loney was informed that he was to close his agency within two or three weeks as the Temporary Relief Act was now operational. On his way back to London, he was asked to visit Strzelecki in Dublin, to inform him of his experiences.[117] Following his work in Ireland, Loney returned to the Navy, sailing as Surgeon on the HMS *Amphitrite* to West Africa in July 1847. The Captain of the ship was Thomas Rodney Eden who had been similarly employed by the British Relief Association.

Captain Frederick of the Royal Navy replaced Lord Butler in looking after Clare and Galway in May 1847. Although at that stage the Temporary Relief Act was in operation throughout much of his district, he was disappointed to find that private charity was being provided in the form of uncooked food. Frederick disapproved of giving uncooked food, fearing it would be resold and this abuse would do a 'moral injury' to the poor.[118] To obviate this possibility, Frederick informed the Committee of the Association, 'I have taken upon myself, to the grants of food lately made by me, to attach the condition of its being in a cooked state'.[119] To this end, he focused his energies on helping to get boilers in place.[120] In mid-June, the areas under his care came fully under the operation of the Temporary Relief Act, Frederick informed the Association that he would be officially retiring from this position. In his final communication with London, his closing comments made clear his dislike of providing gratuitous relief to the poor even in the form of soup, explaining, 'I believe that the sooner the permanent Poor Law supersedes the Temporary Act, the better it will be for the country'.[121]

Following the end of their service in Ireland, the various members of the Royal Navy were thanked for what they had done:

> I am commanded by my Lords Commissioners of the Admiralty to send you herewith, a copy of a letter from the Secretary to the British Relief Association, dated 14 Inst. expressing the acknowledgement of the Committee for the Services of the Officers of the Royal Navy employed in carrying out the objects of the association in Ireland, and my Lords direct me to convey to you the expression of their great satisfaction at this Report and to inform you that a note of the Services you have rendered and the qualifications you have exhibited, whilst executing such Services, will be made in this Office in your favour.[122]

The British Relief Association also expressed their gratitude to the Admiralty in Whitehall:

> As the Committee have deemed it expedient to suspend their operations for the present, and have consequently directed the recall of all the officers employed as their agents in Ireland, they think it right to take this opportunity of expressing the strongest testimony in their power to the energy, zeal, and activity, which have characterized the service of the Naval Officers, who undertook the duty of their agents.

Acting in the true and highest spirit of benevolence, they have in the cause of their duty been exposed to much danger, privation, and suffering, in their endeavours to relieve, as far as lay in their power, the pressure of extreme distress in the districts to which they were severally sent, they have now returned, having fulfilled all the objects of their mission with the utmost ability and discretion.

This Committee feel that they have no means of rewarding such services, but take the liberty of expressing their high admiration of them, in the hope that the conduct of the Naval Officers who have been so employed may not be deemed unworthy of the approbation of their Lordships the Commissioners of the Admiralty.[123]

The British Relief Association

During the transition to the opening of government soup kitchens, the British Relief Association not only increased the number of agents operating in Ireland, but made available a total of £30,000 a month to allow them to assist those who found themselves without access to other forms of relief. The Committee approved these measures, recording they had, 'reason to believe that this measure tended to mitigate the pressure'.[124] This belief was confirmed by their agent in Donegal who informed the London Committee that their interventions 'have materially *assisted* the Government measure of bringing the Unions under the Act of 9 & 10 Victoria, chap. 7, which seems so desirable at the present crisis'.[125] In addition to providing financial aid or relief in foodstuffs in spring 1847, the British Relief Association had sold £18,000 worth of seed oats in the west. The government urged them to do so, even providing them with four war-steamers for this purpose, while the South-Western Railway Company provided free transportation within England. All of the cargoes of seed were disposed of and the Association was later informed that the crops raised were luxuriant and flourishing'.[126]

Government officials were unequivocal about their debt to the British Relief Association in general, and to Strzelecki in particular. In the Westport Union, by 24 April an estimated 8,000 persons were being fed weekly, due to the grants made by the Association; this number was expected to triple in the succeeding weeks. Richard Lynch, an Inspecting Officer for the Poor Law, informed Strzelecki that:

To them [the BRA] this union owes a debt of gratitude, for this as well as the many grants made to them during the last three months; and to you I am personally under great obligation, for putting at my disposal so effective a stimulant to the several Committees to commence the new system of relief. Pray convey my acknowledgement to your truly benevolent Association.[127]

By May, as government soup kitchens started to open, Count Strzelecki advised the British Relief Association that they should prepare to suspend their operations. The Temporary Relief Act was the most successful of all of the measures introduced by the government. By mid-June, Strzelecki reported that there was no longer any starvation in County Mayo. He recommended that the Association reduced its grants and thus preserve its resources, pointing out, 'The Friends are issuing largely, and disposing freely of the supplies which they received from America'.[128] Strzelecki followed this with a visit to the offices of the Quakers to ascertain their plans in the coming months. They informed him that their American supplies amounted to £80,000 in breadstuffs which they had agreed to distribute before harvest. This, together with the Temporary Relief Act and limited agricultural employment, Strzelecki believed, would be sufficient for the needs of the people. He suggested that Association reserve their funds for 'that time when the source of the public bounties will be drained, the Government assistance at an end, and the people left to themselves'.[129]

By the end of June, all of the British Relief Association agents, with the exception of Strzelecki, had been withdrawn from Ireland. The food depots established by the Association had been closed, although this had been carried out gradually, to prevent any sudden need. Regardless of the Association's ending its main activities in the west of Ireland, Strzelecki offered to continue his services, which resulted in his move to Dublin where he was to act as Central Agent for all of Ireland.[130] In this capacity, he worked with the Irish government and the Relief Commissioners, the Association having offered to make their remaining funds available to any distressed district. However, the success of the government soup kitchens meant that few calls were made on him. Instead, the Association used its money to provide assistance in other ways: they gave £1,000 to the Central Board of Health for the relief of the sick poor and £500 for the distribution of free turnip seed in County Mayo.[131]

From the commencements of operations in January to 1 October 1847, the British Relief Association expended almost half a million pounds in Ireland, which included £100,000 in direct grants, £176,000 on the import of foodstuffs, £56,000 for the purchase of food from government depots, £18,000 for the purchase of seed and £14,000 in money grants to various charities. The London Committee modestly recorded that:

> The letters of acknowledgement and gratitude from the Chairmen of Relief Committees, from Clergymen of all denominations and from the gentry of the country, which were addressed to the Committee, afford the most satisfactory evidence that this large expenditure was not unproductive of the desired result.[132]

These humble words did not do justice to how many lives the British Relief Association had saved in the first nine months of 1847.

Supporting the Poor Law

As its name suggested, the Temporary Relief Act came to a close in the autumn of 1847, when it was replaced a more permanent system of relief based on an extended Poor Law. The close was staggered; on 16 August, 56 unions closed their soup kitchens, a further 25 at the end of the month and the remaining 46 by the end of November. Following this date, there was no legislative provision for providing relief in the soup kitchens. The government realized that the closures of the soup kitchens would cause much hardship. In expectation of these privations, they asked the British Relief Association to intervene and 'strongly urged upon them that their remaining-funds could in no other way be so beneficially employed as in the effort to alleviate the difficulties and sufferings which might be connected with the change in the system of Government relief'.[133] The government also appealed directly to Strzelecki:

> There is no doubt but a great deal of immediate distress will be the consequence. Will you, under these circumstances, be prepared to come to the rescue in a very parsimonious manner, to relieve the utterly destitute in a degree, while the local authorities are pressing on their arrangements, as they perhaps will do then, for employment and the establishment of poor-rate systems?[134]

Strzelecki straightaway recommended to the Association's committee that they continue to assist, referring to, 'the need of their immediate and effectual interference'. He pointed that, without foreign relief being available, 'to close that which is in operation without substituting another would have been tantamount to dooming its population to starvation'.[135] Despite their high outlay in the previous months, in August the Association still had funds of £160,000, to which would be added the income from the second Queen's Letter.[136] The second Queen's Letter, however, was to yield a disappointing £30,000.

Charles Trevelyan, who had gained a reputation among relief officials for unnecessary interference, made it clear that he had firm ideas about how the remaining funds of the charity should be deployed. In a letter to the Chairman of the British Relief Association dated 20 August 1847, he directed:

> you should not form any new independent machinery, which you might find difficult to manage, and which would give the impression that the lavish charitable system of last season was intended to be renewed; but that you should select, through the Poor Law Commissioners, a certain number of Unions in which there is a reason to believe that the rate-payers will not be able to meet their liabilities, and that you should appropriate from time to time such sums as the Poor Law Commissioners may recommend for the purpose of assisting in giving *out-door* relief.[137]

Trevelyan's directive was telling, both for his characterization of the system of charity as 'lavish' and because of his determination that the funds of the British Relief Association should be channelled through the Poor Law, which ultimately gave him control of distribution of relief and of expenditure. The committee of the Association, 'after much deliberation', agreed that they would, as Trevelyan had suggested, give relief to those in need in poorest unions 'and especially to mitigate the evils which may temporarily arise during the period in which the new Poor Law may be only partially or incompletely established'.[138] Twenty-two Poor Law Unions, which were officially designated 'distressed', were to be helped in this way. The Association agreed that the assistance provided would be in cooked food only; they also agreed that, unlike in the previous season when they had provided the poor with stirabout or porridge, in the coming months they would give bread. To facilitate this change, the Treasury agreed to pay for the provision and installation of the ovens required.[139]

In September, Strzelecki reported that the closing of the Temporary Relief Act had gone 'smoothly', and that both the British Relief Association and the Society of Friends had decided to reserve their balances for the more advanced season 'when they apprehend very justly that it will be sadly wanted'.[140] On 5 October 1847, Charles Trevelyan visited Dublin. Strzelecki was hopeful of the benefits of his visit. Trevelyan had already agreed that the 22 distressed unions could each have a separate Inspector who would not only look after Poor Law administration, but would undertake to see that the affairs of the Association were properly administered. Strzelecki believed that this move alone 'clears our field of action from the difficulties, apprehensions, and perplexities with which, notwithstanding past experience, our path was beset'.[141]

In the months following the introduction of the Poor Law Extension Act in August 1847, the British Relief Association continued to provide relief to the most distressed unions, particularly assisting those who were being granted temporary outdoor relief. The first calls on the Association under the new system of relief were made in October 1847. In each subsequent month, the number of applications increased. This pattern continued until July 1848, when the Association suspended its work due to lack of funds. During this time, an unexpected claim on the resources of the British Relief Association had been made in April 1848. As a result of the February revolution in France, Irish artisans had been forced to leave France. When they arrived in Dublin, they were given assistance by the Lord Lieutenant Lord Clarendon. At their next destination of Belfast, they were given assistance by the British Relief Association.[142] Between October 1847 and July 1848, the Association had provided £150,000 to supplement the Poor Law, with almost £46,000 having been spent in June 1848 alone. Strzelecki believed that this involvement had been beneficial: 'small as these grants are, they become nevertheless a great auxiliary to the other means which are being taken to administer to the wants and mitigate the sufferings of the people'.[143]

Edward Twistleton, the Irish Poor Law Commissioner, was clear about his debt to the British Relief Association, writing:

> The Commissioners cannot but be sensible that they are under the greatest obligations, as a public body, to the British Relief Association, without whose munificent assistance the new Irish Poor Law would in some Unions of Ireland have been practically a dead letter, *and thousands might have died of starvation.*[144]

Feeding the schoolchildren

In the critical two-year period following the second potato failure, the British Relief Association intervened in Ireland in another vital way. For the most part, both official and charitable relief had been directed towards adults, which meant that children, 'in the general run and scramble for food, have been left behind hungry by the way'.[145] When he arrived in Westport, Strzelecki devised a scheme for giving daily food to children who attended school in the Union. He explained:

> Conscious that schools in general would be the most systematic and beneficial machinery for the issue of such relief, I had placed in the first instance 600 girls of the Roman Catholic persuasion under the charge of the Sisters of Charity, 700 boys of the same persuasion under the superintendence of the Catholic Dean of Westport; and then to the children thus placed, and those I found already in two Protestant schools of Westport and Louisbourg [sic], amounting to 160, I distributed clothing, and secured one meal daily, of which the cost averaged one-third of a penny per head.[146]

Within a few weeks, Strzelecki was successfully providing relief to over 1,000 children of all religious persuasions in this way. The scheme was praised by the Chairman of the Westport Poor Law Union, Lord Sligo. When thanking the British Relief Association, he paid special tribute to this scheme and, 'the maintenance of our juvenile population in the several schools we were enabled to keep open, and thereby not only relieve their physical wants, but extend the blessings of education so necessary to the well-being of society'.[147]

In October 1847, Strzelecki had 'begged' the Committee of the British Relief Association that he be allowed to continue with this scheme and even extend it, due to the 'utter inability' of the Poor Law to provide for children. As before, he wanted to give them clothing and food through the medium of schools.[148] The clothing, he suggested, should be provided through the Dublin Ladies' Reproductive and Industrial Society, while the Inspecting Officers of the Poor Law Unions would control the number of children receiving daily rations of rye bread.[149] The children thus helped were between 5 and 14 years of age. Before being allowed a meal, they were required to wash their face and hands and to comb their hair.[150] The British Relief Association agreed to Strzelecki's suggestion and granted him £12,000 to be spent on clothing.

Strzelecki's scheme proved to be successful and, unlike Poor Law relief, was widely popular. By 1 January 1848, at an average cost of less than four pence per week, 58,000 children were receiving this form of aid. By March, it had increased to over 200,000 children from a total of 27 Poor Law Unions.[151] Regarding the rye bread, Strzelecki was informed 'the children like and delight in eating it'. Strzelecki, in turn, advised the Committee of the British Relief Association that:

> This kind of relief is a charity more striking amongst the people here than that of a general issue of provisions amongst them, and I do hope that the Committee will derive satisfaction from the mode in which it was introduced and accepted by the public.[152]

Reports from the Unions supported these claims. Mr Marshall, Inspecting Officer at Skibbereen, informed Strzelecki:

> You can have idea of the benefit this system is affording to the poor in this Union – you don't see Skibbereen mentioned in the papers – we have no deaths from starvation, although there is less employment here than in any other Union.[153]

Similar claims were made by the government official in the Kilrush Union, which made it clear that the scheme was also helping the families of the children and so was taking pressure off the limited resources of the Poor Law:

> I cannot tell you how much benefit is derived from feeding the destitute children at the Schools: it prevents the little creatures from starving, and improves their habits, and leaves the parents free to seek for their own subsistence; and about here it is fully appreciated by everyone, as a well-timed, judicious charity.[154]

Additional praise for both the British Relief Association and for Strzelecki came from other impoverished areas that had benefitted from their actions. The Guardians of Ballyshannon Union resolved:

> We offer our sincere thanks to the British Relief Association, and to their able and courteous agent, Count Strzelecki, for the great and judicious assistance given to their Union, through the medium of food distributed to the destitute children in Schools, as, independent of the charity to them, it has been of signal service in reducing the pressure for relief both in and

out-door, as many persons who are almost on the verge of destitution, become so relieved by the bread given to the children, that the heads of the families have endeavoured to support themselves.[155]

By the summer of 1848, the funds of the British Relief Association were almost exhausted. In anticipation, Strzelecki had asked the government to promise to continue their work in the schools until harvest.[156] In April, the Prime Minister had issued a Memorandum in which he agreed that the scheme of feeding schoolchildren should continue, paid for by the Treasury.[157] In one of his most heartless interventions, however, Trevelyan refused to allow this expenditure. The failure to meet this commitment not only threw a further burden on the resources of the Poor Law, but also deprived one of the most vulnerable groups – children – of a vital lifeline. On 8 July, the British Relief Association formally ended its involvement in Irish relief and thus 'brought to a close a system of relief which, it is believed, was one of the most satisfactory in its working, of any kind of charity introduced during the period of distress'.[158] They had spent £80,854 on feeding children and £12,000 on clothing them. The grants to the poorest unions in the west amounted to £143,518, making a total of £236,000.

In November 1848, the Committee agreed that the residue of £12,000 should be given to the Poor Law Commissioners for them to use assisting the most distressed unions.[159] In total, between 1 January 1847 and 25 December 1848, the British Relief Association had spent £603,505 in Ireland – raising £269,302 from private subscriptions, £200,738 from the two Queen's Letters and the remainder being derived from income from the sale of seeds and provisions.[160] Regardless of the hard work of Strzelecki and his fellow workers, their reports made dismal reading and chart the deteriorating situation in Ireland. On 5 February 1847, Harston, the Association's agent in west Cork, wrote from Crookhaven, 'Deaths are fast gaining ground, and I most firmly believe that full half of these parishes will fall victims. They are too far gone to recover'.[161] A week later, he recounted, 'The deaths about here are increasing fast, and the people have the most woeful, haggard, starving looks that can be conceived. The labourers we employ are weakened so as to be almost unfit for work'.[162] On 17 February, Harston recorded, 'It appears to me that Crookhaven and Bantry are the *worst places I have yet visited;* but all are now so bad it is difficult to judge between them'.[163] On 14 March, writing from Skibbereen, he admitted that in all the places he had visited, 'I have found the distress, disease, and deaths have very much increased; nothing can exceed the wretchedness that is, and has been existing; it is the spreading so rapidly that now principally horrifies the visitor'.[164] The situation was so bad that Harston contravened the rules of the Association by giving the local relief committees food that they would pay for later. He reassured the London Committee that, 'I apprehend no danger in this arrangement . . . it is of such benefit to poor districts and Committees, I had no hesitation in adopting it'.[165] A few weeks later, Harston reported that he had again departed from the instructions of the British Relief Association and had given provisions to private soup kitchens.[166] His practical approach demonstrated the benefits of private involvement, which repeatedly proved itself more receptive to the needs of the people.

Withdrawal of the British Relief Association

When the British Relief Association had wound up its activities in the summer of 1848, it had raised a staggering £470,041.1s.2d., far more than any other relief organization. Five-sixths of this money, £391,700.17s.8d., had been used to alleviate the suffering in Ireland; the remainder had benefitted Scotland. The valuable contributions made by the British Relief Association and its officers were recognized by the people in Ireland who had benefitted from their selfless efforts. The inhabitants of the Cahirciveen Union, for example, thanked Strzelecki for his 'utmost zeal and self-devotion, combined with great practical ability, in the administration of a noble charity, springing out of the benevolence of Englishmen'.[167] The Skibbereen Guardians paid tribute to the valuable work undertaken by the British Relief Association in the local schools.[168] This sentiment was echoed by the 'Protestant Patrons' of the Skibbereen Union who thanked both the British Relief Association and the 'British Public' for providing such extensive aid, as a result of which, the children were 'not only in a healthy, but in a thriving condition'. They paid especial tribute to Strzelecki for conceiving this idea which they described as 'one of the most judicious methods that could be thought of for affording us the assistance we required'.[169]

The vital role played by Strzelecki was not only acknowledged by people in Ireland, but by the Committee of the Association in London who passed a series of 'warm resolutions' thanking him for 'services equally remarkable for their efficiency as for their disinterested character'. They pointed out:

> That the successful result which has attended the labours of the Committee, the grateful acknowledgements which they have received, as well from the gentry and clergy of all denominations in Ireland as from the recipients of the bounty of the Association, and the full approbation of the measures of the Association expressed by the Lord Lieutenant and the Government in England, have afforded to the Committee the greatest satisfaction, for which they feel that they are largely indebted to the very able and zealous assistance which they have received from the Count de Strzelecki.[170]

The Chairman of the British Relief Association, Samuel Jones-Loyd, who had known Strzelecki before he became employed by the Association, wrote a personal letter of thanks. At the outset of the correspondence, Jones Loyd admitted, 'I feel it difficult to confine myself to the cold and measured language of an official form'. In a letter full of praise for Strzelecki, a naturalized British subject, he added, 'You have indeed established the strongest claim upon the gratitude of the country which you have adopted; long may you live to adorn it by your virtues, and to benefit it by further services which you are capable of rendering it'. Jones-Loyd concluded by describing himself as, 'Your faithful Servant and Friend'.[171] While Strzelecki was singled out for special mention, thanks were also offered to the Poor Law Inspectors who had assisted him. The Committee of the British Relief Association gave them special thanks for their assistance in giving relief to the schoolchildren.[172] Strzelecki's contribution was recognized by the government of the country in which he had made his home. In November 1848, he was made a Civil Companion of the Bath. Trevelyan had received a similar honour six months earlier, which led one Australian newspaper (where Strzelecki was regarded as a folk hero for his expeditions) to comment on the tardiness of his recognition.[173]

The transfer to Poor Law relief in August 1847 was intended to mark an end to government involvement in Famine relief. It also coincided with the drying up of most private charity to Ireland. However, the high levels of emigration, disease and death, together with the great increase in evictions, forced further changes in policy in the form of the Rate-in-Aid acts of 1848 and 1849.[174] Despite evidence of extreme suffering, the government remained unwilling to commit Treasury funds to alleviate the situation. Instead, they sought to reactivate the role of private charity, an admission that the official measures could not copewith. To encourage a renewal of charitable interventions, a private subscription was opened by the government with MPs donating £100, while the Queen gave £500. Strzelecki was asked to return to Ireland to oversee the distribution of these funds, which amounted to £6,400.[175] It was a pitifully small amount in light of the widespread misery in Ireland. Worryingly, when Strzelecki arrived in the west of the country he was dismayed by what he found as, 'the distress of these ill-fated districts presented in June a character of suffering greatly exceeded in severity than that which I witnessed there in the fatal winter of 1846–47'.[176] Throughout June, July, August and early September, Strzelecki had travelled 2,700 miles, spending £3,838 to help those the Poor Law could not reach, £2,500 to supply clothing and £12 for post-office expenses.[177] By October, the money raised by the government was exhausted. Yet again, private charity had been required to intervene to support inadequate government measures and, once more, Strzelecki had come to the assistance of the Irish poor.

When Strzelecki died in 1873, his death received more attention in Australia than in Ireland. His Australian obituary paid tribute to his remarkable role during the Famine.[178] Strzelecki, a Polish nobleman with no connection to Ireland, perhaps more than any other individual personified a spirit of selflessness and sacrifice that had helped to save an untold number of Irish lives. As the next chapter illustrates, his work, and that of his colleagues, would not have been possible without the generosity of thousands of benefactors, drawn from all parts of the world.

9

'The brotherhood of mankind'.[1] Donations to the British Relief Association

The British Relief Association for the Relief of Distress in Ireland and the Highlands of Scotland was financially the most successful of all the famine charities, raising over £400,000, most of which was expended in Ireland. In total, over 15,000 individual donations were made to the Association, coming from all five continents and representing a broad spectrum of the public. A large number were contributed anonymously, or the names and locations of the individual donors are unknown because they were given via a committee. Others were simply signed as coming from 'A Friend of Ireland'. Donations also ranged in amount. One shilling was given by 'A Poor Man', who explained that it was 'part of an unexpected fee', while one of the largest, of £1,000, came from 'An Irish Landlord, for Skibbereen'.[2] Some came with brief explanations, such as one for £1.1s. from 'A Saxon, who loves his brother Pat with all his faults' and £10 from the unknown 'H.M.P. a Saxon, for Ireland'. One of the final donations in the alphabetical list of donors was made by the mysterious 'W. X. Y. Z.' who gave £2.

The first official donor to the Association, and the individual who made the single largest contribution, was Queen Victoria. On 4 January, the Committee recorded receipt of a letter from the British Prime Minister informing them that the Queen was 'pleased to order her name to be inserted as a donor of two thousand pounds towards the object of the fund'.[3] Her early involvement was an important example to her subjects in her vast Empire. Acting on this potential, the Association extended their appeal to 'British communities in India, Singapore and China'.[4] Unexpectedly, however, the appeal spread beyond people of British descent, reaching individuals 'whose sole ties with the people of Great Britain were those of sympathy, humanity, and the brotherhood of mankind'.[5] An early and notable example of this was the contribution of Sultan Abdul Medjid Khan,

Emperor of Turkey, who made a 'noble contribution of 1000*l* for the relief of distress in Ireland'.[6] His was not the only donation from the Ottoman Empire to the British Association. The Conference of the St Vincent of Paul in Constantinople made two donations, of £170 and £113, while a general collection in Constantinople raised £450.11s. These donations were an early indication of how support for the Association cut across religious, geographical and social boundaries.

Following the lead of Queen Victoria, members of the royal family donated to the British Association. The day after Victoria's contribution was made, her Consort, Prince Albert of Saxe-Coburg and Gotha, gave £500.[7] In addition to their donations, contributions were made by members of British nobility and titled dignitaries, usually ranging from £50 to £200. The Marquis and Marchioness of Aylesbury, for example, gave £100 and £50, respectively. Both the Marquis of Bute and the Duke of Cleveland donated £200. The Honourable Mountstewart Elphinstone, Scottish statesman and historian, made a donation of £100. The Duchess of Inverness gave £50. The Dowager Countess of Limerick donated £50, while the servants employed in her establishment gave £1.15s. The Earl of Manvers contributed £100, and the Countess, £20. The Marquis of Westminster gave £200 to each Scotland and Ireland. Sir James Wigram, a judge, gave £100, as did his brother, Loftus, a successful barrister. A third brother, the Reverend Joseph Cotton Wigram, who became Bishop of Rochester, donated £15.15s.

Several of the donors had connections with Ireland. Earl Spencer donated £250, which he asked be used for 'the districts of Castlebar and Mayo'. The Spencer family was related by marriage to the Lucan family, who owned estates in County Mayo.[8] One of the largest individual donations was made by the Duke of Devonshire, who gave £1,000.[9] Devonshire owned the well-managed Lismore estate in County Waterford, but the main residence of successive Dukes was Chatsworth in Derbyshire, England. Traditionally, they were not permanent residents of Lismore Castle, leaving it in the hands of agents, visiting mostly visiting to hunt or fish.[10] Although an absentee, Devonshire was generally regarded as a benevolent landlord.[11] A more obscure claim to fame was that his ancestor, also the Duke of Devonshire, had been Viceroy at the time of the 1740–41 famine and had personally invited the composer, George Handel, to Dublin to take part in a fund-raising concert.[12]

Prominent politicians donated to the British Association. The donations cut across traditional party divisions. The Right Honourable Sir Robert Peel, who throughout his distinguished career had many associations with Ireland – from acting as Chief Secretary between 1812 and 1818, to being Prime Minister when the blight first appeared in 1845 – contributed £200. Lord John Russell, who replaced Peel as Whig Premier in the summer of 1846, donated £300. The Right Honourable Earl Grey, the Secretary of State for Colonial Affairs in Russell's administration, gave £200. In his official capacity, Grey was the recipient of the multiple grants from British colonies to Ireland and Scotland. Lord Heytesbury, a Conservative politician who had served as Lord Lieutenant of Ireland from 1844 to 1846 and had been sympathetic to the suffering of the poor, gave £100.[13] One of the most flamboyant politicians of the time, Benjamin D'Israeli (also spelled Disraeli), donated £21. D'Israeli was a long-term adversary of Daniel O'Connell.[14] Following the split in the Tory Party in 1846, he became one of the most vociferous opponents of the Peelite group. The Right Honourable William Gladstone donated £50. Although Gladstone was later associated with the Liberal Party and Home Rule, in 1847 he was a member of the Tory Party and had remained loyal to Peel following the 1846 split in the Party. The radical MP, George Poulett Scrope, who was frequently outspoken on behalf of Ireland, donated £25. A number of lesser-known members of the British parliament were contributors.[15] The fact that fund-raising for Ireland was receiving cross-party support suggested widespread approval for this sort of charitable intervention. It also was an admission that government relief measures alone would not be sufficient to save lives in Ireland.

Two men who were closely associated with overseeing the distribution of government relief contributed to the British Relief Association. The Chancellor of the Exchequer in Russell's government, the Right Honourable Sir Charles Wood, gave £200. Charles Trevelyan, the leading civil servant at the Treasury, donated £50. These men worked closely together and controlled much of the day-to-day distribution of government finances. Moreover, along with the Home Secretary, George Grey, they favoured a providentialist interpretation of the Famine.[16] The British Relief Association, by choosing to work closely with the government, came under Trevelyan's powerful orbit. Within days of being formed, members of their Committee were meeting daily with him.[17] As a consequence of his involvement, on a number of occasions, the money raised by this private charity was used as a stopgap for deficiencies in government relief measures.[18] Trevelyan's constant meddling in areas that were not his responsibility became a source of frustration to other leading relief officials, including Count Strzelecki, Randolph Routh and Edward Twistleton. They also worried that Trevelyan's view of relief was more limited than was practicable.[19] Trevelyan's dogmatism led an exasperated Earl of Clarendon, the Lord Lieutenant, to exclaim privately:

C. Wood, backed by Grey, and relying upon arguments (or rather Trevelyanisms) that are no more applicable to Ireland than to Loo Choo, affirmed that the right thing to do was to do nothing – they have prevailed and you see what a fix we are in.[20]

In 1848, it was Trevelyan who overrode the promise made by the Prime Minister that the government would continue to feed children in schools, a scheme that had been previously financed by the British Relief Association.[21] It was unfortunate – and possibly, at times, lethal – that a man with such an unsympathetic view of helping the starving Irish should have so much control over both government and private relief.

The idea of a Queen's Letter had been discussed by the Committee of the British Relief Association in January, although its implementation was channelled through the offices of the government and the Archbishop of Canterbury.[22] The proceeds, however, were all to be dispersed by the Association. The call by Queen Victoria for a Fast Day on behalf of the Irish poor, raised money in churches not only throughout Britain, but much further afield. Moreover, it was not only Anglican churches who responded to the Queen but people from all denominations raised funds for the British Association. For example, collections were made in the Moravian Chapel in Fairfield near Manchester, which raised £11, the proceeds of a fast. The German Lutheran Church in the Strand in London gave £22.16s.6d. The High Pavement Chapel in Nottingham, which was a stronghold of the Society of Protest Dissenters, who was known for its charitable and educational work, donated £56.6s.6d.[23] The Unitarian Meeting House in Birmingham raised £106.4s.5d. The Presbyterian Church in Brampton, Cumbria, collected £1.1s.0d. Church Wardens in Whickham in Durham made a door-to-door collection that raised £62.12s.9d. The Lord Bishop of Durham donated £105.

Banks and financial houses in both Britain and Ireland played an important role in acting as conduits for the receipt of donations throughout the Famine. They were also donors in their own right. The directors of the London and Westminster Bank donated £300, while 34 clerks employed there raised £20.17s. Clerks in the Marylebone branch of the bank separately raised £1.12s.6d. The London-based financiers, Cazenove and Laurence,[24] contributed £100. The banking company of Stevenson, Salt & Co., which had opened in Cheapside, London in 1788, donated £100. The long-establishing London banking firm of Strahan, Paul and Bates donated £200. This company was one of the oldest in England, dating back to the reign of Charles II. The bank, which was already struggling in the 1840s, did not survive the British commercial crisis of the mid-1850s, leading them to apply for bankruptcy in 1856.[25] The bankers Willis, Percival and Co. gave £103. Smith, Payne & Smiths gave £1,000. Smith's Bank had the distinction to be the first English bank to be established outside of London – in Nottingham – in the 1650s.[26] These, and similar donations, brought some of the most affluent members of British society indirectly into the lives of the Irish poor.

Many other businesses gave to the British Association. The Office of the Sun Fire and Life Insurance Company, established in London in 1708 had by the 1840s developed into a worldwide business, gave £500.[27] The London-based merchants of Thomson, Bonar and Company gave £100. J. and S. Ricardo and Co., London merchants who, in 1845, had created the Electric Telegraph Company,[28] donated £100. The tea sellers Twining's, who first opened a tea room in London in 1706, gave £200. Additionally, two members of the Twining family, Thomas and Elizabeth, made personal donations of £10 and £1, respectively. John Wilson and Sons, who were based in London and specialized in high quality linens and damasks,[29] donated £52.10s.

The appeal by the British Association met with an overwhelming response in cities, towns and villages throughout Britain, with many holding special collections to raise funds for both Ireland and Scotland. The amounts collected covered a wide financial range: for example, the small parish of Aerise in Kent raised 16s.8d, while a specially formed committee in the fishing and industrial port of Hull raised the large sum of £3,823.19s.3d. The 'Irish and Scotch Relief Committee' established in Bristol, raised £2606.5s.3d., while £1,221.12s.11d. was collected by a relief committee in Exeter. Some of the largest donations came from newly industrialized cities in the north of England, many of which contained large Irish populations. Bradford in Yorkshire established a Committee for Ireland, which raised £1,482.18s.4d. A committee in the nearby industrial town of Leeds contributed £2,500. The city of York raised £1,700. The large sum of £2,052.19s.6d. was given by the town of Huddersfield. The largest single donation came from a committee formed in the adjoining cities of Manchester and Salford, who were at the centre of Britain's industrial revolution. Regardless of a downswing in trade and high unemployment, they raised £7,785.[30] A committee formed in Newcastle-upon-Tyne raised £3,780, and nearby Sunderland, both in the north east of England, gave £1,241.12s.11d. Stoke-on-Trent donated £355.12s.6d, and the town of Wolverhampton, £2,888.7s.6d. Many smaller towns also made collections, some of which represented substantial amounts of money. Beverly in Yorkshire raised £700.8s.2d., while the nearby Bingley committee collected £176.19s. At the opposite end of the country, the town of Yeovil in Somerset contributed £164.17s. In addition to private donations, the Corporation of the City of London gave £2,000. These donations represent only a small portion of the collections made on behalf of the British Relief Association, but they demonstrated the widespread sympathy of ordinary English people for the poor in Ireland.

Oxford and Cambridge

Contributions made through specially formed relief committees were not the only way in which English people gave to the British Association. The city and the University of Cambridge, for example, made multiple contributions on behalf of Ireland. By the 1840s, Cambridge had a population of almost 25,000 and like many towns of the period, contained many dirty streets and courts, in which the poor lived in filthy and overcrowded conditions.[31] In total, 17 local chapels and churches donated, ranging from £21 raised in St Clements' Catholic Church, to £502 from the Baptist Chapel in St Andrews Street. The University had been established in the thirteenth century and, as an 'unreformed University', it still retained jurisdiction over town affairs – a situation dating back to its medieval foundations. By the mid-nineteenth century, it comprised of 17 colleges. Most 'Fellows' of the colleges were not allowed to marry, while various religious tests ensured that Jews and Dissenters were barred from taking degrees.[32] Despite being an overwhelmingly Anglican institution, assistance for Ireland came from a variety of sources. This included £100 from the Provost and Scholars, and £13.13s. from the 'Bachelors', of King's College. The Lady Margaret Boat Club of St John's College raised £44 and the St Peter's College Boat Club, £16. Three separate donations were made from Caius College: £43.6s.6d. from the College Chapel, the same amount from Tutors in the College and £3 from an unidentified 'Student'. Rev William French, Master of Jesus College, gave £10.10s. The Rev William Hepworth Thompson, Fellow and Tutor of Trinity College, who subsequently became Master of the College, gave £10. Undergraduates at this college raised £75.13s.

A number of private donations were made by Joseph Romilly, a Fellow of Trinity and the University Registrar from 1832 to 1861. Romilly was politically liberal and had supported Catholic Emancipation in 1829.[33] He was also an enthusiastic diarist and his writings provide an insight into the motivations for helping the Irish poor and the context in which they took place. Moreover, his fleeting references to Ireland demonstrate how news of the Famine permeated English society and how the responses to this news varied. Romilly noted in January 1847:

> *Sun. 24* . . . Hopkins preached very ably for the starving Irish. Miss Baldrey (in the Hospital) sent 6d by me, M [Romilly's elder sister] sent £2, I gave £5 (having intended only to give £1); £161 collected at the door. The next largest Church collection was at St Andrews, £55. At the Baptist Church I think £400 was collected – the Dissenters altogether raised £600. Hopkins' Text was 'Think ye those men on whom the tower &&.[34]

On the following day, Romilly recorded:

> *Mon. 25* . . . Meeting of Master & Seniors:- we made a subscription for the poor Irish; the Master and Brown gave £50 each. I gave £30, the rest £25.[35]

The circulation of the Queen's Letter resulted in additional sermons on behalf of Ireland, as Romilly's entry on 22 February made clear:

> *Sun. 21* . . . Lucy [his younger sister] went at 2 to St Mary's to hear Henry John Rose (the preacher of the month) preach on the Q's Letter for the Starving Irish . . . M sent £2 by her.[36]

For some in Cambridge, the Famine in Ireland had reawakened deeply held anti-Catholic views. On the day appointed for the National Fast in March,

Romilly and his daughter Lucy attended Trinity Church where the sermon was given by Rev William Carus who was known for his Calvinist tendencies and his dislike of the Catholic Church.[37] Like a number of evangelicals, Carus viewed the Famine as a punishment on Ireland for the giving of a government grant to Maynooth Seminary in 1845. His sermon outraged Romilly:

> Wed. 24 . . . L & I to Trinity Church where Carus preached a most obnoxious political sermon (against the Maynooth grant in particular & Romanism in general). His Text was Jer. XIV. 7.8.9: – Lucy gave £10.10s.; M £2 and I, £1 only. Lucy disliked his sermon so much that she burnt her notes when she came home . . . The sermon was 67 mins![38]

Romilly's support for the Irish poor continued throughout spring. On 27 April, he 'Bought 2 sixpenny pincushions of Fanny Henslow: she & her sisters & Aunts have made £4000!!! for the benefit of the Irish'.[39] His connection with the Famine came in a more oblique manner. In June 1846, Romilly was asked if he would preside at the wedding of his cousin, Peter Thomas Ouvry. Romilly agreed, and the marriage took place in London on 21 July. The bride was Jane Nicholls, daughter of George Nicholls, an English Poor Law Commissioner and the chief creator of the Irish Poor Law. On the evening before the wedding, Nicholls invited the wedding party to tea at his home on Hyde Park Street. Romilly seemed pleased with the wedding itself as there was 'no crying, no giggling'.[40] This sombreness seemed appropriate as George Nicholls, the father of the bride, had been the main moving force behind the draconian Irish Poor Law, upon which so many starving people were being forced to depend. Nicholls made his own donation of £20 to the British Relief Association.

Oxford University was equally responsive to news of Irish distress, with multiple donations being made to the British Relief Association. Between 1834 and 1852, the Chancellor of the University of Oxford was the Irish-born Duke of Wellington. In the 1840s, the university was in some turmoil as a consequence of what was known as the 'Oxford Movement'. This movement was supported by High Church Anglicans, who wished the Church of England to return to some of its Catholic theology and traditions. Its leaders, which included John Newman, John Keble and E. B. Pusey, were associated with Oriel College, Oxford.[41] Members of Oriel College sent £100 to the British Association, to which A. de Butts Esq., added £2. A donation of £500 was given by the University of Oxford, with an additional £5 from the Archdeacon of the University. Other donations from Oxford included £50 from the Bachelor Undergraduates of Brzenose [sic]. The Rev John Watson also of Brasenose College contributed £5. Two hundred pounds was given by the President and Scholars of Magdalen College, to which Dr Charles Daubeny, Professor of Chemistry, made an additional contribution of £10. The Dean and Canons of Christ Church gave £100, followed by a second donation of the same amount. The Master and Fellows of Corpus Christi College donated £50. New College made three individual donations: £10 from the College, £20 from the Warden and £22.6s. collected in the Offertory. The Bachelors and Undergraduates of St John's College sent £70.0s.6d., while the Rev Henry Longueville Mansel, Tutor at the College, gave £2. The Rev John Barnabas of Queen's College, Oxford, gave £5. Junior members of Wadham College collected £106.16s.6d. H. Lopez of Balliol College gave £2 and, from the same college, E. S. Parry Esq. and H. H. Parry Esq., each donated £1, while S. S. Vaughan Esq. contributed £1. George Ridding, then a 19-year-old student at Balliol, gave £1. Ridding went on to have an illustrious career which included being appointed Headmaster of Winchester College and becoming the first Bishop of Southwell.[42] C. H. Stanton also of Balliol College, who was President of the Oxford Union in Hilary Term in 1847, donated £2. He was succeeded as President of the Union by the Earl of Dufferin, a student in Christ Church, who was to forge a close association with Skibbereen and raise money for the starving of that area.[43]

One Tutor at the University of Oxford made a unique contribution to the distressed Irish. In spring 1847, an association was formed in Oxford to urge its residents not to indulge in unnecessary expenditure during a time of such suffering. Arthur Hugh Clough, a Fellow at Oriel College, joined the society and quickly became its most vocal supporter.[44] Clough published an article entitled, 'A Consideration of Objections against a Retrenchment Society at Oxford during the Irish Famine of 1847', which he addressed to undergraduates, renowned for their extravagant lifestyles. Before writing it, he had sought to obtain accurate information from Richard Whately, the Archbishop of Dublin.[45] Clough, who had been born in Liverpool in 1819, was only a little older than many of the students to whom he appealed. In his pamphlet, he reassuring readers that, 'it professes no more than a retrenchment for the sake of the Irish'.[46] In answer to criticism that English men were suffering unemployment and needed help, he pointed out 'If we keep alive Irishmen in their wretched Skibbereens, we shall preserve not only hungry mouths, but also strong hands that will do strong work. In the end, I plead for both'.[47] He urged the students to do more than 'eat and drink and be drunk' but, for Ireland's sake 'abstain, be temperate and save'.[48] To Clough, helping Ireland was 'a matter of pure justice and not generosity, England is bound to share her last crust with Ireland, and the rich men to fare as the poor'.[49] He further enjoined, 'let us not scoff at eternal justice with our champagne and our claret, our breakfasts and suppers, our dinners and desserts, wasteful even to the worst taste, luxurious even to unwholesomeness'. Clough's forthright message attracted attention but provoked mixed reactions. Those who objected did so on the grounds that he appeared to be suggesting that the rights of the poor were equal to those of the rich.[50] However, Clough attracted some support and the Oxford Retrenchment Association donated £70 to the British Association. In 1848, Clough gave up his position at Oxford, which he found stifling, in order to travel and write poetry.[51] He journeyed to Paris where he expressed support for that and other revolutions taking place throughout Europe.[52] Clough died prematurely in 1861 in Florence, where he had visited for health reasons. His donation to the British Association was significant for more than what it represented in monetary terms; Clough saw the starving Irish not simply as victims to be pitied, but as the equals of the privileged people of England.

Diverse donors

It was not only Oxford and Cambridge Universities who raised money for Ireland. Students of the Faculty of Arts in the University College, London contributed £50.5s.6d. The teaching college in St Bartholomew's Hospital in London sent £3. Many schools also made collections. The pupils of the Commercial School in Grosvenor Square, London raised £2.13s.6d., while the boys attending the City Commercial School in Lombard Street in London donated £3.8s.3d. Pupils of the Royal Naval Academy in Gosport in Hampshire donated £3. Boys in the Church of England School in Hackney gave £6. Bruton Grammar School in Somerset contributed £6. Marlborough College in Wiltshire, which had been established in 1843 for the education of the sons of Church of England clergy, made four donations. The Master gave £5, two separate collections raised £6.6s.6d. and £17.10s. respectively, and a collection at the school's Offertory, £12.3s.6d.

A number of public schools actively engaged in fund-raising activities. Pupils in the elite Rugby School, which had been founded in 1567, made donations through their various Houses. Those in the House of the Rev R. B. Mayor gave £8.10s., those in the House of Rev R. Congreve raised £6.13s.6d., those in the House of G. E. L. Cotton £9, while the House superintended by G. G. Bradley donated £4.12s. In addition, a general collection by the schoolboys raised £8.10s. The headmaster of Rugby, the Reverend Archibald Tait, who had held that position since 1842, gave £75.[53] An Offertory in the Chapel of Charterhouse House, a renowned English public school, raised £60.30s.9d. Many other schools held collections including the City of London School, who gave 12 shillings, while £4.4s. was raised by pupils in Clarendon House in Kennington. Harrow School, founded by Royal Charter in 1572, also contributed. The Rev Dr Charles Vaughan, its headmaster, made a personal donation of £50. Vaughan had been elected to that position in 1844, at a low point in the school's history when it had only 60 pupils.[54] At the time of the donation, a former pupil of Harrow was observing the suffering in Ireland first hand. Lord Bessborough, a former pupil who had been appointed Irish Viceroy in 1846 died, in office, in May 1847, at the height of the Famine.[55]

Young people were independent contributors in a number of other ways. The 'three young children of Mrs Courthope' donated three shillings, 'for

Cork'. To this, their mother added £25. Lady Maria Lewis and her husband, George Cornewall Lewis, allowed a 'Juvenile Bazaar' to be held in their home, which raised £203. 'Pence from a School Room and Servants' Hall' provided nine shillings. No details were provided regarding the location of the school. The 'Savings of three children during Lent' raised £1.13s.6d. Children who attended the Sunday School in St George's Church in Bloomsbury donated 2s.6d., while St Dunstan's Sunday School in Stepney raised £1.7s.10d.

The role played by the British Army in Ireland during the Famine has generally been remembered negatively, especially for their part in guarding the large supplies of food being exported from the country.[56] However, members of the British Army throughout the world – both officers and privates – raised large amounts of money to help the suffering in Ireland. Soldiers stationed in locations as far apart as India, Canada, Antigua, Australia and St Helena, sent donations to the British Association. Their commanders also contributed. For example, General Sir William Davy KCB donated £10. Lord Hugh Gough, Commander in Chief of the British Army in India, made a personal donation of £100 to the British Relief Association. He had earlier donated to the Calcutta Relief Fund. Gough, who had been born in Limerick in 1779, was descended from an Anglo-Irish family. In 1829, at the height of O'Connell's campaign to gain Catholic Emancipation, Gough had been sent to Ireland to 'suppress outrages'. In recognition of his services to the British Empire, Gough was elevated to the peerage in 1846.[57]

It was not only the Army that responded generously to the British Association's appeal. Members of the British Navy, who were also scattered around the world, donated. Again, people at all levels of service gave. They included the officers and crew on HMS *Acorn* who contributed £22.9s.6d., those on HMS *Actaeon*, £19.15s.10d., HMS *Gladiator*, £60.3s.11d., while Lieutenant Henry Ainslie of HMS *Stromboli,* £3.3s. Ainslie, who had been born in Lincoln in England and was a younger son of Sir Robert Sharpe Ainslie, had entered the navy in 1826 when aged 13. His long, distinguished career had a less than distinguished ending. In 1882, the Admiralty reported that 'Major Henry Ainslie Alfred Turner having been found unfit for further active service is placed on the Retired List'.[58] These examples represent only a very small portion of the service men who gave to the poor in Ireland.

A number of special fund-raising events were held throughout England, which were as diverse as they were creative. A ball held in Bishop's Stortford in Hertfordshire raised £32.5s., while one held in Wigan in the north of England made £12.5s.11d. A concert in Bridport in Dorset 'by Amateurs', earned £11. Similarly, an amateur performance in Liverpool, organized by the local Licensed Victuallers Association, raised £20.7s. Two amateur productions at St James's Theatre in London, which had opened in 1835, raised £1,113. Some of the fund-raising activities were even more unusual. The Proprietors of the Chinese Collection in London donated £20. The Collection, which was based in Knightsbridge, was the brainchild of Nathan Dunn, Esq., a merchant from Philadelphia, who had lived in Canton for

12 years.[59] The sale of a sketch book in Carrion in Monmouthshire raised £50. The first profits of a song, 'Erin Dear Erin', which totalled £3.5s., were given to the Association. Three sales of foreign coins by a group called 'First feed and then confiscate' raised a total of £4.4s.0d. A commemorative dinner held by officers in Greenwich Hospital brought in £40. The sum of £50.14s.9d. was donated by the Huddersfield Glee Club, the surplus of proceeds of a concert. A lecture on the topic of Italy by J. B. Carter at the Red Lion Inn in Petersfield raised £10. The Village Choir in Shirley and Addington, north of London, gave 7s.6d. The Cogers Society (A 'Society of Thinkers' founded in 1755) raised £14 from their base in Fleet Street in London. Their members included Daniel O'Connell.[60] 'A few friends meeting at the Granby Wine Rooms' in Bedford Square in London raised £11.

During a social evening in Paddington, people were urged to donate half crowns (2s.6d.) for Ireland. In this way, £2.7s.6d. was raised. The Royal Adelaide Gallery in the Strand, London, donated proceeds taken at the door on one day, which amounted to £18.0s.6d. At a performance of the Royal Italian Opera, 19s.6d. was collected. Mrs Lockett of Brighton held an exhibition of her talking canary bird, which raised £10.10s. Entertainment provided by the Elocution Society of the London Mechanics Institution collected £11.17s. The owner of a telescope located at the foot of Blackfriars Bridge in London raised 1s.10d., by allowing people to have 'sundry peeks at the Moon and Jupiter'. Astley's Theatre in Lambeth, London, which had opened in 1773, gave £56.1s.6d. to the Association, the proceeds of one night's performance. The Theatre was home to a circus, the manager of which was William Batty. The 1847 season was notable for the London debut of the flamboyant Pablo Fanqué (real name William Darby), performing equestrian tricks.[61] In addition to being a famous performer, Fanqué won notoriety for becoming the first black circus proprietor in Britain. He was also known for his philanthropy.[62]

Businesses in England proved to be generous. Various members of the Wedgwood family, who were associated with both high quality pottery and anti-slavery, gave a total of £115. The land agents of Messrs Vacher, based in Parliament Street in London, donated £20. Henry Woods, a cotton manufacturer and colliery owner in Wigan, gave £40. Jacob Wrench and Company, seedsmen in London, who were described by the *British Farmer's Journal* as being 'the respectable house of . . .' contributed £20.[63] The London Company of Truman, Hanbury, Buxton & Co, which had been involved in brewing since 1666, made four donations; two on behalf of the company which amounted to £1,105, a further of £50 from clerks employed in the company, and one of £8.10s. from workers in the brewery. Schunck, Souchay and Company, an European-wide printing company, donated £200. The London-based shipping company, Frühling and Goschen, gave £200. William Hardblock, a Director of City Bank in London,[64] made a personal donation of £20, while 164 employers in his business, Hardblock, Clark and Co., who were tanners, curriers and leather merchants, gave £9.0s.4d.[65]

The Company of Thomas Usborne and Sons, London-based Corn and Malt
Factors, gave £100, to which John Usborne added a further £100. This was
not the first time that the family had come to the assistance of Ireland as
'In July 1831, *The Times* reported donations for the "Relief of Famine in
Ireland" as follows: T. Usborne and son: five guineas; Mrs Usborne: two
guineas; The Masters Usborne: 1 guinea; Miss H. M. Usborne: one guinea'.[66]
Professional bodies also supported the British Relief Association. Officers
and Constables of the Metropolitan Police force raised £161.0s.2d. Money
was raised by Chelsea Pensioners, those in both the South London district
and the area surrounding Stockport in the north of England. Together, they
raised just over £8. The Honourable Society of Lincoln's Inn, the famous
Inns of Court in London, gave £247.9s.6d., the result of a collection made
in their chapel.

A number of Anglo-Greek traders assisted the British Association. The
company of Ralli and Brothers, which had bases in London, Manchester
and Constantinople, and traded throughout Europe, gave £100, while the
sister company, Ralli and Mavrojani, donated £20.[67] The five Ralli brothers
were the most successful expatriate Greek merchant businessmen in the mid-
nineteenth century. By the 1840s, they employed 40,000 people.[68] Pandia
Ralli, the third of the brothers and Director of Ralli Brothers, made a personal
donation of £25.[69] The trading and banking company of Rodocanachi Sons
& Co., also founded by members of the Greek diaspora, gave £30, which
they suggested should be used to purchase 'raiment'. Michel Emmanuel
Rodocanachi, the Director of the company, although only in his twenties,
had helped to establish the Bank of Athens.[70] Both the Rodocanachi and the
Ralli families were active members of the Greek Orthodox Church.

The involvement of Anglo-Jews in a various charitable endeavours proved
to be important. The English branch of the Rothschild family, who were
international financiers and renowned philanthropists, were prominent in
these activities. They made an early donation of £1,000. Lionel de Rothschild
was a founding member of the British Association and his younger brother,
Mayer, attended meetings of the Association if Lionel was not available.[71]
Lionel's personal popularity was evident as he was elected to the House of
Commons in 1847 and again in 1849. On both occasions he was disqualified
because he was a Jew. Other Jewish families gave their support to the British
Relief Association. The London bullion brokerage company of Messrs
Mocatta and Goldsmid gave £26.5s. The Mocatta family, who were known
for their charitable work, especially among the Jewish community, also
made individual donations.[72] Benjamin Mocatta gave £5, Isaac Mocatta,
£2, Maria Mocatta, £2.2s., Moses Mocatta, £5.5s. and E. Mocatta, £5. The
Mocattas were not the only notable Jewish family to contribute. Joseph
Mayer Montefiore gave £40, with separate donations of £20 and £10 from
other members of his family. Moses Montefiore, the scion of the family,
had direct experience of Irish affairs, having helped Daniel O'Connell to

establish the Provincial Bank of Ireland. O'Connell, in turn, had been a vocal supporter of Jewish Emancipation (i.e. the right of Jews to sit in the British Parliament). Moses offered to help the starving Irish in a practical way. Within days of the British Association being founded, he volunteered his personal services, offering to undertake a fact-finding mission in the poorest districts in Ireland.[73]

Women were important as both as fund-raisers and as donors, with perhaps as many as a third of Association's donations coming from females. The women were drawn from all social classes. Inevitably, some belonged to the landed elite. The Dowager Lady Lyttelton contributed £20, which she stipulated should go to Castlebar in County Mayo. Lady Lyttelton, formerly Lady Sarah Spencer, was related to the Lucan family of that county. Following the death of her husband in 1837, she had been appointed a Lady of the Bedchamber to Queen Victoria and governess to the royal children.[74] She was not the only member of her family to show concern for the Irish poor. Lady Lyttelton's brother, George Spencer, had given up to his Anglican ministry to convert to Catholicism, and in January 1847 had entered the Passionist Congregation, taking the name, Father Ignatius. In this capacity, he worked with famine immigrants in Aston near Birmingham in England, even catching fever, from which he recovered.[75] Other aristocratic women who supported the British Association included the Countess of Waldegrave, a noted English philanthropist, who gave £100. The Right Honourable Lady Dynevor gave £5 for 'Poor Irish Women and Children'. Lady Isabella Blachford donated £3 and Lady Blunt gave £10. Another woman noted for her charitable donations was the young English heiress, Sarah Esther Touchet. In October 1847, she had married James-Nowell of Ffarrington in Leyland and, 'For several days Leyland went wild with enthusiasm for the young couple: there were sports and a balloon ascent, a treat for 1,500 children, fireworks and an ox roast'.[76] Ffarrington died eight months later.[77] Sarah Touchet donated £100 to the British Relief Association. At the other end of the social scale, 'Widow Cannon' from Eton gave 2s.8d in farthings (a coin that was worth a quarter of a penny). A penny subscription opened by the 'Misses Rushworm' in Southsea near Portsmouth brought in 8 shillings. The 'Misses Moland' gave £35, followed by a second donation of £10 'for Skibbereen'. They gave a further £10 to the Mansion House Committee in Dublin.[78] In Leamington in Warwickshire, a Ladies' Bazaar on behalf of Ireland raised £300.[79]

Newspapers did much to disseminate accounts of the suffering in Ireland. Additionally, their publication of the eyewitness reports from the Quakers and others who distributed relief reassured the British public that early descriptions of the Famine had not been exaggerated. Nonetheless, some newspapers, including the influential *Times*, remained unsympathetic to the Irish poor and even opposed the fund-raising activities. In an editorial on 5 January 1847, just as the British Association's activities were gaining momentum, readers were urged not to support 'so pernicious an expedient'.[80] In contrast, a number of newspapers made their own collections on behalf of the British Association. The proprietors and writers on the *Daily News* raised £137 in total. Compositors in the *Express* newspaper raised £2.2s. Proprietors of the London *Globe* donated £10 and those of the *Illustrated London News*, which had done much to help to expose the suffering in Ireland, contributed £10.10s. Sixty-five members, primarily reporters, of the *London Daily Press*, contributed £68.5s. Compositors of the *Morning Chronicle* gave £2.16s. Reporters on the *Morning Herald* gave £17.17s. Three donations were made by people employed on the *Morning Post*, which amounted to £4.16s.9d. The proprietors of the *Observer* newspaper donated £50. A more surprising donation of £50 came from the owners of *Punch*, a journal which had frequently satirized the Irish and their situation. The owners of the *Record* contributed £50, while 'sundry subscriptions' from its staff raised £201.16s.7d.

Individual donations provided a significant amount of income to the British Relief Association. The portrait artist Walter Vizard gave £20. John Homfray of Penllyne Castle in Wales contributed £5. The astronomer, R. A. Le Mesurier, gave £10.10s.[81] G. W. Lydekker of the Hare Court Law Chambers in London donated £5.5s. William Rothry, a lawyer in London, donated £10.10s.[82] Servants in his household raised an additional £2.5s., upon 'Captain Caffin's Letter being read'. Captain Caffin was Commander of the *Scourge*, which had delivered food supplies to Cork and Bantry on 8 and 9 February 1847.[83] While there, he decided to visit to Schull. His escort was Dr Traill, the local rector. On 15 February, Caffin had written a graphic account of what he had witnessed, which was then republished in a number of newspapers. He admitted that:

> I had read in the papers letters and accounts of this state of things, but I thought they must be highly coloured to attract sympathy, but I there saw the reality of the whole – no exaggeration, for it does not admit of it – famine exists to a fearful degree with all of its horrors . . . In no house that I entered was there not to be found the dead or the dying . . . Never in my life have I seen such wholesale misery, nor could I have thought it so complete.

Caffin's postscript as equally grim:

> P.S. There have been two or three *post mortem* examinations of those who have died, and they find that the inner membrane of the stomach turns into a white mucus, as if nature had supported herself upon herself, until exhaustion of all the humours of the system has taken place.[84]

This letter, like so many personal testimonies, helped to bring the awful realities of the Irish Famine into many British households.

Overseas aid

The majority of the fund-raising efforts in the United States were channelled through the Society of Friends. However, a smaller number of donations were made to the British Relief Association. The company of Ravenshendt and Schumacher in New York sent £20 to them. Robert Tucker of Baltimore gave £5. A more unusual donation came from an American lawyer, who had recently been elected to the U.S. House of Representatives, Abraham Lincoln Esq., who donated £5. At this stage, Lincoln had no direct contact with Ireland; in later years, he admitted that one of his favourite ballads was the poignant, 'The Lament of the Irish Emigrant'.[85] This ballad was based on a poem written by Lady Dufferin, mother of Lord Dufferin, the Oxford student who had visited Skibbereen in 1847.

Many donations to the British Relief Association came from the various provinces in Canada. New Brunswick was in the forefront of these efforts. The local Provincial House of Assembly voted £1,500 for British Association, to which was added £80.10s.11d. collected by Dr Dollard, the Roman Catholic Bishop.[86] The town of Richibucto sent £61.31s.4d. via Sir Howard Douglas, the English-born former Governor.[87] In addition, a number of New Brunswick churches made collections amounting to £66. A donation of £71.74s. came from the inhabitants of the small town of Woodstock in the west of the province. Tellingly, the covering note explaining:

> I regret that the amount collected here has been so small, but there is so much misery and destitution in this country, caused chiefly by the scarcity and dearth of provisions, that many who would have contributed more largely towards the assistance of their fellow-subjects at a distance, have so many urgent claims upon their sympathies by those who come under their own observation, that they are unable to do so much as they would wish, but if the small sum now sent can only be instrumental in saving one destitute family from starvation 'verily we will have our reward'.[88]

A number of donations to the British Association came from Newfoundland, the most easterly province in Canada, where the first and second public collections raised £500 and £350. A third, and private, donation of 10 shillings came from 'Newman Hoggs' (the name of a character in Charles Dickens' novel *Nicholas Nickleby*) from Trinity in Newfoundland. The local Philharmonic Society of St John's contributed £46.10s.

The largest donations from Canada were channelled through the Government House in Montreal. On 28 May, the Earl of Elgin informed Earl Grey, the Colonial Secretary, that he expected their final contribution to be not less than £20,000, which had been raised by people 'of all creeds and origins'. He was especially pleased to point out that 'several of the Indian tribes have expressed a desire to share in relieving the wants of their suffering white brethren'.[89] Other groups, who themselves had little, gave to Ireland. Fishermen in Canada responded to the sad news from Ireland. Employers at the Gaspé Fishery Company in the Bay of Chaleurs Gaspé in Lower Canada contributed £46. Even before the Famine emigration, there had been a large Irish community in Nova Scotia, many of whom had emigrated in the late eighteenth century and were from Ulster and of Scottish descent.[90] A generous donation of £2,655.0s.7d. came from Nova Scotia. In addition, residents in Halifax raised £283, while Pictou, a strong base of Scottish settlement, sent £303.[91] A subscription in Amherst Island in Ontario raised £31.19s for the Irish poor.

Elsewhere, donations to the British Relief Association came from diverse sources, some of the benefactors having no connection with Ireland. An example of this was the members of the German Society of Benevolence and Concord, which had been formed in London in 1817, who raised £20.2s.6d. Other donors had clear links to Ireland. The Irish Peasantry Society of London raised £300. James Ogilby of Pellipar House in County Derry donated £100.[92] His estate was part of the London Companies' Estates granted under the seventeenth century Plantation of Ulster.[93] Stephen Spring Rice, the Honorary Secretary of the British Relief Association, gave £50. His family's estate was in County Limerick. A number of Irish banks provided their services free of charge to the various charitable associations. They also made their own donations. This included the National Bank of Ireland who gave £1,000 to the British Association.

Passengers on board the transatlantic ship, SS *Cambria*, which departed from Liverpool on 12 February 1847, made their own donation.[94] The sponsors included the diminutive 'General' Tom Thumb, who, with his manager, the impresario and circus owner, P. T. Barnum, had been travelling in England. During his visit, Tom Thumb had been a guest of Queen Victoria at Buckingham Palace.[95] Another passenger on the *Cambria* was the Irish-born explorer John Palliser. He wrote of his first encounter with Tom Thumb, who, 'creeping from under shawls and ladies' work baskets, emerged into the saloon, stuck his Lilliputian hands into his little pockets . . . he was the smallest specimen of human nature it has ever been my lot to behold'.[96] Palliser also recalled that:

> About the middle of the passage a conversation arising relative to the sufferings of the poor in Ireland, an American gentlemen suggested a subscription in aid of the funds then raising for their relief; and the proposition having been seconded by a Canadian merchant, the result exceeded our expectations in a collection of over 120*l*.[97]

Thumb, who was aged approximately 17, had headed the list of donations, giving $50. Interestingly, he had already donated £100 when in London.[98] The involvement of the *Cambria* did not end there. On a return journey from the US, Mr Lewis, agent for the Cunard Line, brought 500 barrels of breadstuffs for free distribution to the poor of Ireland and Scotland.[99]

The *Cambria* attracted notoriety only a few weeks later. In April 1847, the vessel carried the escaped slave and champion of abolition, Frederick Douglass, back to the United States. Douglass had visited Ireland at the end of 1845 and the beginning of 1846. He had been appalled by the scenes of poverty he witnessed, everywhere. Writing from Dublin in February 1846, he recounted:

> The streets were almost literally alive with beggars, displaying the greatest wretchedness—some of them mere stumps of men, without feet, without legs, without hands, without arms—and others still more horribly deformed, with crooked limbs, down upon their hands and knees, their feet lapped around each other, and laid upon their backs, pressing their way through the muddy streets and merciless crowd, casting sad looks to the right and left, in the hope of catching the eye of a passing stranger— the citizens generally having set their faces against giving to beggars. I have had more than a dozen around me at one time, men, women and children, all telling a tale of woe which would move any but a heart of iron. Women, barefooted and bareheaded, and only covered by rags which seemed to be held together by the very dirt and filth with which they were covered—many of these had infants in their arms, whose emaciated forms, sunken eyes and pallid cheeks, told too plainly that they had nursed till they had nursed in vain.[100]

During Douglass's return to America, the fact that he was segregated from other passengers led to him write to the London *Times*, 'I have travelled in this country 19 months, and have always enjoyed equal rights and privileges with other passengers, and it was not until I turned my face towards America that I met anything like proscription on account of my colour'. Douglass, who understood so much about degradation and marginalization, attributed much of Irish poverty to intemperance.[101] However, Douglass was able to help the famine poor in a more practical way when, at a meeting of 'colored citizens' in the Philadelphia, it was suggested that all money raised for Ireland should be channelled through him.[102]

Initially, the British Association had expected to raise money only in Britain and among British communities overseas, but an unexpected aspect to the fund-raising was that financial assistance came from all over the world – as far away as India, Australia, China, South America and South Africa. The first international fund-raising activities for Ireland had taken place in Calcutta in late 1845 and their involvement continued into 1847. Following the formation of the British Relief Association, much of this money was channelled through them. These donations included the Honourable East India Company who donated £1,000. The East India Relief Agency at Agra gave £136.10s.11d. The servants employed by the East and West India Dock Company contributed £10.4s.2d. In Agra, donations were received from the Bengal Artillery, totalling £9.9s.8d., and the local Missionary Society gave

£180.9s.7d. A monthly subscription organized by the Honourable Mr and Mrs C. Cameron raised £62.5s.3d. H. W. Reeves of the Indian Civil Service, from his base in Bombay, sent £10. St John's Lodge in Seagoe, Central India raised £21.13s.5d. The largest single collection came from the Bombay Relief Committee, which raised £10,177.14s.8d.

Elsewhere, British people overseas proved receptive to Irish suffering. Contributions were made to the British Consul in Syria, then part of the Ottoman Empire, which raised £143.19s.6d. Collections in the English Church in Amsterdam amounted to £457.15s.11d., and the English church at Antwerp raised £13.7s.8d. A 'Committee of Dutch and English Gentlemen' in Rotterdam sent £245.14s.5d. Donations came from as far away as Australia, which had been used as a British penal colony since 1788, although few convicts were being sent there in the 1840s. The donations included one for £56.0s.6d., the proceeds of a 'Subscription entered by a few parties' in Melbourne. The South Australian Destitution Fund raised £1,000. An Association in Sydney, New South Wales, raised £647.15s.2d. Two remittances were received from Van Diemen's Land (later, Tasmania), a British colony also used as a penal colony. Hobart Town sent £1,101.12s.9d., while the sale of 23 bags of wheat in the district raised £36.13s.4d.

The West Indies

Islands in the Caribbean (known as the West Indies) made a number of donations. Like Australasia, the West Indies were part of the British Empire. In 1833, slavery had been abolished in these islands, although a system of apprenticeship – slavery by another name – had not been finally abolished until 1838. The campaigns to end both slavery and apprenticeship had been spearheaded by an Irishman, Daniel O'Connell.[103] In the Bahamas, collections made in local churches of various denominations totalled £204.15s.2d.[104] The latter included a contribution of £6.10s.2d. from the island's Baptist Chapels, its congregation comprising of large numbers of former black slaves.[105] Donations to the British Relief Association were frequently directed through the local government. The sum of £746.18s.9d. was received from the Bahamas, £500 coming from the Legislature in Nassau, made on behalf of both Ireland and Scotland. When sending the donation, the local Assembly moved:

> ... with feelings of deep commiseration for the extreme destitution, and consequent disease, which are now desolating large areas in Ireland and in the Highlands and Islands of Scotland, cannot permit the present session of the Legislature to close, without an expression of their sympathy with the numerous sufferers under the present calamity, and without an attempt, commensurate in some degree with the ability of the Colony, to aid the benevolence of our fellow colonists and fellow subjects throughout the empire, now so actively and admirably exerted for their relief.[106]

The resolution ended with a request that:

> Her Majesty's Government will apply the same for the relief of our
> destitute fellow subjects in Ireland and Scotland as, from the exigencies
> of the case, may appear to them expedient.[107]

A further £69.12s.11d. came from the islands surrounding the Bahamas,
including £1.3s.5d. and £27.8s.4d., respectively, from the locally based
Royal Artillery and the Second West Indian Regiment.[108]

Trinidad, a British colony since 1802, raised £1457.13s.9d. for the British
Relief Association, while unnamed 'friends at . . .' gave £10. The British
colony of Grenada, also in the Caribbean, donated £564.18s.6d. Lieutenant-
Governor Hamilton described this money as, 'bearing testimony to sympathy
and kind feeling shown by all classes of this community towards those who
are suffering from the severe visitation of sickness and famine'.[109] Four
Catholic clergy in Grenada sent a separate donation through Bishop Smith of
Trinidad.[110] The small island of St Vincent raised £148.8s.3d., while officers
and privates stationed there contributed £34.13s.2d. The Caribbean island
of Dominica, a British colony since 1805, subscribed £44 to the Colonial
Bank, all of which was to go to Scotland. Collections were also made in the
premises of the Colonial Banks on the islands of St Thomas and Dominica,
raising £34, again on behalf of Scotland. Money raised in Antigua amounted
to £444.12s.3d. and £200.10s., which was sent directly to banks in Dublin
and Glasgow. When forwarding this money, the Governor pointed out that
'many of the emancipated race readily united with the other classes of the
community in contributing to this charitable object'.[111]

Barbados had been a British colony since 1625, when it was claimed
on behalf of King James I of England. In Barbados, a specially constituted
relief committee was established to support the work of the British Relief
Association. In mid-February, it informed people that 'subscriptions have
been opened at the office of the Colonial Treasury and at the Colonial and
West Indies bank where the donations of the charitable are most earnestly
supplicated'.[112] An editorial in the main newspaper on the island, commenting
on the fact that the House of Assembly was about to meet for the purpose of
making a donation to Ireland, reminding its members:

> Barbados owes Ireland a great debt of gratitude for substantial aid in
> distress. The princely sum of £20,000 was contributed by the citizens of
> Dublin for our relief after the dreadful hurricane of 1780. What would
> that amount to at present? . . . they are without food. A yam, a quart of
> corn, a dozen eddoes, anything that can be eaten and will reach Ireland
> will be successful . . . Oh how we should rejoice to see a ship sail out of
> Carlisle bay with a cargo of our native provisions, contributed as a free
> will offering of Christian amity by the free peasants of Barbados to their
> distressed brethren in Ireland.[113]

The Barbados committee raised the large sum of £2,650.10s.98d. A high portion of this money, £2,000, had been granted by the local Assembly, who simultaneously passed a resolution that:

> the inhabitants of Her Majesty's ancient and loyal colony of Barbados, impressed with feelings of deep sympathy for their poor, distressed fellow subjects, are desirous, through the Legislature, of testifying the same by the grant from a Public Treasury of the island.[114]

St Andrew's Anglican Church in the north of the island, which had been destroyed by the 'Great Hurricane' of 1831, and was in the process of being rebuilt after 1846, raised an additional £27.17s.5d.

A number of collections were made on the island of Bermuda. The sum of £62 was raised in a general collection, £109.0s.2d. by officers and other in the Naval establishment, and £113.7s.6d. by the Twentieth Regiment. On 21 April, the House of Assembly, which was based in Hamilton and comprised exclusively of large proprietors, voted to give £500.[115] The Minutes of the House stated that 'the sum of £500 be remitted to the Secretary of State for the Colonies to be applied towards the relief of persons suffering from Famine in Ireland, Scotland, or in any other part of the United Kingdom'.[116] Five separate donations came from the island of St Christopher (also known as St Kitts), in the West Indies. St Kitt's had been variously under Spanish, British and French jurisdiction, with the British regaining control of it in 1783. To maintain the island's sugar production, slaves had been brought from Africa, Ireland and Scotland. As part of the British Empire, the island had been included in the 1833 legislation that abolished slavery. On 31 March 1847, two members of the Legislature, Mr Cock and Mr Davoren, raised a motion to give £500 to Ireland and Scotland.[117] Following on their motion, on 8 April, the following resolution was passed, 'That the sum of £500 sterling be voted in aid of the depressed Irish and Scotch and that his honour the president be requested to transmit same to the Right Honourable, the Secretary of State for the colonies'.[118]

The congregation of St George's Anglican Church, in the capital of Basseterre, contributed £80 to the British Relief Association. The church had been destroyed by an earthquake in 1842, followed by a hurricane in 1843. The congregation continued to worship in the ruins of the old one, until a new church was opened in 1856.[119] Other donations from St Kitts included two separate ones from the Church of St Peter, also in Basseterre, of £8.14s. and £21.2s.9d. A more unusual donation was made by 'Negroes belonging to the Congregation under the charge of the Moravian Missionaries'. They raised £15.17s.10d. In the eighteenth century, Moravian missionaries, trained in Saxony, had been sent to the West Indies. Although Protestant, they remained apart from the other Protestant churches.[120] The donation was channelled through the Rev George Wall Westerby, a Yorkshireman, who did much to develop Moravian missionary work throughout the Caribbean.[121]

Multiple donations came from Jamaica, including several ones from British troops stationed there. In addition, the parish of St Ann's raised £50, the result of two separate collections. St Ann's Bay was about 50 miles from Kingston, where the main relief committee was located. The collection was commenced by the local stipendiary magistrate, T. A. Dillon. Dillon, an Irishman, sent a direct appeal to the inhabitants of St Ann's, telling them that 'famine – unmitigated famine – without a parallel in the history of the world, has prostrated an entire nation'. He asked, 'Imagine a dying infant seeking nourishment from the breast of a dead woman'.[122] When forwarding his contributions to the Colonial Secretary, Dillon admitted to a further purpose, namely, 'to bring under Your Lordships observation every circumstance calculated to raise the inhabitants of this island in Your Lordship's estimation'.[123] Other donations from Jamaica included ones from the people of Montego Bay who gave £111, while those of Trelawny contributed £475. The Lord Bishop of the Island contributed £1,360, while the island Legislature voted £500 for distribution between Ireland and Scotland; £300 to the former and £200 to the latter.[124] Individual donations from Jamaica included £4 from Hinton East, £1.1s. from Mrs Dorothy Reddish and £90 from the Honourable G. Shaw. The Kingston Relief Committee raised £1,146.17s.

The island of St Lucia donated £604.0s.11d. The small island of Tobago, which had only been part of the British Empire since 1814, held a meeting in the Scarborough Court House on 30 March, which was attended by local dignitaries, with the island's Governor in the Chair. The meeting decided that all classes of people should be invited to donate as, 'a substantial expression of our sympathy for the sufferings of our fellow subjects'.[125] When forwarding £310.3s.5d. to the Colonial Secretary, the Governor explained:

Although this is only a mite compared in comparison with the gigantic efforts made by the richer provinces for the relief of our destitute fellow countrymen, Your Lordship will learn with pleasure that the negro population of Tobago have come forward on this occasion with much liberality and good feeling.[126]

Aid from afar

It was not only the West Indies that supported the British Relief Association. A public subscription on the island of Mauritius raised £2,800. This was followed by a second donation of £220 that included £111.16s.11d. from the Seychelles Islands and £16.7s from Rodrigues. A public subscription in British Guiana, a British colony located in South America, raised £3,170.5s.8d. Other remittances from Guiana totalled £1,200. When forwarding these donations, Governor Light pointed to the fact that 'among the subscriptions from the districts, those of many Coolies are to be ranked, who have contributed a day's wages cheerfully'.[127] In a further communication, he commented that subscriptions had been made from every 'class, grade and complexion'.[128] St Helena, an island in the South Atlantic and a British colony, which had been rendered famous by Napoleon's exile and ultimate death there in 1821, raised £8.10s. To this sum, the men of the regiment serving on the island, added £40. H. J. Lord of La Guayra [sic], the British Vice-Consul in Venezuela, contributed £10.10s.[129] Contrary to the initial expectations of the British Relief Association, the desire to help the Irish poor extended well beyond the confines of the British Empire. A collection in the Colonial Bank at St Juan, Porto Rico [sic], an overseas Spanish colony, raised £146.13s.4d. British residents in Mexico raised £652.0s.10d. British subjects in Bogotá, the capital of Columbia, raised £140. A collection in Caracas in Venezuela raised £13.4s. Collections were made in Brazil. Residents in Rio de Janeiro contributed £327.7s.6d. The English, German and Swiss inhabitants of Bahia in the north of the country donated £142.15s.3d, while a subscription by British subjects in Pernambuco raised £234.12s.3d.

Thousands of miles away on the Continent of Africa, exertions were made on behalf of the famine poor of Ireland and Scotland. Two collections were made in Grahamstown, situated on the eastern Cape of Good Hope, raising a total of £300. A joint subscription from a public concert and a collection in the St Mary the Virgin's Anglican Church in Port Elizabeth raised £69. This settlement had only been established in 1825 and the Rev Francis McClelland had been appointed its first Colonial Chaplain.[130] Contributions to the British Association were also received from Asia. The British possessions in China of Hong Kong, Shanghae [sic] and Canton – won as a consequence of the aggressive Opium Wars – raised £1,426.15s.8d. A British resident in Hong Kong, John Hylam, gave £4.10s. An Irish Fund, established in Singapore, sent £31 via the banking company of Rawson, Norton and Company. The bank sent its own donation of £100. A remittance of £30 was forwarded from Penang in the Straits of Malacca, a British possession since 1786, via J. Bercher, Esquire.

Multiple donations came from Europe. Germany, which since 1815 had been a loose confederation of 39 states, came to Ireland's assistance. The shipping company of Eimbcke and Shipmann in Hamburg donated £15. Ludwig Leonard Günther, a Nuremberg businessman, gave £1.10s. A collection in the Protestant Episcopal Church in Nuremburg raised £42.10s. A donation of £122.9s. was raised in Berlin and sent via the Earl of Westmoreland, John Fane, the 11th Earl of Westmoreland and the British Ambassador in that city since 1841. The Bishop of Hildesheim in Saxony sent £19.15s.6d., the proceeds of a collection 'in accordance with the Circular Letter of His Holiness the Pope'. Subscriptions from Munich totalled £112. British residents in Wiesbaden in southern Germany gave £67.16s., while a local German resident gave £1.13s.6d. The Rev Thiessen, the pastor of Cologne, sent £3.13s.

Numerous contributions came from France, which had historical and religious links with Ireland. N. Johnston and Sons, china merchants in Bordeaux, sent £217.2s.8d. One of the owners, David Johnston, was the adopted son of a successful Irish merchant. He had been Mayor of Bordeaux from 1838 to 1842.[131] The Johnston family was also famous for its wine cellar, which was described by a travel writer visiting the region as 'a subterraneous wonderland'.[132] English residents in Caen in Normandy gave £17, with a local church raising a further £11. The British Church in Dieppe raised £12 at an Offertory made during Lent. A collection of £17 was collected at Liseaux near Caen. An anonymous donation from 'G.S.' of ten shillings was sent via the British Consul in Calais. British residents in Marseilles gave £71.1s. Yet again, donations cut across traditional religious divides. The English Congregation at Avanches La Manche in Normandy sent £50. The Catholic Order of the Holy Sepulchre in Paris sent £21.11s.3d. The Anglican congregation of St Servin, situated near to St Malo in western France, collected £72, which they sent via their English-born minister, the Rev Samuel Symons.[133] Trustees of the British Protestant Church in Le Havre gave £91. Messrs Lafitte, Blount and Company in Paris sent a remittance of £259.17s.11d. A few years earlier, Edward Blount, an Irishman, had helped O'Connell set up the Provincial Bank in Ireland, assisted by the Anglo-Jewish banker, Moses Montefiore.[134] British residents in Pau in the south of France contributed £295.5s.6d. following a sermon given by their Anglican chaplain, the Rev E. Hedges. Hedges was an admirer of the evangelical Rev Alexander Dallas, who had established a number of proselytizing missions in Ireland. In the following years, Hedges made a number of contributions to the Irish Church Mission Society for the Conversion of Catholics.[135]

Italy, which like Germany comprised of a number of states and king-doms some of which were under foreign control, donated to the British Relief Association. A committee established in Florence raised £500. English servants in that city donated £9.13s.9d. The proceeds of a society ball held at San Donato in Lazio amounted to £891.17s.2d. The ball was hosted by Prince Anitole de Demidoff who had been born in Russia in 1812 and was a wealthy mining and munitions magnate. He spent much of his time between Paris and Florence.[136] Similarly, a ball was held in Rome hosted by Marcus Paterson. It raised £192.12s.10d., which he sent to London via the banking company of Maguay, Pakenham and Smythe.[137] Other donations came from Rome: a general collection raised £67.5s.0d.; a concert for Ireland, £73.17s.6d.; and a collection at an English chapel on the Day of Thanksgiving, £8.13s.8d. The British- and American-owned firm, Gardner, Rose and Co., which owned mines near Palermo in southern Italy, sent £20.[138] The shipping company of Lang and Freeland, from their base in Trieste, sent £100. J. H. Rutherford Esq. of Trieste donated £10.4s.5d. for Ireland, which was in addition to the 100 florins he had already sent to help Scotland. Vito Terni, who was associated with the Naples shipping company of the same name and was of Italian-Jewish origin, gave £25. Madame Harriet Meuricoffre of Naples gave £20. The English-born Harriet was the sister of the Victorian social reformer and feminist, Josephine Butler.[139] A donation of £178.14s.10d. was sent from Palermo.

Many miscellaneous donations came from other places in Europe. Donations from Spain included £20 from James Webster Gordon, a wine merchant in Madeira. Fifty pounds was sent from Lisbon and from the city of Oporto. Smith Woodhouse, a port-producing company founded by Christopher Smith MP in 1784, sent £100.[140] British residents in Copenhagen raised £500.0s.9d. Three collections were made in The Hague, in the Netherlands. In addition to a remittance of £171, an additional £90 came from a collection at a local Episcopal Church, while the sale of a volume of Dutch poetry raised £24. The Garrison and people of Corfu sent £252.6s.0d. A donation of £99.9s. came from Gibraltar, with a further £23.3s.11d. from the Rev Thomas Hall, a Wesleyan minister on the island. Officers and clerks employed in Gibraltar's Commissariat Department donated one day's pay, which amounted to £13.2s. Elsewhere in Europe, the Rev William Sergison, chaplain to the English Congregation at Moines in Belgium, sent £9 on their behalf. A sermon in the British Church in Ostend, also in Belgium, raised £22.0s.7d. The Mediterranean Islands of Malta and Gozo, which had been part of the British Empire since 1814, sent £720.12s.4d. A number of donations came from Russia. The trading company of Messrs Brandt, which operated out of the Russian ports of Archangel, St Petersburg and Riga, donated £100, with a further £100 from their sister company in London.[141] The city of St Petersburg raised the large sum of £2,440.73. The Rev Matthew Camidge of the British Chapel in Moscow sent £26.13s.10d.[142] Camidge, who had trained in England, had travelled to Russia on behalf of the Russia Company.[143]

The contributions of individuals to the British Association were generous and sometimes intriguing. The Danish-born inventor Chevalier Chaussen, then resident in Bruxelles, contributed £5. Chaussen died in 1862, believed to be insane.[144] Henry Gaederty, Lloyd's Agent in Lübeck in the north of Germany, sent £10.[145] The British Consul at Geneva donated £3.8s. The successful Serbian-born shipowner, Speridione Gopčevich, sent £50 from his business base in Trieste, in the north of Italy.[146] The Italian Marquis Raimondo Montecuccoli Laderchi, a descendant of the notorious seventeenth century military leader Raymond Montecuccoli, gave £100. The Marquis de Thuissy and his son, the Comte George, each gave £5. The Honourable Algernon Gray Tollemache, formerly a British MP who had moved to New Zealand where he made a fortune in land speculation, contributed £300.[147] Madame de Polier Vernand from Lausanne, in the French-speaking part of Switzerland, donated £100. During the French Revolution, many French *emigrés* had fled to Switzerland, and Madame de Polier had been personally acquainted with them.[148]

The poor helping the poor

Finally, as was the case with other charitable appeals, a high proportion of contributions came from people who were themselves poor, ordinary workers, with little disposable income. While the amounts they gave to the British Relief Association might appear small in monetary terms, in terms of disposable income, they represented a real sacrifice. Employers in the industries which had fuelled the revolution in Britain responded to the suffering in Ireland. The individual names of these donors have not been recorded, donations often being made collectively, at the workplace. Workers in Wales made multiple contributions; this included ones from those employed on the Aberdare Railway who gave £28, ironworkers in Abergavenny who raised £60.2s., workers in the Clydach Iron Works, £66.0s.9d. and workers in Dowlais Iron Works who donated £176.17s.10d. In Avon in England, workers in the local copper mines raised £30.2s.6d. Workmen in the Cramlington Colliery in Durham collected £4.6s.6d. Workers in the London lathe-making firm of Holtzapffel & Co. raised £1.11s., while the company's owners gave £3.3s. Employers at John W. Pawley's Company donated £1.10s., which they earned by working a night's overtime. The owner of the company added £1 to this. Workmen employed in the Great Grimsby gave £10. Employers in the Great Western Railway made four separate donations: the Carriage Department at Swindon gave two donations of one day's pay that amounted to £60 and £35.7s.2d.; mechanics gave £1.1s.; and officers, £11.6s.6d. Workers on the Wolverhampton, Newbury and Hungerford Railway made their own collection of £24.13s. Dockers in the new Union Dock in Plymouth, a site developed by the engineering genius Isambard Brunel, donated £18.17s.3d.[149]

It was not just industrial workers who responded. Shop assistants in Allisons in Regents St, London gave £4.4s. Robert Allison and Co. were piano-makers.[150]'A few journeymen hatters' contributed 10s.6d. Shopkeepers in Convent Garden, London raised £20. Letter carriers and sub-sorters at the General Post-Office gave a total of £8.18s.6d. Workmen employed by the silver and goldsmiths, Hunt and Roskell, made six weekly donations that amounted to £7.6s.10d.[151] To this, the owners of the company added £20. Servants also gave. Those employed at 'Fairy Hall' gave 11s., while servants from 'Number 41, Harley Street' gave 14s. Servants in the Royal Household of the Dowager Queen contributed £885.14s.6d., while in the Queen's Royal Household made two donations, one of £217.12s, following by a second of £5. An anonymous donation was made by servants who raised £2 as a result of 'self-denial in beer, sugar, etc.' Servants employed in the Victoria Hotel, Euston Square in London, which had been opened in 1837, gave £5. The hotel had been built to serve travellers to the nearby Euston Railway Station. Even workers without permanent employment responded to the appeal of the British Association. 'Day Labourers on a property of a resident landowners' in Crosby Ravensworth near Appleby in Cumbria, donated £6.3s. At a time when the British economy was facing a credit crisis and high unemployment, these donations represented a considerable personal munificence.

A number of donations to the British Relief Association came from groups who were marginalized – and sometimes even demonized – within early Victorian society. Two contributions came from Pentonville, a Home for Penitent Females in London, which had been opened in 1807 as a charity, 'intended to save those whom the vanity, idleness, and the treachery of man have led astray'.[152] A fast by inmates in the institution raised £1.1s., while a collection made on those days by the officers raised £8.17s. Similar sacrifices were made by other impoverished groups. A fast in an unnamed Foundling Home raised £202. Girls in an anonymous Orphan Asylum gave £1. Females in the House of Occupation in Southwark, London donated £3–10s. The House of Occupation was a charitable institution that accepted children (boys and girls) aged 8 to 18 years, educated them and helped them to find apprenticeships.[153] The Chapel in the Foundling Hospital in London donated the proceeds of a day's fast. The Foundling Hospital, which had opened in 1741, was not a hospital but an institution for 'the maintenance and education of exposed and deserted young children'. After 1801, it admitted only illegitimate children. Such institutions had achieved some notoriety in the 1830s, when Charles Dickens published his own fictionalized account of a foundling child, *Oliver Twist*.[154]

Overall, the range of people who gave to the British Relief Association in 1847 was truly remarkable. Donations not only came from all parts of the world, but they cut across all economic, religious and ethnic divides. The British Relief Association recorded over 15,000 individual donations of which the above are only a small portion. Moreover, it was due the selfless and professional approach of members of the British Association in London, and their agents in Ireland led by Strzelecki, that this assistance reached those people in Ireland who most needed it. Why did so many people feel moved to give money for Ireland? For a few, the motivation for giving appears to have been political expediency or religious conviction; for the vast majority, however, the suffering of the Irish poor touched a humanitarian nerve and unleashed fund-raising efforts on a scale never before seen.

10

'Without distinction of creed or party, nation or colour'.[1] American Aid

People in North America proved to be some of the most generous donors during the Famine, with both rich and poor coming together to help Ireland. While close ties had been forged between the two countries as a consequence of emigration, many of those involved in fund-raising had no immediate connection with Ireland. The first failure of the potato crop had been widely reported by the American press. A number of papers had even speculated that external intervention would be necessary. By the end of 1845, however, some reports from Ireland were suggesting that the food deficit had been exaggerated.[2] Moreover, the shortages were only expected to last for one season, as usually had been the case with failures of the potato crop. After spring 1846, America was involved in a controversial war in Mexico, which dominated much press column space. Consequently, the majority of fund-raising efforts in the United States did not commence until after the second appearance of blight.

The Irish community in Boston proved to be an exception. On 6 January 1846, a meeting of the 'Friends of Ireland' took place in Boston. The main speaker was Rev Dr O'Flaherty of St Mary's parish, a Kerry-born physician.[3] The resolutions passed were overtly political and antagonistic to Britain:

By the fatal connection of Ireland with England, the Rich Grain harvest of the former country are carried off to pay an absentee government, and an absent proprietary; leaving uniformly little behind to support the inhabitants but the potato, which is at best a wretched material of subsistence, and which now appears to be totally destroyed.

More pointedly, it was agreed:

> ... this wicked treatment of a brave and patient, and industrious people, by the British Government, is further confirmation, if such were wanting, of the necessity of an immediate severance of that political connection which now exists between unhappy Ireland and her tyrant sister, and we pledge ourselves to Ireland and to our fellow citizens of this great Republic.

The meeting called on people throughout the United States, 'without distinction of creed or party, nation or colour' to come forward on behalf of Ireland. It set an example by collecting $750.[4]

The early reappearance of blight in the 1846 harvest meant that any doubts about the distress in Ireland disappeared. Every packet-ship from the United Kingdom confirmed stories of Irish suffering. Reports from Ireland were suggesting that communities were breaking down as government relief was no longer saving lives.[5] Within the United States, it became increasingly common to contrast the poverty of Ireland with the wealth of America: 'The granaries of this country overflowing, the poorest living luxuriously, speculators realizing fortunes by dealing in wheat and corn, while the curse of famine is brooding over every rood of land in poor Ireland'.[6] For some American politicians and speculators, the food shortages in Ireland, together with the recent repeal of the Corn Laws, represented a bonanza for American exports, not only in the immediate period, but for some years to come. The American Consul in Belfast even suggested that in the longer term, Indian corn from the United States would replace potatoes as the subsistence food of the Irish poor.[7]

A number of American fund-raising committees commenced limited activities in the latter months of 1846, with New York, Boston, Washington and Jersey City being at the forefront. By this stage, Irish immigrants had been sending money back home privately for some months.[8] It was in the early months of 1847, however, that the movement gathered momentum. Newspapers played an important role in ensuring that the Famine in Ireland and the need for external aid was regularly and prominently featured. The National Era, a weekly paper associated with the abolition movement, made a number of direct appeals to Americans to do something for Ireland. On 4 February 1847, in an article entitled 'Famine – Death from Starvation – Plan of Relief', they informed their readers:

> A nation is on the brink of starvation. Why should not public meetings be called, committees of correspondence appointed, and the mode designated by which contributions of corn, flour and provisions, might be concentrated at given points, so as to be conveyed immediately to Ireland? What a beautiful spectacle it would be! Ships freighted with the rich gifts of one nation to the perishing millions of another![9]

The paper went on to suggest:

> Let a public meeting of Congress and Citizens of Washington be called to meet in the Hall of the House of Representatives. Let a Central National Committee of Relief be organized. Let points be designated where the surplus produce of the country might be deposited . . . Let the plan be published in every paper in every State, local and general . . . In this way, without feeling it, the United States might concentrate and direct its magnificent charities, so as to save Ireland from destruction.[10]

Even as this appeal was being made, people throughout the United States were beginning to organize on behalf of the poor of Ireland.

Philadelphia

One of the first meetings to be held in the United States on behalf of Ireland took place in Philadelphia. The organizers published an account of their proceedings, thus leaving a record of the logistical steps that were necessary to raise funds and deliver aid to Ireland. The initial meeting had taken place at the Globe Hotel in Philadelphia on 17 November 1846. It had been convened by John Binns, a former Alderman, and was described as a select gathering of 'gentlemen'. Binns himself had been born in Dublin in 1772 and had participated in the 1798 rebellion.[11] His decision to call the meeting had been motivated by reports made by recent immigrants to the city of the suffering in Ireland. Binns explained:

> It is thought to be the duty of this city, which has so often been among the foremost in works of mercy and charity, to do something for the famishing people of Ireland. What that something shall be, we do not undertake to say.[12]

This meeting, considered to be the first major public meeting in the United States for this purpose, was chaired by Robert Taylor, a local immigration agent and active member of the Friendly Sons of St Patrick.[13] The Friendly Sons, a social organization for Irish Americans, had been founded in 1771. One of its early, and honorary, members had been George Washington. John Binns was also a member.[14] At the meeting, a committee was appointed with the aim of convening a larger public meeting and establishing a Philadelphia Irish Relief Fund. To this end, the committee prepared an appeal, which was issued on 26 November 1846 and addressed, 'To the Inhabitants of the City and County of Philadelphia'. Again, the abundance of the American harvest was contrasted with the situation in Ireland, where:

> All the assistance of the Government, and all the aid of the wealthy and benevolent of their own land, are altogether insufficient, and must very soon become utterly inadequate to meet the necessities and distresses of the

people; and unless prompt and vigorous measures to avert it be adopted by the friends of humanity in other nations, wide-spread famine, with its dire accompaniments of disease and death, are about to depopulate a large portion of the country.[15]

The address concluded by saying:

It appears to be particularly appropriate that this great work of 'brotherly love' should have its commencement in Philadelphia, whose example it is confidently hoped will induce other cities and communities to unite their exertions to ours on behalf of a sister nation now in deep distress.[16]

Subscriptions lists were prepared for the purpose of purchasing grain, flour or Indian corn to ship to Ireland. A separate appeal was made to local clergy, asking them to use their pulpits to encourage donations to the fund.[17] Impressively, the Philadelphia committee did not confine its work to its immediate locality, but extended its appeal to other parts of the US, particularly the southern and western states. The first request was shrewdly timed to coincide with the day appointed by the Governor of Pennsylvania for public thanksgiving and praise for the abundant harvests in the country.[18] A local newspaper, the *Pennsylvanian*, supported these fund-raising efforts by pointing out that George Washington had been 'an *adopted* son of Ireland and was proud to have been so'.[19]

Within a few weeks, the Philadelphia committee had raised $825, which was forwarded to the Society of Friends in Dublin.[20] Money continued to pour in. Unsurprisingly, the Irish community and local Quakers were the first to respond.[21] The donations from Quakers, many of whom had no connection with Ireland, were described as being 'liberal and prompt, and made with the quiet of unostentatious charity'.[22] Despite evidence of widespread sympathy, the committee believed that more needed to be done and, in mid-February, the Mayor, John Swift, convened a town meeting to take place in the Chinese Museum Building in Ninth Street. The meeting was well attended and 'men of all creeds and parties were present'.[23] Binns made an emotional speech in which he contrasted the great nation that America had become since achieving independence with, 'that dark, deep, and general distress, with the gloom of night, overshadows unhappy Ireland; her people perish under the pangs of hunger, and are swept by pestilence; they exist in shelterless cabins, with scant garments to cover them, and fall by thousands into unkept, too often uncovered, graves'.[24] From the outset, a business-like approach was evident. Mayor Swift was appointed to act as President and nine Vice-Presidents were chosen, included the lawyer and former member of the House of Representatives, the Honorable Horace Binney.[25] A Treasurer was appointed, as were collectors to receive contributions, a committee was created to forward receipts to Ireland (breadstuffs as far as possible, otherwise money) and a corresponding committee was also created.[26] In total, seven committees were formed for the districts of Northern Liberties, Kensington, Southwark, Spring Garden, Passyunk and Moyamensing.[27]

A second meeting was held on 18 February in Congress Hall, with Joseph R. Chandler, in the Chair, and a further appeal for money and provisions was made 'to all citizens of the Commonwealth'. A request was made to the managers of all local canals and railroads requesting that provisions for Ireland be allowed to travel free of charge.[28] Offices in the Hall of Independence in the State House were made available for use by the committee, indicating the level of support for the Irish that existed at many levels.[29] Inevitably, Irish groups were at the forefront of these efforts. The Hibernian Society of Philadelphia (originally part of the Friendly Sons of St Patrick) decided unanimously on 10 March that, 'In consequence of the distress that now pervades all of Ireland, a convivial celebration on St Patrick's Day is deemed inappropriate, and it is therefore recommended that the customary anniversary dinner be omitted this year'. This action was deemed appropriate on the grounds that, 'Most of the members of the Hibernian Society are connected by blood and nativity with the people of Ireland, and all of them are bound to the inhabitants of that land by the strongest ties of sympathy'.[30] One member, John Moss, contributed an additional $50 to the money thus raised.[31] When he died on 17 June 1847, tributes were made to his 'humanity and benevolence'.[32]

Money was raised in a variety of ways. The Rev Henry Giles, a Unitarian minister and noted orator, was asked by the Philadelphia committee to deliver a lecture on their behalf. Giles had been born in County Wexford in 1809 and emigrated to the United States in 1840, where he achieved a reputation as a skilled lecturer on topics ranging from Christianity to Shakespeare.[33] The committee recorded that 'a handsome sum accrued from the proceeds of his eloquent discourse'.[34] The profits from a benefit performance by John Collins at a local theatre were also given to the Philadelphia Relief Fund.[35] The performer in question, who had been born in Lucan, near Dublin, and was a tenor, comedian and actor, had emigrated to the United States in 1846.[36] In recognition of his contribution, the local Hibernian Society made Collins an Honorary Member as, 'a compliment justly due to him, from his handsome and generous conduct in giving his professional services in behalf of the Irish Relief Fund, by which the sum of $430 was realized'.[37]

Initially, some money was sent to Ireland in the form of bills of exchange, but the committee quickly realized that sending money simply contributed to an increase in the price of foodstuffs. The committee instead decided to use its funds to buy 'cheap and wholesome' food within the US. This scheme was generously supported by 'warm-hearted' farmers in the state and by the decision of the Pennsylvania Legislature to waive all tolls for the carriage of such items. However, a request to the Secretary of the Navy for a government ship to carry the goods to Ireland was turned down, although the committee accepted that it had been with good reason.[38]

The food from the Irish Relief Fund was transported to a number of locations in Ireland, but it was all put under the charge of the Central Committee of the Society of Friends in Dublin. As with all relief from the US, freight charges for the transatlantic journey were paid by the British government. The shipments from the Philadelphia committee were:

Brig *St George*, to Cork $9,350.00
Barque *John Welsh*, to Londonderry $9,768.24
Barque *Ohio*, to Dublin $12,723.75
Barque *Adle*, to Donegal $6,468.77
Barque *Lydia Ann*, to Limerick $9,282.50
Brig *Islam*, to Galway $11,340.62
Brig *Baracoa*, to Belfast $9,291.50
Brig *Tar*, to Liverpool $3,518.00
Total $71,743.38[39]

All of the cargoes arrived safely. In September 1847, when acknowledging receipt of this bounty, Joseph Bewley and Jonathan Pim informed the Philadelphia committee that while they hoped distress in the following year would not be as general, they were holding on to some of the foodstuffs sent to them 'reserving them for a time of severer pressure, which seems likely to come'.[40]

The Irish Relief Fund in Philadelphia had officially commenced work on 9 February and it ended its operations on 13 May 1847. Like many other fund-raisers in the US, those who managed the Fund believed that assistance to Ireland would not be necessary following the harvest. During their four months' existence, they had raised $48,949.53 in cash and contributions-in-kind, of which only $63.10 had been absorbed by administrative costs, such as stationery and printing.[41] The amount received later rose to over $72,000.[42] Contributions to the Philadelphia Fund had come from a number of other states, including Maryland, Virginia, Ohio, Illinois, Kentucky, Missouri and New Jersey. In contrast to many relief bodies, the Philadelphia committee decided not to publish names of individual donors, on the grounds that, 'such publicity might have been deemed indelicate on the part of the committee, and offensive to the truly charitable feelings of the donors'.[43] However, they did reveal that those who gave were predominantly factory or manual workers, whom they described as being:

... activated by a most benevolent rivalry, to unite their means, and present them for the assistance of the sufferers.

Though the people on whose behalf the appeal for aid was made, were of a single nation, yet the efforts for their relief were not confined to those from that country, or of the same descent; the work was one of general benevolence, and it demanded and received the co-operation of Pennsylvania at large ... and the response was from men and women of all creeds, Jews and Christians, of every variety of religious denominations, Churches, assemblies, philanthropic societies, business communities and even parties of pleasure, found one great and good end presented by the assistance they could render to the cause of humanity.[44]

On 19 October 1847, the Philadelphia committee held a final meeting to report on its business and present an audited account of its transactions. Thanks were offered to all those who had donated 'to the cause of humanity; with special tribute made to the people of Pennsylvania and Ohio'. The works of the Quakers in Dublin was also commended:

> . . . for their fidelity, diligence and exemplary impartiality in distributing among the poor in Ireland, the relief sent to them from Philadelphia. We are aware that exalted and disinterested feelings influenced the Friends in Ireland, with whom we correspond, and that thanks from us formed no part of any reward which they may have anticipated; still it is due to ourselves that we should declare our thankfulness, and we hope that this expression of it may be acceptable to those by whom it is so well deserved.[45]

The local newspapers were thanked for their assistance, as was the local council, which had allowed them to use the Hall of Independence for their meetings. It was decided to publish the committee's proceedings in pamphlet form and then to give their papers to the care of the Hibernian Society. It appears that they – rightly – wanted a permanent record of their generous response.

At the final meeting, special tribute was paid to a local merchant, Allen Cuthbert, for allowing his warehouses on Lombard Street Wharf to be used, free of charge, for the storage of provisions.[46] Additionally, he had undertaken to supervise personally all of the shipments in and out of the city.[47] In honour of his contribution, Cuthbert was presented with a framed letter of thanks, the committee noting, 'Conduct such as this confers honor not only on himself but on the community of which he is a worthy member'.[48] Philadelphia-born Cuthbert was also honoured by the Hibernian Society for his contribution of 'time, money and use of his warehouses', which had been crucial in ensuring that aid got to Ireland in a timely manner. In appreciation, he was elected an honorary member of the Society.[49] In December 1847, the Hibernian Society honoured two other men, Thomas Robins and Thomas Allibone Esquires, who were not members but had worked with the Irish Relief Fund 'with untiring zeal in the good cause . . . and to whom some token of our grateful appreciation of their efficient and disinterested labours in due'.[50]

While the Irish Relief Fund in Philadelphia was the largest committee in that city, funds for Ireland were also raised by other groups. The local Episcopal Church sent breadstuffs to the value of $6,400 to the Archbishops of Armagh and Dublin, to be distributed by them 'without regard to sect'.

Archbishop Whately of Dublin paid tribute to this initiative in the House of Lords, explaining:

> He had received, not long ago, intelligence of the arrival of a large cargo of corn meal, purchased by the contributions of the people of Philadelphia, through the suggestion and instrumentality of Bishop Potter, a Protestant Episcopalian bishop, who announced to him the collection that had been made. He had received intelligence of the arrival of the first cargo, and was also informed that another was on the way ... He trusted he need not assure most of their Lordships that the distribution of those contributions was made in such a manner as would most effectually carry into effect the beneficent purposes of the donors.[51]

The city's Catholic churches raised $3,000 and directed that this be used in the same way. The banks in Philadelphia estimated that private donations sent directly to individuals in Ireland amounted to $311,200. A separate collection was made by committee formed by 'colored citizens' of the Northern Liberties and Kensington. At a meeting held on 12 March, it was agreed:

> an afflicting calamity has befallen the people of Ireland and Scotland, and hundreds are starving to death for the want of the commonest food, and we believing it right to sympathize with and assist our fellow-men of all climes and countries, therefore, be it *Resolved*, That a committee of five be appointed, to collect and receive such contributions as many be made.[52]

A committee was formed consisting of Isaac W. Riggs, James Hallowell, Francis Faucet, John Diton and Moses Davis, with Charles Davis as President and Cyrus Burris as Secretary. They recommended that all the money raised by 'the coloured people of this country' be entrusted to the escaped slave, Frederick Douglass, who had been travelling in Ireland and Scotland.[53] Overall, therefore, the Irish Relief Fund of Philadelphia was only part of a mosaic of charitable aid from the city and its environs. The committee itself estimated that:

> Thousands have been remitted through other channels, of which no information was obtained; and it is therefore deemed a fair calculation, to estimate the public and private contributions from and through Philadelphia, for the relief of the suffering poor in Ireland, at *half a million dollars.*[54]

Brooklyn

As had been the case in Philadelphia, fund-raising for Ireland in Brooklyn commenced in late 1846. At that stage, Brooklyn was a fast-growing city with a population of almost 40,000. The *Brooklyn Eagle,* which between

1846 and 1848 was under the editorship of Walt Whitman, carried many articles describing the unfolding situation in Ireland. As early as May 1846, the paper was including reports from the Irish *Evening Post* appealing for provisions to be sent from America to assist the 'frightful famine' in Ireland. The *Eagle* responded by proposing that a public meeting be convened.[55] However, it was the second, more complete, failure of the potato crop that prompted direct interventions. The first public meeting in Brooklyn for Irish relief took place on 27 November 1846. Although the attendance was small, $133.50 was collected, with individual donations ranging from $25 to 50 cents.[56] A second meeting was held on 1 December. Two days prior to this meeting, the *Eagle* had enjoined its readers:

> While we are all enjoying our Thanksgiving dinners, it were well to think of the meeting which takes place on Friday night for aiding, as far as we can here, in relieving the distress at present prevailing through so many parts of Ireland. Remember on Friday evening! And remember too, that every man must act *himself,* however humble his influence, for every man can (and ought to in this case) do something.[57]

At the third meeting, on the 8 December, the Mayor was nominated Treasurer and five men were appointed in each ward to collect subscriptions.[58]

At the beginning of 1847, news from Ireland remained unremittingly awful. Reports carried by the steamer *Hibernia* prompted the citizens of Brooklyn to convene a further public meeting to assist 'millions of our unhappy fellow beings across the Atlantic'. It was attended by 250 people and described as 'enthusiastic' and 'spirited'. Those present included Mayor Stryker, and a number of ex-mayors, Henry C. Murphy, Joseph Sprague, Jeremiah Johnson, C. P. Smith, Jonathan Trotter, George Hall, the Rev Dr Baugs, Rev Dr Cox and Reverends Farley and Thayer. 'Several ladies' were also present. The opening address by General Johnson was deeply critical of the British government:

> What has Great Britain, the greatest and wealthiest nation on the face of the earth done for them as a nation? They ought to have entirely relieved this suffering, but they have not done it. They have extended sympathy enough, but the Irish people want something more substantial.

Dr Cox, who had no Irish background but had visited Ireland in 1833, endorsed this sentiment, averring that, 'England had thought too much of self and too little of duty'.[59] Stryker also spoke, but his criticisms were directed against the Irish Repeal Association. He referred to money that had been sent for repeal and suggested it had done little good. To ensure that their assistance was wisely used, he suggested they send provisions and not money.[60] One of the outcomes of the meeting was that a 'philanthropic' committee of 13 men was appointed with 'the venerable patriarch of Brooklyn', General

Jeremiah Johnson, as President. The Vice-Presidents were F. B. Stryker, H. C. Murphy, George Hall, J. Sprague, Jonathan Trotter and C. P. Smith, and the Secretaries were, J. Greenwood, A. J. Spooner, A. Campbell and J. M. Van Cott. More unusually, a Brooklyn Ladies' Committee was formed. In the week following the meeting, the ladies of Brooklyn held several tea parties to raise money for Ireland.[61] The women also helped to organize clothing collections. Support was given to the ladies' committees in both Brooklyn and in Ireland by R. J. Todd, a merchant based in Fulton Street, who agreed to sell goods made by Irish women and sent to him through the Dublin Ladies' Committee for All Ireland.[62]

A further meeting was convened in Brooklyn on 5 February in Hall's Exchange Building, home of the Supreme Court since 1838, 'to devise some means of diverting the great calamity with which Providence has seen fit to visit Ireland'. The gathering was described as being without 'regard to sect, party or creed' and 'several eminent individuals' attended.[63] Henry C. Murphy, lawyer and Democratic Congressman,[64] chaired the meeting and Alden J. Spooner, who was regarded as one of the city's most distinguished citizens, acted as Secretary.[65] Murphy described, in detail, the state of Ireland, in order to show 'the imperative claim of that nation upon the charities of a Christian people'. The meeting agreed that the Famine in Ireland was 'unexampled in modern times' that 'no truly enlightened, humane and Christian people can hear such an appeal without making determined efforts to answer it'. It was decided that the committee should publish regular accounts of their progress.[66] By 19 February, over $2,000 had been collected in Brooklyn. This sum included contributions of $250 sent via Judge Hammond, over $600 from a lecture given by Mr Giles in the Institute, $700 from workmen at the dry dock and $500 from private sources. However, the people of Brooklyn were indignant that their donations were being claimed by some newspapers as coming from New York City.[67]

On 20 February, the *Brooklyn Eagle* reprinted a letter from Nicholas Cummins, a Justice of the Peace in Cork, to the Duke of Wellington.[68] Cummins's appeal appeared in several American newspapers.[69] It graphically described the suffering of the poor in the region around Skibbereen. These reports were important in keeping the condition of Ireland in public consciousness. As in Philadelphia, money was raised in Brooklyn number of imaginative ways. On the evening of 23 February, a concert was given by the Alleghanian singers.[70] This singing group had made their first public appearance in New York on 17 June 1846.[71] The *Eagle* encouraged locals to support the concert, adding 'The programme of the songs is very attractive'.[72] Further concerts followed.[73] One of the stars set to appear at a concert to be held on 11 May in Gothic Hall, Miss Julia Northall, had to withdraw due to a sore throat.[74] The singer, a soprano, was the daughter of Dr William K. Northall, dentist, author, playwright and editor of the *Brooklyn Advertiser*.[75]

A number of committees in the United States aimed to raise sufficient funds to fill their own designated relief ship. This was the case in Brooklyn, with donations being used to obtain a 'Brooklyn ship', the *Patrick Henry,* which left for Ireland in early May. The ship contained provisions to the value of $1,166-07 and, while the committee suggested it go to the Newry area, they made it clear that their primary concern was 'that of relieving the greatest distress'. Following the lead of the General Relief Committee in New York, the Brooklyn committee directed their cargo to the care of the Society of Friends in Dublin.[76] The Brooklyn men in charge of this operation were William M. Harris, Freeman Hunt and David Leavitt. They expressed the hope that 'our mite may arrive in time to alleviate the miseries of a few of the many sufferers of your devoted countrymen'.[77] In addition to the *Patrick Henry,* the Brooklyn committee commenced loading a second ship, the British brig *Ann [Amy] Maria,* but were unable to fill it. The New York General Relief Committee agreed to complete the cargo on their behalf.[78] The second ship was destined for the west of Ireland, and it carried 530 lbs of corn meal and 200 bbls of 'navy bread'.[79] A local newspaper commented 'Well has Brooklyn deported herself, under the call from that unhappy island, distant in situation, but close in our hearts'. Bewley and Pim in Dublin responded by acknowledging, 'the deep sense we entertain of the extraordinary kindness and liberality of the American people towards our country in the present season of sore calamity, and how gratefully we appreciate that confidence in us which has led them to so large an extent to select this committee as an almoner of their bounty'.[80]

As in many places, the charitable momentum in Brooklyn was short lived and largely confined to early 1847. Within months of commencement, however, charity towards the Irish poor in Brooklyn had not only dissipated, but the treatment and cost of famine immigrants had become part of wider political divisions, which were played out in the local press over the next few years. The *Brooklyn Advertiser,* which supported the American Whig Party, accused the *Eagle,* a Democratic supporter, of not assisting fundraising efforts, while claiming to be the first local newspaper to intervene on behalf of Ireland. These allegations were strenuously denied by the *Eagle* which retaliated by accusing the *Advertiser* of opposing to Irish repeal and being antagonistic to its (now dead) leader O'Connell.[81] The *Advertiser* reproached the Democrats for allegedly betraying the newly arrived Irish immigrants, claiming that hundreds of these 'penniless, friendless and hungry' people had been forced to seek shelter in the Brooklyn alms house, 'And now, because their sustenance has caused an increase of costs to the county, the *Eagle* is appealing to Irish-born citizens to vote against the Whigs, on the grounds of extravagance'.[82] In turn, the *Eagle* blamed Whig mismanagement rather than Irish immigration for the massive increase in local poor rates.[83] Sadly, both Irish and American politics had entered what had been a magnificent fund-raising effort for the Irish poor, and suffering in Ireland had provided a new platform for political point-scoring in the city of Brooklyn. Nonetheless, the efforts on behalf of Ireland set a standard for later fund-raising. In March 1850, the *Eagle* reported that a ball was to be held in Tammany Hall to raise donations for New York volunteers who had returned from the Mexico War. The paper, pointing to the 'liberal' donations that had been given to the Irish poor in 1847 and to the Hungarian revolutionaries in 1848, asked that the same should now be done on behalf of American citizens.[84]

Charleston, New Orleans, Albany and Boston

People in the South of the United States proved to be generous benefactors to Ireland. Inevitably, perhaps, the sensitive issue of slavery underpinned some of the discussions regarding the poverty of Ireland and her relationship with Britain.[85] In the preceding years, many Repeal Associations had been formed throughout United States, but a number had fallen out with Daniel O'Connell because of his fierce attacks on American slave owners.[86] It was to be expected that the condition of the poor Irish should be compared to that of the slaves – who were not dying of starvation. The Famine provided an opportunity to demonstrate the morality and generosity of people involved in slavery. Successful fund-raising activities took place in Charleston, mostly coordinated by the Charleston Hibernian Society, many members of which were wealthy Protestants.[87] At the time of the Famine, New Orleans was the largest city in the south and the third largest in the nation. Its rapid population growth was due primarily to recent large-scale immigration from Ireland, with many coming to work on building the New Basin Canal. On 5 February 1847, a public meeting was held presided over by Isaac Johnson, the Governor of Louisiana, and Henry Clay of Kentucky, a previous Whig Secretary of State and Presidential candidate. Sargent Smith Prentiss, former Whig Representative for Mississippi and noted orator, also spoke. Prentiss's speech, lasting almost an hour, was described as 'sublime', while keeping his audience 'spell-bound'. During it, Prentiss explained that Ireland had 'given to the world more than its share of genius'. He contrasted this greatness with how 'gaunt and ghastly famine seized a nation with its struggling grasp'. He concluded by imploring the audience to 'look at your family, smiling, in rosy health, and then think of the pale, famine-pinched cheeks of the poor children of Ireland'.[88] The speeches by Prentiss and Clay were reprinted in newspapers throughout the country.[89] During the meeting, a committee was formed chaired by the Abdiel Daily Crossman, the Mayor of New Orleans. A subscription of $15,000 was raised, 'to alleviate, in the most general and equitable manner, the sufferings of the people of Ireland'.[90] This money was then sent to George Bancroft, United States Ambassador to the United Kingdom. He, in turn, forwarded it to the British Prime Minister, Lord John Russell, pointing out in an accompanying letter:

I am compelled to say that the sympathy of the people of the United States with the sudden and overwhelming calamity which has befallen Ireland is earnest and universal, and that, mindful of their European origin, they share the afflictions and rejoice in the prosperity of the nations from which they sprang.[91]

Russell responded immediately by sending the money to the Central Relief Committee in Dublin, which was presided over by Lord Kildare. The Prime Minister added his own personal thanks to the people of New Orleans:

The earnest and universal sympathy of the people of the United States with our distressed countrymen in Ireland is most gratifying to the people of Great Britain and Ireland, and that Her Majesty the Queen has seen, with the highest satisfaction, the manifestations of generosity and charity of a nation sprung from the same origin as ourselves.[92]

The publicity given to the New Orleans's donation was deprecated by one American newspaper, the anti-slavery *National Era*. It described the letters as 'correspondence of much pretension between Mr Bancroft and Lord John Russell', while pointing out:

The hundreds of thousands of alms from other sections of the country can be safely delivered without the diplomatic midwifery of Ministers and Premiers, but the 'magnificent' charity of New Orleans must have as many important aids and witnesses at the delivery as a royal heir.

Why could not Mr Bancroft have ascertained, in a private way, from Lord John Russell or anybody else, to whom to send the gift, and then without further trouble, transmitted it, without calling all the world to witness?[93]

The money raised in New Orleans had included a $300 donation from the small, local Hebrew community.[94] Similar efforts were being made by Jews in New York. On 8 March, Hazan Jacques Judah Lyons addressed a gathering at Shearith Israel for the purpose of raising funds for Ireland. He pointed out that there was one indestructible and all-powerful link with the hungry in Ireland: 'That link, my brethren, is HUMANITY! Its appeal to the heart surmounts every obstacle. Clime, color, sect are barriers which impede not its progress thither'.[95]

The 1840 census return showed that New York City was by far the largest city in the United States with a population of 312,710. Albany, the state capital of New York since 1797, with a population of 33,721 was the ninth largest city. Both cities played a prominent role in fund-raising for Ireland.[96] On 12 February, a meeting was held in Albany, convened by Mayor William Parmelee. People were asked to attend on the grounds that:

The destitution, suffering and absolute starvation which prevail in Ireland, plead with the humane throughout the world, and especially with Americans, for something more than silent regrets and unavailing sympathy. It calls for active, generous and zealous efforts . . . Shall we Americans, surrounded as we are by fruitful fields, and the bounties of a smiling providence, be deaf to the ocean-tongued cries of distress which reach us?[97]

Yet again, the plentitude of America was contrasted with the wants of Ireland. The meeting was described as being 'one of the largest meetings convened for a purely benevolent object'.[98] Only a few days later, on 15 February, the Albany committee issued a statewide appeal asking that every town and ward in New York State should organize a relief committee. The central Committee was chaired by Charles Jenkins, a successful Albany lawyer. Other members included Edward Delavan, a wealthy wine merchant and temperance advocate, bank presidents Thomas Olcott and John Norton, and attorney James Dexter. Another lawyer, John Ford, was appointed the committee's Secretary and Theodore Olcott, Director of the Canal Bank, the Treasurer. In addition, a number of subcommittees were formed. A decision was made that the name of every person who donated more than five dollars would appear in the local press. This ruling was in contrast with the actions of other committees, Philadelphia, for example, which chose not to provide any names. As was the case elsewhere, donations were gathered in imaginative ways; the committee organized 'benefit performances at local theaters, sponsored lectures by famous temperance leaders, and had local papers publish various articles intending to inspire guilt and pity'.[99] The local Hibernian Society raised $600.[100]

Initially, Albany had been part of the Roman Catholic diocese of New York City but, at the request of John Hughes, had gained independent status in April 1847. There were three Catholic churches in Albany and they instigated a 'benevolent race', which raised $5,329.[101] As impoverished immigrants arrived in the US, the nature of charitable benevolence changed. Many Irish fleeing the Famine chose to settle in Albany, which transformed the city from being a predominately Dutch to an Irish city. Some groups, such as the Vincent de Paul Society, which was only established in 1847, focused on working with poor Catholic immigrants, as did Father John McCloskey, the first Catholic Bishop of Albany.[102] The Albany committee also sent its own relief ship to Ireland. In June 1847, approximately $12,200.77 worth of foodstuffs arrived in Dublin on the *Malabar*. By September, $25,354.82 had been collected for Ireland, while $411.12 had been donated to Scotland. Unusually, the Albany committee remained active following the 1847 harvest. The final shipment sent by the Albany Committee sailed in the later part of December, on the *Ashburton*. It was carrying 715 barrels of corn meal and $212.78 in cash. Following this, the Albany committee was dissolved.[103]

Like Albany, Boston had a large community even before the Famine. On 18 February 1847, Boston's leading citizens held a packed meeting at Faneuil Hall in response to news from Ireland. Speakers included Edward

Everett, Dr S. G. Howe and Thomas J. Stevenson. One speech, referring to the affluence of Bostonians, added:

I shall therefore be surprised – I shall be deeply aggrieved – if on the list of contributions for the mitigation of this truly appalling calamity, the name of any place shall, in proportion to its numbers, stand higher than that of Boston.[104]

The meeting agreed to establish the New England Relief Committee for Famine in Ireland and Scotland, with Mayor Quincy as the Chairman. Committees were appointed in all the wards of the city to solicit money, food and clothing.[105] Interestingly, the two men who took the lead in promoting support for Ireland, Josiah Quincy and Robert Winthrop, had no Irish connections but were described as being 'Boston bluebloods'.[106] On the other side of the Atlantic, the New England Committee worked closely with a Liverpool merchant, William Rathbone. Rathbone, a former Mayor of the city, was a well-respected philanthropist who was active in the local abolition movement. His role was to oversee the distribution of charity from New England to relief committees in Scotland and Ireland. He informed the latter that all aid would be given 'free from religious or party differences'.[107]

Within a few months, the Boston Committee had collected $150,000.[108] The donors were drawn from diverse backgrounds. Andrew Carney, who had been born in County Cavan but emigrated to the United States in 1816, donated $1,000.[109] Carney, a tailor, had amassed a fortune in the preceding decade and was a renowned patron of many local charities including the Catholic Church.[110] He was also an early benefactor of Boston College.[111] Patrick Mooney, who owned a Catholic bookshop on Franklin Street and was Sexton of the local church, gave $200. His contribution was particularly praised because he had a large family to support.[112] James Ryan, the Irish-born landlord of the Stackpole House, a tavern which had first opened in 1823, gave $50.[113] Ryan, who was frequently called on for charitable donations, was famed for his generosity, especially to his fellow Irish men.[114] Some of the Boston contributors were nameless, including 'a poor woman who sells fruit at a "stand", corner of State and Congress Streets [and] gave from her hard earnings five dollars'.[115] Other donors chose to be anonymous, such as the donation of $300, from a person who was benefitting financially from the situation in Ireland, 'To the Relief Committee for Ireland: Gentlemen, I enclose my contribution to your funds in Bank Bills, being a part of the pecuniary debt due to *Starvation* for the rise in freights from A Ship Owner, Boston, March 6, 1847'.[116]

Again, a number of fund-raising activities proved to be creative. The employers of the Boston Museum, for example, offered to provide an evening's entertainment on 27 February. The proprietor, the flamboyant Moses Kimball, agreed to his recently rebuilt Museum (whose attractions ranged from mummies to a mermaid) being used free of charge.[117] The

proprietors of the nearby Howard Athenaeum, a local playhouse, offered
their premises for a ball to raise money on behalf of the local relief committee.[118] Less colourfully, a separate collection, coordinated by Bishop John
Fitzpatrick, had raised almost $20,000 by March. To expedite its arrival in
Ireland, Fitzpatrick sent the relief in the form of cash, to be entrusted to the
Archbishops, but to be distributed 'in accordance with the wants of the various localities, and without distinction of creed'.[119]

Chicago, Rochester and elsewhere

As was the case in a number of other American towns and cities, the number
of Irish people in Chicago had grown in the decade before the Famine as
a result of the expansion of the transport system, in this case, the Illinois
and Michigan Canal. Following a pattern in other areas with large numbers
of Irish immigrants, contact had been maintained with the home country
and its political development through the activities of O'Connell's repeal
movement.[120] In Chicago, an Irish Repeal Association had been founded
in October 1842. Dr William Egan, a founding member, was later active
in organizing famine relief.[121] The local Catholic churches also played an
active role. Bishop William Quarter, who had been born in King's County,
appealed to his co-religionists to donate money for Ireland, while asking the
clergy to set aside a day for a special appeal. All the money, he assured them,
would be given to the Chicago committee, which was inter-denominational,
for transmission to Ireland.[122] Sadly, Bishop Quarter died in April 1848,
aged 42, when the Famine was still raging.[123]

The ecumenical nature of the Chicago committee was emphasized by the
fact that they held their first meeting, on 4 March, in a Baptist Church.[124]
It was chaired by Charles Walker, with an Irish-born Protestant, Dr Egan,
as one of the main speakers. William Bradshaw Egan had been born in
County Kerry in 1808. He was a second cousin of Daniel O'Connell. He
commenced medical studies at the age of 15, completing his education in
England, Ireland and Canada, before attending Rutgers Medical School
in New Jersey and gaining his license to practices in 1830. He moved to
Chicago in 1833 and, among other things, worked to promote public health.
He was also an active member of St James' Episcopal Church and had been
elected President of the local Repeal Association.[125] Egan represented a class
of Irish immigrant that was often overlooked – educated, successful, both
Protestant and nationalist. The involvement of such influential men in relief
committees was crucial in appealing to a wide spectrum of donors.

The first meeting of the Chicago committee raised over $1,600.
Furthermore, it estimated that $2,500 had already been sent to Ireland as
private remittances. Like other relief committees, this one approached its
mission with enthusiasm and dedication, appointing an executive committee,
choosing a Treasurer, and selecting people to take responsibility for each part

of the city. The committee also urged people in North Illinois to establish their own committees, they offering to act as a conduit for any relief raised, and to forward it to the General Relief Committee in New York. George Smith, the Treasurer, had already, in February, helped to found a committee to raise money for the Famine in the Highlands and Islands of Scotland.[126] The enterprising young Smith had been born in Aberdeen and had, with fellow Scotsman Alex Mitchell, established the Wisconsin Marine and Fire Insurance Company in 1839.[127] Smith recognized the value of publicity and so decided that the name of every donor, no matter how small their donation (and some were as small as 10 cents), would be sent to the local press, for inclusion. One local young Irish girl, Rosa White, achieved national notoriety and praise for having given all the money she possessed – six dollars – to the relief fund.[128] As with most other relief committees, the Chicago one was most active in the spring of 1847. By mid-May, $3,600 had been contributed both by the city and local communities.[129]

In Rochester in New York State, the local newspapers began to take intense interest in the crisis in Ireland in early 1847, with readers being 'pushed, shamed and encouraged' to do something.[130] In the previous decade, a number of Irish societies had been organized, which had expressed their support of both the temperance and the repeal movements. The organization of the local Irish community had been largely due to the energy of Fr Bernard O'Reilly. As early as 1841, the Rochester Repeal Society had been formed in support of Daniel O'Connell, and O'Reilly had contributed to its funds.[131]

The first formal meeting on behalf of the Famine took place in Rochester on 8 February, the same week as the well-publicized meeting in Washington. As was the case elsewhere, the committee brought together a diverse group of people, the Dublin Quakers being informed that, 'contributions have been from all classes of citizens, rich and poor'.[132] Not only were the local clergy asked to give sermons, but, unusually, every school was visited and encouraged to become involved. The Episcopalian Bishop of the Diocese of Western New York, William H. DeLancey, requested that the clergy in his church hold special collections on 7 March for Famine relief in both Ireland and Scotland. On 17 March, a special St Patrick's ball was held by some young men who sent the proceeds to Bishop John MacHale of Tuam.[133]

The leading members of the committee reflected the inclusive nature of the Rochester appeal. Levi A. Ward, a successful businessman and member of the Council, did much to organize the committee. At this stage, part of his reputation rested on his attempt to enforce licensing laws and curb saloons. The energetic Ward would be elected Mayor in 1849.[134] A few years following his term as Mayor, Ward helped to found the St Peter's Presbyterian Church.[135] Another prominent member was Silas Cornell, a Quaker and an abolitionist.[136] Jacob Gould, another member, was a successful shoe and boot manufacturer. He had been the second Mayor of Rochester and the first Democrat to hold this position.[137] The current Mayor, William Pitkin, was appointed Treasurer of the Relief Committee. Pitkin was President of the Rochester Savings Bank and known for his Whig sympathies and support for abolition. He was also very active in the affairs of St Luke's Episcopal Church.[138] Initially, Cornell had been appointed Chairman, but was replaced by Ward when the former left the area.[139] A number of men who had direct involvement with Ireland and were members of the local Repeal Association were also members of the executive committee, including Patrick Barry, Secretary of the Repeal Association, Garret Barry, James Donoughue, Patrick Doyle and John Allen.[140] Irish-born John Allen, a member of the Whig Party, had been appointed the Mayor of Rochester in 1844.[141] The involvement of these men on the Irish Relief Committee demonstrated how this cause attracted the attention and involvement of some of the most influential leaders of society, regardless of political or religious affiliations.

Within two weeks of being formed, $1,500 had been raised in Rochester. The committee sought the advice of two New York Quakers, Mahlon Day and David Sands, who recommended sending food and money to the Quakers in Dublin via Liverpool. Like other committees, they decided, as far as possible, to send aid in the form of dry food.[142] When the Rochester committee disbanded in November 1847, they had raised over $4,000, which had been used to purchase 988 barrels of cornmeal, 30 barrels of flour, 15 barrels of corn and wheat and 3 boxes of clothing to Ireland. These cargoes had been sent on board six vessels that sailed from New York to Liverpool, and from there to Ireland; the first shipment left the United States on 3 March and the final one on 2 October 1847.[143] When Ward made his final report to the Society of Friends in December 1847, he emphasized the fact that all classes of citizens had joined in the fund-raising and that the donations had 'been most cheerfully made, and with the earnest wish and most ardent prayer of the donors that your country may not again be visited by that dreadful scourge – famine, and its usual attendant, pestilence'.[144]

By 1840, Cincinnati – sometimes referred to as the city of immigrants – was the sixth largest city in the US, with a population of 46,338.[145] By the mid-nineteenth century, Cincinnati had achieved fame and economic success, as the centre of hog-packing – hence one of its nick-names, Porkopolis. Immigrants were also attracted to the area due to employment opportunities on the Miami and Erie Canal. Even before 1845, there was an established Irish community in Cincinnati, some of whom had formed a repeal association that sent regular financial contributions to Daniel O'Connell in Ireland.[146] However, some of the Irish community had also achieved notoriety for participating in intermittent anti-black riots, which led the abolitionist, William Lloyd Garrison, to describe the city as 'vile and despicable'.[147] Richard Allen, a Dublin abolitionist, characterized his countrymen in Cincinnati as, 'that old, degraded, whiskey-drinking class'.[148] Nonetheless, Cincinnati was one of the first cities in the Midwest to form a Famine Relief Committee, and, by mid-March, they had raised almost $9,000.[149] The committee planned to use this money to charter a schooner, loaded with provisions. R. W. Lee, a local pork merchant, offered to contribute $1,000 for this purpose.[150] By the end of the month, over $12,000 had been collected, which was used to fill several ships with provisions.[151]

The activities of the larger relief committees sometimes overshadowed efforts made elsewhere. In addition to the activities in these major American cities, smaller meetings were being held in towns and townships throughout the country to raise voluntary subscriptions for Ireland. At a meeting in Springfield in northern Illinois, held on 6 April, $235 was raised, which was forwarded to the New Orleans Relief Committee. The Ottawa committee of Lazalle County, also in Illinois, sent their donation of $300 directly to the Society of Friends Committee in Dublin. The committee in Galena was one of the most active in the state of Illinois. It had been founded on 9 March, inspired by the meeting in Washington.[152] The Chairman of the Irish Relief Committee was Charles S. Hempstead, a prominent lawyer, who appeared to have no direct contact with Ireland.[153] Hempstead was helped in great part by local women, who were praised in one paper as 'Sisters of Charity'. The committee raised $1,245, which they forwarded to the General Relief Committee in New York City, to be forwarded to the Friends in Dublin.[154] A meeting in Pottsville, near Philadelphia, yielded $506.[155] In Alexandria in the District of Columbia, $2,000 was raised, which included a contribution of $500 by the local Hibernian Society.[156]

The celebrated author, James Fenimore Cooper, famous for, among other things, *Last of the Mohicans* (1826), presided over a meeting at Cooperstown in Otsego County, New York, at which a depot was opened for the reception of provisions.[157] Northampton, a small town in Massachusetts, raised $5,000 in the first few weeks of 1847.[158] In Williamsburg, the outcome of a meeting held in mid-February, 'to devise measures for the relief of Ireland', created a committee of 40, with each person taking responsibility for a part of the village in which to solicit donations. A motion was then passed asking the American government to give immediate assistance.[159] Operatives on the Lowell railway in Massachusetts contributed $262, while factory operatives in Saco in Maine raised $329.[160] In the nearby 'new' town of Lawrence, famous for its textile mills and its large immigrant population, over $2,000 had been raised by March 1847. This amount included over $400 donated by workers in Bay State Mills, who gave the proceeds of one day's labour.[161] In February 1847, students of Georgetown University collected $306 for Irish Famine relief.[162]

In Natchez, Mississippi, a meeting was held on 20 February. At the suggestion of the Mayor, a committee was convened with the purpose of raising money to provide a relief ship to Ireland. Samuel Cartwright who spoke at the meeting, made what was becoming a common theme, namely, that of American debt to Ireland, he stating 'our free and happy land was watered by the blood of Ireland's sons'.[163] The committee was expanded to include some of its neighbouring districts and, by 17 March, had collected over $1,300, a large portion of which had been donated by Protestant congregations. The British Ambassador to the United States personally thanked the people of Natchez.[164] The nearby town of Jacksonville followed this pattern of convening a public meeting at which a fund-raising committee was formed. Their meeting took place on 28 February and, within only two weeks, they had raised $444–50, which they forwarded to New Orleans for the purchase of foodstuffs.[165]

Occasionally, a political dimension entered these charitable activities. This was evident during a meeting in Rutland, Vermont, presided over by Jonathan Dexter, a lawyer, with no clear connection to Ireland.[166] Their multiple resolutions made it clear that they laid the blame for the suffering at the feet of the British government:

> That we feel deep sympathy for the starving millions in Ireland, and while we regret that England is disgracing herself in the estimation of all nations, by suffering tens of thousands of her subjects to die for want of food, we will contribute out 'mite' as individuals, in order to alleviate, in some degree, that terrible suffering and hunger which is daily consigning thousands to an untimely grave . . .
>
> That when any government so far neglects its duty as to suffer tens of thousands of its subjects to die for the want of bread, it becomes a curse to its people and should be denounced by all Christians. . .
>
> That every virtue which is an honour to man, call upon us, the freemen of this land of liberty and plenty, to give bread to the starving and dying subjects of the tyrannical government and institutions of the old world; that we may save them from destruction and teach their masters that Republicans, when humanity calls, will extend 'aid and comfort' to their starving and dying subjects.[167]

The meeting raised $503.67, which was forwarded to the Irish Relief Fund in Boston.[168]

Several appeals suggested that giving to Ireland was a Christian duty. This was the approach of many of the churches and was also the response of some laymen, including Governor Briggs of Massachusetts. In March, he issued a proclamation for a Day of Public Fast, Humiliation and Prayer to give thanks for America's bounty at a time of Famine.[169] Catholic churches, both in the United States and in Ireland, provided a useful conduit for sending money to the poor, although few kept official records of their involvement, which often dated from the first appearance of blight. Large-scale emigration to American in the decade before the Famine had not only increased the Irish presence throughout the country, but also resulted in a wave of church building and the creation of a number of new dioceses. In Chicago, Bishop William Quarter, the first Irish-born bishop in the city, noted 'several who have near relatives in Ireland have sent remittances to their relief. Many of the Catholics of this Diocese have done so'.[170] In Boston, at the beginning of 1847, meetings were held in the basement of the Church of the Holy

Cross.[171] St Peter's Church on Grand Street was the first Catholic parish church in Jersey City until 1829, public places of Catholic worship being against the law in New Jersey. In 1844, Irish-born Fr John Kelly moved to the parish upon returning from missionary work in Liberia. At the time of his arrival at St Peter's, there were estimated to be less than 800 Catholics in Jersey City.[172] Kelly's energy and commitment were largely responsible for the success of the early church.[173] In 1846, he organized a collection for Irish relief. It raised $110, to which he added his own contribution of $53.[174]

Multiple meetings for Ireland took place in early 1847, but the one which attracted most attention was held in Washington on 9 February, presided over by the Vice-President, George Mifflin Dallas. This was not the first public meeting on behalf of Ireland, although it was the most publicized. A few weeks earlier, on 24 November, the Mayor of Washington, Colonel William Winston Seaton, had chaired a meeting at City Hall. A committee of four had been appointed to organize ward-by-ward collections. Walter Lennox, who succeeded Seaton as Mayor in 1850, was Secretary. A collection was made at the meeting with the Mayor donating $25.[175] Seaton, whose family was of Scottish descent, worked tirelessly to collect funds for Ireland and, within weeks, $10,000 had been collected. A ship, the *General Harrison*, was commissioned and laden with provisions. It arrived in the Cove of Cork in early June 1847. The officers and crew were feted wherever they went. In Galway, a banquet was held in their honour and toasts made to Colonel Seaton.[176]

Seaton's early efforts were overshadowed by the meeting in Washington in February, which was held in the Odd Fellows' Hall. In addition to many members of the House of Representatives, the Senate and the Supreme Court, a number of high-ranking officials were present. Many women also attended. Various resolutions were introduced by Daniel Webster, the renowned Whig Senator from Massachusetts, which he prefaced by saying:

A famine, bringing want and distress on a great portion of a whole population, is unprecedented in Christendom in this age. The calamities of Ireland have been heard and read throughout the whole country, and have touched all American hearts. New improvements in communication have brought nations into near neighbourhood with each other, and we hear the cries of suffering Ireland almost as fresh and as strong as if they had come from a part of our own country.[177]

To make this possible, Webster asked 'the inhabitants of all the cities, towns and villages, in the United States, immediately to appoint committees to receive contributions and make collections, to be forwarded to the General Committees in New York and New Orleans'. Subsequently, committees in Philadelphia, Baltimore and Washington agreed to accept and forward donations. Webster recommended that the Mayors or Customs Collectors of these cities assist in arranging for them to be forwarded to Ireland. Senator

Crittenden, who made one of the closing speeches on behalf of Ireland, asked, 'How can we hesitate a moment?'

The Washington Committee included the local Mayor, Senator Edward Hannegan, Hugh White and William Woodworth of the House of Representatives.[178] Following the meeting, they prepared, 'An Appeal to the People of the Nation', dated 10 February 1847. It asked for nationwide involvement, pointing out, 'An awful crisis has arrived in Ireland . . . Let a generous people, we say, come to the rescue'. The appeal included extracts from a much-reprinted letter written by Nicholas Cummins, the Cork magistrate, together with one from women in Dunmanway to 'Ladies of America', and a further one from a clergyman in Coolany, near Sligo, addressed to Baptists in America. The final letter pleaded:

> Hapless people that we are, whither shall we turn? American brethren we turn to you, with confident expectations . . . Brethren, as God has blessed you with both flour and money, send us a small share. We need it, we crave it. We are besieged by famine.[179]

The Appeal ended by warning, 'friends and countrymen, we must not delay. The death-shrieks come louder and louder from that unhappy shore. Hundreds, thousands, may die before our aid can reach them. Instant action may save other hundreds, other thousands'.[180] It was signed by Daniel Webster, E. A. Hannegan, Orville Dewey, Edward Curtis and W. E. Robinson.[181] Even without this encouragement from Washington, meetings were underway in cities in the US, but in its wake, even more were convened.[182] For a short time, it appeared that the whole of the American nation was determined to come to the rescue of the starving people of Ireland. A few weeks after the Washington meeting, Senator John Crittenden, a Whig from Kentucky, introduced a Bill for Congress to provide $500,000 to help Ireland and Scotland.[183] His was not the first attempt to get Federal support for Ireland, but it appeared to be the most promising. Although Crittenden had some cross-party support and the Bill was passed in the Senate, it floundered in the Ways and Means Committee, with even President Polk declaring such an action to be unconstitutional.[184] (see also Chapter Five). The refusal of the American government to provide a large subvention to Ireland threw the burden back on private charity to intervene.

Relief ships

Following the defeat of Crittenden's Bill, the American government showed its support for the Irish poor in an expected way. At the same time that this debate was being played out, on 24 February, Senator Dix, a Democrat from New York, supported by Senator John Fairfield, suggested that the frigate *Macedonian* be put at the disposal of George DeKay of New Jersey and sent to Ireland. At the request of Robert Charles Winthrop, a prominent Whig politician from Boston, Congress also agreed to make the sloop-of-war, *Jamestown,* available for the use of the Boston Committee.[185] On 2 March, the Senate voted 23 for and 12 against this motion. The House passed the Bill the following day. Despite the *Jamestown* and the *Macedonian* being war ships, they were placed under the command of civilians, and their armaments were removed to allow additional room for foodstuffs.[186] In recognition that the vessels were in a poor state of repair, money was granted for refurbishments, which, in the case of the *Macedonian,* amounted to $6,000.[187]

The New England Relief Committee was given charge of the *Jamestown.* They appointed Captain Robert B. Forbes, a veteran sea-farer, to take command of the vessel. Loading commenced on St Patrick's Day, led by the Labourers' Aid Society, most of whom were Irishmen and were working for free. The crew was also made up of unpaid volunteers, Forbes placing an advertisement in the local press stating:

> I shall be glad to ship any *young men who have been in active service at sea at least one year, with or without pay* . . . To such I can produce room to swing a hammock on the gun deck, plenty of bread, and small stores, plenty of hard work under strict discipline, and a return to Boston in about two months.[188]

The *Jamestown* left Boston on 28 March, bound for Cork, and carrying 800 tons of foodstuffs. Forbes was accompanied by Captain Macondry as first officer and Captain Farwell as second officer.[189] One Boston newspaper, describing the ship's departure proclaimed, 'She walked the waters like a thing of life, as if conscious of the nobleness and importance of her errand'.[190] The *Jamestown* made the journey in a record 15 days and three hours. The cargo was unloaded at Haulbowline, a small island in Cork Harbour, which was also a British Naval base and the location of the British government food depots.[191] William Rathbone had travelled from Liverpool to meet Forbes and to help with the distribution of the cargo.[192]

The captain and crew of the *Jamestown* were greeted as heroes. Among those welcoming them was the Cove Temperance Band who boarded the vessel and played music on it all day.[193] During their ten day stay in Ireland, Forbes and his crew helped with the practical distribution of food. He was assisted by Rathbone, who had undertaken to do so on behalf of the New England Irish Relief Committee.[194] Father Mathew, the temperance leader, took Forbes on a tour of some of most distressed areas in Cork City, which included visiting a local soup kitchen. Forbes was upset by the experience and commented in regard to the food in the latter that it would, 'be refused by well-bred pigs in my own country'. Although Forbes wanted no parties in his honour, he did agree to visit the Temperance Institute of Cork. The hall had been decked with Irish, English and American flags. In response to various tributes, Forbes joked that, although he had visited Blarney Castle and consequently had much to say, he was too overcome with emotions to say anything. Nonetheless, he went on to express his admiration for the women of Cork on the grounds that they '*do* shake hands *like* men – no formal touching of the ends of fingers, chilling the heart, but a regular grip of feeling'.[195] The *Jamestown* left Cork on 22 April and completed its return journey in 24 days. Despite receiving many requests to do so, Forbes made it clear that he would not take any emigrants on board his vessel.[196] Before leaving the country, the people of Cork presented Forbes with a solid silver salver measuring 20 by 30 inches, together with a memorial Address adorned with an Irish harp and an American eagle.[197] He was also charged with taking back a print of the *Jamestown,* which was, 'respectfully dedicated to the President, House of Representatives, Congress and people of the United States of America', which was intended to be, 'commemorative of the splendid generosity of the American government in dismantling a ship of war for a mission of peace and charity, & of the noble-hearted citizens who humanely & benevolently responded to the call of Irish distress'.[198]

William Rathbone, in turn, was thanked personally by Mayor Quincy of Boston for his support in the venture. Rathbone's acknowledgement was typically modest and gracious:

> It was a great privilege to my family and myself, though in so humble a way, to be admitted as fellow labourers in a cause … for which the world has reason to bless and thank you … No thanks are needed for helping the Commander of the Jamestown. The obligation was on our side in being allowed the opportunity of association with one who is held in such deserved estimation by his fellow citizens.[199]

Privately, Rathbone confided to Forbes, 'The sojourn in Ireland was one of unmitigating hopeless pain, but how could we do less for part of our own, when you were making such great sacrifices?' He estimated that the distress in Ireland was likely to continue until harvest. In contrast, the Scottish Relief Committee had informed him that the donations 'had been so liberal they hope they will finish with a surplus'.[200]

At the time of the *Jamestown's* return to the US, the *Macedonian* was still in dock in New York. Despite the massive fund-raising activities going on in New York, DeKay had been unable to mobilize sympathy for his proposed voyage. The situation was probably not helped by DeKay's public falling out with the General Relief Committee in the city.[201] Forbes and the Boston committee came to the aid of the *Macedonian,* their interventions enabling the vessel to sail on 19 June, arriving in Cork on 14 July. The news of the relief ship's departure caused excitement, leading the Anglo-Irish novelist, Samuel Lover, to pen a tribute to 'The War Ship of Peace':

> Sweet land of song, thy harp doth hang
> Upon the willows now,
> While famine's blight and fever's pang

Stamp misery on thy brow;
Yet, take thy harp and raise thy voice,
Though faint and low it be,
And let thy sinking heart rejoice
In friends still left to thee.
Look out, look out, across the sea
That girds thy emerald shore,
A ship of war is bound for thee,
But with no warlike store . . .
Yet, even in sorrow, tuneful still
Let Erin's voice proclaim
In bardic praise, on every hill,
Columbia's glorious name.[202]

The Society of Friends took charge of distributing the cargo of the *Macedonian*, with the exception of 50 barrels of foodstuffs that had been promised to Maria Edgeworth.[203] William Rathbone again travelled to Cork to assist in the distribution of the cargo.[204]

DeKay returned to the United States carrying a formal thanks to the American President. The address was dated 29 July and signed by the Mayor, Andrew F. Roche, on behalf of the people of Cork. It stated:

> The American nation, with ready sympathy, came to the rescue, unsolicited, except by their own hearts; they gave food to feed the hungry, to check the famine-fever, and, under the blessing of a merciful God, to restore the sick to health and usefulness . . . the generous aid given by the American public, and sent on peace-making mission in American ships of war, has done more to secure continued harmony between the countries than any armament could effect. Your people, by doing us good, have recognized the ancestral relationship which belongs to us; while we, in our cordial gratitude, will ever use the remembrance of your noble benevolence as the talisman of amity.

Tellingly, while praising American philanthropy, the message said, 'we emulate her independence'.[205] For DeKay, the journey had not been an unmitigated success. He had spent $30,000 of his own money on supplies and in hiring a crew. DeKay applied to Congress for some financial support, but he died in 1849, impoverished and before any decision had been reached.[206]

While the voyages of the *Jamestown* and the *Macedonian* were the most-publicized of the Famine relief ships, they were not the only ones. Thank you dinners were held for the crew of other vessels who brought foodstuffs to Ireland. At the beginning of May, Captain Clarke of the *Victor* was entertained in the Rotunda in Dublin. It was described as a 'complimentary dinner to the gallant representatives of a generous nation'. During the proceedings, Clarke was presented with a green poplin flag of Irish manufacture, part of which depicted an eagle, carrying a sheaf of corn, flying towards Ireland.

It was inscribed 'from the citizens of Dublin'. Unlike similar occasions, much of the content of the speeches was politicized. Interestingly, however, toasts were made to the Queen, followed by one to the President and people of the United States'. The music played included 'God Save the Queen', 'The Star-Spangled Banner', 'Yankee Doodle' and 'My Ancestors were Irishmen'. In his speech, Clarke paid special tribute to the ladies present, noting their beauty and 'sun bright eyes'.[207] The Irish guests at the ceremony included Thomas Francis Meagher and John Mitchel, two supporters of Irish Repeal who, in the following year, would be tried for treason against the British government.[208] Richard O'Gorman, a fellow Repealer, made an overtly political speech:

> We are here in the presence of a man from a nation that won its own freedom, and wears it well . . . I feel almost ashamed of my position as an Irishman – I feel that I belong to a race the most abject, the most degraded, the most servile, of any that has ever blotted the face of this earth . . . We have borne more suffering, we have tamely borne more degradation, we have broken more vows, than any nation that I ever read of . . . if you want to know how Irish prosperity is to be obtained, read the history of American independence (cheers, hissing and slight confusion).

The formal address was no less political, describing the Irish as 'victims of blighting misrule'. In a blistering attack on the British government, it accused them of having, 'Coolly set their economic seers to calculate with fatal precision how safely to their financial resources they may permit whole millions of Irish subjects to wither from the face of nature'.[209] When responding, Captain Clarke admitted that he had not understood all of the inferences made in the preceding speeches, adding, 'I may express a hope that you are mistaken, and that there is no government, when the lives of the people are at stake, would be influenced by the considerations to which you refer'.[210] The evening ended in discord and disarray. Nonetheless, during the evening, American prosperity had been repeatedly attributed to her independence, and expressing gratitude for American charity had been used as an opportunity to berate British misrule.

The relationship between American and Irish abolitionists on the eve of the Famine was another example of the intertwining of charity and politics. Since the late eighteenth century, the anti-slavery movement in Ireland had been strong and well-organized, while Daniel O'Connell had emerged as one of the most influential figures in the transatlantic movement. However, his strong attacks on American slavery had even alienated some of his Irish supporters in the US.[211] In some Southern states, there was a fear that Irish condemnation of slavery might hinder fund-raising activities. At a meeting in Natchez in February, one speaker even felt it necessary to reassure the audience that the Irish people were not opposed to 'our Southern institutions'.[212]

The Boston *Pilot,* both a critic of the abolitionist movement and a supporter of Irish independence, when reporting a donation to Ireland by a 'slave church' in Richmond, Virginia, used it as an opportunity to make two political points:

> What a forcible rebuke is this to those English bigots who say that no slave can live on British soil, and that the Southern slaves would be justified in cutting their masters' throats! We see these slaves enjoying the necessaries, and many of them even the luxuries, of life in abundance, while thousands and tens of thousands of *freemen, yes free Britons,* are perishing for want of a mere sustenance.[213]

Only a week later, the *Pilot* reported that several African churches in Philadelphia had made donations for Ireland.[214]

The *Liberator,* an abolitionist paper founded by William Lloyd Garrison, inevitably took the opposite view. This paper carried many reports on the situation in Ireland, a number of which were drawn from letters written by Richard Allen from Dublin. Garrison informed his readers, 'He [Allen] will be rejoiced to hear that, in all parts of our country, the people are contributing of their substance to send the needed relief'.[215] In April, the paper included a report from Skibbereen, which had been forwarded to Garrison by a woman abolitionist in Bristol, England. Her motive, she explained, was 'to furnish one more commentary on the oppression of the Irish people, and the utter mismanagement of Irish affairs, attributable to grasping absentee proprietors, and to the illiberal policy of the English government through a long series of years. . .'.[216] Garrison encouraged abolitionists to donate money to Ireland, care of Francis Taylor.[217] The Society of Friends in Dublin recorded two donations from Taylor on behalf of American abolitionists of £200 and £73.5s.1d.[218]

Writing to Richard Webb, a prominent Irish abolitionist, at the beginning of March, Garrison admitted:

> The horrid particulars of the famine in Ireland have made a wide and profound sensation in this country. Contributions are pouring in from every quarter and the amount of food, money and clothing that will be contributed, will be very considerable; yet not a fiftieth part that ought to be done. But we must recollect that the idea of human brotherhood is as yet but very imperfectly developed in the world, and that, hitherto, each nation has left other nations to take care of themselves, without being specially concerned for their welfare. . . .[219]

Several abolitionist papers carried reports from Elihu Burritt, the 'Learned Blacksmith', who had travelled to England to attend a Peace Conference, but travelled to Ireland to assist in famine relief.[220] He sent back regular accounts of what he witnessed and made a number of practical suggestions for getting relief to Ireland. He advised that vessels should be sent to Cork, 'an excellent and accessible port', and entrusted either to the British Relief Association or the Friends' Association. He assured them that, once in Cork, the government would provide steam vessels to transfer the cargoes to other Irish ports. Burritt made a direct appeal, asking if:

> any of the Sunday school children in America should be pleased to make me the agent of their little charities, towards particular groups or families of Irish children, I should be happy to appropriate them in a way that should be satisfactory.[221]

Like many visitors to Ireland in 1847, Burritt felt compelled to witness the suffering in Skibbereen first-hand. His experience led him to suggest, 'Let Ireland's extremity be America's opportunity to teach the nations a magnificent lesson in human brotherly love'.[222]

Despite the overwhelming success of American fund-raising, there were a number of criticisms of the way in which some money had been raised. The Baltimore committee had held a 'grand ball' to raise money for Ireland, which brought in $3,000. One Washington newspaper was not impressed, claiming 'When expenses have been paid, the charity will be rather meager. This thing of dancing, while Ireland is starving, is in miserable taste'.[223] A number of prominent men in South Carolina petitioned their General Assembly requesting that they send state aid to Ireland. The proposal was turned down on the grounds that it was 'the duty of every nation to support its own poor and to relieve the suffering of its people'.[224] Even Captain Forbes of the *Jamestown* did not receive universal admiration. The *Chronotype* commented:

> It is not so much to be wondered at as to be deplored that such a man as Captain Forbes should be puzzled to see *why* there should be famine in Ireland. Probably the refined and Christian landlords of Ireland who take the cottagers' pig and half his potato crop for rent, and always have, are puzzled with the same questions. It is a great problem this. Put several millions of people on a fertile island, without letting them own a foot of land in it, to tell why there should be a famine.[225]

Most American fund-raising activities ended in early summer of 1847, in the expectation that the coming harvest would bring an end to the food shortages. Sadly this did not prove to be the case. In November of that year, many relief organizations published accounts of their fund-raising activities. The Irish Relief Committee of Charleston, South Carolina, reported that they had received from:

The City of Charleston and Neck $8,911.53
Collections in churches $3,342

Columbia $1,461
Camden $64.50
Other districts in the state $5,346.58
Georgia $105
North Carolina $236.50
Tennessee $368
Alabama $136
Sale of corn and flour $341.45
Total: $19,912.58

The Irish Relief Committee of Pittsburg reported receipt of contributions of produce from the adjoining counties of Pennsylvania, Virginia and Ohio, which amounted in value to $28,362.12. In addition, they had received cash donations of $10,525.96 and freight remission to the value of $1,599.14. In total, they had raised $40,487.22. The Cincinnati Committee published their report in pamphlet form. They had received donations in cash, provisions, freight and drayage charges that totalled 28,323. A further $2,000 had been raised through other channels, making a total of $30,323.[226] The Chicago Committee sent its final contribution of $237 to the General Relief Committee in New York at the beginning of November. Following this, they disbanded.[227]

A small number of contributions were made after this date. Although the Rochester committee had formally disbanded in November, it sent its final donation in December, prompting its chairman, Levi Ward, to comment 'It is a delightful employment to feed the hungry, and to succor the perishing'.[228] At this time, donations that had gone through the various American ports included:

Boston $174,874
Philadelphia $80,284.38
New York $182,450.13
Baltimore $21,090
Washington $10,300
Richmond $15,000
New Orleans $50,000
Louisville $9,670.14
Cincinnati $30,385
Providence (RI) $6,377
Salem (Mass.) $3,438.97
Nantucket (Mass.) $2,180.69

Added to this were contributions from New Bedford, Vigo County, Pittsburg and Charleston. Private remittances from Irish citizens alone had reached $536,056. According to one paper, the total value of private and public donations from America in 1847, in both money and kind, was in the region of one and a half million dollars.[229]

Although the precise amount of relief sent from the United States in 1847 is not known, and it is impossible to calculate how many lives were saved as a consequence, without these interventions, many more people would have died. The arrival of corn from America in the early months of 1847 had had an immediate impact on the market. By late March, the price of maize had fallen from £19 to £10 a ton.[230] This reduction in food prices coincided with the opening of the first government soup kitchens, making food more affordable to the committees administering them. While donations to Ireland from the United States did dry up at the end of 1847, some of the same people who had been so active in raising money, now used their time and skills in providing succour to the thousands of emigrants who had fled to the United States with few or no resources.

Thanks and controversies

The appreciation of Irish people for the various contributions from the United States was acknowledged publicly. As early as March 1847, the British Prime Minister, Lord John Russell, addressed the House of Commons about the charity being sent from the US:

> I wish to take this opportunity to say, for the satisfaction of my own feelings, that I have observed with great pleasure the noble and munificent subscriptions in the United States of America, for the relief of distress in Ireland (loud cheers). I think it is not improper, in this House, for me, as a British subject, to say that I am extremely gratified that, mindful of our common origin, the people of the United States are making exertions, in a most charitable spirit, to raise large subscriptions for this object (great cheering).[231]

Tribute was paid in the House of Lords by the Archbishop of Dublin, Richard Whately:

> . . . in respect of the gratitude he felt himself bound to express on behalf of the Irish people for the great bounty and genuine liberality of the people of England, and he might add the people of America likewise, towards the Irish people. He had been made the channel of conveying to the people of Ireland a large portion of the contributions that came from America . . . Those liberal contributors, both from the United States and from Canada, and other of our colonies abroad, had been entrusted to his care; and he had, therefore, taken the opportunity of returning thanks for them on behalf of the people of Ireland.[232]

Lord Palmerston, who been British Foreign Secretary since July 1846, wrote to Richard Pakenham, the British envoy in Washington, directing him to:

> take every opportunity of saying how grateful Her Majesty's Government and the British nation at large feel for this kind and honorable manifestation of sympathy by the citizens of the United States for the sufferings of the Irish people . . . the active and energetic assistance which the people of the United States are thus offering to the poor Irish, while it reflects the highest honour upon our transatlantic brethren, must tend to draw closer, and to render stronger and more lasting, those ties of friendship and mutual esteem, which Her Majesty's Government trusts will long continue to exist between the two great branches of the Anglo-Saxon family.[233]

The warm messages were ironic given that successive British governments had been in dispute with successive American governments over possession of territory in Oregon on the Pacific coast of the US. This tension had come to a head during the early years of the Polk administration, with some talk of war. The Irish-born Pakenham had been the main negotiator on behalf of the British government, with the United States being represented by James Buchanan. The issue had only been settled a few months earlier, with the Oregon Treaty (also known as the Buchanan-Pakenham Treaty) signed on 15 June 1846.[234] Both Buchanan and Pakenham had donated to Irish relief. Pakenham's donation of $500 had accompanied by a 'delicately-worded note', to the Treasurer of the Washington committee.[235]

The bullish Lord Palmerston reopened the sensitive issue of Oregon in the summer of 1847, with negative comments about the United States, leading one Washington newspaper to observe:

> He knew, too, that, at the very moment he was holding this insulting language towards the North American States, the Relief Committee of Ireland was publishing to the world, that they had received in money and provisions, from these same States, value to the amount of half a million of dollars, to aid in relieving the distresses of a portion of his own countrymen. Was he anxious to extinguish the kindly feelings which the settlement of the Oregon controversy had occasioned, and which this act of national liberality was strengthening.[236]

Palmerston, who owned estates in County Sligo, had personal knowledge of the impact of the Famine. Even before 1845, Palmerston had been regarded as an 'improving landlord', who had tried to rationalize the subdivision of plots of land on his estate, including by offering assisted emigration to his tenants. The second failure of the potato crop provided further incentive to remove the poorest occupiers. As Dr West, who worked with the local poor, explained in December 1846, 'It would be much less expensive for Lord Palmerston to send out the half if possible of his tenants than have to feed them here and get no rents. . .'.[237] Shortly afterwards, Palmerston financed large-scale assisted emigration from his estates in 1847. The fact that some emigrants arrived in Canada during a freezing winter, without adequate clothing and with no prospects of employment, inevitably led to criticism of his actions.[238] Palmerston's various interventions during the Famine, both personal and political, demonstrate the complexity of transatlantic relations and the willingness to accept charity for the Irish poor while facilitating their departure from Ireland.

A more general thanks to the United States was made at a public meeting held in the City Lecture Room in Finsbury in London on 24 March. Amidst 'loud cheers', a resolution was passed that:

> we feel language to be inadequate to give expression to our gratitude to that noble and independent people; betokening, as it does, to the nations of the earth, whether afflicted by distress caused by providentialist calamities, or internal impolicy, that there is a great and magnanimous people on our globe, ever ready with hope, succor and consolation, in the hour of need, calling forth the overjoyed thanks of this meeting, the lasting gratitude of Ireland, and the admiration of the world.[239]

Gratitude was expressed in Ireland. Father Mathew, 'the apostle of temperance', informed a colleague in America:

> The magnificent humanity evinced by our beloved brethren in the States, for the suffering Irish, has inspired every heart in this island with ardent gratitude. We shall ever regard America as our deliverer in the hour of bitter calamity.

Mathew also spoke of his desire to visit the United States at the earliest opportunity and thank her people personally.[240] At this stage, Fr Mathew was a hero of abolitionists in the US. However, when he finally visited in 1849, he refused to make any public condemnation of slavery. For this stand, he was condemned by many, including Wendell Phillips who, in an open letter, opined, 'We do not allow a foreign birth to absolve any one, whose position gives him influence here, from speaking on behalf of the American slave'. He added:

> According to Father Mathew, while Ireland is starving, all the world not British born must keep silent on the cruel mistakes of Government which have ruined her . . . Did he not summon the world to her [Ireland's] rescue? The American Slave, a-hungered, with none to give him bread, a-thirst, with none to give him drink – sick, and in prison, with none to visit him – asks of the great Irishman the brand of his testimony.[241]

The intertwining of the slavery question with both Irish and American politics was apparent elsewhere. Vice-President Dallas was the recipient of a letter of thanks from William Smith O'Brien MP, on behalf of the Council of the Irish Confederation. The Confederation had been formed in January 1847 by a group often referred to as 'Young Ireland', who had broken away from Daniel O'Connell's repeal movement a few months earlier.[242] At the beginning of April, they sent a long letter to Dallas saying that when they heard of the Washington meeting:

> This intelligence lightened our despondency. We saw the greatest of the new nations of the earth moved by a universal impulse with sympathy for our country; the same men, of all creeds and parties, co-operating in giving effect to this generous sentiment.[243]

A plea was included on behalf of Irish emigrants to the US: 'They have a strong natural bias in favour of America, and all they require is information and experience, to make them a service and a strength to their adopted country'.[244]

This letter was to cause controversy in Ireland. Vice-President Dallas, a member of the Democratic Party, was an aggressive supporter of American expansionism, notably in Texas and Oregon. He was also a supporter of slavery.[245] James Haughton, a member of the Confederation and a leading Irish abolitionist, had repeatedly urged his colleagues not to accept money associated with, 'the blood-stained money of the slave drivers'.[246] Haughton objected to the letter being sent to Dallas on the grounds that the Vice-President was a slave-owner and that 'they [the Irish people] would never gain their own liberty if they were unmindful of the liberties done in the name of liberty abroad'.[247] Three weeks later, Haughton resigned from the Confederation, citing differences over the slave question.[248] He confided to an American friend that, 'A grateful feeling to America has, to a great extent, destroyed our hatred of slavery as it exists among you. You have bought off our condemnation of this wicked system'.[249]

The Corporation of Dublin issued an 'Address to the American People' which was sent to the President of the United States:

> We, the Lord Mayor, Aldermen and Burgesses of the Corporation of the City of Dublin, beg leave to tender to you, and through you, to the Federal Government and Legislature of the United States, our deep and affectionate gratitude for the prompt generosity with which you placed at the disposal of your benevolent citizens the national ships, the *Jamestown* and the *Macedonian,* for the purpose of conveying to our famishing countrymen the supplies of food furnished by the liberality of the noble-hearted people of your Republic.

Tellingly, the address went on to say:

> That the people of Ireland should be so often exhibited to the world as mendicants, receiving the charity of other nations, is deeply humiliating

to us, so that the pleasure of rendering you our thanks is dashed with gloomy and melancholy feeling . . . if there was any country to which the Irish people could feel pleasure in owing and acknowledging an obligation of this character, that country, Sir, would be yours.[250]

Even as the charitable interventions of the American people were in full swing and being publicly acknowledged, there was evidence of a backlash directing at all immigrants, particularly Irish at ones. Meetings were held as far apart as Boston and Charleston to discuss ways of preventing pauper immigration. The paradox of this response was illustrated by one American paper:

There is something to us revolting in these movements. Boston munificently sends the *Jamestown* to Ireland to feed the poor of that country, paying the charges of transportation etc., but when a few of these wretched people come to our shores, would drive them back to starvation and death! One is tempted to suspect a charity which delights in giving bread to the starving in Cork, and stones to the poor emigrant at Boston.[251]

By the end of 1847, fund-raising in the United States had mostly come to an end. Furthermore, in some areas goodwill towards the Irish appeared to have been exhausted as Famine-weary emigrants landed in the main ports of America and were greeted with hostility. The reasons for this attitudinal shift are not fully clear; some, perhaps, mistakenly believing that the Famine was truly over or even questioning the point of sending relief to Ireland. Whatever the reason, the consequence was that, 'the non-sectarian and interdenominational cooperation of 1847 on behalf of the starving in Ireland and Scotland rapidly faded from memory, obscured by the rise of temperance and nativism in the mid-1850s'.[252]

Overall, the charitable interventions on behalf of Ireland after 1846 threw into sharp relief the contrast between America's riches and Ireland's poverty. The abundance of the harvest was apparent in various regions within the British Empire in that year, notably India. The fund-raising activities at times became unwittingly embroiled in party politics, both Irish and American. Within the US, but less so elsewhere, the Repeal question frequently underpinned the response to Ireland's sufferings. When the Corporation of Dublin spoke of the 'humiliation' of Ireland, for having to rely on external charity, it raised the larger question of Ireland's colonial status and her position with the United Kingdom and the British Empire. Finally, the generous donations from America highlighted the issue of publicity versus anonymity; some people gave money possibly because they wanted their names in the paper; others felt that such a motivation was beneath them. For the receivers of this bounty in Ireland, the motivations were probably irrelevant. Charity, whatever its source, could make the difference between life and death. Survival was what mattered, long after names, dates and motivations had faded. Whatever the motivation, this could not negate the fact that, in the early months of 1847, a wave had swept over America that had prompted people, rich and poor, from all religious persuasions, and often with no direct connection to Ireland, to raise money to take food and clothes to Ireland. Undoubtedly, thousands of lives had been saved as a result. Tragically, the people who had survived the shortages of 1847 and remained in Ireland were now confronting a third year of disease, anguish and death.

11

'The most barbaric nation'.[1] Evangelicals and Charity

Religion was a dominant aspect of everyday life in the mid-nineteenth century.[2] Varieties of Protestantism were embraced by the majority of people in England, Scotland and Wales, but not in Ireland. Nonetheless, the Act of Union of 1800 had confirmed the Anglican Church as the state church of the newly created United Kingdom. Ireland, as the only Catholic nation within the Union, did not fit easily into this Protestant framework. By the early nineteenth century, British national identity was most clearly understood in terms of religious affiliation, and 'Protestantism, broadly understood, provided the majority of Britons with a framework for their lives'.[3] Furthermore, Linda Colley has argued, 'the most striking feature in the religious landscape [was] the gulf between Catholic and Protestant'.[4] It was inevitable that some of these tensions should manifest themselves during the Famine.

At the time of the first appearance of blight, approximately seven million Irish people were Catholic, while 970,000 belonged to the Established Anglican Church, 850,000 were Presbyterian and 140,000 were Wesleyan; Congregationalists, Baptists, Moravians, Quakers and other minority religions accounted for around 100,000 people.[5] Charity was not immune from these divisions and, according to Brian Harrison, 'Victorian philanthropists, especially evangelicals, saw philanthropy as an arena in which Protestantism could test itself against Catholicism'.[6] Despite their relatively small size, Protestant churches played a vital role in providing relief. Their involvement, however, was sometimes controversial due to the intertwining of relief with theological and political aspirations. Moreover, as historian Irish Maria Luddy has pointed out, 'the nature of nineteenth-century philanthropy was sectarian, reflecting the sectarianism which existed in society itself'.[7]

Members of the Protestant churches played a significant role in saving lives. Several appeals for assistance, including the two Queen's Letters, were made on grounds of providing Christian charity to the distressed Irish poor. Following the first appearance of blight, the British government recognized the value of working with local religious ministers, their preference being to work with ministers in the Church of Ireland, which was an autonomous part of the Anglican Communion. The fact that ministers, and often their families, were in the front line of providing relief to people who were dying of various famine-related diseases was evident from the fact that in 1847 alone, an estimated 30 Anglican priests died from famine fever.[8] Disproportionately, however, the history of Protestant churches during these years has been dominated by the part played by proselytizers.

The Second Reformation?

Throughout the eighteenth and nineteenth centuries, many evangelicals believed that the social, economic and political troubles of Ireland were attributable to the Catholicism of the overwhelming majority of its population. For evangelicals, conversion, through exposure to the Scriptures, was the solution. Proselytism had a long pedigree of being intertwined with assistance to the poor. This had been particularly evident in medical interventions. According to the historian Laurence Geary, 'Many prominent Dublin doctors of the eighteenth and nineteenth centuries ... were imbued with a strong evangelical zeal, which translated to their hospital presence and practice'.[9] Consequently, Bibles and religious tracts were kept alongside their medicines.[10] The increasing involvement of the state in matters of social welfare in the early nineteenth century was marked by a determination not to discriminate against Catholics. Thus, the Irish Poor Law, introduced in 1838, sought to treat all those who required relief equally and without regard to religion, albeit it did not meet with total success.[11] The attempts by successive governments to be impartial led some evangelical organizations to accuse them of being anti-Protestant.[12]

In contrast to official policy, private attempts at proselytizing gained fresh impetus in the early decades of the nineteenth century. The social and political advances made by Catholics in the years following the Union led many evangelicals to renew their efforts to stamp out Popery by promoting missionary activity in Ireland.[13] These activities were not confined to church organizations. A number of evangelical landlords were enthusiastic supporters of religious conversion. In 1826, Lord Farnham, a landowner in County Cavan, founded an 'association for promoting the Second Reformation in Ireland'.[14] The winning of Catholic Emancipation in 1829, which gave Catholics throughout the United Kingdom the right to sit in the Westminster Parliament, was a major blow to the Protestant Ascendancy. In its wake, the *Evangelical Magazine and Missionary Chronicle* asked, 'How can Ireland ever become Protestant? ... We verily believe she must if she is not *conciliated* ... We rejoice in what has already been done for the spiritual interests of Ireland; but we long to see the day when the strongholds of Popery, in that interesting country, shall be shaken to their very foundation, and when the religion of the Bibles shall enlighten and bless every cabin from one end of the island to the other'.[15]

Many evangelical societies had their roots in the eighteenth century, but a new zeal became apparent following the Act of Union. The attempts to win converts were intensified during periods of food shortages. or widespread disease. In 1814, the Irish Evangelical Society was formed with committees in London and Dublin. The Society's main purpose was to promote the Gospel among the Irish people.[16] It was especially active during the food shortages of 1831 when 57 agents – who spoke both Irish and English – travelled through the distressed districts and distributed £3,759 worth of relief and Bibles.[17] The 1831 famine and cholera epidemic also resulted in districts in County Kerry, including Dingle and Ventry, becoming centres of proselytizing activities. The early proselytizers had been funded by Lord Ventry, an absentee local landlord. The wife of the landlord's agent, Mrs D. P. Thompson, consolidated these endeavours by opening a school for orphaned girls. A subscription collected in England enabled a 'Dingle Colony' to be established, which, by 1840, comprised of 15 cottages.[18] The use of soup kitchens to attract converts resulted in a dispute with a local parish priest who forbade his parishioners from taking the soup from the 'soupers'.[19] Despite the stigma attached to 'souperism' and to taking the soup, the experiences in the decades preceding the Famine had demonstrated that proselytizers were most successful during periods of food shortages.

Famine

For some evangelicals, the repeated failure of the crop after 1845 confirmed their view that Irish Catholics had offended God, while conveniently providing an opportunity to renew their efforts to convert the peasantry.[20] Within the Whig government, an influential group that included Charles Wood, the Chancellor of the Exchequer, also viewed the Famine through a providentialist lens. This interpretation was shared by the Permanent Secretary at the Treasury, Charles Trevelyan.[21] These men were disproportionately important in deciding how government relief was to be distributed as, from the first appearance of blight, the Treasury had been put in charge of the day-to-day administration of relief. Consequently, the starving poor, who were facing an unprecedented period of food shortages, became pawns in other people's spiritual and political agendas.

Not all evangelicals took this opportunist approach to the suffering of the Irish Catholic poor. Asenath Nicholson had first visited Ireland in 1844 with the intention of distributing Bibles and learning more about the lives of the poor. When she returned during the Famine, she made it clear that her primary motive was to provide relief, not to proselytize. Nicholson regarded it as her Christian duty to help the poor. Moreover, she believed that converts gained under such circumstances would have no lasting attachment to the

Bible and its principles, but would return to their own religion, 'when the hunger was appeased and the "blessed potato" should come [and] they could say Mass at home again'.[22] Nicholson firmly rejected the idea that the Famine was a judgement of God on the Irish people asking, 'Was there then a "God's famine" in Ireland, in 1846–49, and so on? No! it is all mockery to call it so, and mockery which the Almighty will expose'.[23]

The appearance of the potato blight demonstrated that anti-Catholicism was ingrained among some sections of the Anglican Church. The *British Magazine*[24] became a forum for Anglican ministers in both Britain and Ireland to discuss how they could best intervene in Ireland. In a long article entitled 'Scarcity' that appeared in the *British Magazine* in February 1847, the author cautioned against allowing Catholic priests to serve on relief committees, accusing them of 'jobbing' (showing favouritism), selling tickets to the starving poor, while looking after their own friends, 'there are few artifices to which they will not resort'.[25] One letter alluded to a priest who had refused to administer the last rites because he knew he would not be paid. The writer urged that charitable donations should be sent only to a Protestant minister:

> and by supplying him with funds, and provisions, and clothing, and seed, enable him to conciliate the affections of the suffering people to the Protestant church. It is, in fact, such an opportunity to doing lasting and extensive good as may never occur again.[26]

He later suggested that there was no need for overt proselytizing, as people would naturally remember their good works.[27]

Thomas Vores, the Curate of St Mary's Church in Hastings, took a different approach. He suggested to the Editor of the *Record* that wealthy Anglican parishes in England should each adopt a parish in Ireland to provide relief. Just as important as providing sustenance though, was his recommendation that they should, where possible, 'place at the disposal of the Minister whose parish we may select, an Irish Scripture-Reader and thus provide bread for the soul as well as the body'.[28] Promises of spiritual succour were sometimes augmented by bodily sustenance in the form of soup. In May 1847, Rev Garret Prendergast, the parish priest of Ardmore in Waterford, accused the local church of Ireland curate, the Rev Arthur Leech, of 'souperism', funded by money from England and aimed at children:

> In order the more effectually to succeed in this unholy work, he estab-lished a soup kitchen in the immediate vicinity of the school to lure the Famine-stricken children from their duty to their legitimate pastors; this soup is bountifully given to all who frequent the school, and also their respective parents, who are starving in their miserable cabins. By these means they have succeeded in kidnapping many of my unfortu-nate children.[29]

An evangelical endeavour established before the Famine and surrounded in controversy was the Protestant Mission in Achill Island, off the coast of County Mayo. It had been founded in 1834 by the Dublin-born Rev Edward Nangle. Nangle had first visited Achill during the food shortages of 1831 and decided to establish a permanent Protestant missionary there. Three years later, he and his family moved to the island. Asenath Nicholson, who also visited the island on the eve of the Famine, regarded Nangle's 'settlement' as fraudulent and criticized both Mr and Mrs Nangle for imposing conversion on the local poor.[30] She included her censure of the colony in her first book describing her time in Ireland.[31] Regardless of the fact that the food shortages had a negative impact on all parts of Ireland, Rev Nangle, like many evangelicals, saw the potato failure as a judgement of God on Catholics, for believing in idolatrous gods.[32] During the Famine period, his colony appeared to flourish. In the winter of 1846, Nangle arranged for a shipload of meal to come to the island. In the spring of 1847, he reported that the colony was giving employment to 2,192 labourers and feeding 600 children a day in the schools.[33] Nicholson revisited Achill during the Christmas holiday period in 1847.[34] In her opinion, not only was Nangle using the poverty of the local poor as a way of winning converts, but the relief that he provided was palpably insufficient:

> He had eleven schools scattered through that region, reading the Scriptures, and learning Irish but all through these parts might be seen the fallacy of distributing a little over a great surface. The scanty allowance given to the children once a day, and much of this bad food, kept them in lingering want, and many died at last.[35]

Nangle, however, appeared to have no shortage of money. In 1850, Nangle's mission purchased two-thirds of the island through the Encumbered Estates' Court. The remainder of the island was purchased by Archbishop MacHale of Tuam and his nephew.[36] At the time of his retirement, Nangle claimed to have made 2,000 converts. Privately, he admitted that 'had it not been for the Famine of '47, his mission in Achill would have been a failure'.[37]

The Irish Relief Association

Not all evangelical charities used the Famine as an opportunity to proselytize. The Irish Relief Association was formed on 2 September 1846, with headquarters at 16 Upper Sackville Street in Dublin. The Association was a reorganized committee that first had been established during the food shortages of 1831 to help distressed areas in the west. Patrons of the new committee included the Duke of Manchester, the Earl of Roden, the Marquis of Downshire and the Archbishop of Dublin, each of whom was involved with a number of other evangelical organizations. One of the Honorary

Secretaries was Lord George Hill from Gweedore in County Donegal, who was renowned, and widely praised, for his 'improving' approach to landowning.[38] Regardless of the ultra-Protestant leanings of some of the founders of the Association, it proved highly effective in providing relief to all denominations.

One of the early actions of the Irish Relief Association was to charter a steamer in Liverpool and load her with breadstuffs for counties Donegal and Mayo, at a cost of £1796.0s.11d.[39] The Mayo cargo, and subsequent ones, were entrusted to Rev Patrick Pounden, the Anglican Rector of Westport. Pounden, with the support of the Marquis of Sligo and the Dowager Marchioness, opened a soup kitchen in Westport at the beginning of 1847.[40] His premature death in April 1847 was attributed by the secretaries of the Association to 'exhaustion'.[41] One of the main contributions of the Irish Relief Association was to provide boilers in which soup could be made. Detailed questionnaires were prepared for this purpose, with a view to, 'Obtaining information as to the amount of distress, the supplies of food available in each district, the local subscriptions and exertions, and the various means to provide food and employment for the starving peasantry'. The Applications were required to be, 'signed by two or three members of the Local Relief Committee, if any such exists, if not, by persons of high respectability'.[42] Furthermore, 'no grants be made in money, but in materials of provisions and their contingencies alone'.[43] However, as heart-rending requests flowed in, the rules were relaxed and grants in money were given, usually for the purchase of food. The Irish Relief Association also distributed clothing, mostly received from ladies' societies in England. In general, the clothes were entrusted to a local minister or ladies' committee for redistribution. A high portion was distributed in the west of Ireland, but parcels were also sent to Dervock in County Antrim (care of Rev F. Dobbs) and Portadown in County Armagh (care of Rev D. Babington).[44] A more unusual gift to the Association came in the form of two chests of cocoa from 'Mr J. Hunter' in Manchester, England. The contents of this curious contribution were divided between ministers in Gorey, Carlow, Dungarvan, Longford, Portadown and Cloyne.[45]

The first request formally processed by the Association was at the beginning of December 1846. By 15 January 1847, they had supplied 123 boilers and were finding it difficult to keep up with applications for additional ones.[46] At this stage, regardless of all of the public and private assistance being provided, the Association reported pessimistically that 'thousands, they believe, *are dying from want of sustenance*'.[47] In the period from 15 January to 15 February, the Irish Relief Association provided a further 273 boilers, at a cost of £819. By 31 March, they had made available a total of 666 boilers.[48] At this stage, the Association had raised £28,223.18s.4d., of which £18,708.8s.6d. had been spent on provisions and £2,074.5s.0d. for boilers, while their office expenses totalled £540.7s.8d.[49] In total, assistance had been provided to over 780 applicants, some of whom had received as many as four separate grants.[50]

In the months following its formation, Irish newspapers carried advertisements regarding the Association's work and appealing for funding.[51] Overseas donations came from a wide geographical range stretching from St Jude's Irish Relief Committee in Liverpool (the church of Rev Hugh McNeile, who was known for anti-Catholic views), to subscriptions raised in Asia. Some assistance was provided in provisions, and cargoes of foodstuffs had been sent from the residents of Selma in Alabama and from Niagara in Canada.[52] Individual subscriptions included ones from Rev Bickersteth in England, who gave £3; Prince George of Cambridge, £50; Arthur Guinness, £200; and the Duke of Manchester, £20. Donations made within Ireland were diverse and cut across social classes: inmates of a refuge for the destitute gave £9; the faculty of Trinity College, Dublin, £300, which included £27 from the students' Commons; servants working in Sir Patrick Dun's Hospital, eight shillings; associates of the Irish Art Union gave £250; and members of the Constabulary who were based in the Phoenix Park donated £58.19s.9d. Large amounts of money were collected in England, including £8,149 from subscriptions in various towns, and £2,803 given by Anglican clergy. Generous subscriptions came from overseas, coming from as far away as India (£2,599), Australia (£2,314) and America, Canada and the Caribbean (£4,702).[53]

Regardless of their evangelical leanings, the Irish Relief Association insisted that the giving of their grants 'should not be influenced by either sect or party, and that a preference should be given in all cases *only* to the most destitute, without religious or political distinction'.[54] Accordingly, they acceded to requests from applicants as diverse as Brother Bernard Garry from the Franciscan Monastery in Errew near Castlebar, Rev Dr Traill, the Church of Ireland rector in Schull, Michael Brannigan, a Presbyterian missionary preacher in Belmullet and Rev Nangle's Mission on Achill Island.[55] Nonetheless, the religious motives underpinning the work of the Association were clear. They described their work, although 'painful and trying' as a 'labour of love', and their aim having been 'that God in all things may be glorified through Jesus Christ, to whom be praise and dominion for ever and ever'. Each report of the Association was ended with a similar religious sentiment.[56] They also issued appeals in the Belfast newspapers pointing out that the existing crisis presented an opportunity 'for conveying the light of the Gospels to the darkened mind of the Roman Catholic peasantry', leading O'Connell to accuse their committee of being 'ultra-Protestant'.[57] The implication was that, by being good Christians, the Irish people could thus become good subjects.

In 1847, the Irish Relief Association published 'The Lapse of Years, or Thoughts suggested by the close of another period of time'.[58] It was an anonymous religious tract concerned with salvation through redemption.

It viewed the events of the previous year through a providentialist prism, but believed that much good would come of the suffering, as it had allowed those who were 'spiritually dead' to pass from death into spiritual life. As a consequence, they believed, '1846 forms an era which will be joyfully remembered throughout an endless eternity'.[59] As 1847 commenced, and presented similar challenges to those of the previous year, the writer recommended, 'primarily, it is the duty of those who have received, to promulgate and bring men under the power and saving influence of the gospel of Christ'.[60] The opportunity presented by the distress to bring the gospel to the Irish poor was explained:

> Ever ready to sympathize in, and lend our aid to remunerate the spiritual condition of heathen lands in distant climes, surely we evidence a dereliction of duty, if we overlook the state of our native country, in which crimes, the result of its demoralizing condition, are daily recurring, which are unsurpassed in any heathen land.[61]

Although the Famine was continuing, 'as annulled in its nature, as it is likely to prove most awful in its results', the writer was convinced 'that it is a judgment for His outraged laws few will deny'. Again, he saw the suffering as punishment for 'crimes unequalled in the darkest ages, or amongst the most barbaric nations'.[62] Repeatedly, the point was made that the Famine presented an opportunity for 'the churches of the Reformation' to exercise everlasting charity in the form of bringing Bibles to the people.[63] Such sentiments seemed at variance with the Irish Relief Association's declared aim to provide relief with no regard to religion.

The Irish Relief Association formally wound up its activities on 4 November 1847, at a meeting chaired by Lord Roden. For two months, they had received no new income, which they attributed to the new relief measures being implemented and the consequent closing of the local relief committees.[64] The committee met again in January. Despite the existence of widespread distress, they believed that the prospects of raising any further funds were 'quite hopeless'.[65] It was decided to give their residual income, which amounted to £2,500, to the Ladies' Relief Association for Ireland, and smaller sums to the Ladies' Industrial Society, both of which had evangelical leanings.[66] On 4 May 1848, a further meeting was held to decide how to dispose of the money left over. Despite having ceased operations some months earlier, they were still receiving applications for assistance. The committee debated whether they should follow the example of the British Relief Association and use what little money they had to feed the schoolchildren, but decided that this would be too difficult to execute. Instead, they decided to bequeath the money to one parish. Significantly, they chose to give it to an evangelical mission, not to a charitable body. Rev Nangle on Achill Island was the beneficiary. He received £500 and the small residue was given to the Ladies' Irish Relief Association.[67] The final, brief meeting of the Association took place in July 1848. A closing statement reinforced their providentialist view of the tragedy and of their charitable labours:

> Conscious that the Lord never does anything in vain. . . they entertain a sanguine hope that the afflicting dispensation that called the Relief Association into existence, will eventually be overruled for good. They trust that a spirit of energy will be engendered, that an improved system of agriculture will more extensively be introduced, and that plans calculated to give a stimulus to exertion will be devised.[68]

The report of this gathering ended simply with 'Amen'.[69]

During their brief existence, the Irish Relief Association had raised £42,446.5s.0d.[70] The hard-working committee had received over 1,500 individual applications, which filled five large volumes. These questionnaires provided detailed accounts both of local suffering and of local sacrifices. The Association's work emphasized the fact that the need for charitable intervention was not confined to the west of Ireland; every county in Ireland had received both boilers and grants, including 18 boilers to both Counties Armagh and Clare, as well as grants of £531.6s.0d. and £475.0s.0d. respectively, indicating that the poor in the north-east were in need of charitable interventions just as much as those in the south-west.[71] More importantly, whatever their views of the Catholic Irish peasantry, in the short term, the Irish Association provided a vital safety net for people who were not being safeguarded by government relief measures.

A charity that operated in parallel to the Irish Relief Association and shared a similar religious outlook was the National Club of London. This society had been established on 17 June 1845, 'in support of the Protestant principles of the constitution and for raising the moral and social condition of the people'.[72] To this end, they issued a number of *Addresses to the Protestants of the Empire*.[73] Following the second failure of the potato, the National Club established a Famine Relief Fund for Ireland and Scotland and, as early as October 1846, was providing grants to distressed areas.[74] By the end of January 1847, they had raised over £9,000.[75] Many of these grants were made to committees and individuals that would later apply to the Irish Relief Association.[76] This had increased to over £16,000 by April 1847.[77] Of this sum, approximately £1,700 went to Scottish relief.[78] In total, the National Club raised almost £20,000 for famine relief.[79] The evangelical aims of the society were clear, but their donations to Ireland saved lives.

Relief from Belfast

There were a number of instances of cooperation between the main Protestant churches. An example occurred in Belfast. On 5 January 1847, the Belfast General Relief Fund was founded by two prominent evangelicals, the Rev Dr Thomas Drew, Anglican minister of Christ Church and Rev

Dr John Edgar, a leading Presbyterian minister. For a number of years prior to the Famine, Drew had been actively involved with several missionary societies that were devoted to taking the Gospels to 'unenlightened parts of the earth'.[80] Within a few weeks, the Belfast Relief Fund had raised over £4,000 in subscriptions which, a few months later, exceeded £7,000. Most of this money was to be expended in the west, a decision that was criticized by the Belfast press who felt that the poor of the town should have first call on these funds. Some financial support came from across the Atlantic. Samuel H. Cox, who was based in Brooklyn, New York, sent donations to Belfast to be distributed between Rev John Edgar DD and the Rev James Morgan DD., whom he recommended for their 'intelligence, philanthropy and faithful care'. Cox, however, stipulated that the relief was not only for the Protestant poor.[81] On 12 May 1847, the Fund decided to close its operations, as the Temporary Relief Act was coming into effect[82] During its brief time in existence, a subcommittee had worked for seven hours each day to keep up with demands on their resources. In total, the Belfast Fund had provided 206 separate grants to all parts of Ireland, including Belfast, exclusively for the purchase of food.[83] Regardless of the evangelical leanings of the two founders, the Belfast Fund had put the physical needs of the poor above spiritual ones. Both Edgar and Drew, however, were involved in a number of other relief projects, with overt missionary objectives.

For Edgar, the Honorary Secretary of the Home Mission of the Irish Presbyterian Church, the Famine provided a unique opening to extend his work in the west of Ireland. By the end of 1846, Edgar and his followers had established 144 schools, primarily in counties Mayo and Sligo. He believed the second crop failure meant that much more could be achieved. To maximize this opportunity, appeals were made to their sister organizations in America and Scotland. Edgar requested that the latter should provide ministers to visit those districts 'which God, in his providence, has so wonderfully opened up to their Evangelistic endeavours'.[84] His words fell on fertile grounds, with Presbyterians in Ireland, Scotland and the United States responding. The Perth Synod answered:

> The recent awful calamity and famine which has overtaken Ireland, and more especially the fact that this calamity has fallen upon the poorest, appeared to be God's way for preparing their hearts for the reception of the truth. The people are now alive to the selfishness of their priests; and instead of looking upon Protestants as their enemies, they now regard them as their friends.[85]

The appeal to the United States made it clear that the Irish Synod was adopting a providentialist interpretation to the crisis:

> We are grateful to the Almighty God while we humbly regard it as an illustration of the industry and general comfort promoted by our beloved

Church, that in Ulster, where our principles are most widely disseminated, the visitation has appeared in a much less aggravated form than in those provinces in which the Romish system still, unhappily, maintains its degrading and paralyzing ascendancy.[86]

Robert Gault, a Presbyterian minister in Balderg, County Mayo, added his own appeal to Edgar's, alleging, 'The whole land is opened before us, if we had only the courage to colonize and the heart to seek its thorough evangelization'.[87] Edgar was also involved with the Belfast Ladies' Relief Association, which was active in providing relief in Connaught.[88] The high-profile activities of Edgar and his supporters alarmed members of the Catholic Church hierarchy in Ireland. A letter from an unnamed priest in County Down to Archbishop MacHale, which was published in the *Belfast Vindicator*, warned: 'Whilst he [Edgar] pretended to busy himself with the temporal wants of the Catholics of the west, he was providing a rich spiritual riposte for the Presbyterians of the north'.[89]

Even more controversial than the work of Edgar and the Presbyterian Missions was the involvement of Rev Thomas Drew, who was a prominent member of 'The Fund for the Temporal Relief of the Suffering Poor of Ireland through the Instrumentality of the Clergy of the Established Church'. The committee of the Temporal Relief Fund admitted that, as a consequence of the food shortages:

> In numerous cases an opening has been made for conveying the light of the Gospel into the darkened mind of the Roman Catholic peasantry thus severely suffering; they have listened with the deepest attention to the ministers of the church proclaiming the way of salvation while humanely engaged in efforts to rescue their bodies from famine and disease. A wide and effectual door is thus thrown open to our brethren in the hitherto benighted parts of Ireland.[90]

The overt proselytizing aims of this body provoked a strong response in the local press. The *Banner of Ulster* accused them of introducing 'a spirit of sectarianism' into relief provisions, adding, 'At a time when such frightful destitution is prevalent, it is surely most unwise to put forth denominational peculiarities in such an offensive form and thus to give the impression that proselytism is to be the basis of charity.'[91]

The *Northern Whig* was no less critical, describing the Temporal Fund as 'the most revolting record we have yet met connected with the visitation'. The paper urged the people of Belfast not to support it:

> It will be a woeful thing if even the open and common field of charity, benevolence and love, be converted into an arena for sectarian conflict. But this will not be permitted in Belfast. People here are deeply impressed with the sacred duty of endeavouring to guard their unfortunate fellow

creatures from starvation, and they will not, on such occasion, sink or put down party feeling, the operations of which, whether they proceed from political difference or religious distinctions, would be alike misplaced and, as we believe, sinful.[92]

Criticism of the Temporal Fund and its supporters was voiced further afield, in Dublin. The *Evening Packet* suggested it had been founded by 'a knot of Belfast fanatics'.[93] An even more powerful detractor was the Anglican Archbishop of Dublin, Richard Whately. He denounced his Belfast co-religionists who gave any encouragement to the Fund, pointing out, 'All the grace of charitable action is destroyed if we present ourselves as seeking to take an ungenerous advantage of misery and convert our benefactions into a bribe to induce men to do violence to their consciences'.[94] Regardless of such vocal opposition, by March 1847, the Temporal Fund had raised over £2,000, which had been used to make 108 grants in 22 counties.[95]

Methodist activities

At the time of the Famine, there were two Methodist churches in Ireland, the Primitive Wesleyan Methodist Society and the larger Wesleyan Methodist Society (also referred to as the Methodist Connexion). The Primitive Methodists had been active during the famine of 1822 when they had worked to 'bring the hungry out of the darkness of Catholicism', mostly by holding field meetings throughout the country.[96] Similarly to other evangelicals, they realized that 'the Irish language was the most powerful instrument to get at the Irish heart'.[97] By 1845, the Primitives had a network of mission stations throughout the country and an estimated 14,372 members.[98] The Wesleyan Methodists had 27,546 members and 162 ministers.[99]

For some Primitive Methodists, the blight was retribution on Roman Catholic, not only for their religious beliefs, but for their political activities: 'This Divine visitation was no doubt, the means of saving this country from the curse of a most fatal civil war'.[100] The idea that the Famine was a punishment from God proved to be pervasive. According to the Rev William G. Campbell, a Primitive Methodist minister in Tullamore, the local starving 'were all willing to acknowledge that the present calamity was judgment from heaven'.[101] Showing more concern for their spiritual than their physical condition, he added:

I visited a family today, some of whom attended our chapel when their clothing permitted them to appear in public, but who are not members of our Society. And O! the scene. The father, a venerable looking man, lay on straw, covered with what was once a man's coat. He declared he had not eaten a morsel but what he had received from some of our houses on the morning of the day before. His cries for pardoning mercy were truly affecting, and I trust the Lord will hear prayer in his behalf . . . the most affecting scene of all is when I went to prayer. Their cries and tears bespoke the anguish of their souls, and I must say that I thought their spiritual concerns had the preponderance in their distress.[102]

At the time of the Famine, Revs Robert Huston and Henderson were already acting as general itinerant missionaries in Ireland, preaching in the streets or nearby fields of many of the main towns.[103] Huston had been preaching in Ireland since the 1830s and had successfully established a number of new chapels, including one in Dundalk on land owned by the Earl of Roden.[104] During the Famine years, he sent regular reports of his work with Henderson, which were reprinted in the London *Watchman* and the New York *Christian Advocate*. Huston admitted that he had entered the most recent mission, 'in weakness, and in fear, and with much trembling', and that doubts had been raised about the efficacy of outdoor preaching in the present state of Ireland, but, 'Thousands of Romanists . . . have heard us gladly', and they had succeeded in converting hundreds of people. He believed that the Famine had undermined the power of the Catholic priests.[105]

Regardless of their small numbers, Methodists' efforts at conversion were facilitated by the itinerant nature of their ministry and the use of field meetings, which obviated the need for permanent chapels. The activities of these missionaries were reported in the British, Irish and American evangelical newspapers. America, with its majority Methodist population, was particularly targeted for financial support. The *Christian Advocate* published regularly on the deteriorating state of Ireland and the starvation of 'a brave but misguided people'.[106] These reports were important in raising funds for the missions. In 1847, Primitive Methodists in Britain raised almost £6,000 on behalf of their colleagues in Ireland.[107] Like those of other evangelical groups, their efforts were directed particularly at children. By 1848, they had established 53 Sunday and 63 day schools.[108]

Not all of the relief provided by the Methodists was concerned with proselytizing. The Methodist societies looked after their own followers who were suffering as a result of the crop failures. The Dublin Wesleyan Relief Committee, headed by the Rev Robert Masaroon, worked with the Central Wesleyan Committee in London to support their destitute members. In February 1847, Masaroon estimated that 6,350 of their members were suffering and that, 'from the accounts we daily receive *this distress is frightfully increasing*'.[109] An appeal made by the London Committee to the international Wesleyan community for special collections in their chapels had, by 9 March 1847, raised £17,000. It was decided to distribute this money, 'without respect to religious opinions and through the Relief Associations previously in existence'. To this end, the following grants were made:

The British Relief Association £5,000
Wesleyan Ministers in Ireland £2,500

Irish Relief Association £1,000
Wesleyan Central Relief Fund £300
Irish and Scottish Famine Fund £500
United Committee for Scotland £500
Established Church of Scotland £250
'Friends' Irish Relief Society £250
Ladies' Irish Clothing Society £250
Baptist Irish Society £100
Irish Evangelical Society £100
Rev Watson, Shetland £25
Miscellaneous Irish localities £80[110]

There were some instances of Methodist ministers cooperating with other churches to provide relief. The Rev James Collier, Primitive Methodist minister on the Castlebar circuit in County Mayo, worked alongside the local Catholic and Anglican priests to open the first soup kitchen in Castlebar, and they each took turns in attending it. However, the desire to combine saving souls with saving lives was compelling and the Rev Fossey Tackaberry of the Sligo circuit admitted that he gave out tracts as he visited the poor of all denominations and, 'told Romanists of Him who made satisfaction for them on Cavalry'.[111]

The Irish Church Missions

In addition to the activities of the evangelicals already working in Ireland, a number of societies were especially formed to take advantage of the crisis, several of which were associated with the Established Church. One scheme to bring about the 'moral, social and civil elevation' to the 'down-trodden and priest-ridden people' was devised by Rev Edward Bickersteth and the English philanthropist and reformer, Lord Ashley (after 1851, the 7th Earl of Shaftesbury). Bickersteth was an English-born evangelical minister, who was active in a number of religious societies involved in conversion.[112] Bickersteth and Ashley worked closely with the Rev Alexander Dallas, an English-born minister in the Established Church who, despite not being based in Ireland, achieved notoriety as one of the most unrelenting of all of the proselytizers. He was a cousin of the American Vice-President George Dallas who, in February 1847, had convened a meeting on behalf of the Irish poor in Washington.[113]

In January 1846, using the newly established 'uniform penny post', Dallas anonymously sent Gospel literature to over 20,000 Roman Catholic homes at a cost of over £80. This, and much of Dallas's work in Ireland, was financed by a wealthy English businessman, Enosh Durant.[114] Dallas was helped in his work by Miss Mason and Fanny Bellingham, both of whom lived in Dublin. Frances Bellingham was a daughter of Sir Alan Bellingham of Bellingham Castle in County Louth.[115] Dallas's introduction to her had come through the brewer and evangelical philanthropist, Arthur Guinness.[116] Dallas confessed to Bellingham that he would, 'gladly meet the martyrdom of a Tipperary bullet' if that would help his mission to end the power of the Roman Church in Ireland.[117] No bullet was forthcoming and Dallas was encouraged to send out a second batch of 16,000 letters.[118] In addition to sending literature, Dallas recruited eight itinerant Protestant Gospel missionaries, or 'Messengers', to travel to Ireland and preach from village to village.[119] At the beginning of 1847, Dallas penned a tract entitled, 'The Food of Man', in which he pointed out that 'as the priests had cursed the food which God had provided for the soul, God had withdrawn his blessing from that which he usually supplied for the body'.[120] It was a bitter message for those hungry people who were being targeted to receive Dallas's spiritual succour.

Rev Bickersteth believed that the failure of the potato crop 'opened a way for efforts to benefit Ireland'.[121] However, he differentiated his work from that of other fund-raisers:

> While Englishmen, in general, felt the plain duty of relieving temporal distress, there were a smaller number of earnest Christians who saw, in this visitation of God, a still louder call to care for perishing souls, and to raise them from the darkness of sin and superstition into the glorious liberty of the Gospel of Christ.[122]

To achieve this objective, a committee was formed at the end of 1846 called, 'A Special Fund for the Spiritual Exigencies of Ireland'. It was headed by Revs Dallas and Bickerseth, together with Durant, their financial backer.[123] The purpose of the Special Fund was 'the collecting of the large sums for Irish distress, to meet the spiritual wants of the land'.[124] By 25 December 1846, over £1,000 had been raised.[125] By January 1847, this had risen to over £4,000. By early March, it exceeded £6,000.[126] The founders made it clear that none of this money was to be used to provide food, 'or temporal benefits of any kind'. Instead, it was solely to 'meet the spiritual exigencies of Ireland'.[127] As people died of starvation, donations raised for Ireland were used to fund 'a phalanx of colporteurs and Scripture-readers [to] read the Word of God to as many as can be persuaded to listen'. They and their benefactors believed that: 'When Ireland shall be redeemed from her intellectual and moral degradation, inflicted by her priesthood, she will be prosperous and happy, but not before'.[128]

Dallas visited Ireland at the end of 1846. In the north, he met with the Earl of Roden, who supported his work.[129] Dallas's early efforts encouraged him to create a permanent base in Ireland, choosing Rooveagh in west Galway, 'a land of darkness', for 'the first missionary effort'.[130] The Galway mission was supported by Hyacinth D'Arcy, the owner of Clifden Castle and an ally of

Dallas.[131] They had been introduced by Fanny Bellingham. D'Arcy was the Chair of the local relief committee, which had been established in 1846, and Chairman of the Clifden Board of Guardians, the workhouse only opening in March 1847. In keeping with his evangelical views, he would not allow any Catholics to be members of the former committee.[132] In 1847, D'Arcy travelled to Dublin to meet with Strzelecki of the British Relief Association to ask him to provide support to Church of Ireland schools in Connemara. For Dallas, these schools provided a further opportunity for introducing the scriptures to schoolchildren.[133] When, due to lack of funds, the British Relief Association withdrew in August 1848, D'Arcy kept his schools open, funded by Dallas.[134] In 1848, Dallas visited the remote parish of Derrygimla near Errismore, because he had been told that a large number of the local people wanted to convert. He was accompanied by D'Arcy.[135] Wherever he travelled, he told the poor that he was bringing them relief – spiritual relief – pointing out to the starving people, 'Man shall not live by bread alone'.[136]

The various schemes to convert poor Catholics were not without critics. Rev Bickersteth was singled out for criticism in the British House of Lords by the liberal peer, Lord Brougham:

> Rev. Mr. Bickersteth, advocating a subscription of 20,000l. to raise a fund for sending missionaries to Ireland, alleging that they should strike while the iron was hot, and that the present period of suffering in Ireland was a favourable moment for converting the Catholics to Protestantism. This was as bad a thing, nay, it was one of the most wicked things, one of the most diabolical devices for sowing dissension where only charity should prevail, that he had ever heard of.[137]

Daniel O'Connell also charged Rev Bickersteth and other proselytizers with taking 'advantage of Irish starvation, for bribing the peasantry to renounce their faith'.[138] In response, Bickersteth recorded in his private journal that his projects had been opposed by 'the Infidel and the Papal Party and by Lord Brougham in the House of Commons'.[139] The 'Infidel' referred to was O'Connell. Some members of the Protestant churches were uncomfortable with the work of the evangelicals. Dr Whately, the Church of Ireland Archbishop of Dublin, criticized the Rev Dallas and his agents for censure in their work with the poor.[140] Some of Dallas's fellow churchmen in England also mistrusted his enthusiasm and zeal for converting Catholics at a time of want.[141]

Regardless of the controversy over Bickersteth and Dallas's methods, money continued to flow in. They had raised almost £7,000 by the beginning of April 1847, which encouraged them to issue a second appeal for funding. By the end of June, £8,021 had been donated. The money was divided between the 'Church Education 'Additional Curates' Societies, 'Irish scripture readers', 'Hibernian Female Schools', 'Cork Pastoral Aid' 'Achill and Dingle Missions' and the 'Irish Islands Society'.[142] In March 1849, Rev

Dallas, supported by Bickersteth and Durant, convened a meeting in London to found the Irish Church Missions to the Roman Catholics, thus creating a permanent base for their proselytizing activities.[143] The suffering of the Irish was thus used as a platform for bringing about permanent changes in their religious beliefs.

Dallas's joy at the creation of the Church Missions was tinged with sadness as shortly afterwards, his friend, fellow evangelical and financial backer, Enosh Durant died.[144] In 1850, Edward Bickersteth also died. In order to sustain the work of the Church Missions Society, regular appeals were made to the 'Christians' of Britain. An appeal in 1850 included an endorsement from Rev John Gregg, Anglican Archdeacon of Kildare and, later, the Bishop of Cork: 'If the friends of the Mission are able to go on supporting it, as they have done, for a few years, I am sure that all the men on earth, and all the powers of Satan, will not be able to put it down'.[145] Another of Dallas's supporters, Hyacinth D'Arcy, was experiencing his own financial difficulties. Ironically, in 1850, Clifden Castle and its demesne, containing 627 acres, were sold in Dublin by the Encumbered Estates' Commissioners.[146] D'Arcy responded by devoting even more time to evangelical work. In July 1851, he became a Church of Ireland minister, working in the Omey district of west Galway. He married Fanny Bellingham in July 1852.[147]

Similarly to its predecessor, the Church Mission Society especially targeted children. The Famine had increased the number of orphans and evangelical organizations took advantage of this fact.[148] Dallas created 'The Connemara Orphans' Nursery', the Rev Gregg donating £1 to assist its opening. Within a short time, it contained 100 orphans.[149] Dallas also established additional ragged schools and homes for orphaned children. These institutions were largely concentrated in West Connemara. Dallas had much larger ambitions, however, admitting to a friend that he aimed at 'nothing less than the Protestantizing of Ireland'.[150] The Connemara Mission attracted a number of visitors from England. An English visitor in May 1852 found the schools to be well attended and that even young children were familiar with the Scriptures. He recommended, 'Many are skeptical with regard to the great work of the Reformation in Connemara, but let them go and see what the Lord is doing there. Although we had heard much of it, we were not disappointed'.[151] Praise, on a more practical level, came from the Rev Gregg, who suggested that without the work of the missions, hundreds of children would have died of hunger.[152]

Proselytizing was not confined to the west of the country. In 1848, two of Dallas's benefactors, Fanny Bellingham and Arthur Guinness, founded 'The Dublin Visiting Mission'. Despite being the capital of Ireland, Dublin accounted for less than three per cent of the country's population, approximately one-quarter of whom belonged to the Established Church. Significantly, a high percentage of the local Catholic population was poor, and poverty and disease had increased in Dublin, as in other towns and cities, after 1845.[153] Bellingham and Guinness employed a number of agents who were directed to focus on 'the poorest and most neglected parts of the city – Cork Street, New Street, Townsend Street, Summer Hill and James Street [and] seek admittance to every house, ascending the staircase and commencing their missionary work with the family living in the highest room'.[154] Despite some opposition, by the end of the year, they had made 86 converts.[155]

Some people in England were watching the work of the proselytizers with admiration. The anti-nationalist *Morning Herald* praised the involvement of people such as Rev Alexander Dallas, while Rev McNeile in Liverpool suggested that their generosity would reconcile the Irish poor to English rule.[156] In contrast, Lord Brougham believed that the work of the proselytizers was damaging that of sincere philanthropists, telling the House of Lords, 'This mixing up religious fanaticism with the cause of charity and benevolence, was one of the greatest curses that could be experienced'.[157]

Responses and legacies

The English physician John Forbes, who visited Ireland in 1852, noted that much of the success of the missions had been due to 'the zeal of Protestant ladies and of Scripture Readers'. He singled out the Ladies' Relief Association for Connaught for special praise because, while they aimed to promote Protestantism, they had also provided practical skills to poor women. He explained:

> Whatever may have been the effect of these schools in making converts to Protestantism, their influence in making converts to civilization and thus improving the social and economical condition of the female part of the population has been immense.[158]

Nonetheless, Forbes sympathized with the frustration of the Catholic clergy at the work of the proselytizers, but believed that an unlooked for consequence had been that the commitment of Catholic priests had intensified as a way of neutralizing the proselytizers.[159]

The successes of the proselytizers clearly alarmed the Catholic Church hierarchy. As early as 1847, the Irish Bishops had protested to the Lord Lieutenant, claiming: 'a large portion of the public charities has been perverted by many into means of proselytism, thus abusing what was destined to save the lives of the starving into the most annoying and vexatious aggression on the faith as well as the morals of the poor'. The Viceroy did not respond to those complaints.[160] One woman who vigorously campaigned against the proselytizers was Margaret Aylward of Waterford, who had been associated with a number of Catholic religious orders and later became Foundress of the Sisters of Holy Faith. Her work with orphans led her to object to the fact that all Irish orphans had to be raised within the Established Church. Aylward described the actions of Dallas and his missionaries as 'pecuniary proselytism'.[161] The Presentation Nuns in Dingle took a more proactive approach, appealing to Dr Cullen for funds to build a Catholic orphanage and warning him of the 'religious peril' resulting from the Famine.[162]

It is impossible to know how many converts were made or how many remained converted. For Canon John O'Rourke, writing in 1874, part of the problem was the fact that the numbers provided by the proselytizers were always exaggerated. Moreover, after the crisis of the Famine was over, many people reverted to their original religion.[163] Concerning the legacy of Rev Nangle and his Achill Mission, Canon O'Rourke mused:

> The quasi-converts of whom Mr Nangle boasted so much, have not remained with the proselytizers; their conversion was more apparent than real. They joined them to keep body and soul together . . . Bribery, pure and simple was the means adopted by Nangle and his agents, which took the shape of food, clothes, house and land – tempting advantages by which to seduce a *famine stricken* people.[164]

The acrimonious legacy left by proselytizers overshadowed the greater reality that the majority of Protestants did not seek to convert the starving Irish in return for food. Moreover, Protestants were major contributors to international fund-raising efforts and most of them gave without regard to religious affiliation. The poor in many parts of the country were assisted by local ministers of all denominations, whose involvement in the front line of providing relief brought considerable risks to their own health. This sacrifice and cooperation had been evident in some of the most distressed districts which had been well served by their Anglican clerics and by non-Catholic relief organizations.[165] Moreover, a number of the smaller Protestant denominations were active in Ireland throughout the Famine, although they received little recognition. The Plymouth Brethren, also known as Bibles Christians, were mostly located in Dublin. Because of the structure of their church, they had no ministers. Nonetheless, they provided the poor with food and clothing, 'not as a bribe, but as an act of Christian charity'.[166] One of the most famous Brethren was Wicklow-born Charles Henry Mackintosh who, in 1844, had opened a school in Westport, which continued to operate throughout the Famine.[167] The Unitarians, also small in number in Ireland, provided relief without proselytizing, which earned them praise from Nicholson. She also liked the fact that they were teetotallers.[168]

Although by the mid-1850s the country was slowly recovering from Famine, the actions of proselytizers continued to be a running sore among many communities, long after the disappearance of blight. Their activities had promoted religious discord between the main churches and among the poorest and most vulnerable members of society. In 1996, Irish historian Patrick Comerford wrote:

> In many provincial and rural areas, the famine also left bitter memories of evangelical missionaries and their fervour. Whether the vigour and vitriol were real or imaginary is irrelevant in many communities, even today; what is real is the bitter, lingering memory.[169]

Clearly, the work of a small group of proselytizers cast a long, dark shadow over the altruistic generosity of many Protestant donors and relief workers during the Famine.

Conclusion: 'Thousands have by this means been saved'[1]

Tháinig blianta an ghorta agus an droch shaoghal agus an t-ocras agus bhris sin neart agus spiorad na ndaoini. Ní raibh ann ach achan nduine ag iarraidh bheith beo. Chaill siad a'dáimh le chéile. Ba chuma cé a bhí gaolmhar duit, ba do charaid an t-é a bhéarfadh greim duit le chuir in do bhéal.

The years of the famine, of the bad life and of the hunger, arrived and broke the spirit and the strength of the community. People simply wanted to survive. Their spirit of comradeship was lost. It didn't matter what ties or relationships you had, you considered that person to be your friend who gave you food to put in your mouth.[2]

The Famine occurred at a time when the consensus of most British political and social commentators was that poverty was the fault of the individual and, consequently, extensive relief was undesirable. In particular, gratuitous relief was disliked for creating a culture of dependency. These attitudes underpinned the amended English and Welsh Poor Law of 1834 and the Irish Poor Law of 1838; both pieces of legislation being framed in terms of the 'deserving' and the 'undeserving' poor. The role of philanthropy was viewed in similar terms, with it being directed towards the so-called deserving poor, that is, those whose poverty had not resulted from their own improvidence.[3] The great expansion of charity – voluntarism – in the mid-nineteenth century was shaped by the belief that such interventions should and could result in the moral improvement of the recipient.[4] The Irish Famine prompted the greatest outpouring of charitable benevolence in the nineteenth century, most of which was concentrated in a single year, 1847. And yet, an overwhelming number of donations were motivated by compassion, with no ideological restrictions or expectations.[5] Furthermore, the donations did not conform to the traditional pattern of the elite (usually white and Protestant) giving to the non-elite, but charity came from some of the poorest and most marginalized groups. This included contributions from the displaced Choctaw Indians in Oklahoma, to convicts on board a prison hulk in Woolwich; their intercessions demonstrated their humanity, morality and agency.

While a limited amount of charity had been sent to Ireland in the wake of the first appearance of potato blight, far more came following the second, more devastating crop failure. News of Irish suffering was transmitted in newspapers, in letters, by word of mouth, throughout the world. A number of appeals were made by individuals and charitable organizations on behalf of the Irish poor, resulting in new committees being established. Within weeks, a network of fund-raising activities, which were spontaneous and largely un-coordinated, covered the world. These activities not only crossed national boundaries, but also transcended social, religious, economic, age and gender differences. The amounts of money given ranged from a few pennies to thousands of pounds, and donors extended from heads of states to prisoners, and all groups in between. The scale of this voluntary philanthropy was unprecedented. Moreover, many of the people who gave had no direct connection with Ireland.

Private charity did not simply act as an auxiliary to official relief. At times, government relief was only able to remain operative because of support from the main charities. After 1845, but most particularly in 1847, private charity not only worked in parallel with official measures, but also acted as a supplement when the latter proved inadequate. As both Peel and Russell's administrations struggled to respond to the demands being placed on them, a variety of relief systems were introduced, each with its own rules and bureaucratic intricacies. In the case of the public works, for example, there were so many administrative checks and balances that they could take more than six weeks to become functional, by which time, many people were beyond being saved. In these extreme circumstances, private relief often provided a safety net for those who fell beyond the reach of government relief. Private charities also provided support during the rocky transitions from one type of relief to another.

Unlike official relief, charity was not only free from the multiple constraints governing official relief, but could be (and often was) provided in a way that acknowledged the dignity and suffering of the recipient. For Asenath Nicholson, who travelled the country distributing relief, there was a clear difference in the way the two relief systems operated, she voicing her criticisms of government officials:

An officer paid by the government was generally well paid. Consequently, he could take the highest seat in a public conveyance; he sought for the most comfortable inns, where he could secure the best dinner and wines; he inquired the state of the people, and did not visit the dirty hovels himself when he could find a menial who would for a trifle perform it; and though sometimes when accident forced him in contact with the dying or dead, his pity was stirred, it was mingled with the curse which always follows – 'Laziness and filth' and he wondered 'why the dirty wretches had lived so long', and he hoped 'this lesson would teach them to work in future, and lay up something as other people did'.[6]

The work of the various charities reveal a more complex view of the Famine than has been traditionally been assumed, especially in regard to their activities in Dublin and Belfast. Even prior to 1845, Irish towns and cities contained numerous poor inhabitants, and the Famine had a devastating impact on them. Many would not have survived without private assistance from bodies such as the Irish Relief Association. Also, while giving food to the poor was a priority of most charities, they recognized that the poor had a variety of needs, providing essentials such as clothing, blankets, coffins, fuel and medicine. In some instances, the aid was more unusual; the poor in a fishing village near Youghal were given four tons of salt to enable them to cure fish.[7] Without the intervention of various charities in providing boilers throughout the winter of 1846 to 1847, the soup kitchens that sprang up all over the country would have been inoperative. Without this resource, it is likely that hundreds of thousands of people would have died during these months.

The largest relief body was the British Relief Association, which had been founded in London in January 1847 by the Jewish Banker, Lionel de Rothschild and the politician, Thomas Baring. They employed a Polish Count, Paul de Strzelecki, to act as an impartial distributor of relief. From the outset, the organization chose to work closely with the government. This occasionally proved to be frustrating for Strzelecki, as Charles Trevelyan of the Treasury sought repeatedly to impose more stringent conditions on giving relief than the Polish man thought practicable or desirable. Nonetheless, on numerous occasions, the British Relief Association came to the rescue of the official relief measures. Despite the important role played by the Association in fund-raising and distributing relief, little has been written about them and they have been the subject of only modest scholarly research. In popular memory, the involvement of the British Relief Association is less well known than that of the Society of Friends.

The Central Relief Committee of the Society of Friends was the second largest charitable body. Its work has been widely praised, deservedly so, both at the time and by later scholars of the Famine. English and Irish Friends put their own lives in jeopardy by playing a front-line role in giving relief. A number died as a result. Yet, providing relief in a way that conformed with one's conscience and yet was effective, did present some challenges. The Friends were gently criticized by two people who had worked closely with them – Asenath Nicholson and Fr Mathew – both of whom, on occasion, found the Quaker's decisions to be arbitrary.[8] The Friends' acceptance of donations from 'slave states' in the United States dismayed several of their own members. While their refusal to accept money from an actress, because they disapproved of the theatre, was criticized by some in Ireland.[9] These reproaches do not detract from the life-saving work of the Quakers, but demonstrate that involvement with charitable relief was fraught and not simply a question of raising money and distributing resources.

Controversies

Most charity to Ireland was contributed in the twelve-month period that followed the 1846 potato failure. The relative absence of blight in the 1847 crop, the change to Poor Law relief and 'donor fatigue' possibly prompted by the appearance of thousands of unskilled, disease-ridden emigrants at ports in Britain and North America, contributed to a drying up in donations. For months, some of the British press, led by the *Times,* had been advocating that the Irish should be forced to depend on their own resources, describing the giving of charity as 'pernicious'.[10] The *Economist,* which, like the *Times,* had opposed the second Queen's Letter, in October 1847, coldly informed its readers, 'Charity seems now exhausted, and if relief cannot be legally obtained by the Irish, there is a probability that in spite of, not in consequence of, all the exertions of the Government, many of them will yet be starved'.[11]

The callousness of some sections of the British press contrasted sharply with the generosity of thousands of British people. Yet, Britain's role in charitable benevolence has proved contentious. Inevitably perhaps, the fund-raising activities were politicized, with a number of nationalists contrasting the perceived parsimony of Britain with the generosity of others. America, a country that had achieved independence, was often held up as a model of political progress and generosity. This theme was evident in a long article that appeared in the *Freeman's Journal* on 3 April 1847:

> In America, there is no overflowing of lip charity, and lack of that which is real – no humanity mongering – no plentitude of sympathetic words, and poverty of sympathetic action, no wallowing in proscriptive action – no recourse to billingsgate abuse of Ireland and the Irish, after the fashion of many parties in England – no churlish, mean, money-lending, politico-economic spirit to guide and to process its progress. No! The conduct of America stands in bright and glorious contrast. In the day of our desolation we have found them the readiest hands – aye – and the most bounteous – stretched to our aid, from the mouth of the St Lawrence to the mouth of the Mississippi, without the flourish of the Pharisee, or the cold-blooded calculation of the legist.
>
> Honour then, to America. In it, the cause of humanity needs no spur from shame, hypocrisy or 'state policy'. In her bosom our exiles found a refuge where they were safe from exterminating landlords and class legislation . . . But never, as much as our hearts yearned towards America as the asylum of our cast out thousands, never, we say, great as was our experience of the generosity with which our countrymen were received on its shores, were we prepared for the surprising acts of humanity and benevolence towards this stricken nation, which mail after mail enables us to record and to bless.[12]

The Dublin *Nation,* the paper of Young Ireland, was even more forthright:

> While English statesmen are devising daily plans for the increase and
> protection of pauperism in this long royal and long suffering province of
> Ireland, American statesmen, regarding this country as, even in its wreck,
> worth being saved, are accumulating their voluntary tributes for the
> relief of our necessities. While the chief journals of the English capital are
> daily teeming with invectives against our people, high and low American
> journals, from Houston down to Eastport, are reviving reminiscences of
> Irish merit, in order to hasten the kindly interference of their country on
> behalf of ours. While the popular divines of England can see in pestilence
> and famine only judgements from an angered Deity, smiting Ireland on
> both cheeks for her idolatry, the favourite preachers of America perceive
> but as an opportunity for the exercise of active charity ... America needs
> friends in Europe and our relations have always been of a friendly kind:
> *but from this year forth no Irishman will willingly pull a trigger against
> her.*[13]

In contrast, the *Anglo-Celt,* a Cavan-based newspaper, praised English aid,
especially in view of the belligerent articles appearing in the *Nation*:

> Dear generous England, how nobly do you refute the calumnies heaped
> upon you by an insensate and malignant press. Neither the taunts of the
> *Nation,* nor the sordid calculations of the *Times,* can dry up the ever-
> gushing current of your inexhaustible charity. One family alone, that of
> the Guerneys, have subscribed to different Irish subscriptions, upwards
> of £2,000.[14]

The anti-nationalist *Nenagh Guardian* was also at pains to point to the
generosity of the English people, despite the separatist statements of what
they described as a minority of Irish people. They predicted, 'Surely such a
manifestation of feeling as this ... must have some considerable effect, both
in making the poor sufferers ashamed for the past and leading them to a
better mind for the future'.[15] This hope was not always fulfilled. Frances
Vane, the Marchioness of Londonderry, visited her estate in 1846 and
provided extensive relief for her poorest tenants. In 1847, she organized a
fund-raising bazaar that raised thousands of pounds for the same purpose.
The Marchioness also oversaw the erection of what was probably the first
monument to the Famine, commanding an inscription to be made at Garron
Point on the Antrim coast. It read:

> Francis Anne Vane, third Marchioness of Londonderry, being connected
> with this province by the double ties of birth and marriage and being
> desirous to hand down to prosperity and imperishable memorial to

> Ireland's affliction and England's generosity in the year 1846–47, unparalleled in the annals of human suffering, hath engraved this stone.

The reference to England's generosity has been long scratched over.[16]

How much relief had been required to save lives after 1846? At the beginning of 1847, one estimate suggested that before the next harvest, to fill the deficiency it would be necessary to supply 4,000,000 quarters of wheat, and this would require 1,750 ships each carrying 500 tons each.[17] If this calculation was accurate, it suggests an intervention that lay far beyond what private charities could provide. Given the palpable reluctance of private enterprise to supply this deficit, and the refusal of the government to close the ports and keep food in the country, how were the Irish people to be fed?

The role of the British government after 1846 has been criticized by nationalists and others who felt that more should and could have been done to save lives. It is hard to absolve them from responsibility, or from 'standing by', while hundreds of thousands perished in the most painful of ways.[18] Although less documented, and less contentious, should other groups be censured for standing by, or for using the Famine as an opportunity to grow rich? This point was made in January 1847, by a leading Whig politician, Lord Bessborough, to the Prime Minister:

> I cannot make my mind up entirely about the merchants. I know all the difficulties that arise when you begin to interfere with trade, but it is difficult to persuade a starving population that one class should be permitted to make a fifty per cent profit by the sale of provisions, while they are dying in want of these.[19]

Moreover, did the moral responsibility for saving lives extend beyond the United Kingdom? Should the United States, a nation which, by its own admission, was so wealthy in produce, have done more to help the starving in Ireland? Despite the generosity of many Americans, at the beginning of 1847, one newspaper berated the rich for not doing enough:

> What miracles might not be wrought by Benevolence such as Christianity enjoins! A few weeks since, a large meeting was called in New York for the purpose of contributing to the aid of Ireland. What, think you, was the sum total of its contributions? Three thousand dollars! Enough to carry relief to about twenty sufferers. A wondrous gift from a city of millionaires! Compare with this grudging charity the benevolence of the poor Irish in that same city, who live by the sweat of their brow.[20]

Almost 150 years later, the historian Timothy Sarbaugh criticized the American government for refusing to give the proposed $500,000 grant to Ireland. He has suggested that they should be added to the list of groups that could have done more, which included the British government, Irish landlords, Catholic clergy and Irish politicians. He asserts, 'The American government must be added to this list of culpability. Perhaps a little more humanity and less self-interest could have helped to alleviate the scope of human suffering'.[21] Applying this reasoning, is any individual, any group, or any government exonerated from culpability? Should the responsibility of the American government be equated with that of the British one, which governed Ireland, legislated for Ireland, and controlled a vast empire of which Ireland was a part?

While most reports praised the generosity of the donors, a few challenged the efficacy of this sort of intervention, even as charitable donations were pouring into Ireland. One New York newspaper, while reporting on mass mortality and mass emigration in the early months of 1847, lamented, 'American benevolence ends in enabling the Irish landlords to export more food in the midst of poverty'. The paper explained:

> While thousands in America have been exerting themselves to raise money, food and provisions for the starving poor in Ireland, the quantities of butter, bacon, wheat, flour, buckwheat, oats, pork, lard, malt, oatmeal, peas, eggs, hams, beans, beef, Indian Corn, oxen calf etc. exported from Ireland to England are really enormous.[22]

In Ireland, two northern newspapers were similarly cynical about the benefits of the overseas benevolence. The *Belfast Vindicator,* a Catholic newspaper that supported Daniel O'Connell, opined:

> The contributions sent from Europe, Asia, and America, to stay the Hand of Death in Ireland, have only filled the pockets of the landholders. While the people were begging and receiving alms, the landlords were driving and collecting rents. The landlords of Ireland have little now to expect from that source.[23]

A Belfast-based liberal paper, the *Northern Whig,* believed there was a more practical reason for some donations not reaching the intended recipient:

> During the late famine in Ireland, many Irish residents in the United States, under the influence of most praiseworthy feelings, sent home money to their friends in Ireland; but there can be no doubt, that very many of the letters containing advices of these remittances, were lost to the parties to whom they were addressed, in consequence of their inability to pay the postage. The present postage of letters to America is one shilling, including both inland and ocean carriage.[24]

Could more lives have been saved if private donations had been handled differently? Asenath Nicholson posed the question, 'why the poor were so

little benefitted by the bounties sent them from abroad'.[25] For her, the fact
that the government insisted that relief workers had to pay for the sacks
which held the imported grain and rice, was important, 'because it involves
a great principle'. She explained:

> The hungry, it should be borne in mind, for whom the donations were
> sent, had no control of what was virtually their own exclusively, but must
> be content to receive it by proxy, or great in small parcels, in a good or
> bad state at the dispenser's option. Consequently, they did not always
> have what belonged to them, and if the meal and rice paid for the sacks,
> as mine were required to do, a great deduction must be made from the
> original account.[26]

This overlooked aspect of famine relief provides a revealing insight into how
government intervention and regulation could hinder rather than facilitate
the giving of charitable relief.

It is not possible to understand the motives of the thousands of people
worldwide who gave help to Ireland.[27] Religion was a powerful force in
early Victorian charity, with its constant search for souls to save.[28] At the
same time, there was a desire to do what was narrowly and vaguely (and in
this context, inappropriately given the trans-denominational nature of the
charity) referred to as 'Christian duty'. Yet donations also came from Jews,
Muslims and Hindus. For some, charity to the Irish poor offered a form
of moral brokerage for future compliance, a sentiment articulated by Rev
Joseph Tuckerman, a Unitarian pastor:

> Misery will subdue the starving Irish; their will broken and their
> dependence heightened, they will be open to 'healing influences of kind
> and helpful advice' . . . tell them plainly, that if material aid must be
> furnished for a time by others, the moral co-operation which alone can
> make it a blessing, and not a curse, must come from themselves'.[29]

For other middle class donors, philanthropy represented 'another form of
internal politics among social elites'.[30] At an extreme level, public displays of
charity were motivated by self-promotion as, 'through the subscription list
one could display one's wealth to public view, co-operate openly with the
aristocracy, and thus buy a place in public life and even a seat in Parliament'.[31]
In the United States, there is no doubt that some of the demonstrations of
public philanthropy by the Whig and Democrat politicians were driven by a
desire to capture the Irish American vote.[32] Such functionalist interpretations
should not overshadow the fact that humanity was undoubtedly a key factor
behind many of the donations, and simple compassion for fellow human
beings who were suffering.[33]

What was the feeling of those who gave, not only their money, but their
time on behalf of Ireland? Did they believe that their efforts had been

squandered? One of the first city and statewide appeals for Ireland had been made in Philadelphia. During the relief committee's official existence from February to May 1847, it raised over $172,000, which was used to buy foodstuffs. In its closing statement in October 1847, the committee admitted:

> It is not easy to fix an estimate upon the value of charitable acts, such as are noted in this Report. The lives of thousands were saved by the timely arrival in Ireland of the remittances of money and provisions, and the hearts of thousands in this country were made to beat with pleasure, in the consciousness of good performed. These were the immediate results of the contributions. Nations of kindred feelings and the same language were made to feel their relationship, and men, separated by an ocean, were taught to recognize each other as brethren. Thus afflictive Providences have been made to work extensive good, and the exercise of the virtue of charity has resulted in enlarged permanent rewards.[34]

The British Relief Association, which understood the difficulties and limitations of providing such large-scale relief, agreed that some good had been achieved. The Association, which of all charities provided the greatest amount of relief, believed that thousands had been saved by private donations. In its final report, it observed:

> ... in the application of this fund, any evils which may have accompanied its distribution have been far more than counterbalanced by the great benefits which have been conferred upon their starving fellow-countrymen. If ill-desert has sometimes participated in this bounty, a vast amount of human misery and suffering has been relieved; if an isolated instance can be shown of idleness engendered, there can also be no doubt, real and permanent good has been effected amongst the poor, and amongst the rising generation more especially. If, indeed, the single good result has been that which the Poor Law Commissioners have deliberately put on record, 'that thousands have by this means been saved from starvation', the Committee will have reason to rejoice in the belief that their labour has been far from vain; and the Subscribers to the Association will be assured that the great trust which they reposed in the Committee has been faithfully administered.[35]

A widely held belief, not confined to evangelical missionaries, was that the Famine was punishment by a retributive god. This explanation took on a political dimension following the coming to power of the Whig Party. As the historian Phillip Williamson has observed, Peel responded to the first year of food shortages with a policy 'not of religious humiliation but human action, in the form of corn law repeal'.[36] The Whigs, in contrast, ordered that a series of state prayer days be held, which culminated in a day of fast and humiliation in March 1847. Contrasting with the providentialist interpretation, the General Relief Committee in New York, when appealing for donations, made it, 'on behalf of suffering caused by no improvidence, caused by no vice, but proceeding immediately, as far as the intricate web of human affairs can be unravelled, from the direct agency of the Almighty'.[37]

In its most extreme form, the providentialist interpretation led to proselytism. Proselytism, or souperism, was not new in Ireland, but the scale and intensity of missionary work after 1846 were unprecedented. Arguably, souperism saved lives and souls. Would such large amounts of money have been raised, if not for the work of the proselytizers? On the other hand, could the money that was spent on bibles, if expended on food, have saved even more lives? In the longer term, souperism split communities and left acrimonious memories regarding the giving of private relief.

Remembering the sacrifice

Although it is impossible to quantify, private relief saved or, in some cases, merely prolonged lives. By providing coffins, private relief also honoured death. Yet, with rare exceptions, few of those individuals who contributed have been remembered or acknowledged. An exception is the Quakers. Many accounts of the Famine have commended the collective work of the Society of Friends, not only for distributing relief, but for doing so without attempting to convert the recipients. An early, and lengthy, example of praise of their involvement came from Richard Cobden, an Anglican English politician, who wrote in 1853:

A famine fell upon nearly one half of a great nation. The whole world hastened to contribute money and food, but a few courageous men left their homes in Middlesex and Surrey, and penetrated to the remotest glens and bogs of the west coast of the stricken island, to administer relief with their own hands. To say that they found themselves in the valley of the shadow of death would be but an imperfect image; they were in the charnel-house of a nation. Never since the fourteenth century did pestilence, the gaunt handmaid of famine, glean so rich a harvest. In the midst of a scene, which no field of battle ever equalled in danger, in the number of its slain or the sufferings of the surviving, these brave men moved as calm and undismayed as though they had been in their own homes. The population sank so fast that the living could not bury the dead; half-interred bodies protruded from the gaping graves; often the wife died in the midst of her starving children, whilst the husband lay a festering corpse by her side. Into the midst of these horrors did our heroes penetrate, dragging the dead from the living with their own hands, raising the head of famishing infancy, and pouring nourishment into parched lips, from which shot fever-flames more deadly than a volley of musketry.

Here was courage. No music strung the nerves; no smoke obscured the imminent danger; no thunder of artillery deadened the senses. It was cool self-possession and resolute will; calculating risk and heroic resignation. And who were these brave men? To what gallant *corps* did they belong? Were they of the horse, foot, or artillery force? They were Quakers from Clapham and Kingston! If you would know what heroic actions they performed, you must inquire from those who witnessed them. You will not find them recorded in the volume of reports published by themselves—for Quakers write no bulletins of their victories.[38]

The work of the Friends would not have been possible without the munificent donations raised in the United States and channelled through the New York General Relief Committee. The man who is indelibly linked with this initiative, Myndert Van Schaick, was of Dutch origin. His name is generally forgotten in histories of the Famine and, when he died in 1865, his long obituary in the *New York Times* made no mention of his invaluable role in providing relief.[39]

Contributions to Ireland were made not only in money, but also in time. From the merchant banker Lionel de Rothschild in London, who spent hundreds of hours working on the committee of the British Relief Association, to workers in various parts of the world, including ex-slaves in the Caribbean, who gave a day's wages, hundreds of people gave their time freely to help Ireland. Numerous selfless people, in offices in places as far apart as Calcutta, Sydney, New York, London and Belfast, worked to ensure that their assistance arrived where it was most needed, and in a timely manner. The names of these people have long been forgotten. During the course of the Famine, only two men received official recognition from the British government. They were a Polish Count, Paul de Strzelecki and an English Civil Servant, Charles Trevelyan. Both were knighted for their roles in providing relief. An American, Captain Robert Forbes, who brought the *Jamestown* to Cork in the spring of 1847, refused to travel to either Dublin or London to receive the official thanks of the British government, seeing such an action as a distraction from his main purpose.[40]

In 1848, both Strzelecki and Trevelyan were made Knight Commanders of the Order of Bath, an honour bestowed on senior civil servants and foreign citizens.[41] Trevelyan, in addition to his normal annual salary of £2,500, also received a bonus of an equal amount, in acknowledgement of 'his extraordinary labours'.[42] Trevelyan's bonus was in marked contrast to Strzelecki's refusal to take any payment for his 18 months labour. The story was repeated in Australian newspapers, the country in which Strzelecki achieved fame as an explorer. The *Sydney Morning Herald* reminded its readers that despite the hardships Strzelecki had endured in Ireland, he had given his labour freely. In the light of this, they believed the government had acted 'somewhat tardily' in recognizing the Count.[43] The people for whom Strzelecki had worked so selflessly did not forget him. According to William

O'Brien, an early historian of the Famine, in the west of Ireland, 'the name of this benevolent stranger was then, and for long afterwards, a familiar one if not a household word, in the homes of the suffering poor'.[44]

US involvement

By far, the largest amount of relief was raised in the US. In April 1847, the Dublin Quakers informed the committee in New York that:

> We can truly say that the munificence of your City and its vicinity, and of the citizens at large in many other parts of the United States as exhibited by the immense supplies of food they are sending for our starving people, surpass all the expectations that we had ventured to form on the subject.[45]

The Dublin Friends also hoped that longer-term benefits would arise from the generosity of the American people:

> This country owes you much for your great liberality and devoted exertions, and we trust they will produce permanent effects by cementing the bond of union between two nations allied by race, language, manners and kindred political institutions, and which, though separated under different governments, can hardly be regarded as forming more than one branch of the great human family.[46]

These hopes proved short lived. The return of good harvests to Ireland in the early 1850s did not mark an end to emigration, with large numbers still leaving the country. The favoured destination continued to be North America. The number of Irish arriving in New York peaked in 1851, with 163,256 arrivals; by 1855, it had fallen to 43,043, the reasons being the Crimea War (which provided an outlet for Irish men), increased and more stringent immigration regulations, and 'political objections to Catholics and the Irish'.[47] Interestingly, in each of these years the number of German immigrants far exceeded that of the Irish.[48] Nonetheless, anti-Irish and anti-Catholic feeling combined and was given a formal outlet in the Know Nothing Party. It was hard to believe that, only a few years earlier, Americans had been at the forefront of fund-raising activities for Ireland.

The cost of the Famine

The 1851 census demonstrated the human cost of the Famine: the population had fallen from 8,175,124 in 1841, to 6,515,794 in 1851. Just as tragically, which nobody could know at the time, the population would continue to

fall. Significantly, while the Irish population had recovered in the wake of
the famine of 1740–41, it never recovered from the demographic shock
associated with the years 1846–52. Responding to the publication of the
1851 Census, an American newspaper commented:

> The most interesting, if most melancholy, information embraced in the
> latest advices from the Old World tell of the wonderful decrease of
> population in Ireland, as developed by the returns of the Irish census for
> the decade ending in 1851. It has thus been made manifest that the land,
> one of the fairest of the globe, preeminent for soil as well as for climate,
> richer than almost any other in the labor of its children, where that labor
> is properly directed and rewarded, as the wonderful improvement of our
> own country by Irish sinews proves, has lost 1,600,000 human beings in
> ten years! Its strength has perished by man's, not God's, hand.[49]

Apart from loss of population, other aspects of Irish life were lost, which
were more difficult to quantify. A report from Newtownards in County
Down lamented:

> The weavers after the Famine were not the same men as they had been
> before it . . . a tone of seriousness pervaded the people. Many of them felt
> that they had something else to live for than to eat, drink and be merry.
> Numbers of old Hymn books, Bibles and Psalm books were fished up
> from all sorts of places.[50]

Moreover, a gloom had descended on the poor who had survived, who
exchanged 'poetical romance' for 'fearful realities':

> The superstitions of the peasantry are more poetical than frightful, and
> they generally turn all supernatural appearances to favourable account.
> But the Famine changed their poetical romance into such fearful realities
> that no time was left to bestow on imagination.[51]

The circle of charity

Further famines followed in Ireland, but none matched the longevity or
devastation of the 1840s. Yet the Great Famine was not the only time
that people throughout the world came to the assistance of the starving
Irish. Following the poor harvests of 1861 and 1862, and 1879 and 1880,
donations again came from all parts of the world.[52] In 1863, the United
States was at the centre of these activities, with the *New York Times* forming
an Irish Relief Committee to coordinate contributions.[53] Following the
disastrous harvest of 1879, members of the Society of Friends again became
involved, including James Hack Tuke, who was still remembered for his

work in 1846–48.[54] Again, support from the United States was prompt and generous. In December 1879, the *New York Herald* announced that it was once again setting up a relief fund on behalf of the starving Irish. Donations came from a wide range of social groups and geographic areas, as far away as Alaska and California. By March 1880, over one million dollars had been raised and more were still flowing in. Moreover, just as had been the case in 1847, Congress allowed a frigate to be used to take emergency aid to Ireland.[55]

Support also came from the other side of the world. Fund-raising committees were organized in Australia, as they had been in the 1840s.[56] In Dunedin in New Zealand, a meeting was convened in 1880 to raise money for Ireland.[57] A Presbyterian minister, the Rev Dr Donald MacNaughton Stuart, now an old man, recalled that, in 1846 as a young teacher at a boys' preparatory school in Windsor near London, seven of his pupils had said they would go without a meal if he would contribute one shilling for each meal missed to Ireland, to which he agreed. Over 30 years later, from his new home in Dunedin, he encouraged that subscriptions be collected for the latest famine in Ireland.[58]

Nor was the giving one way only. In 1853, an American newspaper suggested to its readers that generosity to Ireland had been simply 'Repaying an old debt':

> In A. D. 1676, after King Philip's war, Dr. Mather, of Boston, Massachusetts, 'did by his letters procure a whole ship-load of provisions from the charity of his friends in Dublin, Ireland'. So that, when Boston sent, by R. B. Forbes, Esq., a ship-load of provisions to Ireland, a few years ago, it was but the payment, without interest, of a debt contracted a century and three-quarters before.[59]

One of the first places to give aid to the Irish poor had been India, another British colony. In India, famines were to be a feature of British Imperial rule in the late nineteenth century and they proved to be catastrophic. As had been the case in Ireland in the 1840s, private charity made up for some of the deficit in official relief. During the 1877 famine, an 'Indian Relief Fund' was formed in Ireland, which sent money to the poor of India, just as India had sent money to the poor of Ireland 30 years earlier.[60] In 1943–44, a famine in Bengal resulted in the deaths of between three-and-half and five million people.[61] In July 1945, Taoiseach Éamon de Valera welcomed two Indian students from Cambridge University to Ireland. They had come to offer, 'the grateful thanks of the Indian people for the generous donation of the Irish government for the relief of famine in India'.[62] The circle of giving was again evident in 1992, when eight people from Ireland retraced the 500-mile 'Trail of Tears' from Oklahoma to Mississippi, to repay a longstanding debt to the Choctaw Indian tribe, for their donation to Ireland in 1847. The sponsorship thus raised was donated to famine relief in Somalia.[63]

In 1847, widely remembered as 'Black '47', a letter of thanks was sent to the Sultan of the Ottoman Empire for his donation of £1,000. The Irish authors explained that in this emergency, the people of Ireland had no alternative but to appeal to the kindness and munificence of other countries, in order to save themselves and their families from famine and starvation.[64] As the recipients of the Sultan's benevolence realized, private charity could make the difference between life and death. The message was simple. Without the kindness of strangers, the 'fearful reality' of these catastrophic years would have been far more tragic and – unimaginable as it seems – even more deadly.

NOTES

Introduction

1 There had been international fund raising before, for example when Caracas suffered an earthquake in 1812, during the Greek rising in the 1820s, but nothing on the geographic or financial scale of the Irish Famine.

2 Laurence M. Geary, *Medicine and Charity in Ireland, 1718–1851* (Dublin: University College, 2005), p. 8.

3 Brian Harrison, 'Philanthropy and the Victorians', *Victorian Studies* 9(4), (June 1966), 356.

4 Gertrude Himmelfarb, 'True Charity: Lessons from Victorian England', in Michael Tanner (ed.), *The End of Welfare. Fighting Poverty in Civil Society* (Washington: Cato Press, 1996), pp. 31–2.

5 These attitudes were encapsulated by best-selling author Samuel Smiles in *Self Help* (1859), and its sequel, *Thrift* (1875). In the latter, he argued that misdirected charity did more harm than good.

6 Margaret Preston, *Charitable Words: Women, Philanthropy, and The Language Of Charity in Nineteenth-Century Dublin* (Westport, CT: Greenwood Press, 2004), pp. 69–70.

7 Ibid.

8 For more on these and other differences, see Christine Kinealy, *A Disunited Kingdom England, Ireland, Scotland and Wales 1800–1949* (Cambridge: Cambridge University Press, 1999).

9 Harrison, 'Philanthropy and the Victorians', p. 355.

10 Howard M. Wach, 'Unitarian Philanthropy and Cultural Hegemony in Comparative Perspective: Manchester and Boston, 1827–1848', *Journal of Social History* 26(3), (Spring 1993), 541.

11 Ibid., pp. 546, 548.

12 Abigail Green, 'Sir Moses Montefiore: Religion, Nationhood and International Philanthropy in the Nineteenth Century', *The American Historical Review* 110(3), (June 2005), 648.

13 'An Appeal for clothing the Naked and Destitute Irish, addressed to all classes, and especially to the Women of England', William and Mary Howitt (eds) *Howitt's Journal of Literature and Popular Progress*, Vol. 1 (London: William Lovett, 1847).

14 Count de Strzelecki, Dublin, 1 January 1848, Committee of BRA, *Report of the British Relief Association for the Relief of Extreme Distress in Ireland and Scotland*, hereafter *Report of BRA* (London: Richard Clay, 1849), p. 132.

15 Strzelecki, Westport, 8 February 1847, *Report of BRA*, p. 100.

16 Rob Goodbody, *A Suitable Channel: Quaker Relief in the Great Famine* (Bray, Dublin: Pale Publishing, 1995), p. 78.

17 For more on the negative role played by the press see, Michael de Nie, *The Eternal Paddy. Irish Identity and the British Press* (Madison, WI: University of Wisconsin Press, 2004).

18 Matthew Higgins, Belmullet, 14 April 1847, *Report of BRA*, p. 114.

19 *Report of BRA,* p. 34.

20 Ibid., Captain Hotham, RN, Tralee Union, 16 January 1848, p. 42.

21 Ibid., Quoted by Mr Marshall, Skibbereen Union, 22 December 1847, p. 41.

22 *Report of BRA,* p. 45.

23 Distress in Ireland, *Irish Relief Association for the Destitute Peasantry* (Dublin: P. D. Hardy, 1847), p. 9.

24 Ibid., Appendix 11, p. 11.

25 Report of Mr Foster RN, Wexford, 9 February 1847, *Report of BRA*, p. 126.

26 Ibid., Strzelecki, Belmullet, 10 February 1847, p. 93.

27 Ibid., Higgins, Belmullet, 4 April 1847, p. 114.

28 Ibid., Captain Jones, Letterkenny, 22 May 1847, p. 120.

29 Ibid., Strzelecki, Dublin, 13 February 1848, p. 133.

30 Robin Haines, *Charles Trevelyan and the Great Irish* Famine (Dublin: Four Courts Press, 2004).

31 Trevelyan to Father Mathew, 14 August 1847, quoted in Cecil Woodham-Smith, *The Great Hunger* (London: Hamish Hamilton, 1962), p. 303.

32 Trevelyan to Henry Labouchere, 15 December 1846, in Peter Gray, 'National Humiliation and the Great Hunger: Fast and Famine in 1847', *Irish Historical Studies* 32 (2006–07), 197.

33 *Times,* 12 October 1847.

34 Haines, Trevelyan, pp. 269–70.

35 The *Standard* article was published in full in the *Freeman's Journal,* 15 October 1847.

36 See Haines, *Trevelyan,* pp. 76–7.

37 *Times,* 12 October 1847.

38 William Loney, RN, 14 April 1847, from *Letter Books of William Loney*: http://home.wxs.nl/~pdavis/Famine3.htm, accessed 3 April 2012.

39 *New York Christian Advocate,* 29 September 1847.

40 Ibid., 17 November 1847.

41 Rev Robert McCarthy, *Church of Ireland Gazette,* 11 August 1995.

42 *Tuam Herald,* 9 January 1847.

43 William Curry, Jun., *The Dublin University Magazine*, Vol. 32, August 1848, p. 228.

44 M. Van Schaick, Chairman of Irish Relief Committee, New York, to Central Relief Committee of the Society, 57 William Street, Dublin, 1st of 4th month (April 1847), in General Relief Committee of the City of New York, *Aid to Ireland. Report of the General Relief Committee of the City of New York. With Schedules of Receipts in Money, Provisions and Clothing,* hereafter, Report of GRC (New York: The Committee, 1848), p. 118.

45 Ibid., p. 13.

46 Ibid., p. 70.

47 Asenath Nicholson, *Annals of the Famine in Ireland,* Maureen Murphy (ed.), (Dublin: Lilliput Press, 1998), pp. 47–8.

48 William Patrick O'Brien, *The Great Famine in Ireland: And a Retrospect of the Fifty Years 1845–95 with a Sketch of the Present Condition and Future Prospects of the Congested Districts* (London: Downey and Co., 1896), pp. 156–7.

49 Contemporary accounts were also provided by Charles Trevelyan and Asenath Nicholson, among others.

50 Christine Kinealy, 'Potatoes, providence and philanthropy: the role of private charity during the Famine', in Patrick O'Sullivan (ed.), *The Meaning of the Famine* (London: Leicester University Press, 1997), pp. 140–71.

51 William Curry, Jun., *The Dublin University Magazine*, Vol. 32, August 1848, p. 228.

52 Thomas D'Arcy McGee, *A History of the Irish Settlers in North America* (Boston: Patrick Donahoe 1852).

53 Ibid., p. 137.

54 Ibid.

55 Rev James J. Brennan, *A Catechism of the History of Ireland* (New York: Thomas Kelly, 1878). It cost 50 cents.

56 Christine Kinealy in David Valone and Christine Kinealy (eds) *Ireland's Great Hunger: Silence, Memory, and Commemoration* (University of America Press, 2002).

57 *Irish Canadian*, 7 January 1880.

58 *New Witness and Catholic Chronicle*, 4 February 1880.

59 For a taste of this embittered debate see, *Cork Constitution,* 14 June 1995.

60 *Inangahua Times*, Vol. II, 22 March 1880, p. 2.

61 'Role of Turkey during Famine clarified', *Irish Times*, 6 June 2010.

62 *Ankara-Hürriyet Daily News*, 23 March 2010: http://www.hurriyetdailynews.com/default.aspx?pageid=438&n=irish-president-mcaleese-backs-turkey8217s-eu-bid-2010-03-23, accessed 10 February 2012.

63 *Drogheda Independent*, 14 December 2011.

64 Rev R. W. Fraser, 'Turkey Ancient and Modern. A History of the Ottoman Empire from its period of establishment to the present time' (Edinburgh: Adam and Charles Black, 1854).

65 William Curry, Jun., *The Dublin University Magazine*, vol. 32, August 1848, p. 228.

66 Report of GRC, p. 7.

67 F. K. Prochaska, *Women and Philanthropy in Nineteenth-Century England* (Oxford: Oxford University Press, 1980), p. 7.

68 Harrison, 'Philanthropy and the Victorians', p. 356.

69 Jim O'Donoghue, Louise Goulding and Grahame Allen, 'Consumer Price Inflation Since 1750', *Economic Trends* (2004, No. 604), 38–46, which estimates historic British inflation back to 1750.

70 Report of GRC, p. 30.

Chapter 1

1 *New York Christian Advocate*, 7 April 1847.

2 Terrence McDonough, *Was Ireland a Colony? Economy, Politics, Ideology and Culture in Nineteenth-Century Ireland* (Dublin: Irish Academic Press, 2004).

3 Liam Kennedy and Leslie A. Clarkson, '"Birth, Death and Exile" in Irish Population History, 1700–1921', in B. J. Graham and L. J. Proudfoot (eds), *An Historical Geography of Ireland* (Dublin: Irish Academic Press, 1993), pp. 158–65.

4 David Dickson, *Arctic Ireland: The Extraordinary Story of the Great Frost and Forgotten Famine of 1740–41* (Belfast: White Row Press, 1997).

5 Leslie A. Clarkson and E. Margaret Crawford. *Feast and Famine: A History of Food in Ireland 1500–1920* (Oxford University Press, 2002), p. 274.

6 Boulter to Duke of Newcastle, 17 January 1729, Hugh Boulter, Ambrose Philips, *Letters written by His Excellency Hugh Boulter . . . to Several Ministers of State in England, and some others: Containing an Account of the most Interesting Transactions which Passed in Ireland from 1724 to 1738* (Dublin: G. Faulkner and J. Williams, 1770), p. 274.

7 Padraic O'Farrell, *A History of County Kildare* (Dublin: Gill & Macmillan, 2003), p. 90.

8 Dickson, *Artic Ireland*, p. 78.

9 Jonathan Bardon, *A History of Ireland in 250 Episodes* (Dublin: Gill & Macmillan, 2009).

10 John D. Post, *Food Shortages, Climatic Variability and Epidemic Disease in Pre-Industrial Europe: The Mortality Peak in the Early 1740s* (New York: Cornell University Press, 1985).

11 Christine Kinealy, *A Death-Dealing Famine. The Great Hunger in Ireland* (London: Pluto Press, 1997), pp. 44–5.

12 See, James Kelly, 'Scarcity and Poor Relief in Eighteenth-Century Ireland: The Subsistence Crisis of 1782–4'. *Irish Historical Studies* 28(109), (May 1992), 38–62.

13 Thomas King Moylan, 'Vagabonds and Sturdy Beggars'. *Dublin Historical Record* 1(3), (Sepetember 1938), 65–74.

14 Kinealy, *Death-Dealing*, pp. 44–5.

15 Kelly, 'Scarcity and Poor Relief', p. 38.

16 Thomas Malthus, *An Essay on The Principle of Population as it Affects the Future Improvement of Society* (London: J. Johnson, 1798). The first edition was anonymous.

17 G. Talbot Griffith, *Population Problems in the Age of Malthus* (Cambridge: The University Press, 1926).

18 A Member of a Parochial Poor Relief Committee, 'A Letter to the Prime Minister on the Deplorable Condition of the Helpless Poor in Ireland'. *The Pamphleteer* (London: A. J. Valpy, vol. 29, 1828), 457–83.

19 Ibid., p. 478.

20 Ibid.

21 *An Act for the Amendment and Better Administration of the Laws relating to the Poor in England and Wales,* 4 & 5 Will. IV cap. 76, 14 August 1834.

22 Kinealy, *Death-Dealing*, pp. 38–9.

23 Third Report of His Majesty's Commissioners for inquiring into the condition of the poorer classes in Ireland, with appendix and supplement, British Parliamentary Papers, hereafter BPP, 1836 [43], xxx.

24 Kinealy, *Death-Dealing*, pp. 38–40. For additional background see, Peter Gray, *The Making of the Irish Poor Law, 1815–43* (Manchester: Manchester University Press, 2009).

25 'An Act for the more effectual Relief of the Destitute Poor in Ireland', 1 and 2 Vic. c. 56, 31 July 1838.

26 An Act for the Amendment and better Administration of the Laws relating to the Poor in England and Wales, compared with, 'An Act for the more effectual Relief of the Destitute Poor in Ireland'.

27 An Act for the more effectual Relief . . . 1838.

28 Cormac Ó Gráda, *Black '47 and Beyond: The Great Irish Famine in History, Economy, and Memory* (Princeton, NJ: Princeton University Press, 2000), p. 26.

29 An Act for the further amendment of an act for the more effectual Relief of the destitute poor in Ireland, 6 and 7th Vic. c. 92, 24 August 1843.

30 Geary, *Medicine and Charity in Ireland*, p. 3.

31 Ibid., pp. 3–4.

32 Ibid., pp. 26–7.

33 George Nicholls, *A history of the Irish Poor Law: In Connexion with the Condition of the People* (London: J. Murray, 1856), p. 357.

34 *Seventh Annual Report of Poor Law Commissioners for England and Ireland* (London: Poor Law Commission Office, 1845).

35 For background on the Irish Poor Law, both before and during the Famine, see, Christine Kinealy, *This Great Calamity. The Irish Famine 1845–52* (Dublin: Gill and Macmillan, 2007).

36 *Eighth Annual Report of Poor Law Commissioners for England and Ireland* (London: Poor Law Commission Office, 1846).

37 Report from 'Silliman's Journal of Science and Arts', September 1846, reprinted in *New York Christian Advocate*, 2 December 1846.

38 See Kinealy, *Great Calamity*, for detailed background on these various relief measures.

39 Trevelyan to Baring Brothers, 29 December 1845, Baring Archive, London, HC 3 3.75.

40 *Irish Railway News,* 29 November 1845, reprinted in *Brooklyn Eagle*, 23 December 1845.

41 J. Cummins to Baring Brothers, Baring Archive, 12 January 1846, HC 15 A. 2 (1846–48).

42 Ibid., Trevelyan to Thomas Baring, 2 January 1846, HC 3 3.75.

43 Ibid., Baring Brothers, Liverpool to Baring Brothers, London, 28 April 1846, HC 3 3.75.

44 Christine Kinealy 'Peel, Rotten Potatoes and Providence. The repeal of the Corn Laws and the Irish famine', in Geraint Parry, Hillel Steiner, Andrew Marrison (eds), *Freedom and Trade: Free Trade and its Reception, 1815–1960* (London: Routledge, 1998), p. 50.

45 *Brooklyn Eagle*, 24 November 1845.

46 Christine Kinealy, *Repeal and Revolution. 1848 in Ireland* (Manchester: Manchester University Press, 2009).

47 Lord John Russell, 17 August 1846, *Hansard*, 3, lxxxviii, cc. 772–8.

48 Lord John Russell to Daniel O'Connell, Russell Papers, 30 22 5 B, National Archives of England, hereafter NAE, 14 August 1846.

49 Haines, *Trevelyan*, pp. 43–6.

50 Kinealy, *Death-Dealing Famine*, p. 138.

51 Henry Labouchere, Dublin Castle, to Lord John Russell, Russell Papers, 30 22 5 B, 2 January 1847.

52 Isaac Butt, *A Voice for Ireland. The Famine in the Land* (Dublin: J. McGlashan, 1847).

53 See Kinealy, *Death-Dealing*, Chapter Four.

54 *Tuam Herald*, 23 October 1846.

55 Kinealy, *Death-Dealing*, pp. 83–91.

56 *Cherokee Nation*, reprinted on 1 July 1847.

57 *Fourteenth Annual Report of the Board of Public Works* (London, 1846), 9 December 1846.

58 *Nation*, 28 November 1846.

59 William Bennett, *Narrative of a Recent Journey of Six Weeks in Ireland: In Connexion with the Subject of Supplying Small Seed to some of the Remoter Districts* (London: Charles Gilpin, 1847), p. 9.

60 Extract from the Journal of Lieutenant Telfer, Inspecting Officer, Limerick, for week ending 6 February 1847, BPP, Board of Works, Measures adopted

for the relief of distress: correspondence: Board of Works Series: part I1, p. 252.

61 The prevalence of dysentery was noted by the Quaker George Hancock during his visit to Ireland in February 1847, Central Relief Committee, *Transactions of the Central Relief Committee of the Society of Friends during the Famine in Ireland, in 1846 and 1847* (Dublin: Hodges and Smith, 1852), p. 169.

62 Irish Relief Association, 'Distress in Ireland' (Dublin: P. Hardy and Sons, 1847), Appendix 1, p. 8.

63 *Bell's Messenger*, 9 January 1847; *Cork Constitution*, 7 February 1847.

64 *Cork Examiner*, 25 November 1846.

65 *Times*, 24 December 1847.

66 Strzelecki, Westport, 25 March 1847, *Report of BRA*, p. 97.

67 Joseph Bewley and Jonathan Pim to Reyburn, 18 September 1847, General Relief Committee of the City of New York, *Aid to Ireland. Report of the General Relief Committee of the City of New York. With Schedules of Receipts in Money, Provisions and Clothing*, hereafter, Report of GRC (New York: The Committee, 1848), p. 143.

68 Geary, *Medicine and Charity in Ireland*, p. 187.

69 Ibid., pp. 187–8.

70 Ibid., p. 190.

71 See, Christine Kinealy, *The Great Irish Famine. Impact, Ideology and Rebellion* (Hampshire: Palgrave Press, 2002).

72 Kinealy, *Death-Dealing Famine*, pp. 77–83.

73 Canon John O Rourke, *The History of the Great Irish Famine of 1847* (Dublin: Veritas, 1989, First pub. 1874), Chapter x.

74 Hugh James Rose, Samuel Roffey Maitland, *The British Magazine*, vol. 31, p. 217, London, 1847.

75 Ibid., p. 217.

76 Ibid., p. 218.

77 Ibid., p. 219.

78 *National Era*, 25 February 1847.

79 Treasury Minute dated 10 March, *First Report of Relief Commissioners Constituted under the Act 10 Vic., cap. 7*, BPP, Distress (Ireland), 1847, vol. 17, p. 3.

80 Ibid., p. 4.

81 Quoted in the *Times*, 24 March 1847.

82 *Nation*, 27 March 1847.

83 Strzelecki, Sligo, 14 April 1847, *Report of BRA*, p. 102.

84 Ibid., p. 25.

85 Nicholson, *Annals*, p. 96.

86 *Dublin Evening Mail*, 7 April 1847.

87 *Nenagh Guardian*, 6 March 1847.

88 MR Foster RN, BRA agent for Wexford district, 1 May 1847, *Report of BRA*, p. 127.

89 *Nation*, 5 March 1847.

90 Rations in Ireland, *Hansard*, 25 March 1847, vol. 91, cc. 413–14.

91 Bewley and Pim to Myndert Van Schaick, 3 May 1847, *Report of GRC*, p. 126.

92 *Report of BRA*, pp. 26–7.

93 Ibid., Bewley and Pim to Van Schaick, 3 July 1847, p. 135.

94 Ibid.

95 Ibid.

96 Higgins, Belmullet, *Report of BRA*, 13 April 1847, p. 110.

97 *Bell's New Weekly Messenger*, 28 March 1847.

98 The pen name of Alice French (1850–1934).

99 Octave Thanet, 'An Irish Gentlewoman in the Famine Time', in *The Century*, vol. 41, November 1890 – April 1891 (New York: T. Fisher Unwin, 1891), pp. 344, 146.

100 *New York Christian Advocate*, 10 February 1847.

101 Ibid., 31 March 1847.

102 Ibid., 7 April 1847.

103 Elihu Burritt and Joseph Sturge, *A Journal of a Visit of Three Days to Skibbereen, and its Neighbourhood* (London: C. Gilpin, 1847).

104 Francis M. Carroll, *The American Presence In Ulster: A Diplomatic History, 1796–1996* (Washington: Catholic University of America Press, 2005), p. 47.

105 Ibid., pp. 44, 57, 248.

106 Ibid., p. 56.

107 Guide to the James A. Loughead Family Correspondence, University of Notre Dame Rare Books and Special Collections: http://www.rbsc.library.nd.edu/finding_aid/RBSC-MSNEA0526:25, accessed 3 July 2012.

108 *Londonderry Standard*, 10 December 1847.

109 Mortality in Ireland, *Hansard*, H C, 29 March 1847, vol. 91, cc. 571–5.

110 Maria Edgeworth to Lady Beaufort, 8 May 1847, Letters of Maria Edgeworth: http://www.gutenberg.org/cache/epub/9095/pg9095.txt, accessed 1 May 2012.

111 *NY Christian Advocate*, 21 July 1847.

112 *Nation*, reprinted in *NY Christian Advocate*, 21 July 1847.

113 Colin Rallings and Michael Thrasher, *British Electoral Facts 1832–1999* (London: Ashgate Publishing Ltd, 2000).

114 Kinealy, *Repeal and Revolution*.

115 Three separate acts were passed in June and July 1847. The main changes were embodied in *An Act to make further Provision for the Relief of the Destitute Poor in Ireland*, 10 Vic., c. 31, 8 June 1847.

116 Ibid., c. 9.

117 Memorial by Lord Palmerston to Russell, 20 May 1848, in George Peabody Gooch, *The Later Correspondence of Lord John Russell* (London: Longmans and Green, 1925), p. 225.

118 *NY Christian Advocate*, 3 March 1847, see also Kinealy, *Great Calamity*.

119 Geary, *Medical Charities*, pp. 192–3.

120 Ibid., p. 195.

121 Bewley and Pim to Reyburn, *Report of GRC*, 3 December 1847, p. 146.

122 Nicholson, *Annals*, p. 108.

123 Bewley and Pim to Reyburn, 18 August 1847, *Report of GRC*, p. 139.

124 James Hack Tuke's Visit to Erris, *Transactions*, pp. 205–6.

125 *Report of BRA*, p. 29.

126 *Nation*, 27 October 1849.

127 Ibid.

128 Strzelecki, Dublin, 12 March 1848, *Report of BRA*, p. 135.

129 Trevelyan wrote a letter on this issue to the *Times*, 10 October 1847.

130 Higgins, Westport, 26 April 1847, *Report of BRA*, p. 116.

131 The 1848 Act was ineffective and replaced by: Statute 12 & 13 Vict. c. 77.

132 *Nation*, 2 September 1849.

133 Kerr, *Nation of Beggars*, p. 211.

134 *Times*, 19 October 1849.

135 *National Era*, 14 June 1849.

136 For more on the Rate in Aid and opposition to it see, Kinealy, *Death-Dealing Famine*, pp. 141–6.

137 *Nation*, 27 October 1849.

138 *Nenagh Guardian*, 26 September 1849.

139 *Ballina Chronicle*, 2 October 1850.

Chapter 2

1 *Bengal Hurkaru and the India Gazette*, hereafter *Hurkaru*, 30 December 1845.

2 *Hurkaru*, 12 November 1845.

3 *Friend of India*, 11 and 25 December 1845.

4 Lists of Jurors returned by Collectors of Grand Jury Cess for County of Dublin; Special Jurors' List, 1844; Affidavits filed in Case, Queen v. O'Connell, December 1843, p. 349; Noel Ignatiev, *How the Irish Became White* (London: Routledge, 1996), p. 15.

5 Boston *Pilot*, 12 December 1845.

6 H. A. Crosby Forbes and Henry Lee, *Massachusetts Help to Ireland during the Great Famine* (Mass., Boston: Captain Robert Bennet Forbes House, 1967), pp. 3–6.

7 From *Englishman*, reported in *Hurkaru*, 26 December 1845.

8 Ibid.

9 Abstract of Receipts . . . for the Relief of Distress in the Southern and Western Provinces of Ireland, BPP, Suffering from Scarcity in Ireland between 1822 and 1839 (1846), p. 6.

10 *Hurkaru*, 30 December 1845.

11 Ibid.

12 George Clement Boase, 'Peel, Lawrence', *Dictionary of National Biography, 1885–1900*, Vol. 44 (1895).

13 In 1856, Shaughnessy was knighted by Queen Victoria for his work on the telegraph in India. He is also famous for helping to popularize the use of medical marijuana, *Times*, 21 October 2009.

14 *Hurkaru*, 30 December 1845: *Membership of the Provisional Committee.* The Honourable Sir Lawrence Peel, President; Sir John P Grant; Sir R. W Seeton; The Lord Bishop of Madras; the Most Reverend the Archbishop of Blass; The Venerable Arch-Deacon Draltry; the Honourable C. H. Cameron; R. H. Rattray, Esq. CS; A. Dick, Esq. CS; Evelyn Gordun Tedorn, Esq.; CS; W. Richie Esq.; H. Torrens, Esq. CS; G. T Bushby, Esq. CS; A. RO, Dowes, Esq.; C. Merley, Esq. CS: F. C Sands, Esq.; J. T. Pierson, Esq. MD; Blank Sands, Esq.; W. B. O'Shaughnessy; P. O. Hanlen, Esq.; J. P. McKiligan; G. G. McPherson; Samuel Smith, Esq.; Henry Piddington, Provisional Honorary Secretary.

15 Ibid.

16 *Bengal Catholic Herald*, 17 January 1846.

17 *Indian News*, 21 April 1846, p. 176.

18 *Tuam Herald*, 17 October 1846.

19 Bob Cullen, *Thomas L. Synnott: The Career of a Dublin Catholic, 1830–70* (Dublin: Irish Academic Press, 1997), p. 32.

20 *Freeman's Journal*, 25 April 1846.

21 *Hurkaru*, 10 January 1846.

22 *Bengal Catholic Herald*, 14 February 1846.

23 Ibid.

24 Ibid., 17 January 1846.

25 *Hurkaru*, 9 January 1846.

26 From *Bombay Times*, quoted in *Indian News*, 24 July 1846.

27 *Indian News*, 12 March 1846.

28 *Dublin Evening Post*, 28 April 1846.

29 *Indian News*, 5 June 1846, 24 July 1846.

30 *Freeman's Journal*, 6 June 1846.

31 Ibid., 15 May 1846.

32 For example, Rev Thomas Cahalan, PP of Killimer, recorded thanks for the receipt of £30 in *Freeman's Journal,* 9 July 1846; the Very Rev J. MacHale of Hollymount, received £15, Ibid., 26 July 1846; Ibid., 20 January 1847.

33 Ibid., 3 June 1846.

34 Famine Records in National Archives, Dublin. http://www.nationalarchives.ie/topics/famine/GF.pdf, accessed 10 February 2012.

35 *Freeman's Journal,* 25 November 1846.

36 Ibid., 15 October 1846.

37 Reprinted in the *Connacht Tribune,* 28 March 1975.

38 Charles Trevelyan, *The Irish Crisis* (London: Longman, Brown, Green & Longmans, 1880; first pub. in *Edinburgh Review* in 1848), pp. 84–5.

39 Duke of Leinster, Carton, to Archbishop Murray, 16 January 1847, in *Papers of Archbishop Daniel Murray: 1823–1852. Dublin Diocesan Archives:* http://www.dublindiocese.ie/content/daniel-murray-1823–1852, accessed 4 March 2012.

40 *Nation,* 10 July 1847.

41 *Roscommon and Leitrim Gazette,* 1 May 1847.

42 *The Globe,* 11 January 1847.

43 Extract of letter from Bombay Committee, dated 1 May 1847, reprinted in the (London) *Times,* 7 June 1847.

44 Ibid.

45 Ibid.

46 *Nation,* 19 June 1847.

47 *Freeman's Journal,* 14 November 1877.

48 For more see, Patrick Farrell, *Irish in Australia* (South Bend, IN: University of Notre Dame, 1989).

49 *The Straits Times* (Singapore), 7 November 1846.

50 *Freeman's Journal,* 21 May 1847.

51 Ibid., 7 April 1847.

52 Ibid., 21 May 1847.

53 *The Moreton Bay Courier* (Brisbane), 17 July 1847.

54 *Freeman's Journal,* 7 April 1847.

55 *The Moreton Bay Courier* (Brisbane), 17 July 1847.

56 Ibid.

57 J. B. Standish Haly, BRA, London, 18 April 1848 to Sydney Relief Fund, *Sydney Morning Herald* (NSW), 10 August 1848.

58 Ibid.

59 Ibid., J. B. Standish Haly to George King Esq, Sydney, 5 February 1848, 22 July 1848.

60 Ibid., Francis Scott M. P., House of Commons, to George King, Sydney, 31 March 1848, 22 July 1848.

61 *Sydney Chronicle (NSW)*, 23 September 1848.

62 *Sydney Morning Herald*, 2 October 1846. See also Kinealy, *Great Calamity*, for more on the orphan emigration scheme.

63 *Sydney Morning Herald*, 2 October 1846.

64 *The Australian* (NSW), 7 August 1847.

65 *Sydney Chronicle*, 18 August 1847.

66 Ibid.

67 Ibid.

68 William Sowerby (1799–1875) had been born in Cumberland in England and emigrated to Sydney in 1837. He became the first Anglican minister in Goulburn.

69 William Sowerby, *To the Congregation of St Saviour's Church, Goulburn, at Whose Request it is Published, this Sermon is Respectfully Inscribed to their Faithful Friend and Minister, William Sowerby, July 21, 1847* (New South Wales, Sydney: Kemp and Fairfax, 1847).

70 Ibid., p. 5.

71 Ibid., p. 6.

72 Ibid.

73 Ibid., pp. 7–8.

74 Ibid., p. 8.

75 Ibid. p. 14.

76 Ibid., p. 9.

77 Ibid., pp. 9–10.

78 Ibid., p. 11.

79 Ibid., pp. 12–13.

80 Ibid., pp. 14–15.

81 *South Australian Register* (Adelaide), 28 July 1847.

82 *The Cornwall Chronicle* (Tasmania), 30 January 1847.

83 Denis LeMerchant, Home Office, London, to C. Driscoll, Treasurer, Hobart Irish Relief Fund, 26 October 1847, *The Hobart Town Courier and Van Diemen's Land Gazette*, 6 May 1848.

84 Ibid., 17 July 1840.

85 Ibid., 27 February 1847.

86 Kinealy, *Repeal and Revolution*.

87 William Patrick O'Brien, *The Great Famine in Ireland* (London: Downey & Co., 1896), p. 169.

88 *Times*, 19 March 1847.

89 *Transactions of Society of Friends*, pp. 12, 212.

90 Strzelecki, Clifden, 4 March 1847, *Report of BRA*, p. 96.

91 See, for example, *Anglo-Celt*, 26 February 1847.

92 Circular of Bruff Relief Committee sent to all holding land in area, 29 October 1846. Famine Relief Limerick, National Library of Ireland (hereafter NLI) Ms 8474 (7).

93 Richard Davis Webb to Central Relief Committee, 8 May 1847, *Transactions*, p. 198.

94 Crossthwaite to *Cork Constitution* in Hugh James Rose, Samuel Roffey Maitland, *The British Magazine*, vol. 31, February 1847, pp. 235–6.

95 *Northern Whig*, 12 January 1847.

96 C. E. Carrington, *John Robert Godley of Canterbury* (Cambridge: Cambridge University Press, 1950), p. 30.

97 Donald E. Jordan, *Land and Popular Politics in Ireland: County Mayo from the Plantation to the Land War* (Cambridge: Cambridge University Press, 1994), p. 111.

98 *Londonderry Standard*, 6 February 1847.

99 Kinealy, *Death-Dealing*, p. 97.

100 Dublin Mansion House Committee for the Relief of Distress in Ireland, *Report of the Mansion House Committee on the Potato Disease* (Dublin: J. Browne, 1846), p. 1.

101 Bob Cullen, *Thomas L. Synnott: The Career of a Dublin Catholic, 1830–70* (Dublin: Irish Academic Press, 1997), p. 32.

102 Ibid.

103 *Freeman's Journal*, 4 November 1845.

104 Kinealy, *Death-Dealing*, pp. 42–7.

105 *Freeman's Journal*, 4 November 1845.

106 *Mansion House Report*, p. 3.

107 Ibid., Mansion House Committee to Peel, 7 November 1845, p. 5.

108 *Freeman's Journal*, 4 December 1845.

109 Report of Mansion House Committee, pp. 7–11.

110 *Times*, 3 November 1845.

111 O'Brien, *The Great Famine in Ireland*, p. 58.

112 *Freeman's Journal*, 7 September 1846.

113 Ibid.

114 *Nation*, 26 December 146.

115 *Freeman's Journal*, 31 December 1846.

116 For more on its proceedings and donors, see Ibid., 3 February 1847.

117 Ibid., 9 January, 11 January etc.

118 Ibid., 2 January 1847.

119 Ibid., 7 May 1847.

120 Ibid., 18 January 1847, 26 January 1847.

121 Ibid., 5 January 1847.

122 Ibid., 1 March 1847.

123 Ibid., 18 March 1847.

124 Kinealy, *Repeal and Revolution.*

125 O'Connell died in Geneo before this meeting took place.

126 *Freeman's Journal,* 1 January 1847.

127 For example, in July 1847, he gave £60, Ibid., 5 July 1847.

128 Ibid., 6 February 1847.

129 Ibid., 10 February 1847.

130 Ibid., 9 February 1847.

131 Ibid., 12 January 1847.

132 Ibid., 17 April 1847.

133 Ibid., 5 July 1847.

134 *Report of the Proceedings of the General Central Relief Committee for all Ireland* (Dublin, 1848), pp. 7–11.

135 *Freeman's Journal,* 19 March 1847.

136 *Time*s, 12 May 1849.

137 Ibid.

138 *Nenagh Guardian,* 5 May 1847.

139 Report of General Relief Committee in Belfast, in *Banner of Ulster,* 5 January 1849.

140 *Nation,* 27 March 1847.

141 See Christine Kinealy and Gerard MacAtasney, *The Hidden Famine: Hunger, Poverty and Sectarianism in Belfast* (London: Pluto, 2000).

142 *Banner of Ulster,* 5 January 1849.

143 Ibid.

144 Kinealy, *Hidden Famine,* p. 114.

145 Richard Webb, 5 May 1847, *Transactions,* p. 203.

146 Higgins, Belmullet, 13 April 1847, Report of BRA, p. 111.

147 Boston *Pilot,* 30 January 1847.

148 Thomas Burke, *Catholic History of Liverpool* (Liverpool: C. Tinling & Co. 1910), p. 86.

149 Butler, HMS *Tartarus,* 29 March 1847, *Report of BRA,* p. 85.

150 Campbell Allen Papers (D1558), Public Record Office of Northern Ireland (hereafter PRONI): http://www.proni.gov.uk/introduction__campbell_allen_d1558.pdf, accessed 4 April 2012.

151 *Royal Irish Art Union Monthly Journal,* 1 May 1847.

152 Sir Alfred Comyn Lyall, *The Life of the Marquis of Dufferin and Ava,* vol. 1 (London: J. Murray, 1905), p. 42.

153 Lord Dufferin and the Hon G. F. Boyle, *Narrative of a Journey from Oxford to Skibbereen during the year of the Irish Famine* (Oxford: John Henry Parker, 1847), p. 5.

154 Lyall, The life of the Marquis of Dufferin, p. 43.

155 Ibid., Dufferin to his mother, pp. 42–4.

156 Ibid.

157 Cabinet Memorandum 1 November 1845, in Lord Mahon, *Memoirs of the Right Honourable Sir Robert Peel, Bart., M. P., &c. Published by the Trustees of His Papers, Lord Mahon (now Earl Stanhope), and the Right Hon Edward Cardwell. M. P, Part III: Repeal of the Corn Laws, 1845–6* (London: J. Murray, 1856), p. 145.

158 *Church and State Gazette*, 30 April 1847.

159 Mr T. Duncombe MP, 'Treatment of convicts in the Hulks at Woolwich', *Hansard*, HC. 28 January 1847, vol. 89, cc. 511–28.

160 *Sydney Chronicle*, 6 February 1847.

161 *Public Ledger*, Philadelphia, 19 July 1844.

162 Duncombe, Treatment of Convicts, *Hansard*, cc. 512–18.

Chapter 3

1 Joseph Bewley and Jonathan Pim to Myndert Van Schaick, 3 June 1847, General Relief Committee of the City of New York, *Aid to Ireland. Report of the General Relief Committee of the City of New York. With Schedules of Receipts in Money, Provisions and Clothing* (New York: The Committee, 1848), (hereafter, *Report of GRC*), p. 133.

2 Harrison, 'Philanthropy and the Victorians', p. 359.

3 *Freeman's Journal*, 14 November 1846.

4 R. Goodbody, 'The Quakers and the Famine'. *History Ireland* 6, (Spring 1998), 28–9.

5 William Bennett, *Narrative of a Recent Journey of Six Weeks in Ireland* (London: Charles Gilpin, 1847), hereafter *Six Weeks*, p. 3.

6 *Transactions of the Central Relief Committee of the Society of Friends during the Famine in Ireland in 1846 and 1847* (Dublin: Hodges and Smith, 1852), hereafter *Transactions*, pp. 33–5.

7 *Nation*, 28 November 1846.

8 *Transactions of the Central Relief Committee of the Society of Friends during the Famine in Ireland in 1846 and 1847* (Dublin: Hodges and Smith, 1852), hereafter *Transactions*, pp. 33–5.

9 James H. Tuke, *A Visit to Connaught in the Autumn of 1847, A Letter Addressed To the Central Committee of the Society of Friends, Dublin* (London: C. Gilpin, 1848), p. 29.

10 Bewley and Pim to Reyburn, 3 December 1847, *Report of GRC*, p. 146.

11 *The British Friend*, February 1847, p. 43.

12 *Cork Examiner*, 9 November 1846.

13 *Freeman's Journal*, 19 December 1846.

14 *Nenagh Guardian*, 20 January 1847.

15 The Friends made donations of rice to a number of dispensaries for the same reason, *Anglo-Celt,* 14 May 1847.

16 Report made to Central Relief Committee by the sub-committee appointed for the management of the soup shop, *Transactions,* p. 359.

17 See for example, letter by Jacob Harvey, dated 14 July 1847, printed in *Anglo-Celt,* 6 August 1847.

18 The Quakers in Ireland: http://www.quakers-in-ireland.ie/history/charity/, accessed 12 January 2012.

19 He was brother in law of Joseph Lister, Royal College of Surgeons of England website, 'Sir Rickman John Godlee': http://www.livesonline.rcseng.ac.uk/biogs/E000221b.htm, accessed 18 November 2011.

20 Bennett, *Six Weeks,* pp. 31, 137.

21 *Transactions,* p. 142.

22 Appendix 1, 'Address to Friends in North America from the Committee of the Society of Friends in London, in Committee of Society of Friends, *Distress in Ireland. Third Report of the London Committee with List of Subscriber* (London: Edward Newman, 1848), (hereafter *Distress in Ireland),* pp. 28–9.

23 *Transactions,* p. 142.

24 *Distress in Ireland,* pp. 1–37.

25 *Transactions,* p. 142.

26 Treasurer of Society of Friends, 31 December 1847, *Distress in Ireland,* p. 32.

27 *Distress in Ireland,* p. iii.

28 For example, an account of his first week in Ireland was reprinted in the *American & Commercial Daily Advertiser,* 1 February 1847.

29 *The British Friend,* February 1847, p. 43.

30 *Nation,* 20 March 1847.

31 Ibid.

32 *Report of GRC,* pp. 5–6.

33 Ibid., William Hughes, Assistant Secretary, Minute of Central Relief Committee of Society of Friends, 3 May 1847, p. 127.

34 *Freeman's Journal,* 5 June 1847.

35 *Report of GRC,* pp. 12–13.

36 Ibid., Bewley and Pim to Van Schaick 18 May 1847, p. 130.

37 Ibid., Bewley and Pim to Van Schaick, 3 June 1847, p. 132.

38 Ibid., p. 133.

39 Ibid., p. 13.

40 Ibid., p. 12.

41 *Distress in Ireland,* p. 36.

42 From *British Colonist,* reprinted in *Anglo-Celt,* 21 May 1847.

43 Ibid.

44 Ibid., 19 May 1847.

45 Ibid.

46 Ibid., 4 June 1847.

47 *Freeman's Journal*, 10 September 1847.

48 *Nation*, 11 September 1847.

49 Appendix xxix, *Transactions*, p. 474.

50 Ibid., pp. 475–6.

51 Ibid., pp. 476–9.

52 *Transactions*, p. 50.

53 Charles Trevelyan, Treasury, to Randolph Routh, Commissariat, 6 April 1847, Appendix xiii, *Transactions*, p. 370.

54 Nicholson, *Annals*, pp. 60–1.

55 Ibid., p. 61.

56 *Transactions*, p. 39.

57 James Hack Tuke, *James Hack Tuke: A Memoir* (London: Macmillan, 1899), p. 43.

58 Central Relief Committee, *Distress in Ireland. Extracts from Correspondence* (Dublin: Webb and Chapman, 1847), hereafter, *Distress . . . Correspondence*, p. 3.

59 Ibid., p. 39.

60 Tuke, *A Memoir*, p. 44.

61 *Transactions*, p. 38.

62 Quoted in Jeanne A. Flood, 'The Forster Family and the Irish Famine'. *Quaker History* 84(2), (Fall 1995), 120.

63 O'Brien, *The Great Famine in Ireland*, p. 167.

64 Ibid., p. 169.

65 Joseph Crosfield and Josiah Forster, *A Letter from Joseph Crosfield: Containing a Narrative of the First Week of William Forster's Visit to Some of the Distressed Districts in Ireland* (London: Edward Newman, 1846).

66 W. Alexander, *The Annual Monitor or, Obituary of the Members of the Society of Friends in Great Britain and Ireland* (York: W. Alexander, 1895) p. 153.

67 William Forster and William Dillwyn Sims, *Distress in Ireland: W. D. Sims' Narrative Describing the 5th and 6th Weeks of W. Forster's Journey in the Distressed Districts in Ireland* (London: Edward Newman, 1847).

68 Miller Christy, 'Tuke, James Hack', *Dictionary of National Biography, 1885–1900*, vol. 57 (1899): http://www.en.wikisource.org/wiki/Tuke,_James_Hack_%28DNB00%29, accessed 13 February 2011.

69 Tuke, *A Memoir*, p. 49.

70 Ibid., Tuke, Dunfanaghy, 13 December 1846, p. 148.

71 Nicholson, *Annals*, p. 98.

72 James H. Tuke's Visit to Erris, *Transactions*, p. 205.

73 Ibid., p. 207.

74 Tuke, *A Memoir*, p. 63.

75 Ibid., p. 73.

76 *Transactions*, p. 41.

77 *The British Friend*, 2 April 1847, p. 43.

78 William Lloyd Garrison, Walter McIntosh Merrill and Louis Ruchames, *The Letters of William Lloyd Garrison: I will be Heard, 1822–1835* (Harvard: Harvard University Press, 1971), p. 343.

79 *Transactions*, p. 169.

80 Ibid., Edmunds to Central Relief Committee, 10 March 1847, p. 172.

81 Mangle-wurzel is a 'dual-purpose' vegetable because both the roots and the leaves are edible. It is sometimes known as the 'Yellowbeet', the 'Mangold' the 'Mangold-wurzel' or the 'Manglebeet'. It is closely related to beetroot, silverbeet and sugarbeet, and they all share the same scientific name, *Beta vulgaris)*.

82 *Transactions*, p. 40.

83 Ibid., pp. 385–6.

84 Bennett, *Six Weeks*, p. 2.

85 Ibid.

86 Ibid., p. 5.

87 Ibid., pp. 11–12.

88 Ibid., pp. 26–9.

89 Ibid.

90 Ibid., p. vii.

91 *Transactions*, pp. 194–204.

92 Ibid., James Perry to Central Relief Committee, 28 March 1847, p. 194.

93 Ibid., Webb, Belmullet, 8 May 1847, p. 98.

94 Ibid., p. 208.

95 Ibid., Webb, Belmullet, 2 February 1848, p. 208.

96 Goodbody, *Quakers*, p. 29.

97 Webb to Central Relief Committee, 20 November 1849, *Transactions*, pp. 395–9.

98 For example, *American & Commercial Daily Advertiser*, 1 February 1847 and *The Friend. A Religious and Literary Journal* (Philadelphia), 6 February 1847.

99 *Freeman's Journal*, 2 January 1847.

100 *Distress in Ireland*, p. iv.

101 O'Brien, *The great famine in Ireland*.

102 Strzelecki, Dublin, 18 June 1847, *Report of BRA*, p. 128.

103 Ibid., pp. 132–3.

104 Dublin Committee of Friends to Reyburn, 24 February 1847, p. 178.

105 *Distress in Ireland*, p. v.

106 Ibid., p. v.

107 Ibid., p. iii.

108 Irish Relief Committee, Charleston, 19 February 1847, *Transactions,* p. 231.

109 Ibid., 23 February 1847, p. 231.

110 *Transactions,* p. 478.

111 Ibid., Hibernian Society, Charleston 10 November 1847, p. 250.

112 Goodbody, *Quakers,* p. 24. Daniel O'Connell, a committed abolitionist, had been challenged a few years earlier about his acceptance of money for repeal from slave-holding states, see Kinealy, *The Saddest People.*

113 *Charleston Courier,* 1 February 1847, 8 February 1847.

114 Hannah Maria Wigham, *A Christian Philanthropist of Dublin: A Memoir of Richard Allen* (London: Hodder and Stoughton, 1886), p. 65.

115 Ibid., Allen to members of Central Relief Committee, 29 March 1847, pp. 62–8.

116 Ibid., p. 66.

117 Ibid., p. 67.

118 Henry C. Wright and R. D. Webb, 'SEND BACK THE MONEY', 2 April 1847, in the *Liberator,* 30 April 1847.

119 Boston *Pilot* in the *Liberator,* 24 September 1847.

120 Ibid.

121 Letter from Mrs C. W. Dall, Needham, Mass, to the Editor, 7 August 1847, *Liberator,* 27 August 1847.

122 *Transactions,* pp. 92–3.

123 Ibid., pp. iv–v.

124 Quoted in, Helen E. Hatton, *The Largest Amount of Good: Quaker Relief in Ireland, 1654–1921* (Kingston: McGill-Queens, 1993), p. 163.

125 Jonathan Pim to Committee, 2 September 1847, *Transactions,* p. 313.

126 Ibid., p. 314.

127 Nicholson, *Annals,* pp. 149–50.

128 *Transactions,* p. 376.; The Quaker Perrys: http://www.irishperrys.com/meath.htm, accessed 17 January 2012.

129 R. Goodbody, *A Suitable Channel: Quaker Relief in the Great Famine* (Bray: Pale Publishers, 1995), p. 78.

130 *Transactions,* p. 351.

131 *Report of GRC,* pp. 13–14.

132 Nicholson, *Annals,* p. 54.

133 *Transactions,* p. 473.

Chapter 4

1 General Relief Committee of the City of New York, *Aid to Ireland. Report of the General Relief Committee of the City of New York. With Schedules of Receipts in Money, Provisions and Clothing* (New York: The Committee, 1848), (*Report of GRC*), p. 160.

2 Boston *Pilot*, hereafter *Pilot*, 28 November 1846.

3 *Report of GRC*, p. 7.

4 Gerard T. Koeppel, *Water for Gotham: A History* (Princeton, NJ: Princeton University Press, 1 July 2012), p. 145.

5 'To the Public', 12 February 1847, *Report of GRC*, p. 147.

6 *Report of GRC*.

7 Ibid., p. 149.

8 Ibid., p. 8.

9 The Broadway United Church of Christ: http://www.broadwayucc.org/ history/history/, accessed 1 February 2012.

10 *Brooklyn Eagle*, hereafter *Eagle*, 16 February 1847.

11 *Report of GRC*, p. 8.

12 *Eagle*, 16 February 1847.

13 *Report of GRC*, p. 152.

14 Ibid.

15 Ibid., Speech by Van Schaick, p. 154.

16 Ibid., p. 155.

17 Ibid., p. 156.

18 Ibid., p. 157.

19 Ibid., p. 156.

20 *Freemans* (NY), 16 February 1847.

21 Obituary of Van Schaick, *New York Times*, 3 December 1865.

22 To Van Schaick, New York, 9 April 1847, from Messrs. C. F. Peake, P. Donan, J. M. Portine, Committee of Pensacola, Florida, *Report of GRC*, p. 84.

23 Ibid., Van Schaick to Bewley and Pim, Dublin, 7 April 1847, p. 80.

24 Some of Jacob's papers are held by the American Philosophical Society: http:// www.amphilsoc.org/mole/view?docId=ead/Mss.Film.1111-ead.xml, accessed 4 May 2012.

25 James C. Bell, New York, to Society of Friends, Dublin, 16 May 1848, *Transactions*, p. 327.

26 *Report of GRC*, pp. 17, 149.

27 Perry Belmont, *Public Record of Perry Belmont, a Member of the House of Representatives in the 47th, 48th, 49th, 50th Congress etc* (Albany, NY: Lyon Block, 1898), pp. 80–3.

28 *Report of GRC*, p. 8.

29 Ibid., pp. 14–16.

30 Ibid., p. 91.

31 Ibid., Van Schaick, Primes Building, NY, to Pim and Bewley, 24 February 1847, p. 67.

32 Ibid., p. 69.

33 *Report of GRC*, p. 27.

34 Ibid., p. 43.

35 Ibid., Van Schaick to Bewley and Pim, 29 March 1847, p. 79.

36 Ibid., Van Schaick to Bewley and Pim, 15 April 1847, p. 86.

37 Ibid., Van Schaick to Bewley and Pim, 11 May 1847, p. 88.

38 Ibid., Van Schaick to Bewley and Pim, 22 May 1847, p. 91.

39 *Report of GRC*, p. 54.

40 Ibid., Appendix 2, p. 59.

41 Ibid., Appendix 3, p. 65.

42 *Report of GRC*, p. 83.

43 Ibid., Van Schaick to Mayor of Hartford, 24 February 1847, p. 72.

44 Ibid., Bewley and Pim to Van Schaick, 4 April 1847, p. 118.

45 Ibid., Extract from a letter from Jonathan Pim to Jacob Harvey, Westport, County Mayo, (Ireland), 31 March 1847, p. 120.

46 Ibid., Central Relief Committee of the Society of Friends, 57 William Street, Dublin, 1 April 1847; M. Van Schaick, Chairman of Irish Relief Committee, New York, 19 April 1847, p. 121.

47 *Report of GRC*, p. 3.

48 Ibid., pp. 6–7.

49 Ibid., pp. 5–6.

50 Ibid., Van Schaick to Pim and Bewley, 16 March 1847, p. 82.

51 Ibid., pp. 87–8.

52 Ibid., Van Schaick 29 April 1847 to Bewley and Pim, Dublin, p. 87.

53 See Patrick Hickey, *Famine in West Cork. The Mizen Peninsula and People, 1800–1852* (Dublin: Mercier Press, 2002).

54 Bewley and Pim to Van Schaick, 5 May 1847, *Report of GRC*, p. 130.

55 Diary of Philip Hone, quoted in Merle Curti, *American Philanthropy Abroad* (St Louis: Transaction, 1963), p. 55.

56 *Report of GRC*, p. 149.

57 Ibid., p. 22.

58 Stephen N. Elias, *The Forgotten Merchant Prince* (Westport: Praeger, 1992), p. 165.

59 *Report of GRC*, p. 162.

60 Vera Brodsky Lawrence, George Templeton Strong, *Resonances, 1836–1849* (Chicago: University of Chicago Press, 1995), p. 400.

61 *Report of GRC*, p. 35.

62 Elias, *The Forgotten Merchant Prince*, p. 165.

63 Francis Samuel Drake, *Dictionary of American Biography, Including Men of the Time: Etc.* (Boston: James R. Osgood, 1872), p. 868.

64 Elias, *The Forgotten Merchant Prince*, pp. 164–5.

65 *Eagle*, 16 February 1847.

66 Ibid., 17 February 1847.

67 Todd's premises were at of 83 Fulton Street Brooklyn, *Brooklyn Eagle*, 18 February 1847.

68 Ibid., Van Schaick to Bewley and Pim, *Report of GRC*, 24 February 1847, p. 69.

69 Ibid., Pim and Bewley to Van Schaick, 1 April 1847, p. 119.

70 Ibid., Bewley and Pim, to Van Schaick, 4 April 847, p. 119.

71 Ibid., Reyburn to Bewley and Pim, 13 August 1847, p. 113.

72 Ibid., Appendix 3, pp. 60–1. The ships were *Victor, Fame, Duncan, Boston, New Haven, Lisbon, Bavaria, Europe, Express, Liverpool, Siddons, Minerva* (Albany ship one), *Anna Marie* (Albany ship 2), *Malabar* (Albany ship 3).

73 *Report of GRC*, p. 73.

74 Ibid, p. 119.

75 Ibid., Bewley and Pim to Van Schaick, 19 April 1847, p. 122.

76 Ibid., Bewley and Pim to Van Schaick, 3 May 1847, p. 124.

77 Ibid.

78 Ibid., Bewley and Pim to Van Schaick, 3 May 1847, p. 125.

79 Ibid., Bewley and Pim to Reyburn, 24 February 1848, p. 179.

80 This was possibly Father Patrick Murphy, priest of Barntown, Wexford: http://www.taghmon.com/vol4/chapter07/chapter07.htm, accessed 9 May 1012.

81 See Chapter on the role of women.

82 'Food from America. Return to the House of Commons, dated 7 November 1847 in Appendix of *Report of GRC*, pp. 180–7.

83 *Report of GRC*, p. 9.

84 Ibid., p. 27, 30.

85 Ibid., Van Schaick to Pim and Bewley, New York, 13 March 1847, p. 78.

86 Louis Dow Scisco, *Political Nativism in New York State*, Volume 13, Issue 1 (PhD, Columbia University, 1901), p. 68. (available through Google Books).

87 *Report of GRC*, p. 29.

88 Ibid., p. 46.

89 Ibid., p. 32.

90 Ibid., p. 41.

91 Ibid., p. 38.

92 Ibid., p. 47.

93 Ibid., p. 50.

94 Rev. C. C. Stratton (ed.), *Autobiography of Erastus O. Haven. With an Introduction by the Rev. J. M. Buckley* (New York: Phillips & Hunt, 1883).

95 *Report of GRC*, pp. 24, 33.

96 Ibid., p. 34.

97 Ibid., p. 50.

98 Catherine Elizabeth Havens, *Diary of a Little Girl in Old New York*, second edition (New York: Henry Collins Brown, 1920), pp. 84–5.

99 Appendix No. 1, *Report of GRC*, p. 17.

100 Ibid., p. 21.

101 Ibid., p. 36.

102 Ibid., p. 43.

103 See Kinealy, *Repeal and Revolution*.

104 *Report of GRC*, p. 52.

105 Renwick Gallery, Washington: http://www.eyelevel.si.edu/2011/09/from-defence-to-decoration-the-renwick-gallery-in-the-civil-war.html, accessed 12 November 2011.

106 William Wilson Corcoran, *A Grandfather's Legacy: Containing a Sketch of his Life and Obituary Notices* (Washington: H. Polkinhorn, 1879), p. 3.

107 Ibid., pp. 99–100.

108 Ibid., p. 110.

109 *Report of GRC*, pp. 29–30.

110 Ibid., pp. 31, 36.

111 Vera Brodsky Lawrence, *Resonances*, p. 480.

112 Ibid.

113 *Report of GRC*, p. 31.

114 *Minutes of the Common Council of the City of New York, 1784–1831*, vol. 17 (New York: Common Council), p. 620; *Report of GRC*, p. 41.

115 $10 was received from 'a few poor Christians in Brooklyn', *Report of GRC*, p. 18; Ibid., 'a poor man' gave $3, p. 23.

116 Ibid., passim.

117 Appendix 2, *Report of GRC*, p. 58.

118 *Eagle*, 12 May 1847.

119 Van Schaick to Henry Burch, Esq., Moira, Franklin Co., N. Y, 14 June 1847, *Report of GRC*, p. 96.

120 B. Washburne, *Historical Sketch of Charles S. Hempstead* (Galena: Gazette Book, 1876).

121 *Report of GRC*, pp. 29, 34.

122 Ibid., p. 45.

123 Ibid., p. 36.

124 Albert Clark Stevens, *The Cyclopædia of Fraternities* (New York: E. B. Treat and Co., 1907), p. 300.

125 Scisco, *Political Nativism*, p. 68.

126 *Report of GRC*, p. 40.

127 Ibid., p. 34. For more on Mickle see: the Political Graveyard. A database of American History, http://www.politicalgraveyard.com/bio/micheau-middleswarth.html, accessed 15 December 2011.

128 See Kinealy, *Saddest People*.

129 *Report of GRC*, p. 43.

130 Ibid., p. 51.

131 John D. Crimmins, *St. Patrick's Day* (New York: Published by 'The author', 1902) p. 97.

132 *Report of GRC*, p. 43.

133 Ibid., p. 10.

134 Ibid., p. 44.

135 New Advent. Catholic Encyclopedia: http://www.newadvent.org/cathen/07516a.htm, accessed 9 September 2012.

136 Quoted in Joseph Lee, Marion R. Casey, *Making the Irish American: History and Heritage of the Irish in the United States* (New York: New York University Press, 2006), p. 278.

137 John Hughes, 'On the antecedents of Famine', delivered under the auspices of the General Relief Committee for the relief of the suffering poor of Ireland', in *The Complete Works of the Most Rev John Hughes, D. D., Archbishop of New York. Comprising his Sermons, Letters, Lectures, Speeches, etc.* (New York: American News, 1864), p. 544.

138 Ibid., pp. 556–7.

139 Ibid, p. 556.

140 For more on Irish involvement in abolition see, Kinealy, *Saddest People*.

141 *Report of GRC*, p. 44.

142 *National Era*, 25 March 1847.

143 Ibid., p. 35.

144 Ibid., pp. 41–2.

145 Catholic editing company, *The Catholic Church in the United States of America: Undertaken to Celebrate the Golden Jubilee of His Holiness, Pope Pius X*, vol. 3 (New York: Catholic editing company, 1908), p. 432.

146 History of St Francis of Assisi: http://www.stfrancisnyc.org/history/, accessed 4 May 2012.

147 For example: included the Bridgeport Congregational Church ($83), St Luke's Episcopalian Church in Catskill, Church of the Holy Communion in New York ($403.45), the Norfolk Street Methodist Church ($12), the Church of the Ascension, Fifth Avenue ($645.53 and four barrels of bread stuffs), Trinity Church, New York ($334–82), Protestant Episcopal Free Church of the Holy Evangelists ($95.38), St Paul's Episcopal Chapel ($265.55), Unitarian Church of the Messiah ($481), St John's Church ($556 and $13.60), St Matthew's Episcopal Church on Christopher Street ($83–37), Presbyterian Church of Morris County in New Jersey ($18), Duane Street, Presbyterian Church ($273.31), Second Wesleyan Chapel, Duane Street, New York ($700.75), the Methodist churches in Middletown, Connecticut ($62), St Annis [sic] Church, Fishkill ($40.86), Congregational Society, Meriden, Connecticut ($76.35), the Episcopalian Grace Church in New York City ($1,912.38), St Mary's Catholic Church, Brooklyn ($230), the Catholic churches of St Columba's, the Church of the Transfiguration, St Andrew's in New York City ($435–88, $531 and $276.07 respectively), the Methodist Episcopal Church on Forsyth Street

($102.50), the Commercial Congregation of South Amherst in Ohio ($37), the Episcopal Churches of Southport, Connecticut ($30) and Calvary in New York City ($1 and 375 barrels of the corn meal), Christ Church at Syosset, Long Island ($64), the Reformed Dutch Church on Houston Street, New York City ($37.57 and later, $3), Unitarian Church ($91), Methodist Episcopal Church ($30), Unitarian Universalist Church ($33), North Congregational Church, Connecticut ($171.33), St John's Church ($148), Christ Church ($363), Centre Church ($244.66 for Ireland and $100 for Scotland), Mercer Presbyterian Church ($381.38), St Stephen's Episcopal Church, near Sixth Avenue ($186), St Mark's Church, New York ($250), Christ Episcopal Church in Norwich, Connecticut ($100), St Paul's Church, St Lawrence ($24), St Thomas Episcopal Church on Broadway ($319.38), St Peter's Episcopal Church ($150.62), the Methodist Church on Seventh Street ($35), St John's Episcopal Church in Bridgeport, Connecticut ($120), St John's Episcopal Church, Staten Island ($65.75), St John's Episcopal Church, Stamford, Connecticut ($110), First Presbyterian Church, Mercer Street, New York ($153), St John's Episcopal Church, Delhi, Delaware ($15.36), St Vincent ($150), St John the Evangelist ($61.25), the Methodist Episcopal Church in Cayuga in New York ($15), St Matthew's Episcopal Church, Westchester, Bedford ($10.25), St George's Episcopal Church on Long Island ($23.50), St Paul's Catholic Church, Harlem ($358.86), Reformed Dutch Church on Staten Island ($25.50), St Bartholomew's Episcopal Church, Bowery, New York ($354.25), Christ Episcopal Church in Tarrytown, New York ($115.50), Union Episcopal Church in Humphreysville, Connecticut ($14), Mercer Street Presbyterian Church, New York ($25), Protestant Episcopal Church of the Holy Cross in Troy ($108), Reformed Dutch Church in Kinderhook ($36.80), the Congregational Society and the Methodist Society of Essex in Connecticut ($90.75 and $20.50 respectively), the Baptist Church in Amity Street ($275). See *Report of GRC* for more churches and congregations that gave.

148 *Report of GRC*, p. 9.
149 Ibid., p. 47.
150 William Balch, Dictionary of Unitarian and Universalist Biography: http://www.25.uua.org/uuhs/duub/article/williamstephenbalch.html, accessed 4 June 2011. 25.ch.html http://www2 Biography.
151 *Report of GRC*, p. 44.
152 Ibid., p. 53.
153 Henry C. Whyman, *The Hedstroms and the Bethel Ship Saga. Methodist Influence on Swedish Religious Life* (Carbondale, Ill: Southern Illinois University, 1992), p. 77.
154 *Report of GRA*, p. 37.
155 Whyman, *The Hedstroms and the Bethel Ship Saga*, p. 77.
156 'Sailor's Union Bethel Methodist Church': http://www.federalhillonline.com/tourstop04.htm, accessed 12 July 2011.
157 *Report of GRC*, p. 37.
158 George Lane (1784–1859) was influential in Joseph Smith's founding of the Mormon Church. Larry C. Porter, 'Rev. George Lane. Good Gifts, Good

Grace, and Marked Usefulness'. *Brigham Young University Studies* 9(3), (Spring 1969), 321–40.

159 *NY Christian Advocate*, 24 March 1847.

160 American Jewish Historical Society, *Publications of the American Jewish Historical Society,* Issue 6 (1897), p. 143.

161 Ibid., Vol. III, No. 5, August 1847; *Report of GRC*, p. 40.

162 American Jewish Historical Society, *American Jewish Historical Quarterly*, Volume 27 (reprinted by Nabu Press, 2011), p. 251.

163 'Meeting of the Jewish Population of New York in Aid of Ireland', *The Occident and American Jewish Advocate*, vol. V, No. 1, April 1847.

164 Ibid.

165 Ibid.

166 *Report of GRC,* pp. 24, 30, 35.

167 Ibid., 39.

168 Ibid., p. 48.

169 Ibid., p. 47.

170 Florida's Ante Bellum Plantations: http://www.dejaelaine.com/abplantations. html, access 8 May 2011.

171 Van Schaick to Bewley and Pim, 14 May 1847, *Report of GRC*, p. 103.

172 Ibid., George Barclay to Bewley and Pim, 14 May 1847, p. 104.

173 Ibid., The Milwaukee Committee consisted of Richard Murphy, John White and Rufus King, Reyburn to Pim and Bewley, 14 July 1847, p. 106.

174 *Report of GRC*, p. 47.

175 Ibid., p. 59.

176 Albany Committee for the Relief of Ireland, A Guide to the Albany Committee for the Relief of Ireland Records: http://www.albanyinstitute. org/collections/FindingAids/Albany . . . Irish%20Relief%20CD%20528.pdf, accessed 10 November 2011.

177 Van Schaick, NY, to Bewley and Pim, Dublin, 15 May 1847, *Report of GRC*, p. 89.

178 Ibid., Van Schaick to Charles M. Jenkins, chairman of executive committee or relief of Ireland Albany, 10 April 1847, p. 85 (the real name of the vessel was the British brig *Minerva*).

179 Ibid., Van Schaick to Pim and Bewley, 22 May 1847, p. 91.

180 Ibid., Van Schaick to Pim and Bewley, 26 May 1847, p. 94.

181 Committee for the Relief of Ireland, Albany.

182 Van Schaick to Pim and Bewley, 15 April 1847, *Report of GRC*, p. 86.

183 *Report of GRC*, p. 49.

184 Richard L. Trotter, 'For the Defense of the Western Border: Arkansas Volunteers on the Indian Frontier, 1846–1847'. *The Arkansas Historical Quarterly* 60(4), (Winter, 2001), 394–410.

185 Coolidge was promoted to brevet lieutenant-colonel for faithful and meritorious services during the Civil War: http://www.civilwarmedicalbooks. com/Principles_of_Surgery.html, accessed 4 September 2011. US Army Medical Department, Office of Medical History, http://www.history.amedd. army.mil/booksdocs/civil/gillett2/amedd_1818–1865_chpt4.html, accessed 4 September 2011.

186 *Report of GRC*, Appendix 2, p. 56.

187 Ibid., p. 53.

188 Ibid.

189 Harry Wright Newman, *The Smoots of Maryland and Virginia; A Genealogical History of William Smute, Boatright, of Hampton, Virginia, and Pickawaxon, Maryland, with a History of his Descendants to the Present Generation* (Washington: J. P. Bell, 1936), p. 31.

190 Herman Melville used his experiences to inform his novels *White-Jacket* and *Moby Dick*.

191 George C. Read, U. S. Naval Forces, West Coast of Africa, United States frigate, *United States*, Porto Praya, Cape Verde Islands, to Jacob Harvey, Esq., 14th May, 1847, *Report of GRC*, p. 117.

192 *Report of GRC*, p. 46. Litton had been born in Ireland in 1799: http://www. findagrave.com/cgibin/fg.cgi?page=gr&GSln=Litton&GSiman=1&GScty=135 876&GRid=34690836&, accessed 5 June 2012.

193 Irish Relief Committee, Nashville, Tennessee, 27 March 1847, Appendix V, *Transactions*, p. 238.

194 Ibid.

195 *Report of GRC*, p. 51.

196 Ibid., p. 92.

197 Ibid., Van Schaick to D. Dark, Chairman and Charles Goffland, Treasurer, Memphis Irish Relief Committee, Tennessee, 21 May 1847, p. 90.

198 Ibid.

199 Isaac McKeever, Captain, US. Navy, to Myndert Van Schaick, Esq., 12 March 1847, *Report of GRC*, p. 76.

200 Ibid., Van Schaick to McKeever, 12 March 1847, p. 77.

201 *Report of GRC*, p. 51.

202 For example, *Arkansas Intelligencer*, 3 April 1847, *Niles National Register*, 1 May 1847.

203 Van Schaick to Bewley and Pim, 22 May 1847, *Report of GRC*, p. 92.

204 *Report of GRC*, p. 51; some newspapers gave the figure as $710, for example, *Connecticut Courant*, 24 April 1847.

205 *Nation*, 19 June 1847.

206 *Cherokee Nation*, 6 May 1847.

207 Chief John Ross: http://www.rossvillega.com/cherokee_chief_john_ross.htm, accessed 9 December 2011.

208 *Cherokee Nation,* 6 May 1847.

209 Ibid., 13 May 1847.

210 Ibid., 10 June 1847.

211 Ibid., 15 July 1847.

212 N. Chapman, Philadelphia to Chief John Ross, 11 June 1847 in *Cherokee Nation,* 15 July 1847.

213 These accusations were made by Commander DeKay and published in the *New York Sun, Report of GRC,* pp. 165–6.

214 Resolution of Standing Committee, 10 March 1847, *Report of GRC,* pp. 166–9.

215 Ibid., Letter of GRC, 31 May 1847, pp. 169–74.

216 Ibid., p. 175.

217 *National Era,* 5 August 1847.

218 Reyburn to Bewley and Pim, 13 August 1847, *Report of GRC,* p. 113.

219 *Report of GRC,* p. 59.

220 Ibid., pp. 54, 59.

221 Obituary of Van Schaick, *New York Times,* 3 December 1865.

222 This is a quote from Elihu Burritt, made on behalf of Ireland, *Report of GRC,* p. 15.

Chapter 5

1 The late historian of the Famine, T. P. O'Neill, drew my attention to this ditty in 1995. I remain grateful to him.

2 Frank Prochaska, *The Voluntary Impulse – Philanthropy in Modern Britain* (London: Faber and Faber, 1998).

3 This point has been made by Harrison and Prochaska in regard to Britain, but also see, Thomas Adam, *Philanthropy, Patronage and Civil Society: Experiences from Germany, Great Britain and North America* (Bloomington: Indiana University Press, 2004), p. 99.

4 Queen's Speech, Meeting of Parliament, 19 January 1847, *Hansard,* House of Lords Debates, 19 January 1847, vol. 89, cc. 1–5.

5 Committee of BRA, *Report of the British Relief Association for the Relief of Extreme Distress in Ireland and Scotland* (London: Richard Clay, 1849), hereafter, *Report of BRA,* pp. 9–10.

6 Ibid., p. 11.

7 Charles Wood to Lord John Russell, 6 January 1847, Russell Papers, National Archives, England, hereafter, NAE, 30/22/5F.

8 Ibid., Wood to Russell, 6 January 1847, 30/22/5F, NAE.

9 For more, see Christine Kinealy, in 'Leading by Example', in Patrick O'Sullivan (ed.), *The Meaning of the Famine* (London: Leicester University Press, 1997), pp. 145–52.

10 *Report of BRA,* pp. 10–11.

11 Philip Williamson, 'State Prayers, Fasts and Thanksgivings'. *Past and Present* 200(1), (2008), 121–74.

12 Russell to the Archbishop of Canterbury, 8 September 1846, Russell Papers, NAE, 30/22/5C.

13 Williamson, 'State Prayers', pp. 125–30.

14 Ibid., pp. 121–2.

15 Linda Colley has argued that Protestantism was a defining feature of British society see, *Britons: Forging the Nation 1707–1837* (New Haven: Yale University Press, 1994).

16 For more on this, see Williamson, 'State Prayers', p. 141.

17 *Freeman's Journal,* 20 March 1847.

18 Rev Edward Bickersteth, *The National Fast of 1847, a Help for Duly Observing it* (London: Seeley, Burnside, and Seeley, 1847).

19 *Brooklyn Eagle,* 29 April 1847; John Adams, *Proclamation 8 – Recommending a National Day of Humiliation, Fasting and Prayer,* 23 March 1798.

20 Wood to Russell, 21 December 1846, Russell Papers, NAE, 30/22/5G.

21 Bickersteth, *The National Fast of 1847.*

22 Williamson, 'State Prayers', p. 129.

23 Details of these proceedings were reported as far away as Van Diemen's Land, *Courier* (Hobart), 3 July 1847.

24 Williamson, 'State Prayers', p. 132.

25 Russell in the House of Commons, 'The National Fast Day', *Hansard,* House of Commons Debates, 23 March 1847, vol. 91, cc. 335–7.

26 *Courier* (Hobart), 3 July 1847.

27 Quoted in Williamson, 'State Prayers', pp. 153–4.

28 Peter Gray, 'National Humiliation and the Great Hunger: Fast and Famine in 1847'. *Irish Historical Studies* 32 (126), (November 2000), 193–216, 195.

29 Russell, 'The National Fast Day', cc. 335–7.

30 Ibid.

31 Bright in the House of Commons, 'The National Fast Day', col. 337.

32 *Launceston Examiner,* 8 September 1847.

33 C. H. Gaye, MA, *Irish Famine. A Special Occasion for Keeping Lent in England. A Sermon Preached in Obedience to the Queen's Letter on the First Sunday in Lent 1847 at Archbishop Tennison's chapel, St James Westminster,* Second edition (London: Francis and John Rivington, 1847), pp. 8–9.

34 Ibid., p. 14.

35 Ibid., p. 19.

36 M. E. Bury and D. Pickles (eds), *Rommilly's Cambridge Diary* (Cambridge: Cambridgeshire Records Society, 1994), p. 203.

37 Williamson, 'State Prayers', p. 162.

38 *South Australian Register* (Adelaide), 28 July 1847; Russell in House of Commons, 'The National Fast Day', col 337.

39 *Anglo-Celt,* 30 July 1847.

40 'Cost of Relief (Ireland)', *Hansard,* House of Commons Debates, 28 January 1847, vol. 89, cc. 504–6.

41 Ibid., 'Roman Catholic Relief Bill', 10 May 1825, vol. 13, cc. 486–562; Ibid., 'Disabilities of the Jews', 16 December 1847, vol. 95, cc. 1234–332.

42 Ibid., 'The Queen's Letter (Ireland)', 8 February 1847, vol. 89, c. 942.

43 Lord John Russell to Queen, 14 October 1847, Arthur Christopher Benson and Reginald Baliol Brett Esher (eds), *The Letters of Queen Victoria, 1837–61* (London: J. Murray, 1911), p. 141.

44 Appendix, Williamson, 'State Prayers'.

45 Reprinted in the *Economist,* 16 October 1847.

46 *Report of BRA,* p. 24.

47 The London *Times,* a critic of Ireland, had made it clear from the time of the first Letter that it believed God was punishing the undeserving Irish poor, *Times,* 24 March 1847.

48 *Economist,* 16 October 1847.

49 *Journal des Débats,* reprinted in the *Tablet,* 23 October 1847.

50 J. Cantwell, Mullingar, to Archbishop Cullen, 17 January 1848, Cullen Papers, No. 1514.

51 See chapter on role of British Relief Association.

52 Russell to Clarendon, 23 June 1845, Benson, *The Letters of Queen Victoria,* p. 239.

53 Ibid., Clarendon to Sir George Grey, 14 August 1849, p. 237.

54 Quoted in Donal Kerr, *A Nation of Beggars?: Priests, People, and Politics in Famine Ireland, 1846–1852* (Oxford: Clarendon Press, 1994), p. 203.

55 Ibid.

56 See footnote 1.

57 *Irish Canadian,* 7 January 1880.

58 Stanley Lane-Poole, *The Life of Lord Stratford de Redcliffe* (London: Longmans, Green, 1890), pp. 162–6.

59 Rev R. W. Fraser, *Turkey Ancient and Modern. A History of the Ottoman Empire from its Period of Establishment to the Present Time* (Edinburgh: Adam and Charles Black, mdcccliv (1854), p. 449.

60 Damascus Affair, *Jewish Encyclopedia*: http://www.jewishencyclopedia.com/articles/4862-damascus-affair, accessed 4 November 2011a.

61 *Nonconformist,* 17 February 1847.

62 *Church And State Gazette,* 1 April 1847.

63 Henry Christmas, *The Sultan of Turkey, Abdul Medjid Khan: A Brief Memoir of his Life and Reign, with Notices of the Country, its Army, Navy, & Present Prospects* (London: Shaw, 1854), p. 19.

64 *The Albion. A Journal of News, Politics and Literature*, 21 July 1849.

65 Kinealy, 'Leading by Example', in O'Sullivan (ed.), *The Meaning of the Famine* (London: Leicester University Press, 1997b), pp. 145–52.

66 Ottoman Archives, Ministry of Foreign Affairs, Document no: 1847, Letter to the Ministry of Foreign Affairs to the Sultan, dated 1847. In 1994, copies of these documents were given by the Department Foreign Affairs in Dublin to the National Library.

67 *Ibid., Letter to the Ministry of Foreign Affair to the Sultan, dated 1847, Document No: 1888; Ibid., Annex to Document No. 1888.*

68 *Bell's New Weekly Messenger*, 18 April 1847.

69 *Church And State Gazette*, 23 April 1847.

70 *Bell's New Weekly Messenger*, 25 April 1847.

71 *Times*, 17 April 1847.

72 Christmas, *Sultan*, pp. 20–1. No mention is made of the ships allegedly sent by the Sultan.

73 Address to Emperor of Turkey, Appendix D, *Report of BRA*, pp. 181–2.

74 Ibid.

75 *The Albion*, 21 July 1849.

76 *National Era*, 20 May 1847.

77 *The Sydney Morning Herald* (NSW), 24 February 1849.

78 *Brooklyn Eagle*, 24 September 1849.

79 The *Nation*, 13 October 1849.

80 *Freeman's Journal*, 23 November 1853.

81 Ibid.

82 Henry Barrett Learned, 'Cabinet Meetings under President Polk'.*Annual Report of the American Historical Association for 1914* I, 229–42, 235.

83 In his diaries, Polk notes his attendance at church, or otherwise.

84 Margaret M. Mulrooney, *Fleeing the Famine: North America and Irish Refugees, 1845–1851*(Westport, Conn.: Praeger, 2003), p. 51.

85 Mrs Chapman Coleman, *The Life of John J. Crittenden: With Selections from His Correspondence and Speeches*, vols. 1–2 (Philadelphia: J.B. Lippincott & Co., 1873), p. 284.

86 Ibid., pp. 287–8.

87 Ibid.

88 *NY Weekly Tribune*, 20 February 1847.

89 William T. Young, *Sketch of the Life and Public Services of General Lewis Cass: With the Pamphlet on the Right of Search, and some of his Speeches on the Great Political Questions of the Day* (Detroit: Alexander McFarren, 1852), p. 353.

90 Mulrooney, *Fleeing the Famine*, p. 50.

91 Curti, *American Philanthropy Abroad*, pp. 44–5.

92 Ibid., p. 48. Hannegan is alleged to have said in the U.S. Senate, 'Delendaest Britannia' ('Britain must be destroyed').

93 Ballard C. Campbell, *Disasters, Accidents and Crises in American History* (New York: Facts On File, 2008), p. 87.

94 *National Era*, 4 March 1847.

95 Ibid.

96 Ibid.

97 *Brooklyn Eagle*, 29 October 1847.

98 Ibid., 4 November 1848.

99 Tuesday, 2 March 1847, James K. Polk, *Polk; The Diary of a President, 1845–1849, Covering the Mexican War, the Acquisition of Oregon and the Conquest of California and the Southwest* (New York: Longmans, Green and Co., 1929), p. 396.

100 Ibid., p. 397.

101 Ibid., p. 398.

102 Curti, *American Philanthropy*, pp. 48–9.

103 Boston *Pilot*, 13 March 1847.

104 James Buchanan and John Bassett Moore, *James Henry Buchanan, The Works of James Buchanan: Comprising his Speeches, etc.*, vol. 12 (Philadelphia: Lippincott, 1911), p. 289.

105 Boston *Pilot*, 17 April 1847.

106 Rochester, p. 5.

107 Sickle Biography: http://www.sicklesatgettysburg.com/Sickles_Biography.html, accessed 5 October 2011.

108 'Debate on the Bill for the Relief of Ireland', *Congressional Globe*, 29 Congress, 2nd Session, 3 March 1847, pp. 440–1.

109 Polk, *Diary*, 5 March 1847, p. 408.

110 'F', Boston, 1 March 1847, to Editor of *Tablet*, reprinted in *Sydney Chronicle*, 4 August 1847.

111 *Nation*, 31 July 1847.

Chapter 6

1 The Papal Encyclical, *Praedecessores Nostros*, 25 March 1847, *Papal Encyclicals Online*: http://www.papalencyclicals.net/index.htm, accessed 9 March 2012.

2 *The United States Catholic Magazine and Monthly Review*, vol. 5 (Baltimore: J. Murphy, February 1846), p. 105.

3 Letter from Bishop John Cantwell, Mullingar, reprinted in *Freeman's Journal*, 17 February 1847.

4 For example, William Bennett in *Six Weeks*, made frequent reference to their roles, pp. 35–6.

5 Ibid., p. 51.

6 Quoted in Rev Donal Kerr, *The Catholic Church and the Great Irish Famine* (Dublin: Columba Press, 1996).

7 Nicholson, *Annals,* p. 64.

8 Bernard O'Reilly, *John MacHale, Archbishop of Tuam: His Life, Times and Correspondence,* vol. 2 (New York: F. Pustet, 1890), pp. 65–8.

9 Kerr, *Nation of Beggars,* p. 18.

10 J. T. Gilbert, 'Daniel Murray', in Leslie Stephen, Robert Blake, Christine Stephanie Nicholls (eds), *Dictionary of National Biography,* vol. 13 (Oxford University Press, 1909), p. 1249.

11 *New York Christian Advocate,* 2 June 1847 (information based on 1841 census).

12 This is evident from the correspondence of Cullen etc, see Paul Cullen Papers, Rome, Archives Pontifical Irish College, Rome: http://www.irishcollege. org/wp-content/uploads/2011/02/Cullen-Collection-Master-Catalogue.pdf, accessed 11 December 2011. The Cullen letters cited in this chapter are from this source.

13 O'Reily, *John MacHale,* p. 263.

14 Ibid., p. 202.

15 C. Egan, Killarney, Kerry, to Cullen, 16 February 1848, Cullen Papers, No. 1537.

16 'Pope Pius IX', in New Advent, *Catholic Encyclopedia:* http://www. newadvent.org/cathen/12134b.htm, accessed 8 May 2012.

17 Christopher Duggan, *A Concise History of Italy* (Cambridge: Cambridge University Press, 1994), pp. 135–8.

18 Christine Kinealy, *Lives of Victorian Political Figures: Daniel O'Connell* (London: Pickering and Chatto, 2007), pp. 338–57.

19 Pontificio Collegio Irlandese: http://www.irishcollege.org/college/, accessed 4 June 2012.

20 1122, 19 December 1845, J. Cantwell, Mullingar, to Cullen, 19 December 1845, Cullen Papers, No. 1122; Ibid., E. Maginn, Buncrana, to Cullen, 28 August 1846, No. 1237.

21 Kerr, *Nation of Beggars,* p. 89.

22 Draft notes by Dr Cullen on the subject of Lord Lieutenant Clarendon's letter to Dr Murray, Cullen's New Collection, CUL/NC/4/1847/2: http:// www.irishcollege.org/wp-content/uploads/2011/02/Cullen-Collection-Master-Catalogue.pdf, accessed 11 December 2011.

23 George Clement Boase, 'Harford, John Scandrett', Dictionary of National Biography Online 1885–1900, vol. 24(1890), http://en.wikisource.org/wiki/ Harford,_John_Scandrett_%28DNB00%29, accessed 12 May 2012.

24 Harford's Journal of these months is held in the Bristol Record Office: http:// www.nationalarchives.gov.uk/a2a/records.aspx?cat=002-28048&cid=6-14#6-14, accessed 2 August 2011.

25 *Tuam Herald,* 6 March 1847.

26 Ab. Rosmini, Prep. General dell' Istituto Item della Carita, Stresa to D. Giova. B Pagani, Provinciale dell'Istituto della Carita in Inghilterra, Cullen Papers, 31 December 1846, CUL/NC/4/1846/27.

27 Cullen to Murray, Cullen Papers, 13 February 1847, CUL/144.

28 *Anglo-Celt*, 19 April 1847.

29 The letter was quoted in *Freeman's Journal*, 30 January 1847.

30 Cullen to Murray, 25 March 1847, Cullen Papers, CUL/143.

31 Ibid., 16 January 1847 John Harford [Chairman], Rome, to Cullen, 16 January 1847, CUL/1304.

32 *Tuam Herald*, 6 March 1847.

33 Ibid.

34 For example, Cardinal Bishop of Osimo, to Cullen, 18 June 1847, Cullen Papers, CUL/145, sent money to Cardinal Fransoni 'for suffering Irish'.

35 Ibid., Fransoni to Murray, 30 January 1847, CUL/159.

36 Ibid., M. Slattery, Thurles, to Cullen, 9 April 1847, CUL/1368.

37 Ibid., Catherine Englefield, Rome, to Cullen, 24 January 1847, CUL/1312.

38 A Neapolitan measure that was equivalent to 644 English cubic feet. William Alfred Browne, *The Merchants' Handbook* (London: Edward Stanford, 1879), p. 226.

39 Salvatore Mauri and Agostino (Alimonda) to Cullen, 4 February 1847, Cullen Papers, CUL/1324a.

40 *Sydney Chronicle* (NSW), 23 June 1847.

41 Letter from Secretary of the Congregation of the Index, Rome, to Cullen, Cullen Papers, CUL/140.

42 Ibid., Dr Cullen to Dean Meyler, 13 February 1847, CUL/144.

43 *Freeman's Journal*, 2 September 1847.

44 *Sydney Chronicle*, 23 June 1847.

45 Ibid.

46 Kinealy, *O'Connell*, pp. 338–57.

47 Ibid.

48 *Anglo-Celt*, 19 February 1847.

49 George Fitz-Hardinge Berkeley, Joan Weld Berkeley, *Italy in the Making: June 1846 to 1 January 1848* (Cambridge: Cambridge University Press, 1968), pp. 162–3.

50 Dr Cullen, (Rome) to Murray, 28 February 1847, Cullen Papers, CUL/142.

51 Kerr, *Nation of Beggars*, p. 89.

52 *Church and State Gazette*, 30 April 1847.

53 T. Kirby, (Rome), to Cullen, 8 August 1847, Cullen Papers, CUL/1450.

54 *Times*, 20 May 1847.

55 *Freeman's Journal*, 16 June 1847.

56 E. Maginn, Buncrana, to Cullen, 10 July 1847, Cullen Papers, CUL/1434. Murray had sent his own letter in May thanking the Pope for his Encyclical, Murray Papers, 151, 6 May 1847.

57 Formal address entitled 'The Address of the Catholics of Ireland to His Holiness Pope Pius IX' signed on behalf of the Meeting by the Chairman,

John O'Connell, M. P. for the City of Limerick and City of Kilkenny, Dublin', November 1847, Cullen Papers, New Collection, CUL/NC/4/1847/50.

58 Ibid.

59 M. Chanoine Tanghe, Secretary to the Archbishop of Bruges, to Murray, 29 July 1847, Murray Papers, Dublin Diocesan Archives, No. 78. Murray's papers are available at, Dublin Diocesan Archives: http://www.ulir.ul.ie/ bitstream/handle/10344/1558/Murray%2032-3,1847.pdf?sequence=2, accessed various dates in 2012. The Murray letters cited in this chapter are from this source. A Guide to Murray's Papers is available at, The University of Limerick Institutional Repository: http://www.ulir.ul.ie/handle/10344/1554.

60 Kerr, *Nation of Beggars*, p. 49.

61 Bob Cullen, *Thomas L. Synnott: The Career of a Dublin Catholic, 1830–70* (Dublin: Irish Academic Press, 1997), pp. 32–40.

62 Kerr, *Nation of Beggars*, p. 49.

63 Kay Boardman and Christine Kinealy, *The Year the World Turned. 1848 in Europe* (Newcastle: Cambridge Scholars Publishing, 2007).

64 'Table 1.3 Potato production and consumption and the fall in yields in 1845 and 1846 compared to "normal" years' in, Eric Vanhaute, Richard Paping, and Cormac Ó Gráda, *The European Subsistence Crisis of 1845–1850: A Comparative Perspective* (International Economic History Congress, 2006, Helsinki Session 123), p. 10.

65 M. lc Chanoine Tanghe, Secretary to the Archbishop of Bruges, to Murray, 10 July 1847, Murray Papers, No. 7.

66 Ibid., Louis Joseph Delebecque, Archbishop of Client, to Murray, 5 July 1847, No., 80.

67 Ibid., Cardinal-Archbishop of Malines, Engelbert Sterckx, to Murray, 3 July 1847, 19 July 1847, Nos 86 and 87.

68 Ibid., Van Cannart, Antwerp, to Murray, 26 August 1847, 23 November 1847, Nos 82 and 83.

69 Ibid., Abbe Moriarty, Cure of Derchigny, near Dieppe, to Murray, 27 February 1847, No. 88.

70 Vicar-General of Paris on behalf of the Archbishop to Murray, 30 June 1847, No., 94.

71 Ibid., Carol J. E. de Mazenod, Bishop of Marseilles, to Murray, 14 April 1847, Nos 89 and 90.

72 Ibid., Mgr des Essarts, Bishop of Blois, to Murray, 13 July 1847, No. 95.

73 Ibid., from 'un pauvre domestique de France' to Murray, 30 April 1847, No. 91.

74 Ibid., Letter from J. T. Mooratz, 82 Rue de Rivoli, Paris, to Murray, 17 April 1847, No. 93.

75 Ibid., Peter Richarz, Archbishop of Augsburg, to Murray, 29 October 1847, No. 97.

76 Ibid., Richarz to Murray, 25 December 1847, No. 98.

77 Ibid.

78 Ibid., Wagner and Schoemann, Bankers, to William Arnoldi, Archbishop of Treves (Trier), fowarded to Murray, 7 December 1847, No 99 and 100.

79 Ibid., William Arnoldi, Archbishop of Trier (Treves) to Murray, 3 November 1847, No. 103.

80 Ibid., Francis Arnold Melchers Vicar Capitular of Munster and Suffragan, to Murray, 26 June 1847, 19 July, 14 August, 15 December 1847, 104 and 105, 106, 107.

81 Ibid., Jona Cahn, Bankers, Bonn to Murray, 12 November 1847, No. 102.

82 Bishop of Cartagena (Cardinal Viale Prela) to Murray, Murray Papers, 25 October 1847, No. 126; Antonio Polanzo, offices of the review, *Revisto Catolica*, Tarragona, to Murray. 2 December 1847, No. 127.

83 Rev Dr Henry Hughes, Gibraltar to Murray, 18 March 1847, No. 76.

84 'Dr Henry Hughes, Bishop in Gibraltar', in *Catholic Hierarchy*: http://www. catholic-hierarchy.org/bishop/bhug.html, accessed 11 May 2012.

85 Loreto Education Arrives in Gibraltar: http://www.loreto.ie/archives/ foundations-made-by-m-teresa-ball/188-gibraltar-1845, accessed 11 May 2012.

86 Rev Dr Henry Hughes, Gibraltar to Murray, 18 March 1847, Murray Papers, No. 76.

87 Ibid., Cardinal Placidus Maria Tadini, Archbishop of Genoa, to Murray, 26 May 1847, No. 113.

88 Ibid., Letter to Murray from Aloysius Moreno, Bishop of Ivrea, 23 June 1847, Nos 114 and 115; Ibid., Count Revel, Sardinian Charge d'Affaires, London, to Murray; 20 July 1847, No. 116.

89 Ibid., Dr Modestus Contraltus, Bishop of Acqui, to Murray, 1847, No. 124. 1847.

90 Ibid., Letter from a secretary of Mgr Aloysius Rendu, Bishop of Annecy to Murray, 7 July 1847, No. 125.

91 *Freeman's Journal,* 9 September 1847.

92 MacHale to Murray, Murray Papers, 25 February 1847, No. 47.

93 Ibid., Dr Crolly to Murray, 28 February 1847, No. 48.

94 Ibid., Dr Crolly to Murray, 13 March 1847, No., 51; Ibid., Dr MacHale to Murray, 14 March 1847.

95 Ibid., MacHale to Murray, 27 September 1847, No. 59; Ibid., 65 Dr MacHale to Murray, 19 April 1847, No., 65.

96 Ibid., Dr MacHale to Murray, 27 September 1847, No. 65.

97 Ibid., Mr Fetherston, J. P. Bruree House, Charleville, to Murray, 13 May 1847, No. 134.

98 Ibid., Fr Enright, Castletown Berehaven, to Murray, 23 November 1847, No. 40.

99 Ibid., Elizabeth Fetherston, Bruree House, Charleville, 4 May 1847, No. 16.

100 Ibid., Fr Michael Enright, Castletown Berehaven, to Murray. 21 May 1847, No. 136.

101 *The Literary World,* vol. 49 (1894), p. 512.

102 *Bengal Catholic Herald,* 17 January 1847.

103 Andrew W. Cochran, Chairman of the General Committee, Quebec addressed to Dr Murray, Archbishop of Dublin and Richard Whately, Church of Ireland Archbishop of Dublin, 22 February 1847, Cullen New Collection, CUL/NC/4/1847/10.

104 The *Quebec Saturday Budget*, 13 March 1897.

105 William Walsh, Bishop of Halifax, St Mary's, Halifax, Nova Scotia to Dr Murray, 29 March 1847, Cullen New Collection, CUL/NC/4/1847/20.

106 'William Walsh', in *Dictionary of National Biography Online*: http://www.biographi.ca/009004-119.01-e.php?&id_nbr=4239, accessed 4 June 2012.

107 William Walsh, Bishop of Halifax, St Mary's, Halifax, to Dr Murray, 29 March 1847, Cullen New Collection, CUL/NC/4/1847/20.

108 'Patrick Phelan', in *Dictionary of National Biography Online*: http://www.biographi.ca/009004-119.01-e.php?id_nbr=4133, accessed 3 June 2012.

109 Patrick Phelan, Coadjutor of the Diocese Item of Kingston, Kingston to Dr Murray, 23 April 1847, Cullen New Collection, CUL/NC/4/1847/22.

110 Ibid., C. Curran, Montreal to Dr Murray, 25 February 1847, CUL/NC/4/1847/11.

111 Ibid., John Sweeny, Catholic Missionary, Chatham, Miramichi, New Brunswick to Dr Murray, 26 February 1847, CUL/NC/4/1847/12.

112 Kerr, *Nation of Beggars*, p. 57.

113 'Bishop William Barber Tyler', in *Catholic Hierarchy*: http://www.catholic-hierarchy.org/bishop/btyler.html, accessed 1 June 2012.

114 Boston *Pilot*, 6 March 1847.

115 Dr William Tyler, Bishop of Hartford, to Murray, 17 February 1847, Murray Papers, No. 129.

116 Ibid., MacHale to Murray, 19 April 1847, No. 59.

117 Ibid., J. Bayley, Secretary to Dr John Joseph Hughes, Bishop of New York, to Murray, 1 March, 14 March 1847, No. 130.

118 Boston *Pilot*, 6 March 1847.

119 Central Executive Committee in the State of New York, Albany, New York to Dr Murray, 7 April 1847, Cullen New Collection, CUL/NC/4/1847/23.

120 The *Charlottetown Examiner*, 30 October 1847.

121 Kerr, *Nation of Beggars*, p. 58.

122 John Talbot, Wexford, to Murray, 22 July 1847, Murray Papers, No. 30.

123 'Vicariate Apostolic of Natal', in *Catholic Encyclopedia*: http://www.newadvent.org/cathen/10707a.htm, accessed 28 May 2012.

124 'Bishop Aidan Devereaux', Vicar Apostolic of Cape of Good Hope, Eastern District (Capo de Buona Speranza, Distretto Orientale), in *Catholic Hierarchy*: http://www.catholic-hierarchy.org/bishop/bdever.html, accessed 1 June 2012.

125 *Tablet*, 2 January, 9 January 1847.

126 Dr Griffiths, Vicar Apostolic, London, to Murray, 18 January 1847, Murray Papers, No. 68.

127 Cardinal Wiseman, Oscott College, Birmingham, to Murray, 22, 26, 27, 28 January 1847, Murray Papers, No. 73.

128 Ibid., John Kirke, Lichfield, to Murray 11 January 1847, No. 4.

129 Thomas Burke, *Catholic History of Liverpool* (Liverpool: C. Tinling & Co., 1910), p. 83.

130 Ibid., p. 83.

131 Lord Brougham, House of Lords, 'Distress in Ireland', 28 January 1847, vol. 89 cc. 501–3.

132 H. J. Cullen (nephew), Liverpool, to Cullen, 17 February 1847, Murray Papers, No. 1335.

133 *The Liverpool Commercial List* (London: Seyd and Co. 1866), p. 9.

134 Burke, *Liverpool*, pp. 85–6.

135 Thomas Cullen, Liverpool, to Cullen, Cullen Papers, 23 February 1847, No. 1339.

136 *History of the Faithful Companions of Jesus in Britain and the Channel Isles:* http://www.fcjsisters.org/ep/english/about/history_brit.html, accessed 3 May 2011.

137 Burke, *Liverpool*, pp. 86–7.

138 Ibid., p. 85.

139 English Benedictine Congregation History: http://www.plantata.org.uk/people.php?choice=surname&target=appleton, accessed 2 May 2012.

140 Burke, *Liverpool*, pp. 86–7.

141 *Liverpool Monuments*: http://www.liverpoolmonuments.co.uk/relstatues/pat01.html, accessed 2 May 2012.

142 Kerr, Nation of Beggars, p. 58.

143 Ibid., p. 50.

144 *Nation*, 20 March 1847.

145 From Father Mathew to William Rathbone, 26 February 1848, Rathbone Papers, PRV 1. 67, Liverpool University Archives.

146 *The Cork Examiner*, 7 June 1847.

147 *The Dublin Almanac and general register of Ireland, for 1847*, pp. 337, 759.

148 Kerr, *Catholic Church*.

149 *The Anglo-Celt* (Cavan), 4 February 1848.

150 Kerr, *Nation of Beggars*, pp. 50, 207.

151 Jacinta Prunty, *'Margaret Aylward', 1810–1889: Lady of Charity, Sister of Faith* (Dublin: Four Courts Press, 2011), pp. 23–4, 167.

152 Redmond Peter O'Carroll, Solicitor, Dublin to Murray, 27 May 1847, Murray Papers, No. 138.

153 Cardinal Gerri to M. Jules Gossin, President General of the St Vincent de Paul Society, to Murray, 15 April 1847, Murray Papers, No. 164.

154 Maire Brighid Ni Chearbhaill, 'The Society of St Vincent de Paul in Dublin, 1926–1875' (New University of Ireland, Maynooth, 2008, PhD), p. 9. Available online: http://www.eprints.nuim.ie/1482/, accessed 3 August 2012.

155 History of the Society of the St Vincent de Paul in Ireland: http://www. docstoc.com/docs/2203032/THE-HISTORY-OF-THE-SOCIETY-OF-ST-VINCENT-DE-PAUL-IN-IRELAND, accessed 15 May 2011.

156 Sixth Annual Report of St Vincent de Paul, *Freeman's Journal,* 18 December 1851.

157 Earl of Clarendon to Charles Wood, 2 August 1847, Letter books of Lord Clarendon, Bodleian Library, Oxford.

158 *St James's Chronicle,* 26 October 1847.

159 Kerr, *Nation of Beggars,* p. 51.

160 Kinealy, *Repeal and Revolution.*

161 Tobias Kirby, Tivoli, to Cullen, 19 September 1847, Cullen Papers, CUL/1469.

162 Ibid., Maginn to Cullen, 7 October 1847, CUL/1476.

163 1721, 16 March 1849, Ibid., J. Cantwell, Mullingar, to Cullen, 16 March 1849, Cullen Papers, Meath Collection, CUL/1721; Ibid., 1722, 20 March 1849 J. Cantwell, Mullingar, to Cullen, 20 March 1849, CUL/1722, each letter included sums collected for the Pope and requested that Dr Cullen take them to Gaeta.

164 See chapter on proselytism.

165 Quoted in Niall Ó Ciosáin, 'Approaching a Folklore Archive: The Irish Folklore Commission and the Memory of the Great Famine'. *Folklore* 115(2), (August 2004), 222–32, 227.

166 Ibid., pp. 227–8.

Chapter 7

1 Maria Edgeworth to Mrs Butler, 13 March 1847, Maria Edgeworth, *The Life and Letters of Maria Edgeworth*, Vol. 2: http://www.gutenberg.org/cache/epub/9095/pg9095.txt, accessed 29 May 2011.

2 Eliza Tyndall Pope, *A Ladies Committee in Ireland, 1849,* National Library of Ireland (NLI), Ms. 40, 438 (*Commonplates*, Eliza Tyndall Pope, Reginald's Place, Waterford, 1849). Pope, nee Tyndall, was married to Alexander Pope and appears to have been a young wife and mother living in Waterford when she wrote this poem. See, *Ireland. High Court of Chancery, Ireland. Rolls Court, Ireland. Court of Bankruptcy and Insolvency, Ireland. Landed Estates Court* (Dublin: Hodges and Smith, 1856), p. 66.

3 Harrison, 'Philanthropy and the Victorians', p. 360.

4 Luddy, *Women and Philanthropy,* p. 1.

5 Preston, *Charitable Words,* pp. 69–70.

6 There were notable exceptions. See Chapter Eleven for more on proselytism.

7 The government officials who toured the country noted the important roles played by women. See, for example, Lieutenant Col Douglas to Sir Randolph Routh, *Correspondence Relating to Measures for Relief of Distress in Ireland* (Commissariat Series, Second Part), January–March 1847, BPP, H of C, p. 42.

8 According to the historian Frank Prochaska, 'charity work did more than anything else to expand the horizons of women in the nineteenth century', F. K. Prochaska, *Women and Philanthropy in Nineteenth-Century England* (Oxford: Oxford University Press, 1980), p. 275.

9 Trevelyan to Mr Hewat, Provincial Bank, 1 March 1847, *House of Commons Papers*, vol. 52 (London: Great Britain Parliament, House of Commons), p. 213.

10 Prochaska, Women and Philanthropy, p. 275.

11 'Schedule of Grants, Irish Relief Association, *Distress in Ireland* (Dublin: Philip Dixon Hardy, 1847), pp. 17, 23.

12 Relief Committee of Six Mile Bridge, County Clare to IRA, 15 September 1846, Application No. 148, Minutes of IRA, Royal Irish Academy, 27.Q.24.

13 Ibid., Arklow Relief Association to IRA, 21 December 1846, Application No. 149.

14 Ibid., Baltinglass Committee to IRA, 22 December 1846, Application No. 153.

15 Ibid., Tubrid Parish, Co. Tipperary, to IRA, 12 January 1847, Application No. 259.

16 Minutes of British Relief Association (BRA), NLI, 13 January 1847, p. 45.

17 Ibid, 14 January 1847, p. 46.

18 William Dool Killen, *The Ecclesiastical History of Ireland: From the Earliest Period to the Present Times*, vol. 2 (London: Macmillan, 1875), p. 496.

19 *Transactions*, p. 46.

20 Ibid., Statement Dr Edgar of Belfast, p. 436.

21 Killen, *The Ecclesiastical History*, p. 496.

22 Nicholson, *Annals*, p. 59.

23 Minute of Central Relief Committee, 25 May 1848, *Transactions*, p. 436.

24 Ibid., p. 92.

25 Shaftesbury Society and Ragged School Union, *The Ragged School Union Magazine*, vol. v (London: Patridge and Oakey, 1853), p. 190.

26 *First Report of Belfast Ladies' Committee*, hereafter *Report of BLC*, 6 March 1847 (Belfast: s.n., 1847), p. 1.

27 Ibid., pp. 4–5.

28 Nicholson, *Annals*, pp. 58–60.

29 Mary McNeill, *The Life and Times of Mary Ann McCracken, 1770–1866: A Belfast Panorama* (Dublin: A. Figgis, 1960).

30 Christine Kinealy, *Daniel O'Connell and the Anti-Slavery Movement. The Saddest People the Sun Sees* (London: Pickering and Chatto, 2011).

31 Samuel Rhoads, Enoch Lewis, *Friends' Review: A Religious, Literary and Miscellaneous Journal*, Vol. 27 (Philadelphia: J. Tatum., 1874), p. 747.

32 *National Era*, 4 February 1847.

33 Webb, 2 December 1847, Boston Library digitized Anti-slavery collection: http://www.archive.org/details/lettertomariacha00webb, accessed 10 October 2011.

34 Nicholson, *Annals*, p. 60; Kinealy, *The Saddest People*.

35 William Campbell Allen Papers, Public Record Office on Northern Ireland [D1558/7/1/]: http://www.proni.gov.uk/introduction__campbell_allen_d1558.pdf, access 15 April 2012.

36 *Report of BLC*, pp. 2–10.

37 Ibid.

38 Ibid., Report of Clothing Committee, p. 36.

39 *Report of BLC*, pp. 10–20.

40 Ibid., Report of Operations of Industrial Committee, pp. 27–30.

41 *Report of BLC*, pp. 7–8. See also Kinealy and MacAtasney, *The Hidden Famine*.

42 Ibid., p. 28.

43 Ibid., pp. 20–30.

44 Ibid., Mrs Hewitson, Rossgarrow (incorrectly printed as Rossgarron) 18 February 1847, pp. 17–19.

45 Nicholson, *Annals*, p. 82.

46 Ibid., p. 80.

47 Ibid., p. 83.

48 Ibid., Rev P. Griffiths and Dr Brady, Templecrone, p. 25.

49 Ibid., Rev Griffiths to Ladies' Committee, 4 February 1847, p. 25.

50 Ibid., Mrs Hume, Glen Lodge Killibegs, 3 February 1847, p. 33.

51 William Hume to William Stanley Esquire, 2 April 1847, [Relief Commission Papers, National Archives, Dublin, RLFC 3/2/7/8]: http://www.learnaboutarchives.ie/~learnabo/images/learnaboutarchives/sampledocuments/famine/donegaltranscript1.pdf, accessed 1 May 2012.

52 Ibid., 22 February 1847. William Hume, who was a JP, died in November 1849, *Headstone Inscriptions, St. Columba's Church of Ireland, Glencolumbkille*, http://www.freepages.genealogy.rootsweb.ancestry.com/~donegal/stccofi.htm, accessed 3 March 2012.

53 *Transactions*, p. 46.

54 Nicholson, *Annals*, pp. 72–3.

55 *Cork Constitution*, 30 January 1847.

56 Ibid.

57 *Southern Reporter*, 29 December 1846.

58 Copies survive in the Roberts Forbes Collection in Massachusetts History Society: http://www.masshist.org/findingaids/doc.cfm?fa=fa0039#top, accessed 1 December 2011.

59 *Cork Constitution*, 30 January 1847.

60 *Tuam Herald*, 2 May 1847.

61 Patrick Hickey, *Famine, Mortality and Emigration. A Profile of Six Parishes in the Poor Law Union of Skibbereen, 1846–47*: http://www.home.alphalink.com.au/~datatree/wolf%2053.htm, accessed 3 March 2011.

62 William Maziere Brady, *Clerical and Parochial Records of Cork, Cloyne and Ross* (Dublin, Printed for the author by A. Thom, 1863), p. 249.

63 *Cork Constitution*, 22 April 1847.

64 Assistant Commissary-General Bishop to Routh, 27 January 1847, BPP, *Correspondence Relating to Measures for Relief of Distress*, p. 40.

65 *Report of BRA*, p. 17.

66 W and J. Harvey, Cork, Second Month 1847, *Transactions*, p. 175.

67 Ibid., p. 176.

68 Hugh James Rose, Samuel Roffey Maitland, *The British Magazine*, vol. 31, p. 240.

69 Ibid., p. 240.

70 Ibid.

71 'Schedule of Grants', IRA, *Distress in Ireland*, p. 23.

72 Dunmanyway Ladies' Committee to IRA, Application No 271, 11 January 1847, RIA. 27.Q.24.

73 *National Intelligencer*, 11 February 1847.

74 In 2011, descendants of the Cox family returned the tea service to Dunmanway, Ailin Quinlan, 'Historic silver service returned by Cox descendants to Dunmanway', *The Southern Star*, 21 May 2011. The Dunmanway Historical Society explained:

> This magnificent Service contains a teapot, a water jug, a sugar bowl and a milk jug. It was made in London in the 1840s by William Kerr Reid, a renowned silversmith. Each piece has beautifully engraved patterns on it as well as the Cox Crest, similar to the Crest on the stone plaque in St. Mary's Church, which commemorates the wife of Sir Richard Cox, Lady Mary Cox. The teapot has an inscription on it which reads, "Presented to the MISSES COX of the Manor House, Dunmanway, by the REV. JAMES DOHENY P. P. on the part of their tenants as a small token of their gratitude for the unsolicited renewal of their leases Feb. 1848".

http://www.dunmanwayhistoricalsociety.org/post/Cox-Silver-Tea-Service.aspx, accessed 10 December 2011.

75 Landed Estates Database, NUI Galway: http://www.landedestates.ie/LandedEstates/jsp/estate-show.jsp?id=3056, accessed 10 July 2012.

76 Arklow Ladies' Committee to IRA, Application No. 149, 21 December 1846.

77 Appendix Three, *Transactions*, p. 190.

78 Colonel Strokes to Trevelyan, 6 February 1847, BPP, *Correspondence Relating to Measures for Relief of Distress*, p. 92.

79 The Londonderry Ladies' Association also referred to as 'Working Association' and 'Benevolent Association'.

80 Killybegs, 12 December 1846, *Transactions*, p. 191.

81 Rev Mr Shaw to Commander Kent, 30 January 1847, BPP, *Correspondence Relating to Measures for Relief of Distress*, p. 72.

82 Nicholson, *Annals*, p. 72.

83 These goods were mostly sold by the Brooklyn merchant R. J. Todd, see, for example, *Brooklyn Eagle*, 24 December 1847.

84 *Nation*, 10 July 1847.

85 *Transactions*, p. 46.

86 Luddy, *Women and Philanthropy*, p. 46.

87 Ibid., p. 48.

88 Ibid., pp. 52–3.

89 Ibid., p. 52.

90 Reproduced from an original booklet by the Printing Students, Cork Regional Technical College on the occasion of the XXV International Apprentice Competition, September 1979). http://www.cobhmuseum.com/Exhibitions/IrishLace/IrishLace.html, accessed 3 September 2011.

91 James Perry to Central Relief Committee, 28 March 1847, *Transactions*, p. 194.

92 Sister M. Paula Cullen (Cousin) Mercy Convent, Westport, to Cullen, 31 July 1847, Cullen Papers, CUL/1445.

93 Ibid., M.[other] Teresa Collin's, Convent President, Dingle to Cullen, 13 July 1847, CUL/1436.

94 Ibid., 1571 23 March 1848 M. T. Collis, Presentation Convent, Dingle to Cullen, 23 March 1848, CUL/1571; Ibid., Sr. M. Paula Cullen, Westport, to Cullen, 1 July 1848, CUL/1611.

95 Ibid., Convent President, Tuam, to Cullen, 15 June 1847, CUL/1413.

96 Nicholson, *Annals*, p. 145.

97 Kerr, *Nation of Beggars*, p. 61.

98 *Leaves from the Annals of the Sisters of Mercy in three volumes: Volume i. Ireland: containing sketches of the convents established by the Holy Foundress, and their earlier developments* (New York: The Catholic Publication Society, 1888), p. 354.

99 Ibid., pp. 451–2.

100 Printed appeal sent by D. Murphy, Kinsale, to Cullen, for funds for Kinsale Mercy Convent, 2 February 1848, Cullen Papers, CUL/1523.

101 *Leaves from Annals*, pp. 451–2.

102 The Virtual Archive of the Grey Nuns has been made available by the University of Limerick: http://www.history.ul.ie/historyoffamily/faminearchive/, accessed 29 August 2012.

103 Kerr, *Nation of Beggars*, p. 58.

104 Rev H. Hammond Hamilton, Vicarage, Carrick-on-Suir, 4 January 1847, Hugh James Rose, Samuel Roffey Maitland, *The British Magazine*, vol. 31, p. 241.

105 Maria Edgeworth to Mrs R. Butler, 9 February 1847, *The Life of Maria Edgeworth*.

106 Ibid.

107 Ibid, 22 February 1847.

108 Ibid., 28 April 1847.

109 Grace Atkinson Oliver, *A Study of Maria Edgeworth, with Notices of her Father and Friends* (Boston: A. Williams and Co., 1882), p. 510.

110 Maria to Mrs S. C. Hall, undated, probably 1848, *The Life of Maria Edgeworth*.

111 Ibid., Maria to Mrs Butler, 13 March 1847.

112 It was printed in a number of newspapers including the *Brooklyn Eagle*, 17 April 1847.

113 Ibid.,

114 Timothy Sarbaugh, 'Charity begins at Home': the United States Government and Irish Famine Relief 1845–1849'. *History Ireland* ix (ii), (Summer 1996), p. 35.

115 Maria Edgeworth, 11 June 1847, *The Life of Maria Edgeworth*.

116 Ibid., Edgeworth to Mrs R. Butler, 22 March 1847.

117 Ibid., 26 April 1847.

118 Ibid.

119 Ibid., Maria to Honora Beaufort, May 1849.

120 Maureen Murphy, Introduction, Nicholson, *Annals*, p. 11.

121 Alfred Tessidder Sheppard (ed.), *The Bible in Ireland. Ireland Welcome to the Stranger, or Excursions to Ireland in the Years 1844 and 1845* (London: Hodder and Stoughton, 1926).

122 Margaret Howitt to Alfred Tresidder Sheppard, reprinted in Alfred Tresidder Sheppard, 'Asenath Nicholson and the Howitt Circle', in *The Bookman*, November 1926, pp. 103–5.

123 Nicholson, *Annals*, pp. 27, 73, 76.

124 Murphy describes Asenath as a 'Bible Christian', Nicholson, *Annals*, p. 8; Ibid., Nicholson, p. 48.

125 Ibid., p. 181.

126 Ibid., p. 33.

127 Ibid., pp. 42–3.

128 Ibid., p. 55.

129 Ibid., This was her description of Newport, p. 83.

130 Ibid., p. 48.

131 Ibid., p. 50.

132 Ibid., pp. 55.

133 Ibid., p. 57.

134 *Nation*, 30 January 1847.

135 Lady Lucy Foley (Marseilles) to Murray; 18 February 1847, Murray Papers, No. 8.

136 Printing Students, Cork.

137 Diane Urquhart, *The Ladies of Londonderry: Women and Political Patronage* (London: I. B. Tauris, 2007), p. 49.

138 Catherine Sligo to Hildebrand (the estate's Agent in Westport), 14 January 1846, Letter 34, Lady Sligo Collection of Letters, Arnold Bernhard Library, Quinnipiac University.

139 Ibid., Letter 14, 9 December 1846.

140 Ibid., Letter 34 (1 and 2), 14 January 1846.

141 Elizabeth Fetherston, Bruree House, Charleville, Co. Cork, to Murray, 4 May 1847, Murray Papers, No. 16.

142 *Londonderry Standard*, 23 July 1847.

143 Washington County Seminary for Women or Washington County Female Seminary Sarah Foster Hanna Submitted by Patty Harris: http://www.rootsweb.ancestry.com/~pawashin/seminary/focus-on-washington_vol1/sarah-foster-hanna.html, accessed 3 March 2012.

144 Irish Relief Committee of Brooklyn, in *Report of GRC*, p. 170: Ibid., Anna M. Hifferman, Secretary of the Committee in Brooklyn, p. 22. An Anna M. Hefferman was the daughter of R. T. Todd, of Brooklyn, Esq.: http://www.ied.dippam.ac.uk/records/50065.

145 *Brooklyn Eagle*, 9 March 1847.

146 Ibid., 24 December 1847.

147 Ibid., 27 January 1848.

148 Ibid., 14 February 1849.

149 Harvey Strum, 'To Feed the Hungry'. *Rochester History* LXVIII(3), (Summer 2006), 2–22, 8.

150 J. Harvey, New York, 29 April 1847, Appendix V, *Transactions*, p. 272.

151 Quoted in the *National Era*, 3 June 1847.

152 Ibid., 1 April 1847.

153 Ibid.

154 *Transactions*, pp. 70–4.

155 Trevelyan to Routh, 5 February 1847, *House of Commons Papers*, Vol. 52 (Great Britain Parliament. House of Commons), p. 65.

156 Routh, Dublin Castle to Trevelyan, 8 February 1847, BPP, *Correspondence Relating to Measures for Relief of Distress*, p. 103.

157 *Transactions*, p. 46.

158 Rev G. Gould to Trevelyan, 2 March 1847, House of Commons papers, Vol. 52 (Great Britain Parliament. House of Commons), p. 187.

159 Higgins, Belmullet, 13 April 1847, *Report of BRA*, pp. 111–12.

160 Nicholson, *Annals*, p. 107.

161 *Transactions*, pp. 70–1.

162 Ibid., pp. 72–3.

163 Ibid., p. 73.

164 Ibid., pp. 77–8.

165 Ibid., Appendix 111, p. 168.

166 William Wilde was a member of this committee.

167   *Dublin Quarterly Journal of Medical Science*, vol. 5, 1848, p. 286.

168   Ibid., p. 564.

169   Elizabeth Jane Whately, Richard Whately, *Life and Correspondence of Richard Whately, late Archbishop of Dublin* (London: Longmans, Green and Co., 1866), pp. 212–13.

170   Strzelecki, Dublin, 1 January 1848, *Report of BRA*, p. 133.

171   House of Commons Papers, vol. 52, p. 40.

172   Lieutenant Col Douglas to Sir Randolph Routh, *Correspondence Relating to Measures for Relief of Distress in Ireland* (Commissariat Series, Second Part), January–March 1847, BPP, H of C, p. 42.

173   Captain Harston, 5 February 1848, Appendix, *Report of BRA*, p. 60.

174   Ibid., Lord James Butler, Tuam, 18 April 1847, p. 87.

175   *Transactions*, p. 56.

176   *Cork Examiner*, 21 January 1847.

Chapter 8

1   Count Strzelecki, Sligo, Committee of BRA, *Report of the British Relief Association for the Relief of Extreme Distress in Ireland and Scotland* (London: Richard Clay, 1849), hereafter, *Report of BRA*, 14 April 1847, p. 102.

2   Ibid., *Original Prospectus*, Appendix C, p. 171.

3   Hooper, born in 1791, was President of St Bartholomew's, Director of the Great Central Gas Company and a member of the Vintners' Company. He died in 1854. See "London City" History': http://www.london-city-history.org.uk/biography.htm, accessed 12 December 2011.

4   *Tuam Herald*, 9 January 1847.

5   Minute Book of British Relief Association, 1 January 1847, NLI, Ms 2022.

6   Ibid.

7   Ibid.

8   Barings employed N. J. Cummins to act on their behalf. Much of the correspondence survives in 'The Baring Archive', in London, HC 15 A. 2, 1846–48.

9   Ibid.

10   For more on the role of London bankers in British public life see: Ben Brudney, *Gentlemen Bankers. The Self-Perception of the Financial Elite in the City of London, 1792–1848* (Columbia History Department, 2009): http://www.history.columbia.edu/resource-library/Brudney_thesis.pdf, accessed 23 March 2012.

11   *Report of BRA*.

12   *Jewish Encyclopedia*, at: http://www.jewishencyclopedia.com/view.jsp?artid=89&letter=S#ixzz1W4O0nvl, accessed 3 July 2011b.

13   Green, 'Moses Montefiore', p. 631.

14 Ibid., pp. 650–2.

15 *Minutes of BRA*, 7 January 1847, NLI, p. 16.

16 Ibid., 2 January 1847, pp. 3–5.

17 Ibid., 4 January 1847, p. 8.

18 Niall Ferguson, *The House of Rothschild: Money's Prophets, 1798–1848* (New York: Penguin, 1999), p. 443.

19 *Report of BRA*, Appendix C, pp. 171–7.

20 *Minutes of BRA*, 2 January 1847, NLI, pp. 4–6.

21 *Report of BRA*, pp. 171–2.

22 *Minutes of BRA*, 1 January 1847, NLI, pp. 1–3.

23 Ibid., 4 January 1847, p. 7.

24 Ibid., 5 January 1847, p. 11.

25 'Contributions', *Report of the BRA*.

26 *Minutes of BRA*, 4 January 1847, NLI, pp. 8–9.

27 Ibid, 5 January 1847, p. 12.

28 T. M. Devine, *The Great Highland Famine: Hunger, Emigration and the Scottish Highlands in the Nineteenth Century* (Edinburgh: John Donald, 1988).

29 *Minutes of BRA*, 5 January 1847, NLI, p. 12.

30 Ibid., 8 January 1847, p. 22.

31 Trevelyan to Jones-Loyd, 1 February 1847, *Correspondence Relating to Measures for Relief of Distress in Ireland* (Commissariat Series, Second Part), January–March 1847, BPP, H of C p. 49.

32 Ibid., pp. 10–22.

33 Ibid., 18 January 1847, p. 64.

34 Ibid., 19 January 1847, p. 69.

35 Ibid., 14 January 1847, p. 49.

36 Ibid.

37 *Report of BRA*, p. 13.

38 Ibid., p. 14.

39 Ibid., pp. 15–16.

40 Ibid., p. 14.

41 *Minutes of BRA*, 4 January 1847, NLI, p. 10.

42 *Report of BRA*, p. 16.

43 Ibid., pp. 17–18.

44 *The Voyage of the Jamestown on Her Errand of Mercy* (Boston: Eastburn's Press, 1847), p. 26.

45 Captain Harston R. N., Kinsale, 17 January 1847, 18 January 1847, Appendix A, *Report of BRA*, pp. 55–6.

46 Ibid., 28 January 1847, p. 58.

47 Ibid., 31 January 1847, p. 59.

48 The IRA commenced distributing boilers in November 1846, Minutes of IRA (Royal Irish Academy), 27.Q.24, 2 December 1846.

49 Captain Harston R. N., Kinsale, 17 January 1847, 5 February 1847, Appendix A, *Report of BRA*, p. 60.

50 Ibid., 18 April 1847, p. 69.

51 Ibid., 5 May 1847, p. 69.

52 Ibid., Report of Capt. Rodney Eden, 12 May 1847, p. 69.

53 Ibid., 17 June 1847.

54 Naval Database: HMS *Aphrodite* (1816): http://www.pbenyon.plus.com/18-1900/A/00238.html, accessed 3 May 2012.

55 William Loney R. N., Documents Ships' Logs: http://www.home.wxs.nl/~pdavis/Log_Amphitrite.htm, accessed 5 May 2012.

56 Extracts from Reports of Capt. Whitmore, *Report of BRA*, pp. 72–8.

57 Ibid., Capt. Whitmore, Clonmel, 15 May 1847, p. 77.

58 In the BRA Minutes, the surname was rendered as 'Strelitzski'.

59 S. Jones-Loyd to Count de Strzelecki, London, 21 July 1848, Appendix D, *Report of BRA*, pp. 188–9.

60 *Minutes of BRA*, 20 January 1847, NLI, p. 64.

61 Ibid., 21 January 1847, p. 77.

62 Ibid., 22 January 1847, p. 80.

63 Strzelecki, Belmullet, 10 February 1847, *Report of BRA*, p. 93.

64 Ibid., Strzelecki, Westport, 15 March 1847, p. 97.

65 Ibid., Count Strzelecki, Westport, 29 January 1847, p. 92.

66 Ibid., Strzelecki, Belmullet, 10 February 1847, p. 93.

67 Ibid., p. 20.

68 Ibid., Strzelecki, Belmullet, 10 February 1847, p. 92.

69 Ibid., Strzelecki, Westport, 1 March 1847, p. 94.

70 Ibid., Strzelecki, Westport, 25 March 1847, p. 98.

71 Ibid., Strzelecki, Westport, 25 April 1847, p. 103.

72 Ibid., Strzelecki, Westport, 5 April 1847, p. 99.

73 Ibid., Strzelecki, Westport 8 April 1847, p. 100.

74 Ibid., Strzelecki, Sligo, 14 April 1847, p. 101.

75 Ibid., p. 100.

76 Ibid., Strzelecki, Sligo, 14 April 1847, p. 102.

77 Ibid., Strzelecki, Westport, 18 April 1847, pp. 102–3.

78 Frederic Boase, *Modern English Biography: Containing Many Thousand Concise Memoirs of Persons who have Died during the years 1851 to 1900*, vol. 1 (Truro: Netherton and Worth, 1908), p. 1464.

79 O'Rourke, *History of the Famine*, p. 336.

80 Anthony Trollope, *An Autobiography*, vol. 1 (Edinburgh and London: William Blackwood and Sons, 1883), p. 129.

81 BRA to M. J. Higgins, 31 March 1847, William Loney – Documents: http://www.home.wxs.nl/~pdavis/Famine5.htm, accessed 2 December 2011.

82 Higgins, Belmullet, 8 April 1847, *Report of BRA*, p. 108.

83 Ibid., p. 111.

84 Ibid., p. 109.

85 Ibid., Higgins, Belmullet, 14 April 1847, p. 113.

86 Ibid., Higgins, Belmullet, 13 April 1847, p. 110.

87 Ibid.

88 Ibid., Higgins, Belmullet, 13 April 1847, p. 113.

89 *Times*, 22 April 1847.

90 Ibid.

91 *Report of BRA*, pp. 21–2.

92 Ibid., Higgins, Belmullet, 29 April 1847, p. 116.

93 Ibid., Higgins, Belmullet, 3 May 1847, p. 116.

94 For example, *Melbourne Argus*, 29 September 1868, *Sydney Morning Herald*, 29 September 1868.

95 Pelham [Robert] Clinton, See 'Hansard People', *Hansard*: http://www.hansard.millbanksystems.com/people/lord-robert-clinton, accessed 6 May 2012.

96 Captain Lord James Wandesford Butler (1815–93) of the Butlers of Kilkenny Castle.

97 Lord Clinton, Galway, 17 March 1847, *Report of BRA*, pp. 78–9.

98 Ibid., Lord Clinton, Tralee, 30 March 1847, pp. 79–80.

99 Ibid., Clinton, Limerick, 29 April 1847, p. 80.

100 http://www.hansard.millbanksystems.com/people/lord-robert-clinton.

101 Lord James Butler, Galway, 21 March 1847, *Report of BRA*, pp. 81–4.

102 Ibid., Butler, on board HMS *Tartarus*, Greatman's Bay, 29 March 1847, pp. 85–6.

103 *Report of BRA*, p. 24.

104 Letter Books of William Loney, 14 April 1847: http://www.home.wxs.nl/~pdavis/Famine3.htm, accessed 3 April 2012.

105 Dermot James, John Hamilton of Donegal 1800–84 (Dublin: Woodfield Press, 1998).

106 Drainage Acts, 9 Vic., c. 4; Commissioners of Public Works to Trevelyan, 5 February 1847, *House of Commons Papers*, vol. 52, p. 141.

107 Capt. Lewis Jones RN, Agent for Donegal, Letterkenny, 4 May 1848, *Report of BRA*, p. 117.

108 Ibid., Jones, Rathmelton, 15 May 1847, p. 119.

109 Ibid., Jones, Inishowen, 26 May 1847, Londonderry, 31 May 1847, pp. 120–1.

110 Ibid., Jones, Ballyshannon, 12 June 1847, p. 121.

111 'Lewis Tobias Jones': http://www.pdavis.nl/ShowBiog.php?id=369, accessed 20 April 2011.

112 *United Service: A Monthly Review of Military and Naval Affairs, Volume 14* (Philadelphia: Hamersly & Co., 1895), p. 564.

113 W. *Burnett*, Director-General, to William Loney, 5 March 1847, Loney Documents.

114 Specific instructions of the Association to Dr Loney, 14 April 1847, William Jones R. N. – Documents: http://www.home.wxs.nl/~pdavis/Famine4.htm, accessed 4 May 2012.

115 Life of William Loney: http://www.home.wxs.nl/~pdavis/Life.htm, accessed 5 May 2012.

116 Dr Loney R. N., Sligo, 5 May 1847, *Report of BRA*, p. 122.

117 Full letter in Appendix, BRA to Loney, 12 June 1847, W. Loney Documents: http://www.home.wxs.nl/~pdavis/Famine7.htm, accessed 4 May 2012.

118 Frederick, Galway, 7 June 1847, *Report of BRA*, p. 90.

119 Ibid.

120 Ibid., Frederick, 31 May, 1847, p. 89.

121 Ibid., Frederick, Galway, 14 June 1847, pp. 90–1.

122 W. Hamilton on behalf of Admiralty to Loney, 30 July 1847: http://www.home.wxs.nl/~pdavis/Famine8.htm, accessed 4 May 2012.

123 E. Cane, Hon Secretary, British Association for the Relief of the Extreme Distress in Ireland & Scotland. Committee Room, 14 July 1847, in *Summary of Services of Dr William Loney* (London, 1864): http://www.home.wxs.nl/~pdavis/Pamphlet.htm, accessed 6 May 2012.

124 *Report of BRA*, p. 25.

125 Ibid., Capt. Lewis, Letterkenny, 10 May 1847, p. 118.

126 *Report of BRA*, pp. 25–6.

127 Ibid., Richard M. Lynch to Strzelecki, Westport, 24 April 1847, BRA, p. 104.

128 Ibid., Count Strzelecki, Central Agent in Dublin, Dublin, 15 June 1847, p. 128.

129 Ibid., Strzelecki, Dublin, 18 June 1847, p. 128.

130 Strzelecki's Dublin base was Reynold's Hotel in Upper Sackville Street.

131 *Report of BRA*, pp. 28–9.

132 Ibid.

133 Ibid., p. 29.

134 Ibid., John Burgoyne to Strzelecki, 14 July 1847, p. 130.

135 Ibid., Strzelecki, Dublin, 14 August 1847, p. 130.

136 The second Queen's Letter, which was issued in October 1847, was more widely criticized than the first one.

137 *Report of BRA*, pp. 29–30.

138 Ibid., p. 31.

139 Ibid., p. 33.

140 Ibid., Strzelecki, Dublin, 22 September 1847, p. 131.

141 Ibid., Strzelecki, Dublin, 7 October 1847, p. 131.

142 *Report of BRA*, Strzelecki, Dublin, 9 April 1848, p. 135.

143 Ibid., Strzelecki, Dublin, 20 February 1848, p. 133.

144 *Report of BRA*, p. 34.

145 Ibid., p. 36.

146 Ibid.

147 Ibid., p. 37.

148 Ibid., Count Strzelecki to Committee of BRA, 24 October 1847, pp. 35–9.

149 Ibid., p. 38. The Dublin Ladies' Reproductive and Industrial Society was led by the Hon Mrs Newcombe and Mrs Humphrey Lloyd.

150 Ibid., Regulations regarding relief through Schools, November 1847, Appendix D, pp. 186–7.

151 *Report of BRA*, p. 41.

152 Ibid., pp. 39–41.

153 Ibid., Mr Marshall, Skibbereen Union, 16 February 1848, p. 42.

154 Ibid., Captain R. Mann, Kilrush Union, 14 February 1848, p. 43.

155 Ibid., Matthew Davis, Chairman of Ballyshannon Union, 20 February 1848, p. 44.

156 Ibid., Treasury Minute, 27 June 1848, p. 46.

157 Memorandum by Lord John Russell, National Archives of England, T.64/367 B, 30 April 1848.

158 *Report of BRA*, p. 46.

159 Ibid., pp. 46–7.

160 Ibid., Statements of Receipts and Expenditure, pp. 49–50.

161 Ibid., Captain Harston, 5 February 1847, p. 60.

162 Ibid., 12 February 1847, p. 61.

163 Ibid., 17 February 1847, p. 61.

164 Ibid., 14 March 1847, p. 65.

165 Ibid., 17 March 1847, p. 66.

166 Ibid., 30 April 1847, p. 68.

167 Testimonial of Proprietors and Inhabitants of Cahirciveen Union to the Count de Strzelecki, Appendix D, *Report of BRA*, pp. 182–3.

168 Ibid., Resolution of Guardians of Skibbereen Union, 31 August 1838, pp. 183–4.

169 Ibid., Testimonial to Count de Strzelecki from the Protestant Patrons of the Skibbereen Union, 5 September 1848, pp. 184–5.

170 Ibid., Resolutions of Committee of BRA, Appendix D, pp. 189–90.

171 Ibid., Jones-Loyd to Strzelecki, 21 July 1848, App D, pp. 188–9.

172 Ibid., J. B. Standish Haly, Secretary, BRA, to Strzelecki, 21 July 1848, pp. 190–1.

173 *The Sydney Morning Herald*, 5 May 1849.

174 See Kinealy, *Death-Dealing Famine*, pp. 135–6, 141–6.

175 George Nicholls, *History of the Irish Poor Law* (London: J. Murray, 1856), p. 137; subscription list in *Times*, 16 June 1849.

176 *Nation*, 27 October 1849.

177 *Times*, 19 October 1849.

178 'Sir Paul de Strzelecki', *Obituaries, Australia*: http://www.oa.anu.edu.au/ obituary/strzelecki-sir-paul-edmund-de-2711, accessed 10 August 2011.

Chapter 9

1 Committee of BRA, *Report of the British Relief Association for the Relief of Extreme Distress in Ireland and Scotland* (London: Richard Clay, 1849), hereafter *Report of BRA,* pp. 10–11.

2 These, and all of the donations that follow, come from this source unless otherwise stated. Ibid., Contributions to the BRA, Appendix D.

3 *Minutes of BRA*, NLI, 4 January 1847, p. 7.

4 Ibid., p. 8.

5 *Report of BRA,* pp. 10–11.

6 Ibid., Appendix D, p. 181.

7 *Minutes of BRA*, 5 January, p. 1.

8 Guide to the Lucan Papers: http://www.archives.library.nuigalway.ie/col_level. php?col=P48, accessed 11 May 2012.

9 *Report of BRA.*

10 For more on the Duke of Devonshire and his Irish estates see, Lismore Castle Papers, Co. Waterford Archive: http://www.waterfordcoco.ie/en/media/ archives/pdfs/LISMORE%20CASTLE%20PAPERS%20Final.pdf, accessed 15 May 2012.

11 Des Cowman and Donald Brady, *The famine in Waterford, 1845–1850: teacht na bprátaí dubha* (Dublin: Geography Publications, 1995).

12 The Year of Slaughter, 1840: http://www.bbc.co.uk/northernireland/ ashorthistory/archive/intro123.shtml, accessed 1 June 2011.

13 See Kinealy, *Death-Dealing Famine*, pp. 56–7.

14 For more on the dispute between O'Connell and Disraeli see Kinealy, *Victorian Lives*, pp. 117–26.

15 This group included Joseph Bailey Esq. and Joseph Bailey junior, who gave £200 and £50, respectively. The Bailey family owned a successful iron-foundry in South Wales. Francis Baring donated £50 and John Studholme Brownrigg gave £25. The Honourable Robert Henry Clive gave £100. Edward George Barnard, a ship-builder and representative for Greenwich, donated £20. In the 1847 General Election, Barnard ran against and defeated David Solomans, the latter being a member of the committee of the British Association. Solomans, in addition to his work for the Association, donated £100 for famine relief.

William Forbes, MP for Stirlingshire, gave £50. Sir Thomas Freemantle MP, who had been Chief Secretary for Ireland between 1845 and 1846, donated the same. Thomas Green, MP for Lancaster, donated £100. John Cam Hobhouse, Unitarian, reformer and radical Member of Parliament, donated £200. Lord Hotham, the MP for East Yorkshire gave £100. Sir Fitzroy Kelly, the English-born Tory MP for Cambridge gave £100, as did Henry Kemble, MP for Surrey. Thomas James Agar-Robartes gave £50. In the 1847 General Election, he was elected MP for Cornwall. The Whig MP Hedworth Lambton gave two donations, one of £25 and a second of £20. Charles Shaw-Lefevre, Speaker of the House of Commons, gave £100, as did the historian and Whig politician, Thomas Babington Macauley. Ross Donnelly Mangles, Whig MP for Guilford and Director and later Chairman, of the East India Company, gave £10. Lord John Manners, Conservative MP for Newark, gave £10. The Whig Secretary for War, the Right Honorable Fox Maule, gave £50. The English Whig politician, Viscount Morpeth, made four donations that totalled £400. Osman Ricardo, son of the political economist David Ricardo, who was elected for Worcester in the 1847 General Election, donated £25. George Rice, the long-serving MP for Carmarthenshire, donated £50. To this, his three daughters added sums ranging from 10s to £2. Edmond Wodehouse, who represented Norfolk, donated £5.

16 Kinealy, *Death-Dealing Famine*, p. 68.

17 *Minutes of BRA*, 5 and 6 January 1847, pp. 11–15.

18 This was particularly apparent when public works closed down and during the transfer to the Amended Poor Law – see previous chapter.

19 Woodham-Smith, *Great Hunger*, pp. 366–70.

20 Clarendon to Duke of Bedford, 16 February 1849, Clarendon Letter-Books, Bodleian Library, Oxford.

21 Woodham-Smith, *Great Hunger*, p. 370.

22 *Minutes of BRA*, 12 and 13 January 1847, pp. 26–43.

23 Records of High Pavement Presbyterian (Unitarian) Chapel, Nottingham, 1576–1982, University of Nottingham: http://www.longford.nottingham. ac.uk/Dserve/dserve.exe?dsqIni=Dserve.ini&dsqApp=Archive&dsqDb=Catalo g&dsqSearch=%28PersonCode==NA336%29&dsqCmd=Show.tcl, accessed 9 June 2012.

24 The papers of Cazenove and Company are based in the London Metropolitan Archives: http://www.aim25.ac.uk/cgi-in/vcdf/detail?coll_id=17159&inst_ id=118&nv1=browse&nv2=sub, accessed 13 June 2012.

25 David Morier Evans, *The History of the Commercial Crisis, 1857–1858: And the Stock Exchange*, p. lxxviii.; *The Legal Observer, and Solicitors' Journal*, vol. 51 (London: Law Newspaper Co, 1856), p. 168.

26 J. A. S. L. Leighton-Boyce, *Smiths, the Bankers, 1658–1958* (London: National Provincial Bank, 1958).

27 Records of Sun Fire Office, National Archives, England: http://www. nationalarchives.gov.uk/a2a/records.aspx?cat=076-sun_2–85&cid=-1#-1, accessed 7 June 2012.

28 Steven Roberts, *Distant Writing. A History of the Telegraph Companies in Britain between 1838 and 1868:* http://www.distantwriting.co.uk/ electrictelegraphcompany.aspx, accessed 3 June 2010.

29 Meg Andrews, *Antique Costumes and Textiles:* http://www.meg-andrews.com/ item-details/Lewis-Foreman-Day/6002, accessed 8 February 2011.

30 The despair and poverty of the English poor in these years is captured in Elizabeth Gaskell's *Mary Barton,* which was published in 1848.

31 See Introduction to M. E. Bury and D. Pickles (eds), *Romilly's Cambridge Diary, 1842–1847* (Cambridge: Cambridge Records Society, 1994), p. xv.

32 Ibid., p. xvi.

33 Martha McMackin Garland, *Cambridge Before Darwin: The Ideal of a Liberal Education, 1800–1860* (Cambridge:Cambridge University Press, 1980), p. 20.

34 Bury and Pickles, *Romilly's Cambridge Diary*, p. 191. According to the editors, the text read by [William] Hopkins 'was a popular one for disasters and invited general repentance'.

35 Ibid.

36 Ibid., p. 196.

37 Wilson, Rev William Carus (1791–1859), *A Brontë Encyclopedia,* available online: http://www.blackwellreference.com/public/ tocnode?id=g9781405151191_chunk_g978140515119124_ss57, accessed 12 December 2012.

38 *Romilly's Cambridge Diary*, p. 203.

39 Ibid., p. 209.

40 Ibid., pp. 169–73.

41 'The Oxford Movement', Oriel College: http://www.oriel.ox.ac.uk/content/ oxford-movement, accessed 1 December 2011.

42 Lady Laura Ridding, *George Ridding: Schoolmaster and Bishop, Forty-Third Head Master of Winchester, 1866–1884, First Bishop of Southwell, 1884–1904* (London: E. Arnold, 1908).

43 See Chapter Two.

44 Godfrey Lushington, 'Pamphlet on Retrenchment at Oxford', in Arthur Hugh Clough (ed.), *Letters and Remains of Arthur Hugh Clough* (London: Spottiswoode, 1865), p. 92.

45 Anthony Kenny, *Arthur Hugh Clough: A Poet's Life* (London: Continuum, 2005), p. 109.

46 'A Consideration of Objections against a Retrenchment Society at Oxford during the Irish Famine of 1847', in Arthur Hugh Clough, Blanche Smith Clough (eds), *Prose Remains of Arthur Hugh Clough: With a Selection from his Letters and a Memoir* (London: Macmillan, 1888), pp. 283–304.

47 Ibid., p. 287.

48 Ibid., pp. 292–8.

49 Ibid., p. 293.

50 Kenny, *A Poet's Life*, pp. 110–11.

51 Godfrey Lushington, 'Pamphlet on Retrenchment at Oxford', pp. 93–4.

52 To celebrate the 1848 revolutions, Clough wrote, 'Say not the Struggle Nought Availeth'.

53 Arthur Tompson Michell, *Rugby School Register*, Rugby School, vol. 2 (Rugby: A. J. Lawrence, 1901–02), p. 1.

54 Edmund Whytehead Howson, George Townsend Warner (eds), *Harrow School* (London: E. Arnold, 1898), p. 108.

55 Ibid., p. 168.

56 For example, John Mitchel in *Jail Journal*.

57 'The First Sikh War: Sir Hugh Gough': http://www.britishempire.co.uk/forces/armycampaigns/indiancampaigns/sikhwars/sirhughgough.htm, accessed 5 October 2011.

58 *London Gazette*, 15 August 1882.

59 *Mogg's New Picture of London and Visitor's Guide to its Sights*, 1844. http://www.victorianlondon.org/entertainment/chinesecollection.htm, accessed 17 October 2011.

60 The Cogers Society: http://www.cogers.org/History.html, accessed 4 June 2012.

61 Pablo Fanque's Grave: http://www.mech-eng.leeds.ac.uk/support/images/misc/PABLO_FANQUE.HTML, accessed 11 December 2011.

62 Pablo was the inspiration for John Lennon's 'For the Benefit of Mr Kite' on *Sargent Pepper's Lonely Heart Club Band* Album.

63 *British Farmer's Magazine*, vol. 1 (London: Ridgway and Sons, 1837), pp. 358–9.

64 *The Bankers' Magazine*, vol. 17 (London: Groombridge and Sons, 1857), p. x.

65 Dissolution Agreement, 1854: http://www.london-gazette.co.uk/issues/21604/pages/3036/page.pdf, accessed 4 May 2012.

66 Usborne Family Tree: http://www.usbornefamilytree.com/thomas1769.htm, accessed 4 May 2012.

67 *The Manchester Commercial List* (London: Estell & Co., 1867–75), p. 35.

68 Gelina Harlaftis, *A History of Greek-Owned Shipping: The Making of an International Tramp Fleet* (London: Routledge, 1996), p. 53.

69 Panda Zeus Ralli belonged to the Greek Orthodox Church: http://www.christopherlong.co.uk/gen/vlastogen/fg03/fg03_316.html, accessed 15 May 2011.

70 Stuart Thompstone 'Rodocanachi, Michael Emmanuel', Oxford Dictionary of National Biography.

71 *Minutes of BRA*, 7 January 1847, p. 16.

72 *Jewish Encyclopedia*: http://www.jewishencyclopedia.com/view.jsp?artid=682&letter=M#2309, accessed 16 May 2011.

73 *Minutes of BRA*, 7 January 1847, p. 16.

74 The Lyttelton History: http://www.thelyttelton.com/About/History/, accessed 16 May 2012.

75 Sarah Spencer Lyttelton Lyttleton (Baroness), Lady Lucy Caroline Lyttelton Cavendish et al, *Correspondence of Sarah Spencer, Lady Lyttelton, 1787–1870* (London, J. Murray, 1912), p. 367.

76 Sir Bernard Burke, *A Genealogical and Heraldic Dictionary of the Landed Gentry of Great Britain and Ireland*, vol. 1(London: Harrison, 1862–63), p. 474.

77 The ffaringtons of Worden: http://www.southribble.gov.uk/museum_collection_ffaringtons.asp?catid=301000, accessed 5 April 2012.

78 Appendix D, *Report of BRA.*

79 See Chapter Seven for more on the role of women.

80 For example, the *Times* vociferously opposed the second Queen's Letter, *Times,* 5 January 1847, 2 September 1847.

81 Mesurier revised views on the Planet Uranus, see T. Keith, *A New Treatise on the Use of the Globes; or, Philosophical View of the Earth and Heavens* (London: W. Tegg & Co., 1853).

82 'Rothery, Henry Cadogan', in Dictionary of National Biography (London: Smith, Elder & Co. 1885–1900).

83 HMS *Scourge* service details: http://www.worldnavalships.com/forums/archive/index.php/t-11262.html, accessed 10 July 2011.

84 Ibid., J. Crauford [sic] Caffin, 15 February 1847.

85 Ward Hill Lamon, *Recollections of Abraham Lincoln, 1847–1865* (Chicago: A. C. McClurg and company, 1895), p. 152.

86 Lieutenant Governor W. M. G. Colebrooke, Frederick Town, N. B., to Earl Grey, 27 March 1847, 'Copies of despatches addressed to the Secretary of State from the governor of Her Majesty's colonial possessions relative to money voted and subscriptions raised for the Relief of the destitute Poor in Ireland and Scotland', in *Papers Relative to the Relief of the Destitute Poor in Ireland and Scotland,* hereafter *Copies of despatches,* BPP, HC, (853) vol. LIII, p. 7.

87 New Brunswick Hall of Fame: http://www.new-brunswick.net/new-brunswick/fame.html, accessed 11 December 2011.

88 J. Robertson, Woodstock to Alfred Read Esq 26 March 1847, *Copies of despatches,* Papers Relative to the Relief of the Destitute Poor in Ireland and Scotland (BPP, HC, (184). vol. LIII, 1847), p. 8.

89 Earl of Elgin to Earl Grey, 28 May 1847, *Copies of despatches,*(BPP, HC, vol. LIII, 1847), p. 7.

90 Donald MacKay, *Flight from Famine: The Coming of the Irish to Canada* (Toronto: McClelland & Stewart, 1990), p. 24.

91 In the donor's list, Pictou is incorrectly rendered as Picton.

92 In the list of Contributors provided by the BRA, the house is incorrectly referred to as Pellissar House.

93 London Companies Estates in County Derry: http://www.billmacafee.com/estates/landlords/notescompaniesestates.htm, accessed 9 July 2012.

94 The records of the BRA say the *Cambria* donated £52–10s., but newspapers reports suggest it was higher.

95 Tom Thumb, *Sketch of the Life: Personal Appearance, Character and Manners of Charles S. Stratton, the Man in Miniature, known as General Tom Thumb, and his Wife, Lavinia Warren Stratton, including the History of their Courtship and Marriage . . . Also, Songs Given at their Public Levees* (New York, S. Booth, 1874), p. 6.

96 John Palliser, *Solitary Rambles and Adventures of a Hunter in the Prairies* (London: J. Murray, 1853), pp. 2–3.

97 Ibid., p. 6.

98 *Nation*, 20 March 1847.

99 Ibid.

100 Douglass to William Garrison, The *Liberator*, 27 March 1846.

101 Frederick Douglass, Brown's Temperance Hotel, Liverpool (England), 3 April 1847, Letter to the Editor of the London *Times*; Philip Foner (ed.), *Life and Writings of Frederick Douglass*, vol. I (New York: International Publishers, 1950), p. 233.

102 *National Era*, 1 April 1847.

103 Kinealy, *Saddest People*.

104 Governor Mathew, Government House, Nassau, to Earl Grey, *Reports of despatches*, 9 April 1847, p. 11.

105 James Martin Wright, *History of the Bahama Islands, with a Special Study of the Abolition of Slavery in the Colony* (New York: Macmillan Co., 1905), p. 542.

106 Enclosure in No. 9, Governor Mathew, Government House Nassau to Earl Grey, 8 April 1847, *Reports of Despatches*, p. 12.

107 Ibid.

108 Ibid., C. R. Nesbitt, Government House Nassau, to Earl Grey, 9 May 1847, pp. 12–13.

109 Ibid., Lieutenant Governor Kerr Hamilton, Government House, Grenada, 24 April 1847, p. 14.

110 Ibid.

111 Ibid., Governor Higginson, Government House, Antigua, to Earl Grey, 11 May 1847, p. 16.

112 The *Liberal* pub. in Bridgetown, Barbados, 15 February 1847.

113 Ibid., (editorial).

114 Enclosure in No 11, Governor Reid, Government House, Barbados, to Earl Grey, 15 March 1847, *Reports of Despatches*, pp. 13–14.

115 House of Assembly, Bermuda website: http://www.gov.bm/portal/server.pt?open=512&objID=311&PageID=0&cached=true&mode=2&userID=2, accessed 11 April 2012.

116 The Resolution was read in the House of Assembly on 21 April 1847, with a second reading on 24 April, *Journals of the Bermuda House of Assembly*, Ms. 16/1845/47, pp. 300–7.

117 The BRA records that they received £505-5s.-3d.

118 8 April 1847, *St. Christopher Council Minutes 1843–47, Minutes of the Assembly 1847–1843*. I am grateful to Victoria O'Flaherty, Director of the National Archives, St Kitts, for searching these records on my behalf.

119 Basseterre Past and Present, St Kitts National Archives: http://www.historicbasseterre.com/hs_summation.asp?HSID=10, accessed 28 October 2011.

120 Jeffrey Cox, *The British Missionary Enterprise Since 1700* (London: Routledge, 2008), p. 56.

121 J. E. Hutton MA, *History of Moravian Missions* (London: Moravian Publication Office, 1922), pp. 232–8.

122 Captain Dillon, 'To the Inhabitants of St Ann's and Trelawney'[sic], Copies of despatches, p. 10.

123 Ibid., T. A. Dillon to Right Hon Earl Grey, 20 April 1847, p. 12.

124 Ibid., Hon C. E. Grey, King's House, Jamaica, to Earl Grey, 22 May 1847, p. 9.

125 Ibid., Enclosure No 13, 'Destitution in Ireland and the Highlands', 30 March 1847, p. 15.

126 Ibid., Lieutenant Governor Graeme, Government House, Tobago, to Earl Grey, 4 May 1847, p. 15.

127 Ibid., Governor Light, Government House, Demerara, Guiana, 19 March 1847, to Earl Grey, p. 17.

128 Ibid., 17 April 1847, p. 17.

129 *House of Commons Papers*, vol. 59, p. 125.

130 The Anglican Diocese of St Elizabeth: http://www.anglicandiocesepe.org.za/parishes.php?id=20001, accessed 14 May 2011.

131 A road in Bordeaux is named after David Johnston, see 'Rue David Johnston' at: http://www.bordeaux.360cityscape.com/rue-david-johnston/266/, accessed 15 May 2012.

132 Charles Cocks, *Bordeaux: Its Wines, and the Claret Country* (London: Longman, Brown and Green, 1846), p. 6.

133 George Clement Boase and William Prideaux Courtney, *Bibliotheca Cornubiensis, P-Z* (London: Longmans, Green, Reader and Dyer, 1874–82), p. 697.

134 This may be a transcription error. The Blount Bank, Father and Son, established in the 1830s, was situated on Lafitte Street in Paris, Sir Edward Charles Blount, *Memoirs of Sir Edward Blount* (New York: Arno Press, 1977), pp. 44, 102.

135 Society for Irish Church Missions to the Roman Catholics, *The Banner of the Truth in Ireland: Monthly Information Concerning Irish Church Missions to the Roman Catholics* (London: Wonston, 1852), p. 26.

136 'Anatole de Demidoff' at: http://www.jssgallery.org/Essay/Italy/Demidoff/Demidoff_1st.htm, accessed 3 October 2011.

137 In the list of contributors, Maguay is incorrectly transcribed as 'Magnay'.

138 Gerald Kutney, *Sulfur: History, Technology, Applications & Industry* (Ontario: ChemTec Publishing, 2007), p. 50.

139 Josephine E. Butler, *Personal Reminiscences of a Great Crusade* (London: Horace Marshall, 1896), p. 150.

140 Smith Woodhouse History: http://www.smithwoodhouse.com/, accessed 2 May 2012. This company is still in existence and when I sent a note to the current Directors informing them of their contribution, they responded with a gracious letter.

141 The Brandt family was originally from Hamburg, but established companies in Russia, with a trading house in London. The Emmanual H. Brandt Collection is housed at the University of Illinois: http://www.library.illinois.edu/archives/uasfa/1535050.pdf, accessed 4 December 2011.

142 In the Appendix of Contributors, Camidge is incorrectly referred to as Camilege.

143 Max Robertson (ed.), *The English Reports, Common Pleas,* Volume 4; Volume 134, (Edinburgh: William Green and Sons, 1913), p. 885.

144 *The Country Gentleman,* Volume 20, vol. x, 1862–63 (Albany: Luther Tucker and Son, 1963), p. 291.

145 J. Maurice Dempsey, *Our Ocean Highways: A Condensed Universal Hand Gazetteer and International* (London: Edward Stanford, 1871), p. 269.

146 He was born in Boka Kotorska, which is now Montenegro.

147 Tollemache gained a reputation for assisting new settlers to get property, W. H. Secker, 'Tawa Historical Society': http://www.tawahistory.wellington.net.nz/projects/secker_articles.html, accessed 5 May 2012.

148 Mary Frampton, *The Journal of Mary Frampton: From the year 1779, until the year 1846. Including Various Interesting and Curious Letters, Anecdotes, & c., Relating to Events Which Occurred during that Period* (London: S. Low, Marston, Searle, & Rivington, 1885), p. 285.

149 Millbay Docks: http://www.plymouth.gov.uk/millbay_docks_9-13.pdf, accessed 3 June 2012.

150 Martha Novak Clinkscale, *Makers of the Piano: 1820–1860* (Oxford:Oxford University Press, 1999), p. 7.

151 Hunt and Roskell: http://www.artfact.com/subcollection/hunt-roskell-h1ncvw2d3p, accessed 17 December 2011.

152 'Pentonville', in Walter Thornbury, *Old and New London: A Narrative of its History, its People and its Places* (London: Cassell, Petter, & Galpin, 1878), pp. 279–89.

153 The institution, which was situated on St George's Road, Southwark, was later renamed St Edward's School. Guildhall Library Manuscripts: http://www.history.ac.uk/gh/brhkes.htm, accessed 16 October 2011.

154 Foundling Hospital. UCL Bloomsbury Project: http://www.ucl.ac.uk/bloomsburyproject/institutions/foundling_hospital.htm, accessed 18 October 2011.

Chapter 10

1 Boston *Pilot*, hereafter *Pilot*, 12 December 1845.

2 Brooklyn *Eagle*, hereafter *Eagle*, 23 December 1845.

3 William Byrne and W. A. Leahy, *Archdiocese of Boston* (Boston: Hurd & Everts Company, 1899), p. 67.

4 *Pilot*, 12 December 1845.

5 *Eagle*, 12 November 1846.

6 *National Era*, 4 February 1847.

7 Timothy J. Sarbaugh, '"Charity begins at Home", the United States government and Irish Famine Relief, 1845–49'. *History Ireland*, Summer 1996, p. 31.

8 Harvey Strum, 'To Feed the Hungry. Rochester and Irish Famine Relief', in Ruth Rosenberg-Naparsteck (ed.), *Rochester History*, LXVIII(3), (Summer 2006), p. 4.

9 *National Era*, 4 February 1847.

10 Ibid.

11 John Binns, *Recollections of the Life of John Binns* (Philadelphia: Parry and McMillan, 1854), pp. 14, 80–8.

12 Thomas D'Arcy Magee, *A History of Irish Settlers*, pp. 20–6.

13 Margaret M. Mulrooney, *Fleeing the Famine: North America and Irish Refugees, 1845–1851* (Westport: Praeger, 2003), p. 38.

14 *118th Anniversary of the Hibernian Society of Philadelphia* (Philadelphia: F. McManus jr and Co. 1889), p. 1.

15 To the Inhabitants of the City and County of Philadelphia, *Report of the General Executive Committee of the City and County of Philadelphia Appointed by the Town Meeting of February 17, 1847, to provide Means to Relieve the Sufferings in Ireland*, hereafter, *Report of GEC* (Philadelphia: Crissy and Markley, 1847), p. 6.

16 Ibid., pp. 7–9.

17 Ibid., General Executive Committee to Clergy and Pastors of the City and County of Philadelphia, 26 November 1846, pp. 8–9.

18 Ibid., p. 9.

19 *Pennsylvanian*, quoted in *Eagle*, 26 February 1847.

20 *Report of GEC*, p. 9.

21 Ibid., pp. 3–4.

22 Ibid., p. 5.

23 Ibid., p. 11.

24 Ibid., p. 16.

25 Ibid., Meeting for Relief of Ireland, p. 12.

26 Ibid., p. 14.

27 Ibid., pp. 18–19.

28 Ibid., pp. 20–1.

29 Ibid., p. 23.

30 John Hugh Campbell, *History of the Friendly Sons of St. Patrick and of the Hibernian Society for the Relief of Emigrants from Ireland. March 17, 1771–March 17, 1892* (Philadelphia: Hibernian Society, 1892), p. 206.

31 *Report of GEC*, p. 10.

32 Campbell, *History of Friendly Sons*, p. 206.

33 Obituary of Rev Henry Giles, *New York Times*, 11 July 1882.

34 *Report of GEC*, p. 10.

35 Ibid.

36 John Collins, *Early Actors of the Stage. In Memoriam:* http://www. genealogytrails.com/main/actorsmemoriam.html, accessed 3 May 2012.

37 Campbell, *History of the Friendly Sons*, p. 206.

38 *Report of GEC*, pp. 24–5.

39 Ibid., p. 31.

40 Ibid., J. Bewley and J. Pim, 17 September 1847, p. 39.

41 Ibid., p. 26.

42 Ibid., p. 32.

43 Ibid., p. 27.

44 Ibid., pp. 23–4.

45 Ibid., Report of Irish Relief Committee, 19 October 1847, p. 33.

46 *Report of GEC*, pp. 20–1.

47 Ibid., p. 29.

48 Ibid, p. 33.

49 Campbell, *History of the Friendly Sons*, p. 387.

50 Ibid., p. 206.

51 Statement by the Archbishop of Dublin in the House of Lords, *Hansard,* Poor Relief (Ireland) Bill, HL Debates, 29 April 1847, vol. 92, cc. 60–126.

52 *National Era,* 1 April 1847.

53 Ibid.

54 *Report of GEC*, p. 36.

55 *Eagle,* 6 May 1846.

56 *Pilot,* 12 December 1846,

57 *Eagle,* 25 November 1846.

58 Ibid., 2 December 1846; *Pilot,* 2 December 1846.

59 Ibid.

60 Ibid., 27 February 1847.

61 Ibid.

62 Ibid., 22 January 1848.

63 Ibid., 3 February 1847.

64 Henry Murphy's grandfather had emigrated from Ireland in 1769. In 1842, Henry was elected Mayor of Brooklyn, *New York Times*, 2 December 1882.

65 Spooner (1810–81) stood in the Republican primaries in 1862, *New York Times*, 11 October 1862.

66 *Eagle*, 6 February 1847.

67 Ibid., 19 February 1847.

68 Ibid., 20 February 1847.

69 *National Era*, 4 February 1847.

70 Ibid., 23 February 1847.

71 *New York Daily Tribune*, 25 June 1846.

72 *Eagle*, 23 February 1847.

73 Ibid., 29 April 1847.

74 Ibid., 7 May 1847.

75 Vera Brodsky Lawrence, George Templeton Strong, 'Strong on Music: The New York Music Scene in the Days of George Templeton Strong', in *Resonances, 1836–1849*, vol. 1 (Chicago: University of Chicago, 1988), pp. 293–4.

76 Brooklyn Committee to Bewley and Pim, 11 May 1847, reprinted in *Eagle*, 9 June 1847.

77 *Eagle*, 19 June 1847.

78 Van Schaick to Pim and Bewley, 15 April 1847, *Report of GRC*, pp. 86, 89.

79 Brooklyn committee to Bewley and Pim, 11 May 47, *Eagle*, 19 June 1847.

80 Ibid., Bewley and Pim to Brooklyn committee, 2 June 1847, 19 June 1847.

81 Ibid., 7 July 1847.

82 Article from *Advertiser* appeared in *Eagle*, 20 March 1850.

83 *Eagle*, 20 March 1850.

84 Ibid., 14 March 1850.

85 Howard Strum, 'South Carolina and Irish Famine Relief'. *The South Carolina Historical Magazine* 2, (2002), 130–52.

86 Kinealy, *The Saddest People*.

87 *Charleston Mercury*, 10 February 1847, 17 February 1847 etc.

88 Quoted in David T. Gleeson, *The Irish in the South, 1815–1877* (Chapel Hill: University of North Carolina Press, 2001), p. 104.

89 *Arkansas Gazette*, 20 February 1847.

90 *The Californian*, 15 December 1847.

91 Ibid., Bancroft to Russell, 30 Eaton Square, 28 April 1847.

92 Ibid., Russell to Bancroft, 29 April 1847.

93 *National Era*, 27 May 1847.

94 *Nation*, 20 March 1847.

95 Sermon on the Occasion of the 350th Anniversary Service at Shearith Israel, 12 September 2004: http://www.jewishideas.org/min-hamuvhar/sermon-occasion-350th-anniversary-service-shear.

96 Also see chapter on the work of the General Relief Committee of New York.

97 'Relief to Ireland. Large Meeting in Albany'. Poster, 1847.

98 Ibid.

99 Ibid.

100 *Nation*, 20 March 1847.

101 A Guide to the Albany Committee for the Relief of Ireland Records: http://
www.albanyinstitute.org/collections/FindingAids/Albany . . . Irish%20
Relief%20CD%20528.pdf, 10 October 2011.

102 Brian Greenberg, *Worker and Community: Response to Industrialization in a
Nineteenth-century American City, Albany, New York, 1850–1884* (Albany:
State University of New York Press, 1985), pp. 93, 129.

103 A Guide to the Albany Committee for the Relief of Ireland Records.

104 Edward Everett, '*The Famine in Ireland*', *Orations and Speeches on Various
Occasions*, vol. 2 (Boston: C. C. Little and J. Brown, 1850), p. 537.

105 *Liberator*, 26 February 1847.

106 Robert Hamlett Bremner, *American Philanthropy* (Chicago: University of
Chicago Press, 1988), p. 54.

107 Rathbone to Glasgow Committee, Rathbone Papers, University of Liverpool
Archives, 12 May 1847.

108 Samuel Eliot Morison, *The Maritime History of Massachusetts, 1783–1860*
(Boston: Houghton Mifflin Company, 1921), p. 242.

109 Report by 'F' to the *Tablet*, 1 March 1847, reprinted in *Sydney Chronicle*
(NSW), 4 August 1847.

110 Rev Gerald Treacy, S. J., 'Andrew Carney, Philanthropist', *Historical Records and
Studies*, vol. 13 (United States Catholic Historical Society, 1919), pp. 101–5.

111 Carney Hall (1963) is named after him, Boston College: http://www.bc.edu/
offices/historian/resources/guide/carney.html, accessed 3 July 2012.

112 *The Boston Directory for 1851* (Boston: Sampson & Murdock Company,
1851), p. 176; *Sydney Chronicle*, 4 August 1847.

113 *Sydney Chronicle*, 4 August 1847; David M. Balfour, *The taverns of Boston
in ye olden time*: http://www.usgennet.org/usa/ma/state/suff/hist/tav.html,
accessed 3 December 2011.

114 *Sydney Chronicle*, 4 August 1847.

115 Ibid.

116 *Liberator*, 12 March 1847.

117 *Nation*, 20 March 1847.

118 Ibid.

119 *Pilot*, 6 March 1847.

120 See, Christine Kinealy, *Repeal and Revolution, 1848 in Ireland* (Manchester:
Manchester University Press, 2008).

121 Harvey Strum, 'Famine Relief from the Garden City to the Green Isle', p. 394:
http://www.dig.lib.niu.edu/ISHS/ishs-2000winter/ishs-2000winter388.pdf,
accessed 5 November 2011,

122 Ibid., p. 395.

123 John Kearney, 'Bishop William Quarter – First Catholic Bishop of Chicago', in *Offaly Historical and Archaeological Society*: http://www.offalyhistory.com/articles/228/1/Bishop-William-Quarter-1806-1848-First-Catholic-Bishop-of-Chicago/Page1.html, accessed 3 April 2012.

124 Strum, 'Famine Relief', p. 395.

125 Chicago Medical Society, *History of Medicine and Surgery and Physicians and Surgeons of Chicago, Endorsed by and Published under the Supervision of the Council of the Chicago Medical Society* (Chicago: The Biographical Publishing Corporation, 1922), pp. 31–3. In this biography of Egan, no mention is made of his role in famine relief.

126 Strum, 'Famine Relief', p. 299.

127 American Bankers Association, *Proceedings of the Convention of the American Bankers' Association* (New York: The Association, 1878), pp. 11–12.

128 Strum, 'Famine Relief', pp. 396–7.

129 Ibid., p. 398.

130 Harvey Strum, 'To Feed the Hungry. Rochester and Irish Famine Relief', in Ruth Rosenberg-Naparsteck (ed.), *Rochester History*, LXVIII(3), (Summer 2006), p. 4.

131 Ibid., pp. 6–9.

132 Ibid.

133 Ibid., p. 11.

134 Charles Elliott Fitch, *Encyclopedia of Biography of New York: A Life Record of Men and Women Whose Sterling Character and Energy and Industry Have Made Them Preeminent in Their Own and Many Other States,* vol. 4 (New York: American Historical Society, 1916), pp. 130–1.

135 Blake McKelvey, 'Rochester mayors before the civil war'. *Rochester History*, 26(1), (1964), p. 1.

136 Strum, 'To Feed the Hungry', pp. 6–9.

137 McKelvey, 'Rochester mayors', p. 4.

138 Ibid., p. 11.

139 Ward to Society of Friends Dublin, 10 December 1847, *Transactions*, p. 250.

140 Strum, 'To Feed the Hungry', pp. 9–11.

141 McKelvey, 'Rochester Mayors', pp. 9–10. Sadly, Allen died some years later in poverty and by his own hand.

142 Strum, 'To Feed the Hungry', p. 11

143 Ibid., p. 12.

144 Ward to Society of Friends 10 December 1847, *Transactions*, p. 250.

145 Population history of Cincinnati: http://www.physics.bu.edu/~redner/projects/population/cities/cincinnati.html, accessed 3 December 2011.

146 Christine Kinealy, *Daniel O'Connell and the Anti-Slavery Movement. The Saddest People the Sun Sees* (London: Pickering and Chatto, 2011), pp. 126–30.

147 *Liberator,* 21 January 1842.

148 Ibid., 7 January 1842.

149 *National Era*, 18 March 1847.

150 Ibid., 25 February 1847.

151 Ibid., 1 April 1847.

152 Strum, 'Famine Relief', p. 401.

153 E. B. Washburne, *Historical Sketch of Charles S. Hempstead* (Galena: Gazette Book, 1876), p. 7.

154 Strum, 'Famine Relief', p. 401.

155 *Pilot*, 6 March 1847.

156 *Nation*, 20 March 1847.

157 John Daniel Crimmins, *Irish-American Historical Miscellany: Relating Largely to New York City and Vicinity, Together with Much Interesting Material Relative to Other Parts of the Country* (New York: The author, 1905), p. 194.

158 *National Era*, 25 February 1847.

159 *Eagle*, 23 February 1847.

160 *National Era*, 18 March 1847.

161 *The Merrimack Courier*, 6 March 1847.

162 *The Washington Post*, 8 October 1848.

163 Natchez in Mississippi held a meeting on 20 February, p. 103.

164 Gleeson, *The Irish in the South*, p. 104.

165 Ibid.

166 Miss A. M. Hemenway, 'Biography of Jonathan C. Dexter', *The Vermont Historical Magazine* (Burlington, Vt., 1868), p. 629.

167 *Pilot*, 10 April 1847.

168 Ibid.

169 Curti, *American Philanthropy*, p. 50.

170 *Western Herald*, 2 December 1846, quoted in Strum, 'Famine Relief', p. 389.

171 *Liberator*, 12 February 1847.

172 Rev Henry A. Brann, ' "The Rev. John Kelly", United States Catholic Historical Society', *Historical Records and Studies,* vol. 5 (Catholic Historical Society, April 1909), pp. 348–9.

173 A Short History of St Peter's Parish and Church: http://www.resurrectionparishjc.com/short%20history%20of%20peter.html, accessed 9 May 2012.

174 *St Peter's Annual Report for 1846.* I am grateful to Alan Delozier, Archivist at Seton Hall University, for giving me a copy of the relevant entry.

175 *Pilot*, 28 November 1846.

176 Josephine Seaton, *William Winston Seaton of the 'National Intelligencer', with Passing Notices of his Associates and Friends* (Boston: James R. Osgood and Co., 1871), pp. 280–5.

177 *National Era*, 18 February 1847.

178 Ibid.

179 Ibid.

180 Ibid.

181 Ibid.

182 *New York Spectator*, 20 February 1847.

183 *NY Weekly Tribune*, 20 February 1847.

184 Mulrooney, *Fleeing the Famine*, p. 50.

185 Robert C. Winthrop Jr, *A Memoir of Robert C. Winthrop* (Boston: Little, Brown, and Company, 1897), p. 338; Samuel Eliot Morison, *The Maritime History of Massachusetts, 1783–1860* (Boston: Houghton Mifflin Company, 1921), p. 242.

186 Curti, *American Philanthropy*, p. 49.

187 Debate in Congress, 25 February 1847, in *National Era*, 4 March 1847.

188 *Pilot*, 20 March 1847.

189 Ibid., 3 April 1847.

190 Quoted in *Liverpool Mercury*, 12 April 1847.

191 *Freeman's Journal*, 11 April 1847.

192 *Liverpool Mercury*, 12 April 1847 (some papers reported the journey as taking 13 days).

193 Richard Miller Devens, *Our First Century* (Springfield, Mass: C. A. Nichols, 1876), pp. 482–3.

194 William Rathbone to Mayor of Boston, 18 June 1847, Letter Book. New England Relief Society. RPV. 1, William Rathbone Papers, Liverpool Archives.

195 Devens, *Our First Century*, p. 484.

196 Robert Forbes, *The Voyage of the 'Jamestown' on her Errand of Mercy* (Boston: Eastburn's Press, 1847), pp. x.

197 Ibid., p. 486.

198 W. Scraggs Cork (1847), *US Sloop of War, Jamestown*: http://www.worldcat.org/title/us-sloop-of-war-jamestown, 8 July 2011.

199 William Rathbone to Mayor of Boston, 18 June 1847, Letter Book. New England Relief Society. RPV. 1, William Rathbone Papers, Liverpool Archives.

200 Ibid., 3 June 1847, Rathbone to Forbes re. the *Jamestown*.

201 See Chapter Four.

202 Samuel Lover in *Dublin Evening Post*, reprinted in *National Era*, 2 September 1847.

203 Sarbaugh, 'Charity begins', p. 35.

204 William Rathbone to New England Committee, 18 June 1847. Liverpool Archives.

205 *Eagle*, 2 November 1847.

206 Sarbaugh, 'Charity begins', p. 35.

207 *Nation*, 8 May 1847.

208 P. J. Smyth, also a Repealer and subsequently an MP, was present.

209 *Nation*, 8 May 1847.

210 Ibid.

211 See Kinealy, *Saddest People*, pp. 136–9.

212 Gleeson, *The Irish in the South*, p. 103.

213 *Pilot*, 13 March 1847.

214 Ibid., 20 March 1847.

215 *Liberator*, 26 February 1847.

216 'A letter sent to Mr. Garrison, From the *Bristol Mirror*, England, of 2 January'. The letter is dated 1 December 1846, from Skibbereen, received 'by a lady in Bristol', *Liberator,* 16 April 1847.

217 *Liberator*, 12 February 1847,

218 *Transactions*, p. 477.

219 Garrison to Richard Webb, 1 March 1847, *Garrison Letters*.

220 *National Era,* 4 February 1847.

221 Ibid., 1 April 1847.

222 Elihu Burritt, *A Journal of a Visit of Three Days to Skibbereen and its Neighborhood* (London: Charles Gilpin, 1847).

223 *National Era*, 25 February 1847.

224 Gleeson, *The Irish in the South*, p. 103.

225 *Chronotype* quoted in *Eagle*, 9 August 1847.

226 *National Era*, 25 November 1847.

227 Strum, 'Garden City', p. 398.

228 Strum, 'To Feed the Hungry', p. 3.

229 *National Era*, 25 November 1847.

230 Fr Mathew, Cork, to Mr Weed, US, 31 March 1847, pub in *National Era,* 29 April 1847.

231 Ibid., 29 April 1847.

232 Archbishop of Dublin, House of Lords, *Hansard*, Poor Relief (Ireland) Bill, HL Debates, 29 April 1847, vol. 92, cc. 60–126.

233 Palmerston to Pakenham, 31 March 1847, reprinted in *National Era*, 6 May 1847.

234 Barry M. Gough, The Royal Navy and Oregon Crisis, 1844–1846 in *The British Columbian Quarterly*, Issue 9 (1971): http://ojs.library.ubc.ca/index. php/bcstudies/article/view/689, accessed 10 December 2011.

235 *National Era*, 25 February 1847.

236 Ibid., 12 August 1847.

237 Dr West to Kinkaid, agent to Lord Palmerston, December 1846, in Desmond Norton, 'Lord Palmerston and the Irish Famine Emigration', in Tyler Anbinder (ed.), *Centre for Economic Research Working Paper Series* (Dublin:University College Dublin, 2001), WP01/19, September 2001.

238 Ibid.

239 *National Era*, 29 April 1847.

240 Fr Mathew, Cork, to Mr Weed, US, 31 March 1847, pub. in *National Era*, 29 April 1847.

241 Wendell Phillips, Boston to James Haughton, Dublin, 20 August 1849, in *National Era*, 21 September 1849.

242 See Kinealy, *Repeal and Revolution.*

243 William Smith O'Brien to Vice-President George M. Dallas, 3 April 1847, in *National Era*, 29 April 1847.

244 Ibid.

245 A town in Texas was renamed in his honour in the 1840s. The following biography makes no mention of his role in Irish relief. George Mifflin Dallas, 11th Vice-President (1845–1849), 'United States Senate': http://www.senate.gov/artandhistory/history/common/generic/VP_George_Dallas.htm, accessed 9 June 2012.

246 *Mercury*, 13 April 1847. For more on this debate see, Kinealy, *Saddest People* (London: Pickering and Chatto, 2011b), pp. 136–9.

247 Ibid.

248 *Nation*, 1 May 1847.

249 James Haughton to Samuel May, 30 August 1847, Clare Taylor, *British and American Abolitionists: An Episode in Transatlantic Understanding* (Edinburgh: Edinburgh University Press, 1974), pp. 319–20.

250 'Address to the American People', 24 April 1847, John Gray, Chairman, reprinted in *National Era*, 27 May 1847.

251 *National Era*, 1 July 1847.

252 Strum, 'Famine Relief', p. 406.

Chapter 11

1 Irish Relief Association, *The Lapse of Years, or Thoughts Suggested by the Close of Another Period of Time* (Dublin: William Leckie, 1847), p. 24.

2 This argument is made most convincingly by Boyd Hilton, *The Age of Atonement. The Influence of Evangelicalism on Social and Economic Thought, 1785–1865* (Oxford: Oxford University Press, 1992).

3 Linda Colley, *Britons. Forging the Nation, 1707–1837* (New Haven: Yale University Press, 1994), p. 55. A striking aspect of Colley's book is how little attention she pays to Ireland.

4 Ibid., p. 19.

5 *New York Christian Advocate*, 2 June 1847 (information based on the 1841 census).

6 Harrison, 'Philanthropy and the Victorians', p. 357.

7 Ibid., p. 218.

8 Quoted in Robert McCarthy, 'The Role of the Clergy in the Great Famine', in APCK, *The Great Famine. A Church of Ireland Perspective* (Dublin: APCK, 1996), p. 9.

9 Geary, *Medicine and Charity*, p. 32.

10 Ibid.

11 *1838 Irish Poor Law Act.*

12 *The British Protestant, or, Journal of the Religious Principles of the Reformation* (London: J. F. Shaw), pp. 18–19; *New York Christian Advocate*, 17 November 1847. The *Christian Advocate* began publication in 1826 and by the mid-1830s had become the largest circulating weekly in America with more than 30,000 subscribers and an estimated 150,000 readers.

13 Desmond Bowen, *The Protestant Crusade in Ireland, 1800–70: A Study of Catholic-Protestant Relations Between the Act of Union and Disestablishment* (Dublin: Gill and Macmillan, 1978).

14 William John Fitzpatrick, J. P., *The Life, Times and Correspondence of the Right Rev. Dr. Doyle, Bishop of Kildare and Leighlin*, vol. ii (Dublin: James Duffy, 1861), pp. 1–3.

15 'Catholic Emancipation', in *The Evangelical Magazine and Missionary Chronicle* (London: s.n., 1829), p. 154.

16 Irish Evangelical Society, PRONI: http://www.proni.gov.uk/introduction_irish_evangelical_society.pdf, accessed 9 March 2012. See also, John Owen, *The history of the origin and first ten years of the British and foreign Bible society* (London: Tilling and Hughes, 1816–20), p. 103.

17 J. Newton Brown, Bela Bates Edwards, *Encyclopedia of Religious Knowledge: or, Dictionary of the Bibles* (New York: Lewis Colby, 1851).

18 Canon O'Rourke, *The Battle of the Faith in Ireland* (Dublin: James Duffy, 1887), pp. 531–2.

19 Irene Whelan, 'The Stigma of Souperism', in Cathal Poirteir, (ed.), *The Great Famine* (Cork: Mercier Press, 1995), p. 140.

20 *Christian Advocate*, 29 September 1847.

21 Peter Gray, *Famine, Land and Politics: British Government and Irish Society, 1843–50* (Dublin: Irish Academic Press, 2001), pp. 96–106.

22 Nicholson, *Annals*, pp. 181–2.

23 Ibid., pp. 48–9.

24 Full title, *The British Magazine and Monthly Registers of Religious and Ecclesiastical Information, Parochial History and Documents Respecting the State of the Poor, Progress of Education, etc.*

25 'The Scarcity', in Hugh James Rose, Samuel Roffey Maitland, *The British Magazine*, Volume 31, February 1847, p. 210.

26 Ibid., p. 212.

27 Ibid. p. 213.

28 Ibid., Thomas Vores, curate of St Mary's, Hastings, 30 December 1846, p. 213.

29 Ibid. Eugene Broderick, '*The Famine and Religious Controversy in Waterford, 1847–1850*'. *Decies* 51: 11–24.

30 Alfred Tresidder Sheppard (ed.), Asenath Nicholson, *The Bible in Ireland; Ireland's Welcome to the Stranger, or Excursions Through Ireland in 1844 and 1845 for the Purpose of Personally Investigating the Condition of the Poor* (London: Hodder and Stoughton, 1926), pp. xviii, xix.

31 Ibid.

32 Branach, 'Edward Nangle', pp. 36–8.

33 Ibid.

34 Nicholson, *Annals*, p. 105.

35 Ibid.

36 Branach, 'Edward Nangle', pp. 36–8.

37 Canon O'Rourke, *The Battle of the Faith in Ireland* (Dublin: James Duffy, 1887), pp. 524–7.

38 O'Brien, *The Great Famine in Ireland*, p. 198.

39 *Tuam Herald*, 9 January 1847; Irish Relief Association for the Destitute Peasantry, *'Distress in Ireland'* (Dublin: Philip Hardy and Sons, 1847), p. 8.

40 *The Globe and Traveller* (London), 1 January 1847. The contributors to the Westport Soup Kitchen were: Marquis of Sligo: donation £100, weekly subscription £5. Marchioness of Sligo: donation £10, weekly subscription £3. William Levyston Esq. donation £50, weekly subscription £2. George Glendinning donation £50, weekly subscription £3. Rev. Patrick Pounden donation £10, weekly subscription £1. M. MacDonnell: donation £25, weekly subscription £1. Very Rev. Bernard Burke: donation £10, weekly subscription 10 shillings.

41 *Report of IRA* 1848, p. viii.

42 Applications for relief to the IRA, 3 December 1846, Royal Irish Academy, 27.Q.24.

43 *Distress in Ireland,* p. 8.

44 Ibid., Clothing Account, p. 31.

45 Ibid., p. 31.

46 Ibid., Appendix One, 15 January 1847, p. 9.

47 Ibid., p. 10.

48 Ibid., Schedule of Grants, September to 31 March 1847, pp. 13–30.

49 Ibid., *'Distress in Ireland'*, p. 5.

50 Ibid., p. 6.

51 *Tuam Herald*, 24 October 1847.

52 *Report of the Proceedings of Irish Relief Association* (Dublin: Philip Dixon, 1848), hereafter, *Report of Proceedings*, 1848, p. vi.

53 Ibid., pp. 14–33.

54 Ibid., p. 7.

55 Applications to the IRA, Application numbers 11, 72, 122, 346, IRA, 27.Q.24.

56 *Distress in Ireland*, appendix 11, 15 January to 15 February, p. 12.

57 *Northern Whig*, quoted in Flann Campbell, *The Dissenting Voice: Protestant Democracy in Ulster from Plantation to Partition* (Belfast: Blackstaff Press, 1991), p. 206.

58 Irish Relief Association, *The Lapse of Years*.

59 Ibid., p. 18.

60 Ibid., p. 21.

61 Ibid., pp. 21–2.

62 Ibid., p. 24.

63 Ibid., pp. 26–8.

64 *Report of Proceedings*, 1848, p. iv.

65 Ibid.

66 Ibid., p. x.

67 Ibid., p. xi.

68 Ibid., p. x.

69 Ibid., p. xii.

70 Ibid., p. 34.

71 *Distress in Ireland*, Schedule of Grants, September to 31 March 1847, pp. 13–30.

72 J. F. Smith and W. Howitt, *John Cassell's Illustrated History of England. The Text, to the Reign of Edward 1 by J. F. Smith; and from that Period by W. Howitt* (London: Cassell, 1856–64), p. 624.

73 National Club, *Addresses to the Protestants of the Empire*, November, 1847, to February, 1849 (London: Macintosh, 1849).

74 Report from Newport, Co. Mayo, Applications to IRA, No. 165. RIA, 27.Q.24, 23 December 1846.

75 *Freeman's Journal*, 25 January 1847.

76 Applications to the IRA, RIA, 27.Q.24, 23,

77 *Freeman's Journal*, 7 April 1847.

78 Ibid.

79 J. Smith and Howitt, *John Cassell's Illustrated History of England*, p. 624.

80 Church Missionary Society, *Missionary Register, 1840*, vol. 28 (London: Seeley, Jackson, & Halliday), p. 261.

81 *Brooklyn Eagle*, 7 August 1847.

82 See also Kinealy and MacAtasney, *Hidden Famine*, pp. 114–17.

83 *Banner of Ulster*, 5 January 1849.

84 *News-Letter*, 17 August 1847.

85 *Banner of Ulster*, 26 October 1847.

86 General Assembly of the Presbyterian Church in Ireland to US, *News-Letter*, 20 July 1847.

87 *News-Letter*, 18 May 1847.

88 For more, see Chapter 7, and Kinealy and MacAtasney, *Famine in Belfast*, pp. 126–9.

89 *Vindicator*, 16 December 1846. For more on this controversy see Kinealy and MacAtasney, *Hidden Famine*, pp. 126–30.

90 *News-Letter,* 8 January 1847.

91 *Banner*, 8 January 1847.

92 *Whig,* 7 January 1847.

93 *Dublin Evening Post*, 9 January 1847.

94 *Whig*, 13 February 1847.

95 For more see, Kinealy and MacAtasney, *Hidden Famine*, pp. 131–4.

96 Charles Henry Crookshank, *History of Methodism in Ireland* (Belfast: R.S. Allen, 1885–88), pp. 34–5.

97 *Armagh Guardian*, 18 February 1845.

98 The Stations of the Primitive Wesleyan Methodist Preachers: Dublin—Thomas M'Fann, W. H. Graham, George Revington, Dawson. D. Heather, John Ramsay, Thomas C. Maguire. Waterford—Arthur Connell. Cork—Charles Graham, John White. Bandon—Henry Taylor. Mallow—John Stephenson. Kinsale—Thomas H. Jones. Limerick—William H. Mervyn. Roscrea—Samuel Larminie. Athlone—Geo. Hamilton, Alexander Campbell. Longford—Abraham L. Dobbin. Boyle—Robert Kane. Clones—William Herbert, John S. Evans. Cavan—Robert Campbell, Richard Wilson. Newtownbutler—Robert Wilson, William Graham. Ballyjamesduff—William Burns. Enniskillen—William Craig, John Clendinning. Maguiresbridge—Alexander Stewart, John Heatley. Lowtherstown—Daniel Henderson, James Robinson, sen. Ballyshannon—Joseph Payne, Robert Kerr. Springfield—Adam Ford, Wm. Lendrum. Manorhamilton—Richard Robinson. Londonderry—William Scott, jun. Newtownstewart—James Herbert, John Edwards. Fintona—William Gunn, John Milligan. Charlemont—John Wherry, William Skuse. Armagh—John M'Illroy, Robert Sewell. Tandragee—Abraham Dawson, William Robinson. Belfast—James Griffin, John Graham. Lurgan—Joseph M'Cormick, James Harvey. Downpatrick—Wm. Lindsay, Thomas Abraham. Wicklow—William Stokes, John Henning. New Ross—John Cullen. Youghal—Edward Sullivan. Skibbereen—Thomas Wilson. Kerry—Richard J. Dawson. Clonmel—George H. Irwin. Cloghjordan— Charles Skuse. Mountrath—John Wilson, William Flaherty. Roscommon—Joseph Thomson. Sligo—George Stewart. Kells—James Robinson, jun. Cootehill—Wm. Pattyson, Richard Griffin. Ballyconnell—One to be sent. Omagh— John Thompson. Cookstown—John Taylor. Aughnacloy— Adam L. Ford. Antrim—Edward Addy. Glenavy—Edward Whittle. Lisburn—John Carlisle. Banbridge—Charles Reid. Newry—William Scott, sen. Dundalk—Robert Kingsborough. Ennishowen [sic]—James Moffett.

Armagh Guardian, 5 August 1845; *The Portadown Weekly News, and County Armagh Advertiser*, 16 July 1859.

99 *The Dublin Almanac, and General Register of Ireland, for 1847*, p. 148.

100 Ibid.

101 From *London Watchman*, reprinted in *Christian Advocate*, 31 March 1847.

102 *Christian Advocate*, 31 March 1847.

103 Crookshank, *History of Methodism*, p. 376.

104 Ibid., p. 269.

105 Huston in *Christian Advocate*, 6 April 1847.

106 *Christian Advocate*, 3 February 1847.

107 Crookshank, *History of Methodism*, p. 374.

108 Ibid., p. 385.

109 *London Watchman*, in *Christian Advocate*, 31 March 1847.

110 *Christian Advocate*, 28 April 1847.

111 Ibid., p. 375.

112 Encyclopedia Britannica, 1911. http://www.en.wikisource.org/wiki/1911_
     Encyclop%C3%A6dia_Britannica/Bickersteth,_Edward, accessed 9 October
     2011.

113 See Chapter 10.

114 Dallas, *Incidents in the Life*, p. 335.

115 Sir Bernard Burke, *A Genealogical and Heraldic History of the Landed
     Gentry of Great Britain & Ireland*, vol. 1 (London: Harrison, 1871),
     p. 322.

116 Dallas, *Irish Church Mission*, p. 33.

117 Dallas to F. Bellingham, 1 November 1845, Dallas, *Incidents in the Life*,
     p. 340. In a letter of April 1847, he made a similar quip about meeting a
     'Nenagh bullet', p. 354.

118 Dallas, *Irish Church Mission*, p. 70.

119 Dallas, *Incidents in the Life*, p. 336.

120 Dallas, *Irish Church Mission*, p. 84.

121 Thomas Rawson Birks, *Memoir of the Rev. Edward Bickersteth: late rector of
     Watton, Herts*, vol. 2 (New York: Harper and Bros, 1851), p. 315.

122 Ibid., p. 316.

123 Durant had been a member for some years, Dallas joined in 1846, and they
     invited Bickersteth to join them, Dallas, *Irish Mission Society*, pp. 167–8.

124 Sampson Low Jr, *The Charities of London. Their Origin, Design, Progress
     and Present position* (London: Sampson Low, 1850), p. 426.

125 Anne B. Dallas, *Incidents in the Life and Ministry of the Rev. Alex. R. C.
     Dallas* (London: James Nisbet & Co, 1872), p. 351; Birks, *Memoir of
     Bickersteth*, 25 December 1846, p. 317.

126 Ibid., 7 March 1847, p. 389.

127 Dallas, *Irish Church Mission*, p. 173.

128 *Christian Intelligencer*, quoted in *Christian Advocate*, 31 March 1847.

129 Dallas, *Incidents in the Life*, p. 336.

130 Ibid., p. 352.

131 Ibid., p. 358.

132 Kathleen Villiers-Tuthill, *A Colony of Strangers: the Founding & Early
     History of Clifden* (Galway: Connemara Girl, 2012), pp. 207–8.

133 Dallas, *Irish Church Mission*, pp. 137–42. Dallas mistakenly refers to
     Strzelecki as 'Stralyckie', p. 139.

134 Villiers-Tuthill, *Colony of Strangers*, pp. 220–1.

135 Dallas, *Incidents in the Life*, p. 367.

136 Ibid., p. 367.

137 Lord Brougham, 28 January 1847, 'Distress in Ireland', House of Lords Debates, vol. 89 cc. 501–3.

138 Birks, *Memoir of Bickersteth*, 30 January 1847, p. 318.

139 Ibid., 30 January 1847, p. 317.

140 Bowen, *Protestant Crusade*, p. 295.

141 Dallas, *Incidents in the Life*, p. 359.

142 Birks, *Memoir of Bickersteth*, pp. 219–21.

143 Dallas, *Incidents in the Life*, p. 372.

144 Dallas, *Irish Church Mission*, p. 191.

145 *Society for Irish Church Missions to the Roman Catholics* (London: s.n., 1850), p. 2.

146 *Ballina Chronicle*, 7 August 1850.

147 Burke, *A Genealogical and Heraldic History,* 1871, p. 322.

148 Donald Brady, *Margaret Louisa Aylward 1810–1889* (Waterford Co. Council), p. 6: http://www.snap.waterfordcoco.ie/collections/ebooks/104720/104720.pdf, accessed 10 July 2012.

149 Dallas, *Incidents in the Life*, p. 377.

150 Irish Church Missions: http://www.icm-online.ie/resources/articles/69-alexander-dallas-and-founding-of-the-icm.html, accessed 2 July 2012.

151 'M', *Connemara, Journal of a Tour, Undertaken to Enquire into the Progress of the Reformation in the West of Ireland* (Dublin: G. Drought, 1852), p. 24.

152 John Gregg, *A Missionary Visit to Connemara, and Other Parts of the County of Galway,* (Dublin: Curry, 1849).

153 Cormac Ó Gráda, 'Church of Ireland mortality during the famine', in APCK, *The Great Famine. A Church of Ireland Perspective*, p. 14.

154 Ibid., John O'Rourke, *'Them also': The Story of the Dublin Mission* (Dublin: J. Nisbet & Co., 1866), p. 6.

155 O'Rourke, *Them Also*, p. 8.

156 Reprinted in *Nenagh Guardian*, 20 January 1847.

157 Lord Brougham, 28 January 1847, 'Distress in Ireland', House of Lords, Debates, vol. 89 cc. 501–3.

158 Sir John Forbes, *Memorandums Made in Ireland in the Autumn of 1852,* vol. 2 (London: Smith, Elder, and co., 1853), pp. 20–1.

159 Ibid., pp. 54–5.

160 *Morning Chronicle*, 22 November 1847.

161 Brady, *Margaret Louisa Aylward*, p. 6.

162 Presentation Nuns to Dr Cullen, 15 February 1847, Cullen Papers. CUL/1332.

163 O'Rourke, *Battle for the Faith*, p. 271.

164 Ibid., p. 527.

165 See, for example, Patrick Hickey, *Famine in West Cork*.

166 Nicholson, *Annals*, p. 188.

167 C. H. Mackintosh (1820–96), Biography, in '*My Brethren*': http://www. mybrethren.org/bios/framchm.htm, accessed 2 May 2012.

168 Nicholson, *Annals*, p. 188.

169 Patrick Comerford, 'A Bitter Legacy', in APCK, *The Great Famine*, p. 5.

Conclusion

1 *Report of BRA*, p. 48.

2 Recollections of Máire Ni Grianna, Rannafast, the Rosses, County Donegal. Quoted in S. Deane (ed.), *The Field Day Anthology of Irish Writing* (Derry: Field Day, 1994), pp. 203–4.

3 Carolyn Oulton, *Literature and Religion in Mid-Victorian England: From Dickens to Eliot* (London: Palgrave Macmillan, 2003), p. 180.

4 Ibid., p. 179.

5 The humanitarianism that lay behind famine charity has also been identified by Anelise Hanson Shrout, 'Distressing News from Ireland'. The Famine, the News and International Philanthropy. Unpublished PhD Dissertation (New York: New York University, 2013), pp. 154–5.

6 Nicholson, *Annals*, pp. 60–1.

7 Reports to IRA, 2 December 1846.

8 Ibid., pp. 57, 210.

9 See Chapters Three and Four.

10 *Times*, 5 January 1847.

11 *Economist*, 16 October 1847.

12 *Freeman's Journal*, 3 April 1847.

13 *Nation*, 3 April 1847.

14 Ibid., 8 January 1847.

15 *Morning Herald* reprinted in *Nenagh Guardian*, 20 January 1847.

16 Urquhart, *Ladies of Londonderry*, p. 49.

17 *Brooklyn Eagle*, 16 February 1847.

18 This point was made by former Prime Minister Tony Blair, in 1997.

19 Lord Bessborough, Dublin Castle to Russell, Russell Papers, NAE, 30 22 16A, 23 January 1847.

20 *National Era*, 4 February 1847.

21 Sarbaugh, 'Charity begins at Home', p. 35.

22 *New York Christian Advocate*, 21 July 1847.

23 *Belfast Vindicator* in *Northern Star*, 5 October 1849.

24 *Northern Star*, 21 June 1848.

25 Nicholson, *Annals*, p. 52.

26 Ibid.

27 Harrison makes the point in regard to Victorian philanthropy, 'there are as many philanthropic motivations as there are philanthropists', Harrison, 'Philanthropy and the Victorians', p. 358.

28 Ibid., p. 359.

29 Tuckerman delivered this sermon on 14 March 1847. Quoted in Wach, 'Unitarian Philanthropy', p. 549.

30 Sandra Cavello, 'The Motivations of Benefactors: An Overview of Approaches to the Study of Charity', in Jonathan Barry and Colin Jones (eds), *Medicine and Charity Before the Welfare State* (London: Taylor & Francis, 2007), pp. 46–62.

31 Harrison, 'Philanthropy and the Victorians', p. 364.

32 Curti, *American Philanthropy*, p. 32.

33 This point has been made in Alan Kidd, 'Philanthropy and the "Social History" paradigm'. *Social History* 21(2), (May 1996), 180–92.

34 *Report of the committee of Philadelphia*, p. 38.

35 *Report of BRA*, p. 48.

36 Williamson, 'State Prayers', p. 140.

37 'Appeal to Public', *Report of GRC*, 12 February 1847, p. 148.

38 *Brooklyn Eagle*, 5 March 1853.

39 *New York Times*, 3 December 1865.

40 *Massachusetts Help*, pp. 51–3.

41 Knights Commander of the Order of Bath: http://en.wikipedia.org/w/index.php?title=Category:Knights_Commander_of_the_Order_of_the_Bath&pageuntil=Vickers%2C+Richard%0ARichard+Vickers#mw-pages, accessed 9 October 2011.

42 From *Morning Chronicle* in the *Sydney Morning Herald*, 5 May 1849.

43 Ibid.

44 O'Brien, *The Great Famine in Ireland*, p. 190.

45 Bewley and Pim, 19 April 1847, *Report of GRC*, p. 121.

46 Ibid., Bewley and Pim to Reyburn, 3 August 1847, p. 137.

47 *Brooklyn Eagle*, 2 January 1857.

48 Ibid.

49 *National Era*, 7 August 1851.

50 *Newtownards Independent*, 18 July 1872.

51 Nicholson, *Annals*, p. 191.

52 Strum, 'To Feed the Hungry', p. 3.

53 *New York Times*, 11 April 1863.

54 Tuke, *The Great Famine in Ireland: and a Retrospect of the Fifty Years 1845–95*, p. 180; O'Brien, *Famine in Ireland*, pp. 176–7.

55 Timothy Collins, 'HMS Valorous'. *Journal of the Galway Archaeological and Historical Society* (vol. 49, 1997: 122–42), pp. 130–2.

56 *Sydney Morning Herald*, 7 January 1880.

57 *New Zealand Tablet*, 23 January 1880.

58 Ibid.

59 *National Era*, July 26, 1855.

60 *Freeman's Journal*, 14 November 1877.

61 J. N. Uppal, *Bengal Famine of 1943. A Man-made Tragedy* (Atma Ram & Sons, Delhi, 1984).

62 *Irish Press*, 9 July 1945. The students were Subrata Roy Chowdhury and Dilip Sen.

63 *Austin American-Statesman*, 22 September 1992.

64 *Report of BRA*, p. 221.

APPENDIX

1 The New York Relief Committee, 12 February 1847

Myndert Van Schaick, Wm. Shaw,
Robert B. Minturn, Robert H. Morris,
Stewart Brown, G. G. Rowland,
Mortimer Livingston, Moses H. Grinnell,
James Reyburn, William S. Wetmore,
Thomas Suffern, George Barclay,
Jacob Harvey, Jonathan Sturges,
Thomas E. Davis, Walden Pell,
August Belmont, Pelatiah Perit,
George Griffin, Victor DeLaunay,
John Jay, Philip Hone,
Cornelius W. Lawrence, John Haggerty,
Anthony Barclay, William H. Macy,
Wm. Redmond, George McBroob, Jr
Wm. Barnwall, John L. Aspinwall.

From, Report of General Relief Committee, pp. 149–50.

2 Instruction from BRA to their Agents in Ireland

South Sea House
14 April 1847

The main object of the Committee in appointing Agents is to administer relief, subject to certain general rules, with more rapidity than can be done by a body acting from a distance. It is desirable therefore that having to decide in extreme and peculiar cases without waiting for specific instructions, the Agents should be apprized of the principles on which the Committee proceed.

The distress in Ireland is unfortunately certain to last for several months. The Funds which are or will be at the disposal of the Committee must prove inadequate to effect more than a mitigation of the suffering which is unavoidable. The means being thus insufficient to secure the result which would be wished, it is most desirable to economize them as far as practicable – urgent cases, of necessity must, it is true, be provided for at all hazards; but it must be always remembered that caution to economy at the present time will be the best security against the general spread of famine throughout the Country. The object of your mission being the early relief of distress, the above observation will point out to you that a careful economy of the funds of the Association is the most important rule of administration to be observed.

The economy can be exercised in two ways; first, by inducing the resident Proprietors and others locally interested to purchase provisions at prime cost, instead of looking for Grants; secondly by promoting the establishment of Soup Kitchens and other systems for making available all means of providing food which may actually be found in the Country. The Committee consider the first of these methods the essential duty of an agent; the second as incidental.

The most effectual relief which can be afforded is an increase in the supply of provisions. Now if it were possible at this moment to invest all the subscriptions received by the Association in provisions and distribute the same in the most distressed Districts, the relief afforded would be but temporary and insufficient. But if, on the contrary, such a portion of the provisions can be sold on the spot as may enable the Association to effect further purchases, a continuous stream of food may be poured in. Every effort must therefore be made to induce parties on the spot to *purchase*, as far as their means will allow or to raise (where it has not already been done) a subscription for purchasing; which, being of the nature of a reproduction fund, will subject the Contributors to a loss infinitely disproportional to the good which will be effected.

In cases where you may think fit you are at liberty to make absolute grants of provisions to the amount in values of 1/10th of the local private subscriptions, these grants being placed at the disposal of the Relief Committees. Should any further Grant appear to you advisable under peculiar circumstances, you are to report your opinion to the Committee specially, and in a letter separate from all other matters, stating your reasons to the amount of the extraordinary Grant which you recommend.

The Committee are aware that famine has already established itself in many Districts so undeniably, that it would be a vain attempt on the part of their Agent to define with any accuracy the classes of persons to be relieved out of a free Grant. But they wish you to bear in mind for application, whenever practicable, the principle that few Grants ought to be limited to those who are unable to labour. After the observations which have been made above, it is almost unnecessary to state that you are at liberty to make sales of the provisions under your charge to relief Committees or to any Individuals who you are satisfied will retail them for charitable purposes not for profit. With respect to the latter it will be desirable that you should make it a condition that the food should be retailed at a maximum price fixed by you and acknowledged in writing by the Purchaser.

On the subject of the price at which you are at liberty to make these sales, you will take the prime cost, except in cases where the nearest Commissariat Store may be selling below that price, when you will sell at their value.

You will also bear in mind the necessities of those parts of your District which you may not yet have visited; and not exhaust your Stores before you see an immediate prospect of their being replenished.

Considering the question of Grants and of sales jointly, it is likely that you may often be able to induce the latter, by a conditional promise of the former. A relief Committee may be willing to make an effort to purchase, when they are assured that a Grant will accompany a sale.

Your independent position, both as regards the Government and as regards local influences, may enable you to enforce with effect on the Relief Committees the importance of encouraging the retail local trade. It would be very undesirable that you should attempt to interfere in the details of any such arrangements; but it may be very useful that you should take opportunities of pointing out the importance of the principle.

It is the practice of the Committee to issue blank query sheets to parties applying for assistance with instructions then when filled up, they should be handed to their Agents on the spot. It will be your duty to consider to inform yourself carefully as to such of these statements as may reach you and to forward the same to the Committee with your observations: using your best discretion as to the necessity of taking any steps for affording relief before an answer can be received from hence.

In order to the accurate formation of an opinion upon these documents, the Committee will only observe that as the most necessitous Districts are those which require their first notice, it is desirable to pay especial attention first to the subject of the Poor Law Valuation, both in its proportion to the population and to the acreable extent of the District, as indicative of the local means which exist for meeting the distress; and secondly to the proportion of the population which has been employed on Public Works. For though the amount of distress is not measured by the latter, yet the absence of distress is pretty generally shown by there having been but a small number employed in that manner.

The Committee are desirous that their Agents should be in as frequent communication as possible with the Relief Officers employed under the authority of Government, and you will be at liberty to communicate directly with M. General Sir John Burgoyne, the Chief of the relief department, on any points which may appear to be deserving of his attention. But you will take care to make it fully understood by the Relief Committees and other local bodies with whom you communicate, that you are assisting in the administration of a voluntary Relief Subscription arising from English Charity necessarily limited in extent, and therefore not only justifying, but requiring economy in its distribution, but yet so large to deserve the warmest thanks of the Irish people to the Contributors.

Though it is not within your province or that of the Committee to yet interfere directly with the subject of the non-cultivation of the land, your position will give you opportunities of adverting to it incidentally with great effect.

It is desirable that you should as far as practicable employ the agency of the Relief Committees organized by Government and even in cases where it may be necessary to make a Grant to a specific portion of a Relief District, it is expedient to entrust the administration thereof to the Committee which includes that locality within its sphere of influence. Some instances unhappily exist where from local jealousies or other causes, the relief Committee is inefficient or unworthy of trust and in such cases it will be your duty to form a Committee of not less than three Individuals who may be found fit Administrators of the Charity.

In conclusion, I have to request that you will keep this Committee as fully acquainted with your proceedings as such times of urgency will permit.

I have the honour to be, Sir,
Y^r. obed^t. Servt.
S. Spring Rice
Hon^y Sec^y

3 Instructions from BRA on Closure of their Operations

South Sea House
12 June 1847

Sir

The Committee being of opinion that it is advisable to suspend their operations during the next two months, I am directed to request you will take steps to close your Agency within a fortnight or three weeks if possible.

They entertain no doubt that wherever the Relief Act is in operation, the necessary relief will be afforded through its machinery and the assistance of this Association is therefore now in a great measure superfluous.

In the case of Districts where through any unavoidable circumstances the Act in question has not been carried into operation, though it is expected very few if any such cases will exist after the expiration of the next fortnight, any assistance the Association may feel disposed to give will probably be conveyed through the instrumentality of the Inspecting officers.

I am desired to request that you will be good enough to take an early opportunity of making your arrangements in conformity with this notice and the Committee hope shortly to hear from you that you can retire from the District without further difficulty.

On passing through Dublin be so good as to call upon the Count Strzelecki – Reynolds Hotel Saxville [sic] Street – and give him such explanations regarding the assistance you have afforded and the channels through which it has been given as may be sufficient to enable him fully to understand the circumstances connected with your District, at the time of your retirement from it. This information the Count will require to guide him in the further duties that may devolve upon him in his connection with this Association.

I have the honour to be
Sir
Your obd^t Servt
J. B. Standish Haly
Secretary.

From Report of BRA, pp. 13–36.

BIBLIOGRAPHY

Adam, T. (2004), *Philanthropy, Patronage, and Civil Society: Experiences from Germany, Great Britain, and North America*. Indiana University Press.

Alexander, W. (1895), *The Annual Monitor or, Obituary of the Members of the Society of Friends in Great Britain and Ireland*. York: Alexander.

Allen, C. (n.d.), *Campbell Allen Papers* (D1558), Public Record Office of Northern Ireland. Available at: http://www.proni.gov.uk/introduction__campbell_allen_d1558.pdf. [Accessed April 2012].

American Bankers Association (1878), *Proceedings of the Convention of the American Bankers' Association*. New York: The Association.

American & Commercial Daily Advertiser.

American Jewish Historical Society (2011),*American Jewish Historical Quarterly*, Vol. 27. Charleston, S.C.: Nabu Press.

An Act for the Amendment and Better Administration of the Laws relating to the Poor in England and Wales (14 August 1834), 4 & 5 Will. IV cap. 76.

An Act for the Amendment and Better Administration of the Laws relating to the Poor in England and Wales (1834). London: George Eyre and Andrew Spottiswoode.

An Act for the more Effectual Relief of the Destitute Poor in Ireland (31 July 1838), 1 and 2 Vic. c.56.

An Act for the Further Amendment of an Act for the more Effectual Relief of the Destitute Poor in Ireland (24 August 1843), 6 and 7th Vic. c.92.

An Act to make Further Provision for the Relief of the Destitute Poor in Ireland (8 June 1847), 10 Vic. c.31.

Andrews, M. (2010), *Antique Costumes and Textiles*. [online] Available at: http://www.meg-andrews.com/item-details/Lewis-Foreman-Day/6002. [Accessed 8 February 2011].

The Anglican Diocese of St Elizabeth (n.d.), [online] Available at: http://www.anglicandiocesepe.org.za/parishes.php?id=20001. [Accessed 14 May 2011].

The Anglo-Celt (Cavan).

Ankara-Hürriyet Daily News (Turkey), 23 March 2010. http://www.hurriyetdailynews.com/default.aspx?pageid=438&n=irish-president-mcaleese-backs-turkey8217s-eu-bid-2010-03-23. [Accessed 10 February 2012].

Archibishop Daniel Murray Catalogue. [online]. The University of Limerick Institutional Repository. Available at: http://www.ulir.ul.ie/handle/10344/1554. [Accessed various dates].

Arkansas Gazette.

The Armagh Guardian.

Artfact (n.d.), *Hunt and Roskell* [online] Available at: http://www.artfact.com/subcollection/hunt-roskell-h1ncvw2d3p. [Accessed 17 December 2011].

Austin American-Statesman.

The Australian (NSW).

The Baptist Magazine.

Ballina Chronicle.

The Bankers' Magazine (1857), Vol. 17. London: Groombridge and Sons.

Banner of Ulster.

Bardon, J. (2009), *A History of Ireland in 250 Episodes.* Dublin: Gill & Macmillan.

The Baring Archive, London.

Barry, J. and Jones, C. (2007) *Medicine and Charity Before the Welfare State* London: Taylor & Francis.

BBC (2012), *The Year of Slaughter, 1740.* [online] Available at: http://www.bbc. co.uk/northernireland/ashorthistory/archive/intro123.shtml. [Accessed 1 June 2011].

Belfast Ladies' Committee (1847) *First Report of Belfast Ladies' Committee.* Belfast: s.n.

Bell's New Weekly Messenger.

Belmont, P. (1898), *Public Record of Perry Belmont, a Member of the House of Representatives in the 47th, 48th, 49th, 50th Congress etc.* Albany, N.Y: Lyon Block.

Bengal Catholic Herald.

Bengal Hurkaru and the India Gazette.

Bennett, W. (1847), *Narrative of a Recent Journey of Six Weeks in Ireland: In Connexion with the Subject of Supplying Small Seed to some of the Remoter Districts.* London: Charles Gilpin.

Benson, A. C. and Esher, R. B. B. (eds) (1911), *The Letters of Queen Victoria, 1837-61.* London: J. Murray.

Berkeley, G. F. and Joan, W. B. (1968), *Italy in the Making: June 1846 to 1 January 1848.* Cambridge: Cambridge University Press.

Bickersteth, E. (1847), *The National Fast of 1847: A Help for Duly Observing It.* London: Seeley, Burnside, and Seeley.

Binns, J. (1854), *Recollections of the Life of John Binns.* Philadelphia: Parry and McMillan.

Blount, E. C. (1977), *Memoirs of Sir Edward Blount.* New York: Arno Press.

Board of Public Works (9 December 1846), *Fourteenth Annual Report.* London: Board of Public Works.

Boase, F. (1908), *Modern English Biography: Containing Many Thousand Concise Memoirs of Persons who have Died during the Years 1851 to 1900,* Vol. 1. Truro: Netherton and Worth.

Boase, G. C. and Courtney, W. P. (1874–82), *Bibliotheca Cornubiensis.* London: Longmans, Green, Reader and Dyer.

Boase, G. C. (1890), 'Harford, John Scandrett', in Dictionary of National Biography Online, 1885–1900, Vol. 24. [online] Available at: http://www. en.wikisource.org/wiki/Harford,_John_Scandrett_%28DNB00%29. [Accessed 12 May 2012].

— (1895), 'Peel, Lawrence', in Leslie Stephen (ed.), *Dictionary of National Biography, 1885–1900,* Vol. 44. London: Smith, Elder and Co.

Bombay Times.

The Boston Directory for 1851. Boston: Sampson & Murdock Company.

Boston Pilot.

Boulter, H. and Philips, A. (1770), *Letters Written by His Excellency Hugh Boulter . . . to Several Ministers of State in England, and some others: Containing an Account of the most Interesting Transactions which Passed in Ireland from 1724 to 1738*. Dublin: G. Faulkner and J. Williams.

Bowen, B. (1978), *The Protestant Crusade in Ireland, 1800–70: A Study of Catholic-Protestant Relations Between the Act of Union and Disestablishment*. Dublin and Montreal: Gill and Macmillan.

Brady, D. *Margaret Louisa Aylward 1810–1889* (Waterford Co. Council): http://www.snap.waterfordcoco.ie/collections/ebooks/104720/104720.pdf. [Accessed 10 July 2012].

Brady, W. M. (1863), *Clerical and Parochial Records of Cork, Cloyne, and Ross*. Dublin: Printed for the author by A. Thom.

Branach, N. R. (2000), 'Edward Nangle & the Achill Island Mission'. *History Ireland* 8(3): 35–8.

Brandt, E. H. (1807–42, 1889), *The Emmanuel H. Brandt Collection*. [manuscript] 15/35/50. Urbana: University of Illinois. Available at: http://www.library.illinois.edu/archives/uasfa/1535050.pdf. [Accessed 4 December 2011].

Brann, H. A. (April 1909), 'The Rev. John Kelly', in United States Catholic Historical Society, *Historical Records and Studies*. Vol. 5. United States: Catholic Historical Society, pp. 348–53.

Bremner, R. H. (1988), *American Philanthropy*. Chicago: University of Chicago Press.

Brennan, J. J. (1878), *A Catechism of the History of Ireland*. New York: Thomas Kelly.

British Farmer's Magazine (1837), Vol. 1. London: Ridgway and Sons.

The British Friend.

The British Magazine.

British Parliamentary Papers (1847a), *Correspondence Relating to Measures for Relief of Distress in Ireland*. HC (Commissariat Series, Second Part). January-March.

— (1847b), *First Report of Relief Commissioners Constituted under the Act 10 Vic., cap. 7*, Distress (Ireland).

— (1847c), *Measures Adopted for the Relief of Distress*. Board of Works Series: part I1.

— (1847d), *Papers Relative to the Relief of the Destitute Poor in Ireland and Scotland*. HC, (853) vol. LIII.

— (1847e), *The British Protestant, or, Journal of the Religious principles of the Reformation* [serial]. London: J. F. Shaw.

— (1846), *Suffering from Scarcity in Ireland between 1822 and 1839*.

British Relief Association for the Relief of Extreme Distress in Ireland and Scotland (1849), *Report*. London: Richard Clay.

The Broadway United Church of Christ (2012), [online] Available at: http://www.broadwayucc.org. [Accessed 1 February 2012].

Broderick, E. (1995), 'The Famine and Religious Controversy in Waterford, 1847–1850'. *Decies* 51: 11–24.

Brooklyn Eagle.

Brudney, B. (2009), *Gentlemen Bankers. The Self-Perception of the Financial Elite in the City of London, 1792–1848*. Undergraduate. Columbia University History Department.

Buckley, L. (2010), *Headstone Inscriptions, St. Columba's Church of Ireland, Glencolumbkille*. [online] Available at: http://www.freepages.genealogy. rootsweb.ancestry.com/~donegal/stccofi.htm. [Accessed 3 March 2012].

Burke, B. (1862–63), *A Genealogical and Heraldic Dictionary of the Landed Gentry of Great Britain and Ireland*. London: Harrison.

Burke, T. (1910), *Catholic History of Liverpool*. Liverpool: C. Tinling & Co.

Burritt, E. (1847), *A Journal of a Visit of Three Days to Skibbereen and its Neighborhood*. London: Charles Gilpin.

Bury, M. E. and Pickles, D. (eds) (1994), *Rommilly's Cambridge Diary*. Cambridge: Cambridgeshire Records Society.

Butler, J. E. (1896), *Personal Reminiscences of a Great Crusade*. London: Horace Marshall.

Butt, I. (1847), *A Voice for Ireland: The Famine in the Land*. Dublin: J. McGlashan.

Byrne, W. and Leahy, W. A. (1899), *Archdiocese of Boston*. Boston: Hurd & Everts Company.

The Californian.

Campbell, B. C. (2008), *Disasters, Accidents, and Crises in American History*. New York: Facts On File.

Campbell, F. (1991) *The Dissenting Voice: Protestant Democracy in Ulster from Plantation to Partition*. Belfast: Blackstaff Press.

Campbell, J. (1844), *Memoirs of David Nasmith: His Labours and Travels in Great Britain, France, and the United States, and Canada*. London: John Snow.

Campbell, J. H. (1892), *History of the Friendly Sons of St. Patrick and of the Hibernian Society for the Relief of Emigrants from Ireland, March 17, 1771-March 17, 1892*. Philadelphia: Hibernian Society.

Carrington, C. E. (1950), *John Robert Godley of Canterbury*. Cambridge: Cambridge: Cambridge University Press.

Carroll, F. M. (2005), *The American Presence In Ulster: A Diplomatic History, 1796–1996*. Washington, DC: Catholic University of American Press.

Catholic Editing Company (1908), *The Catholic Church in the United States of America: Undertaken to Celebrate the Golden Jubilee of His Holiness, Pope Pius X*, Vol. 3. New York: Catholic Editing Company.

Catholic Hierarchy (2012a), *Bishop Aidan Devereaux, Vicar Apostolic of Cape of Good Hope, Eastern District (Capo de Buona Speranza, Distretto Orientale)*. [online] Available at: *http://www.catholic-hierarchy.org/bishop/bdever.html*. [Accessed 1 June 2012].

— (2012b), *Bishop William Barber Tyler*. [online] Available at: http://www. catholic-hierarchy.org/bishop/btyler.html. [Accessed 1 June 2012].

— (2012c), *Dr Henry Hughes, Bishop in Gibraltar*. [online] Available at: http:// www.catholic-hierarchy.org/bishop/bhug.html. [Accessed 11 May 2012].

Cazenove and Company (1853–2003), [manuscript]. GB 0074 CLC/B/039. London Metropolitan Archives. Available at: http://www.aim25.ac.uk/cgi-bin/vcdf/ detail?coll_id=17159&inst_id=118&nv1=browse&nv2=sub. [Accessed 13 June 2012].

Central Relief Committee (1852), *Transactions of the Central Relief Committee of the Society of Friends during the Famine in Ireland, in 1846 and 1847*. Dublin: Hodges and Smith.

Charleston Courier.

Charleston Mercury.

The Charlottetown Examiner.

Chearbhaill, M. B. N. (2008), *The Society of St Vincent de Paul in Dublin, 1926–1875*. PhD. New University of Ireland. Available at: http://www.eprints.nuim.ie/1482/. [Accessed 3 August 2012].

Cherokee Nation.

Chicago Medical Society (1922), *History of Medicine and Surgery and Physicians and Surgeons of Chicago, Endorsed by and Published under the Supervision of the Council of the Chicago Medical Society*. Chicago: The Biographical Publishing Corporation.

Christian Advocate.

The Christian Guardian.

Christmas, H. (1854), *The Sultan of Turkey, Abdul Medjid Khan: A Brief Memoir of his Life and Reign, with Notices of the Country, its Army, Navy, & Present Prospects*. London: Shaw.

Christy, M. (1899), 'Tuke, James Hack' [online], *Dictionary of National Biography, 1885–1900*, Vol. 57. London: Smith, Elder and Co. Available at: http://www.en.wikisource.org/wiki/Tuke,_James_Hack_%28DNB00%29. [Accessed 13 February 2011].

Chronotype.

Church and Friary of Saint Francis of Assisi (n.d.), *History*. [online] Available at: http://www.stfrancisnyc.org/history/. [Accessed 4 May 2012].

Church and State Gazette.

Church of Ireland Gazette.

Church Missionary Society. (1840), *Missionary Register,* Vol. 28. London: Seeley, Jackson, & Halliday.

CityScape (2012), *Rue David Johnston.* [online] Available at: http://www.bordeaux.360cityscape.com/rue-david-johnston/266/. [Accessed 15 May 2012].

Civil War Medical Books (n.d.), *The Principles of Surgery.* [online] Available at: http://www.civilwarmedicalbooks.com/Principles_of_Surgery.html. [Accessed 4 September 2011].

Clarendon Papers (1820–70), *Letter books of Lord Clarendon,* [manuscript]. Oxford. Bodleian Library.

Clarkson, L. A. and Crawford, E. M. (2002), *Feast and Famine: A History of Food in Ireland 1500–1920*. Oxford: Oxford University Press.

Claus, P. (2005), *London City History.* [online] Available at: http://www.london-city-history.org.uk/biography.htm. [Accessed 12 December 2011].

Clinkscale, M. N. (1999), *Makers of the Piano: 1820–1860*. Oxford: Oxford University Press.

Clough, A. C. and Clough, B. S. (eds) (1888), *Prose Remains of Arthur Hugh Clough: With a Selection from his Letters and a Memoir*. London: Macmillan.

Cobh Museum (2011), *Irish Lace.* [online] Available at: http://www.cobhmuseum.com/Exhibitions/IrishLace/IrishLace.html. [Accessed 3 September 2011].

Cocks, C. (1846), *Bordeaux: Its Wines, and the Claret Country*. London: Longman, Brown and Green.

The Cogers Society. [online] Available at: http://www.cogers.org/history.html. [Accessed 4 June 2012].

Coleman, A. M. B. (1873), *The Life of John J. Crittenden: With Selections from his Correspondence and Speeches*. Philadelphia: J. B. Lippincott & Co.

Colley, L. (1994), *Britons: Forging the Nation, 1707–1837*. New Haven: Yale University Press.

Collins, T. (1997), 'HMS Valorous'. *Journal of the Galway Archaeological and Historical Society* 49: 122–42.

Colville, D. (2011), *Foundling Hospital*. [online] UCL Bloomsbury Project. Available at: http://www.ucl.ac.uk/bloomsbury-project/institutions/foundling_hospital.htm. [Accessed 18 October 2011].

Committee of Society of Friends (1848), *Distress in Ireland: Third Report of the London Committee with List of Subscriber*. London: Edward Newman.

Committee for the Relief of Ireland, CD 528. Albany Institute of History & Art Library, New York. Available at: http://www.albanyinstitute.org/collections/FindingAids/Albany . . . Irish%20Relief%20CD%20528.pdf. [Accessed 10 November 2011].

Connacht Tribune.

Corcoran, W. W. (1879), *A Grandfather's Legacy: Containing a Sketch of his Life and Obituary Notices*. Washington, DC: H. Polkinhorn.

Cork Constitution.

Cork Examiner.

The Cornwall Chronicle (Tasmania).

Cosgrave, M., Lohan, R. and Quinlan, T. (1995), *Sources in the National Archives for Researching the Great Famine*. [online] Dublin. National Archives. Available at: http://www.nationalarchives.ie/topics/famine/Great_Famine.pdf. [Accessed 10 February 2012].

Courier (Hobart).

Cowman, D. and Brady, D. (1995), *The Famine in Waterford, 1845–1850: teacht na bprátaí dubha*. Dublin: Geography Publications.

Cox, J. (2008), *The British Missionary Enterprise since 1700*. London: Routledge.

Crimmins, J. D. (1902), *St. Patrick's Day*. New York: Published by the Author.

— (1905), *Irish-American Historical Miscellany: Relating largely to New York City and Vicinity, Together With Much Interesting Material Relative to Other Parts Of The Country*. New York: Published by the author.

Crookshank, C. H. (1885–88), *History of Methodism in Ireland*. Belfast: R. S. Allen.

Crosfield, J. and Forster, J. (1846), *A Letter from Joseph Crosfield: Containing a Narrative of the First Week of William Forster's Visit to Some of the Distressed Districts in Ireland*. London: Edward Newman.

Culbert, M. (2012), *Cox Silver Tea Service*. [online] The Dunmanway Historical Society. Available at: *http://www.dunmanwayhistoricalsociety.org/post/Cox-Silver-Tea-Service.aspx*. [Accessed 10 December 2011].

Cullen, B. (1997), *Thomas L. Synnott: the Career of a Dublin Catholic, 1830–70*. Dublin: Irish Academic Press.

Cullen, P. (1821–79), *Paul Cullen Papers*. [online] Archives Pontifical Irish College, Rome. Available at: http://www.irishcollege.org/wp-content/uploads/2011/02/Cullen-Collection-Master-Catalogue.pdf. [Accessed 11 December 2011].

Curti, M. (1963), *American Philanthropy Abroad*. St Louis: Transaction.

Curry, W. (1848), *The Dublin University Magazine*, Vol. 32. Dublin: William Curry Jun. and Company.

Dallas, A. R. C. (1867), *The Story of the Irish Church Missions. Part I.: An Account of the Providential Preparation which led to the Establishment of the Society for Irish Church Missions to the Roman Catholics in 1849*. London: Society for Irish Church Missions.

Dallas, A. B. (1872), *Incidents in the Life and Ministry of the Rev. Alex. R. C. Dallas*. London: James Nisbet & Co.

Davis, P. (n.d.), *William Loney RN—Victorian Naval Surgeon*. [online] Available at: http://www.home.wxs.nl/~pdavis/index.htm.

Deane, S., Carpenter, A. and Williams, J. (eds), (1994), *The Field Day Anthology of Irish Writing*. Derry: Field Day Publications.

Dejaelaine (2004), *Florida's Ante Bellum Plantations*. [online] Available at: http://www.dejaelaine.com/abplantations.html. [Accessed 8 May 2011].

Dempsey, J. M. (1871), *Our Ocean Highways: A Condensed Universal Hand Gazetteer and International*. London: Edward Stanford.

Department of History, University of Limerick, Ireland (2007), 'Grey Nuns Famine Annal', in *Famine Archive*. [online] Available at: http://www.history.ul.ie/historyoffamily/faminearchive/. [Accessed 29 August 2012].

Devens, R. M. (1876), *Our First Century*. Springfield, Mass: C. A. Nichols.

Devine, T. M. (1988), *The Great Highland Famine: Hunger, Emigration, and the Scottish Highlands in the Nineteenth Century*. Edinburgh: John Donald.

Dickson, D. (1997), *Arctic Ireland: The Extraordinary Story of the Great Frost and Forgotten Famine of 1740–41*. Belfast: White Row Press.

Drake, F. S. (1872), *Dictionary of American Biography, Including Men of the Time, Etc.* Boston: James R. Osgood.

Drogheda Independent.

The Dublin Almanac and General Register of Ireland (1847). Dublin: Pettigrew and Oulton.

Dublin Evening Mail.

Dublin Mansion House Committee for the Relief of Distress in Ireland (1846), *Report of the Mansion House Committee on the Potato Disease*. Dublin: J. Browne.

Dublin Quarterly Journal of Medical Science (1848), Vol. 5. Dublin: Fannin and Co.

Ducykinck, E. A., Hoffman, C. F. and Ducykinck, G. L. (eds) (1894), *The Literary World*. New York: Osgood.

Dufferin, Lord and Boyle, G. F. (1847), *Narrative of a Journey from Oxford to Skibbereen during the year of the Irish Famine*. Oxford: John Henry Parker.

Duggan, C. (1994), *A Concise History of Italy*. Cambridge: Cambridge University Press.

The Economist.

Edgar D. D., John. E. (1852) 'Ireland's Mission Field' *A Paper Read at the Sixth Annual Conference of the British Protestant Organization, August 1852*. London: s.n.

Edgeworth, Maria (n.d.), *Letters of Maria Edgeworth*. Project Gutenberg. http://www.gutenberg.org/cache/epub/9095/pg9095.txt. [Accessed 1 May 2012].

Edwards, B. B. (1837), *Fessenden and Co.'s Encyclopedia of Religious Knowledge: or, Dictionary of the Bible, Theology, Religious Biography, all Religions, Ecclesiastical History, and Missions*. Brattleboro, VT: Brattleboro Typographic Co.

Elias, S. N. (1992), *The Forgotten Merchant Prince*. Westport: Praeger.

Encyclopaedia Britannica (1911), 11th edition. London: Chatto & Windus.

English Benedictine Congregation History (2012). [online] Available at: http://www.plantata.org.uk/people.php?choice=surname&target=appleton. [Accessed 2 May 2012].

Enhanced British Parliamentary Papers [online] Available at: http://www.ied.dippam.ac.uk/records/50065.

The Evangelical Magazine and Missionary Chronicle.

Evans, D. M. (1859), *The History of the Commercial Crisis, 1857–1858: And the Stock Exchange.* London: Groombridge and Sons.

Everett, E. (1850), *Orations and Speeches on Various Occasions,* Vol. 2. Boston: C. C. Little and J. Brown.

Eye Level (2011), *From Defense to Decoration: The Renwick Gallery during the Civil War.* [online] Available at: http://www.eyelevel.si.edu/2011/09/from-defense-to-decoration-the-renwick-gallery-in-the-civil-war.html. [Accessed 12 November 2011].

Farrell, P. (1989), *Irish in Australia.* South Bend, IN: University of Notre Dame Press.

Federal Hill Online (n.d.), *Sailor's Union Bethel Methodist Church.* [online] Available at: http://www.federalhillonline.com/tourstop04.htm. [Accessed 12 July 2011].

Ferguson, N. (1999), *The House of Rothschild: Money's Prophets, 1798–1848.* New York: Penguin.

Fitch, C. E. (1916), *Encyclopedia of Biography of New York: A Life Record of Men and Women Whose Sterling Character and Energy and Industry Have Made Them Preeminent in Their Own and Many Other States,* Vol. 4. New York: American Historical Society.

Fitz-Patrick, W. J. (1861), *The Life, Times, and Correspondence of the Right Rev. Dr. Doyle, Bishop of Kildare and Leighlin.* Dublin: James Duffy.

Flemming, D. B. (1860), 'William Walsh' in *Dictionary of Canadian Biography Online.* [online] Available at: http://www.biographi.ca/009004-119.01-e.php?&id_nbr=4239. [Accessed 4 June 2012].

Flood, J. A. (Fall 1995), 'The Forster Family and the Irish Famine'. *Quaker History* 84(2): 116–30.

Foner, P. (ed.), (1950), *Life and Writings of Frederick Douglass.* New York: International Publishers.

Forbes, Sir J. (1853) *Memorandums Made in Ireland in the Autumn of 1852.* London: Smith, Elder, and co., 1853, vol. 2.

Forbes, H. A. C. and Lee, H. (1967), *Massachusetts Help to Ireland during the Great Famine.* Milton, MA: Captain Robert Bennet Forbes House.

Forbes, R. B. (1817–1967), *Robert Bennet Forbes Papers: Guide to the Collection.* [manuscript]. Boston: Massachusetts History Society. Available at: http://www.masshist.org/findingaids/doc.cfm?fa = fa0039#top. [Accessed 1 December 2011].

— (1847), *The Voyage of the Jamestown on Her Errand of Mercy.* Boston: Eastburn's Press.

Frampton, M. (1885), *The Journal of Mary Frampton: From the Year 1779, until the Year 1846, including Various Interesting and Curious Letters, Anecdotes, &c., Relating to Events which Occurred during that Period.* London: S. Low, Marston, Searle, & Rivington.

Fraser, R. W. (1854), *Turkey Ancient and Modern. A History of the Ottoman Empire from its Period of Establishment to the Present Time*. Edinburgh: Adam and Charles Black.

Freeman's Journal.

Freemans (NY).

The Friend. A Religious and Literary Journal (Philadelphia).

Friend of India.

Gann, M. (n.d.), *New Brunswick Hall of Fame*. [online] Available at: http://www. new-brunswick.net/new-brunswick/fame.html. [Accessed 11 December 2011].

Garland, M. M. (1980), *Cambridge before Darwin: The Ideal of a Liberal Education, 1800–1860*. Cambridge: Cambridge University Press.

Garrison, W. L. (1971), *The Letters of William Lloyd Garrison: I will be Heard, 1822–1835*, W. M. Merrill and L. Ruchames (eds). Harvard: Harvard University Press.

Gaye, C. H. (1847), *Irish Famine. A Special Occasion for Keeping Lent in England. A Sermon Preached in Obedience to the Queen's Letter on the first Sunday in Lent 1847 at Archbishop Tennison's chapel, St James Westminster*. Second edition. London: Francis and John Rivington.

Geary, L. M. (2005), *Medicine and Charity in Ireland, 1718–1851*. Dublin: University College.

General Central Relief Committee (1848), *Report of the Proceedings of the General Central Relief Committee for all Ireland*. Dublin: J. Browne.

General Executive Committee for the Relief of Ireland, Philadelphia (1847), *Report of the General Executive Committee of the City and County of Philadelphia Appointed by the Town Meeting of February 17, 1847, to Provide Means to Relieve the Sufferings in Ireland*. Philadelphia: Crissy and Markley.

General Relief Committee (1849), 'Report of General Relief Committee in Belfast', *Banner of Ulster*, 5 January.

General Relief Committee of the City of New York. *Aid to Ireland: Report of the General Relief Committee of the City of New York, With Schedules of Receipts in Money, Provisions and Clothing*. New York: The Committee.

The Globe.

Gilbert, J. T. (1909), 'Daniel Murray', in L. Stephen, R. Blake (ed.), *Dictionary of National Biography*, Vol. 13. Oxford: Oxford University Press.

Gleeson, D. T. (2001), *The Irish in the South, 1815–1877*. Chapel Hill: University of North Carolina Press.

Gooch, G. P. (1925), *The Later Correspondence of Lord John Russell*. London: Longmans and Green.

Goodbody, R. (1995), *A Suitable Channel: Quaker Relief in the Great Famine*. Bray: Pale Publishing.

— (Spring 1998) 'The Quakers and the Famine'. *History Ireland*, 1: 28–9.

Gough, B. M. (1971), 'The Royal Navy and Oregon Crisis, 1844–1846'. *The British Columbian Quarterly* 9: 15–37. Available at: http://www.ojs.library.ubc. ca/index.php/bcstudies/article/view/689. [Accessed 10 December 2011].

Government of Bermuda (2011), *House of Assembly*. [online] Available at: http:// www.gov.bm/portal/server.pt?open=512&objID=311&PageID=0&cached=tr ue&mode=2&userID=2. [Accessed 11 April 2012].

Gray, P. (November 2000), 'National humiliation and the Great Hunger: fast and famine in 1847'. *Irish Historical Studies* 21 (126): 193–216.

— (2001), *Famine, Land and Politics: British Government and Irish Society, 1843–50*. Ireland: Irish Academic Press.

— (2009) *The Making of the Irish Poor Law, 1815–43*. Manchester: Manchester University Press.

Gregg, J. (1849), *A Missionary Visit to Connemara, and other Parts of the County of Galway*. Dublin: Curry.

Green, Abigail (June 2005), 'Sir Moses Montefiore: Religion, Nationhood and International Philanthropy in the Nineteenth Century'. *The American Historical Review* 110(3): 631–58.

Greenberg, B. (1985), *Worker and Community: Response to Industrialization in a Nineteenth-century American City, Albany, New York, 1850–1884*. Albany: State University of New York Press.

Griffith, G. T. (1926), *Population Problems in the Age of Malthus*. Cambridge: The University Press.

Guildhall Library Manuscripts (2006), [online] Available at: http://www.history. ac.uk/gh/brhkes.htm. [Accessed 16 October 2011].

Haines, R. (2004), *Charles Trevelyan and the Great Irish Famine*. Dublin: Four Courts Press.

Hall, S. C. (1841–43), *Ireland: its Scenery, Character, &c.* London: How and Parsons.

Hanna, S. F. (2011), *Washington County Seminary for Women or Washington County Female Seminary*. [online] Available at: *http://www.rootsweb.ancestry. com/~pawashin/seminary/focus-on-washington_vol1/sarah-foster-hanna.html*. [Accessed 3 March 2012].

Hansard.

Hansard People (n.d.), *Lord Robert Clinton*. [online] Available at: http://www. hansard.millbanksystems.com/people/lord-robert-clinton. [Accessed 6 May 2012].

Harford Family (1576–1959), *Deeds and Documents Relating to the Harford Family*. [manuscript] Bristol Record Office. The National Archives. England. Available at: http://www.nationalarchives.gov.uk/a2a/records.aspx?cat=002-28048&cid=6-14#6-14. [Accessed 9 June 2012].

Harlaftis, G. (1996), *A History of Greek-Owned Shipping: The Making of an International Tramp Fleet*. London: Routledge.

Harrison, B. (June 1966), 'Philanthropy and the Victorians'. *Victorian Studies* 9(4): 353–74.

Harvey, J. (n.d.), *John Harvey Papers, 1808–1847*. [manuscript] Available at: http:// www.amphilsoc.org/mole/view?docId=ead/Mss.Film.1111-ead.xml. [Accessed 4 May 2012].

Hatton, H. E. (1993), *The Largest Amount of Good: Quaker Relief in Ireland, 1654–1921*. Montreal: McGill-Queens.

Havens, C. E. (1920), *Diary of a Little Girl in Old New York*, Second edition. New York: Henry Collins Brown.

Hayes, P. (1910). 'John Hughes', in *The Catholic Encyclopedia*. *[online]* New York: Robert Appleton Company. http://www.newadvent.org/cathen/07516a.htm. [Accessed 9 September 2012].

Hemenway, A. M. (1868), 'Biography of Jonathan C. Dexter'. *The Vermont Historical Magazine* 2: 1030.

Hibernian Society (1889), *118th Anniversary of the Hibernian Society of Philadelphia*. Philadelphia: F. McManus Jr. and Co.

Hickey, P. (1993) *Famine, Mortality and Emigration. A Profile of Six Parishes in the Poor Law Union of Skibbereen, 1846–47*. [online] Available at: http://www.home.alphalink.com.au/~datatree/wolf%2053.htm. [Accessed 3 March 2011].

Hickey, P. (2002), *Famine in West Cork: The Mizen Peninsula and People, 1800–1852*. Dublin: Mercier Press.

Hilton, B. (1992), *The Age of Atonement. The Influence of Evangelicalism on Social and Economic Thought, 1785–1865*. Oxford: Oxford University Press.

Himmelfarb, G. (1996), 'True charity: lessons from Victorian England', in M. Tanner (ed.), *The End of Welfare: Fighting Poverty in Civil Society*. Washington, DC: Cato Institute.

History Ireland.

History of the Society of the St Vincent de Paul in Ireland (n.d.), [online] Available at: http://www.docstoc.com/docs/2203032/THE-HISTORY-OF-THE-SOCIETY-OF-ST-VINCENT-DE-PAUL-IN-IRELAND. [Accessed 15 May 2011].

The Hobart Town Courier and Van Diemen's Land Gazette.

Holland, M. C. (n.d.), *History of the Faithful Companions of Jesus in Britain and the Channel Isles*. [online] Available at: *http://www.fcjsisters.org/ep/english/about/history_brit.html*. [Accessed 3 May 2011].

House of Commons (1852), *House of Commons*. London: HMSO.

Howitt W. and Howitt, Mary (eds) (1847) *Howitt's Journal of Literature and Popular Progress*, Vol. 1. London: William Lovett.

Howson, E. W. and Warner, G. T. (eds) (1898), *Harrow School*. London: E. Arnold.

Hughes, J. (ed.) (1864), 'On the antecedents of Famine, delivered under the auspices of the General Relief Committee for the relief of the suffering poor of Ireland', in *The Complete Works of the Most Rev. John Hughes, D. D., Archbishop of New York. Comprising his Sermons, Letters, Lectures, Speeches, etc*. New York: American News.

Hughes, P. (2012), 'William Balch', in *Dictionary of Unitarian and Universalist Biography*. [online] Available at: http://www25.uua.org/uuhs/duub/articles/williamstevensbalch.html. [Accessed 4 June 2011].

Hume, W. (1847), *William Hume to William Stanley Esquire, 2 April 1847*, [manuscript] Relief Commission Papers. RLFC 3/2/7/8. Dublin. National Archives. Available at: http://www.learnaboutarchives.ie/~learnabo/images/learnaboutarchives/sampledocuments/famine/donegaltranscript1.pdf. [Accessed 1 May 2012].

Hutton, J. E. (1922), *History of Moravian Missions*. London: Moravian Publication Office.

Inangahua Times (New Zealand).

Incorporated Council of Law Reporting for England and Wales (1866–1952), *The Weekly Notes*. London: Printed for the Inc. Council of Law Reporting for England and Wales by W. Clowes and Sons.

Indian News.

Institute of the Blessed Virgin Mary (2012), *Loreto Education Arrives in Gibraltar*. [online] Available at: http://www.loreto.ie/archives/foundations-made-by-m-teresa-ball/188-gibraltar-1845. [Accessed 11 May 2012].

Institute for Jewish Ideas and Ideals (2009), *Sermon on the Occasion of the 350th Anniversary Service at Shearith Israel, September 12, 2004.* [online] Available at: http://www.jewishideas.org/min-hamuvhar/sermon-occasion-350th-anniversary-service-shear.

Ireland. High Court of Chancery, Ireland. Rolls Court, etc. (1856), *Irish Chancery Reports.* Dublin: Hodges and Smith.

Irish Canadian.

Irish Emigration Database (2012), *Marriage of Robert Kerr & Ann M. Hefferman, Philadelphia.* [online] Available at: http://www.ied.dippam.ac.uk/records/50065.

Irish Relief Association (1847), *The Lapse of Years, or Thoughts Suggested by the Close of Another period of Time.* Dublin: William Leckie.

Irish Relief Association (1847), *Distress in Ireland.* Dublin: Philip Dixon Hardy, 1847.

Irish Evangelical Society [online], Available at: http://www.proni.gov.uk/.

Irish Press.

Irish Railway News.

Irish Relief Association for the Destitute Peasantry (1847), *Distress in Ireland.* Dublin: P. D. Hardy.

Jackson, L. (n.d.), *Mogg's New Picture of London and Visitor's Guide to its Sights, 1844.* [online] Available at: http://www.victorianlondon.org/entertainment/chinesecollection.htm. [Accessed 17 October 2011].

James A. Loughead Family Correspondence, 1827–1850. Department of Special Collections, Hesburgh Libraries of Notre Dame. Available at: http://www.rbsc.library.nd.edu/finding_aid/RBSC-MSNEA0526:25. Accessed 16 October 2012].

James Hardiman Library (n.d.), *Guide to Lucan Papers.* [online] Available at: http://www.archives.library.nuigalway.ie/col_level.php?col=P48. [Accessed 11 May 2012].

Jay, J., King, J. G. and Brown, S. (1848), *Aid to Ireland: Report of the General Relief Committee of the City of New York, with Schedules of Receipts in Money, Provisions and Clothing.* New York: The Committee.

Jewish Encyclopedia (2011a), *Damascus Affair.* [online] Available at: http://www.jewishencyclopedia.com/articles/4862-damascus-affair. [Accessed 4 November 2011].

— (2011b), *Mocatta.* [online] Available at: http://www.jewishencyclopedia.com/view.jsp?artid=682&letter=M#2309. [Accessed 16 May 2011].

— (2011c), *Salomons.* [online] Available at: http://www.jewishencyclopedia.com/view.jsp?artid=89&letter=S#ixzz1W4O0nvl. [Accessed 3 July 2011].

Jordan, D. E. (1994), *Land and Popular Politics in Ireland: County Mayo from the Plantation to the Land War.* Cambridge: Cambridge University Press.

Journal des Débats (Paris).

Journals of the Bermuda House of Assembly. Hamilton, Bermuda: Bermuda Government Archives.

Kearney, J. (2007), 'Bishop William Quarter – First Catholic Bishop of Chicago', in *Offaly Historical and Archaeological Society.* [online] Available at: '*http://www.offalyhistory.com/articles/228/1/Bishop-William-Quarter-1806-1848–First-Catholic-Bishop-of-Chicago/Page1.html.* [Accessed 3April 2012].

Keith, T. (1853), *A New Treatise on the Use of the Globes; or, Philosophical View of the Earth and Heavens.* London: W. Tegg & Co.

Kelly, J. (May 1992), 'Scarcity and poor relief in Eighteenth-Century Ireland: The subsistence crisis of 1782–4'. *Irish Historical Studies* 28 (109): 38–62.

Kennedy, L. and Clarkson, L. A. (1993), 'Birth, Death and Exile: Irish Population History, 1700-1921', in B. J. Graham and L. J. Proudfoot (eds), *An Historical Geography of Ireland*. Dublin: Irish Academic Press.

Kenny, A. (2005), *Arthur Hugh Clough: A Poet's Life*. London: Continuum.

Kerr, D. (1994), *A Nation of Beggars?: Priests, People, and Politics in Famine Ireland, 1846-1852*. Oxford: Clarendon Press.

— (1996), *The Catholic Church and the Great Irish Famine*. Dublin: Columba Press.

Kestenbaum, L. (2012), *The Political Graveyard: A Database of American History*. [online] Available at: http://www.politicalgraveyard.com/bio/micheau-middleswarth.html. [Accessed 15 December 2011].

Kidd, A. (May 1996), 'Philanthropy and the "Social History" paradigm'. *Social History* 21(2): 180–92.

Killen, W. D. (1875), *The Ecclesiastical History of Ireland: From the Earliest Period to the Present Times*, Vol. 2. London: Macmillan.

Kinealy, C. (1997a), *A Death-Dealing Famine: The Great Hunger in Ireland*. London: Pluto Press.

— (1997b), 'Potatoes, providence and philanthropy: the role of private charity during the Famine', in P. O'Sullivan (ed.), *The Meaning of the Famine*. London: Leicester University Press, pp. 140–71.

— (1998), 'Peel, Rotten Potatoes and Providence. The repeal of the Corn Laws and the Irish famine', in G. Parry, H. Steiner, and A. Marrison (eds), *Freedom and Trade: Free Trade and its Reception, 1815–1960*. London and New York: Routledge.

— (2002), *The Great Irish Famine: Impact, Ideology and Rebellion*. Hampshire: Palgrave Press.

— (2006), *This Great Calamity: The Irish Famine 1845–52*. Dublin: Gill and Macmillan.

— (2007), *Lives of Victorian Political Figures: Daniel O'Connell*. London: Pickering and Chatto.

— (2009), *Repeal and Revolution: 1848 in Ireland*. Manchester: Manchester University Press.

— (2011), *Daniel O'Connell and the Anti-slavery Movement: 'The Saddest People the Sun Sees'*. London: Pickering and Chatto.

Kinealy, C. and MacAtasney, G. (2000), *The Hidden Famine: Hunger, Poverty and Sectarianism in Belfast 1840–50*. London: Pluto.

Knights Commander of the Order of Bath, [online] Available at: http://www. en.wikipedia.org/w/index.php?title=Category:Knights_Commander_of_the_ Order_of_the_Bath&pageuntil=Vickers%2C+Richard%0ARichard+Vickers# mw-pages.

Koeppel, G. T. (2012), *Water for Gotham: A History*. Princeton, NJ: Princeton University Press.

Kutney, G. (2007), *Sulfur: History, Technology, Applications & Industry*. Ontario: ChemTec Publishing.

Lady Sligo Letters, Arnold Bernhard Library, Quinnipiac University.

Lamon, W. H. (1895), *Recollections of Abraham Lincoln, 1847–1865*. Chicago: A. C. McClurg and Company.

Landed Estates Database, NUI Galway (2011), *Cox (Cork and Kilkenny)*. [online] Available at: http://www.landedestates.ie/LandedEstates/jsp/estate-show.jsp?id=3056. [Accessed 10 July 2012].

Lane-Poole, S. (1890), *The Life of Lord Stratford de Redcliffe*. London: Longmans, Green.

Langouet, Λ. (1911). 'Natal', in *The Catholic Encyclopedia*. [online] New York: Robert Appleton Company. Available at: http://www.newadvent.org/cathen/10707a.htm. [Accessed 28 May 2012].

Launcetown Examiner (Tasmania).

Lawrence, V. B. and Strong, G. T. (1995), *Resonances, 1836–1849*. Chicago: University of Chicago Press.

Learned, H. B. (1914), 'Cabinet Meetings under President Polk'. *American Historical Association* 1: 231–42.

Lee, J. and Casey, M. R. (2006), *Making the Irish American: History and Heritage of the Irish in the United States*. New York: New York University Press.

The Legal Observer, and Solicitors' Journal (1856), Vol. 51. London: Law Newspaper Co.

Leighton-Boyce, J. A. S. L. (1958), *Smiths, the Bankers, 1658–1958*. London: National Provincial Bank.

Letters and other Documents relating to Famine Relief Schemes in Limerick and Dublin, 1822–1825 and 1846–1848. [manuscript] Bourke Papers, MS 8474 (7). Dublin: National Library of Ireland.

Lewis, D. (2001), *Liverpool Monuments*. [online] Available at: http://www.liverpoolmonuments.co.uk/relstatues/pat01.html. [Accessed 2 May 2012].

The Liberal (Bridgetown, Barbados).

Liberator (Boston).

Lismore Estate (1750–1969), *Lismore Castle Papers*. [manuscript]. IE WCA PP LISM. Waterford County Archives. Available at: http://www.waterfordcoco.ie/en/media/archives/pdfs/LISMORE%20CASTLE%20PAPERS-%20Final.pdf. [Accessed 15 May 2012].

The Liverpool Commercial List (1866). London: Seyd and Co.

Liverpool Mercury.

London Gazette.

The London Gazette (2012), *Dissolution Agreement, 1854*. [online] Available at: http://www.london-gazette.co.uk/issues/21604/pages/3036/page.pdf. [Accessed 4 May 2012].

Londonderry Standard.

Low, S., Jr (1850). *The Charities of London. Their Origin, Design, Progress and Present Position*. London: Sampson Low.

Luddy, M. (1995), *Women and Philanthropy in Nineteenth-Century Ireland*. Cambridge: Cambridge University Press.

Luscombe, S. (n.d.), *The First Sikh War: Sir Hugh Gough*. [online] Available at: http://www.britishempire.co.uk/forces/armycampaigns/indiancampaigns/sikhwars/sirhughgough.htm. [Accessed 5 October 2011].

Lushington, G. (1865), 'Pamphlet on Retrenchment at Oxford', in A. H. Clough (ed.), *Letters and Remains of Arthur Hugh Clough*. London: Spottiswoode.

Lyall, A. C. (1905), *The life of the Marquis of Dufferin and Ava*, Vol. 1. London: J. Murray.

The Lyttelton History (2012), [online] Available at: http://www.thelyttelton.com/ About/History/. [Accessed 16 May 2012].

Lyttelton, S. S., Cavendish L. C. L. and Leconfield, M. M. (1912), *Correspondence of Sarah Spencer, Lady Lyttelton, 1787–1870*. London: J. Murray.

'M' (1852), *Connemara, Journal of a Tour, Undertaken to Enquire into the Progress of the Reformation in the West of Ireland*. Dublin: G. Drought.

Macafee, W. (2010), *London Companies Estates in County Derry*. [online] Available at: http://www.billmacafee.com/estates/landlords/ notescompaniesestates.htm. [Accessed 9 July 2012].

Machin, G. I. T. (Jan. 1967), 'The Maynooth Grant, the dissenters and disestablishment, 1845-1847', *The English Historical Review* 82(322): 61–85.

McCarthy, K. D. (2001). *Women, Philanthropy, and Civil Society*. Bloomington: Indiana University Press.

MacKay, D. (1990), *Flight from Famine: The Coming of the Irish to* Canada. Toronto: McClelland & Stewart.

Magee, T. D. (1852), *A History of the Irish Settlers in North America*. Boston: Patrick Donahoe.

Malthus, T. (1798), *An Essay On The Principle Of Population as it Effects the Future Improvement of Society*. London: J. Johnson.

The Manchester Commercial List (1867–1875). London: Estell & Co.

McCarthy, R. (1967), 'The Role of the Clergy in the Great Famine', in K. Milne (ed.), *The Great Famine: A Church of Ireland Perspective*. Dublin: Association for Promoting Christian Knowledge.

McKelvey, B. (1964), 'Rochester mayors before the civil war'. *Rochester History* 26(1): 1–20.

McNeile, H. (1847), *The Famine, a Rod of God, its Provoking Cause – Its Merciful Design: A Sermon, Preached in St. Jude's Church, Liverpool, on Sunday February 28, 1847*. London: Seeley, Burnside and Seeley.

McNeill, M. (1960), *The Life and Times of Mary Ann McCracken, 1770–1866: A Belfast Panorama*. Dublin: A. Figgis.

'Meeting of The Jewish Population of New York In Aid Of Ireland' (1847), *The Occident and American Jewish Advocate*, V (1).

Melbourne Argus.

A Member of a Parochial Poor Relief Committee (1828), 'A Letter to the Prime Minister on the Deplorable Condition of the Helpless Poor in Ireland'. *The Pamphleteer*. London: A. J. Valpy 29: 457–83.

Mercury (Liverpool).

The Merrimack Courier (New Hampshire).

Michell, A. T. (1901–02), *Rugby School Register, Rugby School*, Vol. 2. Rugby: A. J. Lawrence.

Minutes of British Relief Association. [manuscript] MS 2022. Dublin: National Library of Ireland.

Moffitt, M. (2006), 'The Society for Irish Church Missions to Roman Catholics: Philanthropy or Bribery?'. *International Bulletin of Missionary Research* 30(1): 32–6.

The Moreton Bay Courier (Brisbane).

Morison, S. E. (1921). *The Maritime History of Massachusetts, 1783–1860*. Boston: Houghton Mifflin Company.

Morning Chronicle (London).

Moylan, T. K. (September 1938), 'Vagabonds and Sturdy Beggars'. *Dublin Historical Record* 1(3): 65–74.

Mulrooney, M. M. (2003), *Fleeing the Famine: North America and Irish Refugees, 1845–1851*. Westport, Conn.: Praeger.

Murray, D. (1823–52), *Papers of Archbishop Daniel Murray: 1823–1852*. Dublin. Diocesan Archives. http://www.dublindiocese.ie/content/daniel-murray-1823-1852. [Accessed various dates].

Murray, K. (2010), 'Role of Turkey during Famine clarified', *Irish Times*, 1 June, *Nation* (Dublin).

National Club (1849), *Addresses to the Protestants of the empire*, November, 1847, to February, 1849. London: Macintosh.

National Era (Washington).

National Intelligencer (Washington).

Naval Database (n.d.), *HMS Aphrodite (1816)*. [online] Available at: http://www.pbenyon.plus.com/18-1900/A/00238.html. [Accessed 3 May 2012].

Nenagh Guardian.

Newman, H. W. (1936), *The Smoots of Maryland and Virginia: A Genealogical History of William Smute, Boatright, of Hampton, Virginia, and Pickawaxon, Maryland, with a History of his Descendants to the Present Generation*. Washington, DC: J. P. Bell.

Newtownards Independent.

New Witness and Catholic Chronicle.

New York Christian Advocate.

New York Spectator.

New York Weekly Tribune.

New Zealand Tablet.

Newry Commercial Telegraph.

News-Letter (Belfast).

Nicholls, G. (1856), *A History of the Irish Poor Law: In Connexion with the Condition of the People*. London: J. Murray.

Nicholson, A. (1998), *Annals of the Famine in Ireland*. M. Murphy (ed.). Dublin: Lilliput Press.

de Nie, M. (2004), *The Eternal Paddy. Irish Identity and the British Press*. University of Wisconsin Press.

Nonconformist.

Northern Star.

Northern Whig.

Norton, D. (2001), 'Lord Palmerston and the Irish Famine Emigration', in T. Anbinder (ed.), *Centre for Economic Research Working Paper Series*, Dublin: University College Dublin, WP01/19.

Obituaries, Australia (2012), *Sir Paul de Strzelecki*. [online] Available at: http://www.oa.anu.edu.au/obituary/strzelecki-sir-paul-edmund-de-2711. [Accessed 10 August 2011].

'Obituary of Van Schaick', *New York Times*, 3 December 1865.

O'Brien, W. P. (1896), *The Great Famine in Ireland: And a Retrospect of the Fifty years 1845-95 with a Sketch of the Present Condition and Future Prospects of the Congested Districts*. London: Downey and Co.

Ó Ciosáin, N. (2004), 'Approaching a Folklore Archive: The Irish Folklore Commission and the Memory of the Great Famine'. *Folklore* 115(2): 222–32.

O'Donoghue, J., Goulding, L. and Allen, G. (2004), 'Consumer price inflation since 1750'. *Economic Trends* 604: 38–46.

O'Farrell, P. (2003), *A history of County Kildare*. Dublin: Gill & Macmillan.

Office of the University Historian, Boston College (2011), *Carney Hall (1963)*. [online] Available at: http://www.bc.edu/offices/historian/resources/guide/carney.html.[Accessed 11 October 2012].

O'Flanagan, P. and Buttimer, C. G. (eds) (1993), *Interdisciplinary Essays on the History of an Irish County*. Dublin: Geography Publications.

Ó Gráda, C. (1996), 'Church of Ireland mortality during the famine', in K. Milne (ed.), *The Great Famine. A Church of Ireland Perspective*. Dublin: Association for Promoting Christian Knowledge.

— (2000), *'Black '47' and Beyond: The Great Irish Famine in History, Economy, and Memory*. Princeton, NJ: Princeton University Press.

Oliver, G. A. (1882), *A Study of Maria Edgeworth, with Notices of her Father and Friends*. Boston: A. Williams and Co.

O'Reilly, B. (1890), *John MacHale, Archbishop of Tuam: His Life, Times and Correspondence*. New York: F. Pustet.

Oriel College (2011), *The Oxford Movement*. [online] Available at: http://www.oriel.ox.ac.uk/content/oxford-movement. [Accessed 1 December 2011].

O'Rourke, J. (1866), *'Them also': The Story of the Dublin Mission*. Dublin: J. Nisbet & Co.

— (1874), *The History of the Great Irish Famine of 1847*. Reprint 1989. Dublin: Veritas.

— (1887), *Battle of the Faith in Ireland*. Dublin: J. Duffy.

Ott, M. (1911). 'Pope Pius IX', in *The Catholic Encyclopedia*. [online] New York: Robert Appleton Company. Available at: http://www.newadvent.org/cathen/12134b.htm. [Accessed 8 May 2012].

Oulton, C. (2003), *Literature and Religion in Mid-Victorian England: From Dickens to Eliot*. New York: Palgrave Macmillan.

Owen, J. (1816), *The History of the Origin and First Ten Years of the British and Foreign Bible Society*. London: Tilling & Hughes.

Palliser, J. (1853), *Solitary Rambles and Adventures of a Hunter in the Prairies*. London: J. Murray.

Papal Encyclicals Online (2012). [online] Available at: http://www.papalencyclicals.net/index.htm. [Accessed 9 March 2012].

Parish of the Resurrection (2012), *A Short History of St. Peter's Parish and Church*. [online] Available at: http://www.resurrectionparishjc.com/short%20history%20of%20peter.html. [Accessed 9 May 2012].

Peel, R. (1856), *Memoirs of the Right Honourable Sir Robert Peel*. London: J. Murray.

Pilot.

Pius, P. (1843), *Identity of Popery & Tractarianism: or Pope Pius IV's Creed, Illustrated by Tractarian Comments*. London: sold by Nisbet, Hatchard, etc.

Plymouth City Council (n.d.), *Millbay Docks*. [online] Available at: http://www.plymouth.gov.uk/millbay_docks_9-13.pdf. [Accessed 3 June 2012].

Polk, J. K. (1929), *Polk; the Diary of a President, 1845-1849, Covering the Mexican War, the Acquisition of Oregon, and the Conquest of California and the Southwest*. New York: Longmans, Green and Co.

Pontificio Collegio Irlandese (2012). [online] Available at: http://www.irishcollege.org/college/. [Accessed 4 June 2012].

Poor Law Commission Office (1845), *Seventh Annual Report of Poor Law Commissioners for England and Ireland*. London: Poor Law Commission Office.

— (1846), *Eighth Annual Report of Poor Law Commissioners for England and Ireland*. London: Poor Law Commission Office.

Pope, E. T. (1849), *A Ladies Committee in Ireland, 1849*. [manuscript] Ms. 40, 438 Dublin: National Library of Ireland.

Porter, L. C. (1969), 'Rev. George Lane. Good Gifts, Good Grace, and Marked Usefulness', *Brigham Young University Studies* 9(3): 321–40.

Post, J. D. (1985), *Food Shortages, Climatic Variability and Epidemic Disease in Pre-Industrial Europe: The Mortality Peak in the Early 1740s*. New York: Cornell University Press.

Preston, M. H., (2004) *Charitable Words: Women, Philanthropy, And The Language Of Charity In Nineteenth-Century Dublin*. Westport, CT: Greenwood Press.

Prochaska, F. K. (1980), *Women and Philanthropy in Nineteenth-Century England*. Oxford: Oxford University Press.

— (1988), *The Voluntary Impulse - Philanthropy in Modern Britain*. London: Faber and Faber.

Prunty, J. (2011), *Margaret Aylward, 1810–1889: Lady of Charity, Sister of Faith*. Dublin: Four Courts Press.

Public Ledger Philadelphia.

The Quaker Perrys [online]. Available at: http://www.irishperrys.com/meath.htm. [Accessed 17 January 2012].

The Quakers in Ireland [online]. Available at: http://www.quakers-in-ireland.ie/history/charity/. [Accessed 12 January 2012].

Quarterly Journal of the American Education Society.

The Quebec Saturday Budget.

Rallings, C. and Thrasher, M. (2000), *British Electoral Facts 1832–1999*. Brookfield, Vt.: Ashgate Publishing Ltd.

Rathbone Family (1721–1971), *Rathbone Papers*, [manuscript] PRV 1. 67. Liverpool: Liverpool University Archives.

Records of High Pavement Presbyterian (Unitarian) Chapel, Nottingham (1576–1982), [manuscript]. University of Nottingham. Available at: http://www.longford.nottingham.ac.uk/Dserve/dserve.exe?dsqIni=Dserve.ini&dsqApp=Archive&dsqDb=Catalog&dsqSearch=%28PersonCode==NA336%29&dsqCmd=Show.tcl. [Accessed 9 June 2012].

Records of Sun Fire Office. [manuscript] MS 11936/555. Guildhall Library. England. National Archives. Available at: http://www.nationalarchives.gov.uk/a2a/records.aspx?cat = 076-sun_2-85&cid = -1#-1. [Accessed 7 June 2012].

Redner, S. (2003), *Population history of Cincinnati*. [online] Available at: http://www.physics.bu.edu/~redner/projects/population/cities/cincinnati.html. [Accessed 3 December 2011].

Rhoads, S. and Lewis, E. (eds) (1874), *Friends' Review: A Religious, Literary and Miscellaneous Journal*, Vol. 27. Philadelphia: J. Tatum.

Ridding, L. (1908), *George Ridding: Schoolmaster and Bishop, Forty-Third Head Master of Winchester, 1866–1884, First Bishop of Southwell, 1884–1904.* London: E. Arnold.

Roberts, S. (2012), *Distant Writing. A History of the Telegraph Companies in Britain between 1838 and 1868.* [online] Available at: http://www.distantwriting.co.uk/electrictelegraphcompany.aspx. [Accessed 3 June 2010].

Robertson, M. (ed.), (1913), *The English Reports, Common Pleas,* Vol. 4; Vol. 134. Edinburgh: William Green and Sons.

Roscommon and Leitrim Gazette.

Rose, H. J. and Maitland, S. R. (eds) (1847), *The British Magazine,* vol. 31, p. 217.

'Rothery, Henry Cadogan' (1885–1900), in Dictionary of National Biography. London: Smith, Elder & Co.

Royal College of Surgeons (2012), *Godlee, Sir Rickman John (1849–1925).* [online] Available at: http://www.livesonline.rcseng.ac.uk/biogs/E000221b.htm. [Accessed 18 November 2011].

Royal Irish Art Union Monthly Journal.

Russell, Lord John Papers, c.1800–1903. 30/22, National Archives of England.

Sarbaugh, T. J. (Summer 1996), '"Charity begins at Home", the United States government and Irish famine relief, 1845–1849'. *History Ireland,* 4(2): 31–5.

Scisco, L. D. (1901), *Political Nativism in New York State.* PhD. Columbia University.

Scott, J. A. (2008), 'John Collins', in *Early Actors of the Stage. In Memoriam.* [online] Available at: http://www.genealogytrails.com/main/actorsmemoriam.html. [Accessed 3 May 2012].

Scraggs, W. (1847), *US Sloop of War, Jamestown.* [print] Cork, Ireland: W. Scraggs, Cork.

Seaton, J. (1871), *William Winston Seaton of the 'National Intelligencer', with Passing Notices of his Associates and Friends.* Boston: James R. Osgood and Co.

Secker, W. H. (2012), *Tawa Historical Society.* [online] Available at: http://www.tawahistory.wellington.net.nz/projects/secker_articles.html. [Accessed 5 May 2012].

Select Committee on Orange Lodges (1835), 'Report from the Select Committee Appointed to Inquire into the Nature, Character, Extent and Tendency of Orange Lodges, Associations or Societies in Ireland', [online transcript] *British Parliamentary Papers* XV (337), Available at: http://www.ied.dippam.ac.uk/records/26813.

Shaftesbury Society and Ragged School Union (1853), *The Ragged School Union Magazine.* London: Patridge and Oakey.

Sheppard, A. T. (1926), 'Asenath Nicholson and the Howitt Circle', in *The Bookman,* pp. 103–5.

— (ed.), (1926), *The Bible in Ireland: Ireland Welcome to the Stranger, or Excursions to Ireland in the Years 1844 and 1845.* London: Hodder and Stoughton.

Shrout, A. H. (2013) 'Distressing News from Ireland.' The Famine, the News and International Philanthropy. Unpublished PhD Dissertation, New York: New York University.

Sims, W. D. (1847), *Distress in Ireland: W. D. Sims' Narrative Describing the Fifth and Sixth Weeks of W. Forster's Journey in the Distressed Districts in Ireland.* London: Edward Newman.

Sisters of Mercy (1888), *Leaves from the Annals of the Sisters of Mercy in Three Volumes*, Volume I. Ireland. New York: The Catholic Publication Society.

Smiles. S. (1907), *Thrift: A Book of Domestic Counsel*. Scotland: J. Murray.

Smith, J. F. and W. Howitt. (1856–64), *John Cassell's Illustrated History of England. The Text, to the Reign of Edward 1 by J. F. Smith; and from that Period by W. Howitt*. London: Cassell.

Society for Irish Church Missions to the Roman Catholics (1852), *The Banner of the Truth in Ireland: Monthly Information Concerning Irish Church Missions to the Roman Catholics*. London: Wonston.

South Australian Register (Adelaide).

South Ribble Borough Council (2010), *The ffaringtons of Worden*. [online] Available at: *http://www.southribble.gov.uk/museum_collection_ffaringtons. asp?catid=301000*. [Accessed 5 April 2012].

Southern Reporter.

Southern Star.

Sowerby, W. (1847), *To the Congregation of St Saviour's Church, Goulburn, at Whose Request it is Published, this Sermon is Respectfully Inscribed to their Faithful Friend and Minister, William Sowerby, July 21, 1847*. New South Wales, Sydney: Kemp and Fairfax.

St James's Chronicle.

St Kitts National Archives (2010), 'St George's Anglican Church', in *Basseterre Past and Present*. [online] Available at: http://www.historicbasseterre.com/ hs_summation.asp?HSID = 10. [Accessed 28 October 2011].

St. Christopher Council Minutes (1843–47), Minutes of the Assembly of St Christopher, 1847–1843. Basseterre, St. Kitts: National Archive.

Stevens, A. C. (1907), *The cyclopædia of Fraternities*. New York: E. B. Treat and Co.

The Straits Times (Singapore).

Stratton, C. C. (ed.), (1883), *Autobiography of Erastus O. Haven. With an Introduction by the Rev. J. M. Buckley*. New York: Phillips & Hunt.

Strum, H. (2000), 'Famine relief from the Garden City to the Green Isle'. *Journal of the Illinois State Historical Society* 93(4): 388–414. Available at: http://www. dig.lib.niu.edu/ISHS/ishs-2000winter/ishs-2000winter388.pdf. [Accessed 5 November 2011].

— (2002) 'South Carolina and Irish Famine Relief'. *The South Carolina Historical Magazine* 2: 130–52.

— (2006), 'To feed the hungry: Rochester and Irish famine relief'. *Rochester History* 68(3): 1–22.

Sydney Chronicle (NSW).

The Sydney Morning Herald.

Symington Family Estates (n.d.), *Smith Woodhouse History*. [online] Available at: http://www.smithwoodhouse.com/. [Accessed 2 May 2012].

Tablet.

Taylor, C. (1974), *British and American Abolitionists: An Episode in Transatlantic Understanding*. Edinburgh: Edinburgh University Press.

Thanet, O. (1891), 'An Irish gentlewoman in the famine time', in Richard Watson Gilder (ed.), *The Century*. New York: T. Fisher Unwin.

Third Report of His Majesty's Commissioners for Inquiring into the Condition of the Poorer Classes in Ireland 1836. (43, xxx) London: HMSO.

Thornbury, W. (1878), *Old and New London: A Narrative of its History, its People, and its Places*. London: Cassell, Petter, & Galpin.

Thumb, T. (1874), *Sketch of the Life: Personal Appearance, Character and Manners of Charles S. Stratton, the Man in Miniature, known as General Tom Thumb, and his Wife, Lavinia Warren Stratton, including the History of their Courtship and Marriage . . . Also, Songs Given at their Public Levees*. New York: S. Booth.

Times.

Treacy, G. (1919), 'Andrew Carney, Philanthropist'. *Historical Records and Studies* 13: 101–5.

Trevelyan, C. (1880). *The Irish Crisis*. London: Longman, Brown, Green & Longman.

Trollope, A. (1883), *Anthony Trollope: An Autobiography*. Edinburgh and London: William Blackwood and Sons.

Trotter, R. L. (Winter 2001), 'For the defense of the western border: Arkansas volunteers on the Indian frontier, 1846–1847'. *The Arkansas Historical Quarterly* 60(4): 394–410.

The True Witness and Catholic Chronicle.

Tuam Herald.

Tucker, L. and Thomas, J. J. (eds) (1862–63), *The Country Gentleman*, Vol. 20. Albany: Luther Tucker and Son.

Tuke, J. H. (1880), *Irish Distress and its Remedies: The Land Question, a Visit to Donegal and Connaught in the Spring of 1880*. London: W. Ridgway.

Tuke, J. H. and Edward F. (1899), *James Hack Tuke: A Memoir*. London: Macmillan.

United Service: A Monthly Review of Military and Naval Affairs (1895), Vol. 14. Philadelphia: Hamersly & Co.

The United States Catholic Magazine and Monthly Review. (1846), Vol. 5. Baltimore: J. Murphy.

University of Leeds (2012), *Pablo Fanque's Grave*. [online] Available at: http://www.mech-eng.leeds.ac.uk/support/images/misc/PABLO_FANQUE.HTML. [Accessed 11 December 2011].

Uppal, J. N. (1984), *Bengal Famine of 1943. A Man-Made Tragedy*. Delhi: Atma Ram & Sons.

Urban, S. (1852), *The Gentleman's Magazine and Historical Review*, Vol. 42. London: John Bowyer Nichols and Son.

Urquhart, D. (2007), *The Ladies of Londonderry: Women and Political Patronage*. London: I. B. Tauris.

US Army Medical Department, Office of Medical History (2009), *Lawson's First Years as Surgeon General, 1836–1845*. [online] Available at: http://www.history.amedd.army.mil/booksdocs/civil/gillett2/amedd_1818–1865_chpt4.html. [Accessed 4 September 2011].

The Usborne Family Tree (n.d.), [online] Available at: http://www.usbornefamilytree.com/thomas1769.htm. [Accessed 4 May 2012].

Valone, D. and Kinealy, C. (eds) (2002), *Ireland's Great Hunger: Silence, Memory, and Commemoration*. Lanham, MD: University of America Press.

Vanhaute, E., Paping, R. and Ó Gráda, C. (2006), 'The European subsistence crisis of 1845–1850: a comparative perspective', in *International Economic History Congress*, Helsinki Session 123 in XIV, Finland.

Villiers-Tuthill, K. (2012), *A Colony of Strangers: The Founding & Early History of Clifden*. Galway: Connemara Girl.

Vindicator (Belfast).

Wach, H. M. (Spring, 1993), 'Unitarian Philanthropy and Cultural Hegemony in Comparative Perspective: Manchester and Boston, 1827–1848', *Journal of Social History* 26(3): 539–57.

Wallace, N. (2003), *Anatole N. Demidoff, 1st Prince of San Donato (1813–1870)*. [online] Available at: http://www.jssgallery.org/Essay/Italy/Demidoff/Demidoff_1st.htm. [Accessed 3 October 2011].

Washburne, E. B. (1876), *Historical Sketch of Charles S. Hempstead*. Galena: Gazette Book.

The Washington Post.

Webb, M. (1847), *[Letter] to Maria Chapman, Dear Friend, 2 December 1847*. [manuscript] Anti-slavery Collection, Boston Library. Available through Internet Archive at: http://www.archive.org/details/lettertomariacha00webb. [Accessed 10 October 2011].

Whately, E. J. and Whately, R. (1866), *Life and Correspondence of Richard Whately, Late Archbishop of Dublin*. London: Longmans, Green and Co.

Whelan, I. (1995), 'The Stigma of Souperism', in Cathal Poirteir (ed.), *The Great Irish Famine*. Dublin: Mercier Press.

Whyman, H. C. (1992), *The Hedstroms and the Bethel Ship Saga: Methodist Influence on Swedish Religious Life*. Carbondale, Ill.: Southern Illinois University.

Wigham, H. A. (1886), *A Christian Philanthropist of Dublin: A Memoir of Richard Allen Richard Allen*. London: Hodder and Stoughton.

Williamson, P. (2008), 'State prayers, fasts and thanksgivings: Public worship in Britain 1830-1897'. *Past and Present* 200(1): 121–74.

Winthrop, R. C. Jr. (1897), *A Memoir of Robert C. Winthrop*. Boston: Little, Brown, and Company.

Woodham-Smith, C. (1962), *The Great Hunger*. London: Hamish Hamilton.

World Naval Ships (2012), *HMS Scourge Service Details*. [online] Available at: http://www.worldnavalships.com/forums/archive/index.php/t-11262.html. [Accessed 10 July 2011].

Wright, J. M. (1905), *History of the Bahama Islands, with a Special Study of the Abolition of Slavery in the Colony*. New York: Macmillan Co.

Young, W. T. (1852), *Sketch of the Life and Public Services of General Lewis Cass: With the Pamphlet on the Right of Search, and some of his Speeches on the Great Political Questions of the Day*. Detroit: Alexander McFarren.

INDEX

Lightning Source UK Ltd.
Milton Keynes UK
UKHW022033030521
383060UK00007B/1422